Managing Workplace Diversity and Inclusion

Managing Workplace Diversity and Inclusion bridges the gap between social science theory and research and the practical concerns of those working in diversity and inclusion by presenting an applied psychological perspective. Using foundational ideas in the field of diversity and inclusion as well as concepts in the social sciences, this book provides a set of cognitive tools for dealing with situations related to workplace diversity and applies both classic theories and new ideas to topics such as United States employment law, teamwork, gender, race and ethnicity, sexual orientation, and other areas. Each chapter includes engaging scenarios and real-world applications to stimulate learning and help students conceptualize and contextualize diversity in the workplace. Intended for upper-level undergraduates as well as graduate students, this textbook brings together foundational theories with practical, real-world applications to build a strong understanding of managing diversity and inclusion in the workplace.

Rosemary (Lowe) Hays-Thomas is Professor Emerita at the University of West Florida in Pensacola, where she developed the university's first course in Workforce Diversity and was psychology department chair. She has published widely, consulted, and held elected office and fellow status in several psychology organizations. She also holds a lifetime certification as a Senior Professional in Human Resources and for many years was a licensed psychologist.

Managing Workplace Diversity and Inclusion

A Psychological Perspective

Rosemary Hays-Thomas

Routledge
Taylor & Francis Group

NEW YORK AND LONDON

First published 2017
by Routledge
711 Third Avenue, New York, NY 10017

and by Routledge
2 Park Square, Milton Park, Abingdon, Oxon, OX14 4RN

Routledge is an imprint of the Taylor & Francis Group, an informa business

Library of Congress Cataloging in Publication Data
Names: Hays-Thomas, Rosemary, author.
Title: Managing workplace diversity and inclusion : a psychological perspective / Rosemary Hays-Thomas.
Description: New York, NY : Routledge, 2017. | Includes bibliographical references and index.
Identifiers: LCCN 2016030858 | ISBN 9781848729834 (hardback : alk. paper) | ISBN 9781138794269 (pbk. : alk. paper) | ISBN 9780203127049 (ebook)
Subjects: LCSH: Diversity in the workplace—Management. | Multiculturalism. | Personnel management. | Psychology, Industrial.
Classification: LCC HF5549.5.M5 H395 2017 | DDC 658.3008—dc23
LC record available at https://lccn.loc.gov/2016030858

ISBN: 978-1-84872-983-4 (hbk)
ISBN: 978-1-138-79426-9 (pbk)
ISBN: 978-0-203-12704-9 (ebk)

Typeset in Baskerville
by Keystroke, Neville Lodge, Tettenhall, Wolverhampton

In memory of Cliff

Contents

Preface

This book addresses the subject of organizational diversity and inclusion, one that has grown over the last half-century as employees and managers adapted to changes in the composition of the workforce, laws about fairness and discrimination, jobs, and work organizations. The field of diversity and inclusion (D&I) grew out of human resources, management, law, and other fields, often without connection to highly relevant advances in psychology and other social sciences. This book attempts to bridge the gap between social science theory and research and the practical concerns of those working in D&I by presenting an applied psychological perspective on the field. The book is targeted at graduate students, advanced undergraduates, and professionals interested in improving D&I at work. It aims to provide a foundation for those entering the field of D&I as well as those who have moved into this work from other areas of management and human resources. Though D&I is of concern in other industrialized countries, our focus is on applications in the United States, largely because of legal provisions and cultural context unique to the US. The book was in production at the time of the 2016 national election in the US.

Chapters cover a wide variety of material, moving from foundational conceptual ideas in D&I management (Part I) and basic social science concepts (Part II) to practical applications in targeted areas (Part III) and possible solutions (Part IV). Despite an attempt at comprehensive treatment, only a subset of the many relevant ideas and studies could be presented. Classic theories and research have been mentioned as well as recent ideas and empirical results. Older work is cited to emphasize that some of these ideas have been studied for quite some time by social scientists. Discussion of recent work aims to provide a current perspective on the many controversies in the field rather than an extensive review of literature. Excellent reviews by others have been cited frequently but the many excellent sources exceeded the space available to discuss them. Reference list citations with asterisks are recommended for those who want to read more about various topics. I hope that readers will find this work exciting and useful, as I have in pulling it together for you.

Special thanks go to colleagues who have assisted in various ways, especially Marc Bendick, Laura Koppes Bryan, Steven Kass, Kim LeDuff, Valerie Morganson, Julie O'Mara, Belle Rose Ragins, Bruce Swain, Stephen Vodanovich, and Susan Walch. Graduate students Kimber Bougan, Sijia Li, and Sadie O'Neill provided valuable assistance. The faculty and staff of the Department of Psychology and the Pace Library at the University of West Florida also provided important support. Preparation of the book was greatly assisted by a SAGES grant from the Society for the Psychological Study of Social Issues, which supports the application of social science to practical challenges of everyday life. Finally, I am grateful to my own teachers, faculty colleagues, and students who have taught me about social interaction and organizations, to friends and family for their patience and encouragement, and to Anne Duffy for getting me started.

Part I

Basic Concepts, Tools, and Information

Chapter 1

Diversity and Inclusion in Organizations

Basic Concepts

Diversity and inclusion (D&I) are central concepts in contemporary workplaces. Miscommunication often results from the fact that people use the same words but do always not mean the same thing. Therefore we begin by defining terms we will use throughout this text. What is diversity, what is inclusion, and how are they different from some other familiar terms?

Diversity and *Inclusion*—Where Do We Get These Terms?

When the word *diversity* first became popular in the 1980s, it referred to changes in demographic characteristics of the labor force and work organizations, particularly race, ethnicity, and sex. The workforce was expected to be more variable in the future in these demographic characteristics, and diversity seemed a good word to convey these differences. Later, some thought it would be useful also to consider other bases for diversity such as education levels, geographic background, language, value system, and other attributes. We can think of the first meaning as a *narrow* definition, and the expanded meaning as *broad*.

Subsequently, diversity managers and scholars have also begun considering *inclusion*. Early diversity work emphasized the process of *bringing into the work organization* those who were different than current employees in important ways. This is called *representational diversity*. However, practitioners and researchers began to see a pattern: women and ethnic minorities were hired but seldom progressed in the organization, and some even left in a fairly short time. Merely hiring people from underrepresented groups clearly is not sufficient to maintain diversity. Employers must also consider processes and factors that lead people of difference to become fully accepted and equally productive and rewarded at work. This state is called *inclusion*, without which newcomers, especially if from underrepresented groups, may feel like the *outsider within* (Collins, 1986); they may experience special stresses, resign prematurely, remain stagnated at entry levels in the organization, or even be terminated.

Some definitions of inclusion focus on how the employee feels and others refer to characteristics of the work organization, such as its processes and climate. Shore and her colleagues have reviewed the literature on inclusion and offer a definition incorporating both aspects: inclusion is "the degree to which an employee perceives that he or she is an esteemed member of the work group through experiencing treatment that satisfies his or her needs for belongingness and uniqueness" (Shore et al., 2011, p. 1265). This definition also highlights both a wish to be accepted as part of a group and a need for uniqueness. We'll settle on working definitions of diversity and inclusion after we consider how diversity is defined in different situations.

Why a Narrow Definition of Diversity?

There are several good reasons. First, the narrow usage refers to differences among people, such as sex, race, or disability, that have historically been the basis for important power differences and serious discrimination and hostility. Some of these differences are called *protected categories* because membership in these groups entitles one to legal protection against illegal discrimination. Some think these are the most common and most important bases for mal-treatment, and if the definition is expanded our focus on these historically significant and very serious differences will be diluted.

In addition, the narrow usage generally refers to *surface diversity*, meaning attributes of people that can easily be seen and thus often become the basis for stereotyping and misunderstanding. These dimensions are often important in social interaction and are familiar to most of us as potential bases for difficulties at work. They are also widely studied by social scientists.

Most of these differences relate to *ascribed status*: social position that is accorded to people because of who they are rather than what they have achieved. Most of these attributes are not under the person's control and cannot be changed at will through energy, effort, or talent. Some, such as sex and race, typically do not typically change throughout one's life, although we do get older and some of us may become disabled.

Some problems occur with this narrow definition, however. If everything in the diversity program seems to deal with women or ethnic minorities, it may be difficult to garner support from those in the more numerous or favored majority, typically White males, who see nothing positive, and even potential losses, for themselves. Diversity activities may become marginalized and seen only as relevant to *others*.

Another problem is that a narrow definition of diversity may lead to confusion of this term with others such as Equal Employment Opportunity (EEO) or Affirmative Action (AA), which have legal definitions and may be disliked or even reviled by those with negative experiences they attribute to these programs. The term EEO came into use in the Civil Rights era of the 1960s. An employer identifying as an Equal Opportunity Employer is stating publicly that all qualified applicants will have an equal chance for employment without fear of discrimination based on race, sex, religion, color, or ethnicity, the factors covered in Title VII of the Civil Rights Act of 1964. EEO ensures equal consideration, not preferential hiring.

AA means that an employer will conduct various kinds of outreach to find and attract qualified job applicants from underrepresented groups. AA is a requirement for the federal government and for any organization that contracts to do a significant amount of business with the federal government. Like EEO, AA does not require an employer to hire anyone, certainly not anyone unqualified for the job.

EEO is a *passive* statement saying only that an employer will not discriminate unfairly. AA is an *active* statement that the employer will act *affirmatively* or proactively to attract qualified applicants from groups that in the past were victims of unfair exclusion and discriminatory treatment. Although the terms AA and EEO are related to the idea of D&I, they mean something different. EEO and AA are addressed more fully in Chapters 2 and 7.

Why a Broad Definition?

First, many types of differences within organizations can cause problems in communication and interaction to which diversity concepts can be applied. Some examples are an employee's functional area (department or specialization), organizational level, geographic origin or accent, or personality and work style; any of these can be the basis for serious stereotyping and prejudice. Thinking of these as diversity issues improves our understanding of workplace dynamics and leads us to a broader range of research literature and techniques for addressing problems. For example, many studies exist on homogeneity vs. heterogeneity in problem-solving groups, based sometimes on sex but often on other types of differences.

A broader definition also encourages people to recognize that diversity initiatives can be beneficial for everyone. Often programs targeted at one group later become helpful to others. For example, mentoring programs or assistance with children's day care or elder care might first be designed for women but later prove very helpful for men as well. The broad definition also reduces confusion of diversity with EEO or AA, and it encourages us to think about differences whether or not they are addressed by fair employment law.

Finally, a broader definition reminds us that differences are *socially constructed*, meaning that what we consider "different" arises from social interaction and is context-relevant. The situation determines what differences are noticed and considered important. At work we may not even notice whether someone has brown eyes, but we usually are aware of a person's brown skin.

The major argument *against* using a broad definition of diversity is that it suggests all kinds of differences are equally important and worthy of our attention and resources. Surely, more damage has resulted from discrimination against ethnic minority individuals and women than from differences in personality, functional area, or work style. The late Elsie Cross, a widely respected diversity consultant, recounted the humiliation and pain of being unable to use the bathrooms in bus terminals during long trips because of her race. She saw a driver threaten a Black soldier with being shot for sitting in the front of a bus and persevered through many discriminatory educational and employment barriers that did not occur for most White women. Cross said, "When people today tell me that managing diversity is about 'all kinds of difference' I just look at them with amazement. Obviously, all difference is not treated the same" (2000, p. 23). From this perspective, it is a mistake to use diversity resources to address all kinds of difference rather than to correct the results of illegal and harmful discrimination.

The capable diversity manager will consider the context of a particular organization and chart a course for D&I that takes into consideration both the broad and the narrow views. Each is appropriate in some situations.

Diversity, Diversity Management, and Inclusion: Working Definitions

From a psychological perspective on diversity management, our concerns are the behaviors and feelings of different people and how organizations and managers can most effectively deal with these issues. Therefore, we will use the term *diversity* to mean "differences among people that are likely to affect their acceptance, performance, satisfaction, or progress in an organization" (Hays-Thomas, 2004, p. 12). Thus, diversity includes whatever differences are most significant in a particular organizational setting. *Managing diversity* concerns how organizations design processes and structures to make these differences into assets and sources of strength rather than liabilities and sources of weakness. More specifically, *diversity management* refers to planned and systematic programs and procedures designed to (a) improve interaction among diverse people; and (b) make this diversity a source of innovation and increased effectiveness rather than miscommunication, conflict, or obstacles to employees' performance, satisfaction, and advancement. *Inclusion* refers to one result of good diversity management practices: the acceptance, satisfaction, and progress of different groups of people. It applies especially to individuals and groups differing in sex, ethnicity, culture, ability status, sexual orientation, or other ways that are important in a particular organization.

Valuing Diversity

This term refers to activities or procedures intended to highlight in a positive way the uniqueness of various groups or individuals. For example, organizations may call attention to holidays or religious periods that are recognized by people of different faiths, ethnicities, or national origins. *Cinco de Mayo* celebrations are a common example. Although ethnic meals, dance exhibitions, and informative displays are interesting and positive in tone, they generally do little to address diversity conflicts that may exist in the employment setting. They can surely be part of a diversity management program, but by themselves they are not enough. Other things organizations can do are discussed in later chapters.

Why is Diversity Important?

Why should a manager, CEO, or HR staffer be concerned about diversity in the organization's workforce? The short answer is that workforce diversity affects every HR function in the organization as well as outcomes for employees (see Kossek & Lobel, 1996). Diversity relates to nearly every chapter in the typical industrial-organizational (I-O) psychology or management textbook.

Job Analysis and Design

One of the first steps in making decisions about employees is to identify what must be done in each job and how jobs relate to each other. In new or very small organizations, this is often done on an *ad hoc* basis, using "common sense" or judgment based on what the founder or owner has in mind. However, in existing or larger organizations, typically this is done through *job analysis*, which involves observing, interviewing, or surveying job incumbents and people in related jobs. For example, the job analyst might collect information from the supervisor or someone in another job who interacts frequently with the incumbent to accomplish work. A good job analysis produces a list of tasks, including those considered *essential functions*, as well as the list of the knowledges, skills, and abilities (KSAs) to be sought in applicants during the next process of *selection*.

Diversity should be considered in the job analysis process. For example, job analysis and KSAs may be suspect if they are not based on a representative sample of incumbents of different demographic characteristics. Furthermore, some attributes may be required because of how one job relates to others; for example, it would be useful for a supervisor to be able to speak some Spanish if she or he will supervise a number of Latino employees. Finally, in some cases incumbents in a particular job may be homogeneous in terms of race, ethnicity, sex, or other attributes. Separating the tasks and KSAs that characterize these people from the ones that are really needed to do the job well can be difficult. Perhaps other attributes or backgrounds not currently represented would lead to equal or better performance.

Selection

The hiring or selection function involves choosing people who have or can learn the necessary KSAs for the job in question. Diversity should be considered in this process for several reasons. First, sometimes an organization actively tries to diversify its pool of employees. Perhaps the company's customer base includes persons who differ from its employee group in primary language, racio-ethnicity, sex, religion, or other attributes, and product development or marketing could be improved by including these perspectives within the organization. Some organizations are following an AA plan or engaging in corrective action after an investigation or a lawsuit alleging discrimination.

Second, the measurement of job-relevant attributes may be affected by test-takers' backgrounds. Some commonly used tests may not accurately or fairly assess job-related skills if the individual possesses a disability or comes from a minority ethnic group with a background different than that of majority employees. For example, it is well documented that cognitive ability tests when used alone may underestimate the ability of minority employees to perform jobs like those of public safety employees (Outtz & Newman, 2010). This occurs because cognitive ability test scores are affected by things (such as test-taking skill) that are not associated with job performance. This problem can lead to elimination of racial minorities from hiring pools and result in discrimination charges or lawsuits. Alternative ways of measuring KSAs may be needed in the selection process to assess individuals accurately when they are from a different background than previous employees.

Third, organizations may find that their applicant pools are more diverse than in former years, and the selection process may require adaptation to take this into account. For example, in some settings it would be appropriate to provide testing instructions in various languages. In fact, increasing diversity in the nation's workforce is an important factor that led to the diversity movement.

Training and Socialization

When a newly hired employee joins an organization, or when an incumbent moves to a new job, typically he or she must learn about specific requirements of the new job as well as relevant policies, culture, and norms. *Training* refers to learning experiences specifically designed to focus on the job and work policies. Training may be provided for newcomers and for incumbents when a job is changed significantly or new policies are instituted. *Socialization* generally refers to the process of learning the culture, norms, and patterns of work behaviors and usually applies to informal experiences of those entering a work setting. Socialization may also be addressed through mentoring programs, employee orientation sessions, or written materials, but in some cases, it is simply assumed that the new employee will adapt by figuring these things out on his or her own. How is diversity related to these processes?

With respect to training, existing systems or programs may need to be adapted to the educational backgrounds, language capabilities, or learning styles of new employees who are different in important ways from the employees of the past. As another example, organizations may need to develop training experiences for new types of interpersonal interaction that are required by shifting customer bases or different employee attributes. One illustration is the *culture assimilator* (Fiedler, Mitchell, & Triandis, 1971), a training program developed to prepare those assigned to work in another country to interact effectively by learning how to behave appropriately and without giving offense.

Concerning organizational socialization, if a new employee comes from a background similar to those already employed—same college education, same sex or racio-ethnic group, for example— the person may already have absorbed some of the informal social knowledge about what is expected, how to dress, speak, and relate to others within the social system of the work organization. However, for the first person of color ever to serve in a particular role, the first woman to lead a particular work group, or a person from a religious or ethnic background that is unusual for the organization, some of those informal understandings may be difficult to anticipate or to master. One way to overcome this difficulty is a mentoring program in which a senior person knowledgeable about nuances of organizational life is partnered with a newcomer so that a broad range of career and psychosocial issues is part of discussions between them over time (Kram & Hall, 1996). Training and mentoring are discussed in Chapter 13.

Performance Appraisal/Evaluation

This term refers to the evaluation of *work performance*: how well people are doing their jobs. Performance reviews should be based on work assigned to employees. In larger organizations, there may be an annual cycle of formal performance evaluation; often it is part of a larger process that includes planning or goal-setting for a particular time period, evaluation of performance with respect to those goals, and decisions about performance-based monetary or other rewards (such as promotions, raises, bonuses, or awards). In a well-functioning organization, this formal system is supplemented by frequent informal feedback on things that are being done well and situations that require correction or, perhaps, discipline. Performance feedback is more helpful when one receives it shortly after the relevant behavior or event; this gives the employee guidance about what to continue or increase, and how to improve while there is still time to do so. How is diversity related to this process?

Most importantly, the performance appraisal process should not be biased by the sex, race, ethnicity, age, religion, or other attributes of workers that are not job-related. Many grievances and lawsuits have been filed, and some of them won, because employers evaluated and rewarded the job performance of men and women, or workers from majority groups and people of color, differently and unfairly, sometimes without realizing they were doing so. Furthermore, an employee who feels unfairly evaluated based on sex, ethnicity, or other non-job-related attributes will likely be dissatisfied and resentful and may respond with reduced effort and performance, poor attendance, or perhaps even dysfunctional behaviors such as theft.

Employees from a different background may not recognize the importance of aspects of work performance that are commonly understood among those who are more typical of the organization's members. For example, the importance of meeting deadlines or arriving at work on time varies among cultural groups with different interpretations of time. Expectations should be clear at the beginning and supervisors should be careful in making assumptions about what "everybody understands."

It's an organizational truism that people do those things for which they are rewarded. Therefore the performance appraisal and reward structure should be designed to emphasize what is important to the organization. If the work setting truly values diversity and the importance of inclusion and career development for workers of different backgrounds, then performance expectations and rewards for managers should explicitly reflect this expectation. In some organizations, how a manager deals with issues of D&I may be part of his or her work assignment and performance evaluation.

Job Evaluation and Compensation

The term *job evaluation* refers to a system for assigning worth to *jobs*, as distinguished from evaluation of the work performance of employees previously discussed. In larger organizations, there is usually a system for arranging jobs in a hierarchy based on job factors such as necessary skill and effort, difficulty of working conditions, or responsibility for people or money. The job evaluation process is designed to produce an ordering of jobs that is linked to compensation with the most important, difficult, and highly paid jobs at the top. However, this hierarchy is usually distorted by the fact of *occupational segregation*: in most organizations there is a pattern of certain jobs, job categories, or departments being filled predominantly by women or by men, or by people of color vs. Whites (Hegewisch, Liepmann, Hayes, & Hartmann, 2010; Jacobs, 1999). This results in part from explicit discrimination in the past, demographically-linked individual choices in education and careers, socialization patterns and role expectations typical for different groups of people, and other factors. Judgments about skill and other job factors can be biased by knowledge of the kinds of people who typically occupy a job or the typical level of pay for that work (Grams & Schwab, 1985). The term *wage gap* refers to the well-documented difference between annual earnings of men and women (or of Whites and ethnic minorities) working year-round and full-time. Though there are many reasons for this gap, one factor recognized by most experts is the influence of deliberate or unintentional bias based on demographic attributes of job incumbents. Examples abound: teaching, child or elder care, and secretarial, janitorial, and housekeeping work.

The point is that judgments about the importance of jobs, and related decisions about compensation, are often biased by the demographic attributes of the workers who perform those jobs. This topic is discussed in more detail in Chapter 4.

Group Processes and Leadership

When groups or teams are composed of people who differ from one another in important ways, two types of results may occur. First, differences in experience, demographic characteristics, personality, ability, or other attributes may lead to more effective work and a better product. For example, perhaps the task requires different types of expertise which would not be found in a homogeneous group. A diverse group may produce more creative ideas about how to approach tasks or problems. On the other hand, differences among people may also lead to communication problems or to conflicts related to different goals or expectations. Often the difference between harmony and productivity on the one hand, and conflict and crisis on the other, is how differences in a group are understood and managed. Important differences which are ignored or which are simply expected to be irrelevant are likely to be a source of difficulty among co-workers.

Leadership refers to processes of goal-oriented influence in group and organizational settings. Many different styles and leadership behaviors can be successful depending on factors like the nature of the task and the context, available resources, and expectations of followers. With respect to diversity, often there are differences in access to leadership positions or behavior and success in that role among people who are male or female or vary in age or racio-ethnicity. Effective leadership behavior may vary with follower characteristics, and the same leader behavior may be received differently when the leader is a member of a majority versus an underrepresented group. The effects and management of heterogeneity within work groups and the process of leadership are discussed in Chapter 8.

Organizational Change and Development

This term refers to processes and techniques that occur when leaders, consultants, or members of organizations attempt to improve internal relationships and success in accomplishing important goals. Sometimes organizational development (OD) techniques are used to diagnose and remedy problems among people or groups that impede the organization's success. At other times they are used when organizations are doing well but want to do better. How is this related to diversity?

As one example, consider two organizations that are merged. Perhaps one has bought out the other and the two cultures, employee groups, and work processes must be combined. This is even more difficult because some number of executives, managers, and employees are likely to lose their jobs in the process. One aspect of a successful merger is managing impacts on people when the organizations are combined.

Another example is, in fact, the management of diversity itself. Good diversity management is a form of OD. Some organizations may attempt to become more diverse in response to changes in customer base, applicant pools, or stakeholder expectations. In other cases, an organization becomes more diverse in ethnicity, age, sex, or other member attributes as circumstances change, and continued effectiveness may require different procedures or behaviors so that this increasing diversity is a source of strength for the organization. Chapter 14 addresses the use of OD techniques for improved diversity management.

Why is Diversity Important Now?[1]

After the major 1960s Civil Rights legislation discussed in Chapter 7, work organizations attended more to hiring of various demographic subgroups, particularly women and members of ethnic minorities. Processes such as AA resulted in increased demographic diversity at work. When employers found they could be sued for alleged discrimination, many put into place programs and processes that were required or that would reduce the likelihood of lawsuits.

The corporate world's emphasis on diversity management increased during a period in the 1980s when integration slowed as a result of conservative appointments to the judiciary, unfavorable court decisions, challenging legal procedures, and inadequate remedies. According to Paskoff (1996), "Diversity programs came into being in part as a response to this legal vacuum. Astute business people realized there were problems of discrimination in the workplace, and the law was not then a significant force in addressing them" (p. 47).

Other drivers of the diversity movement were real and perceived demographic changes in the workforce, changes in the structure of our economy and in the organization of work, and the development of the *business case* for diversity.

Actual Demographic Changes in the Workforce

The 2000 and 2010 census counts confirmed that the labor force was becoming more ethnically diverse. Since the 1990 census, the relative numbers of those identified as Hispanic (of any race) and Asian have increased. Non-Hispanic Whites, though still in the majority, have dropped proportionally and Blacks/African Americans have remained relatively constant. In 2000, for the first time respondents could indicate more than one race. Ten years later, the 2010 census showed an increase in this multiracial demographic identity. In addition, the age cohorts of the workforce are changing; the median age is rising and a generation of experienced workers is reaching retirement (SHRM, 2013). These patterns are discussed in more detail in Chapter 2.

(Mis)perceptions of Demographic Change

One major impetus for the diversity movement was the publication of *Workforce 2000* by the nonprofit Hudson Institute (Johnston & Packer, 1987). This book was widely claimed to show dramatic demographic changes to come. However, its huge impact actually resulted from a misinterpretation of the book's statistical portrayals, which was erroneously and widely repeated in the media.

Four trends were discussed in the book: (a) the economy would grow; (b) the manufacturing sector would shrink and service industries would increase; (c) many of these new service jobs would require higher levels of skill; and (d) the labor force would slowly become larger and would include more older workers, more females, and relatively fewer Whites. An illustration titled "Most New Entrants to the Labor Force Will be Non-White, Female, or Immigrants" (Figure 3.7, p. 95) showed percentages of the 1985 labor force in six demographic groups along with a bar graph for the same six groups labeled "Increase, 1985–2000." This was widely misunderstood (DiThomaso & Friedman, 1995). The second bar graph actually showed the percentage of *net* new entrants by 2000 for each demographic group, not the percentage of new entrants. *Net new entrants* refers to those in a particular group who join the labor force, minus those from that group who retire, die, or leave the workforce. The graph was inaccurately understood to show that only 15% of the *2000 workforce* would be "native white males," when actually it meant that 15% of the *net new entrants* would be in that category.

White males (WM) were the largest group of both current and new workers, and most were already in the labor force. Thus most WMs entering the workforce would simply replace others who were leaving, which was not true for other demographic categories. As a result, although WMs were increasing, their growth would be slower than that of the other categories, which were and remained smaller although drawing proportionally more new entrants. The confusion overstated the expected increase in diversity and led to the widespread belief that without extensive training, managers would have difficulty with this dramatically changed workforce. The movement quickly gathered steam as consultants rushed to provide workshops, articles, training materials, and trade books on *managing diversity*.

Changes in the Nature of Work

The contemporary focus on D&I has also been influenced by several work trends. These include globalization, the shift from manufacturing to service work, the electronic technology revolution, increased organization of work around teams rather than individual jobs, increased reliance on contingent workers, and several factors leading to greater instability in employment for many people.

Increased globalization means that today's work organizations function internationally or worldwide more than those of the past (Sweet & Meiksins, 2008). In Europe, national boundaries are more permeable due to the European Union and removal of many barriers to commerce and travel. More people work for US subsidiaries of foreign companies than ever before (Foulkes, Vachani, & Zaslow, 2006). Outsourcing or offshoring of jobs from the US to other countries has become commonplace, and even companies housed in the US do increased business in other countries (Farrell et al., 2005). For example, in 2013 the iconic American auto company, Ford, employed over 180,000 people with operations on every continent except Antarctica (Ford Motor Company, 2014). Competition occurs across national boundaries and US companies may own or be owned by foreign brands (Nestlé, 2014; Pepsico, n.d.). As a result, workers in the US increasingly collaborate with those in other countries; managers receive international assignments and travel across national borders to conduct business. The implication for diversity management is that customers, employees, and executives increasingly encounter others from different countries and cultures. (For an interesting example, see the shaded box.)

Beers Around the World

Know any Bud drinkers? This classic American beer is made by Anheuser-Busch, which was founded in 1852 in St. Louis (Anheuser-Busch, n.d.). In 2008 Anheuser-Busch was bought by the Belgian brewing company InBev and became part of the larger global company Anheuser-Busch InBev (ABInBev, 2008). This huge brewer advertises three *global beers* (Stella Artois, Corona, and Budweiser), three international labels (Leffe, Hoegaarden, and Beck's), and numerous *local champions* such as Bohemia, Bud Light, Labatt, and Löwenbräu.

Already the half-owner of Grupo Modelo, the Mexican company that makes Corona Beer, Anheuser-Busch InBev bought the other half in June 2012. Thus the maker of Budweiser expanded its beer labels and became a company with 150,000 employees in 24 companies around the world and annual sales of $47 billion! CEO Carlos Brito said, "There is tremendous opportunity from … expanding Grupo Modelo's brands worldwide through AB InBev's extensive global distribution network" (Sterling, 2012). With this sale, InBev's brands were introduced into the Mexican market. In November 2015 the company announced anticipated acquisition of SABMiller, a South African company, to become a "truly global brewer" (Bray, 2015).

To access the company's websites, one must be of legal drinking age. Because this varies by country, the viewer must enter his or her country as well as birthdate. This is just one minor complication resulting from the globalization of the brewing of beer!

Another change in recent years is shrinking of the manufacturing sector and growth in the service sector in this country. In 2014, about 13% of the workforce were found in production of nonagricultural goods while approximately 80% were in service jobs (Henderson, 2015) and this was expected to increase by 2024. In addition, even in manufacturing firms there are many service workers, such as those in human resources, housekeeping, or accounting. The growth of service work has major implications for diversity management.

Those who manufacture may seldom see or interact with those who use their product. However, service providers interact directly with the consumer (Gutek, 1995). To provide good service, the provider must be able to understand customers' needs and communicate clearly with them. Consider the difficulty of providing good diagnostic and health care services when patient and provider come from different cultures. Effective teachers must use language that their students understand; professionals, salespersons, and waitstaff must communicate effectively with clients and customers or sales and tips will suffer. Bridging diversity is critical in service work.

Another trend, the phenomenal growth in electronic communications across geographical boundaries and time zones, means that information can be exchanged 24 hours a day across language groups, geographic regions, and cultural divides (SHRM, 2013). Workers collaborate with others they have never met personally, virtual groups make decisions and solve problems, and less opportunity exists for the face-to-face interaction that leads to the development of group norms and interpersonal trust. Teleworking is more common, and managers may supervise people they seldom see. Anyone who has used electronic mail knows the increased possibility of misunderstanding due to lack of visual and vocal cues as well as body language. Texting, twittering, and other electronic postings may be so abbreviated that contextual cues are greatly reduced. In addition, socioeconomic class differences in technological access and competence at home and at work correlate with education and income levels.

In contemporary organizations work is increasingly likely to be organized around teams rather than individual jobs (Kozlowski & Bell, 2003). These may be short-term project teams or longer-term self-managing teams. Often they include people with diverse skill sets; cross-functional teams are deliberately constructed to include representatives from different functional areas that have a stake in the team's product. Teams are thought to have motivational, productivity, and quality advantages, and some believe they result in increased efficiencies (Cordery, 2003). The diversity implication is that group interaction across differences will increasingly be required.

At the same time, a significant portion of US workers have jobs with only tenuous connections to a particular workplace or group of co-workers (Barley & Kunda, 2006). *Contingent workers*, at minimum about 8% of the labor force, are those who do not have a contract for ongoing employment, either implicit or explicit, and often are short term. As many as 30–31% of employees are *contingent or alternative workers* when this term includes independent contractors, on-call workers, employees of temporary help agencies, or employees of contract firms that place them with another company (US Government Accountability Office, 2015). Some also include in the contingent work category the large group of voluntary or involuntary part-time employees, some of whom may have more than one job. Labor statistics show that almost one-quarter of those working in 2015 were part-timers (US Bureau of Labor Statistics; USBLS, 2016). From the diversity perspective, contingent and alternative employees have little time to learn to adapt to a new work setting and develop trust in co-workers. Adaptation is more challenging even for the core non-contingent workforce as others come and go. In addition, differences in pay or benefits of regular and contingent/alternative employees may be a source of potential friction.

Finally, compared to the post-World War II generation, today's workers experience employment as less stable. In January 2014, the median length of employment with current employer was only 4.6 years, rising slightly from 2008 due to job losses among those with least seniority (USBLS, 2014). According to the BLS (USBLS, 2015), US workers born between 1957 and 1964 held an average of 11.7 jobs from ages 18 to 48. Job instability increased due to the 2008 recession, and technological change has led to skill obsolescence and needs for retraining or replacement of employees. Organizations have reduced their employment rolls by downsizing or merging with other companies. As people move through jobs more frequently, there is increased need for flexibility in adapting to new faces at work.

The *Business Case* for Diversity

As the field matured, practitioners and scholars saw that if diversity initiatives were to succeed in work organizations, a convincing business rationale would be needed to show that this work should receive resources and administrative support. Robinson and Dechant (1997) explain that, "Other business initiatives that present more compelling, factual evidence of payback on investment win out over diversity initiatives, which seem to offer less predictable and tangible benefits" (p. 21). This led to development of the D&I *business case* that good diversity management leads to increased company profitability. This is also called the *bottom line* argument because it claims that good diversity management will improve the organization's bottom line on the profit and loss balance sheet. A related term, the *value-in-diversity* perspective, proposes that diversity is good for organizations, in contrast to the view that diversity is harmful to cohesion, communication, and productivity. The effective diversity manager must be able to articulate a business case for activities needed to manage D&I effectively in her or his company. What are the arguments for the business case?

Cox (1997) outlined conceptual arguments to justify diversity management efforts in terms of organizational profitability. He proposed several factors leading to increased revenue for an organization that manages diversity well. Note that these are not just arguments in favor of *diversity*; they argue for good *diversity management*.

1. Marketing strategy. Companies that are internally diverse will be more effective in understanding their increasingly more diverse customer/client base and probably make fewer ethnicity-related public relations blunders. A public relations advantage consists of being seen as a company that "does diversity well." (For another perspective on marketing, see the shaded box.)

Misunderstanding the Business Case Can Be Costly

Focusing on simple demographic diversity without considering inclusion can be a big mistake for businesses that may succeed in increasing representational diversity but in a way that creates unfair discrimination against members of underrepresented groups. Economists Marc Bendick, Jr., Mary Lou Egan, and Louis Lanier show how this can easily happen when employers engage in the "perverse practice" of matching employees to customers and markets similar to them in terms of ethnicity or sex (2010).

Bendick et al. dissected one aspect of the business case: that increasing diversity will improve a company's ability to market effectively to a more diverse customer base. They argued that focusing on diversity alone, rather than workplace inclusion, is a serious error that can place a company at legal risk. How can this happen, if one supposed benefit of diversity is reduced harassment, discrimination, and legal challenge? These authors gave actual examples from their research with a large grocery chain and from data on the advertising industry. Here's how it could happen.

"Neighborhood Stores" (a fictitious name for a real company) did a very good job of recruiting African Americans into entry-level management positions, showing much better results than the industry average. However, the corporation seemed to assume that these ethnic minority managers would do especially well in stores located in neighborhoods with many African American residents. These managers were much more likely to be assigned to minority neighborhoods (including Latino or Asian), and less likely to work in White and/or more affluent neighborhoods than their actual numbers would suggest. They were not matched to their customers in socioeconomic class, income, residence, and sometimes even ethnicity, which likely reduced the supposed marketing advantage of hiring them.

But more troubling was the fact that this assumption led to African American managers being disproportionately assigned to "career killer" stores with lower square footage, lower total sales, higher rates of theft by customers and employees, and more danger from crime and stress. Sales and shrinkage (loss of inventory, e.g., from theft) were important for performance ratings and bonuses. In addition, these managers were more likely to be overworked and thus less likely to complete assigned training exercises that were required for promotion! According to Bendick et al., "African American managerial employees on average received lower performance ratings, earned less, took longer to be promoted, and voluntarily quit the company sooner than their white counterparts" (p. 475). Eventually this led to a class action lawsuit, which the corporation settled quickly in order to reduce their financial risk and avoid losing public good will. The African American employees received considerable compensation and company employment practices were changed.

The authors pointed out another flaw in the company's diversity strategy. Because these employees were likely to resign before reaching store management, regional, and corporate levels, the presumed benefit of their ethnic knowledge was lost and they did not contribute to innovation, flexibility, or creativity.

Bendick and his colleagues also analyzed data from the advertising industry consistent with "the assumption that African Americans can be useful in advertising only in dealing with African American consumers and . . . associated products" (2010, p. 478). African Americans in advertising are likely to work in agencies with predominantly non-White employees and which specialize in targeting minority markets. When in other agencies, they are less likely than Whites to hold powerful and prestigious positions and to earn high incomes. (This was also true for women in comparison to men.) "Managers appear willing to credit white individuals with flexible or generic skills applicable in promoting a range of products to a range of market segments . . . (but for African Americans) discount such general skills, instead basing hiring, promotion, and assignment decisions solely on these employees' presumed understanding of their own racial group" (p. 479). This occurs despite the fact that these advertisers do not resemble their target audience in education, socioeconomic status, skill, or experience. According to the authors, "the guiding mindset is: All blacks know blacks, and they know nothing else" (p. 480).

These examples of "diversity without inclusion" (p. 481) show the problems that result from failure to incorporate those from underrepresented groups on the same terms as majority individuals. In an inclusive workplace, everyone is treated fairly and is equally able to access resources and opportunity and thus contribute to the success of the organization as well as themselves. Perhaps we should talk about the *business case for inclusion* as well as for diversity.

2. Resource acquisition. Talented minority applicants—and others—may be more likely to accept employment with a company that has a reputation for being *diversity friendly*. Employment benefits and procedures to address concerns of underrepresented groups may also be attractive to high ability employees from other backgrounds.

3. Better problem solving. Varied experience and knowledge of diverse employees should lead to a wider range of information and alternatives and better critical analyses. Group dynamics must be carefully managed for this to happen.

4. More creativity and innovation. This also should follow from the wider range of information and experience, but only if group processes are managed so that innovative ideas can emerge and compete for adoption.

5. Greater *system flexibility* (Cox & Blake, 1991). This term derives from Open Systems Theory, discussed in Chapter 2. An organization that is more diverse internally should be able to adapt more quickly to changed external conditions such as competition, changes in the economy or the labor market, or new laws or regulations.

Cox (1997) also proposed that well-managed organizational diversity can reduce an employer's costs, thus leading to an increase in profitability.

1. Lower absenteeism and turnover. Although diversity has been shown to increase withdrawal behaviors for minority individuals, if it is managed well this should shrink.
2. Reduced barriers to communication. In a well-managed diverse organization, sexism and racism should be lower and more opportunity should exist for members of underrepresented groups and others to contribute meaningfully.
3. More efficient and effective communications. Good diversity management should help avoid losses due to differences in language, communication style, and openness to feedback. Unmanaged, these can lead to dysfunctional silences and serious impairment in information flow.
4. Reduced harassment. Costs in lost productivity, absenteeism, turnover, and conflict can be very high. If intergroup relations are harmonious and harassment seldom or never occurs, costs should be lower.
5. Fewer discrimination lawsuits. Even if a company wins a legal challenge, costs are incurred for attorneys' fees, time required to deal with the situation, and stressful work environments. If the employee's case is strong, very large costs may be involved in settling the case or paying fines or damages. Fair and open treatment of employees regardless of protected class status should reduce these costs.

Arguments like these suggest that paying attention to management of differences among employees should be a cost-effective strategy. Anyone who has ever worked in a conflictual, inflexible work environment will find truth in that statement. Some of these predictions are borne out by studies of small groups in laboratory settings, but when researchers try to test these ideas in actual organizations, they sometimes but not always find support for the predictions.

We should not underestimate how difficult it is to establish convincing empirical evidence for the economic success of diversity management initiatives in actual work organizations. In laboratory experiments, treatments can be applied systematically and outside events can be controlled. In contrast, D&I initiatives are implemented in the messy real-world setting. Many things are going on simultaneously (e.g., changes in the economy, technology, key people, or product lines), so it is difficult to determine the factors that alone or in combination may have caused various outcomes. Benefits from D&I interventions can be undone by other events such as a new IT system or increased competition. The same intervention, such as diversity training, may be implemented differently each time it is offered as a function of the particular individuals involved and the dynamic contexts in which they work. With this in mind, what is the evidence for the business case?

First, surveys of HR and diversity professionals usually show that they believe programs for D&I are effective. For example, in a survey of HR professionals by SHRM and *Fortune* magazine, a majority reported benefits to organizational culture, employee recruitment, client relationships, creativity and productivity, and lower interpersonal conflict as a result of diversity initiatives (Bowl, 2001). Although these results are encouraging, they are opinions of people who may be responsible for managing the programs they are evaluating.

Turning to financial results, a group of business professors examined announcements of awards for outstanding AA programs by the US Department of Labor (DoL), and other announcements of financial damages awarded in the settlement of discrimination lawsuits. They found that stock prices of corporations rose after AA awards and declined following discrimination-related penalties (Wright, Ferris, Hiller, & Kroll, 1995). In another study (Richard, 2000), racial or cultural diversity alone were unrelated to measures of firms' financial performance. However, those firms with a growth strategy were more successful when more diverse. For firms that were downsizing, higher racial diversity was associated with lower productivity. This suggests that diversity's effects may depend on contextual factors in the organization, such as increasing opportunities associated with company growth.

Several studies have found that gender or racial diversity within a company is related to other positive outcomes. For example, Frink et al. (2003) found that firm performance increased as employment of women reached 50%, after which it decreased; thus maximum diversity was associated with best performance. In their second study, firms' income profitability (but not their productivity) was positively associated with the percentage of female employees, but only in service and sales organizations. Like the studies above, this suggests that the relationship of diversity to financial results is complex and limited by contextual factors.

Another example of focus on financials is a study by Catalyst (2004), a nonprofit corporate membership organization focusing on women and business. In that year Catalyst published research ranking 353 Fortune 500 companies based on representation of women in higher management. When the top and bottom fourths of these companies were compared, those with more women at the top showed over 30% higher financial performance in terms of dollar returns to shareholders! Although the measure of diversity was a narrow one, and the study does not tell us *why* the results occurred, in this case better financial performance did correlate with having more women in top management. A later study in 2007 also found this result (Joy, Carter, Wagner, & Narayanan, 2007).

A different research method was used by Herring (2009), a sociologist who analyzed survey data from a national sample of business organizations collected in 1996–1997. He found that racial diversity was associated with higher sales revenue and market share, more customers, and greater relative profit. Gender diversity was associated positively with sales revenue, customer, and relative profits. This study was archival (meaning that data had been collected previously and not specifically for the research purposes of his study) and therefore Herring's ability to investigate the *reasons* for his results was limited.

Complex results were also found by researchers who examined racial and gender diversity and business performance in four large firms in a study sponsored by the Diversity Research Network (Kochan et al., 2003). They found few direct effects of diversity on performance, either positive or negative. However, evidence showed that (a) racial diversity could enhance performance if the organization encouraged learning from diversity; (b) gender diversity sometimes had positive effects; (c) negative effects of diversity could be reduced by training and development activities; and (d) gender diversity was associated with fewer problems than racial diversity (however, women were generally more numerous than racial minorities). They concluded that attempts to manage diversity had generally worked to reduce negative outcomes, and that under some conditions well-managed diversity may improve performance. Eagly (2016) also cautioned that better understanding is needed of conditions that lead to positive or negative diversity effects and the social justice gains diversity may produce.

Deborah Litvin (2006) tried to "make space for a better case" for D&I by challenging the assumption that it must be justified in financial terms. She criticized studies of financial benefit and suggested that management of D&I should be justified on the basis of learning, personal development, and happiness of those working in organizations. A related ethical or moral argument is that *it's the right thing to do*.

Similarly, on the basis of their extensive study described above, Kochan et al. (2003) recommend revising the business case: "Diversity is a reality . . . today. To be successful . . . requires a sustained, systemic approach and long-term commitment. Success is facilitated by (considering) diversity to be an opportunity . . . to learn from each other . . . and an occasion that requires a supportive and cooperative organizational culture as well as group leadership and process skills" (p. 18). In other words, representational diversity does not by itself make an organization more profitable. However, diversity is a reality, and its potential negative impacts can be alleviated and sometimes reversed by climate, leadership, and interactional skills. This is a good transition to the rest of our text.

Looking Forward

In the following chapters, we will cover additional fundamental concepts and information related to D&I (Part I), followed by consideration of how organizations work in terms of their structure and process (Part II). Next these ideas are applied in contexts such as legal challenges, teams and work groups, and diversity based on various dimensions of difference (Part III). Our text concludes by considering possible solutions for managing D&I effectively (Part IV).

Note

1   This section draws heavily on Hays-Thomas (2004).

References

ABInBev (2008). *Press release: InBev completes acquisition of Anheuser-Busch.* Retrieved from www.ab-inbev.com/content/dam/universaltemplate/abinbev/pdf/press-releases/public/2008/11/20081118_1_e.pdf

Anheuser-Busch. (n.d.) *Great people make a company great.* Retrieved from http://anheuser-busch.com/index.php/our-company/about-anheuser-busch/

Barley, S. R., & Kunda, G. (2006). Itinerant professionals: Technical contractors in a knowledge economy. In E. E. Lawler & J. O'Toole (Eds.), *America at work: Choices and challenges* (pp. 173–191). New York: Palgrave Macmillan.

Bendick, M., Jr., Egan, M. L., & Lanier, L. (2010). The business case for diversity and the perverse practice of matching employees to customers. *Personnel Review, 39,* 468–486.

Bowl, K. (2001, July). Diversity means good business, survey says. *HR News, 46,* 12.

Bray, C. (2015, November 11). Anheuser-Busch InBev completes agreement for SABMiller. *The New York Times.* Retrieved from www.nytimes.com/2015/11/12/business/dealbook/anheuser-busch-inbev-sabmiller-deal.html?_r=0

Catalyst. (2004). *The bottom line: Connecting corporate performance and gender diversity: Executive summary.* Retrieved from http://catalyst.org/knowledge/bottom-line-corporate-performance-and-womens-representation-boards

Collins, P. H. (1986). Learning from the Outsider Within: The sociological significance of black feminist thought. *Social Problems, 33,* S14–S32.

Cordery, J. (2003). Team work. In D. Holman, T. D. Wall, C. W. Clegg, P. Sparrow, & A. Howard (Eds.), *The new workplace: A guide to the human impact of modern working practices* (pp. 95–114). Hoboken, NJ: Wiley.

Cox, T., Jr. (1997). Linkages between managing diversity and organizational performance. In T. Cox, Jr., & R. L. Beale (Eds.), *Developing competency to manage diversity: Readings, cases & activities* (pp. 35–43). San Francisco, CA: Berrett-Koehler Publishers.

Cox, T. H., Jr., & Blake, S. (1991). Managing cultural diversity: Implications for organizational competitiveness. *Academy of Management Executive, 5*(3), 45–56.

Cross, E. Y. (2000). *Managing diversity: The courage to lead.* Westport, CT: Quorum Books.

DiThomaso, N., & Friedman, J. J. (1995). A sociological commentary on Workforce 2000. In D. B. Bills (Ed.), *The new modern times: Factors reshaping the world of work* (pp. 207–233). Albany: State University of New York Press.

*Eagly, A. H. (2016). When passionate advocates meet research on diversity, does the honest broker stand a chance? *Journal of Social Issues, 72,* 199–222.

Farrell, D., Laboissiére, M., Pascal, R., de Segundo, C., Rosenfeld, J., Sturze, S., & Umezawa, F. (2005, June). The emerging global labor market. *McKinsey Global Institute.* Retrieved from www.mckinsey.com/insights/mgi/research/labor_markets/the_emerging_global_labor_market

Fiedler, F. E., Mitchell, T., & Triandis, H. C. (1971). The culture assimilator: An approach to cross-cultural training. *Journal of Applied Psychology, 55,* 95–102.

Ford Motor Company (2014, March 13). *2013 Annual Report: Employment data.* Retrieved from http://corporate.ford.com/ar/annual-report-2013/doc/ar2013-employment_data.pdf

Foulkes, F. K., Vachani, S., & Zaslow, J. (2006). Global sourcing of talent: Implications for the U.S. Workforce. In E. E. Lawler & J. O'Toole (Eds.), *America at work: Choices and challenges* (pp. 257–273). New York: Palgrave Macmillan.

Frink, D. D., Robinson, R. K., Reithel, B., Arthur, M. M., Ammeter, A.P., Ferris, G. R, . . . & Morrisette, H. S. (2003). Gender demography and organizational performance: A two-study investigation with convergence. *Group and Organization Management, 28,* 127–147.

Grams, R., & Schwab, D. P. (1985). An investigation of systematic gender-related error in job evaluation. *Academy of Management Journal, 28,* 279–290.

Gutek, B. A. (1995). *The dynamics of service: Reflections on the changing nature of customer/provider interactions.* San Francisco, CA: Jossey-Bass.

Hays-Thomas, R. (2004). Why now? The contemporary focus on managing diversity. In M. S. Stockdale & F. J. Crosby (Eds.), *The psychology and management of workplace diversity* (pp. 3–30). Malden, MA: Blackwell.

Hegewisch, A., Liepmann, H., Hayes, J. & Hartmann, H. (2010, August). *Separate and not equal? Gender segregation in the labor marker and the gender wage gap* (IWPR C377). Retrieved from www.iwpr.org/publications/pubs/separate-and-not-equal-gender-segregation-in-the-labor-market-and-the-gender-wage-gap

Henderson, R. (2015, December). Industry employment and output projections to 2024. *Monthly Labor Review.* Retrieved from www.bls.gov/opub/mlr/2015/article/industry-employment-and-output-projections-to-2024-1.htm

Herring, C. (2009). Does diversity pay? Race, gender, and the business case for diversity. *American Sociological Review, 74,* 208–224.

Jacobs, J. A. (1999). The sex segregation of occupations: Prospects for the 21st century. In G. N. Powell (Ed.), *Handbook of gender & work* (pp. 125–139). Thousand Oaks, CA: Sage.

Johnston, W. B., & Packer, A. H. (1987). *Workforce 2000.* Indianapolis, IN: Hudson Institute.

Joy, L., Carter, N. M., Wagner, H. M., & Narayanan, S. (2007, October 15). *The bottom line: Corporate performance and women's representation on boards.* Retrieved from http://catalyst.org/knowledge/bottom-line-corporate-performance-and-womens-representation-boards

Kochan, T., Bezrukova, K., Ely, R., Jackson, S., Joshi, A., Jehn, K., . . . Thomas, D. (2003). The effects of diversity on business performance: Report of the Diversity Research Network. *Human Resource Management, 42,* 3–21.

Kossek, E. E., & Lobel, S. A. (Eds.) (1996). *Managing diversity: Human resource strategies for transforming the workplace.* Cambridge, MA: Blackwell.

Kozlowski, S. W. J., & Bell, B. S. (2003). Work groups and teams in organizations. In W. C. Borman, D. R. Ilgen, & R. J. Klimoski (Eds.), *Handbook of Psychology: Industrial and organizational psychology* (Vol. 12, pp. 333–375). New York: Wiley.

Kram, K. E., & Hall, D. T. (1996). Mentoring in a context of diversity and turbulence. In E. E. Kossek & S. A. Lobel (Eds.), *Managing diversity: Human resource strategies for transforming the workplace* (pp. 108–136). Cambridge, MA: Blackwell.

Litvin, D. R. (2006). Diversity: Making space for a better case. In A. M. Konrad, P. Prasad, & J. K. Pringle (Eds.), *Handbook of workplace diversity* (pp. 15–94). Thousand Oaks, CA: Sage.

Nestlé. (2014). *Nestlé: About us.* Retrieved from www.nestle.com/aboutus

Outtz, J. L., & Newman, D. A. (2010). A theory of adverse impact. In J. L. Outtz (Ed.), *Adverse impact* (pp. 53–94). New York: Routledge.

Paskoff, S. M. (1996). Ending the workplace diversity wars. *Training, 33*(8), 42–47.

Pepsico. (n.d.). *Pepsico: Who we are.* Retrieved from www.pepsico.com/Company

Richard, O. C. (2000). Racial diversity, business strategy, and firm performance: A resource-based view. *Academy of Management Journal, 43,* 164–177.

Robinson, G., & Dechant, K. (1997). Building a business case for diversity. *Academy of Management Executive, 11,* (3), 21–31.

Shore, L. M., Randel, A. E., Chung, B. G., Dean, M. A., Ehrhart, K. H., & Singh, G. (2011). Inclusion and diversity in work groups: A review and model for future research. *Journal of Management, 37,* 1262–1289.

Society for Human Resource Management. (2013, May). *SHRM workplace forecast.* Retrieved from www.shrm. org/research/futureworkplacetrends/documents/13-0146%20workplace_forecast_full_fnl.pdf

Sterling, T. (2012, June 30). InBev to buy out Modelo for $20.1B. *Pensacola News-Journal,* p. 6C.

Sweet, S., & Meiksins, P. (2008). *Changing contours of work: Jobs and opportunities in the new economy.* Thousand Oaks, CA: Pine Forge Press.

US Bureau of Labor Statistics (2014, September 18). *Employee tenure summary: Employee tenure in 2014.* Retrieved from http://data.bls.gov/cgi-bin/print.pl/news.release/tenure.nr0.htm

US Bureau of Labor Statistics (2015, March 31). *Number of jobs held, labor market activity, and earnings growth among the youngest baby boomers: Results from a longitudinal survey.* Retrieved from www.bls.gov/news.release/pdf/nlsoy. pdf

US Bureau of Labor Statistics (2016). *Current Population Survey: Household data annual averages* (Table 8.). Retrieved from www.bls.gov/cps/cpsaat08.pdf

US Government Accountability Office. (2015, April 20). *Contingent workforce: Size, characteristics, earnings, and benefits.* Retrieved from www.gao.gov/assets/670/669766.pdf

Wright, P., Ferris, S. P., Hiller, J. S., & Kroll, M. (1995). Competitiveness through management of diversity: Effects on stock price valuation. *Academy of Management Journal, 38,* 272–287.

* Recommended for advanced reading.

Chapter 2

Conceptualizing and Measuring Difference

The preceding chapter showed the importance of increased workforce diversity in the growth of the D&I movement. Demographic diversity, especially sex and race, is probably the diversity that people notice most quickly and most often. However, it is not the only diversity that is important for inclusion, productivity, and organizational success. Before discussing other diversity dimensions, we will consider how diversity is understood in work organizations. Not everyone agrees on the meaning of diversity and what should be done about it.

Models: Clarifying What We Mean

Sometimes to understand a complex situation, a *model* can illustrate clearly and simply the variables believed to interact in that situation. Models are usually proposed by scholars as a statement of what they think is important based on research or experience. Because models simplify, they are necessarily incomplete. They may also be more or less accurate and should be tested as they are applied. A good model helps by:

1. Identifying factors and relationships thought to be important.
2. Communicating these ideas clearly to others.
3. Helping us to remember the important variables.
4. Estimating or predicting what will happen if something changes, and guiding actions taken to alter the situation.
5. Suggesting things that have been overlooked or not fully understood.

The "Culinary Model" of Organizational Diversity

An early metaphor for diversity was the "jelly bean model" described by Roosevelt Thomas (1996), who imagined a jar of jelly beans that are all one color. Next jelly beans of other colors are added. Is this diversity? According to Thomas, some people identify the new colors as the diversity in the jar. He said instead that diversity refers to the *whole mixture of different colored beans*. Someone concerned with diversity will consider not only the new and different persons, but the entire social system and the differences represented within it. Which jelly beans are "diverse"? The red, yellow, or black ones? No—the mixture itself is diverse.

Thomas's jelly bean metaphor clarifies that diversity pertains to the collective, but is inadequate on another point. When we add jelly beans of different colors to the jar, each bean retains its own color and flavor and is not affected by its proximity to other beans. However, in social settings people who are different *do* influence one another. People learn, react positively or negatively, conform, develop friendships or cliques, and in other ways develop or reject relationships with others who are different. Thus this simple metaphor identifies an important aspect that has been omitted.

Jelly beans can be eaten one at a time, maintaining the separate flavor of each color. But in a *salad*, the lettuce, cucumbers, tomatoes, and other ingredients are tossed and usually eaten together, accented by a dressing that unites them. Ingredients contrast with and complement each other. Most diners would probably find a bowl of lettuce less interesting than a good tossed salad; the various components make the mixture more diverse, colorful, and tasty. Components retain their own shape, color, and texture; still, someone who *really* did not like cucumbers could pick them out of the salad. This diversity metaphor shows that components, though better in combination, retain their own individuality and in some sense remain separate. Is this what diversity means?

Consider, in contrast, a bowl of stew or chunky soup. The meat and vegetables have been cooked together so the various parts are still identifiable in taste and texture. However, unlike a salad, each is affected by the presence of the others in a way that cannot be undone by removing one of them. The delicious gravy is the product of the collective simmering and gives character to the mixture that is *different* from that of the individual ingredients. Even if onions are removed, their pungent flavor would already have affected the taste of the other components and the gravy. This is yet another image of organizational diversity.

Compare this with tomato sauce, in which the ingredients have been combined and cooked together until they blend into one homogenous thick substance differing from any of the components. Tomatoes and onions and garlic can't be found any more; they have been completely blended or assimilated into the new substance. The *melting pot* expression implies that new ingredients (people) are absorbed into the sauce or culture of the old so that their original attributes are no longer recognizable.

Which best represents organizational diversity? Some organizations behave as if it is sufficient to just add new people who are different, like jelly beans. Nobody has to change, or even interact much with others. In other settings the salad bowl version of diversity seems applicable because different kinds of people are *represented* but don't really have to adapt to be part of the larger group; they still retain a high degree of separateness. In other cases, diversity means that people with differing backgrounds join together in a way that maintains some aspects of individuality and separateness while creating a new milieu to which all contribute, like a good stew. Sometimes diversity is expected to eliminate major differences among people so that everyone becomes equally a part of the wider whole, like a tomato sauce. In other cases *assimilation* is only expected for newcomers or certain kinds of people in the organization who are not from the predominant group. (After all, it's called *TOMATO* sauce, which identifies the "dominant majority" in this combination.) A key variable is the *process* by which people become part of the larger group: Who is expected to change, and to what degree? This simple culinary model highlights a basic puzzle in the field of diversity management.

Scholarly Models of Organizational Diversity

Early models categorized organizations on their approach to D&I; usually categories differed in how diversity was conceptualized and the dominant process by which newcomers changed. Later more complex models proposed a set of interacting processes that produced outcomes relevant to D&I. In contrasting the simple models in this first group, consider (a) the desired end state that is implied; (b) the process and direction by which change occurs; and (c) whether the organizational types seem to be *stages*. In psychology this word implies *qualitatively different periods* occurring in a *fixed chronological order and rate*. In normal development there is usually *no provision for "going back"* or regressing once one has attained a particular stage.

Three Organizational Conditions: R. Roosevelt Thomas, Jr.

In his earliest book (1991) Thomas described three strategies for incorporating women and ethnic minorities into the business world. At that time, diversity issues were defined narrowly in terms of gender and race, and theoretical perspectives on diversity were just beginning to develop.

The first strategy, *Affirmative Action (AA),* assumes that women and ethnic minorities have been excluded from full participation in organizations due to prejudice and that such restrictions are not economically sound, moral, or good public policy. This strategy implies that without intervention, that condition will not change. Therefore, some degree of coercion by laws and social norms is needed to effect change. Executives may work to eliminate blatant prejudice and comply with legal requirements, relying on AA training for White men and a "color-blind" approach (*passive scenario*). Or, out of concern about corporate social responsibility as well as legal requirements, they may increase outreach and programs aimed at assimilation of underrepresented groups (*pipeline scenario*). If this does not improve retention, they may develop stronger AA and special programs to deal with bias in the organization's policies and procedures (*upward mobility scenario*).

Thomas's second strategy is called *Valuing Differences (VD),* and builds upon an AA environment with activities to increase awareness of and respect for difference. Diversity is seen as an asset and the goal is increased knowledge, acceptance, and tolerance. The VD approach could include *diversity days* highlighting food or culture of various ethnic groups, or activities emphasizing increased self-understanding and other-acceptance. However, these do not change the fundamental ways in which the organization operates.

The third strategy, *Managing Diversity (MD),* recognizes that existing organizational systems (e.g., recruiting, hiring, performance appraisal) may prevent full incorporation of and benefit from people who are different from the majority. Still recognizing the need for legal compliance and AA, this strategy asks what must be changed for the organization to work smoothly and productively for everyone regardless of gender, ethnicity, or other bases of diversity. The MD strategy is a form of *organizational development.* Because it requires systemic changes in fundamental procedures and policies, this strategy takes more time, commitment, and expertise than the other two strategies.

The AA, VD, and MD strategies reflect different levels of understanding and motivation to work with diversity as a basis for the organization's competitive advantage. Do they seem like stages in development of an organization's diversity responsiveness? Can an organization function at the MD level without passing through AA and VD first? Can an organization regress, and having functioned well at MD, later slip back into VD or AA? Who or what is the focus of change in each strategy? Figure 2.1 shows some questions that illustrate these strategies and might help an HR manager or diversity professional determine which best characterizes his or her organization.

1. Diversity is a non-issue in my organization.
2. In my organization, there's an emphasis on whether people will "fit in."
3. If a woman or non-White man is hired or promoted into a responsible position in my organization, people are likely to say it was because of affirmative action rather than the person's qualifications.
4. Our training on these issues focuses mainly on what's legally required or prohibited.
5. My organization's diversity efforts focus on improving the quality of interpersonal relationships among employees.
6. Our training focuses on appreciating cultural differences, such as music or food.
7. Management in my organization believes that we will get better ideas and more innovation if we hire people who are different from those already on board.
8. People of color are employed at all levels in my organization.

Key: items 1–2 indicate a pre-Affirmative Action organization; 3–4 Affirmative Action; 5–6 Valuing Diversity; and 7–8 Managing Diversity. Where does your organization fall? A diversity mature organization would probably fit items 7 and 8.

Figure 2.1 Diversity Diagnosis: Organizational Diversity Strategies

Three Organizational Paradigms: Thomas and Ely

The premise of this model (1996) is that how diversity is managed and its implications for the organization depend on the perspectives or *paradigms* of organizational leaders. The *Discrimination-and-Fairness* paradigm emphasizes fairness and legal compliance as reasons to change the organization's employees and structure to become more representative of society. Recruitment and retention of diverse employees are used as indicators of success. According to Thomas and Ely (1996), this paradigm reflects leaders' emphasis on equal treatment and due process and a top-down approach to implementing change, as well as a clear and solidly established culture. Although this paradigm may lead to increasing employee diversity and more equitable treatment, its emphasis on assimilation and "culture-blindness" may also prevent the organization from learning and benefiting from its increasing diversity.

In the *Access-and-Legitimacy* paradigm, leaders work to increase diversity, thinking that it will improve access and response to diverse customer bases, leading to better customer service and thus more business success. This paradigm is most likely when success depends on ability to respond to increased external diversity in potential employees or customers. This *bottom line* emphasis means that diversity initiatives will make sense to employees and likely have their support. On the other hand, it may lead to emphasizing observable characteristics of certain employees and assigning them to specialized work (e.g., AA officer or sales agent for minority accounts). Thus others do not learn from their expertise, and some employees may feel the organization is profiting from their difference by confining them to certain types of work or positions.

Some employers evolve to a more nuanced perspective on diversity, allowing them to benefit in expanded ways through the *Learning-and-Effectiveness* paradigm. Like *Discrimination-and-Fairness*, this paradigm promotes equal opportunity and fairness. Like *Access-and-Legitimacy*, it attends to those aspects that differentiate people in useful ways. But it goes beyond these paradigms by "internaliz(ing) differences among employees so that (the organization) learns and grows because of them" (Thomas & Ely, 1996, p. 86). Thus diversity's benefits extend throughout the organization as it becomes truly multicultural. Factors needed for an organization to use the *Learning-and-Effectiveness* paradigm include organizational leadership and culture, and a structure that encourages innovation and sharing of new ideas.

Three Organization Types: Taylor Cox

A more complex perspective was suggested by Cox (1991, 1993/1994). Key to understanding Cox's typology are four types of *acculturation* (Cox & Finley-Nickelson, 1991). Acculturation refers to change in norms, expectations, and other aspects of the cultures of two or more groups as they combine and adjust. First, in *assimilation*, members of the minority community are expected to adapt to the dominant group's culture, leaving their own behind. This has been an important form of acculturation in the history of the US. For example, immigrant groups have been expected to enter the American melting pot, give up their native languages, and adopt the culture of communities they entered. Forced assimilation also occurred with Native Americans and with Africans imported to this country as slaves.

In contrast, when *separation* occurs, an incoming group resists adaptation and continues to function without significant change within pockets of the larger system. Some immigrant groups settle in *ethnic enclaves* and maintain their language and customs while interacting only minimally with the broader culture—often until the next generation. In the third acculturation process, change occurs in both directions; each group adapts in some ways to the culture of the other. We might think of a good marriage or friendship as embodying this type of adjustment, which for clarity we will call *mutual adaptation*. Finally, the primary or receiving culture may weaken and be displaced by a confusing, chaotic, and unstable new reality through a process called *deculturation*.

Cox proposed that with respect to internal diversity climate, three types of organizations differ in the pattern by which the minority is incorporated into the majority. First, Cox (1991, 1993/1994) described the *monolithic* organization as internally homogeneous in terms of culture and demographic characteristics. The few people who differ in sex or race are likely to be located together in certain parts or job categories of lower status in the organization. Organizational systems and norms reflect those of the dominant majority (usually White men), and others are expected to *assimilate* to this biased environment. For this reason, conflict is infrequent. In the US today, this form is probably rare, at least among large organizations subject to fair employment legislation or AA requirements. However, it may exist among small businesses or in private or religious institutions.

A second type, which Cox proposed is typical among large US organizations today, is the *plural* organization. Superficially diverse, this type has more members of different races and sexes, but they are likely to work mainly in certain areas or levels of the organization and socialize only on a limited basis across these divides. The organization may be technically compliant with AA and fair employment practices and have programs to recruit, hire, and develop persons from underrepresented groups. However, its HR systems remain biased. Influential managers are predominantly White males and others are still expected to assimilate and adapt. Cultural differences and resulting resentments among employees, both majority and minority, produce tension and conflict. Though Cox does not say this, it seems likely that in this type of organization there may also be separation as subgroups maintain their own ways while conforming superficially to the most important and public expectations of the dominant majority.

Third, in the true *multicultural* organization, which Cox believed is seldom fully realized, diversity is valued and appreciated. HR systems show little or no cultural bias; as different types of people spread throughout the organization formally and informally, both they and the organization change in a process of two-way acculturation or mutual adaptation. Because diversity is valued and managed well, there is minimal conflict. The multicultural organization results from a conscious and deliberate pattern of two-way change as people and systems adapt to support an inclusive environment. This is probably an organizational ideal rather than a frequent accomplishment among work organizations.

Cox's model highlights processes by which different people move within parts of the organization. *Informal integration* refers to social and casual inclusion of different others into the organization, and *structural integration* refers to their placement in a variety of areas (e.g., departments, jobs, levels) within the larger entity. When informal integration is high, people of different ethnicities, races, and ages would be found eating lunch together, socializing at company events, or participating together in organizational athletic or community service activities. With high structural integration, women or persons of minority demographic backgrounds are spread throughout the jobs, departments, decision-making bodies, and layers of the organization, including those which are most prestigious and highest paying.

Cox's Interactional Model

These ideas are part of a complex model depicting how diversity in an organization impacts career outcomes of individuals and overall effectiveness of the organization. This *Interactional Model* (Cox, 1993/1994) has been reproduced in Figure 2.2, slightly modified as described below.

Cox proposed that Diversity Climate (DC) consists of three factors: behavior and characteristics of individuals (*Individual Level*), relations among organizational subgroups (*Group/Intergroup Factors*), and aspects of the organization as a whole (*Organizational-Level Factors*). DC affects Career Outcomes for Individuals, which in turn influences Organizational Effectiveness. The effect of DC on organizational effectiveness is *indirect* (shown by short interior arrows) because it works *through* impacts on individuals in the *Equal Opportunity and Motivation to Contribute* process. That is, DC leads

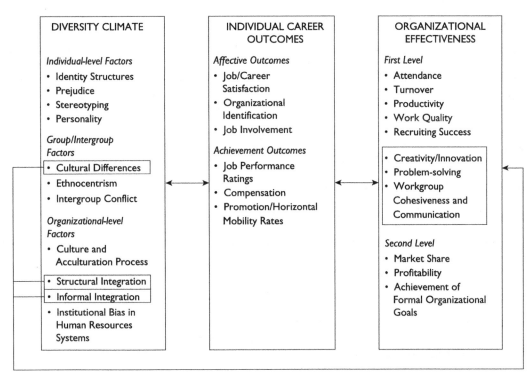

DIVERSITY CLIMATE	INDIVIDUAL CAREER OUTCOMES	ORGANIZATIONAL EFFECTIVENESS
Individual-level Factors • Identity Structures • Prejudice • Stereotyping • Personality *Group/Intergroup Factors* • Cultural Differences • Ethnocentrism • Intergroup Conflict *Organizational-level Factors* • Culture and Acculturation Process • Structural Integration • Informal Integration • Institutional Bias in Human Resources Systems	*Affective Outcomes* • Job/Career Satisfaction • Organizational Identification • Job Involvement *Achievement Outcomes* • Job Performance Ratings • Compensation • Promotion/Horizontal Mobility Rates	*First Level* • Attendance • Turnover • Productivity • Work Quality • Recruiting Success • Creativity/Innovation • Problem-solving • Workgroup Cohesiveness and Communication *Second Level* • Market Share • Profitability • Achievement of Formal Organizational Goals

Figure 2.2 An Interactional Model of the Impact of Diversity on Individual Career Outcomes and Organizational Effectiveness. Adapted and reproduced by permission from Cox (1993/1994). *Cultural diversity in organizations: Theory, research, and practice.* San Francisco, CA: Berrett-Koehler Publishers.

to Career Outcomes that consist of feelings *(Affective Outcomes)* and objective success *(Achievement Outcomes)* for individuals, which in turn influence overall organizational effectiveness.

In addition, some aspects of DC and Organizational Effectiveness are shown within small boxes to indicate *direct* impacts. That is, Cultural Differences and Structural and Informal Integration also have direct impacts on Organizational Effectiveness by altering Creativity and Innovation; Quality of Problem-solving; and Cohesiveness and Communication of Workgroups. This direct effect operates through the *Value in Diversity* route and is indicated by the long external arrow around the bottom of the model.

But couldn't some effects be bidirectional? This possibility is shown by the double-headed interior arrows (modified from Cox, 1993/1994). For example, if achievement outcomes are low for individuals from underrepresented groups, this could impact Prejudice, Stereotyping, Intergroup Conflict, Structural and Informal Integration, and other DC factors. Further, any diversity-related changes in turnover rates, recruiting success, or profitability might influence things like individuals' Job Satisfaction and Levels of Compensation, which in turn affect aspects of DC.

Together, the Cox models (1991, 1993/1994) present a typology of organizations and describe processes by which diversity in organizations (or the lack thereof) impacts the level of success of individuals *and* of the entire organization. The Interactional Model identifies factors and indicators that could be used to test the effects of increased organizational diversity. Acculturation processes are highlighted as a critical indicator of DC and the models show that diversity creates many and complex effects at different levels within the organization.

How do they differ from the earlier models? How would the Interactional Model operate in the three organizational types? Could these models be used to diagnose diversity strengths or problems in an organization? Is anything missing or unnecessary?

Scholarly Models of Diversity Management

The models discussed above conceptualize how diversity functions in an organization. Other models of processes in management of D&I are discussed in later chapters. These include models of *diversity competence* for individuals and organizations (Cox & Beale, 1997) and organizational change models (Agars & Kottke, 2004; Cox, 2001). Next we turn to ideas about different sorts of diversity.

Diversity Constructs: The Nature of Diversity

Surface- vs. Deep-level Diversity

Early models implicitly conceived of diversity as based on demographic characteristics such as racio-ethnicity or sex. However, some scholars considered diversity more broadly. Social psychologists Jackson, May, and Whitney (1995) distinguished between easily detectable differences and underlying attributes with implications for the group's task, internal relationships, or both. Their organizing framework showed how *content* (the differences themselves, e.g., age, skill) and *structure* (how differences are distributed) could change individual and social processes, thus altering behaviors and outcomes. Management researchers Milliken and Martins (1996) differentiated between diversity in observable characteristics and diversity in attributes that appear only with extended interaction (e.g., functional background, personality) and modeled how diversity could affect outcomes for individuals, groups, and organizations.

This distinction between apparent and underlying differences was popularized by Harrison, Price, and Bell (1998) in their study of *surface-* and *deep-level* diversity and social cohesion of small work groups. Surface-level diversity referred to visible differences among people (e.g., age, disability status), and deep-level diversity concerned differences that became apparent as individuals interacted, such as personality, cognitive skills, attitudes or values. In hospital and deli-bakery settings, work group cohesion was *negatively* related to surface diversity (age, sex, racio-ethnicity) for short-term groups. However, when groups worked together longer, the effect of surface diversity declined and deep-level diversity became more important in understanding work group cohesion. Think about a group situation in which you did not know the people very well. What were your initial impressions of others? On what were they based? Did your views of others and your relationships change over time?

Separation, Variety, and Disparity

As more research on diversity's effects was published, results were inconsistent. Sometimes diversity led to better group performance, sometimes not. Inconsistent research results occur when hypotheses are simply wrong; when important variables have been omitted or treated in different ways; or when further conceptualization is needed. Harrison and Klein (2007) suggested it was time to step back and reconceptualize what diversity meant.

First, Harrison and Klein (2007) clarified that "diversity" applies to a group or collection, not to an individual. If someone says "30% of our students are diverse," it suggests the speaker is not well informed about D&I. (Usually the person means that 30% are people of color.) "Diverse" does not mean "minority." Consider that most students at a historically Black college or university (HBCU) are Black, but some HBCU student bodies are not very diverse.

Harrison and Klein described three types of diversity, called *separation, variety,* and *disparity. Separation* occurs when people differ *quantitatively* along one dimension, such as liking for football (or a particular team). Separation usually characterizes attitudes, opinions, or values with which people may agree or disagree to different degrees. Harrison and Klein predicted high separation, especially about group goals or values, would result in interpersonal conflict, lack of trust, and lower task performance. *Variety* occurs when there are *qualitative* differences among group members, usually in knowledge, skill, or information. For example, one member writes very well, another has much technical knowledge, and a third is experienced in managing people. High variety was predicted to lead to more creativity, innovation, flexibility, and higher quality decisions, but more conflict about the task. Third, *disparity* occurs when some individuals have much more of a resource valued within the group, such as money, power, status, or authority. Wide disparity was expected to produce competition, resentment, and withdrawal by some members. Harrison and Klein showed that inappropriate conceptualization of diversity could lead to misleading measurement and inconsistent research results.

The lesson for the diversity manager is that diversity has complex effects. Diversity in attitudes and values implies emotional conflict in the group's interaction, but skill or information diversity has quite different and potentially positive effects. Inequality of valued assets may lead to powerful or deferential behaviors. In the Harrison and Klein framework, demographic diversity is considered a proxy for one or more of these types of diversity, meaning that people *assume* that demographic difference implies other differences. That is, we often assume that surface demographic differences indicate different attitudes and values, skills and information, or power and other valued assets. In other words, we stereotype.

Investigating Various Types of Diversity

This section reviews several sources of information about types of diversity of interest to diversity professionals, and some methods used to study them. Research discussed in this text uses these sources and methods to investigate how best to manage D&I in a work organization. Because demographic variables are central in the diversity movement, we begin with methods and sources of data about racio-ethnicity, sex, age, disability status and religion, all topics of later chapters. Diversity professionals should be knowledgeable about several different demographic measures:

- The overall population of the US.
- Projections or estimates of how the population is expected to change in the future.
- The labor force, which includes only adults. Because of age cohort differences between groups, the labor force is not simply a smaller version of the population.
- Labor force participation (LFP) rate, which varies for different sexes and ethnicities.
- Projections of LFP based partly on current trends for different demographic groups.

Demographic Information about the US Population

The US Census Bureau (USCB) is the source of a wealth of information about residents of the US. This bureau is part of the US Department of Commerce and collects data in the Decennial Census, the American Community Survey, the Economic Census, and other surveys. The USCB also conducts the Current Population Survey (CPS) for the Bureau of Labor Statistics (BLS) in the Department of Labor (DoL), and the BLS itself manages the monthly Current Employment Statistics survey. Aggregate data from these sources provide snapshots of the demographic, business, or economic makeup of a local area, region, or state as well as the country as a whole.

Diversity professionals will find this information useful in many situations. For example, data on labor force characteristics can be used to compare one's organization with the local area and with other businesses, estimate availability of various kinds of workers, plan business locations near centers of available labor or customers, and estimate future training needs. Affirmative Action Plans (AAPs) use information about availability of different categories of employees based on demographic, educational, and other data. Table 2.1 summarizes these surveys and the kinds

Table 2.1 Useful Federal Government Data Sources about People and Work

	Decennial Census	American Community Survey (ACS)	Economic Census	Current Population Survey (CPS)	Current Employment Statistics
When?	Each ten years	Yearly	Each five years in years ending in 2 and 7	Monthly	Monthly
About whom?	Entire country	Sample of households	Large, medium, and multi-site businesses and sample of small businesses	Sample of households	Sample of nonfarm businesses and government agencies
What?	Short form: demographic information Long form: more details	Demographic questions; many items about how people live	Information about businesses	Employment and unemployment; earnings; labor force characteristics	Employment, work hours, earnings
Publishing Agency?	US Census Bureau (USCB, n.d.-b; 2016)	US Census Bureau (USCB, n.d.-a)	US Census Bureau (USCB, 2012, Jan.)	Census Bureau, for the Bureau of Labor Statistics (USBLS, n.d.-b)	US Bureau of Labor Statistics (USBLS, n.d.-a)
Why?	Reapportionment of US Congress, state legislatures; allocation of federal funds; siting of public facilities, and more (USCB, 2016)	More frequent updates, more detailed information than Census (USCB, 2015)	Forecasting and operation of business and economy	Frequent snapshots of current labor force	Frequent snapshots of economy

of information they provide. The USCB and BLS websites give overall tabulations and other tables broken down by age, sex, and other variables, as well as periodic reports on relevant topics.

The surveys mentioned here are collected and analyzed nationally and also compiled for regions or local areas. State and local agencies use these data sources and may also collect their own data. These sources provide extensive and very useful information, but data collection follows a standard format and may not conform to the specific needs of individual diversity managers. In addition, time is required to conduct analyses before new reports become available, and due to the schedule for conducting the various surveys, specific types of information may not seem current at the time they are needed. When sociologists and other social scientists conduct extensive analyses of Census information, their articles may not be published until several years after data were collected.

The US Census is the basis for population estimates of racio-ethnic groups discussed in this chapter. Census categories also suggest the general cultural understanding of these distinctions in the US at ten-year intervals. For the first time in 2000, the Census allowed respondents to indicate multiracial status by choosing more than one alternative. Respondents could check whether they were *Spanish/Hispanic/Latino*. If so, they could choose from *Mexican/Mexican American/Chicano, Puerto Rican, Cuban*, or *Other Spanish/Hispanic/Latino* and could print in the name of a group not listed. The next question asked about "one or more races" with alternatives of *White*; *Black/African American/Negro*; *American Indian/Alaska Native*; or 11 categories of Asian origin (e.g., Asian Indian, Chinese, Filipino, Native Hawai'ian). American Indians and Alaska Natives were asked to print their tribes, and there were spaces for names of other categories of *Asian/Pacific Islander* or other races (USCB, 2000).

Ten years later, the 2010 Census form specifically noted that Hispanic origins did not imply "race" but otherwise used the same questions to assess Latino heritage. The race item provided the same choices as the 2000 Census form but provided several examples of *Other Asian* (e.g., Hmong, Laotian, Thai, Pakistani, Cambodian) and *Other Pacific Islander* (e.g., Fijian, Tongan). As in 2000, the Census form allowed one or more race boxes to be checked (USCB, 2010). In the 2010 Census, for those reporting one race, the largest population group was White (78%). Blacks constituted 13%, with smaller percentages choosing Asian (5.1%), American Indian/Alaska Native (1.2%), and Native Hawai'ian/Other Pacific Islander (0.2%). Hispanics (of any race) were about 17% and 2.4% chose Two or More Races (USCB, 2012, December 12).

Two things are noteworthy: (a) the increasing variety of responses expected from people asked to identify their own racio-ethnicity; and (b) the USCB's distinction between Hispanic/Latino ethnicity and the several "race" categories. In designing the questionnaire the CB queried the public about various terms. Some objected to the word "Negro" but many of African descent preferred that option. Black respondents were given no way to indicate whether they were (a) an American descendant of slaves; (b) from a Caribbean Island or other place; or (c) born in Africa or descended from Africans not enslaved in the US. Those of Hispanic and Asian heritage had many options. What could be the rationale for listing many alternatives for those of Latino or Asian heritage but not for Blacks?

The 2010 Census found that the US population was almost evenly divided between males (49.2%) and females (50.8%), unchanged since the 2000 Census (Howden & Meyer, 2011). The population grew in size about 9–10% for both sexes during that time. All age groups except those 25–44 increased in size from 2000–2010. The population also became older, with median age rising from 35.3 years in 2000 to 37.2 in 2010. Fastest growth from 2000–2010 was in the 45–64 year age group.

In telephone surveys of households in the 2008 American Religious Identification Survey, about 75% of the US population identified themselves as some form of Christian. Among Christians, the largest groups were Catholic (33%) and Baptist (22.5%). Many other Christian affiliations represented smaller percentages of the population. Almost 4% identified another non-Christian religion (e.g., Jewish, Muslim, Buddhist), about 15% specified no religion, and the remaining 5% declined to respond (USCB, 2012). The Census does not ask about disability status, but other surveys by the USCB (Brault, 2012) found that in 2010, approximately 18.7% of the civilian non-institutionalized population reported a disability, about two-thirds of which were severe. Considering only the working-age population (ages 21–64), 16.6% reported a disability and more than 40% of these individuals were employed. Almost three-quarters of those with nonsevere disabilities (71.2%) were employed compared to about one-quarter of those with severe disabilities (27.5%).

Population Projections

Based on the 2010 Census, the US population is expected to become older and more racio-ethnically diverse during the next 50 years (USCB, 2012, December 12). The percentage of the population that is White alone (including Whites of Hispanic heritage) is expected to drop from 78% in 2012 to 69% in 2060 but percentages of all other groups are expected to increase over that time.

- Hispanics (of any race): from 17% to 31% of population by 2060. Most rapidly growing single racio-ethnic group.
- Two or More Races: from 2.4% to 6.4%.
- Asians: from 5.1% to 8.2%.

- Blacks: from 13% to 15%.
- American Indian/Alaska Natives: from 1.2% to 1.5%.
- Native Hawai'ian/Other Pacific Islanders: 0.2% to 0.3%.

Many things could alter these estimates, including changes in fertility, life span, immigration policy, or death rates from various causes.

Projections indicate that in 2043, the country will probably become majority-minority for the first time. Around that year, non-Hispanic Whites will remain the largest single category, but all other groups combined will be more than half the population. By 2060, the total minority population (including Hispanics who are White) is estimated to be 57%. The percentage of working-age people, currently 62.7 %, will decline to 56.9% by 2060. The proportion of older people is increasing faster than that of younger people, with those 65 and older expected to outnumber those under 18 for the first time by 2056. Based on the trajectory of changes in life expectancy for women and men, the USCB projects that the 2012 ratio of 98.9 men to 100 women in the working-age population (18–64) will increase to about 104.1 men per 100 women in 2060 (USCB, 2012, December 12).

The US Labor Force

The USCB defines the labor force as consisting of the civilian population 16 years of age or older, who are not institutionalized (in a medical or care facility or in prison), and are working or looking for work. Although both employed and unemployed persons are included, the labor force does not include students, retirees, active duty military, or others not looking for work due to illness, disability, choice, or because they are *marginally attached* (USBLS, 2015, November). This term applies to persons who are available for work, want to work, and have looked for work within the preceding year but not in the four weeks preceding the CPS data collection. Some of the marginally attached are *discouraged workers* who have been looking unsuccessfully for employment but, finding none, have given up. Because of age and labor force participation differences for men and women in various racio-ethnic categories, the labor force has a different demographic distribution than the population as a whole.

Data on US labor force composition show:

- 46.8% women and 53.1% men in 2014 (Toossi, 2015, December).
- In 2014, 79% White, 12% Black, 6% Asian, 1% American Indian/Alaska Native, and a smaller percentage Native Hawai'ian/Other Pacific Islander; about 2% two or more races; about 16% Hispanic or Latino ethnicity (USBLS, 2015, November). Percentages do not add to 100% because Latinos may be of any race.
- Among Hispanics in 2014, most of Mexican descent (62%), with Central American heritage 10%, Puerto Rican 8%, South American 7%, Cuban 4%; 9% Other. Mostly White (89%); 4% Black, 1% Asian (USBLS, 2015, November).
- 13.7% aged 16–24, 64.6% aged 25–54 (slightly more over 45), and 21.6% in age group 55 and older (about half under 65) in 2014 (Toossi, 2015, December).
- Approximately 3.7% of the labor force persons with disabilities (USBLS, 2015, June 16).

Labor Force Participation, Unemployment, and Educational Levels

Within each racio-ethnic group the rate of LFP is the percentage of that group that is working or looking for work. Differences across racio-ethnic groups occur for many reasons: geographic concentrations and access to employment, education levels, employment in different occupations and industries, socioeconomic and other factors. The highest levels of LFP in 2014 were for Native Hawai'ian/Other Pacific Islanders (67.6%) with slightly lower rates for Hispanics (66%), Asians

(63.6%), and Whites (63.1%). LFP for Blacks (61.2%) and American Indians/Alaska Natives (60.9%) was lower still (USBLS, 2015, November).

Unemployment rates in 2012 also varied across the racio-ethnic groups. The DoL defines as *unemployed* those who were not employed during the week of data collection and have looked for work during the preceding month or were waiting to be recalled to a job from which they were laid off. Unemployment rates were highest for Blacks (11.3%) and American Indians/Alaska Natives (11.3%), intermediate for Hispanics (7.4%) and Native Hawai'ians/Other Pacific Islanders (6.1%), and lowest for Whites (5.3%) and Asians (5%) (USBLS, 2015, November). These rates occurred during a period of only partial recovery from the serious job losses of the 2008 recession. Besides socioeconomic characteristics of various racio-ethnic groups, unemployment rates reflect the availability of different kinds of jobs in which these groups usually work. For example, the largest employment category for Whites and Asians was managerial work, whereas Blacks and Hispanics were more evenly divided between sales and office, managerial, and service (including public sector) jobs. Blacks and Hispanics were also more likely than others to hold jobs in manufacturing and transportation (USBLS, 2015, November).

Sex interacts with racio-ethnicity in employment patterns. For example, labor force participation and unemployment rates vary by sex within racio-ethnic groups (USBLS, 2015, November). In 2014, for men age 20 or older:

- LFP highest for Hispanics (81%), lower for Asian (75.8%) and White men (72.2%).
- Lowest LFP shown by Black men (67.3%).

LFP was different among adult women:

- Highest LFP (61.6%) for Black women.
- Slightly lower LFP for White (57.9%), Hispanic (58.7%), and Asian women (58%).

However, unemployment rates were:

- Highest for Black men (11.3%) and women (9.8%)
- Lower for Hispanic men (6.1%) and women (7.5%)
- Lower and similar for White men (4.9%) and women (4.8%) as well as Asian men (5.1%) and women (4.5%).

LFP for the sexes also varies with age. Overall, in 2014 for those over 16 years of age the LFP for men was considerably higher (69.2%) than for women (57%). This percentage peaked around ages 25–44 for men (80 to 90%) and for women over a longer period, ages 25–61, (63–74%; Toossi, 2015, December). Unemployment also varies by age. Highest unemployment rates during 2012 were for teenagers, particularly Black teenagers (33%). Rates were also high for Hispanic (22.5%), White (17.3%), and Asian teenagers (14%; USBLS, 2015, November).

LFP is considerably lower for those with a disability. For men with disabilities over the age of 16 in 2014, about 22.9% were employed or looking for work. For adult women with a disability, LFP was 16.6%. The unemployment rate for those with disabilities was 12.5% in 2014, as compared to the rate of 5.9% for those without a disability, and was similar for women and men (USBLS, 2015, June 16).

With respect to education, about 90% of Blacks, Whites, and Asians over the age of 25 had completed at least high school in 2014. Only 72% of Hispanics had done so. Asians were most likely to have completed college; 60% had a bachelor's degree or higher. In contrast, 38% of Whites, 27% of Blacks, and 19% of Hispanics had attained a bachelor's degree or higher (USBLS, 2015, November).

Labor Force Projections

Demographers and labor economists make projections of the future size and characteristics of the labor force as well as the population. Estimates are based on relative sizes and growth rates of demographic groups and on LFP rates for various groups, sizes of age cohorts in these groups, and changes in jobs and the economy. For example, baby boomers born between 1946 and 1964 are less likely than others to be employed as they reach retirement age. Using CPS data and Census projections, the BLS estimates that by 2050, the labor force will age with the over-54 age group representing about one-quarter of the workforce. More people will be in the labor force in all racio-ethnic groups; however, Whites will grow more slowly than other groups. By 2050, the labor force is estimated to be 75% White, 12% Black, 8% Asian, and 5% other groups (compared to 81%, 12%, 5%, and 2% in 2010, respectively). The relative size of the Hispanic labor force will double from 15% in 2010 to about 30% in 2050. Projections are that between now and 2050 the LFP rate for women and men will become more similar, especially after prime child-bearing years. By 2050, men's LFP is expected to be 64.6% and women's 52.7% (Toossi, 2012, October; compare this with the within-race percentages given above.)

Other Sources of Information

In addition to federal, state, and local governmental agencies, a wide variety of trade and professional organizations publish reports of interest to diversity professionals. Many nonprofits (e.g., Institute for Women's Policy Research, Pew Research Center) provide reports free of charge or for a nominal fee. Other organizations (e.g., Catalyst, Diversity Inc., or the Society for Human Resource Management (SHRM)) provide some materials to the general public but reserve other documents to member individuals or organizations. Diversity professionals will probably find it useful to join networks and organizations that provide information about populations of interest and about other organizations' management of D&I.

Data about Individual Organizations

The types of data discussed above are useful for understanding national and regional demographic patterns in the labor force. However, to manage D&I in their own organizations, diversity and HR professionals also need data on a smaller scale. In addition, often they are involved in preparing summaries of the employer's workforce overall or for parts of the organization. Diversity or HR professionals may have responsibility for preparing *EEO-1 reports* and AAPs, both of which use information on employee demographics. These documents can also be used as guides in developing programs for managing D&I.

An employer's EEO-1 report is an annual survey of the racio-ethnicity and sex of occupants of different job categories. It must be submitted by federal contractors with 50 or more employees and a federal contract of at least $50,000, and by companies with 100 or more employees who are covered by Title VII of the Civil Rights Act of 1964 whether or not they are federal contractors (US Equal Employment Opportunity Commission, EEOC, n.d.). Information provided to the EEOC is used to evaluate compliance with Executive Order 11246 and Title VII (see Chapter 7), but in most cases is not publicly available. Instructions and sample forms are available electronically and filing is completed on line. The EEOC uses data from these reports to analyze patterns of employment by women and members of ethnic minority groups and for civil rights enforcement. The Office of Federal Contract Compliance (OFCCP) also selects organizations for compliance reviews based on information on EEO-1 forms.

The AAP is a document that must be completed or updated annually by covered employers (generally those with a minimum of 50 employees and $50,000 federal contracts) or those who are subject to a court order as a result of discrimination litigation. Some contractors may be required to *take affirmative action* although not to prepare a written AAP (SHRM, 2015). However, affirmative action would probably be difficult to do in good faith without an AAP of some type. The organization is not required to submit the AAP but should keep it on file to be produced in case of a compliance review or filing of a complaint of discrimination. The AAP includes data on the demographics of employees in various job categories and on the relevant workforce. By comparing this with availability of qualified women or ethnic minorities, the employer identifies areas of underutilization and develops goals, timetables, and a narrative description of how any problems will be addressed through expanded outreach, targeted recruitment, training, or other activities (USDoL, n.d.).

Many organizations conduct internal surveys of their workforce to assess employee engagement, job satisfaction, ideas for improvement or other responses that may be useful in managing the organization well. An employee survey that specifically focuses on experiences of inclusion, discrimination, or other topics related to diversity management is called a *culture audit* (see Chapter 14) and is often the first step in designing a program for managing D&I. Surveys can also be part of needs assessment and evaluation of diversity training activities. Good survey design and administration requires knowledge and technical skill; diversity managers without a background in this area should rely on other qualified staff or work with a consulting firm or independent consultant. Important issues in conducting surveys relevant to D&I include sampling, confidentiality, appropriate question wording, and the format and disclosure of results.

Studying Surface- and Deep-level Diversity

This textbook frequently refers to research by social scientists or management researchers who have investigated questions of interest to diversity professionals. The empirical research is of two main types: experimental and correlational designs. Either may be conducted in the lab or the field. After many studies have been completed on the same topic, narrative or meta-analytic reviews are conducted to draw overall conclusions that are considered more reliable than the results of any single study. There is no perfect study, but internal and external validity of a research design are helpful guidelines for evaluating its quality. A complete discussion of research design is beyond the scope of this text, but some definitions of key terms are presented here as a refresher. For more detailed information, readers should consult a good textbook in social psychology, industrial-organizational psychology, or another social science field.

Box 2.1 Key Terms in Social Science Research

- Empirical research: work that actually measures variables (as opposed to theoretical research developing conceptual frameworks to summarize and guide understanding).
- Experiment: research that alters or manipulates one or more variables, holds other variables constant, then measures the results. Because experiments attempt to rule out alternative explanations in this way, they are usually the most suitable method for drawing conclusions about *causes* of certain outcomes.
- Correlational research: study that measures two or more variables to find out the extent to which they are related. These designs are often used when it is difficult or impossible (e.g., for practical or ethical reasons) to manipulate proposed causal variables. Reliable correlations can be very useful in predicting what will happen later even if reasons for this relationship are unclear. Although most correlational designs cannot establish inferences about causality because of uncontrolled variables, some very sophisticated designs and analyses may be able to approximate the level of causal inference of an experiment.

- Internal validity: degree of confidence that study results actually show what the researcher concluded. Internal validity is high when competing explanations are ruled out by selection of participants or by control (through design or statistical analysis) of other variables that might explain results. Generally very simple studies have low internal validity, but those with high internal validity may seem artificial and unrealistic.

- External validity: degree to which results of a study can be generalized to other populations, environments, or ranges of the variables studied. Usually studies with high external validity seem realistic, but this may come at the cost of uncontrolled variables. When external validity is low, the results are probably not generalizable. External validity is usually established through a program of several well-controlled studies with different populations, environments, or different levels of variables. This is costly and time-consuming.

- Lab and field settings: *laboratory* refers to an artificial environment in which aspects of the situation can be controlled. It may be an actual lab or a classroom or other setting to which participants come for research purposes. Generally they are aware of participation in research and their informed consent is obtained. *Field* refers to the real-world environment in which the behavior in question naturally occurs. Studies in actual organizations are usually field research. Most commonly, experiments occur in lab settings and field research is correlational. However, there are correlational designs in laboratory settings as well as field experiments.

- Narrative review: compilation of several studies on the same general topic, in which the reviewer draws conclusions based on how well the studies seem to have been conducted and how strong their results seem to be. Conclusions are based on the reviewer's professional knowledge and expertise.

- Meta-analytic review: compilation of many studies on the same general topic, in which the reviewer categorizes studies on dimensions that seem important (e.g., design of study, characteristics of participants, lab or field setting, sex of researcher). Statistical analysis (not reviewer expertise alone) is used to determine overall results and whether the strength of conclusions varies with any of these classifications.

- Survey: when this term refers to a type of research, it generally means that a specified sample of people have been asked questions either by interviewers or by written or computer-presented questionnaires.

Everyday Conceptions of Difference

To manage an ethnically diverse workforce successfully, one should have some knowledge of historical and cultural contexts of interaction involving members of different groups represented among employees and applicants. Later chapters address several important dimensions of diversity and provide contextual information about each, but understanding of history is perhaps most important when considering present-day ideas about racio-ethnicity. Therefore, this chapter concludes by illustrating how the history of intergroup relations is relevant for the management of D&I in today's work organizations. More extensive historical background about major racio-ethnic groups in today's US workforce is discussed by Takaki (1993), Tatum (1997), and Hays-Thomas (2015).

Social science offers general recommendations about managing inter-ethnic relations. However, in a particular employment setting, work relationships occur among specific racio-ethnic groups with particular *legacy* issues. These are biases, expectations, understandings, and behavior patterns resulting from the history of a relationship. *Macro-legacy* issues arise from the history of a relationship between racio-ethnic groups, e.g., Israelis and Palestinians in the Middle East. In contrast, individuals also experience *micro-legacy* issues, which concern each person's unique history of interracial relationships. Has the person experienced close and positive relationships, friendship, and trust, with those of other racio-ethnicities? Exclusion and discrimination? Victimization by others' criminal behavior? Perhaps no interracial experiences at all? Many of us come to a diverse work environment without experiencing discussion of these issues comfortably across divides that separate people of different groups. For many employees, the workplace is the most likely setting for social interactions with those of different racio-ethnicities, and it may seem taboo to discuss inter-ethnic topics at work. Why is this topic relevant for those working in D&I?

First, co-workers with a strong racio-ethnic identity experience work interactions through the lens of historical and cultural issues relevant to their group. We can interact more effectively if we understand how others experience the world. Macro-legacy issues for American Blacks include slavery, Jim Crow laws, and segregation. Latino Americans may be concerned about the use of Spanish in the workplace or the stereotype of "illegal aliens." Asian Americans, even those who are US-born, may be treated and feel like *forever foreigners* because of their facial characteristics and confront the *Model Minority* stereotype (see Chapter 10). Whites may be sensitive to long-standing prejudices about Southerners or Northerners rooted in Civil War history. For other examples of macro-legacy issues related to racio-ethnicity, see the shaded box.

Why It Helps to Know Some History

What are some macro-legacy issues to consider in contemporary American workplaces? For American Blacks, macro-legacy issues include the experience of slavery (and destruction of culture and tribal/family ties); repressive Jim Crow laws, sharecropping, peonage, and convict leasing; widespread segregation and denial of opportunity in employment and education; AA and systemic and interpersonal discrimination that affect present-day levels of education, income, and opportunity. Indigenous populations of Native Americans and Alaska Natives have been victims of genocide through war and illness; loss of land and subsistence way of life; repeated treaty violations; and destruction of culture through removal to reservations, forced removal of children, and bans on use of native languages. For Asian Americans, legacy issues include the history of war and invasion involving Japan and China, Japan and Korea, Vietnam and China; varying legal restrictions over time on immigration to the US; and the *Model Minority* myth. In addition, widespread religious, cultural, language, educational, physical appearance, and socioeconomic differences exist among Asian American groups. These include persons whose heritage includes the Far East (e.g., China, Japan, Korea), Southeast Asia (e.g., Vietnam, Cambodia, Thailand), the Pacific Islands (e.g., Samoa, Guam), South Asia (e.g., India, Pakistan, Nepal), West Asia (e.g., Iran, Afghanistan, Turkey), and the Middle East (e.g., Iraq, Jordan, Palestine).

Latinos or Hispanics are also very diverse and are formally considered an ethnic, not a racial group. Latinos include Mexican Americans (Chicanos), Puerto Ricans, Cubans, and persons from anywhere in Central or South America. Important legacy issues for these heritage groups include language, segregation and discrimination, forced relocations, erratic and inconsistent US immigration policies and enforcement, the assumption of so-called illegal alien status, and lingering effects of political disputes and military conflicts. Puerto Ricans are US citizens, Cuban immigrants have privileged immigration status (as a result of Cuban Communism), and many Chicanos are descended from families that have lived in US territory longer than the families of most US Whites. Each of these groups has its own issues, but the burdens of exclusion, poverty, and discrimination are a common theme.

For most Whites of European American heritage, legacy issues may seem less obvious due to their greater assimilation into the general US culture, but in some areas with little outmigration there may still be strong ethnic identifications, rural/urban differences, or prejudices based on regional origin (e.g., North vs. South). Some Whites have strong views about holding or rejecting a sense of collective responsibility for the legacy of slavery or of the destruction of Native American culture. Some ethnic legacy issues are related to religion, such as Jewish heritage. Whites have been the most numerous and dominant group in the US for so long that rising numbers of ethnic minority groups may present special challenges as more areas become "majority-minority." For example, Whites were fewer in number than all minority groups combined in 11% of the counties in the US as of July 2011. The District of Columbia and four states were majority-minority, including Hawai'i, California, New Mexico, and Texas (USCB, 2012, May 17). Majority-minority US cities in 2010 included Houston, Los Angeles, New York, San Antonio, San Diego, San Francisco, and San Jose (Czekalinski & Nhan, 2012). For majority Whites, this presents a new reality.

Second, contemporary and historical conflicts between groups can affect relations among individuals. It is very easy to give offense without realizing it. For example, those whose families experienced "the Troubles" in Northern Ireland may be sensitive to issues of religion or Irish/British affiliation (Beattie, 2013; Hammer, 2009); those of Taiwanese heritage may not appreciate being called "Chinese" (Albert, 2016); or persons from Austria may take offense at being thought of as "German" because they sound "German" to North Americans. Southerners or those from Appalachia may not think jokes about those US regions are funny.

Third, rightly or wrongly, some ethnicities are seen as associated with particular religions. For example, persons from the Middle East may be Muslim but may also be Catholic, Jewish, or of other faiths. Those with limited knowledge may confuse nationality, ethnicity, and religious faith. Finally, it is wise to remember that some supposedly typical American things may only characterize one part of US culture. Not everyone recognizes Sunday as the day of worship and people of color often face challenges unimaginable to their White co-workers. Many readers of this text have experienced fairly homogeneous environments in terms of school, residence, church, or social interactions. Social and work environments of the future will probably include a wider range of racio-ethnicities, and knowing something about the histories of other groups will be useful.

Racial Distinctions

The concept of "Whiteness" is a fairly recent invention, going back to the time of the establishment of the African slave trade in the 1700s (Omi & Winant, 2007; Painter, 2010). In Western history, many racio-ethnic groups have experienced slavery and indentured servitude (a time-limited contractual arrangement in which the servant received passage, room, and board in exchange for several years' work). In fact, 300,000 to 400,000 White people, about one-half to two-thirds of the immigrants from Europe to the British colonies in the 1600s, were indentured servants (Painter, 2010).

The earliest Black Africans in North America came as indentured servants in the early 1600s (Painter, 2010; Public Broadcasting System, n.d.) but by mid-century, the demand for cheaper labor and the seemingly endless supply of those kidnapped from Africa led colonial landowners to enact slave laws pertaining to Africans. The idea of "Whiteness" apparently began in the late 1600s and 1700s as a way to explain and justify enslavement of Blacks, who became the basis for the colonial plantation economy and categorized apart from European indentured servants. Around the same time, indigenous Indian populations were racialized to justify appropriation of their land in the New World (Grimsley, 2004). To maintain order and prevent revolt in colonial society, landowners distinguished poor free persons of European descent from those forcibly brought to America as slaves (Buck, 2007). The original notion of Whiteness was associated with the promise of land at the end of the indenture period. However, over time the moneyed classes used status based on

Whiteness as a "psychological wage" instead of higher wages or parcels of land. This hierarchal distinction from Black slaves gave lower-class Whites increased social status and privilege compared to Blacks. By the late 1700s these boundaries were firmly in place, embedded in an institutional system that enforced social and economic segregation of Blacks from everyone else and continues in some ways today.

Census Categories as a Snapshot of "Race"

US Census categories over the years show the social distinctions that identified those who have been considered *not-White*. Each 10 years from 1790–1860 the Census distinguished between White and Black males and females, usually between Blacks who were free and those enslaved. From 1850–1880, categories included Mulatto (mixed Black and White) and in 1890 there were also categories for Quadroon (one-quarter Black) and Octoroon (one eighth Black). Beginning in 1870, American Indians and Chinese were distinguished and Japanese were added in 1890. The three enumerations beginning in 1900 simply asked for *color or race*. Beginning in 1930, complexity increased with additions of Mexican, Filipino, Hindu, and Korean (as well as Indian tribes). A category for Hawai'ians was added in 1970. Ten years later several other categories were listed (Vietnamese, Asian Indian, Guamanian, Samoan, Eskimo, Aleut). *Spanish or Hispanic descent* was also included for the first time with listings of Mexican, Puerto Rican, Cuban, and Other. In 1990 there were ten options for those of Asian or Pacific Islander descent and several options for Spanish or Hispanic (Racebox, n.d.).

In 1819 Congress required shipmasters to provide lists of those immigrating and by 1840, almost 750,000 persons had arrived. By 1850, over 1,700,000 more entered the US and the Census that year first distinguished between native-born and immigrant residents (Open Collections Program, n.d.). Millions immigrated each decade until immigration peaked between 1901 and 1910. About this time, the pattern of immigration shifted from predominantly Northern and Western Europe (e.g., Scandinavia, British Isles) to Southern and Eastern European countries (e.g., Italy, Poland). Restrictions on immigration increased and each decade from 1911 to 1940 added 4 to 5 million immigrants. Since the 1960s, most immigrants have come from Latin America (about half) and Asia (about one-quarter) (Pew Research Center, 2013, January 29).

At times of increased US immigration, those who were poor, rural, neither Protestant nor English-speaking were perceived as non-White. This included immigrants from Eastern and Southern Europe (e.g., Poles, Greeks) and especially Jews (Brodkin, 2007; Painter, 2010). Impoverished and rural Irish immigrants escaping the potato famine in the 1840s were considered a different race and cartooned as animals (Knobel, 1986). Racialization was a justification for exploitative treatment of Native Americans, drastic limits on immigration from Asia and much of Europe between 1924 and 1927, and deportation of US citizens of Mexican descent during the Great Depression (Digital History, 2012).

Whites, especially male landowners, based the new US on their own social and cultural values. Many institutions and policies that we take for granted in this country were designed and operated to the benefit of the initial landed elite and others who, by "race," have come to be seen as part of the privileged White group. Many policies, described by Katznelson (2005) as Affirmative Action for Whites, operated to their benefit and were critical to development of the middle class. These included laws and administrative decisions that deliberately and systematically excluded Blacks from benefits of union legislation, working hours, minimum wage, Social Security, support for veterans and the poor, and post-World War II programs such as educational benefits of the GI Bill and VA home loans. These exclusionary policies amplified the consequences of legal segregation. Key to understanding contemporary race relations is the recognition that Whites' socioeconomic status has risen significantly due to public policies designed to their benefit over other racial groups, especially Blacks. As time passes, these policies, political decisions, and institutions are forgotten or become accepted as normal without acknowledgment of the degree to which they have benefited Whites over others.

Although seldom openly discussed, these events are remembered by many of today's workers or their parents and form the context for their understanding of treatment at work. Today people of color are generally underrepresented in high-level positions and desirable occupations and overrepresented in departments and positions with low pay and authority, in part because of historical policies of exclusion. This may go largely unrecognized by majority employees. Work settings are often culturally "White" and many people of color are skilled at bicultural *shifting* or alternation of behavior and attitudes from work to social or family environments (Jones & Shorter-Gooden, 2003).

Someone of minority status (e.g. racio-ethnicity, gender, religion) who inquires or complains about potentially discriminatory situations risks being seen as overreactive or trouble-making. However, ignoring the situation allows it to continue unexamined, unexplained, and uncorrected. An easier course in such cases is to withdraw partially or completely by leaving the organization. Managers and employees who recognize these special stresses affecting those of minority status will be better prepared to mitigate their effects.

This chapter has reviewed intuitive and scholarly conceptualizations of diversity and their implications, as well as major types of surface- and deep-level diversity and methods of measuring them. Because of the emphasis on racio-ethnic diversity in today's workforce, historical background and legacy issues of several groups were also briefly reviewed. Next we turn to psychological processes affecting relationships in contemporary US organizations.

References

Agars, M. D., & Kottke, J. L. (2004). Models and practice of diversity management: A historical review and presentation of a new integration theory. In M. S. Stockdale & F. J. Crosby (Eds.), *The psychology and management of workplace diversity* (pp. 55–77). Malden, MA: Blackwell.

Albert, E. (2016, August 11). *China–Taiwan relations.* Council on Foreign Relations. Retrieved from www.cfr.org/china/china-taiwan-relations/p9223

Beattie, G. (2013). *Our racist heart.* New York, NY: Routledge.

Brault, M. W. (2012, July). *Americans with disabilities: 2010.* Current Population Reports, P70–131. Retrieved from www.census.gov/prod/2012pubs/p70-131.pdf

Brodkin, K. (2007). How Jews became white folks and what that says about race in America. In P. S. Rothenberg (Ed.), *Race, class, and gender in the United States* (pp. 38–53). New York, NY: Worth Publishers.

Buck, P. D. (2007). Constructing race, creating white privilege. In P. S. Rothenberg (Ed.), *Race, class, and gender in the United States,* (pp. 32–38). New York, NY: Worth Publishers.

Cox. T., Jr. (1991). The multicultural organization. *The Executive, 5*(2), 34–47.

Cox, T., Jr. (1993/1994). *Cultural diversity in organizations: Theory, research, and practice.* San Francisco, CA: Berrett-Koehler Publishers.

Cox, T., Jr. (2001). *Creating the multicultural organization.* San Francisco, CA: Jossey-Bass.

Cox, T., Jr., & Beale, R. L. (1997). *Developing competency to manage diversity: Readings, cases & activities.* San Francisco, CA: Berrett-Koehler Publishers, Inc.

Cox, T., & Finley-Nickelson, J. (1991). Models of acculturation for intra-organizational cultural diversity. *Canadian Journal of Administrative Science, 8,* 90–100.

Czekalinski, S., & Nhan, D. (2012, July 2). 7 of 15 most populous U.S. cities are majority-minority. *National Journal.* Retrieved from www.yahoo.com/news/7-15-most-populous-u-cities-majority-minority-121534120.html

Digital History. (2012). *Repatriation during the Great Depression.* Retrieved from www.digitalhistory.uh.edu/disp_textbook.cfm?smtid=3&psid=3699

Grimsley, M. (2004, January). *Warfare and the construction of White identity in the United States, 1675–1865.* Presented at the annual meeting of the American Historical Association, Washington, DC. Retrieved from http://h-net.msu.edu/cgi-bin/logbrowse.pl?trx=vx&list=h-war&month=0401&week=c&msg=qfGphKLjR5oZ6PaPMZxYTA&user=&pw=

Hammer, J. (2009, March). *In Northern Ireland, getting past the Troubles.* Retrieved from www.smithsonianmag.com/people-places/Getting-Past-the-Troubles.html

*Harrison D. A., & Klein, K. J. (2007). What's the difference? Diversity constructs as separation, variety, or disparity in organizations. *Academy of Management Review, 32,* 1199–1228.

*Harrison, D. A., Price, K. H., & Bell, M. P. (1998). Beyond relational demography: Time and the effects of surface- and deep-level diversity on work group cohesion. *Academy of Management Journal, 41,* 96–107.

Hays-Thomas, R. (2015). Building diversity competence through historical and demographic knowledge: Helpful information for managers. *The Psychologist-Manager Journal, 18,* 121–152.

Howden, L. M., & Meyer, J. A. (2011, May). *Age and sex composition: 2010: 2010 Census briefs.* Retrieved from www.census.gov/prod/cen2010/briefs/c2010br-03.pdf

Jackson, S. E., May, K. E., & Whitney, K. (1995). Understanding the dynamics of diversity in decision-making teams. In R. R. Guzzo, E. Salas, & Associates (Eds.), *Team effectiveness and decision making in organizations* (pp. 204–261). San Francisco, CA: Jossey-Bass.

Jones, C., & Shorter-Gooden, K. (2003). *Shifting: The double lives of Black women in America.* New York, NY: Harper-Collins.

Katznelson, I. (2005). *When Affirmative Action was White.* New York, NY: W.W. Norton & Co.

Knobel, D. T. (1986). *Paddy and the Republic: Ethnicity and nationality in antebellum America.* Wesleyan University Press: Middletown, CT.

Milliken, F. J., & Martins, L. L. (1996). Searching for common threads: Understanding the multiple effects of diversity in organizational groups. *Academy of Management Review, 21,* 402–433.

Omi, M., & Winant, H. (2007). Racial formations. In P. S. Rothenberg (Ed.). *Race, class, and gender in the United States* (pp. 13–22). New York, NY: Worth Publishers.

Open Collections Program. (n.d.). *Immigration to the US 1789–1930.* Retrieved from http://ocp.hul.harvard.edu/immigration/timeline.html

Painter, N. I. (2010). *The history of White people.* New York, NY: W.W. Norton & Co.

Pew Research Center. (2013, January 29). *A nation of immigrants.* Retrieved from www.pewhispanic.org/2013/01/29/a-nation-of-immigrants/

Public Broadcasting System. (n.d.). *Indentured servants in the U.S.* History Detectives. Retrieved from www.pbs.org/opb/historydetectives/feature/indentured-servants-in-the-us/

Racebox. (n.d.). *The U. S. Census since 1790.* Retrieved from http://racebox.org/

Society for Human Resource Management. (2015, November 9). *Affirmative Action: General: When would my company need to have an affirmative action program?* Retrieved from www.shrm.org/templatestools/hrqa/pages/whenisanaapneeded.aspx

Takaki, R. (1993). *A different mirror: A history of multicultural America.* Boston, MA: Little, Brown and Company.

Tatum, B. D. (1997). *"Why are all the Black kids sitting together in the cafeteria?" and other conversations about race.* New York, NY: Basic Books.

Thomas, D. A., & Ely, R. J. (1996). Making differences matter: A new paradigm for managing diversity. *Harvard Business Review, 74*(5), 79–90.

Thomas, R. R., Jr. (1991). *Beyond race and gender: Unleashing the power of your total work force by managing diversity.* New York, NY: AMACOM.

Thomas, R. R., Jr. (1996). *Redefining diversity.* New York, NY: AMACOM.

*Toossi, M. (2012, October). Projections of the labor force to 2050: A visual essay. *Monthly Labor Review.* Retrieved from www.bls.gov/opub/mlr/2012/10/art1full.pdf

Toossi, M. (2015, December). Labor force projections to 2024: The labor force is growing, but slowly. *Monthly Labor Review.* Retrieved from www.bls.gov/opub/mlr/2015/article/labor-force-projections-to-2024.htm

US Bureau of Labor Statistics. (n.d.-a). *Current employment statistics—CES (National).* Retrieved from www.bls.gov/ces

US Bureau of Labor Statistics. (n.d.-b). *Labor force statistics from the Current Population Survey.* Retrieved from www.bls.gov/cps/

US Bureau of Labor Statistics. (2015, June 16). *Persons with a disability: Labor force characteristics–2014.* Retrieved from www.bls.gov/news.release/pdf/disabl.pdf

US Bureau of Labor Statistics. (2015, November). *Labor force characteristics by race and ethnicity, 2014.* Report 1057. Retrieved from www.bls.gov/opub/reports/race-and-ethnicity/archive/labor-force-characteristics-by-race-and-ethnicity-2014.pdf

US Census Bureau. (n.d.-a). *American Community Survey.* Retrieved from www.census.gov/programs-surveys/acs/

US Census Bureau (n.d.-b). *What is the Census?* Retrieved from www.census.gov/2010census/about/

US Census Bureau. (2000). *Major differences in subject-matter content between the 1990 and 2000 census questionnaires.* Retrieved from www.census.gov/population/www/cen2000/90vs00/index.html

US Census Bureau. (2010). *United States Census 2010 Informational Copy.* Retrieved from http://www.census.gov/schools/pdf/2010form_info.pdf

US Census Bureau. (2012). *The 2012 Statistical Abstract of the United States.* Table 75. Retrieved from www.census.gov/prod/2011pubs/11statab/pop.pdf

US Census Bureau. (2012, January). *The Economic Census: How it works for you.* Retrieved from www.census.gov/econ/census/pdf/ec_brochure.pdf

US Census Bureau. (2012, May 17). *Most children younger than age 1 are minorities, Census Bureau reports.* Retrieved from www.census.gov/newsroom/releases/archives/population/cb12-90.html

US Census Bureau. (2012, December 12). *U.S. Census Bureau projections show a slower growing, older, more diverse nation a half century from now.* Retrieved from www.census.gov/newsroom/releases/archives/population/cb12-243.html

US Census Bureau. (2015, June). *Why was I selected?* Retrieved from www.census.gov/programs-surveys/acs/about/why-was-i-selected.html

US Census Bureau. (2016, February). *About the Bureau.* Retrieved from www.census.gov/about/what.html

US Department of Labor. (n.d.) *Executive Order 11246: EEO and Affirmative Action Guidelines for federal contractors regarding race, color, gender, religion, and national origin.* Retrieved from www.dol.gov/ofccp/regs/compliance/fs11246.htm

US Equal Employment Opportunity Commission. (n.d.). *EEO-1 frequently asked questions and answers.* Retrieved from www.eeoc.gov/employers/eeo1survey/faq.cfm

* Recommended for advanced reading.

Part II

People and Organizations

Structure and Process

Chapter 3

Privilege, Social Construction, Attribution, and Fairness

We have seen why D&I are important topics for contemporary organizations, especially in light of demographic changes affecting the labor force. Next we consider social interaction in organizational settings, beginning with assumptions that people often make and their habits of thinking, feeling, and acting as they interact with others who may be different in important ways.

Privilege—An Invisible Obstacle

Often conflict in organizations can occur as a result of factors we do not clearly see or understand. One of these is *privilege*, which is invisible to those who have it but very obvious to those who don't. In this context, the term privilege refers to a set of unearned resources or assets, many of which come to a person as a result of gender, ethnic, class, or other groupings into which the person is born. A person may be privileged by being born physically and mentally healthy to a stable family in an industrialized country, with access to good health care, educational, and financial support, opportunities to travel, a comfortable home, and other assets. This accident of birth leads to many outcomes that differentiate this person from others in less fortunate circumstances.

Dr. Peggy McIntosh of Wellesley College is credited with the development of this conception of *privilege* in a widely cited 1988 article which has become a classic in gender and ethnic studies. Privilege is now considered a fundamental idea in the study of many dimensions of status such as race, gender, sexuality, religion, and social class (Case & Iuzzini, 2012).

McIntosh (1998, reprinted) refers to White privilege as an invisible knapsack of understandings and resources that people of European American heritage in the US carry with them throughout life, generally without realizing it. For individuals with this background, these benefits seem "normal." Most of those with whom they associate share these assets so it is easy to overlook the fact that many others do not. McIntosh's additional insight is that we who are privileged do not notice it partly because society is organized and designed so that we do not. The most powerful or *dominant* group in a society sets norms and controls social institutions such as laws, educational systems, and the media; this group's understanding of the world is portrayed as typical, normal, and desirable.

Because the privileged do not easily see these institutional controls and have always had privileged status, they do not realize the degree to which this status is responsible for how others treat them and the good things that come their way. To the contrary, it seems as though they are earning the things that come to them, and are *entitled* to these things. This way of thinking leads to the assumption of *meritocracy* which pervades our culture: an understanding that in society, good things come on the basis of *merit* to those who are talented and capable and work hard to deserve them.

McIntosh wrote about White privilege in the US, but the concept also applies to other dimensions of dominant status. For example, Roy Jacques (1997) illustrates male privilege by saying "As a straight white man, I find that the norms I encounter in terms of social expectations about the 'good' scientist, the 'good' manager . . . conform closely to the norms of the identities within which I have been socialized. Were I a woman, gay, African American . . . (I would have) a cross-cultural experience . . . learn(ing) to be judged by norms originating in a group different from mine" (p. 81). This is the experience of people of difference within organizations in which they are the minority. For a widely cited example of the operation of class-based privilege, see the shaded box.

The Other Side of Privilege

Many people employed in professional or managerial jobs have little or no understanding of the difficulty of surviving on minimum wage employment alone. During the period of "welfare reform" in the 1990s, with its discourse about what would "break the cycle" of poverty, journalist Barbara Ehrenreich decided to see what low-wage employment looked like from the other side. Although well educated and financially comfortable, she temporarily abandoned her privileged identity and life and worked in several places around the country in whatever minimum wage employment she could find. Her jobs included waiting tables, cleaning houses, working as a hotel maid and a nursing home aide, and as a salesperson for the country's largest discount big-box retailer. Ehrenreich quickly found that working in jobs like these is extremely demanding, physically and mentally. Because of low wages and the amount of time required to earn those wages, it is nearly impossible to make any forward progress financially without external assistance. For Erhenreich, this period of bare subsistence employment led to a *New York Times* best-selling book, *Nickel and Dimed: On (not) Getting by in America* (2008). Most other low-wage workers are not so well rewarded.

Before the 2008 recession, reading her book would have given many upper and middle class Americans a shock to see how the working poor live. After 2008, many individuals and families who formerly enjoyed financial stability slipped toward poverty as a result of job loss, difficulty in finding employment, depletion of savings, and home foreclosure. In this context, the privilege of those who are really well-off stands in stark contrast.

A few words about terminology: the term *dominant* may be used to refer to the group or groups which exercise the most influence, power, and control over how a society operates. Those who come from groups whose opportunities are reduced or denied because of these societal institutions are said to be *oppressed*. From the vantage point of the privileged who see their own situation as typical and merited, lower conditions of other groups may seem to result from undesirable personal habits or deficiencies and members of these target groups may seem less than human. Dehumanization leads to "the unjust or cruel exercise of authority or power" by which a more powerful group dominates others (Mor Barak, 2011, p. 156). This domination is called *oppression* and in the extreme is illustrated by slavery and human trafficking, the Holocaust, and the appropriation of land and resources seen in the colonization of America, Africa, and India. Advocates for excluded groups also consider oppression to include systematic unjust institutionalized practices and structures that work to the detriment of marginalized groups. For example, formal laws and informal practices that contribute to gender and racial wage gaps discussed in Chapter 4 would be considered oppressive.

In the broad societal context, the terms "dominance" and "oppression" do not necessarily imply that dominant groups exercise control intentionally or through force or violence, although there are certainly historical and contemporary examples of that. According to Jacques (1997), "Dominance need not – and most often does not – presume the conscious desire to dominate. The dominance resides in the structuring of social interaction" (p. 81). Control can be exercised and privilege maintained through subtle but very effective means such as advertising, media portrayals, public services, location of facilities, and aspects of the political or legal system. Here are some examples of control:

- appearance of models and actors in ads and in high-profile TV or movie roles
- legal penalties: for possession of different types of drugs, white collar vs. blue collar crime
- community location of landfills, sewage treatment plants, or factories vs. parks, schools, hospitals, or shopping
- unavailability of public transportation or parking facilities in certain areas
- procedures and requirements for seeking employment, such as use of the Internet for applications
- access to free or reasonably priced quality education, and support for education from tax revenues vs. tuitions paid by the learner (based partly on student loans)
- formal or informal restrictions on where various kinds of people can live.

Within a society, such things are part of the institutions that structure the lives of everyone. However, they are usually designed to support needs and desires of whatever group(s) are more influential in the society. Often people who benefit do not realize that they have an advantage over the less fortunate simply because of the way their environment is designed. This is the nature of privilege. However, people who are shut out of opportunity as a result notice these inequities; for oppressed groups in today's society, development of gender, ethnic, or other minority identity includes learning to interpret inequality in terms of institutional sources of oppression rather than only in terms of personal deficiencies of the oppressed or prejudices of those who are dominant.

How is this relevant to work? It is important to recognize that organizations exist within, reflect, and often reinforce the social and cultural environment of the surrounding social system in which some are privileged and others are not. Those who benefit from these institutional structures often interpret the resulting social inequality in terms of the "disadvantage" of others resulting from their shortcomings, poor choices, or undesirable behaviors. Social psychologists have shown that interpreting inequality in terms of other-group disadvantage vs. own-group privilege can have important consequences in terms of self-esteem and other psychological responses (Lowery, Knowles, & Unzueta, 2007). For example, White American college students were asked to read about examples of social inequality between Blacks and Whites in the US. When these differences were framed in terms of White privilege, participants scored higher on a measure of collective guilt and lower on a measure of racism than when the *same* examples were framed in terms of Black disadvantage (Powell, Branscombe, & Schmitt, 2005). Framing apparently affected how students attributed blame or responsibility for inequality.

The Framing of Inequality

Here are two versions of an item from the study by Powell et al. (2005):

- "White Americans can easily rent or purchase housing in any area where they can afford to live."
- "Black Americans often have difficulty renting or purchasing housing, even in areas where they can afford to live." (p. 511).

Do you feel differently reading these two versions of the item? Is this related to your racio-ethnic identification?

In addition, interpretation of discrimination as the result of group-based oppressive societal structures is more likely to result in collective action to change the situation than if one accepts it as justified on the basis of deficiencies of one's own talent or motivation (Branscombe & Ellemers, 1998; Ellemers & Barreto, 2009). For example, a woman who finds she is underpaid may interpret this in terms of her own lack of ability or assertiveness, or of others' prejudices or lack of understanding; from this perspective, any coping responses would likely be aimed at changing individuals—herself or others. However, if her sense of gender identity as a woman is high, she may be more likely to see underpayment in feminist terms as a manifestation of historical and cultural processes. This institutional interpretation is more likely to lead to collective action such as membership in woman-supportive activist groups, advocacy for changes in law, and organized attempts to change the *status quo*, particularly if action is expected to be effective. For an example of the value of a collective identity, see the shaded box.

Home-Workers: The National Domestic Workers Alliance

Housecleaners, nannies, and personal caregivers (who are not employees of a firm) generally work in private homes, often without co-workers, and under nonstandard working conditions. They are not protected by most labor laws covering other workers and are especially vulnerable to abuse by employers because of isolation, lack of information, and perhaps undocumented status. Many are ethnic minority women.

A survey of more than 2,000 domestic workers in 14 cities by the National Domestic Workers Alliance (NDWA) revealed that wages are low, employment benefits are rare, work can be hazardous, working conditions are unregulated and variable, and abuse and disrespect are common (Burnham & Theodore, 2012). For example, 23% of surveyed workers are paid below their state's minimum wage. More than 90% work for employers who do not pay Social Security taxes on their behalf although this is required by law. Most do not have an employment contract. If injured on the job, they are not covered by Worker's Compensation.

Home-workers in New York formed the Domestic Workers United (DWU) in 2000 as a membership organization to advocate for fair working conditions, respect, and power regarding their work standards. As part of a coalition, the DWU succeeded in passing the first Domestic Workers Bill of Rights in New York State in 2010. This law requires days of rest, an eight-hour work day, minimum wage protection, and protection from harassment and discrimination for privately employed domestic workers (DWU, n.d.).

DWU is affiliated with the NDWA, which has now grown to a collection of 35 local affiliates with more than 10,000 members in 12 states and 18 cities (Burnham & Theodore, 2012). Organizations such as these provide a framework for collective action and advocacy for individual workers who otherwise would be virtually powerless to improve their own working conditions. In the case of domestic workers who work by themselves in private homes, this sense of collective identity can be especially significant.

We have already noted that the privileged often do not notice inequality, especially if they are not harmed by it. When they *do* notice unequal outcomes, understanding this as due to choices, behaviors, or lesser abilities of the disadvantaged leads to feeling less collective guilt and less responsibility to correct the situation. This framing also reinforces a sense of identity as part of the (privileged) group and negative attitudes or prejudices against those in the other (unprivileged) group.

Here are some real-world examples of interpretations of social reality influenced by sense of privilege:

- Discussions of the gender wage gap often include statements that the gap is due to women's choices, poor negotiating skills, lack of interest in promotions, and other attributes of women. Although these characteristics apply to some employed women, they surely apply to some men as well. These arguments ignore structural and institutional reasons for the wage gap, discussed in Chapter 4.
- Explanations for lack of advancement of employees from minority groups often refer to the supposed quality of their preparation or their level of motivation. Structural impediments to education and training and the de-motivating effects of lack of similar role models or mentors are often ignored.
- Job performance of some groups (e.g., those with disabilities) may be interpreted in terms of their lack of ability to perform certain tasks. However, equipment, environments, and work clothing are designed for capabilities of persons without disabilities, sometimes in arbitrary and unnecessary ways. For example, women soldiers have been assigned to drive small vehicles because men objected to them driving big trucks when they could not reach the pedals comfortably. This totally overlooks the effects of this limitation on morale and women's ability to contribute on the same basis as men. What about using pedal extenders?

In contrast, if dominants understand inequalities as resulting in part from unearned privilege denied to the other group, they may experience more sense of responsibility for inequality, more obligation to address it, and less prejudice or negativity toward "others." For example, over the term of a class in diversity, students became more aware of male privilege, less sexist, and more supportive of affirmative action (Case, 2007). In this case, recognizing privilege was associated with less prejudice and more support for remedial action.

Entitlement, Meritocracy, and Institutional "isms"

Entitlement

As we saw earlier, those who are privileged often do not realize that their good fortune is at least partly responsible for opportunities available to them. Instead it seems as if their talents and efforts—their "merits"—justify these opportunities; this is referred to as a sense of entitlement. Although this may be valid to some extent, privileged ones tend to underestimate how much of their success is actually due to luck or to help from others. This sense of entitlement may also lead to feeling unfairness when opportunities do not come as expected. Jacques (1997) describes a striking example of a White male senior executive whose son had not been admitted to his preferred medical school on the West Coast and instead was enrolled at a school across the country, far from his home. This executive was seen as relatively progressive, and was meeting with Jacques to discuss expanding employment opportunities for women in his company. Despite this, he began the meeting by expressing his frustration with his son's situation, stating that 40% of those admitted to the preferred medical school were Asian Americans!

Jacques noted that this percentage is not at all surprising, given the demographic makeup of the state and the fact that students of Asian descent are more likely to complete college than those in other ethnic groups. Jacques said *"The executive was not complaining that his son could not get into medical school, but that he could not get into the school of his choice.* Such is the sense of entitlement among those of us with dominant identities that we are likely to judge *any* failure to achieve our goals as evidence of structural inequity" (1997, p. 87, emphasis in original). This sense of entitlement is likely to be part of the rationale underlying some claims of "reverse discrimination" by Whites or men who see opportunities go to minorities or women that they think should have gone to them.

Meritocracy

Powerful cultural forces in the US and some other societies lead to a pervasive acceptance of the idea of meritocracy. Survey research has shown that people believe this is not only how things *should* work, but also that organizations and our society *do* operate in this way: Good things come to those who have ability and work hard (Castillo & Benard, 2010). Meritocracy also implies that persons who lack attainment (by the standards of the dominant group) are unsuccessful because of their lack of ability, motivation, or both. It is instructive, however, to consider how and by whom "merit" is defined. Evaluative criteria are usually developed by the group or people in charge and are likely to reflect a biased perspective rather than an objective one. Once again, the consequences of privilege and structural impediments are overlooked. For example, some schools evaluate teachers on the basis of their students' scores on standardized tests. Whose perspective is reflected in this view? How is merit defined in the case of teachers? Is this fair?

Institutional "isms"

Often we use the terms "racism" or "sexism" to refer to prejudice against others of minority or gender status. However, *institutional* racism and sexism (and other "isms") also exist. These terms refer not to the prejudice of individuals, but to the negative consequences for non-dominant groups of living and working within a culture designed by and for those in the dominant group. The history of voting in the US illustrates well the operation of institutional racism and sexism. From the founding of our country until after the Civil War, only White men who owned property were able to vote—not women, and not men of other races or non-landowners. After the Civil War, the 15th Amendment granted the vote to all men, including Blacks (although there were still many obstacles to their voting, such as violence, poll taxes, and literacy tests). Not until 1920 with the passage of the 19th Amendment were women able to vote! And only in 1965 with passage of the Voting Rights Act were racially discriminatory restrictions on voting targeted by law ("Voting Rights Act," 1965; n.d.). Its protections have subsequently been significantly eroded through actions of some state governments and the US Supreme Court (Brennan Center, 2015). This historical example illustrates how institutions of government operate to assure that major decisions affecting the public are made by certain dominant segments of the population rather than by the populace as a whole. Such discriminatory laws and procedures probably do originate in deliberate or thoughtless race and gender prejudice of individuals, which may seem rational and "normal" in its historical context. However, once institutions begin to operate, they constrain behaviors of everyone in a society, whether or not individuals themselves hold prejudiced views. Persons of privilege who are advantaged by existing institutions may not realize the degree to which these barriers limit the opportunity of others. Prior to the 2012 national election, there were attempts to combat "voter fraud" by use of restrictive forms of voter ID, easily available to working age people who drive cars, were born in hospitals, or travel abroad—but very difficult to obtain for some persons who are poor, young, elderly, disabled, or geographically isolated.

Deliberate action is required to confront and change societal institutions and even after they are changed, their effects may be long lasting. Consider, for example, the laws that forbade the teaching of reading and writing to slaves ("An Act" . . ., 2004), the system of racial segregation of education in the US that was only outlawed with the 1954 *Brown v. Board of Education* Supreme Court decision, and the *de facto* educational segregation that still exists today in many communities as a result of patterns of residence.

The institutions of a work organization include policies and procedures and governing structures as well as strong norms and customs. In some work organizations, these may lead to *systemic* discrimination (i.e., throughout the organizational system) even in the absence of intentional prejudice and deliberate discrimination by members of the organization. One important task of a diversity manager is analyzing organizational institutions for any unwarranted differential and negative impacts on some groups of employees, and correcting this where possible. For example, the common practice of hiring new workers by referral from present employees results in limiting the applicant pool to demographic groups already represented in the organization. If different groups of people are not recruited into the hiring pool, they surely will not be hired!

The Social Construction of Difference

Opposed to my three "Contradicts, but..."

Our assumptions and habits of thinking are also affected by the process of *social construction*. This term refers to an important contemporary perspective about how we come to "know" the physical and social world around us. Most of us feel as if we live our daily lives discovering reality as it already exists, independent of ourselves. In contrast, *constructivism* asserts that we actively create our understanding of reality as we give meaning to the world we encounter (Berger & Luckmann, 1966; Hare-Mustin & Maracek, 1988). Furthermore, this reality we perceive is largely constructed out of our interactions with others, hence the term "social construction." Within a culture or a subculture, we share a common sense of reality as well as a common set of signs which we call language, which is needed for communication about this shared reality. Often we feel things are more *real* when we can put them into words. For example, think of how we search for the right words to convey our emotions.

Within the field of psychology, Gergen (1985) has discussed assumptions underlying most constructionist thought, including the following:

1. What we experience as our knowledge of the world does not actually arise from systematic study of reality.
2. Our knowledge actually comes from social inventions such as language, customs, historical accounts, or religious or political frameworks.
3. The interpretations that persist are not necessarily those that are more "valid" in portraying reality accurately. Instead, prevailing perspectives are those that are more successfully communicated, negotiated, or socially supported.
4. These dominant interpretations are critically significant because they often lead to actions of individuals, groups, and societies.

One point should be emphasized about the social constructionist perspective as it applies to differences based on group membership, which are central to our understanding of diversity in organizations. Besides being inherently social, the social construction process relies upon *language*. Those in power in a society have greater influence than others upon development of language, how ideas are communicated through public media such as television, film, and print, and the sharing of ideas that we call education (Hare-Mustin & Maracek, 1988). In US society, those in power have usually been White, able-bodied, heterosexual males, especially those with property and financial resources. Thus, this group has had greater influence on the nature of the social reality we all experience and how it is communicated through language and media.

For example, in the US, we commonly hear the term "working mother" to refer to a woman with children who is employed outside the home. But what is a "non-working mother"? Does this mean that a woman whose primary activity is the care of her family and household is not "working"? Where does this expression come from?

The genesis of this social construction probably goes back to the Industrial Revolution when "work" moved from the home and into the factory. Over time, the term work came to be applied to labor that produced money (Padavic & Reskin, 2002). At times married women were not allowed or not likely to be employed outside the home; for example, during the Great Depression, women whose husbands worked in government jobs were often laid off so their jobs could be held by men (Blackwelder, 1997). This understanding of work is embedded in our Social Security system that provides benefits for spouses on the assumption that they will be female and without lifetime earnings to support retirement. Measurement of the gross domestic product (GDP) of our economy leaves out home-work that does not *produce* something that is sold. This understanding is also embedded in our gender roles and the ideas that men need more earnings than women because they have families to support, that unemployment is worse for men than for women, that women should not work outside the home while their children are young, and even in titles of magazines! In this example, society's institutions devalue "home-work" and the care of one's own children. This social construction has important implications for D&I in contemporary US organizations, such as management of work/family issues (see Chapters 9 and 13). Volunteer activities are often disregarded as qualification for paid employment despite the fact that valuable skills and work habits can certainly be learned in this context. In the US, lack of access to paid parental leave or flexible schedules reflects the socially constructed devaluation of home-based duties. So do the extremely demanding and family-unfriendly schedules that are part of the path to advancement in certain professions such as law, medicine, and finance.

How is this relevant for management of D&I at work? A good diversity manager considers how common assumptions resulting from social construction lead to requirements or procedures that are unnecessary or even harmful to some individuals, or to understandings that may not be shared by employees from different backgrounds. For example, are "requirements" (e.g., strength) for certain jobs really justified? Are criteria for evaluating jobs or appraising employees' job performance (e.g., tardiness) actually useful and appropriate, and are they carefully explained or simply assumed to be widely understood?

Gender: The Social Construction of Sex

Have you been asked to check "male" or "female" to describe your "gender" on a questionnaire or application? Not long ago, the word "gender" referred only to a grammatical property of a noun or pronoun such as "he" or "she." Now it is widely used as a synonym for "sex," perhaps because people believe this is more politically correct (or because they try to avoid confusion with "sexual behavior"). Actually this usage is misleading. In social science, many prefer to use the word "gender" to refer to the social understanding of what it means to be biologically male or female, with "sex" referring to the category associated with one's biological characteristics. For example, in a study comparing the responses of males and females, we would speak of "sex comparisons." On the other hand, when comparing role expectations, normative behaviors, or attributes thought to be characteristic of males or females, we would use the word "gender," such as in the term "gendered leadership." Note that this distinction is *not* based on whether the difference is thought to be *caused* by biology vs. social factors; most differences, in fact, stem from combinations of biology and environment. Instead, the distinction rests on whether we are categorizing people on the basis of anatomical differences vs. the societal meanings of maleness or femaleness. In this text, we will use the term "gender" to refer to the social construction of sex in a particular societal and cultural context.

To understand how powerful social construction can be, try this exercise: See how many arguments you can come up with for the proposition that "there are more than two sexes." (In some cultures, there have been more than two.) Why do we think that there are only two sexes, and that everyone must be one or the other? Why do we speak of the "opposite" sex rather than the "other" sex? For more information, see the shaded box here and in Chapter 9.

A Third Sex? Or Gender?

Judith Lorber has written extensively about the social construction of gender. In an excerpt (2007) from her 1994 book, *Paradoxes of Gender*, she discusses how the idea of gender is construed differently in contemporary Western societies than in some others. "Some societies have three genders—men, women, and *berdaches* or *hijras* or *zaniths* [who are] biological males who behave, dress, work, and are treated in most respects as social women ... There are African and American Indian societies that have a gender status called *manly hearted women*—biological females who work, marry, and parent as men; their social status is 'female men.'" What makes them men is not masculine behavior or dress, but "enough wealth to buy a wife"! (p. 56). The famous biologist Anne Fausto-Sterling also writes of these other conceptions of gender and concludes, "What is important ... is that the existence of other systems suggests that ours is not inevitable" (2000, p. 109).

Many criteria could be used to determine whether someone is male or female: internal or external genitalia (i.e., testes and penis; ovaries and vagina); sex chromosomes (XY or XX); sense of identity as man or woman; physical appearance such as height, body shape, or hair distribution (secondary sex characteristics); social identity as man or woman; or even masculine or feminine personality traits or behaviors. We generally assume that for a given person all these dimensions will coincide, producing two categories of people. However, many individuals do not fit this consistent pattern. Some women have no ovaries, some are very tall, some behave in ways considered "masculine." Some men are employed in careers predominantly occupied by women such as teaching or nursing, some have very little body or facial hair, some behave in gentle and nurturing ways that we associate with women. Some have disguised themselves as members of the other sex in order to do something they could not otherwise have done: fight in a war, work in a profession, publish or perform creative works, or take care of their own children, as actor Robin Williams did in the film *Mrs. Doubtfire*. Homosexual persons are attracted to sexual partners of the same sex. Transgender persons appear to be one sex on the basis of biological factors but feel strongly that they are really the other sex.

Thus, what appears at first to be a simple two-category system of female and male is actually a more complex distinction based on many dimensions. Although women and men are more similar to each other than they are to other animals, our social construction of sex is in terms of *difference* (Hare-Mustin & Maracek, 1988; Lorber, 1998). Much discourse about gender—whether by politicians, the public, or social scientists—concerns whether there are differences between the sexes, and if so, how large the differences are, why they exist, and what if anything is to be done about them. Lorber (1998) argues that the idea of "difference" is itself a social construction: "Bodies differ in many ways physiologically, but they are completely transformed by social practices to fit into the salient categories of a society, the most pervasive of which are 'female' and 'male'" (p. 34).

How is this relevant to behavior in a diverse organization? It is wise to recognize that abilities, skills, interests, and motivations for various sorts of work vary with the individual and are not always predictably associated with one sex. Because we focus on difference, it is easy to assume that women and men should be sorted into work situations in a way that enacts society's construction of gender. We should remember that what is thought to be masculine or feminine varies with history, geography, class, and culture. Our conception of the "traditional" role of women—as mothers whose main task is care of their home and children instead of employment outside the home—in fact has only characterized a relatively small group of middle- and upper-class European and American women during part of the 19th and 20th centuries. For immigrant women, frontier women, slave women, working-class women, and most women in other times and places, this was not the norm. Another example is the idea of *men's jobs* and *women's jobs*. Why is it more acceptable for a man to be an EMT than a nurse? Why do we speak of a "female dentist" when a man is just a "dentist"? Two hundred or more years ago a clerk or secretary was a man with some chance of upward mobility at work; today the job of secretary or clerk is generally held by women, often without college degrees, and seldom leads to career advancement.

The Social Construction of Race

People commonly think of others in terms of categories we call "race," such as those described in Chapter 2. Many people could list physical characteristics of each racial category, perhaps even personality traits, typical skills or interests, or speech patterns. And, as with sex, they probably understand the term "race" to refer to a system of classifying people based on biological characteristics.

What about the biological basis for racial distinctions? So-called racial distinctions are conventionally made on the basis of skin color, hair texture, or shape of facial features such as eyes, nose, or lips. However, two things should be noted: first, choosing the cue on which we will rely is strictly arbitrary—how often do we classify races by eye color? And second, classifying people using one biological trait such as skin color will produce different results than using a different characteristic such as blood type or digestive enzymes (Begley, 1995). Genetic and other differences among individuals of the same race are greater than differences between races (Zuckerman, 1990; Phinney, 1996; Whitfield & McClearn, 2005); current genetic research does not find that races are genetically distinct (Bonham, Warshauer-Baker, & Collins, 2005).

Even skin color, a common basis for racial categorization in the US, is exceedingly variable within a so-called race. Many "Blacks" are lighter than some of south European or Middle Eastern ancestry. Someone from India who is "White" or "Asian" in the US would be "Black" in Great Britain; "in Brazil, however, anyone with any degree of Caucasian appearance is regarded as White" (Zuckerman, 1990, p. 1298). Asians are extremely variable in skin color, from some darker persons from the Indian subcontinent to the very fair East Asians from China, Korea, or Japan. Furthermore, it is more obvious each day that many individuals are biological blends of different "racial" groups and cannot easily be categorized. The American golfer Tiger Woods, son of a Thai mother and an African American father, describes himself as "Cablinasian." More precisely, he is one-eighth Native American, one-eighth African American, one-quarter White, one-quarter Chinese, and one-quarter Thai (McCormick & Begley, 1996).

The concept of race is actually a way of categorizing people on the basis of how others respond to them and the "implications of such responses for one's life chances and sense of identity" (Phinney, 1996, p. 919). For example, consider the widespread racial identification of Barack Obama as "the nation's first Black President." It is generally known that President Obama's Midwestern mother was "white as milk" and his Kenyan father "black as pitch" (Obama, 2004, p. 10; Halberstadt, Sherman, & Sherman, 2011). He is as much White as Black. However, it is quite clear that others respond to him and that he identifies himself as a Black/African American person, and that this categorization has had many implications for his "life chances," though not in the way it does for most African Americans.

The importance of racial distinctions and even the nature of the distinctions themselves have varied widely across time and geography (Rothenberg, 2007). From ancient times to the 17th century, diverse peoples were assimilated physically into conquering societies and "no significant social meanings were attached to their physical differences" (Smedley & Smedley, 2005, p. 18). The idea of distinct races is a recent social invention, dating from the time when European explorers sailed the globe and came into contact with natives of the Far East or the New World (Omi & Winant, 2007). Race arose in the 1600s and 1700s as a biological justification for exploitation of one group by another and coincides historically with African slavery and encroachment on the lands of the Native Americans. Those considered less than human can more easily be enslaved, their families and cultures broken, and their belongings appropriated. Genocide of European Jews during the Holocaust was also facilitated by consideration of Jews as a subordinate race (Brodkin, 2007).

In the American colonies, persons of mixed European/African ancestry, called "mulattoes," were not always considered "Black." In some parts of the pre-Civil War South, they might be considered White or a racial combination (Cose, 1995). Until the late 1700s, physical differences between African and poor European indentured servants did not prevent social interaction and marriage. When the African slave trade grew to replace indentured servitude around that time, the understanding of separate races developed. New legal restrictions prevented intermarriage and offspring of mixed unions were defined as Black (Buck, 2007).

After the Civil War, racial classifications became more stringent in the laws of many states; persons with any sub-Saharan African ancestry would be called "Negro" or Black. The *rule of hypodescent* or the *one-drop rule* developed as a social convention by which a person of mixed heritage was assigned to the racial category lower in the societal hierarchy. Thus anyone known to have Negro ancestry was also considered Negro. This social construction was "an invention, which we in the United States have made in order to keep biological facts from intruding into our collective racist fantasies" (Harris, 1964, p. 56).

To understand the power of this distinction, consider the case of Susie Guillory Phipps, a Louisiana woman who was the descendant of a Black slave and an 18th-century White landowner. In 1982–1983, she sued the Louisiana Bureau of Vital Records to change the racial classification on her birth certificate from Black to White. The Court upheld a 1970 law requiring that anyone with one-thirty-second "Negro blood" was Black, and Ms. Phipps lost her case! In 1986, the Supreme Court let this ruling stand although later the state law was repealed (Cose, 1995; Omi & Winant, 2007). Today in this country people are identified as Black when they choose that self-identity and/or when others see them as Black (Reid, 1994).

Hypodescent still affects our racial perceptions under some circumstances (Peery & Bodenhausen, 2008). Participants in one lab study were shown racially ambiguous faces; some received information about the targets describing their multiracial backgrounds in biological and/or cultural terms. When participants had to choose quickly among categories (Black, White, both, neither), they were more likely to select "Black" when multiracial information was provided. However, with more time to provide a categorization freely using the same multiracial information, a "multiracial" description was more likely. It is encouraging that when people have time to reflect, they make more nuanced judgments about ambiguous faces. However, quick reflexive responses occur often in interactions, lead to stereotypic thinking, and influence how social relationships develop. When we don't have time to ponder, we seem to attend most to the aspect of a multiracial person that indicates subordinate status—a modern version of hypodescent. "It may be that only when perceivers are both motivated and able to reflect upon others in a deliberate manner are they able to escape simplistic, monoracial categorizations of racially complex social targets" (Peery & Bodenhausen, 2008, p. 977).

Some psychologists believe that hypodescent may also be at least partly a result of basic processes of attention and learning. A study of White New Zealanders (Halberstadt et al., 2011), found that someone who grows up surrounded by features of majority groups pays attention to aspects of appearance that distinguish minorities, and this connection will be strong because of the distinctiveness from majority individuals. Then when a racially ambiguous face is encountered, "minority" aspects are noticed and more strongly influence racial categorizations.

Ethnicity: The Social Construction of Race?

Most social scientists today have abandoned the idea of reliable biological distinctions among races, and indeed the notion of "race" itself. Some prefer the related term "ethnicity," referring to broad groupings of people who vary in terms of culture of origin as well as what we conventionally think of as "race" (Phinney, 1996). We need a different word to remind us that our ideas about racial characteristics have a social and cultural rather than a biological basis. Just as gender is the social construction of the distinction between the sexes, so ethnicity is the socially defined counterpart of "racial" distinctions. In both cases an artificial set of categories is imposed on a complex underlying set of variations.

According to Phinney (1996), three central aspects of ethnicity may account for its psychological significance: (a) the collection of attitudes, behaviors, and cultural values that characterize ethnic groups; (b) the sense of ethnic identity that members of an ethnic group share; and (c) the consequences of being in the ethnic group. For example, those in non-dominant ethnic groups experience powerlessness, discrimination, or deprivation, while dominants experience privilege and power.

Other Examples of Social Construction

Other aspects of difference are also socially constructed, such as disability, age, and social class. Although these are discussed in later chapters, at this point you might consider how these characteristics are represented (or not represented) in contemporary media, humor, political rhetoric, and general discourse. Our interactions with individuals at work are conducted in the social context of society's interpretations of their apparent characteristics. Sometimes it is difficult to see persons as *individuals* apart from how their characteristics are socially constructed, but we are more likely to have empathic and effective interactions with others if we do. For another example of social construction relevant to judgments at work, see the shaded box.

What's the Matter with Quotas?

In thinking about opportunities at school and at work, we sometimes use the term "quota." On this Semantic Differential scale, how would you evaluate "quotas"?

Very Good	Good	Neither good nor bad	Bad	Very bad
1	2	3	4	5

Many people think quotas are unfair and probably would rate the term 4 or 5 on this scale. Knowing that quotas have a negative connotation, politicians sometimes equate Affirmative Action (AA) with imposition of quotas. They know this will often rouse the public to support bans on AA such as those in Florida or California. If you rated quotas negatively, consider why the word has that connotation. What is wrong with quotas?

Here is a list of several examples of quotas.

- Quotas for various kinds of foods in weight loss programs
- Drafts of new players by athletic teams
- Immigration quotas based on country of origin
- Trade or import quotas
- Relative numbers of in-state and out-of-state students admitted to public universities
- Allocation of Senators and Representatives in Congress
- Restrictions on how often the same person can publish a Letter to the Editor

- Number of concert tickets that a person can buy at one time
- Number of seats in college stadiums allocated to students, alumnae, the public
- Sales or production quotas for certain periods of time

Why are quotas used in these situations? Is this acceptable? Why do we have a negative view of quotas?

Thinking about *Why* People Do What They Do

Among our assumptions and habits of thinking are *attributions* we make about *why* a person behaved in a particular way and why certain outcomes followed. *Attribution theory* concerns how we come to understand causes of behavior. Because we are likely to respond quite differently toward others depending on judgments of their abilities, motivation, and the circumstances of their behavior, attribution theory is clearly relevant to management of D&I. Applications of attribution research to work environments have been extensively reviewed by Martinko (2004).

An attribution is an assumption about causality. We attribute personality traits or abilities to people based on what they do and the circumstances and consequences of their behavior. For example, we attribute acting talent to Tom Hanks or Meryl Streep because we have seen them in many important roles and they have received praise and awards for their work.

One basic attributional distinction is between *internal* and *external* causes of behavior and its consequences (Heider, 1958). In a study relevant to work-family conflict for parents, a sample of over 250 university alumni reacted to situations in which they faced time-based conflict between work and family responsibilities (Poposki, 2011). Over half attributed the conflict externally rather than internally to themselves; external attributions were more likely to refer to work rather than family as the source of conflict. Those who made external attributions were likely to report feeling frustrated or angry, but did not express more guilt or shame.

When we think someone was hired because of high ability and motivation, we make a *dispositional* (or internal) attribution and are likely to react differently to the person than if we think hiring was based on luck, social connections, demographic fit, or other *situational* (or external) factors. Dispositional attributions often lead us to expect that the person will continue to perform at the same level, but situational attributions suggest that when the circumstances change, the person will behave differently.

Attribution researchers have pointed out that we are more likely to notice and make attributions about behaviors that are unexpected, when they have positive or negative consequences for us, or when the person is important to us in some way (Harvey & Weary, 1984). Furthermore, although this process of drawing causal conclusions could be rational, often it is not. We make errors in the attribution process for "cognitive" reasons: perhaps we have been careless in observing or do not have all the information needed to attribute accurately, or perhaps we do not use available information logically (e.g., overweighting some and disregarding other). We also make attributional mistakes for "motivational" reasons, because we are too involved to reason objectively or distort information because of our own needs and goals.

One attributional habit is so common that it is called the *fundamental attribution error:* a very strong tendency to overestimate the degree to which someone else's behavior results from internal causes (Ross, 1977). A related concept is the *actor-observer effect*, which means that for our own behavior (actor), we focus on external or situational factors. However, when we observe another's behavior, we focus on internal causes. This can be explained in rational and cognitive terms: thinking of our own behavior, we are very conscious of the environmental factors that provide context for our acts, but when observing others' behavior we generally do not have full access to this information. Thus we tend to think that internal causes produce their behavior. What do these habits imply about the attributions we make about others in a diverse work environment?

When making attributions about behavior of members of underrepresented groups, these tendencies may lead us to over-attribute to personality and motivation and underestimate the effect of environmental factors. In the interest of more effective interaction, we might try to discover if situational obstacles such as transportation or responsibilities at home account for tardiness, and what might be done about that. In general, it is helpful to try to understand situations as others see them; empathic understanding is a particularly important skill when the workforce is diverse and the experiences of our co-workers may be quite variable as a function of their demographic characteristics.

Consider a situation in which you apply for a job opening that would be a promotion for you. Another applicant is chosen who is of a different sex or racio-ethnic group than you. In this situation you are likely to make attributions because the selection affects you directly. How would you interpret this outcome if you knew very little about the other person? What if there were no other employees of the same sex or racio-ethnicity as the person chosen? Would it matter if the person was of minority status? What if you had applied as a "stretch," thinking you might not be qualified? What if you had expected to be chosen on the basis of your relationships with those higher up in the organization? The rationality and accuracy of your attributions depends on how much relevant information you have and how carefully and objectively you make use of it.

In addition to making attributions about others, we also draw causal inferences about our own behavior, successes and failures. *Self-serving biases* are self-attributions about success or failure that are distorted in ways that protect our self-esteem. For example, when your project turns out well, it often seems that this is due to your hard work, skills, and talents. On the other hand, if a competition is lost or a goal is not accomplished, it feels as if obstacles were simply too great, time was too short, resources were inadequate, directions misleading, co-workers incompetent or unmotivated, or the evaluation unfair. Harvey and Martinko (2009) found that respondents with a strong sense of entitlement were more likely than others to use a self-serving attributional style, especially if their need for cognition (i.e., motivation to seek out and think about relevant information) was low.

When someone is hired or promoted, the person's qualifications should be publicly known. When someone from the majority group is chosen and there are minority candidates in the pool, this should prevent perceptions of unfair discrimination. When the chosen candidate comes from an underrepresented group, this information should reduce the likelihood that others will assume an "unqualified" person was chosen for demographic reasons. Selection of a woman/man or member of an ethnic minority is likely to be noticed in situations where this is unusual; others, particularly if they feel a sense of entitlement, may assume the choice was based on "AA requirements" to hire an unqualified person. AA does not require selection of unqualified persons just on the basis of race or sex—in fact, this would likely be illegal discrimination. Nevertheless, many people believe that this happens. Part of the strength of this perception stems from attributional processes we have considered.

Thinking about What's Fair

Another pattern of thinking about relationships in organizations concerns perceptions of the fairness or justice of decisions and their consequences. Much research in organizational science has focused on how we perceive fairness or unfairness and how we react to these perceptions. Clearly this work has much relevance for the management of D&I because many situations in diverse organizations deal with what people think is fair or not fair.

Organizational applications of justice research began with Equity Theory (Adams, 1965), a social psychological theory that deals with feelings of fairness in social situations. Equity Theory involves three basic ideas:

1. The essence of a fairness judgment is social comparison of oneself with a relationship partner. Thus Equity Theory is inherently social and comparative.
2. We feel that a situation (e. g., a job, friendship, marriage) is fair when the ratio of our inputs to outputs is equal to the ratio of our chosen comparison person (e.g., co-worker, friend, spouse). Inputs and outputs need not be the same for the two people to generate a sense of fairness, but they should be proportional. For example, if I put in a lot and receive a lot, but the other puts in a little and gets only a little back, that should be fair. However, if I am doing most of the work and receiving little in return, but the other is doing very little yet getting the same reward as I am, that seems unfair.
3. Input/output ratios that are different produce an uncomfortable emotional state of *inequity* that motivates the person to do something to correct the situation: increase or reduce inputs or outputs, leave the relationship, distort evaluations of inputs and outputs, or change the comparison person. Strong feelings of unfairness can sometimes lead to turnover, low effort, sabotage, theft, work slowdowns or stoppages, bad publicity, and even lawsuits as people attempt to correct or respond to outcomes they see as unfair (e.g., Greenberg, 2009).

Theoretically, attempts to correct inequity should happen when one feels *overrewarded* as well as *underrewarded*. Although empirical support exists for both predictions, studies have found more consistent and predictable results about reactions to underreward (Muchinsky, 2006). Overreward is easily justified by thinking of other contributions one is making to the relationship, without working harder to make it seem fair. Feeling underrewarded often leads to reduced input in the form of tardiness, turnover, or reduced effort and is harder to justify cognitively without devaluing one's contributions. Consider feeling underpaid vs. overpaid in a job. Which would feel worse?

Two things should be noted about Equity Theory. First, it deals with *distributive justice* (DJ), that is, how rewards are allocated or distributed. This is also called *outcome justice*. Second, Equity Theory reflects an individualistic and meritocratic understanding of fairness, one that seems quite reasonable in the US in economic relationships and sometimes in social ones. But proportionality or equity-based allocation is not the only standard of fairness: in some situations, and in some other cultures, people feel that things should be distributed *equally* or even on the basis of *need*. For example, generally in unionized situations, organized labor favors an *equality rule* which is likely to increase solidarity and decrease competition and harmful comparisons among co-workers. As another example, in situations of natural disaster, we may think that supplies should be distributed to those who are in greatest need. The requirement for a minimum wage and the "living wage" movement also illustrate attempts to allocate at least partly on the basis of need. None of these three allocation rules (equity, equality, and need) is inherently *right* or better than others, and in some cases rewards can be distributed using more than one rule. For example, employees in the same job might be paid equally in terms of salary, but be eligible for additional pay based on measurement of performance or amount produced/sold (Cropanzano, Bowen, & Gilliland, 2007).

During the 1970s and 1980s, researchers considered a form of justice judgment based on the fairness of the *procedures* that are used to make decisions about outcomes. Leventhal (1980), one of the earliest to distinguish distributive from procedural justice (PJ), proposed six rules for fair procedures:

• Consistency: Procedures should be the same for everyone and across time.
• Bias suppression: Procedures should be objective and not affected by personal self-interest or preconceived ideas.
• Accuracy: Information should be as good, complete, and error-free as possible.
• Correctability: Decisions made in error should be reversible; an appeal process should exist.

- Representativeness: The allocation process should reflect the interests of relevant or important constituencies.
- Ethicality: Procedures should follow commonly accepted moral values and not involve deception, bribery, invasions of privacy, or other unethical behaviors.

Researchers found that judgments about fairness were indeed affected by these structural aspects of procedure, but another important factor was how people are treated. Bies (1987) developed the idea of *interactional justice* or the fairness of interpersonal interaction in the context of significant decisions. Two aspects were identified: *informational justice*, adequacy of information or explanations provided about decisions (also called *social accounts*); and *interpersonal justice*, the degree to which treatment of those affected is respectful and tactful (Bies, 2005). Scholars disagree about whether these two types of organizational justice are independent, but wide consensus exists that perceptions of fairness and people's emotional reactions and behavior are often affected by the timeliness and quality of explanations they receive about decisions affecting them, and by the respect or disrespect with which they are treated in the process.

Besides identifying factors affecting feelings of fair treatment, researchers also studied how judgments about outcomes and procedures interact (Brockner & Wiesenfeld, 2005). For example, for some responses such as accepting decisions, feelings about the outcome itself may matter less when PJ is high. If you were not the winning job candidate but you think the process was open and fair, your disappointment would probably be less than if you think the judgment was biased. PJ can also enhance the effect of favorable outcomes on someone's self-esteem. If you were hired through a process that was widely agreed to be fair, you will probably feel better about yourself than if it was sloppy or biased. Researchers agree that it is usually best to arrange things so that people believe both the outcomes and the procedures have been fair. However, if people will see the outcome as unfair but nothing can be done about this (as in layoffs, for example), it is best to strive for fairness in procedures: Treat people humanely, give good explanations, use a process that is open (Konovsky & Brockner, 1993). In unionized environments, collective bargaining agreements often contain provisions about how layoffs will be implemented (even when none is expected). This process is agreed to by both labor and management before it is needed; this should result in a greater sense of PJ than if management had simply implemented its own process—especially when people are not happy about the outcome.

How do these ideas apply to D&I in organizations? First, people sometimes react strongly to outcomes that are undesirable or unfair, and to procedures that they feel violate principles of just treatment. Those responsible for making and implementing decisions should take this into account when choosing who will receive certain outcomes, how these decisions are made and communicated to employees, and how people feel they are treated in the process. Here are some examples of situations that can be managed more effectively by considering DJ and PJ:

1. Decisions impacting outcomes of others should be made by considering their views, in some cases by actually asking them in advance about what is important to them. In a diverse environment, managers may be less familiar with perspectives of employees from different backgrounds.
2. Not every employee values things in the same way and incentive allocations that seem fair to managers and some employees may seem unfair to others. This is probably more the case when employees are diverse. *Cafeteria benefits* offered by some employers address this variability in the circumstances of different people. In a cafeteria plan, different employee benefits (e.g., paid time off, sick leave, different kinds of insurance, child or elder care assistance) may be offered and employees can select the one(s) that best suit their personal circumstances in a way that equalizes cost to the employer. An employee without dependents might value additional time off, a parent might value child care assistance, and others may choose educational assistance.

3. Jobs, promotions, overtime work, developmental and other opportunities should be allocated through procedures that are clearly and openly described ahead of time, understandable and accessible, and designed to reduce bias. Search committees and other groups that make selection recommendations or decisions should include representatives of relevant stakeholder or employee groups and individuals who understand or advocate for perspectives of underrepresented groups.

4. Criteria should be examined for evidence of deliberate or inadvertent bias, such as being based on stereotypes or characteristics of those selected in the past that may not really be job relevant (e.g., height, some educational requirements). Selections should be based on advertised criteria and not on subjective judgments or favoritism.

5. Remedial procedures (such as AA) should be explained and implemented in a manner that conveys why they are necessary. Qualifications of those selected, whether majority individuals or those from underrepresented groups, should be emphasized to assure that people believe that advertised procedures were followed and those selected are qualified.

6. Employees should consistently be treated with respect, and managers should create opportunities for employees to share their perspectives rather than ignore or make assumptions about what they think or prefer.

This chapter has discussed basic assumptions such as privilege and entitlement, socially constructed meanings of difference such as sex and race, our attributional habits, and our feelings of fairness in social interactions. The next chapter considers how the structure of organizations can constrain behavior of employees and advance or limit outcomes they experience. For example, the chapter discusses effects of organizational structure on compensation of employees—a topic that illustrates entitlement, social construction, attributions, and fairness.

References

Adams, J. S. (1965). Inequity in social exchange. In L. Berkowitz (Ed.), *Advances in experimental social psychology* (Vol. 2, pp. 267–299). New York: Academic Press.

An act prohibiting the teaching of slaves to read. (2004). Reprinted in P. S. Rothenberg (Ed.), *Race, class, and gender in the United States* (6th ed., pp. 455–456). Retrieved from www.historyisaweapon.com/defcon1/slaveprohibit.html

Begley, S. (1995, February 13). Three is not enough. *Newsweek*, 67–69.

Berger, P., & Luckmann, T. (1966). *The social construction of reality*. Garden City, NY: Doubleday.

Bies, R. J. (1987). The predicament of injustice: The management of moral outrage. In L. L. Cummings & B. M. Staw (Eds.), *Research in organizational behavior* (Vol. 9, pp. 289–319). Greenwich, CT: JAI Press.

Bies, R. J. (2005). Are procedural justice and interactional justice conceptually distinct? In J. Greenberg & J. A. Colquitt (Eds.), *Handbook of organizational justice* (pp. 85–112). Mahwah, NJ: Lawrence Erlbaum Associates.

Blackwelder, J. K. (1997). *Now hiring: The feminization of work in the United States, 1900–1995*. College Station, TX: Texas A & M University Press.

Bonham, V. L., Warshauer-Baker, E., & Collins, F. S. (2005). Race and ethnicity in the genome era: The complexity of the constructs. *American Psychologist, 60*, 9–15.

Branscombe, N. R., & Ellemers, N. (1998). Coping with group-based discrimination: Individualistic versus group-level strategies. In J. K. Swim & C. Stangor (Eds.), *Prejudice: The target's perspective* (pp. 243–266). San Diego, CA: Academic Press.

Brennan Center. (2015, August 4). *The Voting Rights Act: A resource page*. Retrieved from www.brennancenter.org/analysis/voting-rights-act-resource-page

Brockner, J., & Wiesenfeld, B. (2005). How, when, and why does outcome favorability interact with procedural fairness? In J. Greenberg & J. A. Colquitt (Eds.), *Handbook of organizational justice* (pp. 525–553). Mahwah, NJ: Lawrence Erlbaum Associates.

Brodkin, K. (2007). How Jews became white folks and what that says about race in America. In P. S. Rothenberg (Ed.). *Race, class, and gender in the United States: An integrated study* (7th ed., pp. 38–53). New York, NY: Worth Publishers.

Buck, P. D. (2007). Constructing race, creating white privilege. In P. S. Rothenberg (Ed.), *Race, class, and gender in the United States: An integrated study* (7th ed., pp. 32–38). New York, NY: Worth Publishers. Reprinted from *Worked to the bone*. Monthly Review Press.

Burnham, L., & Theodore, N. (2012) *Home economics: The invisible and unregulated world of domestic work*. New York, NY: National Domestic Workers Alliance. Retrieved from www.domesticworkers.org/pdfs/Home EconomicsEnglish.pdf

Case, K. A. (2007). Raising male privilege awareness and reducing sexism: An evaluation of diversity courses. *Psychology of Women Quarterly, 31,* 426–435.

Case, K. A., & Iuzzini, J. (2012). Systems of Privilege: Intersections, awareness, and applications. *Journal of Social Issues, 68* (whole issue).

Castillo, E. J., & Benard, S. (2010). The paradox of meritocracy in organizations. *Administrative Science Quarterly, 55,* 543–576.

Cose, E. (1995, February 13). One drop of bloody history. *Newsweek, 70,* 72.

Cropanzano, R., Bowen, D. E., & Gilliland, S. W. (2007). The management of organizational justice. *Academy of Management Perspectives, 21*(4), 34–48.

"Domestic Workers United." (n.d.). Retrieved from www.domesticworkersunited.org

Ellemers, N., & Barreto, M. (2009). Collective action in modern times: How modern expressions of prejudice prevent collective action. *Journal of Social Issues, 65,* 749–768.

Ehrenreich, B. (2008). *Nickel and Dimed: On (not) getting by in America*. New York, NY: Holt Paperbacks.

Fausto-Sterling, A. (2000). *Sexing the body: Gender politics and the construction of sexuality*. New York: Basic Books.

Gergen, K. J. (1985). The social constructionist movement in modern psychology. *American Psychologist, 40,* 266–275.

Greenberg, J. (2009). Everybody talks about organizational justice, but nobody does anything about it. *Industrial and Organizational Psychology, 2,* 181–195.

Halberstadt, J., Sherman, S. G., & Sherman, J. W. (2011). Why Barack Obama is Black: A cognitive account of hypodescent. *Psychological Science, 22,* 29–33.

Hare-Mustin, R. T., & Maracek, J. (1988). The meaning of difference: Gender theory, postmodernism, and psychology. *American Psychologist, 43,* 455–464.

Harris, M. (1964). *Patterns of race in the Americas*. New York, NY: Norton.

Harvey, J. H., & Martinko, M. J. (2009). An empirical examination of the role of attributions in psychological entitlement and its outcomes. *Journal of Organizational Behavior, 30,* 459–476.

Harvey, J. H., & Weary, G. (1984). Current issues in attribution theory and research. *Annual Review of Psychology, 35,* 427–459.

Heider, F. (1958). *The psychology of interpersonal relations*. New York: Wiley.

Jacques, R. (1997). The unbearable whiteness of being: Reflections of a pale, stale male. In P. Prasad, A. J. Mills, M. Elmes, & A. Prasad (Eds.), *Managing the organizational melting pot: Dilemmas of workplace diversity* (pp. 80–106). Thousand Oaks, CA: SAGE Publications.

Konovsky, M. A., & Brockner, J. (1993). Managing victim and survivor layoff reactions: A procedural justice perspective. In R. Cropanzano (Ed.), *Justice in the workplace: Approaching fairness in human resources management* (pp. 133–153). Hillsdale, NJ: Lawrence Erlbaum Associates.

Leventhal, G. S. (1980). What should be done with Equity Theory? New approaches to the study of fairness in social relationships. In K. J. Gergen, M. S. Greenberg, & R. H. Willis (Eds.), *Social exchange: New advances in theory and research* (pp. 27–55). New York: Plenum Press.

Lorber, J. (1994). *Paradoxes of gender*. New Haven, CT: Yale University Press.

Lorber, J. (1998). The social construction of gender. In P. S. Rothenberg (Ed.), *Race, class, and gender in the United States: An integrated study* (4th ed., pp. 33–45). New York: St. Martin's Press.

Lorber, J. (2007). "Night to his day": The social construction of gender. In P. S. Rothenberg (Ed.), *Race, class, and gender in the United States: An integrated study* (7th ed., pp. 54–65). New York, NY: Worth Publishers.

Lowery, B. S., Knowles, E. D., & Unzueta, M. M. (2007). Framing inequality safely: Whites' motivated perceptions of racial privilege. *Personality and Social Psychology Bulletin, 33,* 1237–1250.

Martinko, M. J. (2004). *Attribution theory in the organizational sciences: Theoretical and empirical contributions*. Greenwich, CT: Information Age Publishing.

McCormick, J., & Begley, S. (1996, December 9). How to raise a Tiger. *Newsweek,* 5256.

McIntosh, P. (1998). White privilege: Unpacking the invisible knapsack. In P. S. Rothenberg (Ed.), *Race, class, and gender in the United States: An integrated study* (4th ed., pp. 165–169). Also in *Peace and Freedom,* July/August 1989, pp. 10–12. Retrieved from www.cirtl.net/files/PartI_CreatingAwareness_WhitePrivilegeUnpackingthe InvisibleKnapsack.pdf

Mor Barak, M. E. (2011). *Managing diversity: Toward a globally inclusive workplace.* Los Angeles, CA: SAGE.

Muchinsky, P. M. (2006). *Psychology applied to work* (8th ed.). Belmont, CA: Thomson Wadsworth.

Obama, B. (2004). *Dreams from my father: A story of race and inheritance.* New York, NY: Three Rivers Press.

Omi, M., & Winant, H. (2007). Racial formations. In P. S. Rothenberg (Ed.), *Race, class, and gender in the United States: An integrated study* (7th ed., pp. 13–22). New York, NY: Worth Publishers. Reprinted from *Racial formations in the United States: From the 1960s to the 1980s.*

Padavic, I., & Reskin, B. (2002). *Women and men at work.* Thousand Oaks, CA: Pine Forge Press.

Peery, D., & Bodenhausen, G. V. (2008). Black + White = Black: Hypodescent in reflexive categorization of racially ambiguous faces. *Psychological Science, 19,* 973–977.

Phinney, J. S. (1996). When we talk about American ethnic groups, what do we mean? *American Psychologist, 51,* 918–927.

Poposki, E. M. (2011). The blame game: Exploring the nature and correlates of attributions following work-family conflict. *Group & Organization Management, 36,* 499–525.

Powell, A. A., Branscombe, N. R., & Schmitt, M. T. (2005). Inequality as ingroup privilege or outgroup disadvantage: The impact of group focus on collective guilt and interracial attitudes. *Personality and Social Psychology Bulletin, 31,* 508–521.

Reid, P. (1994, August). *Gender and class identities: African Americans in context.* Paper presented at the American Psychological Association Convention, Los Angeles.

Ross, L. (1977). The intuitive psychologist and his shortcomings: Distortions in the attribution process. In L. Berkowitz (Ed.), *Advances in experimental social psychology* (Vol. 10, pp. 174–221). New York: Academic Press.

Rothenberg, P. S. (2007). *Race, class, and gender in the United States: An integrated study* (7th ed.) New York, NY: Worth Publishers.

Smedley, A., & Smedley, B. D. (2005). Race as biology is fiction, racism as a social problem is real: Anthropological and historical perspectives on the social construction of race. *American Psychologist, 60,* 16–26.

Voting Rights Act, 1965. (n.d.) www.ourdocuments.gov/doc.php?flash=true&doc=100

Whitfield, K. E., & McClearn, G. (2005). Genes, environment, and race. *American Psychologist, 60,* 104–114.

Zuckerman, M. (1990). Some dubious premises in research and theory on racial differences. *American Psychologist, 45,* 1297–1303.

* Recommended for advanced reading.

Chapter 4

Organizational Structure and the Problem of Pay In-Equity

The concept of *organizational structure* is important in understanding dynamics of D&I. Structure refers first to *formal* boundaries within and among parts of an organization, and second to *informal* boundaries. Formal structure might consist of departments, such as Manufacturing or Marketing; divisions, like those organized around different products or geographical areas; or position groupings, e.g., unionized vs. non-unionized employees, exempt vs. nonexempt employees (under the Fair Labor Standards Act, FLSA), regular vs. contingent (part-time or temporary) employees, or administrative/technical/support personnel. Formal structures may result from decisions by the organization's Board of Directors or top management, or may be distinctions required by law or regulation. For example, the FLSA requires documentation of hours worked and payments for overtime beyond the standard 40-hour work week for employees who are non-exempt (that is, covered by the Act). Informal boundaries develop spontaneously, e.g., employees using the lunchroom and those going out for lunch, or those who play golf together and those who do not.

Formal structural boundaries may also define eligibility for benefits such as pension plans, work hours and flexibility, and representation or participation in various internal or external groups. Formal structure also usually defines areas that differ in power, knowledge of organizational affairs, prestige, salary, and promotion opportunities—all of great consequence, implying differences in inclusion. Both formal and informal structures affect patterns of communication and influence within an organization. For example, employees will be more likely to hear about a job opening or other opportunity if they work in a particular department or if they carpool with others who know about it.

Faultlines are separations among employees based on attributes such as race, sex, age, or longevity in the organization (Lau & Murnighan, 1998). Like geological faults, these "cracks" are based on individual differences in development, may be hidden and dormant for periods of time, and are areas of structural weakness along which a group may break under the pressure of some external event. Faultlines are stronger, and the structure thus more fragile, when differences on various dimensions coincide, for example, if most people of color are newly hired and most Whites are long-time employees. Often in organizations, faultlines also match up with formal or informal structural boundaries. As an illustration, consider the typical situation in which a faultline exists based on sex. Women are likely to be clustered in certain jobs and departments (formal structure) and also to socialize together off the job (informal structure). Organizations may be structurally "weaker" in an organizational sense if faultlines, formal boundaries, and informal structures coincide.

Structure and Process

This chapter focuses on organizational structure and some of its consequences. However, structure and process (covered in the next two chapters and elsewhere in this text) constantly interact and influence each other. For example, communication (a process) is channeled by organizational structures such as physical locations or organizational units. Furthermore, processes such as power or communication can create or change structures, as when managers create a task force to work on a particular problem. Sometimes it is useful to consider structure and process independently, but in practice they constantly interact to bring about organizational outcomes. First we focus on structure, examining organizations from two different perspectives.

Formal Vertical Structure: Looking Up and Down

If we look upward in an organization from the lowest levels (or down from the top), we see "layers" dividing the organization in terms of authority, responsibility, power, salary, control of budget, and other attributes. Large or traditional bureaucratic organizations may be *tall* with many layers; in recent years, as organizations have downsized and attempted to become more efficient, many have cut out layers of management and become *flatter* organizational structures. Only the smallest organizations can operate on a totally egalitarian basis without some hierarchal vertical structure. Most organizations of any size have policies or institutional processes that determine how and whether someone can move upward through organizational layers.

Relevant to diversity, frequently there are demographic differences among the layers, with more White men at higher levels and most women and people of color clustered at lower levels. Two popular terms describe this pattern: the *glass ceiling* and the *sticky floor* (Albelda & Tilly, 1997). The glass ceiling originally referred to an invisible but seemingly impermeable barrier that kept most women from advancing beyond a certain point in upper levels of organizations. The sticky floor captures effects of discriminatory practices, short career ladders, and systematic societal inequality that keep women "stuck" near the bottom of the organizational structure, not even within sight of the glass ceiling. Using another metaphor, the *labyrinth (or maze)*, Eagly and Carli (2007) acknowledged that "obstacles that women face have become more surmountable, at least by some women some of the time" (p. 6). They argue that the glass ceiling metaphor is misleading for several reasons. For example, besides implying that women cannot break through this barrier, the image also suggests that women do not realize it exists until they are close enough to run up against it. The metaphor presents a picture of a single hidden, surprising, and impenetrable obstacle, thus oversimplifying the circuitous and varied routes that some women follow on the way to advancement to the highest levels of organizations. For other reasons why the glass ceiling metaphor is misleading, see the shaded box.

Seven Reasons the Glass Ceiling Metaphor is Misleading

1. Erroneously implies that women have equal access to entry-level positions.
2. Erroneously assumes presence of an absolute barrier at a specific high level in organizations.
3. Erroneously suggests that all barriers to women are difficult to detect and therefore unseen.
4. Erroneously assumes that a single, homogeneous barrier exists and thereby ignores complexity and variety of obstacles that women leaders can face.
5. Fails to recognize diverse strategies that women devise to become leaders.
6. Precludes possibility that women can overcome barriers and become leaders.
7. Fails to suggest that thoughtful problem solving can facilitate women's paths to leadership.

Eagly and Carli (2007, p. 7)

The Glass Ceiling

This term became popular in the 1980s after two journalists used the metaphor in a *Wall Street Journal* article (Hymowitz & Schellhardt, 1986). Soon researchers at the Center for Creative Leadership published their work on "The Executive Women Project" based on interviews with 76 women at or slightly below the level of general management, as well as 22 higher-level executives in 25 of the largest US companies (Morrison, White, Van Velsor, & The Center for Creative Leadership, 1987, updated 1992). They defined the glass ceiling as a barrier which "applies to women as a group who are kept from advancing higher *because they are women"* (1992, p. 13). At the time of their research in the 1980s, Morrison and her colleagues had difficulty finding women at their chosen criterion level of management, and the ones they did identify were often the first and/or only woman at that level in the company. These women differed from their male peers because of three types of pressure they had faced throughout their careers: from the job itself, from being a pioneer, and from trying to balance work with family life. The Executive Women Project produced several recommendations for women, which still resonate today not only for women but also for people of color. They include building one's competence, thinking strategically, and connecting with others for mutual benefit. These recommendations are listed in more detail in Box 4.1.

Box 4.1 Recommendations from The Executive Woman Project

Lesson 1: Learn the Ropes. How good you are is only one part; you must also understand the rules in order to survive (p. 75). Don't threaten others; do well in work that is seen as important; succeed at managing men and minorities; trust feedback from your superiors; understand limits.

Lesson 2: Take Control of Your Career. No one else will do this for you, neither the system's natural processes nor a mentor (p. 85). Aim at the "right" jobs as soon as possible; be proactive; make your goals and needs clear; avoid career derailment, such as by failing to pick your fights (pp. 90–91).

Lesson 3: Build Confidence (p. 92). Take reasonable risks in jobs, perhaps with a boss who encourages this, and perform well in them. See how you compare to a broad range of other managers.

Lesson 4: Rely on Others (p. 100). Identify mentors, sponsors, role models, peers and networks who can help with different things, both in and outside the company; learn how to manage others well; seek and use constructive feedback.

Lesson 5: Go for the "Bottom Line" (p. 106). Figure out what is important and focus on results in that area; be willing to make tough decisions; follow good business practices; be authentic to your own values.

Lesson 6: Integrate Life and Work (p. 112). Recognize the difficulties of combining multiple roles and work out a solution that fits your priorities; understand that it is generally more difficult for women to combine a demanding career with marriage and children than it is for men.

Extras: 1. Build credibility that is clear to those higher up by working closely with higher-ups, taking and succeeding in high-visibility roles, or doing well in professional or community organizations.

2. Build on your competency to find advocates higher up.

3. Sheer luck. Recognize opportunities but resist others' attributing your success to luck rather than ability (pp. 127–136).

Morrison, A. M., White, R. P., and Van Velsor, E. (1992, updated edition)

The popularity of the glass ceiling metaphor prompted Congress to include in the Civil Rights Act of 1991 a provision to set up a bipartisan Federal Glass Ceiling Commission to study and prepare recommendations about eliminating "artificial barriers to the advancement of *women and minorities*" (emphasis added) and increasing opportunities and developmental experiences for these groups to improve their advancement into managerial decision-making positions

(PL 102-166, Nov. 21, 1991, Title II, sec. 203[1][a]). More specifically, the Commission was to deal with (a) policies and practices for filling higher-level positions; (b) developmental and training procedures for "moving up"; (c) compensation and reward structures; and (d) use and enforcement of existing pertinent laws.

So by this time, the term "glass ceiling" had come to refer to underrepresented groups, both women and minorities. Meanwhile the term "diversity" had come into usage in the business community to apply to inclusion of underrepresented groups. The findings of the Glass Ceiling Commission led to recommendations that still pertain many years later in the context of managing diversity.

The 1995 Commission report identified barriers at three levels that impede the progress of women and people of color in organizations. In *society at large*, the "supply barrier" of lack of opportunity and the "difference barrier" of stereotypes and bias were noted. *Government barriers* included lack of vigorous and consistent monitoring and law enforcement, weaknesses in the collection of employment-related data, and inadequate reporting of glass ceiling issues. Barriers *internal to business structure* included inadequate outreach and recruitment, hostile or unsupportive corporate climates, and problems in moving women and minorities through the internal pipeline to upper management (US Glass Ceiling Commission, 1995).

The Commission made several recommendations for the Federal government, including:

1. Lead by example.
2. Improve data collection for monitoring vertical movement of underrepresented groups in organizations.
3. Develop ways to make publicly available on a voluntary basis demographic statistics currently collected from federal contractors and publicly-held corporations by the Equal Employment Opportunities Commission (EEOC) and the Federal Securities and Exchange Commission.
4. Enforce anti-discrimination laws more strongly.

Recommendations for business included demonstration of CEO commitment to workforce diversity, including diversity in all business plans, and holding managers accountable for meeting advancement goals for underrepresented groups through commitment to affirmative action as a tool. Qualified individuals should be selected, promoted, and retained; women and people of color, in addition to White men, should be actively prepared for senior management positions and the corporate workforce should be educated about glass ceiling issues. Companies were advised to initiate Work/Life and family-friendly policies and adopt "high performance workplace" practices such as participation, training and education, and attention to issues of compensation, security, and workplace environment. These are still good recommendations for management of D&I.

Since 1992 the Office of Federal Contract Compliance (OFCCP) in the US Department of Labor (DoL) has conducted "glass ceiling audits" or Corporate Management Reviews as part of the routine Affirmative Action (AA) reviews of federal contractors. These audits focus on patterns of recruitment and placement, development and performance appraisal programs, compensation plans, and support for equal opportunity at the highest levels of the company (FordHarrison, 2016; USDoL, 2013).

Understanding Causes and Planning Solutions

Solutions proposed for a problem such as lack of advancement of women and other underrepresented minorities often depend upon how the problem is framed. Gutek (1993; Nieva & Gutek, 1981) identified four general explanations for the glass ceiling. Those accepting the *individual deficit model* believe that underrepresentation at high levels occurs because candidates do not possess the necessary preparation and skills for promotion to higher levels, or the skills or knowledge to work effectively at higher levels. The *structural model* instead proposes that barriers result from how the company's structure affects behavior, and from institutionalized processes considered the route to advancement. In the *sex role model*, the problem is defined as society's expectations about appropriate behavior for and stereotypic ideas about women or men. Finally, the *intergroup model* proposes that advancement is limited by dynamics of the relationships between women and men (or the majority and nonmajority groups), including hierarchy and status, prejudiced attitudes, and discriminatory or exclusionary behavior. These explanations were first applied to the status of women in organizations, but they also apply to other marginalized and underrepresented groups.

Framing lack of advancement using the individual deficit model naturally leads to the recommendation for "specialized" training for underrepresented groups. The structural model suggests examination and modification of the organization's standard practices and procedures, such as recruiting, performance evaluation, benefits (e.g., day care), typical career paths, or developmental opportunities. Following the sex role model, an organization might see its "inability to find qualified applicants" from underrepresented groups as something to be remedied by the larger society—or, it could question its own assumptions about what it means to be "qualified," particularly if these attributes are related to gender or minority status. Finally, the intergroup model suggests that an organization should look for and try to remedy any stereotypic beliefs, prejudice, and offensive or discriminatory behavior based on group membership, leading to unjustified differences in power or access to resources. These four frames are not mutually exclusive and may co-exist in the same organization. Diversity managers should explore or "diagnose" the organization for evidence of operation of one or more of these models in order to identify remedies most likely to address the problem.

Is the Gender Glass Ceiling Weakening?

According to Powell (1999), who reviewed information on this topic, in 1970 38% of women were in the labor force but the proportion in management was only 16%, where it had been for a decade. Participation of women in top management was not systematically studied in those days, and an attempt to study them was abandoned because so few could be identified! Things improved during the 1970s and 1980s; in 1990, 45% of women were employed and of those, 39% were in managerial positions at various levels. Data from government sources do not describe top management, but according to Powell, the proportion of women at executive levels in large corporations as reported by private surveys hovered around 1–3% during those years. The nonprofit business research membership organization Catalyst has surveyed large corporations and reported some improvement from 1995 till reaching a plateau around 2006–2007. For example, in the Fortune 500 (the 500 largest public corporations in terms of assets and revenue) the percentage of CEOs who were female rose from 0.2% (1996) to 3% (2009), 4.8% (2014), and 4% (2016). Fortune 500 Board seats held by women rose steadily from 9.6% (1995) to 16.9% (2013) and 19.2% (2014), with female Corporate Officers (the very top level of jobs) rising from 8.7% (1995) to hover around 15–16% (from 2002 to 2008; Catalyst, 2014, 2016a, 2016b). For comparison purposes, consider that women were about 46–47% of the labor force and 48–51% of those in managerial, professional, and related positions during that period. Women are half the labor force, yet hold only 3–4% of the top jobs and about 16% at executive levels in business.

Contrary to most reports, Powell and Butterfield (1994) found that women fared equal to or better than men in competition for promotion to Senior Executive Service (SES) positions in a cabinet-level department of the federal government, taking into consideration their smaller numbers in the applicant pool. The authors attribute these results to procedures for promotion: public announcement of openings, standard procedures for making decisions, and requirements for record-keeping, as well as the government's concern for equal employment opportunity and the possibility that women applicants, on average, may have been better qualified. These promotional procedures are often recommended to reduce subjectivity and bias and advance D&I. In public sector employment, most aspects of personnel procedures are open. In the private sector, the situation is sometimes quite different.

In a companion study, Powell and Butterfield (1997) considered the role of race in promotions to SES positions, finding that applicants of color, particularly men, were less likely to make the cutoff for further consideration. However, little evidence was found that prejudicial views or race-related biases in processing information about candidates were responsible for this pattern. Instead, men of color were less likely to be employed in the department that was hiring, had more years of work experience (perhaps suggesting they had "plateaued" or reached their highest level of success), but lower degrees of education (although they met the necessary qualifications). Thus, the authors concluded that *indirect* effects of race on job-related factors accounted for the pattern of results for men of color. Women of color were more likely to be working in the hiring department, and perhaps for this reason did not experience negative effects of race. Federal procedures and climate were also mentioned in this study as important contextual factors.

Some Related Terms

Sociologists who have studied the relative progress of women and men have also used the term "glass escalator" to refer to the greater chances of upward mobility for men working in female-dominated fields (Williams, 1992). Using archival (existing) data, Maume (1999) found that considering the occupations represented, the same factors (e.g., higher pay and more hours worked annually) predicted movement into a management position for women and men. However, as percentage of females in the occupation rose, men were *more* likely but women *less* likely to move into management; for each 10% increase in percentage of women, men's odds of promotion *increased* 11% but women's *decreased* 6%! Several possible explanations for this effect have been offered. For example, Williams (1992) suggested that tension may result from a man working in a "woman's job," sometimes because clients prefer certain services to be provided by women. This tension could be reduced by promoting the man to management. Further, gender-role stereotypes, including those held by female co-workers, may suggest that men are more suited to supervision than to the direct services provided by women and, if promoted, would negotiate more effectively on behalf of their female subordinates. Employees may also assume that a man enters a woman's field because he is interested in management rather than the substance of the work itself. Another possibility is that, because there are few male co-workers in women's fields, men have more in common with male supervisors and form mentoring relationships that enhance their promotion opportunities. Williams also found that some males actually reported choosing women's occupations because the route to management would be faster!

Maume's (1999) data set was large but may not have included a representative sample of occupations, and analyses for men and women in male-dominated jobs were not presented. Two later studies have examined this situation. Using a large nationwide survey, Budig (2002) found that men had an advantage in wages, growth of wages over time, and promotion in *all* situations studied: female-dominated, male-dominated, and gender-balanced occupations. In fact, men's advantage in promotions was actually *smaller* in "women's" jobs than in other settings, and thus did not appear to be a result of their token status. A later study by Hultin (2003) analyzed archival data in Sweden to consider promotion rates for women and men in jobs that were held predominantly by one sex or were of mixed composition. In this study, the rates of promotion to supervisory roles were very similar for men in "women's jobs" or in jobs held by both men and women. But surprisingly, rates were almost as high for women in "men's jobs"! Substantially lower rates of promotion were found for women in mixed and female-dominated jobs, and for men in "men's jobs." Two things should be noted about this research. First, it was conducted in Sweden, which has a recent history of political efforts to enhance gender equality. Second, by definition, these beneficial promotion rates only affected *small* numbers of women, because very few women were working in these male-dominated jobs. It is possible these women were atypical in ways other than their career choice. Other considerations include the cultural expectations and legal environment within which job opportunity and progress occurs. As another example of possible limitations on the glass escalator, Wingfield (2009) presented qualitative evidence from interviews with 17 African American male nurses in the southeastern US. In her research, these minority males reported a very different experience from that of White male nurses. For example, instead of receiving rapid promotion, sometimes they were mistaken for custodians or janitors, were received coolly by White female nurses, and were attracted to caring and nurturing aspects of their work as well as opportunity to benefit their minority community.

Finally, another study of the nursing profession found little evidence of a glass escalator using a large national sample as well as in-depth interviews with a smaller sample of female and male nurses (Snyder & Green, 2008). Based on data from six occasions over a 23-year period, researchers did not find that men were overrepresented in administrative or supervisory positions. Instead, they found strong evidence of disproportionate horizontal clustering of men into "gendered specialties" such as intensive care, surgery (including anesthesia), and emergency care; compared to other specialties, these are perceived as providing more "autonomy, technical complexity, decision-making authority, and . . . physical intensity and risk" (p. 294). Often, but not always, these specialties provided higher levels of pay than balanced or female-clustered specialties such as labor and delivery.

A possible explanation for a glass escalator is that, on average, men focus more than women on maximizing their compensation—or perhaps upper administrators *think* they do. If so, men might be more motivated or have more opportunity than women to move into management or more lucrative gendered specialties (which could vary from one setting to another). As always, organizations should avoid relying on stereotypical generalizations and consider people as individuals when making personnel decisions.

So, is there a "glass escalator"? In social science research, typically there are differences in study outcomes at different times and with different settings, sample type and size, and methodologies. A body of research over a period of time is necessary to show the overall picture. At this point, studies show that a glass escalator certainly *does* exist in some settings but is probably not a universal or even widespread phenomenon. It's certainly something for the diversity manager to consider.

Another term, *glass cliff*, has also come into use by researchers who are interested in roles of women and men in organizations. This expression refers to the observation that, in comparison to men, women seem more likely to be chosen for leadership positions in a challenging and perhaps career-threatening organizational crisis. Perhaps experienced male executives are more wary of such situations and this creates opportunity for ambitious women. The glass cliff has been documented by Ryan and Haslam (2007) using both experimental and archival data (real-world records of actual promotions). A glass cliff has been found when participants were asked to choose candidates for an executive position in a declining company, a representative for a music festival with dropping popularity, the lead lawyer for a case expected to generate negative publicity and criticism, and candidates for actual political office for a highly contested rather than a "safe" seat. This pattern may result from perceptions that women possess qualities more effective in managing crises, or may be a form of hostile sexism in choosing women for jobs in which they are doomed to fail. Women may also be chosen to signal a big change designed to turn an organization around.

Strictly speaking, neither the glass escalator nor the glass cliff refers to a *structural* feature of organizations such as the glass ceiling. Instead they imply *processes* of discrimination that produce structural effects but are mentioned here because of the similarity in the terminology to the glass ceiling. They also illustrate the interaction of structure and process within organizations.

Formal Horizontal Structure: Looking Sideways

In addition to structural barriers to upward movement in an organization, another dimension affects career progress and job outcomes of employees. Looking across the "horizon" of an organization, what do we see? "Glass walls" separate different structural areas of the organization. They are barriers that limit movement from one area of a company to another, making lateral and functional moves difficult if not impossible. This may result from organizational policies specifying how promotions or transfers occur, narrow job descriptions, highly specialized skill sets, or lack of cross-training that prevent employees from learning about or performing other jobs. Many organizations, for example, have policies or customs that identify departments in the company from which employees are promoted to mid- and executive management. Often glass walls result from the fact that people working in one area of the structure have no opportunity to learn information and skills required for movement to positions elsewhere in the company.

A relatively impermeable horizontal structure will usually influence opportunities and outcomes for people within the structure. Besides opportunities for lateral movement or promotion into other departments, such a structure may limit knowledge of organizational affairs, input into decision-making, and level of income. Often glass walls are vertical barriers that coincide with faultlines. For example, it is common for jobs in Human Resources (HR) to be filled predominantly by women and for other departments such as Finance or Manufacturing to be occupied to a greater extent by men. Commonly HR is seen as less important strategically and has less organizational power than departments such as Finance or Manufacturing, even though many companies may say that their people are their most important resource! It would not be surprising to find a different salary structure and income level in areas of a company separated by glass walls. In fact, as we shall see, this leads to the strongest explanation for the stubborn differences in median annual income between women and men, namely occupational and job segregation.

Occupational Segregation

The term *occupational sex (or race) segregation* refers to the degree to which people of different sexes or races hold different categories of jobs or different occupations. To some extent, organizations' demographic structures resemble those within broader society, reflecting such things as numbers of people of different ethnicities or sexes in the labor force or working in various fields. Occupational segregation describes such a pattern; it exists within our society and also within our work organizations, although individual organizations may vary from the predictable pattern depending on unique policies, products, locations, or circumstances.

For the most part, women and men do not work in the same jobs, occupations or industries (Jacobs, 1999; Hegewisch, Liepmann, Hayes, & Hartmann, 2010). Prior to the 1964 Civil Rights Act and the protections of Title VII, it was legal to advertise employment openings in terms that today seem at best quaint, and at worst, sexist or racist. Terms like "attractive young woman" could be used in ads and often were linked with stereotypically feminine jobs such as receptionist or secretary. Furthermore, organizations' policies were not expected or required to be gender- or race-neutral, and often there were clear and deliberate practices of assigning and paying people differently based on race or sex. These processes created a structure which today still frames our expectations about appropriate employment for different kinds of people, and about the nature of different kinds of jobs. We still hear "male nurse" or "female astronaut" much more often than "female teacher" or "male governor."

Sociologists and labor economists calculate a statistic called "Duncan's D" or the Index of Dissimilarity to measure how differently groups of people (e.g., men and women) are distributed across different job categories. Recent calculations show that just over 50% of US workers would have to change jobs in order for men and women to be distributed in the same pattern, and this

Table 4.1 Twenty Most Common Occupations for Women and Men, Full-Time Workers, 2015

Women's Jobs	Workers who are Women	Men's Jobs	Workers who are Men
Elementary & middle school teachers	80.6%	Driver/sales workers & truck drivers	96.1%
Registered nurses	88.3%	Managers, all other	61.3%
Secretaries & administrative assts	94.4%	First-line supervisors of retail sales workers	55.7%
Nursing, psychiatric, & home health aides	88.4%	Laborers & freight, stock, & material movers, hand	84.7%
Customer service representatives	65.3%	Retail salespersons	60.4%
Managers, all other	38.7%	Construction laborers	97.9%
First-line supervisors, Retail sales workers	44.3%	Janitors & building cleaners	72.3%
Cashiers	69.4%	Software developers, applications & systems software	82.0%
First-line supervisors, office/ administrative support workers	66.5%	Sales representatives, wholesale & manufacturing	74.1%
Accountants & auditors	57.8%	Grounds maintenance workers	95.5%
Receptionists & information clerks	91.6%	Cooks	62.1%
Office clerks, general	83.2%	Carpenters	98.8%
Retail salespersons	39.6%	Chief executives	72.9%
Maids, housekeeping cleaners	84.7%	Automotive service technicians & mechanics	97.7%
Bookkeeping, accounting & auditing clerks	88.7%	Stock clerks & order fillers	63.4%
Secondary school teachers	58.2%	First-line supervisors of production & operating workers	83.0%
Financial managers	51.0%	Production workers, all other	76.0%
Teacher assistants	92.2%	Electricians	97.1%
Waiters & waitresses	64.9%	General & operations managers	75.5%
Personal care aides	81.2%	Accountants & auditors	42.2

Source: Adapted from Hegewisch and DuMonthier (2016b, April). IWPR calculation of data from US Department of Labor, Bureau of Labor Statistics (2016) "Household Data, Annual Averages. Table 39."

number has not changed much since 1996 (Hegewisch et al., 2010). These numbers are calculated from the US Census every ten years, but sometimes other sources of data are used such as EEO-1 reports to the federal government (e.g., McTague, Stainback, & Tomaskovic-Devey, 2009) or industry surveys (e.g., Snyder & Green, 2008).

Note that Duncan's *D* does *not* indicate the percentage of men—or women—in a particular occupation, which is a different way of describing occupational segregation. Table 4.1 provides a list of the most common occupations for women and men.

Reskin and Roos (1990) described the pattern of occupational segregation in the US and characterized it as "one of the most enduring features of the US labor market" (p. 4). Segregation by sex and by race show different patterns. For example, sex segregation in occupations did not change between 1900 and 1960. After World War II during the 1940s, occupational segregation *by race* dropped markedly, especially for women, but sex segregation persisted; despite women's role in defense and other industries during World War II, patterns readjusted after the War. It was not until the 1970s after the decade of Civil Rights legislation that sex segregation began to change as women moved into some—but not all—traditionally male occupations. Still, in 1980 almost one-half of women and over one-half of men worked in occupations with more than 80% people of their own sex. Sex segregation among Blacks had dropped so that they showed a level of sex segregation similar to that of Whites by 1981.

Research has examined changes during the period after the passage of Civil Rights legislation in the 1960s. By 2003 only 1% of workplaces were single-sex, and single-race establishments (Black or White) dropped to about 15%. (For Hispanics this figure was 19%.) Tomaskovic-Devey et al. (2006), using EEO-1 reports to the federal government (from employers with more than 100 workers), found that although sex segregation by occupation declined dramatically during this period, this drop slowed during the 1980s. Some apparent early improvement was actually due to changes in size of various industries: the less-segregated service sector grew while manufacturing shrunk. On the other hand, desegregation for Blacks and Whites was uneven across regions of the country and seemed to halt during the 1980s.

A later study using Census data from the monthly Current Population Survey (1972–2002) clarifies more recent patterns (Hegewisch et al., 2010). Gender composition of some occupations changed significantly (e.g., mail carriers, photographers, dentists, lawyers, pharmacists) but others remained dominated by one sex (e.g., hairdressers, dental assistants, pre-K and kindergarten teachers, registered nurses; and machinists, carpenters, electricians, civil engineers). They also found that the Index of Dissimilarity for sex fell from 68% in 1972 to 50% in 2002, but within that period the trend of decreasing sex segregation seems to have halted around 1996. This stall in desegregation by sex appeared for jobs of different skill/education levels and for different age cohorts of workers. Typically younger workers show a pattern of lower occupational segregation by sex, but this trend has even reversed since 2002! In 2009, gender segregation within races was still more pronounced than racial segregation within sexes (Hegewisch et al., 2010).

Several measurement issues are involved in calculation of D statistics. One important point is that level of segregation appears lower when broad occupational categories are compared. When smaller and more detailed categories (perhaps occupied mostly by one sex) are combined into broader groupings with categories dominated by the other sex, the two patterns cancel each other out. For example, jobs in elementary and secondary education tend to be held most often by women; in higher education there are more male employees. If all these jobs are combined into "education," the broader category seems more integrated than a more detailed analysis would indicate. To understand job segregation most accurately, we really should look at who holds jobs in particular workplaces (Bielby & Baron, 1984), but such data are hard to collect and sometimes not available through government sources. Think about the restaurants you visit frequently. In some establishments, servers are both male and female. However, in some eating places, servers' jobs are held mostly or exclusively by men; in others the servers are mostly women. The same could be said of people of different racio-ethnicities.

Another measurement problem is that workplaces that are *homogeneous* in terms of sex or race— not very common any more—are *not* included in calculations of D (Tomaskovic-Devey et al., 2006). Therefore, calculated D's are *underestimates* of the actual amount of occupational segregation because *totally segregated* workplaces are left out. Differences in D may also occur based on source of the data (e.g., EEO-1 reports vs. Census data), region of the country, time period, and particular industry groupings that are studied. Nevertheless, experts generally agree that occupational segregation by *sex* has decreased considerably in recent years—perhaps because it started out so large! Desegregation by racio-ethnicity seems to follow a different trajectory, and even differs depending upon the particular racial or ethnic group studied. For example, desegregation for Hispanics compared to Whites seems very sensitive to factors in different local communities, but Black–White desegregation appears to vary with region and industry and to have stalled after about 1980. In fact, after 1995 some industries (e.g., mining, construction, manufacturing) even showed evidence of resegregation (Tomaskovic-Devey et al., 2006).

Why is this relevant for advancing D&I in organizations? First, it's important to understand that some of what occurs within a particular organization is a function of patterns in the broader society. Furthermore, we are less likely to notice and question patterns that are very familiar—"just the way it is!" Finally, what appears in the popular media about these issues is often presented superficially and sometimes inaccurately, perhaps based only on anecdotes from a few interesting cases. The conventional wisdom may be a very distorted understanding of what's really going on in a broader sense. To the person from a marginalized group who is frustrated by lack of progress, the effects of these societal factors may seem very personal. This may affect his or her motivation, retention, and contributions. Deliberate action by managers and executives may be required in order to change these patterns in a particular employment setting.

Explanations for Occupational Segregation

What produces these patterns? Surely individual choices are important as people move into different educational fields and levels, careers, jobs, and organizations. Access to information about job openings, habitual assumptions and institutionalized processes for career counseling, recruitment and hiring, and subtle or outright discrimination and harassment all play a role. Political factors that affect the enforcement of civil rights protections have also been found. For example, it has been suggested that the slowdown in job desegregation during the 1980s was a response to the election of President Reagan and the drop in federal enforcement efforts and pressure from Congress (Stainback, Robinson, & Tomaskovic-Devey, 2005; Tomaskovic-Devey et al., 2006) as well as weakness of OFCCP oversight of federal contractors and attainment of goals in Affirmative Action Plans (AAPs) (McTague et al., 2009).

Sociologists Barbara Reskin and Patricia Roos (1990) went beyond analysis of archival government data and took a qualitative approach to studying processes that lead to changes in sex segregation of jobs. Though this study is not recent and specific details may have changed, the processes they identified are probably still valid. With several colleagues, they conducted detailed case studies of 11 occupations among 33 that had shown the largest increase in women workers between 1970 and 1980. For each occupation, they studied published historical documents and interviewed incumbents, and also observed some jobs. In this way they identified several factors that seemed to lead to "feminization" of these jobs. The factors included:

1. Labor shortages of male workers. Occupations expanded more than could be filled by available men, and/or male workers left the profession following changes in technology, work processes, or reward structure. Examples: baking, pharmacy.
2. Sex-specific demand for women. Anti-discrimination law and affirmative action opened opportunity for women, female clients increased (suggesting a need for female service providers), aspects of "women's work" in the occupation increased, and/or employers reduced wages for jobs, leading men to depart. Examples: banking, insurance adjusting and examining.
3. Changing social attitudes and declining discrimination. Employers enacted equal opportunity, early pioneers received favorable media attention, and/or some women's aspirations changed. Example: bartending.
4. Declining resistance by male workers. Opportunities expanded in some fields, unionization decreased, and/or men became less able to exclude women. Example: typesetting.
5. Women's labor supply and preferences. Employers needed workers and women were available to respond to new and expanding opportunities.

Unfortunately, women's movement into formerly "male jobs" often occurred as wages in these desegregating fields were dropping. As a result, these women pioneers improved their income relative to women who stayed in "women's jobs," but they did not erase the wage gap with men. According to Reskin and Roos (1990), masculinization of "women's" jobs occurs only rarely, for example when immigrant males displace native-born females. One exception is the field of medicine, which became a man's field in the 19th and 20th centuries as medical schools grew and the work became professionalized, excluding women.

Reskin and Roos (1990) developed a "Queueing" model proposing that employers rank-order possible employees, and employees rank alternative kinds of jobs, into queues in terms of characteristics they think are desirable. For example, employers might prefer men over women, and men might prefer jobs with relatively higher wages. The pattern of people actually in various occupations results from a matching process in which workers at the front of the employer's queue get the employment they prefer. Lower-ranked workers take less desirable jobs, and employers who cannot find enough preferred workers begin to hire those seen as less desirable workers. Reskin and Roos suggested that composition of occupations will change when (a) the pattern of jobs or workers changes (e.g., technology changes or men are away at war); or (b) employers' or workers' preferences or strength of preferences change (e.g., with more female clients, employers decide to hire more women, or workers decide to go back to school).

Why Does this Matter? The Example of Pay Equity

A persistent characteristic of our economy is the gap in wages between women and men, even those working full-time and year-round. In 2014, women's annual earnings were 78.6% of men's (Hegewisch & DuMonthier, 2016a). Over a lifetime, this gap would amount to over a million dollars for a female college graduate (Murphy, 2005)!

The wage gap is often calculated based on median annual earnings for men and women who work full-time and year-round. This is done to permit the longest comparison over years (Hartmann, Gault, & Hegewisch, 2014) and make the comparison "cleaner" because many women work part-time or part-year, either voluntarily or because (a) many "women's jobs" such as teaching are designed that way, or (b) some employers may be more likely to place women in less than full-time work. The published gap actually underestimates the *real* sex difference in take-home pay (what the worker can spend) because so many women earn less than the annual full-time amount for their sex. Pay rates for the sexes are more similar than their take-home pay.

Another point: *annual compensation* gives a better picture than using hourly or weekly wages. The wage gap looks smaller with hourly or weekly wages (i.e., women earn a higher percentage of men's pay) because data for these shorter time periods exclude many workers and may not include overtime pay and bonuses. Also, only those with an hourly wage are directly included in the hourly comparisons, which leaves out professionals, managers, executives, and others; weekly wages only include those working during a particular week. Often media discussions of the wage gap focus on hourly or weekly wages, perhaps because they suggest more progress than is actually happening.

There are many reasons for this gender wage gap, but one major factor is occupational segregation of the type just discussed. "Women's" jobs pay less than jobs held predominantly by men, and little evidence exists that this pattern is changing. Hegewisch et al. (2010) reported that regardless of jobs' skill levels, pay levels drop as the percentage of women increases. Analysis of middle-skill (ms) jobs by pay and gender showed that female-dominated ms jobs pay only 66 cents per dollar paid in male-dominated ms occupations (Hegewisch, Bendick, Gault, & Hartmann, 2016). Recommendations are made for employers, policymakers, and workforce developers to increase the number of women in good ms jobs *where worker shortages exist*. Recommendations include outreach and education, design of equipment and work policies, and monitoring and accountability— all consistent with ideas presented in this text.

Job Evaluation

Although many claim that market forces of supply and demand affect compensation, today's wage structures still show the effects of historical differences between women's and men's jobs. Many organizations use a form of *job evaluation* to evaluate skill, responsibility, and other attributes of jobs so they can be arranged in a hierarchy for the purpose of setting wages. Job evaluation was developed over 100 years ago during a period when occupations were highly segregated, and became widely accepted after World War II (Wittig & Lowe, 1989). In one common form of job evaluation, *compensable factors* or job characteristics are identified on which pay will be based. Each factor (or subfactor) is defined and allocated a certain number of points, usually based on subjective judgments of how important that factor is thought to be. For example, a factor such as "responsibility for money" usually carries more points and thus is weighted more heavily than a factor dealing with "working conditions." Although it is possible to use the same system of job evaluation to rate *most jobs* in an organization—the federal government has done this for many years—commonly in private industry separate job evaluation systems are designed for different major job groupings such as managerial, clerical, or manufacturing. It was claimed that this practice of separate systems, with different factors and weights, better characterized each group of jobs. See the shaded box for an historical example of the deliberate use of job evaluation to create a lower wage structure for female employees.

How Women's Wages Became Depressed

After the Civil Rights Act of 1964, an employee union and a class of past and present female employees at a Westinghouse plant in New Jersey brought a suit against the company alleging that women's wages had been systematically and unfairly lowered in comparison to those of men. Wages were based on a job evaluation system that awarded points for scores on compensable factors. This system was claimed to be sex-neutral, but jobs were segregated by sex. During the suit, Westinghouse's 1939 *Industrial Relations Manual* was entered as evidence because the methods described had continued until the Civil Rights Act became effective. It contained the following section:

> The occupations or jobs filled by women are point rated on the same basis of point values for Requirements of the Job and Responsibility, with the same allowance for Job Conditions, as are the jobs commonly filled by men . . .
>
> The gradient of the women's wage curve, however, is not the same for women as for men because of the more transient character of the service of the former, the relative shortness of their activity in industry, the differences in environment required, the extra services that must be provided, overtime limitations, extra help needed for the occasional heavy work, and the general sociological factors not requiring discussion herein.
>
> The rate or range for Labor Grades do not coincide with the values on the men's scale. Basically, then, we have another wage curve or Key Sheet for women below and not parallel with the men's curve. (Westinghouse, 1938)

In the suit, the plaintiffs claimed that this system deliberately discounted the measures of women's jobs. They argued that when the company combined the key sheets for women's and men's jobs, new labor grades were created at the bottom of the list, and that most of the "women's jobs" were assigned to the new grades at the bottom.

Before the case was finally heard, Westinghouse and the plaintiffs settled the case. Back pay was awarded and the women's jobs were upgraded in the system (Heen, 1984, pp. 213–214; *IUE v. Westinghouse*, 1980).

When different systems are used for different groups of jobs, there is no way to assure that all jobs are being evaluated in the same way. In fact, they usually are not. In the example above, managers would likely be men, and clerical employees would usually be women; using two different systems would be like evaluating boys on speaking ability and girls on reading—there is no "crosswalk" or way of calibrating the two systems to assure they are equivalent. It is very easy to overlook—or to hide—unfair discounting of the value of women's work when separate job evaluation systems are used. Many other kinds of possible bias exist in these job evaluation systems so that the characteristics of men's jobs ("responsibility for money or equipment") are weighted more heavily than attributes of women's jobs ("responsibility for people"). See the shaded box for other examples of bias in traditional job evaluation systems (Remick, 1984; Wittig & Lowe, 1989; England, 1992; Ames, 1993).

Examples of Bias in Job Evaluation Systems

How to Subvert an "Objective" System

1. Different systems of factors and weights may be used for "men's" and "women's" jobs, supposedly to model more closely the types of work that are done. This makes it impossible to check for equivalence in ratings.

2. Job analyses and descriptions on which the job evaluation is based may be inaccurate, incomplete, too general, or biased by gender stereotypes. For example, some things that women do look "easy" and may be omitted.

3. Job evaluators may be biased in their judgments by knowledge of incumbents' race or sex or of wages currently paid to the positions.

4. Compensable factors may not be clearly defined and are often double-counted in systems used for "men's jobs," particularly managerial ones.

5. Definitions of factors may be slanted to represent how they appear in "men's" jobs; for example, "lifting heavy objects" may not include lifting people or lifting smaller things more frequently.

6. Weighting of different factors may be slanted to favor "men's jobs."

7. The existing wage structure may be used to "validate" the results of a job evaluation system. In other words, the system is considered accurate if it reproduces existing differentials. If the old system is discriminatory in effect, the new one will be too.

Based on Remick (1984), Wittig and Lowe (1989); England (1992, Ch. 4), Ames (1993).

Another problem in reducing the wage gap is pay secrecy policies. Though common in the private sector, these policies often violate the National Labor Relations Act; however, this is not widely known, and enforcement and penalties are weak (Dreisbach, 2014). Such policies provide that an employee can be disciplined or even terminated for discussing salary with other employees or inquiring about others' salaries. Some claim that managers' decisions would be challenged or employees would be upset if information about pay differences were known. However, for government workers and those under collective bargaining agreements pay information is widely available without these results. Clearly if an employee cannot find out how her or his salary compares with others' pay, existing law cannot be used to correct pay discrimination. One famous example is described in the shaded box on Lilly Ledbetter and the Fair Pay Act that bears her name.

Lilly Ledbetter and the Fair Pay Act of 2009

In 1998 after 19 years of employment, Lilly Ledbetter was one of few female managers at the Goodyear Tire and Rubber Plant in Gadsden, Alabama, when someone left her an anonymous note saying that men holding the same job were being paid much more than she. When Ledbetter was hired, her salary was the same as the men's, but over the years their pay had become very different. Ms. Ledbetter knew that this long-term pay discrimination had affected not only her take-home pay but also Social Security and retirement pension benefits based on her salary. In 1999, after taking a retirement buyout just a few months short of a 20-year milestone, Ledbetter filed suit against Goodyear alleging violations of the Equal Pay Act, Title VII of the Civil Rights Act, and the Age Discrimination in Employment Act (Ledbetter, 2012). As legal action progressed, some initial claims were denied but a jury awarded her a total of over $3 million in back pay and damages for violation of Title VII. This award was reversed in 2005 by the Eleventh Circuit Court of Appeals, after which Ledbetter's legal team appealed to the US Supreme Court. In May 2009, the Court found *against* Ledbetter in a 5–4 decision, arguing that she should have complained within the 180-day limit following the first discriminatory paycheck! Justice Ruth Bader Ginsberg, then the only female on the Court, read her strong dissent from the bench (an unusual event) in which she pointed out that pay discrimination typically occurs in small increments that may not be noticed, especially by nontraditional employees who are trying to succeed in their work, and that this Court decision did not reflect the realities of the workplace. In addition, in some workplaces pay secrecy policies may result in people being fired for inquiring about or comparing their pay. How is one to find out about unfair pay discrimination without inquiring? The Court's decision also overturned a long-time precedent in Title VII pay discrimination cases, namely that each discriminatory paycheck "resets" the 180-day clock (NWLC, 2013).

A firestorm of public reaction ensued because of the apparent unfairness of this unrealistic decision. As a result, in 2009 Congress passed and President Obama signed the Lilly Ledbetter Fair Pay Restoration Act to reinstate the pre-*Ledbetter* interpretation deadlines for filing pay discrimination charges under Title VII, the Age Discrimination Act, and the Americans with Disabilities Act (EEOC, n.d.).

In 2012, Lilly Ledbetter's account of her years of discrimination and sexual harassment appeared in the book *Grace and Grit*. It is a very revealing look at how a web of small and large discriminatory events takes a physical and mental toll on the victim, and how difficult it is to challenge discrimination through legal action. Although Ms. Ledbetter did not win redress at the Supreme Court, she has become a nationally known figure, a public advocate and well-known symbol for equal pay, and the namesake of a law that is designed to prevent her experience with a Title VII suit from happening again to others.

Equal Pay and Pay Equity

But what about "equal pay"? Don't we have that in the US? The answer is yes, and no. The major law addressing pay differences for men and women is the Equal Pay Act of 1963 (EPA), also discussed in Chapter 7. The wording of this law prohibits discrimination in pay on the basis of sex for "equal work on jobs the performance of which requires equal skill, effort, and responsibility, and which are performed under similar working conditions . . ." [29 U.S.C. 206 (d)]. These four factors of skill, effort, responsibility, and working conditions were incorporated into this law because in the 1960s they were major compensable factors found in most job evaluation systems and thus were an accepted (but not scientifically determined) way of measuring the worth of jobs for the purpose of setting pay.

Note that this law uses the word "equal." Courts have interpreted this to require that for the EPA to apply, two comparison jobs must be "substantially equal"—not just in job evaluation points, but also in substance of work. As we have just seen, men and women usually are not doing the same work! Due to high levels of occupational segregation by sex, the EPA has been limited in addressing the wage gap. The other important law that addresses pay discrimination, Title VII of the Civil Rights Act of 1964, is worded differently but also has not been interpreted by courts to require equal pay for jobs of "comparable worth," that is, jobs that are different in substance but equivalent in job evaluation points. Therefore Title VII has also been of limited use in addressing the significant part of the gender and race wage gap due to occupational segregation.

Other legislation has been proposed (but not yet passed) that would begin to address this part of the wage gap. The Fair Pay Act would have expanded the EPA to comparisons among jobs when "composite of skill, effort, responsibility, and working conditions are equivalent in value, even if the jobs are dissimilar" (NCPE, n.d.). The Paycheck Fairness Act, most recently introduced but not passed by Congress in 2015 ("S. 862: Paycheck Fairness Act," 2015), would: (a) prohibit retaliation for sharing information on salaries; (b) improve remedies and make class action suits easier; (c) provide negotiation skills training for girls and women; (d) provide assistance and awards to businesses for doing pay equity well; and (e) improve federal agencies' research and enforcement by collecting better data from employers on salaries and sex (NPWF, 2015; NWLC, 2015).

During the 1980s, opponents of comparable worth including the 1984 Chair of the US Commission on Civil Rights, Clarence Pendleton, made fun of the idea that different jobs could be compared, calling it "looney tunes" and claiming that this was like comparing apples and oranges (Hutner, 1986). Actually, we often do compare apples and oranges, deciding which to buy based on price, freshness, taste, nutritional value, and other qualities. Though informal, this is very like the process of conducting a job evaluation to compare two jobs. Unfortunately, this caricature of the comparable worth term caught hold, so for political reasons proponents began using the term "pay equity" to refer to fair pay across jobs that were different in content. Today the term "equal pay" properly refers to consistent pay for men and women who are doing the same or very similar work, and "pay equity" means that discrimination and unfairness can and should be addressed even when men and women are doing different work. (Many people, even some politicians who speak about women's pay, do not understand or make this distinction.) We will return to this important issue in discussing major federal laws addressing employment discrimination and gender issues in later chapters. The Lilly Ledbetter Fair Pay Act actually pertains to equal pay, not pay equity.

Actually, it is not "looney" to develop a mechanism for improving wage equity among jobs that differ in content. One example is the work of the Pay Equity Commission in the Province of Ontario, Canada (Pay Equity Commission, 2016).

Many of the processes and structures that produce a gender wage gap also disadvantage ethnic minorities. Significant occupational segregation occurs by race as well as sex. Recent comparisons show that median weekly earnings of Latina women are only 61% of those of White men; for African American women the gap is 66.8% (Hegewisch & DuMonthier, 2016a). Though education and skill levels are also important factors, one reason for this gap is the fact that "minority jobs" pay less than those occupied by majority workers. The issue of pay equity is usually associated with the male–female rather than the ethnic wage gap because major advocacy organizations on this issue (e.g., the National Committee on Pay Equity, NCPE) have focused mainly on gender issues. Groups advocating for ethnic and other minorities' rights have addressed issues of discrimination in housing, education, credit, hiring, and other issues as well as employment discrimination. Nevertheless, the depressing effect of occupational segregation on wages occurs similarly for ethnic minorities and for women. For useful ideas to work toward wage fairness for yourself and others, see Murphy (2005) and the WAGE Project website (n.d.).

Changing Organizational Outcomes through Structure (and Process)

We have covered the nature of organizational structure and shown how it is created by and also limits effects of organizational processes, focusing on the example of gender and racial pay equity. How can those concerned with improving D&I make use of this knowledge? Here are some ideas. You may think of others.

1. Examine the organization for structures and processes (institutionalized policies, procedures) that may limit D&I. Work to eliminate, change, supplement, or work around them.

2. Consider structures that could be established to overcome some of the barriers. Some organizations have used Quality Circles, cross-functional teams, or other groups to bring together people who might not ordinarily interact so they can contribute more effectively and organizational goals can be better accomplished. Quality Circles are based on the idea that the people who best know how to improve productivity are those doing the actual production of the organization. These discussion and analysis groups are voluntary, meet on company time, and set up outside the existing organizational structure for the purpose of studying how production occurs. Although they were not developed specifically to address D&I, it seems likely that participants would feel more engaged and respected as a result of their participation, especially if their suggestions for improvement are accepted.

   Cross-functional teams are temporary structures (like task forces) set up to handle specific projects or problems that are most effectively addressed by people with different sorts of expertise in the organization (Northcraft, Polzer, Neale, & Kramer, 1995). For example, if a new product is being developed, it might be helpful to have an engineer, a design specialist, a marketing professional, and someone with financial expertise involved as a group. This creates a forum for contributions from diverse knowledge and skill areas and may lead to greater commitment from various departments or constituencies in the organization. When occupational racial or gender segregation is high, this would also create communication (a process) across informal faultlines as well as formal structures.

   Another structural intervention to improve inclusion is the *affinity group* or Employee Resource Group (ERG). Many organizations allow or encourage employees to organize groups around interest areas (e.g., environmental concerns, hobbies) or identity groups based on demographic attributes (e.g., ethnicity, sex). ERGs are discussed in more detail in Chapter 13.

3. Use communication processes or mechanisms to link or cross structural barriers. Job rotation or temporary assignments, formal mentoring programs, or organizational communication mechanisms can be very helpful. In job rotation, an individual is assigned for varying periods of time to different jobs or locations within the employer's operation, gaining experience working on different tasks and with different people. In formal mentoring programs, the employer matches junior-level employees with more experienced employees so that two-way learning can occur. These processes are discussed in Chapters 13 and 14.

Most contemporary organizations have employee communication mechanisms such as daily email lists of announcements, internal websites, newsletters, or face-to-face meetings. The diversity manager can use these communication tools to advance D&I. Employer policies relevant to D&I can be explained. New employees can be introduced and welcomed. Informative messages about aspects of various cultures represented among employees can be included. Employees can be thanked for specific contributions to organizational functioning. Developmental or promotional opportunities can be announced. Soliciting suggestions for improvement (each of which receives an acknowledgment) may also be helpful, along with employee surveys to solicit input on relevant decisions and activities. In these and other ways, structures and processes of the organization can help advance D&I goals.

References

Albelda, R., & Tilly, C. (1997). *Glass ceilings and bottomless pits: Women's work, women's poverty*. Boston, MA: South End Press.

Ames, L. (1993). *Erase the bias: A pay equity guide to eliminating race and sex bias from wage setting systems*. Washington, DC: National Committee on Pay Equity.

Bielby, W. T., & Baron, J. N. (1984). A woman's place is with other women: Sex segregation within organizations. In B. F. Reskin (Ed.), *Sex segregation in the workplace: Trends, explanations, remedies* (pp. 27–55). Washington, DC: National Academy Press.

Budig, M. J. (2002). Male advantage and the gender composition of jobs: Who rides the glass escalator? *Social Problems, 49*, 258–277.

Catalyst. (2014, June 10). *Women in the United States: Quick take*. Retrieved from www.catalyst.org/knowledge/women-united-states

Catalyst. (2016a, February 1). *Women CEOs of the S&P 500*. Retrieved from www.catalyst.org/knowledge/women-ceos-sp-500

Catalyst. (2016b, February 3). *Women in S&P 500 companies*. Retrieved from www.catalyst.org/knowledge/women-sp-500-companies

Civil Rights Act of 1991. (1991, November 21). PL 102–166. 42 U.S.C. 1981.

Dreisbach, T. (2014, April 13). 'Pay Secrecy' policies at work: Often illegal, and misunderstood. Retrieved from www.npr.org/2014/04/13/301989789/pay-secrecy-policies-at-work-often-illegal-and-misunderstood

Eagly, A. H., & Carli, Linda L. (2007). *Through the labyrinth: The truth about how women become leaders*. Boston, MA: Harvard Business School Press.

England, P. (1992). *Comparable worth: Theories and evidence*. Hawthorne, NY: Aldine de Gruyter.

Equal Employment Opportunity Commission. (n.d.) *Notice concerning the Lilly Ledbetter Fair Pay Act of 2009*. Retrieved from www.eeoc.gov/laws/statutes/epa_ledbetter.cfm

Equal Pay Act. [29 U.S.C. 206] (d) (1963).

FordHarrison. (2016). *Affirmative Action/OFCCP/Diversity*. Retrieved from www.fordharrison.com/Affirmative Action

Gutek, B. A. (1993). Changing the status of women in management. *Applied Psychology: An International Review, 43*, 301–311.

Hartmann, H., Gault, B., & Hegewisch, A. (2014, April 10). *6 things Washington Post's Glenn Kessler missed about the gender wage gap*. Retrieved from www.iwpr.org/blog/2014/04/10/6-things-washington-posts-glenn-kessler-missed-about-the-gender-wage-gap/

Heen, M. (1984). A review of federal court decisions under Title VII of the Civil Rights Act of 1964. In H. Remick (Ed.), *Comparable worth and wage discrimination* (pp. 197–218.) Philadelphia, PA: Temple University Press.

Hegewisch, A., Bendick, M. Jr., Gault, B., & Hartmann, H. (2016). *Pathways to equity: Narrowing the wage gap by improving women's access to good middle-skill jobs*. Retrieved from http://womenandgoodjobs.org/

Hegewisch, A., & DuMonthier, A. (2016a, March). *The gender wage gap: 2015 earnings differences by race and ethnicity* (IWPR Fact Sheet #C437). Retrieved from www.iwpr.org/publications/pubs/the-gender-wage-gap-2015-earnings-differences-by-race-and-ethnicity

Hegewisch, A., & DuMonthier, A. (2016b, April). *The gender wage gap by occupation 2015 and by race and ethnicity*. (IWPR Fact Sheet #C440). Retrieved from www.iwpr.org/publications/pubs/the-gender-wage-gap-by-occupation-2015-and-by-race-and-ethnicity

Hegewisch, A., Liepmann, H., Hayes, J., & Hartmann, H. (2010). *Separate and not equal? Gender segregation in the labor market and the gender wage gap* (Report No. IWPR C377). Washington, DC: IWPR. Retrieved from www.iwpr.org/publications/pubs/separate-and-not-equal-gender-segregation-in-the-labor-market-and-the-gender-wage-gap

Hultin, M. (2003). Some take the glass escalator, some hit the glass ceiling? *Work and Occupations, 30*, 30–61.

Hutner, F. C. (1986). *Equal pay for comparable worth: The working woman's issue of the eighties*. New York, NY: Praeger.

Hymowitz, C., & Schellhardt, T. C. (1986). The glass ceiling: Why women can't seem to break the invisible barrier that blocks them from top jobs. *Wall Street Journal*, March 24, special supplement, 1, 4.

IUE v. Westinghouse Electric Corporation, 631 F.2d 1094 3d Cir. 1980.

Jacobs, J. A. (1999). The sex segregation of occupations: Prospects for the 21st century. In G. N. Powell (Ed.), *Handbook of gender & work* (pp. 125–141). Thousand Oaks, CA: SAGE.

Lau, D. C., & Murnighan, J. K. (1998). Demographic diversity and faultlines: The compositional dynamics of organizational groups. *Academy of Management Review, 23*, 325–340.

Ledbetter, L. (with L. S. Isom). (2012). *Grace and grit: My fight for equal pay and fairness at Goodyear and beyond.* New York, NY: Crown Publishing Group.

Maume, D. J., Jr. (1999). Glass ceilings and glass escalators: Occupational segregation and race and sex differences in managerial promotions. *Work and Occupations, 26*, 483–509.

McTague, T., Stainback, K., & Tomaskovic-Devey, D. (2009). An organizational approach to understanding sex and race segregation in U.S. workplaces. *Social Forces, 87*, 1499–1527.

Morrison, A. M., White, R. P., Van Velsor, E., and the Center for Creative Leadership. (1987, 1992 updated edition). *Breaking the glass ceiling: Can women reach the top of America's largest corporations?* Reading, MA: Addison-Wesley Publishing Company.

Murphy, E., with E. J. Graff. (2005). *Getting even: Why women don't get paid like men—and what to do about it.* New York, NY: Simon & Schuster.

National Committee on Pay Equity. (n.d.) *Questions and answers on the Fair Pay Act.* Retrieved from www.pay-equity.org/info-Q&A-Act.html

National Women's Law Center. (2013). *Lilly Ledbetter Fair Pay Act.* Retrieved from http://nwlc.org/resources/lilly-ledbetter-fair-pay-act/

National Women's Law Center. (2015, May). *How the Paycheck Fairness Act will strengthen the Equal Pay Act.* Retrieved from http://nwlc.org/wp-content/uploads/2015/08/how_the_pfa_will_strengthen_the_epa_may_2015.pdf

National Partnership for Women & Families. (2015, November). *The Paycheck Fairness Act.* Retrieved from http://nwlc.org/wp-content/uploads/2015/08/how_the_pfa_will_strengthen_the_epa_may_2015.pdf

Nieva, V. F., & Gutek, B. A. (1981). *Women and work: A psychological perspective.* New York, NY: Praeger.

Northcraft, G. B., Polzer, J. T., Neale, M. A., & Kramer, R. M. (1995). Diversity, social identity, and performance: Emergent social dynamics in cross-functional teams. In S. Jackson & M. Ruderman (Eds.), *Diversity in work teams* (pp. 69–96). Washington, DC: American Psychological Association.

Pay Equity Commission. (2016). Retrieved from www.payequity.gov.on.ca/EN/Pages/default.aspx

Powell, G. N. (1999). Reflections on the Glass Ceiling: Recent trends and future prospects. In G. N. Powell (Ed.), *Handbook of gender & work* (pp. 325–345). Thousand Oaks, CA: SAGE.

Powell, G. N., & Butterfield, D. A. (1994). Investigating the "glass ceiling" phenomenon: An empirical study of actual promotions to top management. *Academy of Management Journal, 37*, 68–86.

Powell, G. N., & Butterfield, D. A. (1997). Effect of race on promotions to top management in a federal department. *Academy of Management Journal, 40*, 112–128.

Remick, H. (1984). Major issues in *a priori* applications. In H. Remick (Ed.), *Comparable worth and wage discrimination* (pp. 99–117). Philadelphia, PA: Temple University Press.

Reskin, B. F., & Roos, P. A. (1990). *Job queues, gender queues: Explaining women's inroads into male occupations.* Philadelphia, PA: Temple University Press.

Ryan, M. K., & Haslam, S. A. (2007). The Glass Cliff: Exploring the dynamics surrounding the appointment of women to precarious leadership positions. *Academy of Management Review, 32*, 549–572.

S. 862: Paycheck Fairness Act. (2015). Retrieved from www.govtrack.us/congress/bills/114/s862

Snyder, K. A., & Green, A. I. (2008). Revisiting the glass escalator: The case of gender segregation in a female dominated occupation. *Social Problems, 55*, 271–299.

Stainback, K., Robinson, C., & Tomaskovic-Devey, D. (2005). Race and workplace integration: A politically mediated process? *American Behavioral Scientist, 48*, 1200–1229.

Tomaskovic-Devey, D., Zimmer, C., Stainback, K., Robinson, C, Taylor, T., & McTague, T. (2006). Documenting desegregation: Segregation in American workplaces by race, ethnicity, and sex, 1966–2003. *American Sociological Review, 71*, 565–588.

US Department of Labor Office of Federal Contract Compliance Programs. (2013, February 28). *Procedures for Reviewing Contractor Compensation Systems and Practices.* Retrieved from www.dol.gov/ofccp/regs/compliance/directives/dir307.htm

US Glass Ceiling Commission. (1995). *Glass Ceiling Commission—A solid investment: Making full use of the nation's human capital.* Retrieved from http://digitalcommons.ilr.cornell.edu/cgi/viewcontent.cgi?article=1117&context=key_workplace

WAGE Project. (n.d.) Retrieved from www.wageproject.org/

Westinghouse Industrial Relations Manual: Wage Administration, November 1, 1938, and February 1, 1938, cited in Brief for Appellants, Appendix, 110-62, 158. *IUE v. Westinghouse Electric Corporation*, 631 F.2d 1094 3d Cir. (1980).

Williams, C. L. (1992). The glass escalator: Hidden advantages for men in the "female" professions. *Social Problems, 39*, 253–267.

Wingfield, A. H. (2009). Racializing the glass escalator: Reconsidering men's experiences with women's work. *Gender & Society, 23*, 5–26.

Wittig, M. A., & Lowe, R. H. (1989). Comparable worth theory and policy. *Journal of Social Issues, 45*, 1–21.

* Recommended for advanced reading.

Chapter 5

Identities

Who We Are, and Why That Matters

Employees come from different backgrounds bringing with them existing identities based in previous life experience. In the context of D&I, identity means self-image or sense of who one is. Identity may be *personal*, meaning one's sense of traits, physical attributes, skills, and other characteristics. Or, identity may be *social*, based in feelings of relationship to others. As people continue working in an organization they develop or modify aspects of identity based on such things as assignments, interactions with others, developmental experiences (e.g., training), length of employment, or location in the organizational structure. These social identities have important effects on work attitudes and behaviors (Blader & Tyler, 2009).

An influential perspective in conceptualizing diversity, inclusion, and groups is that of Social Identity Theory (SIT; Tajfel & Turner, 1979). In SIT, our very sense of who we are, including our sense of self-esteem and self-worth, is understood to derive from membership of social groups. In work organizations, social identity may be based in one's employer, occupation or department, work location, or shift. Additionally, the whole person also experiences other aspects of identity grounded in gender or ethnicity, age range, religious affiliation, disability status, family role, or other dimensions. For some, sense of connection with an entity outside the employment setting (e.g., sports team, educational institution) is also a powerful part of identity.

SIT defines *social identity* as aspects of self-image deriving from social categories to which the person perceives that he or she belongs (Tajfel & Turner, 1979). The theory assumes (a) that people want to maintain or improve self-esteem; (b) positive or negative evaluations are associated with membership in various identity groups; and (c) we evaluate our own groups through a process of *social comparison* with other relevant groups. Although originally SIT emphasized self-esteem as a motive for identifying with groups, later research expanded this emphasis to consider social identity as a way of understanding the social world by clarifying and reducing uncertainty about the social environment (Hornsey, 2008).

SIT clarifies people's behavior with respect to groups forming the base for positive social identity, particularly within work organizations (Ashforth & Mael, 1989). Employees of Company A will feel good about themselves when they believe Company A is a good place to work, especially in comparison with marketplace competitors or alternative places of employment. They feel a sense of pride when company products or services, financial health, and reputation are widely respected. If their employer falls behind competitors, engages in unethical or illegal behavior, or otherwise suffers a tarnished reputation, employees will feel negative effects as well. These feelings are stronger to the extent that this employment setting is important in social identity.

SIT proposes that we try to maintain self-esteem, rooted in our group membership; thus a threat to our group is perceived as a threat to us. If perceived value of our group is low or drops, we are motivated to do something to protect self-esteem, and this motivation is stronger when we identify strongly with the group. Group-based self-esteem, when threatened, can be protected in three main ways. First is *mobility*, actually physically leaving the group or somehow psychologically dissociating from it. Many individuals have changed their family names to avoid association with their ethnic background (as with some European Jews, out of fear for their lives). People may withdraw from organizations, change religions, or avoid discussing family backgrounds, and mixed-race individuals may "pass" as White in a segregated society (see shaded box).

Second is *social competition*, working to make our group stronger or better in comparison with others. Often we work harder to bring success to groups with which we identify.

Walter Francis White: Strengthening Black Identity by Passing as White

In the context of SIT, we might consider ethnic *passing* as a way of dissociating oneself from an identity group; it can also be a way of strengthening that identity and thus a better example of "competition" than of "mobility." Walter Francis White (1985–1955) was very light-skinned with light hair and eyes but considered "Black" in the South because he was descended from African American slaves. After graduating from Atlanta University he worked for an insurance company and became secretary of the National Association of Colored People (NAACP). While employed there, he investigated race riots, lynchings, and the Ku Klux Klan while passing as a White man. His 1929 book described his research in this role. Eventually White became NAACP chief executive and subsequently recruited Thurgood Marshall, who later argued *Brown v. Board of Education* before the Supreme Court (and later himself became a Supreme Court justice). As head of the NAACP, White was considered an outspoken but non-militant advocate for the rights of African-Americans (Spartacus Educational, 2014).

Photo available on websites: www.biography.com/people/walter-white-9529708 or http://spartacus-educational.com/USAwhiteWF.htm

Roots?

Third is *social creativity* or cognitively redefining the comparison of our group with others. Instead of actually leaving or improving the group, we mentally readjust so that our self-esteem is still protected. This might be done by changing the dimension on which we evaluate our group ("Well, I would like to earn more, but this is a great company"), changing the way we value attributes so the comparison becomes positive ("Company size and recognition is not so important—we make a better product"), or choosing another group—lower in status—as the benchmark comparison ("This is a great place to work, especially compared to other opportunities here").

Significance of work as a source of identity becomes apparent when a person becomes un-employed (e.g., Wanberg, 2012) or retires and loses social connections with former co-workers. On some social identity dimensions, we experience significant change over time. We become older, become parents or spouses/domestic partners, or recognize a change in sexual orientation, health, religion, or physical ability. Some experience a major shift in identity upon losing a spouse or partner through death or divorce. Other foundations for identity, including some very fundamental ones like ethnicity, typically do not change over one's lifetime.

SIT helps us understand how people react when an important social identity base such as gender or ethnicity is devalued in an organization, particularly when they cannot actually leave the group and join a higher-status alternative. Employees may psychologically dissociate themselves from sources of identity, work to improve the actual status of their identity group, or change the social comparison of their group with others as described above. Can you think of examples of responses when important bases of social identity are challenged at work?

How is this relevant to management of D&I in organizations? For the diversity professional, social identity research has at least three major implications. First, SIT directs our attention to processes occurring within and between groups when people think of one another in categories (reviewed in Dovidio & Gaertner, 2010). Recognizing these predictable effects can help us more effectively manage intra- and intergroup dynamics in organizations. Second, many differences exist among co-workers in social foundation for identity; individuals also differ in level of development and importance of these identities. We can interact more effectively with others and be more respectful of them when we are aware of significant aspects of their identities. Third, identities are relevant to organizational socialization and role conflict. Attraction to an organization and decisions to remain with or to leave it are affected in part by perceptions of compatibility between aspects of one's own identity and the policies, climate, and culture, and opportunities in the organization (Highhouse, Thornbury, & Little, 2006).

Identity-based Processes Within and Between Groups

The Minimal Groups Effect

One important discovery of SIT research is that very little is required for people to perceive that they belong to a group. This sets in motion several important processes within that group, as well as discrimination and bias between it and other groups (Tajfel & Turner, 1979). In the famous "boys camp" experiment at Robbers Cave (Sherif, Harvey, White, Hood, & Sherif, 1961), young campers were assigned to separate groups that participated in several competitive intergroup exercises. The resulting conflict between the groups quickly became very strong and unpleasant. Afterwards, simply removing competition did not reduce hostility, nor did intergroup contact such as watching movies or eating together. Eventually Sherif's team reduced intergroup frictions through a series of arranged but apparently real and serious problems on which groups had to work together to reach an important goal requiring everyone's participation. For example, during an outing the truck became "disabled," and all the boys had to work together to get it running again. This type of goal became called a "superordinate goal" because it transcended bounds of group membership.

Tajfel and Turner (1979) made the important point that *competition is not necessary to create a sense of "group."* In fact, just the experience of group assignment is sufficient to trigger in-group and out-group effects. In early SIT studies with children or adults, participants were *randomly* classified as members of two different groups. According to Tajfel and Turner, "intergroup discrimination existed in conditions of minimal group affiliation, anonymity of group membership, absence of conflicts of interest and absence of previous hostility between the groups" (p. 34). In this *minimal group paradigm*, it is consistently found that members favor other members of their own group and discriminate against members of the other group. These effects occur even when the bare minimum of "groupness" or entativity exists. Now imagine what happens when people perceive themselves to be members of groups already in competition and/or with a long history of conflict and hostility. Ethnic and religious conflicts around the world and our own US history amply illustrate destructive intergroup relations with long-lasting effects. In work situations, this minimal group effect can easily occur whenever people strongly identify with one or more groups; effects are stronger when groups are seen to be in competition with each other for resources, assignments, power, or opportunity.

In-group and Out-group Effects

Once people perceive themselves to be members of a group, very predictable processes begin to develop as people think of "us" vs. "them," and this sense of identification becomes stronger if there is a perception of threat or devaluation (Arndt, Greenberg, Schimel, Pyszczynski, & Solomon, 2002; Castano, Yzerbyt, Paladino, & Sacchi, 2002; Leach, Mosquera, Vliek, & Hirt, 2010). First, we tend to see both in- and out-group as homogeneous or internally alike. Differences between groups on characteristics distinguishing one from the other are perceptually accentuated so that groups appear more different from each other than they actually are (Rubin & Badea, 2007). Second, a reliable "out-group homogeneity effect" (OH) develops, such that members of the other group seem very similar to one another (Ostrom & Sedikides, 1992). Further, they are often perceived in stereotypical terms, especially negative ones. The in-group is usually perceived as more heterogeneous or varied than the out-group, perhaps in part due to greater familiarity and more interaction with members of one's own group. Motivational factors may also produce this perceptual bias; for example, it is easier to behave negatively toward "others" who are seen as depersonalized and "all alike." However, this OH effect may be limited or even reversed by factors such as relative power of the groups or their sizes (e.g., Rubin & Badea, 2007). For example, if another group is very powerful, it behooves one to know a lot about them as individuals! As an example, in the Civil Rights-era American South, Black housekeepers usually had more detailed and personal knowledge about their White employers than vice versa. A third consistent effect is that members show favoritism toward those in their own group and a pattern of bias and discrimination toward out-group members. We perceive our in-group members more positively, expect more positive behaviors from them, and trust them more. If they behave badly, we are more likely to give them the benefit of the doubt by attributing their unpleasant behavior to external and unstable causes (Hewstone, 1992; Kramer, 2001). And fourth, a pattern of cooperation is likely to occur within each group (Tyler & Blader, 2001) with competition developing against the out-group.

In employment settings, these intra- and intergroup effects often occur among work teams, departments or parts of the organization, different locations, or other organizational subgroups. For diversity managers, often the most challenging group identities are those based in demographic characteristics such as sex, racio-ethnicity, or age group.

Development and Importance of Group-based Identities

Though each of us has a complex sense of identity rooted in several dimensions that are important to us, research on group-based identity relevant to organizations has tended to focus on demographic bases such as gender or ethnicity, and to study these various identity bases separately (Frable, 1997). This separate focus happens partly because researchers usually study identity in samples of individuals sharing one particular gender or ethnic identity. Identity research is also fragmented because gender identity has been studied by gender researchers; racio-ethnic identity has been studied by those interested in that characteristic; and so on. In addition, according to Frable, gender identity research generally has focused on middle class individuals and excluded racial and ethnic minorities, and racio-ethnic identity research usually has not considered gender and sexual identity. However, each individual experiences identity as a complex interplay of gender, racio-ethnicity, sexual orientation, social class, and other dimensions of personal significance, and relevance of these aspects may vary with context. (See later section on *intersectionality*.) This chapter discusses identity based on racio-ethnicity, gender, and sexual orientation; other aspects of these and other dimensions of diversity are considered in later chapters.

Racial Identity Development

One theme in research on racio-ethnic identity is the idea that sense of identity develops and changes over time. In developmental psychology, physical and psychological growth is sometimes described in terms of *stages* or periods that are qualitatively (rather than quantitatively) different over time. These periods are thought to occur (a) in fixed and relatively predictable forward order; (b) generally without movement "backwards" to earlier developmental stages. Racial or ethnic identity development has been studied extensively by counseling psychologists seeking to understand and facilitate adjustment of their clients. People move through stages as they mature; over time, changes occur in how they come to think and feel about their racio-ethnic identity (e.g., Cross, 1971;

Helms, 1990a). One implication for diversity professionals is that people from the same racio-ethnic background may have very different understandings of this aspect of identity if they are at different developmental periods.

These theories have emphasized racial development of minority individuals, particularly Blacks; racial identity development was thought to be more complex for persons born into a society in which their own racial group is less numerous, powerful, or privileged. For minority persons, one developmental task is coming to understand the distinction of themselves from the majority. In contrast, racial identity development of those in the dominant majority is often considered typical and not particularly significant, especially when majority persons are unaware of their privilege (Ponterotto & Park-Taylor, 2007). For diversity professionals, another lesson is that salience of racio-ethnic identity is quite variable for different people, depending upon their background and experience.

Janet Helms is a counseling psychologist of African American descent whose ideas about racial identity development are probably the best known among diversity scholars. She defined racial identity as "quality or manner of one's identification with the respective racial groups" (1990b, p. 5) that develops as a system of beliefs about racial group membership. In discussing Black identity, Helms focused on racial rather than ethnic identity because she believed that contemporary society emphasized "Africanness" for Blacks rather than cultural differences among them. Derived from an earlier theory by Cross (1971), her stages in racial identity development for Blacks (and later for People of Color) were:

- *Pre-encounter*, general sense of acceptance through conformity through ideas consistent with those of the dominant White culture;
- *Encounter*, usually resulting from a striking event that makes clear that the person will always be considered Black and therefore inferior;
- *Immersion-Emersion*, when a new identity is formed by idealization of Black heritage ("Black pride") and devaluation of White culture;
- *Internalization*, when the person develops a complex and mature understanding of positive Black racial identity, including rejection of racism.

Later, (e.g., 1995), Helms considered these periods to be "statuses" or phases rather than stages, through which one could pass while developing an increasingly mature and complex understanding of racial identity. Earlier periods might continue to be experienced occasionally and influence identity at later periods. The Black Racial Identity Attitude Scale (RIAS-B) was developed by Parham and Helms (1981) to assess strength of beliefs associated with the four stages/statuses listed above. Sample items are shown in the shaded box.

Black Racial Identity Attitude Scale (RIAS-B)—Sample Items

The 1990 version of the RIAS-B includes items representing four stages or statuses. These items illustrate the four themes on the scale (Helms, 1990c, pp. 33–47).

Pre-encounter: I believe that White people look and express themselves better than Blacks.
Encounter: I find myself reading a lot of Black literature and thinking about being Black.
Immersion-Emersion: I have changed my style of life to fit my beliefs about Black people.
Internalization: I feel good about being Black, but do not limit myself to Black activities.

Helms also considered how these stages might apply to development of Whites, who in the US are members of the dominant socio-political and economic group. What does racial identity development mean in this context? For them, Whiteness would seem to be the norm and indeed might not even be noticed. Helms noted that Whiteness becomes salient only when Whites come in contact with people of color. Otherwise, they can choose to ignore race and its effects on how they are seen and treated by others (1990d). If you are White, consider whether you have experienced phases in your understanding of Whiteness; if you do not consider yourself White, ask that question of White people you know.

In Helms's Theory of White Racial Identity Development (1990d, 1995; Thompson & Carter, 1997), maturity involves coming to recognize the reality of individual and institutional racism and oppose it while simultaneously becoming aware and accepting of Whiteness as a positive part of one's identity. Helms identified six statuses falling into two major phases describing how the developing individual processes information about racial identity:

- Recognizing and considering racism

  o *Contact* status: one is naïve and unaware;
  o *Disintegration* status: one begins to recognize Whiteness and racism and feel conflicted about it;
  o *Reintegration* status: one consciously accepts social reality, justifies it, and may experience fear or anger toward minorities.

- Rejecting racism and developing a positive White identity

  o *Pseudo-independent* status: one begins to recognize racism as unjustified and question one's responsibility to address it;
  o *Immersion-Emersion:* one actively seeks out new information and experiences in a growing understanding of race relations;
  o *Autonomy* status: one shows flexibility and curiosity in a continued openness to new and positive understandings of one's own racial identity.

Helms and Carter (1990) developed the White Racial Identity Attitude Scale (WRIAS) to measure five stages included in an early version of Helms's theory of White identity development (immersion-emersion is not included). Fischer and Moradi (2001) reviewed studies of this scale and describe some of its limitations, including the fact that it focuses on Whites' attitudes about Blacks but not other racial groups.

White Racial Identity Attitude Scale (WRIAS)—Sample Items

WRIAS-B items appear in Appendix III in Janet Helms's 1990 book but are not identified by subscale. Items are identified with scales (except for the Pseudo-Independent Scale) only in the 1990 chapter by Helms and Carter.

Contact: I think it is exciting to discover the little ways in which Black people and White people are different.
Disintegration: I feel depressed after I have been around Black people.
Reintegration: I believe Blacks are inferior to Whites.
Pseudo-Independent: —
Autonomy: I think I understand Black people's values.

Helms and Carter (1990, pp. 67–80 and Appendix III, pp. 249–251)

Helms continued to refine her ideas over the years and descriptions of her theories vary slightly in different sources. Thompson and Carter (1997) summarized her views and showed how they apply in clinical settings as well as diversity training and other organizational interventions. Her conceptualizations and measuring instruments resonate with many psychologists and have been widely used in counseling psychology despite some criticisms (summarized by Cokley, 2007; Ponterotto & Park-Taylor, 2007). Other scales of racial identity for various groups have been have reviewed by Fischer and Moradi (2001) and Cokley (2007).

These theories emphasize progression of racial identity across the lifespan and highlight variation among people of different racial backgrounds and among those of similar backgrounds at different periods of identity maturation. The theories were developed to apply to US populations with interaction among different racio-ethnic groups (e.g., college students). The experience of Blackness and Whiteness would clearly be very different in other cultures and where racio-ethnic compositions differ, such as sub-Saharan Africa, the Far East, or the Indian subcontinent. Even within the US, racial identity may develop differently in very homogeneous communities, schools, or employment settings, or in places where representation of various racio-ethnic groups is changing rapidly due to immigration or migration patterns.

Ethnic Identity and its Measurement

The distinction between "racial" and "ethnic" identity is not always clear, which is consistent with earlier discussion about the Social Construction process. Helms and others have written about racial identity, but Jean Phinney is probably the best known of those who have studied *ethnic identity*. Phinney defined this as an experience of identity that a person shares with others in the same ethnic group, a "multidimensional, dynamic construct that develops over time through a process of exploration and commitment" (Phinney & Ong, 2007, p. 271). In her view, ethnic identity involves a sense of connection with "people who see themselves and are seen by others as having a common ancestry, shared history, shared traditions, and shared cultural traits, such as language, beliefs, values, music, dress, and food" (Cokley, 2007, p. 225). Ethnic Identity is distinct from *National Identity* or identification with one's nation of residency or citizenship; and from *Racial Identity*, identification with a supposed biologically based heritage group.

Phinney developed an instrument to measure ethnic identity across many ethnic groups rather than within one particular group (as was the case with the racial identity scales described above). The Multigroup Ethnic Identity Measure (MEIM; Phinney, 1992) began by asking the respondent to identify his or her own ethnic group. In her early work with adolescents, Phinney (1992) included items concerning *attachment or belonging, achieved identity,* and *involvement in ethnic practices.* The scale was refined and shortened to the MEIM-R (Phinney & Ong, 2007) containing six questions measuring constructs of *exploration* (learning about one's ethnicity, e.g., "I have often talked to other people in order to learn more about my ethnic group") and *commitment* (attachment and a positive view of one's ethnicity, e.g., "I have a strong sense of belonging to my own ethnic group"). From this new perspective, ethnic identity begins with an early diffuse lack of clear ethnic identity. It develops in one of two ways: stopping with *foreclosure* (commitment to an ethnicity one knows little about) or progressing through *moratorium* (continued exploration). With continued maturity, one reaches *ethnic identity achievement,* a fairly stable sense of belonging to a particular ethnic group. Even in adulthood, a person may continue to explore the experience of his or her ethnicity. Chae and Larres (2010) reviewed development of the MEIM instrument and recent research with Asian American and multi-ethnic samples. A review by Miville (2010) summarizes its use with Latina/o participants.

The MEIM is a very popular instrument in research, but in most cases it has been used to investigate development and structure of ethnic identity in samples of adolescents and young college-age adults rather than employees. These studies often find that a secure and positive sense of ethnic identity is related to psychological well-being or adjustment, particularly among ethnic minorities (e.g., Ghavami, Fingerhut, Peplau, Grant, & Wittig, 2011; Yoon, 2011). For employed adults in the context of organizational diversity, relevance of MEIM-R research is mainly to emphasize that people differ widely in terms of the significance of their ethnic identity. Some find ethnic identity irrelevant. Others are emotionally committed to an ethnicity without knowing much about it, or they may be very well-informed and continue to explore history, culture, language, and other aspects of ethnicity. The MEIM-R could be useful in training experiences designed to lead to discussion of ethnic identity and its significance to different people.

In fact, research indicates that the concept of ethnic identity as captured in scales such as the MEIM-R is more meaningful to those of ethnic minority status or the minority of Whites (perhaps international students) who identify strongly with a particularly ethnicity (Popp, Landau, Brink, & Thomas, 2002). For most young people who are not ethnic minorities, the very meaning of ethnic identity may be different. Those who are managing D&I should recognize that ethnic identity can be a central part of identity for some employees, particularly those of ethnic minority heritage, and relatively meaningless for others, perhaps even those of second-generation or later. Managers are likely to be more effective when they expect and value diversity in ethnic identity as well as in racio-ethnicity itself.

Self-Identified Ethnic Identity—The MEIM

The early (1992) version of the MEIM opened with a paragraph giving examples of ethnic groups such as Asian American, Black, White, and others considered minority ethnic groups in the US. "Euro-American" was not one of the examples, nor were terms such as "Irish," "German," or "Italian" (common ethnicities of earlier generations of US immigrants). The respondent could provide whatever answer seemed best to the first question "In terms of ethnic group, I consider myself to be _____." How would you answer this question about yourself?

This version of the 20-item MEIM included 14 items written to embody three themes Phinney thought were part of ethnic identity. Examples were "I am happy that I am a member of the group I belong to" and "I feel a strong attachment towards my own ethnic group"* which measured *Affirmation and Belonging*. Items such as "I have spent time trying to find out more about my own ethnic group, such as its history, traditions, and customs"* and "I have a clear sense of my ethnic background and what it means to me" addressed the concept of *Ethnic Identity Achievement*. Two items measured *Ethnic Behaviors*: "I am active in organizations or social groups that include mostly members of my own ethnic group" and "I participate in cultural practices of my own group, such as special food, music, or customs." Six items measured *Other-group Identification* such as "I like meeting and getting to know people from ethnic groups other than my own" and "I often spend time with people from ethnic groups other than my own." Responses were chosen from a 4-point scale from "strongly agree" to "strongly disagree" and a high score indicated a strong ethnic identity. You may want to see how you answer these questions and how high or low your score might be.

The scale ended with three other items asking the person to choose his or her ethnicity from a list of seven ethnic minority groups, including "mixed" and "other." The person was also asked to indicate mother's and father's ethnicity. Thus Phinney could compare the free-response answer in the first item to the answer chosen from the census-like checklist. In the Popp et al. (2002) study, some White students did write in a more specific national heritage, and researchers found that those students tended to have higher ethnic identity scores than other students who simply answered "White."

[handwritten margin note: Behavior later dropped]

Subsequent research led Phinney to revise her thinking about the nature of ethnic identity. The MEIM-R (Phinney & Ong, 2007) was much shorter (six substantive items with the best psychometric properties) and contained only two scales. *The two items shown above with asterisks were retained and illustrate new scales of *Commitment & Attachment* and *Exploration*. Items on the third and fourth subscales were dropped because they described behaviors rather than aspects of identity. Current thinking about the MEIM-R is that it involves two aspects of attachment and exploration. Ethnic (1) behavior is one indicator and correlate of the internal cognitive structure that we call identity. Attitudes (2) toward other groups are a separate variable that may in some cases be related positively or negatively to one's own sense of ethnic identity.

Other researchers have studied ethnic identity and some have developed scales for measuring this concept both across and within specific ethnic groups. Fischer and Moradi (2001) provide information on scales developed to address identity for specific ethnicities. They note a scarcity of research exploring various ethnic identities and the importance of distinctions among Native American tribes and among separate ethnicities considered "Asian," or "Hispanic." Most of these instruments conceptualize ethnic identity as involving aspects such as cultural understanding, acceptance, and positive feelings. Conceptualization and measurement of identities based in gender or sexual orientation have also been considered by some researchers. For information on these identities, see the shaded box.

Development of Identity Related to Gender, Sexuality, and Feminism

Study of gender identity, the idea of oneself as female or male, has focused predominantly on childhood and adolescent development. However, identity development in early and later adulthood may include changes in ideas about oneself as a woman or man (feminist identity, womanist identity), and as a sexual being (sexual orientation identity). Feminist identity refers to viewing oneself as a person who values equality between the sexes while recognizing and working against societal and cultural barriers to this goal. Womanist identity is a similar term used by Helms and others (Carter & Parks, 1996) to refer to attitudes of women toward themselves as women. (In ethnic and women's studies, the term may also refer to the feminist orientation of women of color who focus on fighting for equality; K. M. Thomas, 2005.) Sexual orientation identity addresses processes by which one comes to see oneself as a gay, lesbian, transgender, bisexual, or heterosexual person (e.g., Walters & Simoni, 1993). Several approaches to these identities have been based on ideas of Helms and others about development of self-identity through various periods, in part in reaction to treatment by others and in society at large. For example, the Feminist Identity Scale (Bargad & Hyde, 1991; see also Baird, Szymanski, & Ruebelt, 2007; and Fischer, Tokar, Mergl, Good, Hill, & Blum, 2000) grew from an earlier model of women's feminist identity development, itself based on Cross's earlier work (1971) on African American identity development.

Kecia Thomas (2005) identified several themes common to these approaches as well as models of racial and ethnic development. All identify different developmental periods although approaches differ in flexibility and whether periods are truly sequential stages or simply different phases that may be re-entered. All emphasize importance of critical experiences or encounters (with racism, sexism) in triggering changes in one's thinking. These models also describe movement from passive acceptance of external definitions of group-based identity to a more internally directed sense of self.

How are these perspectives relevant for those interested in D&I? Organizational climates may be more or less accepting of different identities. Recruitment decisions by employers and candidates may be related to the level of compatibility, tolerance or support that is experienced. After hiring, employees' reactions to organizational policies and procedures, relations with supervisors, and sensitivity to perceived prejudice and discrimination may vary with their level of identity development in these areas (Chrobot-Mason & Thomas, 2002, 2004). In some cases, employees may hide aspects of their identities or their views about racism or sexism in order to "get along" in an organization. Over time, employees who feel inauthentic at work may be less productive or satisfied and may even leave the organization for a setting that feels more supportive.

Although research cited above deals with identities based on gender, sexual orientation, or feminist views, the same process is likely to occur based on factors such as religion, political views, parenthood, or other important dimensions. Treatment of employees based on race, color, religion, nationality, or sex, as well as disability and age, may run afoul of federal anti-discrimination laws; differential treatment and acceptance of people related to their expressions of aspects of identity is more complex and subjective and less likely to be reached by legal prohibitions.

Most research on ethnic identity has used standardized scales such as the MEIM-R or the Ethnic Identity Scale (EIS; see Yoon, 2011), which focus on differences among ethnic or age groups and scores relevant to particular theoretical accounts of ethnic identity. A different and qualitative approach to ethnic identity, *grounded theory*, was used by Charmaraman and Grossman (2010) to explore meanings of ethnic identity for adolescents of Asian, Black, Latino, and multiracial backgrounds. Like other ethnic identity research, this study found great variability in how important this theme was to different people. It also showed the complexity of ethnic identity, including both positive and negative aspects and focusing on acceptance of others who are different and on discrimination associated with one's ethnicity.

The meaning of ethnic identity varies greatly with cultural and historical context. For example, compare the meaning of "Japanese American" immediately post-World War II with its meaning today. Being Irish American in the US today is a positive attribute that elicits images of happy people wearing green and adorned with shamrocks. Being Irish in the US in the 1800s was quite different.

"Everyone is Irish on St. Patrick's Day!"

In a 1999 film, *The Boondock Saints*, one character says, "Yeah, it's St. Patty's Day. Everyone's Irish tonight! Why don't you just pull up a stool and have a drink with us?" (Khurana, 2013). Today being Irish conjures up pictures of parades, music, green beer, and Irish step dancing—but not in the 1800s!

When the Potato Famine hit Ireland, poor rural people faced great hardship and starvation. Between 1846 and 1855, 1.8 million people emigrated from Ireland to the US, Canada, Australia, and England (Doyle, 2006). Earlier Irish immigrants to the US had included skilled laborers and prosperous tradesmen and farmers, mostly Protestants from what is today Northern Ireland. However, Famine-era immigrants were mostly the poorest of rural people from Catholic Southern Ireland. Many were subsistence farmers who had relied on the potato as their main source of food. They arrived in the US during the "nativist" movement (also called the "Know Nothings") which sought to elevate the status of "native" Americans—meaning not American Indians, but those second-generation offspring of earlier waves of immigration. Those born and reared in the US were said to be immediately recognizable from their appearance and character, which of course were said to be superior to those of immigrants (Knobel, 1986)!

Irish immigrants were seen as "stereotypically illiterate and uneducated, degraded and depraved" (Knobel, 1986, p. 130). In 1865 the Irish American editor Phelim Lynch described the Know-Nothing view of the Irish as "impudent and voracious ... ignorant, turbulent, and brutal ... controlled by ... clergy (and) willing subjects of a foreign prince, the Pope ... drunkards and criminals ... fill(ing) the workhouses and prisons ... heap(ing) up taxes on industrious and sober and thrifty citizens" (quoted in Knobel, 1986, pp. 132–133). The Irish were racialized, dehumanized, and portrayed in cartoons as having the "lantern-jawed, low-browed" facial structure of apes. Despite stereotypes that they were lazy, unambitious, and sought to live on handouts, labor history shows they in fact worked very hard, often in jobs that others would not take. Irish women dominated domestic service as washerwomen, maids, nannies, and cooks, and many Irish men worked to their deaths in road, canal, and railroad construction (Golway, 1997). During these years, even some earlier Irish immigrants and their descendants tried to distance themselves from this stereotyped negative identity by calling themselves "Scots-Irish"(Doyle, 2006; Miller, 2006).

One hundred years later, Japanese in America were subjected to forced relocation and loss of property at the time of World War II out of fear that they would support Japan and threaten the safety of the US, especially if the West Coast were attacked or invaded (Independence Hall Association, 2013). President Roosevelt signed Executive Order 9066 in 1942 authorizing a military-enforced ban from residing within approximately 60 miles of the Pacific Coast (History Matters, n.d.). More than 127,000 of Japanese ancestry, two-thirds of whom were US citizens born in this country, were required to move to internment camps in barren areas of Arizona, Utah, Colorado, Idaho, Wyoming, and interior California. Most sold their orchards and farms, homes, stores, and other assets, often at great financial loss, not knowing if and when they could return. (Smaller numbers of those of German and Italian descent were also interned.) Despite exemplary US military service of some Japanese Americans during the War and absence of disloyal actions, when the relocation order was rescinded many communities demanded that those interned not return to their former homes. Thus many Japanese Americans moved into other areas across the country. Today the image of Japanese Americans is quite different, suggesting polite industriousness, intelligence, technical expertise, deference, and delicious food.

Research cautions us not to make assumptions about importance or content of ethnic identity to different people, even those who share the same ethnic heritage. Organizationally relevant identities are also likely to reflect this complexity.

Ethnic Identity of Multiracial Individuals

US residents are increasingly likely to identify as more than one race. Census data showed that from 2000 to 2010, the number of people who identified as both Black and White increased by 134% to 1.8 million (Saulny, 2011)! Fully 7.5 million people reported being White and some other race(s) in the 2010 Census (Humes, Jones, & Ramirez, 2011). This increase is due in part to the fact that more children now have parents of different heritages; however, the increase has also occurred because people who formerly would have identified as "Black" are now acknowledging biracial descent, and recent Census forms have made this possible. In contrast, the most popular measures of ethnic identity and conceptualizations of its development over time have emphasized monoracial identities and given little attention to mixed racio-ethnic heritage. Research on this topic is increasing (see Shih & Sanchez, 2009). Its current status has been summarized by Rockquemore, Brunsma, and Delgado (2009):

> The following four patterns emerge for identity development within the mixed-race population: (a) racial identity varies; (b) racial identity often changes over the life course; (c) racial identity development is not a predictable linear process with a single outcome; and (d) social, cultural, and spatial context are critical (pp. 20–21).

Rockquemore and Brunsma (2002) have studied Black-White biracial identity by conducting qualitative interviews and collected quantitative survey information from a sample of Black-White biracial college students at a Midwestern Catholic university. Most respondents fell into one of four categories in terms of how they understood their own biracial identity:

- *Border Identity:* the largest group (58%) saw themselves existing between two socially distinct racial groups. In some cases, border identity was socially validated or acknowledged as something different than Black or White, but in other cases (called "Tragic Mulattos") the border identity was rejected by others who saw the person as Black. (In 19th century literature the term "Tragic Mulatto" was sometimes applied to biracial persons, light enough to "pass" as White, who eventually met with hardship because society considered them to be Black; Nittle, n.d.)
- *Singular Identity*: the second largest group (about 17%) experienced one identity, most often Black.
- *Transcendent Identity*: 13% believed race was a non-issue and a false categorization. Given society's strong emphasis on minority racial categorization, maintaining such an identity is likely to be accompanied by some tension.
- *Protean Identity*: smallest group (about 4%), whose behavior and experienced identity adjusted to various social contexts. ("Protean" means "changeable," referring to the Greek God of the Sea, Proteus, who was able to change forms.)

Reviewing racial identity development among multiracial individuals, Shih and Sanchez (2005) found that psychological adjustment was similar to that of monoracial individuals. Past research suggesting adjustment problems was usually conducted with clinical samples, that is, persons who had sought counseling or therapy. In an earlier review of theories of biracial identity development (Kerwin & Ponterotto, 1995), this theme appears among three "myths" or inaccurate beliefs about biracial children: (a) they will have problems due to their mixed racial heritage; (b) they must choose to identify with one group; and (c) they do not want to discuss their racial identity. Making stereotyped generalizations such as these is risky.

Roccas and Brewer (2002) identified four different patterns in research on bicultural identity and how an individual moves from one identity group to another. These are (a) "hyphenated identities" in which the person's in-group is a blended cultural combination different from either of the separate groups; (b) "cultural dominance," in which one identity is subordinated to the other; (c) "compartmentalization," in which the person alternates identities among different settings and is culturally competent in all of them; and (d) "integrated biculturalism," which combines identities of different cultures into a more inclusive group identity. This categorization derives from a different body of research focusing on immigrant adaptation to new cultures, but it resembles the four groups that emerged in Rockquemore and Brunsma's research (2002) with Black/White biracial students.

Kevins Stencl
for Sarah

Most of us adjust our language, clothing, and topics of conversation as we move from one setting (such as school) to another (such as older relatives' homes or churches). These small and usually well-learned transitions may even seem automatic. However, members of minority cultures within a society who are employed in a typical organization may have to make larger adjustments as they move from the work environment to their homes and neighborhoods. In some cases this *code-switching* or change of identity is so pronounced that it resembles that of moving from one country to another and requires serious and concentrated effort.

This challenge of moving among ethnic cultures resembles other cultural transitions such as being part of the first generation in one's family to attend college, entering an occupation or profession that is unusual for one's demographic characteristics, being gay or lesbian and not "out" at work, returning to college after a military career or as an older student, or even changing jobs when employment cultures are very different. Sometimes the person leaves one cultural surrounding and enters another, but in other cases the individual moves back and forth many times. What happens to identity under these circumstances? Can you think of a time when you have made a life transition that felt like moving from one culture to another? What would have made this transition easier or more difficult?

Bicultural Competency

Diane de Anda (1984) has suggested factors that are likely to support fluid bicultural competency even when the person does not make a clean break from one ethnic culture to another. This is probably the typical situation for most people in work settings who experience complex aspects of identity. Factors are:

1. Degree of cultural overlap between two cultures on values, habits, etc. Moving to another similar culture is easier than moving to one that is very different.
2. Availability of cultural translators, mediators, or models. A translator is someone from one's own culture who has already made the cultural transition successfully and thus knows both cultures, whereas a mediator is someone from the second culture who is familiar with both. Translators and mediators can explain or teach; models are individuals observed and imitated because they have mastered the second culture.
3. Amount and style of corrective feedback as one learns the new culture. Empathetic, tactful, and supportive explanations facilitate adaptation to a new culture.
4. Degree of bilingualism. Transitioning among cultures is probably more difficult when language (or jargon) is quite different and unfamiliar to the learner, or when an accent is very noticeable.
5. Degree of dissimilarity in physical appearance. Transitioning among cultures is more challenging when someone is distinct and different in appearance.

Although de Anda's list was developed in the context of moving from one macro-culture to another as many immigrants do, these items seem quite reasonable in other contexts that are likely to apply to employees in work organizations. In fact, managers might consider this list as a guide to socialization of new employees into organizational culture, even when those employees come from the same background as those already employed.

Intersectionality

Thus far we have focused separately on different aspects of social identity. This contradicts how a complete identity is actually experienced by each of us. No one has *only* ethnic or gender identity; each person experiences an individual pattern of identity structure. This pattern may involve to differing degrees the sense of gender, ethnicity, religious affiliation, age group, family relationships, sexual orientation, social class, region of origin—as well as aspects that have to do with work-related attributes such as occupation, employment history, or level and type of education.

The concept of *intersectionality* in ethnic and women's studies (African American Policy Forum, n.d.; Cole, 2009) concerns this type of identity complexity. In recent years this idea has been popularized by the African American lawyer Kimberlé Williams Crenshaw (Carastathis, 2014), who discovered that intersectional identity had blocked Black women from the protection of Title VII in a 1976 discrimination case against General Motors. Prior to 1964, Black women were not hired by the automaker, and later they found it hard to obtain office jobs that were open to White women as well as the manufacturing work open to men. When a layoff came, these women were "last hired, first fired" and therefore were treated differently than either White women or Black men. Thus race had different effects for the two sexes, and sex was treated differently depending upon race. This made it difficult to present convincing evidence of either straightforward race or sex discrimination and the court decided that interactive discrimination was not covered by Title VII. Although this situation has been interpreted differently in some later cases (see Powell, 1996), this *DeGraffenreid v. General Motors* (1976) case illustrates some difficulties of intersectional discrimination.

As another illustration, Black women are claimed to provide a "two-fer" in the case of Affirmative Action (AA) compliance. In other words, hiring a Black woman allows the employer to "check two boxes" with only one hire when reporting on employment of minorities. (If this dynamic actually provided an advantage to Black women, we would expect to see more of them hired and more in prestigious jobs than is actually the case.)

The point is that occupying two or more marginalized identity statuses (e.g., minority sexual orientation and race; disability and sex) can elicit different reactions: (a) unfavorable treatment could be *similar*, e.g., discrimination toward gay people does not vary with their ethnic background; (b) *additive*, e.g., effects of race and sexual orientation discrimination are combined into double discrimination (or double jeopardy); (c) *multiplicative* or *interactive*, e.g., when minority racial status amplifies (or decreases) the effects of minority sexual orientation status; (d) or just *different*, when the intersectional category leads to qualitatively different treatment than either or both of the separate categories combined. Possibilities are even more complicated when an individual holds privileged status (e.g., highly educated or professional) along with a marginalized one such as minority race or sex (Cole, 2009). For example, how do we react to upper-income ethnic minority athletes or entertainers? Female physicians? A faculty member with a disability?

Considering multiple identities from the perspective of the person, Roccas and Brewer (2002) have defined *social identity complexity* as "an individual's subjective representation of the inter-relationships among his or her multiple group identities" (p. 88). They suggested this complexity may take different forms: (a) intersection, when identity is defined by an area of overlap between two in-groups, such as a female/lawyer; (b) dominance, when one identity is clearly more central, such as a person who considers herself a lawyer who happens to be female; (c) compartmental-ization, when the person expresses different identities in different contexts or situations, such as an individual whose social class is salient at home but whose educational and professional identity takes predominance at work; and (d) merger, when the person experiences anyone who shares any dimension of identity as an in-group member. Roccas and Brewer found that those with more complex social identities were more tolerant of out-groups and suggested that complexity may have a buffering or protective effect when one experiences a painful event or threat to one identity dimension. A later study by Brewer and Pierce (2005) also found more tolerance in persons with more complex and cross-cutting social identities. Evidence shows that greater out-group contact is associated with a more complex perception of one's own group, leading to greater tolerance and less bias. On the other hand, experiences focusing on differences between groups ("distinctiveness threat") tend to produce a simpler conception of in-group identity, which is associated with less tolerance and more bias (Schmid, Hewstone, Tausch, Cairns, & Hughes, 2009).

As organizational diversity has increased and management of D&I has become more sophisticated, diversity professionals have found themselves dealing with increasing intersectionality and social identity complexity. The idea that employees "check their identities" when they walk in the door of the work setting seems very outdated. Many employers, recognizing interconnections between family roles and work performance/satisfaction, have developed "work-family" or "work-life" programs (see Chapter 13). The quality of interpersonal relationships at work can be seriously affected when supervisors or co-workers react to aspects of worker identities (e.g., religion or family role) with respect vs. disdain or harassment. On the other hand, employees must manage various aspects of their identities so that they do not interfere with employers' legitimate expectations for completion of work and productive relationships with others.

Acculturation and Socialization Processes

Earlier we described several factors that may facilitate development of bicultural competency when entering a new and different cultural context (de Anda, 1984). Joining a new work organization and adapting to its culture share many aspects of the process faced by immigrants entering a new country. This process is probably more challenging for individuals whose socioeconomic or racio-ethnic backgrounds differ from those of the majority of current employees. In social science, *acculturation* refers to changes resulting from contact with a dissimilar sociocultural environment (Schwartz, Unger, Zamboanga, & Szapocznik, 2010).

 Usually the process of adopting or modifying identities when joining work organizations is understood in terms of *recruitment, attraction, selection, and socialization.* Employers reach out through advertising, job fairs, a web presence, and other approaches to *recruit* potential employees, who may be more or less *attracted* to various organizations for reasons such as type of work, salary, location, organizational culture or reputation, or a perception of "fit." Organizations *select* applicants based on qualifications for particular job openings as well as other factors such as perceived compatibility with the environment and other employees. Once hired, the new employee goes through a *socialization* period to learn about formal and informal aspects of the job and the organization. How does employee diversity fit into these processes? What should diversity professionals know about managing them effectively?

Conceptualizing Socialization: The ASA Model

One useful way of thinking about these processes is the *ASA model* developed by Benjamin Schneider (1987, 1995). The model's name is an acronym for "Attraction-Selection-Attrition" and it emphasizes the role of similarity between the potential employee and those already in the organization. Schneider proposed that personality and style of organization founder(s) have a strong impact upon its original culture. Others similar in goals, values, attitudes, and personality are *attracted* to that organization; this is consistent with the extensive literature in social psychology showing a strong link between similarity and attraction or liking. At the same time, the organization will also tend to *select* new members who are similar because of a perception of better fit.

In addition, processes that organizations often use to choose new employees are based on identifying attributes of successful employees and hiring others with those characteristics. More specifically, employers are advised to use selection criteria (such as tests, resumé items, interview questions) that have been *validated*. This usually means that they have been found to predict successful job performance by those already in the organization. However, the very meaning of "successful performance" is affected by the existing culture and values of the organization. For example, companies vary in the degree to which they emphasize quantity or quality of work, sales volume, collegiality and teamwork, attendance, innovation, or other aspects of performance. Although use of valid predictors is good advice from measurement and legal perspectives, it does mean that employers are likely to hire people like the ones already working for them. Might there be other attributes not currently represented among employees that would also be associated with or lead to success? For example, there was a time when almost all doctors were men.

The *attrition* aspect of the ASA model explains that those not compatible with the organization will be likely to leave either through resignation or termination because they do not "fit." The combined effect of these three ASA processes is that, over time, the organization becomes more homogeneous. Schneider (1987) suggested that although this may be beneficial in the short run, the organization may be unable to adapt if its environment changes. New technologies, political or economic challenges, competition, or changes in availability of potential employees are problematic if the organization becomes too rigid to adapt.

The ASA model implies that the natural course of things is for organizations to become more homogeneous internally, unless something intervenes. For example, in the US enactment of Civil Rights laws since the 1960s and the policy of AA had the effect of interrupting this "natural" tendency for increasing internal similarity. Advocating for diversity can also be understood as an active strategic force bringing into organizations people who are different from those already there. Sometimes organizations try to make themselves look appealing to members of underrepresented groups in the recruiting process. One example of an unfortunate attempt to do this is illustrated in the shaded box.

Phantom Diversity

The University of Wisconsin-Madison's 2001–2002 undergraduate application book showed enthusiastic students cheering wildly at an athletic event. Among the happy faces was one young African American man, smiling broadly. A student newspaper reporter pondered the cover and wondered why the pattern of sunlight looked different on the Black face than on the White ones. It turned out that university staff had digitally inserted into the cheering crowd a photo of an African American student taken at another event to give the impression of diversity in the student body. In reality, at the time only 10% of the student body consisted of students of color (Durhams, 2000; Mikkelson, 2014).

Things became even worse for the University when the inserted face was identified as that of a well-known campus activist working to increase diversity on campus who had never been to a UW football game! University officials said they had spent months looking without success for an appropriate photo to suggest diversity among students, and finally decided to create one. They publicly apologized to the young African American man and the campus community and printed a new batch of booklets at a cost of $64,000. The story also received widespread news coverage.

How many brochures, booklets, websites, and other materials have you seen that prominently feature students (or employees) of color? One interesting example is an annual report from a large utilities company featuring many employees of color, including a smiling and attractive African American man in a hard hat. Several years ago this company lost a famous and widely cited Title VII race discrimination lawsuit!

Diversity and Socialization

When an employee joins an organization, the process of *socialization* begins. This refers to formal and informal processes occurring as the newcomer learns skills, knowledge, attitudes, and contextual information needed to function as a productive employee. Socialization often starts with orientation during which the new employee learns about such things as procedures, rules, benefits, and key people in the organization. Its length and formality can vary widely from simple introductions and guidance from co-workers to a planned series of experiences involving on-the-job training, completion of workshops or short courses, direct teaching about tools and equipment, mentoring, or a variety of other components. Socialization has traditionally been understood to include mastery of tasks, understanding of worker roles, and knowledge about the work environment. Research has shown that people who are proactive in asking for feedback and actively building relationships with co-workers and supervisors generally report increased clarity of work roles, commitment to the organization, and acceptance by others (e.g., Gruman, Saks, & Zweig, 2006).

Recently, researchers have also begun to think of socialization as including the development of relationships with other employees and a sense of the organization as a supportive place (Allen & Shanock, 2013); this idea is consistent with the emphasis on *inclusion* in contemporary thinking about diversity. In this view, effective socialization leads not only to mastery of tasks, roles, and environmental knowledge, but also to *embeddedness* in a network of social relationships and a sense of *positive organizational support (POS)*, that is, feeling that one's contributions and well-being are valued by the organization. Employees who are socially embedded and experience POS should feel more emotional commitment to the organization and be less likely to leave prematurely.

Work organizations also increase their employees' human, social, and cultural capital through socialization (Allen & Shanock, 2013). *Human capital* is based on knowledge, experience, education, or skill; *social capital* refers to connections with other people; and *cultural capital* involves a common understanding of values and culture (Yoon & Lawler, 2006). In a college environment through interactions with others, successful students increase all three types of capital. Human capital involves the college degree and the knowledge and skills that are mastered, social capital concerns connections that can be important in life after graduation, and cultural capital is the understanding of what it means to be a college-educated person in terms of career aspirations, interests, and participation in society. Learning experiences focused on *content*, such as mastering specific information, skills, or tasks, will increase employees' human capital. Socialization focused on *interactions* such as role modeling, mentoring, or development of social relationships with experienced others should increase social capital. And socialization experiences that occur in a carefully planned social *context* alongside other people (rather than informally or in isolation) should lead to more cultural capital (Allen & Shanock, 2013).

Can you think of examples of these three types of capital in your experience? Have they increased during your higher education? Students in the first generation of their family to attend college or graduate school may notice these changes even more than those whose family members have already earned college, graduate, or professional degrees.

How is this related to D&I? A new employee with different demographic or educational background or experience may face greater challenges in acquiring human, social, and cultural capital that comes more easily to others. Aspects of socialization intended to develop interpersonal connections and cultural knowledge are especially important. Effective diversity managers will take this into account in planning constructive orientation and socialization experiences without relying on stereotyped assumptions about new employees. Newcomers may be more proactive during socialization when they perceive themselves to be similar to others in the organization. In a study of recent college graduates, perceptions of similarity in terms of education and sex (but not other types of similarity) led to more proactive on-the-job socialization behavior (Kammeyer-Mueller, Livingston, & Liao, 2011). Interestingly, those who saw themselves as *different* in age from others in the work group were also more likely to be proactive.

This framework suggests that if people of difference are to become committed to the organization and remain productive and satisfied employees, their socialization experiences must be designed to lead to embeddedness and a sense of POS. In a complex study of more than 500 new employees at various locations across the US, Allen and Shanock (2013) found that all three types of socialization (content, social, and context) were associated with higher levels of POS. Both content and social experiences predicted higher levels of embeddedness. Furthermore, employees who reported more POS and more embeddedness were more emotionally committed to the organization and less likely to leave voluntarily. This supports the importance of socialization experiences leading to a sense of connection with others in the organization and a feeling of being valued for one's contributions. Special challenges exist when developing these subtle and subjective responses with employees from backgrounds very different than those of more typical employees.

Even more challenging is development of knowledge and skill, interpersonal relationships, and values that are necessary in the organization without suppressing significant aspects of employees' identities—assuming those aspects are legal, ethical, and consistent with a diverse and inclusive work environment. In a survey of more than 200 employed adults, those reporting more effort to suppress a group identity perceived more discrimination and also reported lower job satisfaction and higher intentions to leave. Conversely, those who reported openly discussing and expressing important aspects of identity at work (e.g., through language, food, pictures, or holiday celebrations) also saw less discrimination, were more satisfied with their jobs, and reported lower intentions to leave (Madera, King, & Hebl, 2012).

The next chapter turns to topics of stereotyping, prejudice, and discrimination, which underlie many tensions occurring in organizations as they become more diverse. Our focus is on understanding implications of well-supported theories and empirical research with special consideration for how they apply in diverse work organizations.

References

African American Policy Forum. (n.d.) *A primer on intersectionality.* Retrieved from www.whiteprivilegeconference.com/pdf/intersectionality_primer.pdf

Allen, D. G., & Shanock, L. R. (2013). Perceived organizational support and embeddedness as key mechanisms connecting socialization tactics to commitment and turnover among new employees. *Journal of Organizational Behavior, 34,* 350–369.

Arndt, J., Greenberg, J., Schimel, J., Pyszczynski, T., & Solomon, S. (2002). To belong or not to belong, that is the question: Terror management and identification with gender and ethnicity. *Journal of Personality and Social Psychology, 83,* 26–43.

Ashforth, B. E., & Mael, F. (1989). Social Identity Theory and the organization. *Academy of Management Review, 14,* 20–39.

Baird, M. K., Szymanski, D. M., & Ruebelt, S. G. (2007). Feminist identity development and practice among male therapists. *Psychology of Men and Masculinity, 8,* 67–78.

Bargad, A., & Hyde, J. S. (1991). A study of feminist identity development in women. *Psychology of Women Quarterly, 15,* 181–201.

Blader, S. L., & Tyler, T. R. (2009). Testing and extending the group engagement model: Linkages between social identity, procedural justice, economic outcomes, and extrarole behavior. *Journal of Applied Psychology, 94,* 445–464.

Brewer, M. B., & Pierce, K. P. (2005). Social identity complexity and outgroup tolerance. *Personality and Social Psychology Bulletin, 31,* 428–437.

Carastathis, A. (2014). The concept of intersectionality in feminist theory. *Philosophy Compass, 9,* 304–314. Retrieved from www.academia.edu/4894646/The_Concept_of_Intersectionality_in_Feminist_Theory

Carter, R. T., & Parks, E. E. (1996). Womanist identity and mental health. *Journal of Counseling and Development, 74,* 484–489.

Castano, E., Yzerbyt, V., Paladino, M-P., & Sacchi, S. (2002). I belong, therefore, I exist: Ingroup identification, ingroup entativity, and ingroup bias. *Personality and Social Psychology Bulletin, 28,* 135–143.

Chae, M. H., & Larres, C. (2010). Asian American racial and ethnic identity: Update on theory and measurement. In J. G. Ponterotto, J. M. Casas, L. A. Suzuki, & C. M. Alexander (Eds.), *Handbook of multicultural counseling* (3rd ed., pp. 253–267). Los Angeles, CA: SAGE.

*Charmaraman, L., & Grossman, J. M. (2010). Importance of race and ethnicity: An exploration of Asian, Black, Latino, and Multiracial Adolescent Identity. *Cultural Diversity and Ethnic Minority Psychology, 16,* 144–151.

Chrobot-Mason, D., & Thomas, K. M. (2002). Minority employees in majority organizations: The intersection of individual and organizational racial identity in the workplace. *Human Resource Development Review*, *1*, 323–344.

Chrobot-Mason, D., & Thomas, K. M. (2004). Managing racial differences: The role of majority managers' ethnic identity development on minority employee perceptions of support. *Group & Organization Management*, *29*, 5–31.

Cokley, K. (2007). Critical issues in the measurement of ethnic and racial identity: A referendum on the state of the field. *Journal of Counseling Psychology*, *54*, 224–234.

Cole, E. R. (2009). Intersectionality and research in psychology. *American Psychologist*, *64*, 170–180.

Cross, W. E., Jr. (1971). The Negro-to-Black conversion experience: Toward a psychology of Black liberation. *Black World*, *20*(9), 13–27.

de Anda, D. (1984). Bicultural socialization: Factors affecting the minority experience. *Social Work*, *29*, 101–107.

DeGraffenreid v. GENERAL MOTORS ASSEMBLY DIV., ETC. (1976). 413 F. Supp. 142 (E.D. Mo.)

Dovidio, J. F., & Gaertner, S. L. (2010). Intergroup bias. In S. T. Fiske, D. Gilbert, & G. Lindzey (Eds.), *Handbook of social psychology* (Vol. 2, 5th ed., pp. 1084–1121). New York, NY: Wiley.

Doyle, D. N. (2006). The remaking of Irish America, 1845–1880. In J. J. Lee & M. R. Casey (Eds.), *Making the Irish American: History and heritage of the Irish in the United States* (pp. 213–252). New York: New York University Press.

Durhams, S. (2000, September 21). Altered photo forces UW-Madison to reprint 100,000 brochures. *The Milwaukee Journal Sentinel*, p. A2.

Fischer, A. R., & Moradi, B. (2001). Racial and ethnic identity: Recent developments and needed directions. In J. G. Ponterotto, J. M. Casas, L. A. Suzuki, & C. M. Alexander (Eds.), *Handbook of multicultural counseling* (2nd ed., pp. 341–370). Thousand Oaks, CA: SAGE.

Fischer, A. R., Tokar, D. M., Mergl, M. M., Good, G. E., Hill, M. S., & Blum, S. A. (2000). Assessing women's feminist identity development. *Psychology of Women Quarterly*, *24*, 15–29.

Frable, D. E. S. (1997). Gender, racial, ethnic, sexual, and class identities. *Annual Review of Psychology*, *48*, 139–162.

Ghavami, N., Fingerhut, A., Peplau, L. A., Grant, S. K., & Wittig, M. A. (2011). Testing a model of minority identity achievement, identity affirmation, and psychological well-being among ethnic minority and sexual minority individuals. *Cultural Diversity and Ethnic Minority Psychology*, *17*, 79–88.

Golway, T. (1997). The work: Where the Irish did apply. In M. Coffey (Ed.), *The Irish in America* (pp. 135–178). New York: Hyperion.

Gruman, J. A., Saks, A. M., & Zweig, D. I. (2006). Organizational socialization tactics and newcomer proactive behaviors: An integrative study. *Journal of Vocational Behavior*, *69*, 90–104.

Helms, J. E. (Ed.) (1990a). *Black and White racial identity theory: Theory, research, and practice*. Westport, CT: Greenwood.

Helms, J. E. (1990b). Introduction. In J. E. Helms (Ed.), *Black and White racial identity theory: Theory, research, and practice* (pp. 3–8). Westport, CT: Greenwood.

Helms, J. E. (1990c). The measurement of Black racial identity attitudes. In J. E. Helms (Ed.), *Black and white racial identity: Theory, research, and practice* (pp. 33–47). Westport, CT: Greenwood.

Helms, J. E. (1990d). Toward a model of White racial identity development. In J. E. Helms (Ed.), *Black and white racial identity: Theory, research, and practice* (pp. 50–66). Westport, CT: Greenwood.

Helms, J. E. (1995). An update of Helms's White and People of Color Racial Identity models. In J. G. Ponterotto, J. M. Casas, L. A. Suzuki, & C. M. Alexander (Eds.), *Handbook of multicultural counseling* (pp. 181–198). Thousand Oaks, CA: SAGE.

Helms, J. E., & Carter, R. T. (1990). Development of the White Racial Identity Inventory. In J. E. Helms (Ed.), *Black and White racial identity theory: Theory, research, and practice* (pp. 67–80). Westport, CT: Greenwood.

Hewstone, M. (1992). The "ultimate attribution error"? A review of the literature on intergroup causal attribution. *European Journal of Social Psychology*, *20*, 311–335.

Highhouse, S., Thornbury, E. E., & Little, I. S. (2006). Social-identity functions of attraction to organizations. *Organizational Behavior and Human Decision Processes*, *103*, 134–146.

History Matters: The U. S. Survey Course on the Web. (n.d.). *Executive Order 9066: The president authorizes Japanese relocation*. Retrieved from http://historymatters.gmu.edu/d/5154

Hornsey, M. J. (2008). Social Identity Theory and Self-Categorization Theory: A historical review. *Social and Personality Psychology Compass*, *2/1*, 204–222.

Humes, K. R., Jones, N. A., & Ramirez, R. R. (2011). *Overview of race and Hispanic origin: 2010; 2010 Census Briefs.* Retrieved from www.census.gov/prod/cen2010/briefs/c2010br-02.pdf

Independence Hall Association. (2013). *U.S. History: 51e. Japanese-American internment.* Retrieved from www.ushistory.org/us/51e.asp

Kammeyer-Mueller, J. D., Livingston, B. A., & Liao, H. (2011). Perceived similarity, proactive adjustment, and organizational socialization. *Journal of Vocational Behavior, 78,* 225–236.

Kerwin, C., & Ponterotto, J. G. (1995). Biracial identity development. In J. G. Ponterotto, J. M. Casas, L. A. Suzuki, & C. M. Alexander (Eds.), *Handbook of multicultural counseling* (pp. 199–217). Thousand Oaks, CA: SAGE.

Khurana, S. (2013). *Boondock Saints Quotes.* Retrieved from http://quotations.about.com/od/boondocksaints quotes/a/BoondockSaints3.htm

Knobel, D. T. (1986). *Paddy and the Republic: Ethnicity and nationality in antebellum America.* Middletown, CT: Wesleyan University Press.

Kramer, R. M. (2001). Identity and trust in organizations: One anatomy of a productive but problematic relationship. In M. A. Hogg & D. J. Terry (Eds.), *Social identity processes in organizational contexts* (pp. 167–179). Philadelphia, PA: Psychology Press.

Leach, C. W., Mosquera, P. M. R., Vliek, M. L. W., & Hirt, E. (2010). Group devaluation and group identification. *Journal of Social Issues, 66,* 535–552.

Madera, J. M., King, E. B., & Hebl, M. R. (2012). Bringing social identity to work: The influence of manifestation and suppression on perceived discrimination, job satisfaction, and turnover intentions. *Cultural Diversity and Ethnic Minority Psychology, 18,* 165–170.

Mikkelson, D. (2014). *Photo finish.* Retrieved from www.snopes.com/college/admin/uwmadison.asp

Miller, K. A. (2006). Ulster Presbyterians and the "Two Traditions" in Ireland and America. In J. J. Lee & M. R. Casey (Eds.), *Making the Irish American: History and heritage of the Irish in the United States* (pp. 255–270). New York: New York University Press.

Miville, M. L. (2010). Latina/o identity development: Updates on theory, measurement, and counseling implications. In J. G. Ponterotto, J. M. Casas, L. A. Suzuki, & C. M. Alexander (Eds.), *Handbook of multicultural counseling* (3rd ed., pp. 241–251). Los Angeles, CA: SAGE.

Nittle, N. K. (n.d.). *Tragic Mulatto myth.* Retrieved from http://racerelations.about.com/od/history ofracerelations/g/tragicmulattomyth.htm

Ostrom, T. M., & Sedikides, C. (1992). Out-group homogeneity effects in natural and minimal groups. *Psychological Bulletin, 112,* 536–552.

Parham, T. A., & Helms, J. E. (1981). The influence of Black students' racial identity attitudes on preference for counselor's race. *Journal of Counseling Psychology, 28,* 250–257.

Phinney, J. (1992). The Multigroup Ethnic Identity Measure: A new scale for use with diverse groups. *Journal of Adolescent Research, 7,* 156–176.

Phinney, J. S., & Ong, A. D. (2007). Conceptualization and measurement of ethnic identity: Current status and future directions. *Journal of Counseling Psychology, 54,* 271–281.

Ponterotto, J. G., & Park-Taylor, J. (2007). Racial and ethnic identity theory, measurement, and research in counseling psychology: Present status and future directions. *Journal of Counseling Psychology, 54,* 282–294.

Popp, E. C., Landau, H. I., Brink, K. E., & Thomas, K. M. (March, 2002). *Shades of White identity: Self-labels, White ethnic identity, and attitudes toward others.* Presented at annual conference of the Southeastern Psychological Association, Kissimmee, FL.

Powell, M. E. (1996). The claims of women of color under Title VII: The interaction of race and gender. *Golden Gate University Law Review, 26,* 412–436. Retrieved from http://digitalcommons.law.ggu.edu/cgi/viewcontent.cgi?article=1677&context=ggulrev

*Roccas, S., & Brewer, M. B. (2002). Social identity complexity. *Personality and Social Psychology Review, 6,* 88–106.

Rockquemore, K. A., & Brunsma, D. L. (2002). *Beyond black: Biracial identity in America.* Thousand Oaks, CA: SAGE Publications.

Rockquemore, K. A., Brunsma, D. L., & Delgado, D. J. (2009). Racing to theory or retheorizing race? Understanding the struggle to build a multiracial identity theory. *Journal of Social Issues, 65,* 13–34.

Rubin, M., & Badea, C. (2007). Why do people perceive ingroup homogeneity on ingroup traits and outgroup homogeneity on outgroup traits? *Personality and Social Psychology Bulletin, 33,* 31–42.

Saulny, S. (2011, March 24). Census data presents rise in multiracial population of youths. *New York Times.* Retrieved from www.nytimes.com/2011/03/25/us/25race.html?_r=0&pagewanted=print

Schmid, K., Hewstone, M., Tausch, N., Cairns, E., & Hughes, J. (2009). Antecedents and consequences of social identity complexity: Intergroup contact, distinctiveness threat, and outgroup attitudes. *Personality and Social Psychology Bulletin, 35*, 1985–1098.

Schneider, B. (1987). The people make the place. *Personnel Psychology, 40*, 437–453.

Schneider, B. (1995). The ASA Framework: An update. *Personnel Psychology, 48*, 747–773.

Schwartz, S. J., Unger, J. B., Zamboanga, B. L., & Szapocznik, J. (2010). Rethinking the concept of acculturation. *American Psychologist, 65*, 237–251.

Sherif, M., Harvey, O. J., White, B. J., Hood, W. R., & Sherif, C. W. (1961). *Intergroup conflict and cooperation: The Robbers Cave experiment.* Norman, OK: University Book Exchange.

Shih, M., & Sanchez, D. T. (2005). Perspectives and research on the positive and negative implications of having multiple racial identities. *Psychological Bulletin, 131*, 569–591.

*Shih, M., & Sanchez, D. T. (2009). The landscape of multiracial experiences. *Journal of Social Issues, 65.* (Whole issue.)

Spartacus Educational. (2014). *Walter Francis White.* Retrieved from http://spartacus-educational.com/USAwhiteWF.htm

Tajfel, H., & Turner, J. (1979). An integrative theory of intergroup conflict. In W. G. Austin & S. Worchel (Eds.), *The social psychology of intergroup relations* (pp. 33–47). Monterey, CA: Brooks-Cole.

Thomas, K. M. (2005). *Diversity dynamics in the workplace.* Belmont, CA: Thomson Wadsworth.

Thompson, C. E., & Carter, R. T. (1997). An overview and elaboration of Helms' Racial Identity Development. In C. E. Thompson & R. T. Carter (Eds.), *Racial identity theory: Applications to individual, group, and organizational interventions* (pp. 15–32). Mahwah, NJ: Lawrence Erlbaum Associates.

Tyler, T. R., & Blader, S. L. (2001). Identity and cooperative behavior in groups. *Group Processes and Intergroup Relations, 4*, 207–226.

Walters, K. L., & Simoni, J. M. (1993). Lesbian and gay male group identity attitudes and self-esteem: Implications for counseling. *Journal of Counseling Psychology, 40*, 94–99.

Wanberg, C. R. (2012). The individual experience of unemployment. *Annual Review of Psychology, 63*, 369–396.

Yoon, E. (2011). Measuring ethnic identity in the Ethnic Identity Scale and the Multigroup Ethnic Identity Measure—Revised. *Cultural Diversity and Ethnic Minority Psychology, 17*, 144–155.

Yoon, J., & Lawler, E. J. (2006). Relational cohesion model of organizational commitment. In O. Kyriakidou & M. F. Ozbilgin (Eds.), *Relational perspectives in organizational studies (*pp. 138–162). Cheltenham: Edward Elgar.

* Recommended for advanced reading.

Chapter 6

The Big Three

Stereotypes, Prejudice, and Discrimination

This chapter turns to processes that most people probably think they understand very well: stereotyping, prejudice, and discrimination. However, common sense is often not supported by empirical research, and empirical conclusions are sometimes unexpected. We now consider research on these familiar processes and their implications about managing D&I effectively.

Stereotypes, Prejudice, and Discrimination

Psychologists have defined "attitude" in two major ways. The traditional "tripartite" or three-part definition defines attitude as composed of thoughts or beliefs (cognition), feelings or evaluations (affect), and tendencies to behave (conation) toward an attitude object (Crano & Prislin, 2008). Others reserve "attitude" for the evaluative component only, a "learned predisposition to respond in a consistently favorable or unfavorable manner . . . to a given object" (Fishbein & Ajzen, 1975, p. 6). Regardless of definition, it is widely recognized that stereotypes are mainly cognitive, prejudices are predominantly affective, and discrimination is behavioral. All are important in our interactions in diverse environments.

An early assumption about attitudes was that we act in harmony with our beliefs and feelings. We often feel as if our beliefs and emotions *lead to* our behavior. Much diversity management activity in organizations also seems based on this assumption. For example, often diversity training programs begin by trying to reduce stereotypes, on the assumption that this is necessary to reduce prejudice and improve interactions (Caudron, 1993b).

Although this seems reasonable, social psychology research challenges its effectiveness (Park & Judd, 2005). It is quite common for us to behave in ways that could not have been anticipated from our stereotypes or attitudes, and sometimes our behavior implies beliefs or feelings we do not have. Research shows that stereotypes and attitudes sometimes lead to behavior, behavior sometimes leads to new stereotypes or attitudes, and often the two seem independent of each other because of other variables.

The intuitive explanation which seems to underlie much diversity training assumes that stereotypes lead to prejudices, which lead to discriminatory behavior.

Stereotypes → Prejudices → Discrimination

If that's correct, then it really is necessary to address stereotypes first to reduce prejudice and discrimination. However, there are alternatives (Schneider, 2004). For example, stereotypes may lead us to behave differently toward a category of people, even though we may not hold prejudices for or against them. Simply recognizing a category may elicit behaviors strongly associated with that group of people. This possibility is depicted below.

Stereotypes → Discriminatory Behavior

In other cases, discriminatory behavior results from environmental factors, e.g., laws, norms, or others' behavior. The person who is discriminating may have neither strong stereotypic beliefs nor prejudicial attitudes. The behavior may simply be habitual and occur without much thought or feeling, as shown below.

$$???? \rightarrow \text{Discriminatory Behavior}$$

Finally, stereotypes and prejudice could develop *as a result of* discriminatory behavior, rather than the reverse. The person may unintentionally behave in a way that is perceived as offensive or thoughtless, and this behavior may elicit a negative reaction from another. The first person then interprets that negative behavior as characteristic of the second person's group, leading to negative stereotypes and feelings. (This also happens with positive behaviors.)

$$
\begin{array}{l}
\text{Discriminatory Behavior} \rightarrow \text{Stereotypes} \\
\text{OR} \\
\text{Discriminatory Behavior} \rightarrow \text{Prejudices}
\end{array}
$$

Why does this matter to the diversity professional? First, in attempts to improve relationships in organizations, we should consider what is *really* important. Unpleasant or discriminatory behavior toward others is more likely to be a problem in work organizations than stereotyped thinking or negative feelings alone. Beliefs and feelings create problems when expressed in ways that interfere with professional, congenial, and productive interpersonal relationships. Thus it is more efficient, and probably more effective, to focus diversity management work not on stereotypes but on changing *behavior* so that it is respectful, neutral or positive, and focused on accomplishing the organization's work.

A second reason to focus on behavior rather than stereotypes is that people's beliefs and feelings often change *as a result of their behavior;* that is, altering behavior can produce changes in stereotypes and prejudices as well. Third, in some circumstances merely discussing the content of stereotypes or prejudices can create additional problems by suggesting the presence of discrimination, whether or not it actually exists (Caudron, 1993a).

Stereotypes

Stereotypes are categories into which we classify people on the basis of some *defining attribute* such as occupation, national origin, religious or political affiliation, fraternity/sorority. A stereotype includes *associated attributes*, those traits or behavioral characteristics thought to be true of all or most category members. These cognitions of individuals are called *personal stereotypes*. Shared understandings also exist within a group or society about attributes supposedly characterizing others. For example, popular ideas exist about surfers, bankers, long-haul truck drivers, or US Marines. These are called *cultural stereotypes* and are recognized even by people who do not personally believe them.

Unless otherwise specified, in this text the term "stereotype" refers to personal beliefs about categories of people. First someone categorizes others based on a salient or noticeable characteristic (the defining attribute); next the perceiver learns or assumes a set of other characteristics (the associated attributes) thought to apply to people in that category. Once formed, the stereotype filters perceptions of and reactions to others who seem to fit the stereotypic category. Later, when the perceiver encounters someone who fits that category based on defining attribute, an inference is drawn that this person also has associated attributes. This cognitive process is efficient in dealing with complex social environments because we can begin processing information about and behaving toward someone in a way that often is appropriate. For example, what would you talk about with a business major or a student in the performing arts? Stereotypes are a shortcut or *heuristic* for applying past learning about people to a new situation (McGarty, Yzerbyt, & Spears, 2012).

The term "cognitive miser" refers to our tendency to economize on the mental work of understanding the complex world, including diverse people we encounter. The stereotyping heuristic quickly simplifies new information and connects it with information we have already processed about others, and for that reason it's useful and socially adaptive (Hamilton & Sherman, 1994; Schneider, 2004). Thus, trying to eliminate stereotyping seems like a mistake, and probably is doomed to fail.

Instead, we should try to understand how stereotypes operate so that we can avoid pitfalls in their use. In forming and using stereotypes, we experience both *information loss* and *information gain* (Hamilton & Sherman, 1994) as we omit or simplify available information and infer other information. We leave out *individuating information* (unique to that individual), focusing on a few salient characteristics, and assume things about a person on the basis of what we believe about the category.

Three major dangers result from stereotyping, especially in a diverse environment:

- Stereotypes may prevent us from attending to and learning unique information about others because stereotypic beliefs are strong. This may not matter much in one-time superficial interactions but can be a major problem in developing significant or enduring relationships, such as at work.
- Stereotyping may imply we are not paying attention to an individual with whom we are interacting; that person may be offended.
- As generalizations about a group, stereotypes are inaccurate as description of any single individual in that category.

Categorizing

"Natural" or "primitive" categories such as race, gender, and age are widely and habitually used to categorize people. These are broad classifications, immediately apparent when we meet someone, useful in capturing socially and behaviorally relevant distinctions. Eye color is noticeable but usually not diagnostic of important social distinctions in the way that gender is. We also categorize others using categories that:

1. We use frequently: e.g., students vs. faculty, or those in different majors;
2. Distinguish groups to which we belong: "my" team vs. others;
3. Involve differences that are important in a particular situation or context: salesperson vs. customer; or,
4. Capture some way in which someone deviates from the norm we expect in a certain situation, such as minorities or women in upper management (Hamilton & Sherman, 1994).

Category-based (i.e., stereotypic) information processing is most likely when we must make judgments (a) under time pressure; (b) under complex mental demands (called *cognitive load*) from a large amount of information or distracting conditions; (c) when stereotyping is easy and we are not highly motivated to be accurate, perhaps because the judgment does not seem important; (d) when very little individuating information is available; and (e) when we are tired or inattentive (Bodenhausen, 1990; Beike & Sherman, 1994). Stereotyping is especially likely in making decisions about people we do not know well, such as job applicants. Interview and selection processes often embody these characteristics.

Effects of Stereotypes

Attention and memory are affected by stereotypes. We perceive new information in a manner consistent with our stereotype, especially if information is ambiguous. We may not notice contradictory information, or may discount it as "the exception that proves the rule." Contradictory information may also lead us to form *subtypes* such as "female scientist" vs. females in general. Our stereotype about women's abilities remains intact: female scientists are considered unusual women, not typical. Stereotypes are remarkably resistant to change in response to contradictory information (Hamilton & Sherman, 1994). Diversity managers should expect that stereotypes will ordinarily be difficult to change.

Sometimes contradictory information actually receives *more* attention as we try to resolve the inconsistency with expectations. If circumstances permit us to process unexpected information, we may actually recall it better as a result. But if limited time, information complexity, or our own cognitive limitations or distractions prevent this additional mental work, we will remember it less well. When time and cognitive resources are limited, we remember best information matching our stereotypes; we tend to overlook, ignore, filter out, or explain away contradictory information (Hamilton & Sherman, 1994; Hilton & von Hippel, 1996). One implication for diversity managers is to assure sufficient time and minimal distractions when important decisions are being made about people.

Because memory is reconstructive, we may think we are "remembering" something when in fact we are constructing it partly from stereotypes. We may not distinguish between what we have learned and remember from a particular occasion and what we *think* we remember because our prior expectancies have filled in an informational void. With time, it becomes harder to distinguish information actually learned from inferences based on expectations. In gathering information to make decisions about people, good contemporaneous notes will aid in remembering things accurately and completely.

Furthermore, our standards often shift as new information is interpreted consistent with expectancies for the person's category. The same behavior may seem "dynamic" when done by a man, but "too aggressive" when performed by a woman. This *shifting standards* process has been extensively documented by Biernat (2009) and her collaborators (e.g., Biernat, Manis, & Nelson, 1991). To illustrate, if students are asked to rank their peers in terms of height, they commonly rank women in terms of whether they are "tall for a woman" rather than by actual height. If this occurs even when the dimension (height) can be measured easily and accurately, what happens when we assess more subjective variables such as interpersonal skills, motivation, or strategic thinking as would be done in a work setting? To avoid shifting standards, we should define ahead of time in behavioral terms what is meant by "motivation" and other subjective terms, and apply the same behavioral definitions to all candidates.

Stereotypes also affect attributions. Behavior that matches expectation is likely to be taken as an indication of personality or ability, but stereotype-inconsistent behavior is often attributed to the situation. For example, if we believe ethnic minority employees tend to be lazy and have a poor work ethic, we may see persistent lateness as confirmation that this stereotype applies to our minority co-worker. We may not consider that the person is working two jobs, caring for a sick child or elderly parent, or unable to arrange reliable transportation to work. We also may resist assigning a "cause" to someone's behavior when it does not match our stereotype; such information is difficult to understand because it violates expectations. Someone's behavior seems unpredictable or unreliable when it doesn't match expectations for the stereotypic category (Hilton & von Hippel, 1996).

Navy Lt. Kara Hultgreen was one of the first two women qualified to fly carrier-based F-14A fighter jets. When Hultgreen was killed while attempting to land on an aircraft carrier in October 1995, the incident received widespread attention. Allegations of pilot error were made and some claimed the Navy had lowered its standards to permit unqualified women to fly these jets—a claim seldom heard about men who crash even when pilot error is involved. This claim of incompetence is consistent with the stereotype that women are unsuited for combat missions. Investigation showed engine failure as cause of the accident, but allegations of pilot error continued. Her commanding officer said she was clearly qualified and rebutted critics (Patterson, 2006). Contemporary news reports recounted not only stereotypes about women in the military, but alleged harassment and discrimination of which they were victims.

Are Stereotypes Accurate?

Many diversity professionals believe that stereotypes are usually inaccurate, negative, and a barrier to effective interaction in diverse environments (Cox, 1997). This claim of inaccuracy has proven to be surprisingly difficult to evaluate convincingly (Jussim, Cain, Crawford, Harber, & Cohen, 2009). Empirical literature suggests a more nuanced understanding.

Stereotypes cannot be *completely* accurate about all members of a target group, simply because they are generalizations that cannot apply equally to all members of a group unless those members are very much alike indeed. Furthermore, stereotypes often concern subjective attributes that are not easily measured; to determine accuracy of a stereotype, we must compare it with what really exists, and this is sometimes difficult to know.

What is the evidence about stereotype accuracy? Stereotypes are said to contain a "kernel of truth" representing an accurate description of how a group compares with others, but exaggerating differences between groups. Schneider's (2004) review concluded that substantial accuracy exists in many stereotypes; the issue of exaggeration has not been widely investigated, but often people actually *underestimate* objective differences between groups. According to Schneider, people can be "moderately accurate, at least" in stereotypes about groups such as gender, nationality, race or ethnicity, college majors or dorm residents (p. 331). Jussim et al. (2009) reviewed empirical research on accuracy of ethnic, racial, and gender stereotypes and concluded that *cultural* stereotypes are often accurate, especially for comparisons *between* groups. Stereotype accuracy for differences *within* a group or about the *absolute level* of some characteristic is somewhat less; *personal* stereotypes, though often accurate, tend to be less accurate overall than cultural stereotypes. These researchers warned that stereotypes about religion and social class have not been extensively investigated, and that many studies have been conducted with college students rather than older employed persons. Nevertheless, they concluded that "the most appropriate generalization based on the evidence is that people's beliefs about groups are usually moderately to highly accurate, and are occasionally highly inaccurate" (p. 221).

What does stereotype accuracy research imply for those experiencing or managing diversity in work organizations? First, even if a stereotype is accurate, this is not useful for substantive interactions with individuals who may or may not fit that stereotype. We should try to base our behavior on *individuating information*, that is, information distinguishing a particular individual from others. Second, even when one group shows more of some characteristic than another group, this attribute may still be relatively infrequent even within that group. For example, sickle cell anemia is statistically more common among African Americans and people of Mediterranean heritage, but thankfully it is infrequent even within those groups. Finally, in work organizations it is inappropriate and perhaps illegal to make a decision about an individual based on information about demographic group membership.

Valuing Diversity vs. Stereotyping?

Valuing Diversity activities celebrate uniqueness of groups or individuals. Examples are ethnic meals or music, informative events about the culture of a particular group, or dressing in the traditional costume of the ethnicity being celebrated. Such activities are intended to draw positive attention to the heritage and contributions of various groups of people.

Black History Month, observed every February, was started to draw attention to accomplishments of African Americans in the US. The idea came from Dr. Carter G. Woodson, son of former slaves and the second African American PhD graduate in History from Harvard University. In 1926, "Negro History Week" was chosen to include birthdays of Abraham Lincoln and Frederick Douglass. It was expanded in 1976 to African American History Month and has been recognized by Presidential proclamations each year since then (Biography.com, n.d.; Scott, n.d.).

In 1968, Hispanic Heritage Month was designated for the month between September 15 and October 15, including anniversaries of independence in Costa Rica, El Salvador, Guatemala, Nicaragua, Mexico, and Chile, as well as Columbus Day in the US. A 1988 federal law acknowledged this remembrance ("About National Hispanic Heritage Month," n.d.). The Smithsonian Institution also recognizes Women's History Month in March, Asian Pacific American Heritage Month in May, and American Indian Heritage Month in November (Smithsonian Education, 2014).

Such activities draw attention to the significance of these groups, but not everyone believes they are a good idea. Why is there need for a special month focused on history of a particular ethnicity? Why isn't this simply a part of history everyone is exposed to? Another argument is that emphasizing a particular group works against the aim of incorporating these groups into the fabric of our society. Some also think this may encourage stereotyping of groups rather than emphasize the uniqueness of each person, no matter what his or her demographic background.

According to Cox (1997), three important points distinguish Valuing Diversity activities from encouragement of stereotyping. First, educating others about characteristics of various groups should be based on careful research on actual differences, while stereotyping is often an outgrowth of folklore, media portrayals, and misleading or biased sources. Second, stereotypes often emphasize negative characteristics, but differences among cultures may be positive or at least value-neutral. And third, because stereotyping involves categorization, it overlooks important differences *within* culturally distinctive groups. Valuing Diversity work should make clear that everyone in the highlighted group is not the same, even on dimensions distinguishing one group from another.

What do you think about this distinction? Can we emphasize differences between cultures or subcultures without stereotyping? If your group heritage is featured by the Smithsonian Institution, what is your reaction? Why do we not have "White History Month"? Can you say who Abraham Lincoln was? Frederick Douglass?

Stereotyping and Illusory Correlation

Although cognitive heuristics such as stereotypes appear to work well much of the time, sometimes they lead to errors in inference. One example is *illusory correlation (IC)*, a concept especially relevant to inferences about minorities. IC is the tendency to overestimate association between two things (e.g., a group and a characteristic) that are not closely related (Chapman, 1967). This may happen because we notice and remember things that are consistent with our existing biases. Another explanation of IC is based on a cognitive shortcut called the *distinctiveness heuristic*: noticing and remembering things that stand out because they are unusual. Presumably such information catches our attention and requires mental work, increasing its accessibility to memory later on. Membership in an unusual or small group is another kind of distinctive data about someone. Distinctive information about someone in a distinctive category is likely to be noticed and thought about more. Later we overestimate the degree to which the unusual attribute characterizes the unusual group (Hamilton & Gifford, 1976). This is more likely with negative than positive attributes (Mullen & Johnson, 1990; Stroessner & Plak, 2001).

How does this apply in a diverse work environment? Someone from an underrepresented group of people is likely to be noticed and remembered, as are unusual attributes of this person. Later the connection is overestimated as characteristic of that group (rather than that person). Furthermore, existing expectations lead us to notice information confirming our beliefs. For example, suppose a woman joins a predominantly male engineering work group. Others may assume that any other unusual characteristics noted about her—such as an accidental mistake—would also be true of other "female engineers." This is probably more likely to occur when perceivers do not know her well, have had little past experience of women working as engineers, and are thus more susceptible to stereotypic thinking.

Given the barriers to accomplishment by minority individuals in traditional organizations, examples of failure and negative results probably exceed those of dramatic and unusual success; thus IC is one mechanism by which negative stereotypes of underrepresented groups are reinforced. Distinctive negative information is likely to be understood as characteristic of the whole group rather than a foible of the individual. Often distinctive positive information is interpreted as an exception.

Stereotyping and the Self-fulfilling Prophecy (SFP)

Sociologist Robert Merton (1948) first identified the *self-fulfilling prophecy* as the process of assuming something about another, then behaving toward that person as if this incorrect assumption were true. This treatment actually evokes the very behavior that was erroneously predicted. That is, we actually cause the very behavior we wrongly expected of the other person—which of course confirms the expectation! For example, suppose you worry a co-worker may make errors on a new or complex task. Perhaps you scrutinize her work so carefully that you make her very nervous. As a result, she makes an error, "confirming" your prophecy.

Ample empirical evidence shows this process can and does occur. For example, teachers' expectations about children's performance have been shown to affect their intellectual abilities and school grades (Rosenthal & Jacobson, 1968; Jussim & Eccles, 1992). In work settings, researchers have considered both the *Pygmalion effect* in which positive expectations lead to improved behaviors and outcomes and the *Golem effect* (after Hebrew slang) in which negative expectations about someone lead to lowered performance. A meta-analysis of 17 experiments on the Pygmalion effect in organizations found "fairly strong" effects in some cases; stronger effects were found in military environments and when both supervisor and worker were men. In addition, the effect was stronger in studies that raised supervisors' initial low expectations for performance (e.g., for underachievers) in an attempt to avert the Golem effect (McNatt, 2000). The SFP shows us how expectations can lead to behavior that affects how others respond. Even when not category-based, SFPs function like stereotypes. Research shows that both positive and negative expectations have consequences, as do stereotypes.

Stereotypes can also affect performance through *stereotype threat*, a process by which salience of an unfavorable stereotype can depress performance of someone in a stigmatized group. The shaded box discusses stereotype threat and how to combat it.

Stereotype Threat

Suppose you were the first woman to hold an important position in management in your company, the first of your racio-ethnicity hired into a high pressure job, or the first from your average-quality school admitted to a prestigious graduate program. If you were from a background not associated with success in this challenging activity, and you knew others expected you to perform poorly for that reason, would this affect you? Would you feel nervous? Concerned about performing well?

Stereotype threat is "a situational threat . . . that . . . can affect the members of any group about whom a negative stereotype exists" (Steele, 1997, p. 614). Steele and others demonstrated stereotype threat for African American students taking standardized verbal tests and for women working on math problems. When someone is reminded of membership in a group associated with lower performance, the person generally does less well than when this stereotype is not primed (e.g., Steele, 1997). Stereotype threat may also lead to avoidance of the stereotyped domain of activity and changes in the person's self-concept.

Steele and others have broadened this idea to *social identity threat*: an uncomfortable psychological state experienced when one is made aware of an unfavorable *individual or group* reputation in a situation where one's behavior might confirm that negative expectation (Aronson & McGlone, 2009). In this sense, identity threat is like the self-fulfilling prophecy—it may be based on a stereotype of your group, but the same process can occur when the reputation is just about you!

Performance losses from stereotype-based identity threat have been documented with many groups: Latinos and Native Americans, poor White college students in France, elderly individuals when age-related memory declines are mentioned, Black or White racial groups for different types of athletic performance, women asked about political knowledge, and even highly math-proficient White male students who expected to be compared with more talented Asians (summarized by Aronson & McGlone, 2009). At work, this probably occurs more often with persons from underrepresented and stigmatized groups, but contemporary research shows that it can happen with anyone who is reminded of a stereotype or expectation of lower performance. Priming of stereotype threat can occur very easily when people are asked to indicate race, sex, age, or other group memberships *before* their performance is evaluated—often the case in testing and hiring situations. Stereotype threat researchers generally recommend that demographic information be collected at the *end* of the performance situation if possible in order to avoid priming a stereotype threat (e.g., Nguyen & Ryan, 2008).

Priming alone seems insufficient to create the ill effects of stereotype threat. The person must also know about the negative stereotype and see a connection between it and the task at hand, but performance losses can occur even when the person does not accept or agree with the stereotype. The task must be somewhat difficult, and the task domain must be one that is important to the person (Roberson & Kulik, 2007).

Several possible explanations have been offered for how social identity threat can impair performance. First, increased anxiety may make it harder to produce at one's typical level. Self-reported anxiety, but more generally, measures of blood pressure, have been related to stereotype-related performance decrements (e.g., Blascovich, Spencer, Quinn, & Steele, 2001). Second, attention may be distracted from the task by thoughts of the stereotype, others' performance, or other task-related worries. This mental work may distract from memory and other cognitive processes needed for high performance. Other suggested explanations, such as lowered expectations or reduced effort, have received less research support (Aronson & McGlone, 2009).

Fortunately, researchers have identified ways to avert effects of social identity threat. Effects have been reduced or eliminated in lab studies using pamphlets or other forewarnings of how performance can be depressed by stereotype threat, task distraction, or test anxiety. Warnings accompanied by instructions to think self-affirming thoughts about one's abilities (Cohen, Garcia, & Master, 2006) or a different positive identity (e.g., I am in the top third of the class) also can be effective (McGlone & Aronson, 2007). Participants can be persuaded that a test is not stereotype-relevant (Spencer, Steele, & Quinn, 1999) or that it measures an ability that is changeable and can improve with practice (Aronson, Fried, & Good, 2002). Testing or performance situations can be accompanied by presence of or information about very successful role models from the same stereotyped group (McIntyre, Paulson, & Lord, 2003). Advising or teaching about behavioral strategies is also effective. For example, Kray, Thompson, and Galinsky (2001) warned women about stereotypes that females' negotiation success is hampered by unassertive and less self-interested strategies. Women were able to alter their behavior and become more assertive and successful negotiators. Strategies for overcoming effects of stereotype threat are summarized by Aronson and McGlone (2009) and by Roberson and Kulik (2007).

Stereotype Automaticity

Some mental processes are "automatic" or unintentional, and others are "controlled" or deliberate, under conscious control. In 1989 Patricia Devine applied this distinction to cultural stereotypes widely recognized within a society. She concluded that *activation* of these stereotypes is largely automatic when one encounters something (e.g., a word, picture, or sound) connected with the stereotype, but that once activated, these cognitive responses can be intentionally controlled. In her early studies, Devine found stereotype activation for both high and low prejudiced people. Both groups knew the content of a cultural stereotype and relied on it for further judgments unless for some reason they had the opportunity to think more carefully about their personal views (Schneider, 2004). However, under conditions of controlled processing, less prejudiced participants showed less stereotypic thinking.

Well-learned stereotypes can be *primed* very easily. A prime might be words such as "black" or "white;" other physical, mental, or personality attributes that are part of a stereotype; or photos of unknown people, settings, or items associated with a particular group. In research, primes are sometimes shown at a speed or illumination so that participants do not realize they have "seen" it. (This is called *subliminal* because it is below the *limen* or threshold at which something can be seen with conscious awareness.) Even under these circumstances, stereotypic thinking can result.

Although Devine initially proposed that stereotype activation was automatic and inevitable, we now know that several things affect how easily activation occurs. For example, activation is more likely (a) if the individual notices the prime and perceives it as a person or social object; (b) if the person is not unduly distracted and has enough available cognitive resources to notice and pay attention to the stimulus; and (c) for some people more than others, sometimes related to their levels of bias or egalitarian values (Devine & Sharp, 2009). Nevertheless, stereotype activation is often automatic and unintentional.

In lab settings, stereotype activation can be reduced by extensive training in use of non-stereotypic associations or categories, or by repeated practice in identifying and negating stereotypic associations (Kawakami, Dovidio, Moll, Hermsen, & Russin, 2000; Jones & Fazio, 2010). Some success in reducing automatic stereotyping has also been found with Situational Attribution Training consisting of extensive practice in seeking situational explanations for stereotypic behavior that would otherwise be attributed to internal or personal causes. Laboratory research by Stewart, Latu, Kawakami, and Myers (2010) found that training to "consider the situation" was successful in reducing automatic activation of negative stereotypic attributes, and that this experience generalized to other negative stereotypes not specifically included in training. This is good news! However, considerable training was required, and the research did not address whether reduced activation continued outside the laboratory or over time.

Schneider (2004) noted that most automaticity studies have investigated cultural rather than personal stereotypes, which may not match. It's not known how consistently personal stereotypes are automatically activated. Nevertheless Schneider concluded that "it is still true that for many of us stereotypes are automatically activated, despite our intentions to the contrary" (p. 425). For diversity managers, this implies that stereotyping is very likely to occur.

Stereotype Suppression

Because stereotyping is often understood as a negative process, many people may try *not* to stereotype or may be urged by others not to do so. This is problematic for at least two reasons. First, stereotyping is a fundamental and automatic social cognition process, often helpful in making sense of a complicated social reality. Second, trying to suppress stereotyping may not work, and may in fact result in stronger categorical thinking!

The effect of suppressing stereotypes was studied by Macrae, Bodenhausen, Milne, and Jetten (1994). In general, they found that participants followed instructions to avoid stereotypic thinking, but that in a later task, levels of stereotyping were higher than when no such instructions were given. One interpretation of these results is that suppression requires two mental processes: one to monitor thought for stereotypic items, and a second to depress these items when they occur. This is cognitively taxing and ironically makes the stereotypic information *more* accessible; later when the restriction is removed and monitoring/suppression are not enacted, the stereotype *rebounds* to an even stronger level.

Although the stereotype rebound effect seems reliable, Margo Monteith and others have studied boundary conditions limiting its appearance. For example, low-prejudice persons and those who are highly motivated internally to think non-stereotypically are less likely to show a rebound effect. For them, suppression does not seem to require as much cognitive effort. Furthermore, if social norms against stereotyping are strong and remain in place, suppression sometimes becomes less demanding as a result of practice, even for prejudiced persons (Monteith & Mark, 2009). Regardless, according to Schneider, "unfortunately those people who are most responsive to rebound effects are probably the very people (highly prejudiced) who cause more than their share of mischief by using their stereotypes, and whose stereotypes we would most like to see suppressed" (2004, p. 429). The implication for diversity managers is that it is very difficult to suppress stereotypes, and sometimes this even makes them appear more strongly when we are off-guard.

Other Ways to Control Stereotypes and their Effects

Activating a stereotype is not the same as using it. Given the difficulty of preventing stereotype activation, can we prevent destructive effects by recognizing when stereotypes are aroused and preventing ourselves from acting on them thoughtlessly? Research indicates that under some circumstances, we can.

First, we can reduce the impact of categorical thinking by obtaining and using *individuating information* about the target person. For example, when a job candidate from an underrepresented ethnic or gender category is being considered, the effect of category membership is reduced if reviewers have and are instructed to use much information about the candidate's personal accomplishments and other dimensions of identity (Bodenhausen, Todd, & Richeson, 2009). In organizational decision-making, this is an appropriate way to try to overcome bias in judgment resulting from stereotypic thinking.

Second, we may be able to make a decision without knowing candidates' category membership. Sometimes called *blinding*, this strategy is often part of an affirmative action and equal opportunity approach to applicant selection: information that informs about sex, race or ethnicity is removed from an application and each person is identified only by number. In a clever analysis of symphony orchestra auditions and membership over a period of about 40 years, Goldin and Rouse (2000) found that when a screen hid the performer during an audition, it was more likely that a woman would be advanced in competition and hired as an orchestra member. If judges did not know group membership (e.g., sex) of a candidate, then stereotypes about that group could not bias judgments about the person. Unfortunately, this precaution is not feasible when decisions are made about people already known to decision-makers, or when category membership is inextricably intertwined with other relevant information (e.g., when a candidate is a graduate of a school associated with a particular sex or race). On job applications, it may be difficult to remove information about demographic background without weakening the application.

Third, when recognizing we are stereotyping, we may be able to correct for our category-based inferences (Schneider, 2004). For example, we might try to obtain additional information. We could arrange a "tryout," request a work sample, or provide a short-term probationary opportunity during which more relevant information can become available. Correcting for stereotypical inferences may not be feasible in many superficial interactions but surely could be done in organizational settings when important decisions are about to be made. One problem with this approach is determining how and by what amount one should correct judgments potentially affected by stereotypes.

Fourth, the perceiver can try to see a situation as the (stereotyped) other would see it, and emphasize what the perceiver and target have in common (Dovidio et al., 2004). Such *perspective-taking* can lead to a breakdown in perceptions of group boundaries and a decrease in both activation and application of group stereotypes (Galinsky & Moskowitz, 2000).

Fifth, being exposed to counterstereotypic examples or actively generating counterstereotypic imagery can sometimes be successful in reducing automatic stereotype activation (Blair, 2002). To reduce bias in selection, organizations often include members of underrepresented groups (e.g., women, ethnic minority individuals) on screening committees. One reason for doing so is to create a peer group including qualified individuals as counterstereotypic examples.

Both activation and application of stereotypes can also be influenced by the perceiver's goals and motives. Kunda and Spencer (2003) summarized studies showing that use of stereotypes may be reduced if the person is highly motivated to understand another person accurately, maintain a personal identity as unbiased and egalitarian, or comply with external social norms against stereotypic thinking. The diversity manager should stress the importance of perceiving and judging accurately and ask evaluators to explain or justify decisions by evidence to avoid stereotypic influence on decisions.

Stereotypes and Diversity Training

How can an astute diversity manager use this research-based information? One way is to rethink diversity training (DT), addressed in Chapter 13. In the context of training for multicultural management, Egan and Bendick (2008) illustrated how stereotypes can be learned and strengthened by ways in which cultural differences are discussed. Often in DT, an early (and perhaps the only) activity is an exercise in which participants discuss stereotypes about various groups. This can be engaging because everyone has something to contribute. However, good evidence suggests NOT to do this in DT. First, by listing stereotype content, participants are actually *rehearsing* this material and sometimes *learning* new stereotypes from other people. Both processes will likely make stereotyping *more* rather than *less* frequent! Reactions of others in discussions may also strengthen stereotype expression. For example, when research participants discussed stereotypic impressions of a hypothetical group, discussion led to stereotype polarization even when group members also read counterstereotypic information (Brauer, Judd, & Jacquelin, 2001). Further, in a study of communication's role in maintaining stereotypes, Lyons and Kashima (2003) used the game of "telephone" in which a stereotype-relevant story was repeated through a chain of four people. As the story was passed along, it became more stereotype-consistent; this was more pronounced when communicators actually believed the stereotype, and when they thought others agreed with the categorical belief. This highlights the importance of social acceptance in expression of stereotypic descriptions.

Second, public listing of stereotype content may imply that the organization's culture and the views of individuals will lead or have led to unfair discrimination. In a widely publicized lawsuit against Lucky Stores, notes from stereotype discussions became evidence in a legal claim that the company had discriminated illegally, and the employer suffered major financial penalties as a result.

Lucky Stores Case

Trainers led an exercise with managers from Lucky Stores, a California grocery chain, in which the group discussed well-known stereotypes of minorities and women (Caudron, 1993a). Their goal was to use the exercise to increase trainees' awareness of stereotyping and increase their effectiveness in supervising employees.

In a subsequent class action suit against the company, *Stender v. Lucky Stores* (1992), female employees contended that the employer had violated anti-discrimination laws in its personnel practices, resulting in extreme gender segregation and underrepresentation of women in managerial positions. Evidence was presented about lack of implementation of an Affirmative Action Plan (AAP) and statistical analyses showing sex differences in job level. Evidence also included notes taken by managers during DT sessions that recorded unfavorable stereotypic comments about women. For example, women were said to be uninterested in working late shifts and to lack motivation for advancement. These statements were admitted by the Court as evidence of discriminatory attitudes, and were part of the basis for the decision against the company, which lost the suit and tens of millions of dollars!

Instead of discussing stereotype content, it would be more effective to discuss what stereotypes are, why they are helpful or adaptive, and how hard it is to prevent stereotyping. Rather than trying to influence participants NOT to stereotype (which will probably not be effective anyway), trainees can be taught ways to recognize when a stereotype has been activated and to control its application through techniques described above.

Stereotypes Get a "Bad Rap"

Often an author states that stereotypes led to negative effects in a situation when, in fact, stereotypes were neither manipulated nor measured. The intuitive explanation of stereotypes as a cause of prejudice and discrimination is widely held; managers, researchers, textbook writers, and others often assume a stereotype is operating when prejudice or discrimination are observed, and that if only we could stop stereotyping, bad consequences would disappear. Focusing on stereotypes as the explanation for dislike, hostility, or unfair behavior targets an adaptive and learned cognitive habit that is difficult or impossible to change, instead of ways to alter undesirable behaviors directly through training or other interventions. Problematic behavior is probably easier to change than stereotypes (if they exist), and we may even find that stereotypes change after people begin to act differently.

Prejudice and Discrimination: Hard to Disentangle

Earlier we described prejudice as emotional and discrimination as behavioral. Although this distinction is conceptually useful, in research and in organizations they often occur and are measured together and are difficult to separate. Diversity professionals will have difficulty identifying prejudiced feelings apart from discriminatory behavior, negative speech, or avoidance; in fact, prejudice may not matter as long as it does not lead to inappropriate behavior. Thus most explanations and recommended strategies do not address prejudice and discrimination separately. Recall that sometimes people behave unfairly not because of prejudice but due to habit, organizational procedures, or commonly accepted norms. Discrimination can occur even without underlying negative prejudicial feelings.

Often the term "discrimination" is used when the speaker actually means *illegal* discrimination: potentially unlawful differential treatment based on protected category membership. Such discrimination, of concern to top management because of potential cost of complaints or litigation, is discussed in Chapter 7. But much discrimination is not illegal. Social science research on "discrimination" deals with any behavior that distinguishes in a meaningful way between or among people, usually negatively. We might sit farther away from someone, make offensive or unpleasant comments, avoid contact or not speak, or withhold information. Such behaviors cause distress and interfere with inclusion and productivity in organizations and are worthy of diversity professionals' attention—even if not against the law.

Finally, in many situations "discrimination" is appropriate and necessary. In employee selection, promotion, or compensation, it is important to discriminate (i.e., distinguish) on the basis of knowledge, skill, ability, or performance justifying an employment decision. Tests, interviews, application blanks, and performance evaluation procedures are all designed to discriminate appropriately based on qualifications. Employees may see that members of one group are more often successful and assume that this pattern is due to (illegal) discrimination when in fact it may be quite justified.

To summarize, we have discrimination that (a) is useful and perhaps necessary; (b) is undesirable but probably not illegal; and (c) is or may be a violation of the law. One should clarify how this term is used if there is any danger of misunderstanding.

Explanations for Prejudice and Discrimination

In social science, prejudice and discrimination have been extensively studied for many years and found to occur for many reasons. Some say that to change discriminatory behavior we should design a strategy addressing the *reason* for the behavior. However, in work organizations, the diversity or HR manager will sometimes find it necessary to address discrimination or harassment directly and consistently following organizational policies, regardless of how the pattern has developed. Both perspectives have merit. This chapter emphasizes social science remedies, relying heavily on an extensive list modified and updated from Ashmore (1970a, 1970b); some reappear in later chapters as practical organizational remedies.

Societal vs. Individual-level Explanations

Some explanations are framed at the *macro* level, accounting for hostilities between or among groups in a society, and others at the *micro* level, addressing why a particular individual shows prejudicial attitudes and/or discriminatory behavior. Generally societal-level (macro) explanations rest on the history of *intergroup relations* in a particular culture; they also apply to discord rooted in intergroup relations between companies, working groups, neighborhoods, or competing teams. Classic studies of Social Identity Theory (Tajfel & Turner, 1986; see Chapter 5) and of intergroup contact (e.g., Sherif, 1966; Pettigrew & Tropp, 2000; Stephan & Stephan, 2001) illustrate this perspective, in which the root of problems lies in the history of groups more than the experiences of individuals. Diversity professionals will benefit from understanding these group-based approaches because often they account for legacy effects that influence employees' identities and interpersonal relations in an organization, and other situations such as post-merger relations.

In contrast, individual-level (micro) explanations are applied to relationships *among individuals* within a society or other collectivity. These approaches emphasize individual experiences producing differences in prejudice among people in the same society. These explanations are relevant for diversity professionals because they address some common sources of interpersonal problems among individual employees in work organizations.

Societal-level Explanations

Of two major types of "macro" explanations relevant to intergroup relations in diverse societies and organizations, the first is *Exploitation*. In this process, one group takes advantage of another for economic or other advantage because it is more powerful and can easily do so. Historical examples include the Holocaust in 20th-century Europe, apartheid in South Africa, and countless invasions and wars based on control of land and wealth. Probably the two most obvious examples of exploitation in the US are slavery and its after-effects (segregation and continuing inequality); and the devastation inflicted upon Native Americans by Europeans and their descendants. Another contemporary example concerns treatment of immigrants, particularly Latinos, in the US political and economic system. Many have been unable to take advantage of paths open to European, Cuban, and other immigrants of past decades and thus are easily exploited by an economic and business system that profits from their labor, unofficial status, and powerlessness.

The second major societal-level explanation is *Realistic Group Conflict*. This applies when two or more groups compete for scarce or limited resources. The intergroup conflict is realistic in the sense that one group can only profit at the other's expense. Shortages may exist in land, water, housing, jobs, promotions or raises in an organization. Often realistic intergroup conflicts occur in organizations for limited space, equipment, or financial resources.

Exploitation applies most clearly when one group is much more powerful than the other. Attempts to improve conflicts based on power disadvantage include humanitarian or moral appeals to fairness, dignity, and other ideals. In some cases, the low-power group may become so desperate that violence or revolution erupts in an attempt to overthrow the dominant order. Can you think of examples of this process in contemporary organizations? *(Think "minimum wage.")*

The second explanation, Realistic Group Conflict, applies when the focus is on limited resources and there is no motivation to cooperate. At least two common approaches attempt to improve relationships from this perspective. The first relies on expanding the universe of scarce resources, e.g., discovering new sources of land, energy, housing, or jobs. The second approach tries to unite competing groups in response to challenge from another group or external threat, e.g., in wartime, competing factions within a society unite in their joint opposition to the enemy. Does this apply in workplaces today? *(Think budget for D&I.)*

Individual-level Explanations

In contrast to societal-level accounts, these focus on processes leading someone to be prejudiced or discriminatory. These explanations are *social* (i.e., involving interaction with others), but they are not *societal* because they emphasize behavior of individuals rather than historical, cultural, or other large-scale processes or events. They aim to explain differences in prejudice or discrimination among people in the same setting.

Individual-level: Environmental or Experience-based Accounts

These explanations conceptualize discriminatory behavior as a learned response to environmental events, or a result of lack of information or learning. The implication for diversity professionals is that, if the environment created the behavior pattern, then changing the environment is probably the way to address it.

First, some tensions are based on *lack of information or misinformation* about another group. This can lead to discomfort in new situations and inappropriate or offensive comments or exclusionary behavior by employees who may be uncomfortable around people from unfamiliar backgrounds. Most of us feel anxious in unfamiliar situations, especially when stakes are high.

Diversity managers sometimes provide Valuing Diversity experiences in part to overcome lack of information or familiarity. These can be helpful, especially if members of the featured group are involved in planning and presenting material. Such experiences provide interesting cultural information but are unlikely to address deeper sources of intergroup organizational static. Possibly the most effective way to learn about another group is to talk openly with someone from that group in a setting that is nonjudgmental, casual, and respectful. Friendships or comfortable work associations across group boundaries often lead to seeing the world from the other person's perspective.

A second explanation is *learning*: the prejudiced person has been taught feelings or behavior by association of negative things with the disliked group, direct instruction, or experience of negative consequences as a result of behavior toward someone. For example, children may be told not to associate with "those people." Teenagers may have been bullied by aggressive peers from a particular group. Adults may have experienced awkward, unpleasant, or even dangerous situations associated with members of another group. People "fit in" by copying or modeling others, including those who may have behaved in exclusionary or negative ways toward another group. Remedies for learned discriminatory behavior include modeling or demonstrating inclusive behavior and reinforcing positive behaviors toward others. Employees may be helped to see that negative intergroup experiences in high school do not necessarily imply bad experiences with an adult from that group at work. Organizational policies should outline behaviors that are expected and others that are unacceptable, and appropriate consequences should follow.

A third experience-based explanation is that people may discriminate because of unquestioned *norms or practices*. Perhaps in the past these patterns arose from animosity toward another group, but later they may simply be followed out of habit. The excluded person may be very aware of the offensive behavior but the person doing it may not, especially if from a privileged group. A recent example is the case of gay people in the US military. From 1993 until 2011, the *Don't Ask, Don't Tell* policy subjected gay and lesbian military personnel to discharge if they acknowledged their sexual orientation. Despite warnings of dire consequences if this policy were removed, there was very little negative reaction when it was changed. Even some aspects of racial desegregation in parts of the US during the 1950s and 1960s illustrate the power of norms. Many Whites followed segregated seating patterns on public transportation out of conformity to established pattern rather than strong prejudice. Today we might question why they did not object, but this disregards the strength of normative pressure in the situation. Although Rosa Parks and other African Americans faced racist retaliation for violating segregated seating patterns, in other cases once initial resistance was broken, there was remarkably little negative reaction.

To change norm-based behaviors, direct or indirect intervention is generally required. In some cases, simply asking why people act a certain way or modeling a new behavior may be enough to produce changes. In other situations, direct instruction, policy changes, or laws may be needed to break established discriminatory patterns. Diversity managers can also schedule attractive events or programs aimed at disrupting established patterns, with encouragement for attendance and reinforcement of new, more inclusive behaviors. The shaded box describes a program to change lunchroom norms, based on intergroup contact research discussed in a later section.

"Mix It Up at Lunch Day"

Teaching Tolerance is a project of The Southern Poverty Law Center (SPLC), a nonprofit civil rights organization in Montgomery, Alabama. The SLPC is well known for its work in bringing civil legal actions against perpetrators of serious hateful and bigoted attacks on minority victims. In addition to this reactive strategy after events, the SPLC has developed its proactive *Teaching Tolerance* project to "reduce prejudice, improve intergroup relations and support equitable school experiences for our nation's children" ("About Us," n.d.). This work is based partly on surveys of students, who identified cliques as an important issue in schools and cafeterias as places where these divisions are clearly evident ("What is," n.d.).

Mix It Up at Lunch Day is designed to "identify, question and cross social boundaries" by breaking the norm—if only for one day—of sitting only with people in your own group and thus leaving some people out. According to the SPLC, "when students interact with those who are different from them, biases and misperceptions can fall away" ("What is," n.d.). Pictures on the *Teaching Tolerance* website show diverse groups of students enjoying this new activity, which is sanctioned by school authorities and carefully designed to produce positive interactions that are fun as well as informative for students ("Mix It Up," n.d.). Considerable social science research supports the use of intergroup contact designed to reduce stereotypes, prejudice, and discrimination as well as barriers between groups.

Individual-level: Cognitive Accounts

These explanations rely on habits of thinking—the mental shortcuts or heuristics we use in understanding the social world. *Stereotyping* is one such process. Another, *belief prejudice*, refers to dislike or avoidance of someone whose beliefs or values are dissimilar to ours (Rokeach, Smith, & Evans, 1960). Even people similar in ethnicity, socioeconomic status, and other ways can react negatively when they recognize others do not share their beliefs. In organizations, belief-based prejudices may occur when co-workers differ in strong views about political issues, religion, union membership, or other topics. The diversity professional's goal should be to prevent belief-based interpersonal tensions from disrupting productive and appropriate work behavior. Employees should be expected to set appropriate boundaries for discussion of controversial topics and refrain from assertive campaigns of persuasion that offend others. The norm at work should be that employees are expected to work together effectively even when strong personal beliefs are in conflict.

Another cognitive account is *"putting two and two together"* or simple inference. This occurs most often in an unfamiliar situation, such as when someone is forming social relationships in a new environment. Observing that certain individuals or those in a particular group receive differential treatment, one might conclude that there is good reason for this. (*"They must have done something to deserve this treatment."*) The notion of a "just world" in social psychology (Lerner & Miller, 1978) is a similar idea: we assume the world is just, so poor outcomes must be deserved. *Attributional errors* such as the actor-observer effect or the fundamental attribution error are also cognitive explanations for prejudice and discrimination. Inappropriate non-inclusive behavior based in cognitive factors can sometimes be altered by careful discussions in which participants feel safe from retribution. Tactfully questioning differential treatment may lead to correction of inappropriate norms.

Individual-level: Personality or "Symptom" Theories

These explanations consider hostility toward others to be a symptom of internal personality dynamics. From this perspective, prejudice is the external expression of what is going on inside; addressing prejudice directly will be ineffective—or even make it worse—unless internal dynamics are also considered. Most of these explanations are based on a psychoanalytic or Freudian approach to personality development but can also be understood in terms of contemporary personality theories. Their relevance for the diversity professional lies in possible remedies.

Prejudice may be explained as *scapegoating* or *displacement of hostility* from one target onto another, e.g., anger toward an unpleasant boss is suppressed and redirected toward others. In *projection*, the person defends against recognizing something unpleasant or threatening about him-/herself by "projecting" that attribute onto another, who is then rejected.

A third, more complex symptom approach, widely accepted in the US after World War II, is the *Authoritarian Personality* theory developed to account for the extreme hostility of the Holocaust (Adorno, Frenkel-Brunswik, Levinson, & Sanford, 1950). A syndrome of nine personality traits was identified in those who were highly *authoritarian*. In addition to scapegoating and projection, these included exaggerated respect for authority, overzealous respect for conventional values, aggressive reactions to those who disagree, and rigid and stereotypic thought processes.

Contemporary research in this tradition focuses on *right-wing authoritarianism* (RWA), but those on the political left-wing may also share some aspects of authoritarianism. RWA includes (a) authoritarian submission; (b) authoritarian aggression; and (c) conventionalism (Altemeyer, 1994). Those high on this scale often show generalized prejudice against many other groups such as Native Americans, Arabs, immigrants, GLBTs, feminists, and fat people—especially groups viewed as contradicting traditional values and rejected by authority figures. Psychological attributes underlying this pattern include cognitive rigidity, a strong tendency to see the social world in terms of in-groups and out-groups, lack of interest in new experiences and information, and a view that the world is threatening and dangerous.

Sample Items from RWA Scale

Right-Wing Authoritarianism is usually measured with a 32-item scale. Similar to the original F-Scale measuring the Authoritarian Personality, the RWA scale contains items measuring *authoritarian submission, authoritarian aggression,* and *conventionalism.* Sample items for each cluster include:

Authoritarian Submission

It is always better to trust the judgments of the proper authorities in government and religion than to listen to the noisy rabble-rousers in our society who are trying to create doubt in people's minds.

Authoritarian Aggression

The situation in our country is getting so serious, the strongest methods would be justified if they eliminated the troublemakers and got us back to our true path.

Conventionalism

The "old-fashioned ways" and "old-fashioned values" still show the best way to live.

(Altemeyer, 1998, pp. 49–51)

The updated concept of RWA evolved from personality disturbance to a cluster of interrelated attitudes. Another contemporary variable, Social Dominance Orientation (SDO), also involves a pattern of attitudes functioning together as a stable attribute on which people differ and which is correlated with a variety of behaviors and other attitudes.

Social Dominance Orientation

Inequality, oppression, and intergroup prejudice seem to exist everywhere. Jim Sidanius and Felicia Pratto (1993) theorized that to minimize destructive class- and group-based conflict, societies develop ideologies that are widely accepted and in this way make group-based inequality seem legitimate. These *legitimizing myths* are socially constructed in a society and support the privileged position of those who have the larger portion of the society's resources, particularly money and power.

For example, in the popular British Masterpiece Classic series, *Downton Abbey*, most household staff and estate tenants support societal norms of vastly unequal class-based behavior and use of resources. The *myth of meritocracy* is a contemporary ideology that justifies allocation of opportunity, jobs, financial and other resources on the basis of "merit," but leaves unexamined the processes by which "merit" is defined and assessed. Those who accept this ideology are unlikely to challenge it.

Pratto, Sidanius, Stallworth, and Malle (1994) studied the concept of SDO, defined as "the extent to which one desires that one's in-group dominate and be superior to out-groups" (p. 742). They construed SDO as a personality variable at the core of people's attitudes toward many aspects of intergroup relations. Some sample items from their 16-item scale have been modified here to apply in organizations:

> Some groups of people are simply inferior to other groups in work organizations.
> If certain groups stayed in their place in work organizations, we would have fewer problems.
> We should strive to make incomes as equal as possible in work organizations.
>
> (Reverse-scored item, p. 763)

In four studies including almost 2000 college students, Pratto et al. (1994) found that those high in SDO tended to have lower scores on measures of Altruism, Empathy (especially Concern for Others), and Communality (inclusion of others). They also ranked higher on anti-Black racism, nationalism, beliefs in sexism and cultural elitism, and support for military programs; were more likely to oppose social programs, racial policies, and women's rights; and generally endorsed political conservatism. SDO was also related to the type of work the students expected to do after graduation; lower SDO was associated with choice of helping professions such as social work or counseling and higher SDO with career choices in law enforcement, politics, and business. Jost and Thompson (1999) later showed that SDO scale items fell into two groups or factors: group-based dominance (the belief that one's own group should be at the top of the hierarchy); and general opposition to equality (the belief that those currently at or near the bottom should remain there).

Summarizing SDO research, Whitley and Kite (2006) reported that members of more powerful and influential groups (i.e., men, Whites, heterosexuals, and wealthy persons) scored higher on SDO than others (Sidanius & Pratto, 1999). In many countries higher SDO scores have been associated with greater reported prejudice against a variety of other groups such as immigrants, lesbians and gay men, Native Americans and other ethnic minorities, and feminists. Finally, Whitley (1999) found evidence that persons high in SDO, prejudiced against other groups, develop *legitimizing myths* that include stereotypes against these out-groups. Thus, stereotypes provide justification for prejudice that occurs as part of the high-SDO personality. This suggests that a personality constellation leads to prejudice, which then leads to the construction of stereotypes justifying negative feelings toward out-groups. Personality-based prejudice leads to stereotypes, rather than the reverse.

Other research has shown that when people move into more prestigious professions or are randomly assigned to a higher-power role in an experiment, their SDO scores tend to rise (e.g., Guimond, Dambrun, Michinov, & Duarte, 2003). This research finds more support for the Group Socialization Model (GSM) than for the view that SDO functions simply as a personality variable. That is, occupying a dominant social position leads one to develop SDO views, which are justified by the development of bias against other group(s) in that situation. An alternative explanation is that occupying a dominant social position leads to the development of specific biases, which then lead to the pattern of SDO.

SDO and RWA are both associated with prejudice against other groups. They differ in that RWA emphasizes accepting the views of authority figures, whereas SDO focuses on favoring group-based inequality and dominance over other groups. They are usually positively but not strongly correlated, indicating they are different but related concepts. Measures of SDO and RWA in combination are highly correlated with measures of prejudice against Blacks, women, and gay people.

For the diversity manager, this research implies that some prejudices against groups with lower achievement or prestige actually indicate deep-seated belief that inequality and hierarchy among groups is expected and desirable. Some prejudices and stereotypes in organizations function to maintain the person's status or position above others in the organization. Simple education campaigns or even carefully designed intergroup contact activities are unlikely to change this view. The diversity professional might consider whether intergroup attitudes are products of aspects of the organization that emphasize hierarchy, rather than simply an outgrowth of individuals' personalities.

Authoritarianism, RWA, and SDO imply that with some individuals it is not feasible to try to change deep-seated prejudices in isolation without understanding and addressing the rest of the attitude or personality structure. This may be beyond the responsibility or capability of the diversity manager. Policies should clarify the nature of unacceptable behavior (e.g., harassment) and the consequences that will follow. In some cases, an employee may be helped to understand why animosity exists toward another person(s) and to correct it. In more serious cases, if expressed prejudice stems from significant personality or attitude patterns, referral to an Employee Assistance Program or another source of counseling or therapy may be useful. In extreme cases, progressive discipline and eventual termination may be warranted.

Improving Relationships through Intergroup Contact

A common recommendation for improving relationships between groups in conflict has been to arrange interpersonal contact among members of the groups. However, contact does not always reduce intergroup hostility and in fact, sometimes makes it worse! Research has shown that characteristics of contact are important in the quality of subsequent relations. For the diversity professional, this research is relevant for designing intergroup events as well as analyzing qualities of existing relationships to understand why they work or don't work, and how they might be changed to improve intergroup relationships.

The *Intergroup Contact Hypothesis* was first advocated in classic studies by Gordon Allport (1954, 1958) and Muzafer Sherif (Sherif, Harvey, White, Hood, & Sherif, 1961), and studied by Thomas Pettigrew (e.g., Pettigrew & Tropp, 2000, 2005) and many others. This body of work, one of the richest in social psychology, includes both laboratory and field research, with situations involving everything from experimenter-contrived tasks to integrated housing and school desegregation in the real world.

Pettigrew and Tropp (2005) reviewed the history of this hypothesis, summarizing Allport's 1954 view that four factors were necessary for intergroup contact to have positive effects: (a) equal status contact; (b) shared goals; (c) cooperative relations; and (d) support from laws, norms, or authorities. Pettigrew (1998) also reviewed a large number of studies, finding success for contact even when *all four* of these factors were not present. He added a fifth factor: (e) the *friendship potential* which exists when there is *time* and *opportunity* to learn about others as individuals. Pettigrew listed four processes that may produce positive changes when intergroup contact includes these qualities. These processes were (a) opportunities to learn about the other group; (b) changes in behavior in the new intergroup setting; (c) generation of emotional ties through reduced anxiety and development of mutual empathy; and (d) reappraisal or changed understanding of the nature of one's own and other groups. In the "ideal" intergroup contact situation, positive effects of contact generalize to other situations, to other members of the contacted group, and even to members of other groups (e.g., other ethnicities). He also formulated what we might call *Pettigrew's Paradox*: "given real differences between groups, those most likely to have intergroup contact are atypical of their groups. Yet contact effects generalize best when the participants are typical group members. Thus, people most likely to engage in intergroup contact are the least likely to evoke changes that generalize to their groups" (p. 74). For diversity professionals, this implies that activities in the workplace as well as modeling of appropriate inclusive behavior should be structured to involve *typical* members of each group and to encourage "voluntary" associations in the workplace. Such associations provide an environment in which effects of intergroup contact should be most positive and enduring. These principles can be built into activities designed to overcome group divisions, such as the *jigsaw classroom* (Aronson & Patnoe, 2011).

The Jigsaw Classroom

In the 1970s, University of Texas social psychology professor Elliott Aronson was contacted by a former student, a school administrator responsible for implementing school desegregation in an Austin public school. It was not going well (Aronson & Patnoe, 2011). Aronson and his graduate students conducted school observations, then designed and implemented a cooperative learning project called the *jigsaw classroom* because learning occurred as if students were putting together pieces of a puzzle. This project's success led to its popularity as a simple but very powerful way to produce positive results in a diverse setting.

In a jigsaw classroom, students are placed in diverse groups of about six members and each is given responsibility for learning and contributing a key part of the information needed for the group to succeed in mastering the material or completing the project. No one in the group can succeed without listening to and perhaps helping others in the group. Interaction takes place in the supervised environment of the classroom. No leader is appointed and each student has an equal amount of material to learn and contribute to the group's task.

According to Aronson and his colleagues, "students in the jigsaw groups showed a decrease in prejudice and stereotyping and an increase in their liking for their groupmates, both within and across ethnic boundaries . . . performed better on objective exams and showed a significantly greater increase in self-esteem than children in traditional classrooms . . . (and) far greater liking for school" (Aronson, Wilson, & Akert, 2007, p. 453). In addition, students in the schools with jigsaw classrooms showed more cross-racial interaction on the school grounds, suggesting that positive effects occurred beyond the boundaries of the jigsaw groups. A later study with 10-year-olds also found that children with experience in a jigsaw classroom showed greater empathy as measured by ability to put themselves in the situation of others (Bridgeman, 1981). Empathy is an important ability for work in today's diverse work environments.

No social psychology textbook today would be complete without discussion of the jigsaw classroom as a way to improve not only the learning environment, but also relations between members of groups in conflict. Can you find the elements of Pettigrew's recommendations in this design? How could this technique be extended to the work environment?

In their 2005 article, Pettigrew and Tropp presented results of a meta-analysis of 515 studies of intergroup contact in 38 nations from the 1940s to 2000. Main findings were that (a) greater levels of intergroup contact were associated with more reduction in prejudice; (b) results were stronger in more rigorous studies; and (c) results usually generalized from other-group individuals to other members of the same group. The largest prejudice reduction occurred among those of differing sexual orientation, but reduced prejudice also occurred across racio-ethnic and age groups. Prejudice reduction was strongest when contact was structured to develop friendship, or when it included all four of Allport's original factors. Their analysis also determined that about one-quarter of the prejudice reduction was attributable to reduced anxiety among participants.

In a "reformulation" of Contact Theory, Pettigrew (1998) offered a longitudinal model to explain beneficial effects of intergroup contact. He proposed that the five situational factors of equal status contact, common goals, cooperative relations, external support, and friendship potential, when effective, lead to a three-phase process. First, participants *decategorize* or deemphasize group boundaries. Second, some degree of *salient categorization* remains so that participants do remember that interaction includes representative members of the other group (i.e., not "exceptions"). And third, a new, more inclusive formulation develops though *recategorization* emphasizing commonalities among members of this larger new group.

The Common Ingroup Identity Model

Other psychologists have also explored processes accounting for success of intergroup interaction in improving relations. Gaertner and Dovidio's (2000) Common Ingroup Identity Model (CI^{2}M) complemented and extended Pettigrew's ideas. The CI^{2}M emphasizes cognitive factors in intergroup bias and stresses *recategorization* or "development of group categorization at a higher level of category inclusiveness" (p. 46). Similarly, Brewer and Miller (1984) emphasized the role of *decategorization* or weakening of perceived boundaries separating the groups. For diversity professionals, these models all imply that intergroup relations improve when participants relax psychological boundaries between groups but still recognize that individual participants are typical members of the other group. When interaction is successful, a new inclusive sense of group identity develops. Interaction is most likely to succeed when it builds in the five elements of Pettigrew's approach. Informal arrangements encouraging cooperation and friendship across group boundaries in the context of work relationships (e.g., community volunteerism, picnics) can be very constructive.

Focusing on Behavior Change

This chapter emphasizes conceptual and practical reasons to focus on changing discriminatory behavior rather than stereotypes or prejudiced feelings. For several reasons, we can expect to change people's behavior directly without addressing stereotypes or attitudes first; in fact, often behavior change actually leads to altered beliefs and attitudes. These processes have been studied extensively and are well grounded in empirical research in social psychology (Eagly & Chaiken, 1993).

- *Social Learning theory* (Bandura & Walters, 1963). Behavior change through *observational learning* or *modeling:* watching behavior of others. Learning new cues for established behaviors, new behaviors themselves, and/or consequences that follow from a behavior. Especially likely when model is perceived as powerful or respected.
- *Cognitive Dissonance theory* (Festinger, 1957). Unpleasant tension (*dissonance)* results from holding two conflicting ideas. Tension motivates change, which is easier for private attitude than public behavior already enacted and/or supported by other motivations (e.g., salary, others' approval). Change most likely when incentives for counter-attitudinal behavior are barely enough to change behavior, which is experienced as voluntary, not coerced.
- *Self-perception theory* (Bem, 1972). Same predictions for prejudice reduction but without relying on the concept of cognitive dissonance to explain the results. Attitude merely an inference drawn from observation of one's own behavior.
- *Role play* (Hovland, Janis, & Kelley, 1953). Persuasion research at Yale University after World War II. Male participants assigned to speak or write *counter-attitudinal message* disagreeing with their original attitude. Through *improvisation,* opinion moved away from original opinion in direction of speech or essay. Due mainly to *biased scanning*: looking for convincing evidence to persuade others in the process persuades oneself. Corresponds to *central route* to persuasion in Petty and Cacioppo's Elaboration Likelihood Model (1986), and *systematic processing* in Chaiken's Heuristic-Systematic Model (1987).

These theories have several implications for the diversity professional. When employees see managers, executives, or respected peers behaving inclusively toward members of underrepresented groups, they are likely to behave in an inclusive manner as well. To encourage positive attitudes toward others, we should use barely enough influence to get the person to act as if that *were* his or her attitude, preferably publicly. Opportunities for cross-group interaction should be voluntary but expected, rather than required. Forcing people to do things they really do not wish to do—instead of producing dissonance—may create *reactance,* a negative tension that can lead people to be more resistant as they attempt to assert their original position (e.g., Brehm & Brehm, 1981). However, in some circumstances it may be appropriate to *require* behavior; legal or safety requirements are two examples.

For diversity professionals, this work implies that someone induced to interact with other-group members may be motivated to do a good job and thus seek out positive aspects and new information about others. Over time (especially if interaction includes other Contact Hypothesis factors), attitudes toward other-group members may change in a positive direction as new relationships are learned and reinforced. We should expect changed attitudes as a *result* of changed behavior, not as a *requirement* for it. These perspectives do not conflict with each other in terms of recommendations for work in organizations; they are simply different explanations for changes in feelings and thoughts occurring a *as a result of behavior change,* rather than a cause of it. Scholars may differ over which theoretical positions are most satisfactory, but for diversity professionals this implies there are *many* reasons to focus on behavior first. In work settings, employees' behavior is more critical than their thoughts or feelings.

Conclusion

Some interactions are not positive, some intergroup contact is unsuccessful, and prejudices and stereotypes may be associated with unpleasant or exclusionary behavior. It may be necessary to remove some employees or separate them from others with whom they are in conflict in order for work to progress. Nonetheless, legal and ethical reasons exist for including members of previously underrepresented groups along with majority employees. Many cases will bear out predictions of the research discussed here: Change behavior first, and attitudes often change to support the new behavior.

This chapter summarizes a substantial research literature about interactions among people and groups in conflict. Instead of comprehensively reviewing the latest findings, the chapter presents recommendations for diversity management drawn from social science research. Later chapters discuss stereotypes, prejudices and discriminatory behavior of special concern to particular identity groups such as women or ethnic minorities.

References

About National Hispanic Heritage Month. (n.d.). *National Hispanic Heritage Month*. Retrieved from http://hispanicheritagemonth.gov/about

About Us. (n.d.). *Teaching tolerance*. Retrieved from www.tolerance.org/about

Adorno, T., Frenkel-Brunswik, E., Levinson, D., & Sanford, N. (1950). *The authoritarian personality*. New York: Harper.

*Allport, G. W. (1954, 1958). The nature of prejudice (abridged edition). Garden City, NY: Doubleday & Co., Inc.

Altemeyer, B. (1994). Reducing prejudice in right-wing authoritarians. In M. P. Zanna & J. M. Olson (Eds.), *The psychology of prejudice* (pp. 131–149). Mahwah, NJ: Erlbaum.

Altemeyer, B. (1998). The other "Authoritarian Personality." In M. P. Zanna (Ed.), *Advances in experimental social psychology*, (Vol. 30, pp. 47–92). San Diego: Academic Press.

*Aronson, E., & Patnoe, S. (2011). *Cooperation in the classroom: The jigsaw method*. London: Pinter & Martin Ltd.

Aronson, E., Wilson, T. D., & Akert, R. M. (2007). *Social psychology* (6th ed.). Upper Saddle River, NJ: Pearson Prentice Hall.

Aronson, J., Fried, C., & Good, C. (2002). Reducing the effects of stereotype threat on African American college students by shaping theories of intelligence. *Journal of Experimental Social Psychology, 38*, 113–125.

Aronson, J., & McGlone, M. S. (2009). Stereotype threat and social identity threat. In T. D. Nelson (Ed.), *Handbook of prejudice, stereotyping, and discrimination* (pp. 153–178). New York: Psychology Press.

Ashmore, R. D. (1970a). The problem of intergroup prejudice. In B. F. Collins (Ed.), *Social psychology: Social influence, attitude change, group processes, and prejudice* (pp. 245–296). Reading, MA: Addison-Wesley.

Ashmore, R. D. (1970b). Solving the problem of prejudice. In B. F. Collins (Ed.), *Social psychology: Social influence, attitude change, group processes, and prejudice* (pp. 297–339). Reading, MA: Addison-Wesley.

Bandura, A., & Walters, R. H. (1963). *Social learning and personality development*. New York: Holt, Rinehart, & Winston.

Beike, D. R., & Sherman, S. J. (1994). Social inference: Inductions, deductions, and analogies. In R. S. Wyer, Jr., & T.K. Srull (Eds.), *Handbook of social cognition: Basic processes* (Vol. 1, 2nd ed., pp. 209–285). Hillsdale, NJ: Lawrence Erlbaum Associates.

Bem, D. J. (1972). Self-perception theory. In L. Berkowitz (Ed.), *Advances in experimental social psychology* (Vol. 6, pp. 1–62). San Diego, CA: Academic Press.

Biernat, M. (2009). Stereotypes and shifting standards. In T. D. Nelson (Ed.), *Handbook of prejudice, stereotyping, and discrimination* (pp. 137–152). New York: Psychology Press.

Biernat, M., Manis, M., & Nelson, T. E. (1991). Stereotypes and standards of judgment. *Journal of Personality and Social Psychology, 60*, 485–499.

Biography.com. (n.d.). *Carter G. Woodson biography*. Retrieved from www.biography.com/people/carter-g-woodson-9536515

*Blair, I. V. (2002). The malleability of automatic stereotypes and prejudice. *Personality and Social Psychology Review, 6*, 232–261.

Blascovich, J., Spencer, S. J., Quinn, D. M., & Steele, C. M. (2001). Stereotype threat and the cardiovascular reactivity of African-Americans. *Psychological Science, 12,* 225–229.

Bodenhausen, G. V. (1990). Stereotypes as judgmental heuristics: Evidence of circadian variations in discrimination. *Psychological Science, 1,* 319–322.

Bodenhausen, G. V., Todd, A. R., & Richeson, J. A. (2009). Controlling prejudice and stereotyping: Antecedents, mechanisms, and contexts. In T. D. Nelson (Ed.), *Handbook of prejudice, stereotyping, and discrimination* (pp. 111–135). New York: Psychology Press.

Brauer, M., Judd, C. M., & Jacquelin, V. (2001). The communication of social stereotypes: The effects of group discussion and information distribution on stereotypic appraisals. *Journal of Personality and Social Psychology, 81,* 463–475.

Brehm, S. S., & Brehm, J. W. (1981). *Psychological reactance: A theory of freedom and control.* San Diego, CA: Academic Press.

Brewer, M. B., & Miller, N. (1984). Beyond the Contact Hypothesis: Theoretical perspectives on desegregation. In N. Miller & M. B. Brewer (Eds.), *Groups in contact: The psychology of desegregation* (pp. 281–302). New York: Academic Press.

Bridgeman, D. L. (1981). Enhanced role taking through cooperative interdependence: A field study. *Child Development, 52,* 1231–1238.

Caudron, S. (1993a). Employees use diversity-training exercise against Lucky Stores in intentional-discrimination suit. *Personnel Journal, 72*(4), 52.

Caudron, S. (1993b). Training can damage diversity efforts. *Personnel Journal, 72,* 50–61.

Chaiken, S. (1987). The heuristic model of persuasion. In M. P. Zanna, J. M. Olson, & C. P. Herman (Eds.), *Social influence: The Ontario symposium* (Vol. 5, pp. 3–39). Hillsdale, NJ: Erlbaum.

Chapman, L. J. (1967). Illusory correlation in observational report. *Journal of Verbal Learning and Verbal Behavior, 6,* 151–155.

Cohen, G., Garcia, J., & Master, A. (2006). Reducing the racial achievement gap: A social-psychological intervention. *Science, 313,* 1307–1310.

Cox, T., Jr. (1997). Distinguishing valuing diversity from stereotyping. In T. Cox, Jr. & R. L. Beale (Eds.). *Developing competency to manage diversity: Readings, cases, & activities* (pp. 80–82). San Francisco, CA: Berrett-Koehler Publishers, Inc.

Crano, W. D., & Prislin, R. (Eds.) (2008). *Attitudes and attitude change.* New York, NY: Psychology Press.

Devine, P. G. (1989). Stereotypes and prejudice: Their automatic and controlled components. *Journal of Personality and Social Psychology, 56,* 5–18.

Devine, P. G., & Sharp, L. B. (2009). Automaticity and control in stereotyping and prejudice. In T. D. Nelson (Ed.), *Handbook of prejudice, stereotyping, and discrimination* (pp. 61–87). New York: Psychology Press.

Dovidio, J. F., ten Vergert, M., Stewart, T. L., Gaertner, S. L., Johnson, J. D., Esses, V. M., . . . Pearson, A. R. (2004). Perspective and prejudice: Antecedents and mediating mechanisms. *Personality and Social Psychology Bulletin, 30,* 1537–1549.

Eagly, A. H., & Chaiken, S. (1993). *The psychology of attitudes.* Fort Worth, TX: Harcourt Brace Jovanovich College Publishers.

*Egan, M. L., & Bendick, M., Jr. (2008). Combining multicultural management and diversity into one course on cultural competence. *Academy of Management Learning & Education, 7,* 387–393.

Festinger, L. (1957). *A theory of cognitive dissonance.* Stanford, CA: Stanford University Press.

Fishbein, M., & Ajzen, I. (1975). *Belief, attitude, intention, and behavior: An introduction to theory and research.* Reading, MA: Addison-Wesley.

*Gaertner, S. L., & Dovidio, J. F. (2000). *Reducing intergroup bias: The Common Ingroup Identity Model.* Philadelphia, PA: Taylor & Francis Group.

Galinsky, A. D., & Moskowitz, G. B. (2000). Perspective-taking: Decreasing stereotype expression, stereotype accessibility, and in-group favoritism. *Journal of Personality and Social Psychology, 78,* 708–724.

Goldin, C., & Rouse, C. (2000). Orchestrating impartiality: The impact of "blind" auditions on female musicians. *The American Economic Review, 90,* 715–741.

* Guimond, S., Dambrun, N., Michinov, N., & Duarte, S. (2003). Does social dominance generate prejudice? Integrating individual and contextual determinants of intergroup cognitions. *Journal of Personality and Social Psychology, 84,* 697–721.

Hamilton, D. L., & Gifford, R. K. (1976). Illusory correlation in interpersonal perception: A cognitive basis of stereotypic judgments. *Journal of Experimental Social Psychology, 12,* 392–407.

Hamilton, D. L., & Sherman, J. W. (1994). Stereotypes. In R. S. Wyer & T. K. Srull (Eds.), *Handbook of social cognition: Applications* (2nd ed., Vol. 2, pp. 1–68). Hillsdale, NJ: Lawrence Erlbaum Associates.

Hilton, J. L., & von Hippel, W. (1996). Stereotypes. *Annual Review of Psychology, 47*, 237–271.

Hovland, C. L., Janis, I. L., & Kelley, H. H. (1953). *Communication and persuasion: Psychological studies of opinion change.* New Haven, CT: Yale University Press.

Jones, C. R., & Fazio, R. H. (2010). Person categorization and automatic racial stereotyping effects on weapon identification. *Personality and Social Psychology Bulletin, 36*, 1073–1085.

Jost, J. T., & Thompson, E. P. (1999). Group-based dominance and opposition to equality as independent predictors of self-esteem, ethnocentrism, and social policy attitudes among African Americans and European Americans. *Journal of Experimental Social Psychology, 36*, 209–232.

Jussim, L., Cain, T. R., Crawford, J. T., Harber, K., & Cohen, F. (2009). The unbearable accuracy of stereotypes. In T. D. Nelson (Ed.), *Handbook of prejudice, stereotyping, and discrimination* (pp. 199–227). New York: Psychology Press.

Jussim, L. J., & Eccles, J. S. (1992). Teacher expectations: II. Construction and reflection of student achievement. *Journal of Personality and Social Psychology, 63*, 947–961.

Kawakami, K., Dovidio, J. F., Moll, J., Hermsen, S., & Russin, A. (2000). Just say no (to stereotyping): Effects of training in the negation of stereotypic associations on stereotype activation. *Journal of Social and Personality Psychology, 78*, 871–888.

Kray, L. J., Thompson, L., & Galinsky, A. (2001). Battle of the sexes: Gender stereotype confirmation and reactance in negotiations. *Journal of Personality and Social Psychology, 80*, 942–958.

Kunda, Z., & Spencer, S. J. (2003). When do stereotypes come to mind and when do they color judgment? A goal-based theoretical framework for stereotype activation and application. *Psychological Bulletin, 129*, 522–544.

Lerner, M. J., & Miller, D. T. (1978). Just world research and the attribution process: Looking back and ahead. *Psychological Bulletin, 85*, 1030–1051.

Lyons, A., & Kashima, Y. (2003). How are stereotypes maintained through communication? The influence of stereotype sharedness. *Journal of Personality and Social Psychology, 85*, 989–1005.

Macrae, C. N., Bodenhausen, G. V., Milne, A. B., & Jetten, J. (1994). Out of mind but back in sight: Stereotypes on the rebound. *Journal of Personality and Social Psychology, 67*, 808–817.

McGarty, C., Yzerbyt, V. Y., & Spears, R. (2012). Social, cultural and cognitive factors in stereotype formation. In C. McGarty, V. Y. Yzerbyt, & R. Spears (Eds.), *Stereotypes as explanations: The formation of meaningful beliefs about social groups* (pp. 1–15). Cambridge: Cambridge University Press.

McGlone, M. S., & Aronson, J. (2007). Forewarning and forearming stereotype-threatened students. *Communication Education, 56*, 119–133.

McIntyre, R. B., Paulson, R. M., & Lord, C. G. (2003). Alleviating women's mathematics stereotype through salience of group achievement. *Journal of Experimental Social Psychology, 39*, 83–90.

McNatt, D. B. (2000). Ancient Pygmalion joins contemporary management: A meta-analysis of the result. *Journal of Applied Psychology, 85*, 314–322

Merton, R. K. (1948). The self-fulfilling prophecy. *The Antioch Review, 8*(2), 193–210.

Mix It Up at Lunch Day successful nationwide (n.d.). *Teaching Tolerance.* Retrieved from www.tolerance.org/blog/mix-it-lunch-day-successful-nationwide

Monteith, M. J., & Mark, A. Y. (2009). The self-regulation of prejudice. In T. D. Nelson (Ed.), *Handbook of prejudice, stereotyping, and discrimination* (pp. 507–523). New York: Psychology Press.

Mullen, B., & Johnson, C. (1990). Distinctiveness-based illusory correlation and stereotyping: A meta-analytic investigation. *British Journal of Social Psychology, 29*, 11–28.

Nguyen, H-H. D., & Ryan, A. M. (2008). Does stereotype threat affect test performance of minorities and women? A meta-analysis of experimental evidence. *Journal of Applied Psychology, 93*, 1314–1334.

Park, B., & Judd, C. M. (2005). Rethinking the link between categorization and prejudice within the social cognition perspective. *Personality and Social Psychology Review, 9*, 108–130.

Patterson, M. R. (2006). *Kara Spears Hultgreen: Lieutenant, US Navy.* Arlington National Cemetery Website. Retrieved from www.arlingtoncemetery.net/hultgrn.htm

Pettigrew, T. F. (1998). Intergroup contact theory. *Annual Review of Psychology, 49*, 65–85.

Pettigrew, T. F., & Tropp, L. R. (2000). Does intergroup contact reduce prejudice? Recent meta-analytic findings. In S. Oskamp (Ed.), *Reducing prejudice and discrimination* (pp. 93–114). Mahwah, NJ: Erlbaum.

Pettigrew, T. F., & Tropp, L. R. (2005). Allport's Intergroup Contact Hypothesis: Its history and influence. In J. F. Dovidio, P. Glick, & L. A. Rudman (Eds.), *On the nature of prejudice* (pp. 262–277). Malden, MA: Blackwell.

Petty, R. E., & Cacioppo, J. T. (1986). *Communication and persuasion: Central and peripheral routes to attitude change.* New York: Springer-Verlag.

Pratto, F., Sidanius, J., Stallworth, L. M., & Malle, B. F. (1994). Social Dominance Orientation: A personality variable predicting social and political attitudes. *Journal of Personality and Social Psychology, 67,* 741–763.

Roberson, L., & Kulik, C. T. (2007). Stereotype threat at work. *Academy of Management Perspectives, 21,* 24–40.

Rokeach, M., Smith, P. W., & Evans, R. I. (1960). Two kinds of prejudice or one? In M. Rokeach (Ed.), *The open and closed mind* (pp. 132–168). New York: Basic Books.

Rosenthal, R., & Jacobson, L. (1968). *Pygmalion in the classroom.* New York: Holt, Rinehart & Winston.

*Schneider, D. J. (2004). *The psychology of stereotyping.* New York: Guilford Press.

Scott, D. M. (n.d.). *February is African American History month.* Retrieved from www.africanamericanhistorymonth. gov/about.html

Sherif, M. (1966). *In common predicament: Social psychology of intergroup conflict and cooperation.* Boston, MA: Houghton Mifflin.

*Sherif, M., Harvey, O. J., White, B. J., Hood, W. R., & Sherif, C. W. (1961). *Intergroup conflict and cooperation: The Robber's Cave experiment.* Norman, OK: University of Oklahoma, Institute of Group Relations.

Sidanius, J., & Pratto, F. (1993). The dynamics of social dominance and the inevitability of oppression. In P. Sniderman & P. E. Tetlock (Eds.), *Prejudice, politics, and race in American today* (pp. 173–211). Stanford, CA: Stanford University Press.

Sidanius, J., & Pratto, F. (1999). *Social dominance: An intergroup theory of social hierarchy and oppression.* New York: Cambridge University Press.

Smithsonian Education. (2014). *American Indian Heritage Month.* Retrieved from www.smithsonianeducation. org/heritage_month/aihm/index.html

Spencer, S. J., Steele, C. M., & Quinn, D. M. (1999). Stereotype threat and women's math performance. *Journal of Experimental Social Psychology, 35,* 4–28.

Steele, C. M. (1997). A threat in the air: How stereotypes shape the intellectual identity and performance. *American Psychologist, 52,* 613–629.

Stender v. Lucky Stores. 803 F. Supp. 259 (N. D. Cal. 1992).

Stephan, W. G., & Stephan, C. W. (2001). *Improving intergroup relations.* Mahwah, NJ: Erlbaum.

Stewart, T. L., Latu, I. M., Kawakami, K., & Myers, A. C. (2010). Consider the situation: Reducing automatic stereotyping through Situational Attribution Training. *Journal of Experimental Social Psychology, 46,* 221–225.

Stroessner, S. J., & Plak, J. E. (2001). Illusory correlation and stereotype formation: Tracing the arc of research over a quarter century. In G. B. Moskowitz (Ed.), *Cognitive social psychology* (pp. 247–259). Mahwah, NJ: Lawrence Erlbaum Associates.

Tajfel, H., & Turner, J. C. (1986). The social identity theory of intergroup behavior. In W. G. Austin & S. Worchel (Eds.), *Psychology of intergroup relations* (2nd ed., pp. 7–27). Chicago, IL: Nelson-Hall.

What is Mix It Up at Lunch Day? (n.d.). *Teaching tolerance.* Retrieved from www.tolerance.org/mix-it-up/ what-is-mix

Whitley, B. E., Jr. (1999). Right-wing authoritarianism, social dominance orientation, and prejudice. *Journal of Personality and Social Psychology, 77,* 126–134.

*Whitley, B. E., Jr., & Kite, M. E. (2006). *The psychology of prejudice and discrimination.* Belmont, CA: Thomson Wadsworth.

* Recommended for advanced reading.

Part III

Applications

Chapter 7

Diversity, Inclusion, and the Law

The previous chapter discussed approaches to changing stereotypes, prejudices, and discriminatory behaviors. In organizations, often the most direct way to strengthen inclusive behaviors and eliminate existing undesirable patterns is simply to state what is expected, why it's important, and *that people are expected to comply.* Sometimes that is enough. A stronger version of this strategy is to develop and announce a policy covering the situation, describing what is expected and *what will happen* if people do not comply. For example, a policy might state that the organization does not tolerate harassment of co-workers, and anyone found to be harassing others will receive a warning, followed by termination if the behavior continues. The policy should define harassment and give examples so the nature of prohibited behavior is clear. Most human resources experts would advise having a policy in place *before* difficult situations arise rather than waiting until something happens. Existing policies guide managers in handling various situations and can reduce personal attributions and interpersonal stress involved in doing so. Changing behavior becomes a matter of following company policy rather than specific arbitrary and personal requirements of individual managers.

Behavior change can also be attempted by *modeling* or demonstrating the desired behavior. This is especially effective when the model is powerful, attractive, credible, or similar to the target person(s). For example, if managers and executives demonstrate inclusive behaviors and support for diversity, those who work for them are likely to adopt these behaviors. This is unlikely to happen if an organization preaches about valuing diversity but it is clear that managers and top executives rarely act on the issue.

Sometimes undesirable behaviors are so engrained and well established that they are very difficult to change. Norms may be so strong that they are very hard to overcome. When consequences of norms or customs are widespread and harmful to others or to society at large, it may be necessary to address the problem head-on through laws *requiring* people or organizations to change by performing *prescribed* behaviors or by discontinuing things that are *proscribed* or prohibited.

Legal Approaches to Diversity Management

The legal route to D&I goals has advantages and disadvantages. Laws can call attention to and define as unacceptable some behaviors that might otherwise be overlooked; laws state what is required and specify sanctions for noncompliance. They can change undesirable conditions faster than other means. However, enacting law is often lengthy, difficult, and expensive, especially with issues resisted by powerful or monied interests. Furthermore, sometimes laws are widely disregarded. If enforcement is lax or if penalties are insignificant, laws will not be effective. Also, people may feel forced to change and may react strongly or be resentful about being required to comply. This can create problematic conditions, such as the societal upheaval associated with school desegregation in the US.

Another problem with most *Equal Opportunity Employment* laws in the US is that they are *complaint-based.* This means that in most cases the government does not routinely oversee compliance to assure that employers follow legal requirements. Instead, the person who thinks she or he is victim of an illegal act must file a complaint or initiate a lawsuit to require the employer to follow the law. This legal process is often unpleasant, costly, and lengthy; it requires great emotional investment because employers do not react well to being sued and co-workers may be unsupportive or even hostile. In addition, there is no assurance that the *plaintiff* will win a lawsuit, even if the law has been violated; employers usually have more resources to defend against a suit than employees have to bring one. Employees may not know or have access to information that would provide sufficient evidence of employer guilt. Finally, even if plaintiffs win, *remedies* may be such that they feel it was not worth major costs associated with bringing the lawsuit. Consider being sexually harassed by your manager and fired because you complained about it. Would you decide to sue if you had only the manager's word against yours, the suit would be lengthy and costly, and all you could win was your old job back?

Warning: Some Things to Consider

1. This material is technical and detailed. Terms have specific meanings.
2. Legal requirements change constantly. New laws are passed or old ones are amended. An important court decision may occur at any time and set a *precedent* for how later courts should apply the law.
3. Things are not always consistent. States have different laws, such as those requiring minimum wage. Laws vary in requirements or remedies; for example, lawyers may recommend filing a discrimination lawsuit under state vs. federal law depending on evidence required and remedies available. Federal and state laws are not identical; for example, at this time there is no legal protection under federal law against employment discrimination on the basis of sexual orientation, but several states such as California, Massachusetts, Nevada, and the District of Columbia do have such prohibitions (Law & Hrabal, 2010; Nolo, 2016). Federal law may be interpreted differently across judicial regions if courts in different circuits (group of states) do not agree.
4. What seems *not right* or *unfair* may be immoral or wrong, but it may not be *illegal*. For example, at this time federal law prohibiting age discrimination does not apply to young people—only those 40 or older. In most places there is no law against employment discrimination on the basis of physical appearance, e.g., attractiveness or beauty, weight, piercings, tattoos. We may think such discrimination is wrong, not job-related, and should not occur, but unless a law applies, there is no legal recourse.

One final point: nothing in this chapter should be taken as legal advice! This material provides useful information relevant to management of D&I, but if a problem arises, one should consult an attorney.

The Logic of the Legal System

Most anti-discrimination laws can be understood in terms of several aspects, as described by Gutman, Koppes, and Vodanovich (2011). To understand how a law operates, you should understand these terms:

1. Protected classes: Groups protected under the law. For example, the Age Discrimination in Employment Act (ADEA) protects only those aged 40 or older. Laws prohibiting sex discrimination protect both men and women and thus seem to cover everyone; however, for the law to apply it must be shown that the offending practice was based on sex.

2. Covered entities: Types of employers who must comply with the law. Often there are exceptions for organizations below a certain size. Some laws apply only to private sector employers (i.e., not government entities). Most laws we discuss do not apply in the same way to the US military.

3. Covered practices: Types of decisions or actions that are prescribed or proscribed (e.g., discrimination, segregation, or retaliation). A practice may seem unfair but if it cannot be shown to be a covered practice, the law does not apply.

4. Administrative procedures: Details such as how long after a covered action the law still applies (the *statute of limitations*) and the agency responsible for enforcement.

5. Remedies: What happens if a *defendant* (usually the employer charged with violating the law) loses. Remedies might include monetary damages (e.g., back pay), requirements to file reports or change procedures, re-hiring or promotion, or ceasing the offending practices.

6. Scenarios for evidence and proof: Patterns of evidence courts have required in past suits under a particular law. These develop over time as cases are tried and decided, forming *case law*. Scenarios usually specify types of evidence the plaintiff must provide and what the defendant must do to refute that evidence. Sometimes arguments go back and forth until a case is concluded.

Sources of Legal Constraint

So far, we have been talking loosely about *the law*, but this includes several sources of restriction on employment practices. These include the US Constitution and its Amendments; federal and state statutes (laws) and regulations issued by responsible agencies; case law; Executive Orders (EOs); the *Uniform Guidelines*; and contracts resulting from collective bargaining. These differ in terms of how they originate, covered entities, what is required to change them, and remedies.

Constitutional Provisions

The US Constitution contains a few clauses that have been interpreted as authority for federal legislation concerning workplace issues, such as the *Commerce Clause* in Article I which is the foundation for federal regulation of private sector employment. However, most constitutional protections relevant to work come from the Amendments, especially the 5th, 11th, 13th, and 14th, which have been used to enforce employment fairness on the basis of race (Gutman et al., 2011). These outlaw slavery, guarantee equal protection to all citizens, and provide for private citizens to sue the federal government as an employer. They are also the basis for determining whether a federal law applies to states as employers: unless a law specifically includes public employers, courts may conclude it does not apply to states. This happened, for example, with ADEA and the Americans with Disabilities Act (ADA). The Supreme Court found that because of their wording, these laws did not permit lawsuits by *private* individuals against state employers for age or disability discrimination. The Equal Employment Opportunity Commission (EEOC) may, however, bring suit against states under these statutes.

One important feature of protections under the Constitution and amendments is that these documents are very difficult to change. The usual process for amending the Constitution requires passage of both houses of Congress by a two-thirds majority, plus ratification by three-quarters of the states (currently 38). This level of agreement is difficult to obtain. Therefore, constitutional rights are considered relatively stable.

Statutory Law

In contrast to the stability of constitutional protections, state and federal *statutes* or laws can be passed, amended, or repealed by legislative bodies. These bodies can give a right and later take it away, especially if election produces a major change in composition of the legislative body. Usually laws are written to include such information as protected classes and covered entities, what is required or proscribed, remedies, and effective dates. This chapter addresses federal statutes such as Title VII of the Civil Rights Act (CRA) of 1964, the ADA, the Equal Pay Act (EPA), and others.

Regulations

Federal agencies issue formal documents asserting how a law will be interpreted and what it requires. Employers are guided by these regulations. Often professional societies, such as the Society for Human Resource Management or the Society of Industrial-Organizational Psychology (SIOP) follow the process of regulation development and keep members informed on opportunities to comment or how final regulations affect their work.

For federal law, the EEOC enforces laws forbidding employment discrimination on the basis of sex, race, color, national origin, religion, disability, genetic information, and age. The Office of Federal Contract Compliance Programs (OFCCP) of the Department of Labor (DoL) enforces Affirmative Action (AA) provisions and discrimination claims under EO 11246. Another part of DoL enforces the Family and Medical Leave Act (FMLA; EEOC, 2010).

Case Law

Legislative bodies enact laws or local ordinances, but the full meaning of these documents is only revealed as lawsuits are brought by people who make a claim or disagree about interpretation of a law. *Case law* refers to the body of law which develops as a result of decisions made by judges and juries. For example, what types of evidence are necessary to prove or defend a case? What is the meaning of "employer"? What is a "disability"? Decisions by higher courts usually form *precedents* that are taken as guidelines for later courts in that circuit to follow as they hear subsequent suits. Supreme Court decisions become precedents for all lower courts. One commonly cited example of a precedent in employment law is *Griggs v. Duke Power* (1971), the basis for *adverse impact* cases under Title VII of CRA64.

Each of the 12 judicial regions of the US federal courts comprises several states. The losing side in a federal case can appeal the decision to a Federal District (Circuit) Court of Appeal within its region, and the decision at this level becomes precedent for that circuit. Sometimes Courts of Appeal disagree, in which case appeal can be made for Supreme Court review. The Supreme Court also decides disputes among states or citizens of different states or when the federal government is party to a suit, and lawsuits that involve constitutional interpretation of laws (Law.Com, 2012). The Supreme Court only reviews (grants *certiori*) to a small percentage of the cases that come to it (75–80 out of 10,000 annually), so in many cases the decision of the Circuit Court of Appeal or lower court stands. There is no appeal after a Supreme Court decision (Supreme Court of the United States, n.d.).

However, Supreme Court interpretations of *laws* can in effect be "reversed" if Congress enacts a later law clarifying or changing its interpretation. CRA91 and the ADA Amendments Act of 2008 are two such examples. Congress cannot undo a decision of the Supreme Court that is based on *constitutionality*; a constitutional amendment is required. However, a new law can be enacted that is carefully drafted to clarify or alter an earlier law.

Executive Orders

The President and state governors are "chief executives" of the governments they head and administer the Executive branch of government. In that role, they can enact EOs which are statements about how the public employer and its employees and contractors must behave as they carry out the state's business. An EO affects only the government employer headed by the elected official enacting the order. The executive can also rescind an EO that she or he has enacted, or one issued by a predecessor.

The most widely known example of an EO related to employment is EO 11246, which requires AA in employment by the federal government and by most employers who contract with the federal government. This widely misunderstood provision requires certain things such as reports and various programs to correct imbalances in the race or sex in the workforce which are assumed to have resulted from prior discrimination, either deliberate or unintentional. It does NOT require hiring unqualified persons just because of demographic characteristics, although this is widely and erroneously believed. AA is discussed in detail later in this chapter.

The Uniform Guidelines

With passage of civil rights legislation and AA provisions, several federal agencies became responsible for regulation and enforcement. From the perspective of employers, requirements of different agencies did not always agree. Thus, in 1978, after collaboration among the EEOC, Civil Service Commission, DoL, and the Department of Justice (DoJ), the *Uniform Guidelines on Employee Selection Procedures* were jointly published by the four agencies. The title conveys intent to present a *uniform* statement about how employers should act to be in compliance with federal law and regulation regarding fair employment. In subsequent years, courts have given *great deference* to the *Guidelines*, although they are not law and did not require Congressional approval.

Since 1978 many advances have come about in scientific understanding about measurement of employment-related attributes, particularly in assessment and documentation of *validity*, i.e., evidence that a technique (such as a test) is actually measuring what it is said to measure. In light of current scientific evidence and accepted professional practice, some of the *Guidelines'* statements now seem out of date and there have been calls for its revision (McDaniel, Kepes, & Banks, 2011). However, such revision is highly controversial and would present numerous difficulties to various stakeholders; some authors think revision is unnecessary or imprudent (e.g., Tonowski, 2011; see also articles in SIOP, 2011, and Biddle, 2008).

Contracts

In some employment settings, non-managerial employees may be unionized. If so, a legal document called a *collective bargaining agreement* (CBA) is in force which represents an agreement between employer and employees about *terms and conditions of employment*. CBAs include procedures for hiring, layoff, and termination; salaries and benefits; provisions for employee discipline; filing of grievances; and many other issues that in a non-unionized environment are considered the prerogative of management. CBAs are renegotiated periodically and can be changed or overruled. They are considered a legal document that can be enforced.

In addition, in many non-unionized settings, there may be an employee *Handbook* stating policies that govern behavior of management and employees. Workers can be disciplined for violating these policies, and companies can be challenged for violating them. Courts may consider an employee handbook to function as an implied contract between labor and management.

Major EEO Laws Relevant to Diversity Management

Any diversity manager or human resources officer should be knowledgeable about requirements under federal and state law and any local ordinances dealing with fairness on the basis of sex, race/ethnicity, age, disability, national origin, sexual orientation, and other employee characteristics. Two very important reasons are: (a) the company's policies for managing diversity, as well as all its other human resources (HR) policies, should follow the law; and (b) as an employee and possibly an advocate for other employees, the diversity manager should be knowledgeable of workers' rights and procedures for correcting violations or breaches that might occur inadvertently or intentionally. In some cases, actions that may seem reasonable to accomplish the goals of your company's diversity policy may unfortunately open your employer to legal *exposure*, meaning possibility of a lawsuit.

The major federal laws will be covered in an order reflecting their substance. The shaded box lists them in historical order to show the sequence in which Congress addressed various sorts of discrimination. Our coverage reflects general provisions currently in effect for each law, but the complete picture is more detailed and may change at any time as a result of court decisions or Congressional action.

Anti-Discrimination Historical Timeline

1963	Equal Pay Act
1964	Civil Rights Act of 1964
1965	Executive Order 11246 (Affirmative Action)
1967	Age Discrimination in Employment Act
1978	Pregnancy Discrimination Act (amendment to Title VII)
1980	EEOC Guidelines on Sexual Harassment
1986	Immigration Reform and Control Act of 1986
1990	Americans with Disabilities Act
1991	Civil Rights Act of 1991
1993	Family and Medical Leave Act
2008	Amendments to ADA

The Equal Pay Act of 1963

Protected classes under EPA are the sexes, both men and women. A claim under this law must show that *sex was the basis for discrimination*. The EPA says nothing about other bases of discrimination and the only covered practice is wage discrimination. Most important, wording in this law renders it largely unable to address the gender wage gap described in Chapter 4. The law specifies that comparisons only apply to "equal work on jobs the performance of which requires equal skill, effort, and responsibility, and which are performed under similar working conditions . . ." Courts have interpreted this to mean that EPA applies if men's and women's job titles differ (e.g., male *tailors* vs. female *seamstresses*) but the work is basically the same. Courts have also found that work must be *substantially equal*, that is, a few duties can differ. But the EPA does not reach far enough to include comparisons between nurses and house painters, clerical workers and repair technicians, or most other male–female job comparisons. Because most of the gender wage gap results from high levels of occupational sex segregation into *different* but often *comparable* jobs, the EPA has been extremely limited in its ability to reduce the gap, as discussed in Chapter 4.

Covered entities under EPA include public and private employers regardless of size (Gutman et al., 2011); even small employers must comply. It is now administered by the EEOC and complaints must be initiated within two years of the discriminatory action (three years if willful). A plaintiff who wins an EPA suit may be entitled to two years of back pay (the difference between what should have been paid and what was paid) and an *injunction* against the employer ("Don't do that any more!"). However, if the violation is shown to be *willful* (i.e., intentional), financial damages can be much higher.

Often sex-based wage discrimination complaints are brought under both EPA and Title VII (discussed below) because EPA does not prohibit the *gender segregation* which is often the basis for wage differences, and because remedies may be stronger under EPA or Title VII in a particular case. EPA also provides that no one's pay may be *lowered* to achieve equal pay.

Under EPA legal scenarios, the *employee* must first show that pay is unequal for persons of different sexes, and that jobs are substantially equal in skill, effort, responsibility, and working conditions. If that claim is successful, the *employer* may use one of the four *affirmative defenses* written into the law. That is, the employer may claim that pay disparities are due to differences in (a) seniority; (b) merit; (c) quality or quantity of production; or (d) *any other factor other than sex* (FOS). This phrase has sometimes included defenses that the employer was paying market wage or relied on the person's prior salary to set current salary. Generally the so-called *market forces* argument has failed as a FOS defense, but the success of using prior salary has varied depending on the case and the court. If the employer succeeds with an affirmative defense, then the plaintiff can try to prove that this was merely a *pretext* (excuse) for sex discrimination in pay.

Title VII of the Civil Rights Act of 1964

If the EPA is narrowest, "Title 7" is the broadest of the EEO laws. Classes protected under Title VII are race, color, religion, sex, and national origin. Covered entities are the federal government, educational institutions, private employers, and state or local governmental bodies with 15 or more employees for at least 20 weeks of the year. This includes labor organizations, employment agencies, and joint labor/management committees. Religious organizations are exempt, but only with respect to discrimination based on religion. Indian tribes and private tax-exempt membership clubs are also exempt.

Title VII prohibits discrimination in hiring, discharge, compensation, or other "terms, conditions, or privileges of employment" as well as actions to "limit, segregate, or classify" employees or applicants in a discriminatory manner (sec. 703-a). Retaliation against employees or applicants who complain under this law is also prohibited (sec. 704-a). Notably, Title VII also specifies that preferential treatment is *not* required because of an imbalance in sex, race, or other covered attributes (sec. 703-j). Finally, the law establishes the EEOC to enforce its provisions. Title VII charges must be filed with the EEOC (or a state or local agency, if applicable) within 180 days of the alleged discrimination, or 300 days if the violation is also covered by state or local laws (EEOC, 2009a). Remedies under Title VII include injunctions, up to two years back pay, or other *equitable relief.*

Two major judicial scenarios have developed under Title VII: *disparate treatment* and *adverse impact.* Disparate treatment concerns differential treatment that is considered *intentional* because a decision was made to treat similarly situated people differently. Prior to Title VII, it was common for jobs to be advertised as *women only* or *men only*; often Blacks were explicitly excluded from jobs, labor unions, or training opportunities. Such practices are clearly prohibited by Title VII. A more complex situation is one in which an employee or applicant is treated differently than someone in another category. In an early Title VII case, *McDonnell Douglas v. Green* (1973), a Black man employed by McDonnell Douglas was part of a reduction in force after which he participated in illegal labor actions. The company later began re-hiring for Green's previous position as a mechanic. Green applied, was not hired, and sued on grounds of race discrimination. The Supreme Court's decision emerged as the classic disparate treatment legal scenario: plaintiff belongs to a protected category, applies for a job for which he is qualified, and is rejected. Subsequently the job stays open to other similarly qualified applicants. If the plaintiff shows these facts, then the employer must describe (i.e., articulate) a legal reason for rejecting the candidate. In the *Green* case, the company said Green was not re-hired because of his illegal labor activities while laid off. The plaintiff could then show that this argument was merely a *pretext* for illegal discrimination. Green was unable to do this and was not re-hired. However, his name is now famous to lawyers because of this important early suit.

This sequence of claims and evidence has been elaborated by many later lawsuits but remains the basic outline for a disparate treatment case (Gutman et al., 2011).

In some disparate treatment cases, the employer may use the *BFOQ* defense, that is, a claim that sex, national origin, or religious discrimination should be allowed as a *bona fide occupational qualification*. For example, the Supreme Court allowed the State of Alabama to exclude women from work as prison guards in a maximum security setting where many inmates were convicted sex offenders based on logic that this would be a threat to safety (*Dothard v. Rawlinson,* 1977). BFOQs are allowed only narrowly; for example, the Court did not allow Johnson Controls to exclude fertile women from jobs in which they would be exposed to lead, asserting that women had been warned, might not become pregnant, and should make such employment decisions themselves (*Automobile Workers v. Johnson Controls,* 1991). Race cannot be a BFOQ under Title VII, and customer preference is not a valid reason for discrimination prohibited by the law (Gutman et al., 2011).

Some cases involve both legal and illegal reasons for an employment decision. These *mixed motive* cases are more complex and follow a scenario like that of the *Price Waterhouse v. Hopkins* (1989) case. Ann Hopkins was a successful account manager at a large accounting firm but was rejected for promotion to partner in this mostly male job. She had evidence that powerful senior partners had made disparaging gender-biased statements about her lack of femininity; the employer claimed her abrasive personality was the reason her career had stalled, which would not be illegal.

As the case progressed through lower courts, Hopkins won on grounds that she had shown that an illegal reason (sex discrimination) had motivated the negative decision, and that the employer had failed to provide enough evidence of the legal reason for its decision. The Supreme Court sent the case back to the lower court to be retried, saying that the company did not need to meet such a stringent level of proof of legal motive. However, the district court retried the case and found again in favor of Hopkins even with the lower level of required proof by the employer (Gutman et al., 2011). Later mixed motive cases have further developed this scenario. It was also clarified by CRA91 which stated that in order to prevail, the plaintiff had only to *demonstrate* that race, sex, color, religion, or national origin was a factor that *motivated* an employment practice, even if there were also other (legal) factors involved. That is, the plaintiff has to show an illegal reason for unfair treatment. The employer must then show that the decision was based *instead* on a legal reason, after which the employee must show this was only a pretext.

In some disparate treatment cases involving multiple individuals, a claim is made that an employer follows a *pattern or practice* of illegal discrimination, demonstrated by statistical evidence that decisions systematically favor one group over another or by multiple individual disparate treatment claims (as in the *EEOC v. Mitsubishi,* 1996, sexual harassment case). The pattern and practice argument is often the basis for so-called *reverse discrimination* lawsuits (Gutman et al., 2011), in which those complaining of discrimination are actually in the majority. This is most likely to arise when an employer is trying to correct processes that have disadvantaged minorities.

A second legal scenario under Title VII, *adverse* or *disparate impact,* applies to situations in which an employer's action seems fair on first examination, such as a minimum height requirement for applicants. However, this *facially neutral* practice is shown to have *adverse* or more detrimental effects on one protected group than on others. For example, minimum height requirements often screen out women or members of ethnic groups (e.g., Asians, Latinos) who are shorter than typical White males. Such policies can lead to discriminatory outcomes that become apparent when employment records are analyzed for statistical patterns. Requirements producing adverse impact are only allowed if the employer can show they are really necessary for acceptable job performance. Often requirements seem reasonable, but turn out to be based on assumptions or stereotypes rather than data on effective job performance. Adverse impact discrimination is usually called *unintentional* because *proof of intent* to discriminate is not required.

The first and most famous adverse impact case was *Griggs v. Duke Power* (1971), which arose when Duke Power Company changed requirements for promotion from low-wage manual labor positions into operations jobs. The company had routinely hired Blacks for low-wage positions but not higher-wage operations work. Before 1955 Duke had frequently promoted Whites *without diplomas* into operations work. When Title VII became law in 1965, Duke changed its policy to require new operations employees to have a high school diploma and pass two cognitive tests. However, Whites hired before 1955 without diplomas could be promoted on the basis of cognitive tests alone. This gave the appearance that Duke was trying to limit the number of Blacks in operational jobs.

When the Supreme Court heard this case, evidence showed that both diploma and cognitive tests screened out a much higher proportion of Black candidates than Whites. At that time in North Carolina 34% of Whites graduated from high school, but only 12% of Blacks! In addition, over half (58%) of Whites but only 6% of Blacks passed the test. In combination, these two requirements screened out virtually all Blacks from operations jobs (Gutman et al., 2011).

This *Griggs* case set the pattern for adverse impact cases: first plaintiff must prove existence of adverse impact, after which defendant must either disprove the adverse impact claim, or prove that despite adverse impact, the practice being challenged is clearly related to the employment in question. Usually this involves presenting evidence that the practice is *valid*, meaning that success on the measure predicts success on the job. In the *Griggs* case, the employer could not provide such evidence and the Court struck down both requirements. However, if employer does present evidence of acceptable validity and job-relatedness, then plaintiff can show that other equally valid techniques with less adverse impact could have been used instead. Often decisions in such cases depend on technical details of validation and measurement qualities of various alternative techniques. Although the logic of adverse impact cases is reasonable, many technical problems exist in validating selection procedures and adverse impact is often difficult to avoid. An illustration is the *Ricci* case discussed in Chapter 10.

Good business practice suggests that hiring or promotion decisions should be based on evidence of applicants' job-related abilities assessed with valid selection techniques. However, some companies may choose to avoid being sued by not using tests at all, or by hiring enough people from underrepresented groups regardless of qualifications, so that adverse impact cannot be demonstrated. This may prevent an adverse impact lawsuit, but it often results in hiring or promoting people who are not able to perform well. Ironically, if an unqualified minority is hired and then terminated because he or she is not successful, this strengthens the stereotype that *these people just can't do the job!* The real problem in this case is that the employer did not do *its* job and chose unqualified people to avoid possible legal consequences.

Note that no legal requirement exists that employment decisions must be made based on valid selection devices. The only time an employer must present evidence of validity is in an adverse impact lawsuit. Hiring people on the basis of gut instinct, unvalidated interviews, relationship to the boss, or physical appearance alone is not against the law, but it is not smart business practice!

EEOC Guidelines on Sexual Harassment

After passage of Title VII, courts were unclear about whether and how sexual harassment (SH) should be considered a violation of that law, although case law had established that race harassment was illegal. In 1980 the EEOC issued *Guidelines* (EEOC, 1980), clarifying that SH violated Title VII. Unwelcome sexual advances, requests for sexual favors, and other verbal or physical conduct of a sexual nature violated the law when the behavior was (a) unwelcome; (b) related to employment decisions; or (c) of a nature that interfered with the work environment or created an intimidating, hostile, or offensive working environment. These *Guidelines* were not law but stated the EEOC's interpretation of the law at that time. (The EEOC issued further policy guidance in 1990 and 1999.) Good advice for employers is found in a Q&A document (EEOC, 2009b) covering such topics as supervisor's liability, what supervisors should do to prevent and correct harassment, recommended content for a policy prohibiting SH, and how complaints should be handled and investigated.

SH occurs in two forms. In *quid pro quo* harassment (in Latin, *this for that*), the victim is pressured to perform some sexual behavior under threat of firing, demotion, or some other *tangible employment consequence*. In *hostile environment harassment*, the harasser creates an abusive environment that interferes with another's job performance through persistent offensive joking, pranks, aggressive taunts, posting of pictures or information, denial of necessary work information, or other means. Because work environments and workers vary considerably in terms of what is considered offensive, it is generally recommended that a victim clearly and assertively inform the harasser that this conduct is offensive, unwelcome, and should stop.

If *quid pro quo* harassment is committed by a supervisor, the employer is liable whether or not it condoned, was aware of, or should have been aware of the misbehavior; in such cases the supervisor is considered an agent of the employer. In hostile environment harassment by the supervisor, the employer is also liable unless it can show that there was a policy in place and the victim unreasonably failed to use it. However, if there is a compelling reason why the victim did not use the policy (e.g., harasser is the person to whom harassment was to be reported, or victim fears retaliation for reporting harassment) the employer still may be liable. If harassment results from behavior of co-workers or customers, the employer is generally liable if it *knew or should have known* of harassment and took no corrective action (Gutman et al., 2011). An example is harassment of a restaurant hostess by customers, which is often tolerated by employees and even by management on grounds that it is important not to offend customers. However, this is inappropriate. The restaurant should have a harassment policy in place, and if an employee complains, management should correct the situation even if it means the customer never returns! Additional discussion of SH appears in Chapter 9.

Important court rulings have clarified application of SH law. Evidence exists that some behaviors are considered harassing by women but not by men (Gutek & O'Connor, 1995; Rotundo, Nguyen, & Sackett, 2001). However, the Supreme Court has decided that the standard for harassment is what a *reasonable person* (not a *reasonable woman*) would consider intolerable (*Harris v. Forklift*, 1993). Sex-based harassment of someone by another of the same sex has also been considered SH (*Oncale v. Sundowner*, 1998). In this case the plaintiff was a heterosexual male of small stature who worked in the hypermasculine environment of an oil rig. The key fact was that harassment occurred *because of the sex of the victim*, which can happen regardless of sexual orientation of those involved. Another case, *Pennsylvania State Police v. Suders* (2004), established that *tangible employment actions* could include something called *constructive discharge*. This term means that the situation is so intolerable that the ordinary person would see no alternative but to resign, a frequent reaction to discrimination and harassment.

The Pregnancy Discrimination Act of 1978 (PDA)

The PDA is an amendment to CRA64, incorporating "pregnancy, childbirth, or related medical conditions" into the law's meaning of "sex." Under this law, pregnancy is to be treated as would any other time-limited disability or condition that limits someone's work. For example, employees may be hurt in auto accidents, suffer heart attacks, break limbs, or require surgery. Policies applying to such situations (e.g., leave provisions, holding the job while the employee is out) should also apply to pregnancy-related conditions. No special provisions are required for pregnancy or childbirth by the PDA (but note that the FMLA also applies to childbirth situations). If the employer provides health insurance, it is not required to provide coverage for abortion unless the mother's life is endangered or medical complications have resulted from abortion or miscarriage.

It is simply not legal to fire, refuse to hire, or refuse to promote someone due to pregnancy. However, it may still occur.

Affirmative Action

Probably no other EEO provision is more misunderstood and controversial than AA (e.g., see Kravitz & Platania, 1993). AA was originally conceptualized as a *remedial* action to reverse long-standing effects of discrimination, which was legal and widespread prior to CRA64. It was not enough just to make discrimination illegal and assume that would fix the problem; something *affirmative* or proactive was required.

The basis for *voluntary* AA in employment is found in federal EOs, not laws. *Court-ordered* AA may also be required as part of the penalty when an employer loses a discrimination lawsuit; these cases typically involve clear and outrageous violations of anti-discrimination law. AA may also be part of an out-of-court settlement when an employer agrees to certain terms in order to resolve a lawsuit, e.g., when the employer believes it will lose the case or that fighting will be more expensive than settling. AA has also been used in the practice of *set-asides* in awarding government contracts for projects to minority-owned businesses and by educational institutions to increase diversity in student bodies. Our focus here is on AA in employment settings and case law that is relevant there; for further information on AA in admissions or set-asides, see Gutman et al. (2011).

The form of AA required by EO 11246 applies *only to* the federal government and employers holding federal contracts of $10,000 or more. Virtually any large employer or government has a federal contract over this amount. However, some private employers, such as religious organizations or small businesses, do not fall under this EO if they do not have federal contracts. Employers who want to avoid AA can decline to take government-paid work. This EO is enforced by the OFCCP, not the EEOC. Covered employers are prohibited from discriminating on the basis of race, color, religion, sex, and national origin (as under Title VII). They are also required to use AA in recruiting for these *preferred groups*. Notably, the OFCCP interprets *minority* to include Blacks, Hispanics, Native Americans, and Asian Americans. Other requirements include posting information about employment and including an EEO statement in job ads.

Larger contractors with 50 or more employees must file *EEO-1 Reports* showing race and sex of employees in various job categories. An employer with contracts for $50,000 or more must develop an *Affirmative Action Plan* (AAP) to address any *underutilization* of minorities or women. An AAP compares the employer's pattern of applicants and employees with what might reasonably be expected based on the appropriate pool of potential applicants or employees. If the current pattern varies considerably from what might be expected, the employer must set reasonable goals and timetables for achieving them. The employer must also describe actions to try to correct the imbalance so that the workforce better represents the pool of qualified people who might reasonably apply if the job were widely advertised. Some hiring pools may be national or international, but others may be much smaller—within a certain commuting distance, for example—depending on the type of job.

To enforce AA requirements, OFCCP conducts *compliance reviews* examining the employer's reports and AA data. If major problems are found, the agency tries to get the employer to agree to remedy the situation. An employer who remains noncompliant can lose its privilege of doing business with the government, experience loss or suspension of current contracts, or be publicly identified as a noncompliant employer. When it appears that laws have been violated, the OFCCP can refer the case to the EEOC or the DoJ for possible legal action (Gutman et al., 2011).

AA focuses on outreach and recruiting so that the applicant pool is more representative; it does *not* require or even permit preferential hiring or promotion decisions except in rare circumstances. The first AA strategy, targeted recruiting, is generally uncontroversial. Examples include expanded recruitment efforts in locations or institutions from which qualified minorities or women might come, such as historically Black colleges and universities, or advertising through media used frequently by minorities or women. Word-of-mouth recruiting through current employees should not be relied upon for applicants because majority employees are most likely to know people like themselves. Because AA focuses on recruiting and is not a selection procedure, *reverse discrimination* claims do not apply.

Second, an employer should attempt to identify and remedy any discriminatory obstacles to applications from minorities or women (e.g., company transportation from certain neighborhoods, work schedules). Third, an employer could explore and improve its reputation in the minority community. A company with a history of exclusion or discrimination against minorities will probably find it difficult to recruit qualified persons of color. Studies of employee attitudes and behaviors might uncover patterns of prejudice or discrimination that should be addressed. Finally, *tie-breaking* is used infrequently when individuals are *equally qualified*, giving preference to an applicant from a historically underrepresented or excluded group.

Many people believe that AA requires hiring unqualified minorities or women in order to meet *quotas*. This is not correct. In fact, it is contrary to the law. Why is this so widely believed? Perhaps some hiring authorities are reluctant to tell applicants that they are not as well qualified as a woman or minority who was hired instead of them. Saying "I had to hire a woman" is easier than telling a man that he was less qualified than she. In other cases, relying on stereotypes, people may assume that when a minority or woman is hired, the decision is not based on qualifications. Sometimes a person feels entitled to a position and deals with resentment when not selected by concluding that the person chosen was an *affirmative action hire*. In some cases, if managers' incentives depend on meeting diversity goals, they may give preference to less qualified women or minorities. Misguided good intentions to provide opportunities or lack of training in EEO law may lead someone to choose an unqualified applicant. But in none of these cases was this wrong-headed decision *required* by AA procedures. In fact, discrimination on the basis of race, sex, or other protected categories is forbidden by Title VII and *rigid quotas* are ruled out by OFCCP regulations (Gutman et al., 2011). It is no favor to unqualified people to hire them instead of better candidates; their likely lack of success will be taken as proof that *those people just can't do this work!* Additional information about AA appears in Crosby (2004) and Kravitz et al. (1997). The shaded box discusses public views about individual rights.

Affirmative Action and Public Opinion

Public support for AA programs has been assessed by numerous surveys over the years. Results of these efforts have varied based on how the questions were asked, the time when surveys were conducted, and demographic characteristics of respondents. In terms of question wording, a critical factor is inclusion (or not) of the words "preferential treatment." When these words are used, support for AA programs is reduced, especially among non-minorities. If more generic wording is employed without mentioning preferential treatment (e.g., helping minorities get better jobs and education), support rises even among Whites.

Issues regarding survey construction aside, eight states have banned the use of AA programs in public employment and education on the basis of various factors (e.g., race, color, sex, national origin, ethnicity) with the majority of these bans being approved by voters. Support for these bans may have been affected by wording of the amendments—all of those approved contained the words "preferential treatment." For example, the wording of the law banning affirmative action in Michigan (Proposition 2) stated that the amendment would, in part:

> Ban public institutions from using affirmative action programs that give *preferential treatment* to groups or individuals based on their race, gender, color, ethnicity or national origin for public employment, education, or contracting purposes. Public institutions affected by the proposal

include state government, local governments, public colleges and universities, community colleges and school districts.

The Michigan law was challenged and reached the Supreme Court in *Schuette v. BAMN* (2014). In this case, the Court upheld Michigan's ban on the use of AA. Essentially, the justices determined that there was no legal reason to invalidate a state law where voters chose to eliminate use of racial preferences by governmental agencies. Specifically, the Court found that the Michigan law did not result in specific harm to racial minorities, and it was not adopted with the intent to discriminate on the basis of race. As a consequence, the Court determined that there was no violation of the 14th Amendment's Equal Protection Clause.

Notably, the Supreme Court's decision in *Schuette v. BAMN* did not decide on the legality of AA. Indeed, the mission of the OFCCP, the federal agency responsible for enforcing AA programs via Executive Order (EO) 11246, remains intact. Consequently, organizations with federal government contracts over $10,000 (including many public universities) must still comply with EO 11246. It is still legitimate to have AA programs as long as (a) a compelling government interest exists; (b) the procedure is narrowly tailored to reach the stated goal; and (c) there are no other race-neutral alternatives that will meet the stated goal. From a larger perspective, courts have not always upheld public opinion in other arenas, such as gay marriage. Here, the Supreme Court ruled that gay marriage is a fundamental right covered by due process and equal protection clauses of the 14th Amendment. Constitutional rights are not a matter of public opinion.

Stephen J. Vodanovich

Civil Rights Act of 1991

In 1989, the Supreme Court handed down several decisions which appeared to contradict precedents under CRA64 such as the *Griggs* pattern of evidence and proof in adverse impact claims. Congress passed CRA91 to clarify its intent about enforcement of Title VII, returning to precedents that existed before these Supreme Court decisions. Other aspects of this law have had major impacts relevant to D&I: provision of jury trials and compensatory and punitive damages for *intentional* discrimination or harassment, and the prohibition of *subgroup norming*, explained below. Title II of this law, the Glass Ceiling Act, was described in Chapter 4.

Addition of jury trials and increased monetary damages for intentional discrimination and harassment cases is important because some plaintiffs and their attorneys now find it more reasonable to bring lawsuits in such cases. Jury trials are thought to favor the plaintiff because jurors may be able to imagine themselves in the victim's position and may be more sympathetic than a judge would be (Kalven & Zeisel, 1966). Furthermore, a victim of harassment might think that suing is not worth the emotional and financial expenditures if the only remedy is to be rehired with limited back pay. These changes may account for the increase in claims of harassment since passage of CRA91. The EEOC reports that 15,200 charges of harassment were filed with it or state and local agencies during 1992 (EEOC, n.d.-d). From that date on, almost every year the number of harassment charges has increased. Over 30,000 such charges were reported each year from 2008 to 2011 (EEOC, n.d.-c). Charges received by the EEOC alone are approximately 27,000 each subsequent year (EEOC, n.d.-b).

The 1991 CRA also prohibits *subgroup norming*, which shows the difficulty of balancing goals of diversity, inclusion, and fairness. In the 1980s, the US Employment Service (USES) used a statistical adjustment called subgroup norming to refer more racial minorities while still using valid measures of merit. USES performed screening tests on applicants for blue collar jobs and referred to employers a limited number of persons who scored well on screening. This method identified *many* people predicted to be successful if hired, but only a limited number could be referred. The problem was that as a group the White applicants scored higher than minorities, which produced adverse impact. Because many more Whites than minorities applied, qualified minorities seldom scored high enough to be referred although their scores predicted success if hired. To avoid adverse impact yet use valid selection, USES used subgroup norming (also called *within-group norming*) to make referrals. Candidates from the two groups were placed on separate lists in top-down order within each group. Applicants were chosen for referral beginning at the top of each list in proportion to the number who had applied from that group. This resulted in proportional referral of the most qualified members of both subgroups, *all of whom were qualified* for the job based on a valid test.

However, this method was criticized because it resulted in referral of some minorities whose actual score was lower than that of majority candidates not chosen for referral. This seemed unfair to those in the majority group. Critics began calling the technique *race norming*, and such a controversy arose that Congress prohibited the practice in CRA91:

> It shall be an unlawful employment practice . . . to adjust the scores of, use different cutoff scores for, or otherwise alter the results of, employment related tests on the basis of race, color, religion, sex, or national origin. (Sec. 106)(1)

In the words of measurement and legal experts, "The method known as within-group percentiles, dual lists, or 'race norming' simultaneously maximizes validity and reduces adverse impact (except that it is not legal)" (Cascio, Jacobs, & Silva, 2010, p. 282). So we are left with a situation in which Congress and the courts have said we cannot discriminate or create adverse impact, but we can't use a statistically reasonable method to deal with this problem. There is no easy answer. Another controversial technique, *banding*, has been suggested but requires careful implementation to minimize legal challenge and may not always be successful in reducing adverse impact (Cascio et al., 2010). Nevertheless, employers should check for adverse impact in selection measures and use appropriately validated measures.

The Age Discrimination in Employment Act of 1967

ADEA prohibits age-based discrimination or harassment against those 40 years of age or older, and retaliation against those filing complaints under this law. Exemptions exist for mandated retirement ages for some *bona fide executives*, firefighters or law enforcement officers (if a state or locality requires it), and policy-level elected or appointed officials if the law requires. Administered by the EEOC, ADEA applies to private employers with 20 or more employees as well as local and federal agencies. Because of legal interpretations of the law's wording, *individuals* may not sue state governments under ADEA, but the EEOC may sue on their behalf. Title VII legal theories apply (disparate treatment, adverse impact), but the mixed motive scenario is not allowed. That is, the illegal factor of age must be the *major* factor, not merely a *motivating* factor. Employers can defend against an age discrimination claim by showing that a decision was based on a *reasonable factor other than age* (e.g., performance, job tenure) or a *bona fide seniority system*. Also, in some cases a BFOQ defense may be used under ADEA. The law does not exempt Indian reservations or religious organizations (though an exception for ministers may apply); as amended in 1984, ADEA also covers overseas subsidiaries of US corporations.

Age discrimination can occur among persons who are all 40 or older; that is, hiring someone 45 instead of 60 can be a violation. Remedies include injunctions, reinstatement, and monetary damages including back or front pay (in lieu of reinstatement, pay that a person would have earned had discrimination not occurred) and legal fees. Penalties are greater when discrimination is shown to be *willful*. Age discrimination is most common when older individuals are not hired or when they are laid off at higher rates than younger employees. This may seem reasonable to the employer because salaries and benefit costs are often higher for older workers. Employers may believe older workers are less productive or can simply retire.

Evidence of age discrimination that will prevail in court is difficult for a plaintiff to obtain. Most employers who hire a younger rather than older person will not *say* that age is the reason. Nevertheless, the EEOC has filed suit against the Texas Roadhouse restaurant chain on the basis of a pattern or practice of age discrimination in hiring for jobs in which employees would interact with the public (EEOC, 2011).

The Texas Roadhouse Case

An EEOC press release in October 2011 announced a lawsuit against the national restaurant chain Texas Roadhouse. The EEOC alleged a pattern or practice of age discrimination going back at least to 2007 in hiring of *front of the house* employees such as bartenders, servers, and hosts. The press release states that the chain "hired significantly few 'front of the house' employees 40 or older in age. In addition (it) allegedly instructed its managers to hire younger job applicants ... (and) emphasized youth when training managers about hiring employees ... All of the images of employees in its training and employment manuals are of young people" (EEOC, 2011).

Some statements allegedly made to older applicants were "there are younger people here who can grow with the company," "you seem older to be applying for this job," "we are looking for people on the younger side," "how do you feel about working with younger people?" and "do you think you would fit in?" In its suit, the EEOC sought financial settlements for those denied employment because of age, strong policies and procedures against age discrimination, and training of managers on nondiscriminatory procedures. The suit was filed after EEOC's conciliation process was unsuccessful in reaching a settlement with the restaurant chain.

In 1990 Congress amended ADEA with the Older Workers Benefit Protection Act (OWBPA) because it was recognized that benefits for older persons are often more costly, which is an incentive to hire younger applicants. An employer may provide reduced benefits based on age, if the *cost* of these benefits is the same as for younger workers. Voluntary early retirement plans are permitted, especially if financial incentives are included, but maximum ages for these plans are illegal. Prior to OWPBA, those taking early retirement were often asked to sign waivers of their right to sue under ADEA. OWPBA lists eight specific requirements for waivers to be legally binding (e.g., waiver agreements must recommend in writing that the employee consult an attorney before signing; they must be understandable by the typical person eligible to participate; EEOC, n.d.-a, 2009-c; Gutman et al., 2011).

The Americans with Disabilities Act of 1990

Federal attempts to prevent employment discrimination against individuals with disabilities have a long history (Gutman et al., 2011). A precursor to ADA was the Rehabilitation Act of 1973, which required both nondiscrimination *and AA* by the federal government and many federal contractors. With ADA, anti-discrimination protection (but not the AA requirement) was extended to private sector and municipal employers with a minimum of 15 employees. As with ADEA, although private individuals cannot bring suit against *state governments,* the EEOC can sue on their behalf. ADA case law generally follows the disparate treatment scenario; administrative procedures and remedies are those of Title VII.

Those protected under ADA are individuals *qualified for the job in question* who have an enduring physical or mental impairment that substantially limits one or more major life activities, a *record* of such impairment, or are *regarded as* impaired. Confinement to a wheelchair or possession of visual or hearing deficit illustrates the first part of this definition. Cases of a cancer survivor or recovering alcoholic exemplify the second. Someone regarded as impaired—though not actually impaired—might be an individual who is disfigured or the caretaker of someone with AIDs. One must also be qualified to perform the *essential* functions of the job either with or without *reasonable accommodation*. Several conditions are excluded from coverage under ADA: transvestitism, transsexualism, gender identity disorders, compulsive gambling, kleptomania, pyromania, or *current* substance abuse. Temporary disabilities (e.g., broken limb, recovery from surgery) are not included.

A strange paradox developed as cases were tried under ADA as originally written. The Supreme Court interpreted the law to require that individuals *prove they were disabled* before discrimination could be evaluated for legality. If the person possessed a condition that could be managed or corrected (e.g., with medication or eyeglasses), the Court did not consider them disabled because they could perform activities listed in the Act. Therefore the law did not apply and discrimination was allowed!

This was partly addressed by the ADA Amendments Act of 2008 (ADAAA) which expanded the definition of *major life activities* and also clarified that a condition would be considered a *disability* and thus covered by ADA even if it could be corrected by *mitigating measures* such as insulin (for diabetes) or medication (for blood pressure). Further, employers now must consider applicants' *corrected* vision unless uncorrected vision is "job-related and consistent with business necessity." In other words, those needing prescription glasses are not considered *disabled* but also cannot be discriminated against because they require glasses. Episodic conditions or those in remission are considered a disability if they would qualify when active (EEOC, n.d.-e).

Employers should perform a job analysis *before* a job is advertised. The job analysis should identify *essential functions* of the job, that is, activities or duties which are *required* and cannot be dropped or altered without changing the job's core nature. Employers are not required to hire a person with a disability, but such a person cannot be rejected because of the disability. Employers are required to provide *reasonable accommodation* if needed for a qualified but disabled individual to perform the job. Such adjustments might include making the workplace accessible, modifying equipment (e.g., raising desk height to accommodate a wheelchair), or purchasing assistive devices such as amplification for a telephone or special software to alter the size or illumination of computerized visual information. Other reasonable accommodations are modification of work schedules, restructuring of non-essential parts of the job, or reassignment to a vacant position, if available. Accommodations that would place *undue hardship* upon the employer due to cost or difficulty are not required. Accommodations reasonable for a large employer might constitute undue hardship for a smaller company.

Employers can and should ask *all* applicants if they are able to perform essential functions of the job, but private employers should not inquire about disabilities or accommodations, which might give the appearance of discrimination. (However, employers subject to AA requirements of the Rehabilitation Act or the Vietnam Era Veterans' Readjustment Act must invite applicants to self-identify; EEOC, 1995; Schoenfeld, 2013.) Employers should assume no disability that would affect job performance exists unless disability is disclosed and accommodation requested. Parties are expected to *flexibly interact* to determine appropriate accommodations. Certain accommodations may be required even if not directly linked to essential job functions (Duggan, 2013). Medical or psychological exams, including personality tests, may not be administered until after an employment offer is made, and only if all employees are required to have such exams.

Though in most cases, ADA provisions do not create major difficulties for employers, some challenges occur. Some disabilities are psychiatric conditions which may be episodic or vary over time in terms of how well they are controlled by psychoactive medications. As another example, when accommodations such as increased time limits are provided for pre-employment testing, test validity may be called into question. Employers are not required to accommodate disabilities that present a risk to the health and safety of others.

The Family and Medical Leave Act of 1993

FMLA applies to all public employers, public and private schools, and companies with at least 50 employees. However, only certain employees are eligible. One must have worked for the employer for 12 months, including at least 1,250 hours of work during that time, and at a location within 75 miles of which the employer has at least 50 employees. Thus FMLA does not cover small employers; seasonal, temporary or short-term employees; and some part-time employees. In addition, *key employees* are not included if they are among the top company earners and their absence would harm the employer economically.

FMLA is different in substance than other laws we have discussed. Instead of specifically prohibiting discrimination or other practices, it requires that up to 12 weeks of *unpaid l*eave be provided during the year for pregnancy and childbirth, adoption or foster care placement; the employee's own serious health condition; or care of the employee's spouse, child, or parent with a serious health condition. Special expanded provisions apply to military family members. During FMLA leave, the employer must keep in place any health coverage ordinarily available to the worker. Employees returning from FMLA leave must be placed in their former job or an equivalent position, without changes in pay, benefits, or other terms of employment. The 12 weeks may be taken in a block or intermittently when medically necessary (e.g., if a family member receives periodic chemotherapy treatments). Employers may require that FMLA leave be taken concurrently with paid leave. Even if this is not required by the employer, the employee may elect to do so. This might result in less leave time overall, but some leave would be paid. Employees must provide 30 days notice for FMLA leave if possible. Individuals may file a complaint with the DoL which enforces FMLA, or may bring a private lawsuit.

Although the name of this law suggests that it is a great help to those with family responsibilities, its effect is limited by the fact that required leave is *unpaid*. Many households would be severely stressed by missing three months' pay. Another limitation is that the *family* includes only the spouse, child, or parent of the employee—not parents-in-law or unmarried domestic partners. For employers, FMLA presents challenges when keeping accurate records of the types of leave used and relevant timelines.

The Immigration Reform and Control Act of 1986 (IRCA)

This law predates current controversies about employing those not in the US legally. IRCA requires employers to verify employment eligibility *for everyone hired* using the I-9 form based on required documentation (e.g., passport, birth certificate, visa showing employment eligibility). Undocumented immigrants should not have these, but often workers present bogus or forged papers, and sometimes employers hire them mistakenly or because they need low-wage workers. Employers who violate IRCA are subject to fines or a six-month prison sentence if the pattern is persistent. IRCA is enforced by the Immigration and Nationalization Service and the DoJ.

IRCA also prohibits discrimination against anyone authorized to work in the US. An employer who refuses to hire non-natives, assuming they are or may be undocumented, is discriminating illegally under IRCA and possibly also violating the national origin provision of Title VII. IRCA violations also include requiring more documentation after appropriate information has been provided and requiring documentation of some employees (e.g., Latinos) but not others. Civil penalties for discrimination in violation of IRCA are fines of $250–10,000 depending on circumstances (Economic Research Service/USDA, n.d.; US DoJ, 1986).

Taking the Legal Approach

An employee who believes that illegal discrimination has occurred has several alternatives. Often the employer's HR office is the place to begin; problems can sometimes be resolved informally through mediation by a professional staff member. If mediation is unsuccessful or if the employee is not comfortable contacting someone working for the same organization, the EEOC or a state or local Fair Employment Practices agency (sometimes called Human Relations Commission) can be contacted directly. An employment or civil rights attorney should also be consulted early in the process. Strict filing deadlines exist, such as 180 days from the date of the alleged discrimination, and there may be no legal recourse for complaints filed after the deadline. The shaded box in Chapter 4 about Lilly Ledbetter (p. 76) describes this situation in disputes over salary discrimination.

From the perspective of the employer concerned with D&I, it is important to be well informed about legal requirements concerning recruitment, selection, and management of employees from protected classes. Laws and cases reviewed in this chapter provide a minimum threshold for an environment that is procedurally fair for members of underrepresented groups as well as those in the majority. However, the capable diversity manager will likely decide to do more than the law requires in an effort to develop and maintain an inclusive environment. In this process, understanding legal context is important for developing programs and policies that are proactive but still compliant with the law.

The Diversity Paradox

In doing D&I work, we try to create an environment in which each person is valued as an individual, particularly in terms of the diversity of her or his possible contributions to the organization. In this case, employees are respected for their unique individualities, and their membership in demographic groups becomes less important. However, anti-discrimination law requires first that someone be shown to be a member of a protected class. That is, these legal remedies rest upon the very demographic group identifications that our efforts for D&I may be trying to de-emphasize. This is a paradox in managing D&I.

References

Automobile Workers v. Johnson Controls, Inc. 499 U.S. 187 (1991).

Biddle, D. A. (2008). Are the *Uniform Guidelines* outdated? Federal guidelines, professional standards, and validity generalization (VG). *The Industrial-Organizational Psychologist, 45*(4), 17–23.

Cascio, W. F., Jacobs, R., & Silva, J. (2010). Validity, utility, and adverse impact: Practical implications from 20 years of data. In J. L. Outtz (Ed.), *Adverse impact: Implications for organizational staffing and high stakes selection* (pp. 271–288). New York: Routledge.

Crosby, F. J. (2004). *Affirmative action is dead; long live affirmative action.* New Haven, CT: Yale University Press.

Dothard v. Rawlinson 433 U.S. 321 (1977).

Duggan, S. J. (2013, October 7). No link required between job essential function and reasonable accommodation. *Fair Measures, Inc.* Retrieved from www.fairmeasures.com/enews/essential-reasonable-accommodation/

Economic Research Service/USDA. (n.d.). *Immigration Reform and Control Act of 1986.* Retrieved from www.ers.usda.gov/media/536063/ah719f_1_.pdf

EEOC. (n.d.-a). *Age discrimination.* Retrieved from www.eeoc.gov/eeoc/publications/age.cfm

EEOC. (n.d.-b). *All charges alleging harassment: FY 2010–FY 2015.* Retrieved from www.eeoc.gov/eeoc/statistics/enforcement/all_harassment.cfm

EEOC. (n.d.-c). *Harassment Charges EEOC and FEPAs Combined: FY 1997–FY 2011.* Retrieved from www1.eeoc.gov//eeoc/statistics/enforcement/harassment.cfm

EEOC. (n.d.-d). *Harassment Charges FY 1992-FY 1996.* Retrieved from www.eeoc.gov/eeoc/statistics/enforcement/harrassment-a.cfm

EEOC. (n.d.-e). *Titles I and V of the Americans with Disabilities Act of 1990 (ADA)*. Retrieved from www.eeoc.gov/laws/statutes/ada.cfm

EEOC. (1980). *Equal Employment Opportunity Commission's Guidelines on Sexual Harassment*. 45 FR 74677, Nov. 10, 1980. Retrieved from www.gpo.gov/fdsys/pkg/CFR-2012-title29-vol4/pdf/CFR-2012-title29-vol4-sec 1604-11.pdf

EEOC. (1995, October 10). *ADA enforcement guidance: Pre-employment disability-related questions and medical examinations.* Retrieved from www.eeoc.gov/policy/docs/preemp.html

EEOC. (2009a). *Federal laws prohibiting job discrimination questions and answers.* Retrieved from www.eeoc.gov/facts/qanda.html

EEOC. (2009b). *Questions and answers for small employers on employer liability for harassment by supervisors.* Retrieved from www.eeoc.gov/policy/docs/harassment-facts.html

EEOC. (2009c). *Understanding waivers of discrimination claims in employee severance agreements.* Retrieved from www.eeoc.gov/policy/docs/qanda_severance-agreements.html

EEOC. (2010). *Workplace laws not enforced by the EEOC.* Retrieved from www.eeoc.gov/laws/other.cfm

EEOC. (2011). *Texas Roadhouse refused to hire older workers nationwide, EEOC alleges in lawsuit.* Retrieved from www.eeoc.gov/eeoc/newsroom/release/10-3-11.cfm

EEOC v. Mitsubishi Motor Manufacturing of America, Inc. 102 F.3d 869 (1996).

Griggs v. Duke Power Co. 401 U.S. 424 (1971).

Gutek, B., & O'Connor, M. (1995). The empirical basis for the reasonable woman standard. *Journal of Social Issues, 51*, 151–166.

Gutman, A., Koppes, L. L., & Vodanovich, S. J. (2011). *EEO law and personnel practices* (3rd ed.). New York, NY: Routledge.

Harris v. Forklift Systems, Inc. 510 U.S. 17 (1993).

Kalven, H., & Zeisel, H. (1966). *The American jury.* Boston, MA: Little, Brown.

Kravitz, D. A., Harrison, D. A., Turner, M. E., Levine, E. L., Chaves, W., Brannick, M. T., Denning, D. L., Russell, C. J., and Conard, M. A. (1997). *Affirmative action: A review of psychological and behavioral research.* Bowling Green, OH: Society for Industrial and Organizational Psychology.

Kravitz, D. A., & Platania, J. (1993). Attitudes and beliefs about affirmative action: Effects of target and of respondent sex and ethnicity. *Journal of Applied Psychology, 78*, 928–938.

Law, C. L., & Hrabal, E. A. (2010). Sexual minorities in the workplace: The status of legal and organizational protection. *The Industrial-Organizational Psychologist, 47*(4), 37–42.

Law.Com. (2012). *Supreme Court.* Retrieved from http://dictionary.law.com/Default.aspx?selected=2072

McDaniel, M. A., Kepes, S., & Banks, G. C. (2011). The *Uniform Guidelines* are a detriment to the field of personnel selection. *Industrial and Organizational Psychology: Perspectives on Science and Practice, 4*, 494–514.

McDonnell Douglas v. Green 411 U.S. 792 (1973).

Nolo. (2016). *Sexual orientation discrimination: Your rights.* Retrieved from www.nolo.com/legal-encyclopedia/sexual-orientation-discrimination-rights-29541.html

Oncale v. Sundowner Offshore Services, Inc. 523 U.S. 75 (1998).

Pennsylvania State Police v. Suders 542 U.S. 129 (2004).

Price Waterhouse v. Hopkins 490 U.S. 228 (1989).

Rotundo, M., Nguyen, D., & Sackett, P. R. (2001). A meta-analytic review of gender differences in perceptions of sexual harassment. *Journal of Applied Psychology, 86*, 914–922.

Schoenfeld, S. (2013, November 12). *"Are you disabled?" Asking about disabilities without breaking the law.* Retrieved from http://hr.blr.com/HR-news/Discrimination/Disabilities-ADA/zns-Asking-about-disabilities-without-breaking-law/#

Schuette v. BAMN 134 U.S. 1623 (2014).

Society for Industrial and Organizational Psychology. (2011). *Industrial and Organizational Psychology: Perspectives on Science and Practice, 4.* (Section on the *Uniform Guidelines*, pp. 494–570.)

Supreme Court of the United States: Frequently asked questions: General Information. (n.d., version 2009–0). Retrieved from www.supremecourt.gov/faq.aspx#faqgi9

Tonowski, R. F. (2011). The *Uniform Guidelines* and personnel selection: Identify and fix the right problem. *Industrial and Organizational Psychology: Perspectives on Science and Practice, 4*, 521–525.

US Department of Justice. (1986, November 6). *The Immigration Control and Reform Act of 1986*. Retrieved from www.justice.gov/sites/default/files/eoir/legacy/2009/03/04/IRCA.pdf

Chapter 8

Making the Most of Diversity in Teams

Much work is done by people in small groups or teams. Some is inherently teamwork (e.g., playing football), some predominantly independent (e.g., call center employees, retail sales) but labeled a team for administrative reasons. Some jobs require both interdependent and independent work (e.g., restaurant servers, surgeons). Jobs involving no work in groups are hard to find and informal groups occur in most work organizations.

The terms *group* and *team* are widely used, sometimes interchangeably, but they have specific definitions for social scientists. A group is a bounded collection of people who are interdependent, share common purpose, participate in social interaction with one another, and see themselves as a group. In organizational psychology, the word team also implies common purpose of responsibility for accomplishing a particular task or set of tasks (Jex & Britt, 2014). *Pseudo-team* (West & Lyubovnikova, 2012) is a better term when boundaries, common purpose and responsibility, or other team characteristics are not present. Teams are part of a larger organizational system, linked in complex ways with other units in the structure (Kozlowski & Ilgen, 2006).

Why should diversity professionals and managers know about team research? Most managers work with or in a team that is internally diverse, or with several teams that work interdependently. Second, employees are often expected to work productively with others they may not know, have not chosen, or may not like. Third, the team setting provides an opportunity for diversity professionals to encourage adaptive learning, attitude change, and development or strengthening of positive relationships that affect other situations in and out of the work setting. Fourth, diversity professionals may sometimes be called upon to advise others about issues involving team dynamics. Thus, knowledge about positive and negative processes and outcomes of teamwork is helpful so that diversity can be used adaptively, as strength instead of weakness.

For many years social psychologists have studied small groups in a subfield called *group dynamics*. Some early research used *ad hoc* groups, i.e., those formed for research purposes for a limited time period and studied in laboratory settings with task, time, and other constraints. Field studies (e.g., Sherif's Robber's Cave research) and case studies were also conducted, such as the *Groupthink* studies of public policy decision-making fiascoes in the context of strong conformity pressures (Janis, 1972). Recently more research has been conducted by organizational psychologists and management researchers studying actual work teams (Levine & Moreland, 1990), e.g., self-managing, cross-functional, top management, or virtual teams meeting only through electronic technology. These studies often occur in natural work settings with pre-existing teams.

Teams have both *structure* and *process*. *Structure* is a static snapshot of relationships among group members at a particular point in time. *Process* refers to dynamic ways in which relationships change over time, such as leadership that occurs in different ways as the team matures or proceeds with its task. Process (e.g., roles, communication, leadership/influence) generally emphasizes *task* interactions or *socio-emotional* interactions concerned with maintaining relationships among members (Bales, 1950). Over time, both emphases are needed for most groups to be successful: the task must be accomplished, and members must work effectively together and remain satisfied and in the group. To understand the difference between structure and process, consider slide show vs. video. Each slide presents structure at a particular point in time whereas video focuses on changes from one moment to the next. Both structure and process can be *formal* (i.e., officially designated) or *informal* (i.e., what actually occurs). We begin with two models for organizing information about team structure and process.

Two Perspectives

Systems Theory

This framework developed in the physical sciences during the 1930s and became a cross-disciplinary perspective on physical and social systems of all kinds (Laszlo & Krippner, 1998). Organizational psychologists think of teams and organizations as *open systems* characterized by (a) a semi-permeable boundary; (b) interdependent internal parts or subsystems, so that change in one produces ripples of change in others; (c) inputs from the environment, internal processes, and output into the environment; and (d) dependency upon the external environment for sustaining resources and to use output. (A closed system, like a conventional watch or clock, does not receive continual environmental inputs and eventually winds down unless it is wound or the battery is replaced.) Applying this definition to teams, membership is usually specified. Team members are interdependent and if one leaves or is replaced, others must re-adjust. From the organizational environment the team receives task assignments, members, and resources for processing work, which becomes output into that environment. Output also concerns meeting needs of members and the team's viability so that members continue with the team (Hackman, 1987). If the task is completed and no new task adopted, resources disappear, or new members do not replace those who leave—or if the environment ceases to accept the team's output—the team is unlikely to survive without adapting. This perspective highlights the team's relationship with its organizational environment and interdependency among members, both important in team effectiveness. Figure 8.1 illustrates these concepts.

The system perspective helps clarify successes and difficulties of work teams. For example, often we attribute outcomes to individuals and think that if they were replaced or behaved differently,

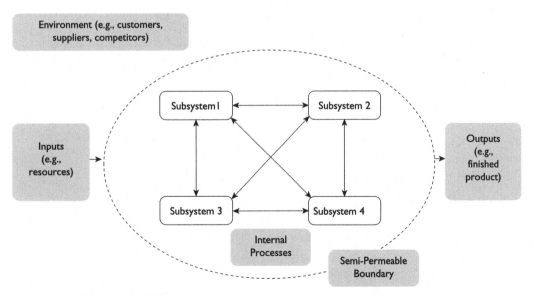

Figure 8.1 An Organizational System

results would change. However, frequently individual behavior and results of team efforts are constrained by factors in the team's environment. Does the team receive sufficient appropriate inputs? Do internal processes operate effectively? Is output accepted by the organizational environment? In addition, because the team is interdependent internally and with other organizational structures, changes elsewhere will produce adjustments in the team.

The Steiner GPM Model

Another useful framework for understanding teams is the Group Productivity Model (GPM) developed by Ivan Steiner (1972). Though published many years ago, GPM is still useful for considering how teams can function more effectively. GPM proposes that *Actual Productivity* of a team depends upon two things: *Potential Productivity* (the *best* a team can do, determined by *task* and available *resources*), and *process losses*, if any (due to member *motivation* and *coordination)*, as shown in Figure 8.2.

Steiner's GPM does not specifically address the organizational *environment* within which work teams operate, but GPM can be combined with a systems perspective. For example, if a team does not receive sufficient *resources*, perhaps its goals do not align with those of the larger organization. Also not specifically included in the GPM are effects of *time* on team process. For example, with repeated interaction teams often learn to deal more effectively with diversity that presented problems for interaction in the beginning. Surface-level diversity exerts its strongest influence early in a team's life but deep-level diversity becomes more important at later stages (Harrison, Price, & Bell, 1998; Harrison, Price, Gavin, & Florey, 2002). More complex models of team effectiveness present a more comprehensive approach to teamwork (see Ilgen, Hollenbeck, Johnson, & Jundt, 2005; Jex & Britt, 2014). However, when supplemented by the systems perspective and effects occurring over time, the Steiner GPM framework is a powerful lens for understanding effects of diversity in teams.

Reviews (e.g., Horwitz & Horwitz, 2007; Bell, Villado, Lukasik, Belau, & Briggs, 2011) have shown inconsistent effects of diversity, partly due to great variety in tasks and contexts, and to ways in which diversity has been conceptualized and measured. Evidence shows that diversity on task-relevant factors (e.g., functional expertise) can have positive effects on quality and quantity of performance on some tasks. Socio-demographic diversity is also claimed to produce better performance, although empirical evidence on this point is weaker and sometimes negative effects are found (Bell et al., 2011). This chapter considers when and why diversity should make a difference in terms of the work of teams so it can be managed more effectively. Diversity is a fact of life in contemporary organizations, and at times diversity should be sought because it is likely to produce better results.

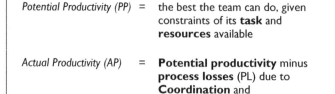

Figure 8.2 Steiner Group Productivity Model

"What Differences Make a Difference?"

An article by this title drew conclusions from more than 50 years of research on effects of differences within small teams. Elizabeth Mannix and Margaret Neale (2005) found that effects of surface diversity on team processes are inconsistent. Diversity in tenure (experience with team or organization) is the most likely to create problems in communication, conflict, and group cohesion; effects of age diversity are weaker and least consistent. In contrast, deep-level diversity is more likely to impact the team positively if and when internal process is carefully managed. For example, diversity in functional area is likely to create conflict about the task, but this can have positive or negative effects. When working with diverse teams, Mannix and Neale recommended considering (a) *organizational context;* (b) underlying *processes* in the team; and (c) how diversity is *understood and measured.*

One effect of *context* is whether cooperativeness or competitiveness characterize the team's reward structure and culture and its organizational environment. Diversity is more likely to be beneficial when cooperation and collective effort are emphasized. Concerning underlying *process,* Mannix and Neale cautioned that demographic variables should not be used as "proxies" for attitudes, values, skills, or other deep-level factors. Such inferences are often wrong, and also prevent us from searching for more fundamental explanations in terms of group process. Finally, what seems to result from surface demographic diversity may actually result from more basic deep-level differences such as level of emotionality or mood, which would be overlooked with a narrow *understanding and measurement* of diversity.

Mannix and Neale made three suggestions about managing diversity within teams.

1. Consider team task and goals. Diversity is more beneficial when the team focuses on *exploration,* i.e., solving problems, innovating, trying out various ideas, creating something new. A variety of skills, knowledge, and experience is likely to be helpful in this situation. For assignments that involve *exploitation* such as productive and efficient application of established methods of work, diversity may be less advantageous.
2. Focus on leadership and group process to use and coordinate differences among team members. For example, if team process emphasizes conformity and agreement, those with different perspectives may not express them and the team will not benefit from their ideas. Another faulty process is *information sampling bias* (Stasser & Titus, 1985), a common pattern of focusing discussion only on information members have in common. This is often dysfunctional because it leads teams to overlook information and ideas held only by a minority of members. Mannix and Neale recommended processes that bridge differences among members by creating comfort and trust through social connections. For example, the team's superordinate identity can be emphasized by stressing what members have in common and their commitment to collective values. Leaders can also try to avoid these problems by not expressing their own preferences, appointing a devil's advocate, or specifically directing conversation to new information or viewpoints.
3. Strengthen influence of minority viewpoints by acknowledging member expertise, specifically requesting alternative ideas, or striving for consensus rather than deciding by majority vote. Voting seems democratic but it produces winners and losers, which can be dysfunctional for a team. Voting should be avoided if a modified or hybrid decision can be reached with which most participants can agree.

This review confirms that the promise of diversity for team and organizational outcomes will not be realized unless it is *managed* by appropriate leadership and group process in a culture of learning and effectiveness (Thomas & Ely, 1996; Van der Vegt & Bunderson, 2005) that supports different identities and perspectives. Because process is a focus of the Steiner Model, the GPM framework (modified to consider system perspective and effects of time) will be used to review some ways in which diversity (or lack of diversity) can make a team more or less effective. This framework can be used to diagnose how well a team is working to make the most of diversity.

Applying a Modified Group Process Model

Teams or Individuals?

This should be the first question a manager asks before assigning a task to a team (Hackman, 2002). Often tasks are routinely assigned to teams without careful consideration of whether the work could be better accomplished by one person, subdivided and assigned to different people, or given to people who work separately and whose work is then combined. In the terms of the GPM, *does an individual have the resources (e.g., information, skill) needed to complete the task?* If the answer is yes, then the job should probably be given to that person unless there is a good extra-task reason for involving a team. (For example, for political reasons it may be necessary to include representatives from different constituencies.)

However, if the answer is no, and no single individual can do the job well, then it should be assigned to a team. But how large? Steiner (1972) summarized the effects of group size on process and productivity:

1. As size increases, Potential Productivity (PP) rises because of increased resources brought by additional members. However, with increasing size, improvement in PP slows because new members add little that is new and unduplicated. Four people have more resources than three people, but the benefit of increasing from 12 to 13 is probably small.
2. As size increases, process losses (PL) increase as well. Unlike PP, as size increases PL increase at a faster rate. Problems in coordinating and maintaining motivation for a 12-member team are greater than for a team of three.
3. The result is that as team size increases, Actual Productivity (AP) rises at first and then starts to drop as process losses outweigh the value of increased resources. The key is to form a team large enough to capture advantages of additional members without having too many. This magic number varies with the task but for interdependent and interactive problem-solving or decision-making teams it is probably only five or six (Hackman, 2002).

How does this apply in the D&I context? Concerning resources, some tasks benefit from including perspectives of people differing in experience and knowledge, assuming that team processes permit those perspectives to be expressed and receive attention. With respect to motivation and coordination, heterogeneous teams often present greater challenges than teams of similar people or individuals working alone. As noted by Mannix and Neale (2005), effects of surface diversity are sometimes problematic. The manager who forms a diverse team should plan to manage team processes carefully in order to avoid problems from surface diversity and obtain positive effects of deep-level diversity.

Additional unique *resources* are not the only reason for forming a team. Other rationales include *detection of error* as well as *inclusiveness* and *demonstration of respect* for perspectives of underrepresented groups. Members from different constituencies can provide *broader support* for implementation of team recommendations. Sometimes team membership gives important *developmental experiences* to those who would otherwise be left out. Finally, membership on a continuing team provides a *context for interaction* among those who would not ordinarily become acquainted across sociocultural or functional divides. Type of task, management of team process, and context for work are all important factors to consider. This is a matter of judgment, without a single right answer.

Tasks: Type

Team functioning is constrained by the task(s) for which members are collectively responsible, and the fact that these may change over time (Tannenbaum, Mathieu, Salas, & Cohen, 2012). Important factors are how an assignment is chosen, by whom, and how clearly task is defined in terms of goals, methods, and speed or quality requirements. Is the work *unitary*, meaning that it cannot be subdivided, or is it *divisible* in ways that permit assignment of different parts to different people (Steiner, 1972)? Divisible tasks allow for a wider variety of assignments, possibly matching different people to parts they do best. Is the goal to do as much as possible as fast as possible, a *maximizing* task? Or is it more important that quality be as high as possible, an *optimizing* task? Assigning more people will probably work well when only speed or quantity is important as long as members do not get in each other's way. Optimizing tasks require more care in selection of the persons who are most capable, and in design of process so their talents are best used.

Many work teams have *discretionary* tasks that can be done in different ways with choice of process up to the team or its leader. If members differ in knowledge, skill, or personal attributes (such as reliability), the team will do best when process makes the most of everyone's strengths while managing around their weaknesses. When member interaction is likely to produce positive effects (e.g., learning, increased motivation, error checking), and when PL from motivation and coordination is negligible, then collective action is a good choice. If differences present a serious challenge for face-to-face interaction, work can sometimes be subdivided among people who co-act rather than interact. Alternative processes for design of the team's work should be considered rather than simply assuming everyone will work together. This becomes more important when there are major concerns surrounding D&I.

Tasks can also be classified based on their goal-directed activities. For example, teams may *generate, choose, negotiate,* or *execute* (McGrath, 1964). Generation usually involves cooperative motivation while negotiating is likely to involve conflict and competition. Choosing and executing probably involve both cooperation and conflict to varying degrees. The most effective internal processes vary with task type as well as team diversity.

For example, in *generation* tasks when success is determined by number of ideas produced, results will be best when members work separately and their answers are later combined (see shaded box).

A Note on Brainstorming—and Other Techniques

Brainstorming has been widely recommended as a way of "unleashing" creativity in a group by asking participants to generate as many ideas as they can think of, build on others' ideas, and refrain from criticizing or evaluating any of the ideas (Osborn, 1957). Hearing another's suggestions supposedly stimulates more ideas when criticism is forbidden. Afterwards ideas are evaluated, combined, and refined to produce more and better ideas and good, creative final solutions.

However, researchers found that these rosy predictions were overstated. Four-person brainstorming groups were contrasted with four participants given brainstorming instructions but working independently (*nominal groups*). Even after duplicate ideas were removed, nominal groups produced *more* ideas and *more creative* ones than brainstorming groups (Taylor, Berry, & Block, 1958). Brainstorming's supposed advantage was probably due to several people working on the problem rather than group process itself. Most studies comparing brainstorming individuals with brainstorming groups of the same number of participants have found similar results (Diehl & Stroebe, 1987; Mullen, Johnson, & Salas, 1991). Nevertheless, group brainstorming is still recommended by people who may not be aware of these results, or may decide to use brainstorming anyway because it is fun or for other reasons.

Why would group brainstorming depress number and quality of ideas compared to those produced by the same number of brainstorming individuals? Several explanations have been examined. In a group, participants tend to build on or react to ideas they have just heard rather than think independently. This is called *production blocking* (Diehl & Stroebe, 1987). Working alone, people think more divergently and overall the number of unduplicated ideas is usually greater.

Other explanations come from social psychological processes within groups, e.g., anxiety about contributing, pressures to conform, or censorship by evaluating before sharing (Mullen et al., 1991). Opportunity to contribute (*floor time*) is less when interacting than when recording ideas separately. Free-riding and social loafing have also been suggested. Mullen et al. meta-analyzed studies comparing brainstorming and nominal groups. They found most support for anxiety, self-censorship, and conformity pressures, some support for production blocking and floor time explanations, and *least* empirical support for social loafing or free-riding processes. Social facilitation research has shown that people working *separately* but in the presence of others are more focused and productive than when working alone because of arousing and motivational influence of co-actors (Zajonc, 1965).

Van de Ven and Delbecq (1971) developed a *round-robin* technique in which several individuals first privately record responses to a problem. Next, a trained facilitator elicits and records one answer at a time from each participant, going around the group until no one has additional ideas to contribute. The group discusses ideas, after which a private vote, ranking, or response is collected and the facilitator determines the "group decision." This technique is sometimes called the *Delbecq method* although this terminology is not used consistently.

A similar method, the *Delphi technique*, was developed in the 1950s and 1960s at the Rand Corporation (Cantrill, Sibbald, & Buetow, 1996). It is best used in complex decision-making situations when knowledgeable experts cannot interact directly. (Today teleconferencing or other virtual decision tools could be used.) Another use is when face-to-face interaction is problematic because of differences in language, time zones, strongly held preferences, interpersonal disagreements, conformity pressures, or other factors. The Delphi technique begins with an anonymous survey of participants who separately consider the problem and background information and make recommendations. An expert facilitator processes responses to create a second-round survey to which all respond. This process continues until an acceptable solution is reached.

Nominal groups, round-robin sessions, and the Delphi technique are all ways of making use of unique resources of diverse individuals while minimizing loss due to faulty process. Brainstorming is useful when the task is idea generation, but it is likely to be more productive with co-acting *individuals* than an interacting group.

When the task is to *choose* and product quality is important, well-managed process can lead diverse team members to find and correct errors, an area in which groups are often superior (Hill, 1982). The team can specifically elicit and consider critiques. In choice tasks, sometimes the best answer is obvious. In other cases the best alternative may be unclear and choice may be unduly influenced by people who are more powerful. If it is important that the best alternative be chosen, process must be managed to control power dynamics so that diverse perspectives are expressed and fully considered. Pros and cons of each alternative can be solicited from everyone until the best choice becomes clear.

In *negotiating*, conflict is inherent because parties' preferences are likely to be different or contradictory. For tasks of *execution* or enacting a procedure, often process is discretionary. The team will do best when process is controlled to make the most of available resources without sacrificing success to motivation or coordination losses. Some techniques for controlling group process are discussed later in this chapter.

Tasks: Interdependence

How work is interconnected among team members can vary greatly depending on task design. In *pooled interdependence,* contributions of different individuals (or other units) are simply combined to make the product (Thompson, 1967). In *sequential interdependence,* one person's output becomes input for the next person, as on an assembly line. The second person can only work as fast and accurately as the first person's work allows. In *reciprocal* interdependence, individuals actually work together, with influence flowing back and forth among members of the team. As degree of interdependence increases, managing process smoothly becomes more difficult. Interdependence presents a challenge for all teams but is amplified when faultlines and differences exist. Interdependence also occurs between or among teams sharing responsibility for a larger goal.

How does this relate to D&I? The more task interdependence in a team (or between teams with interconnected work), the more important it is that communication and cohesion be strong. With highly interdependent tasks, potential disruption from differences among people or teams is high as well. High levels of task interdependence place a premium on good diversity management.

Tasks: Mental Models

How team members *think* about their work and their team are critical factors in process and effectiveness (Kozlowski & Ilgen, 2006). One important type of team cognition is the *Team Mental Model (TMM),* a shared understanding about team, work, and environment. With strong TMM, members agree about membership, roles, task, process for accomplishing it, timeframe, how the team relates to other teams and the organization, and other key factors. The TMM concept was first popularized by Cannon-Bowers and Salas (1990) based on extensive work with military teams, whose work is often complicated and conducted in an uncertain and changing environment. Mohammed, Ferzandi, and Hamilton (2010) reviewed TMM research, finding that agreement on TMM is important for team performance for criteria like client satisfaction, safety, decision quality, and winning in competition. In addition, shared TMMs characterize teams that remain strong and grow over time. TMMs can be clarified and strengthened by leader behavior and by team training. The shaded box presents more information.

Team Mental Models

Team Mental Models (TMMs) are schemas or understandings shared among members about (a) the task itself, including goals, procedures, strategies, and goal requirements; (b) available and appropriate tools and technology; and (c) the team and its members, e.g., individual skills, responsibilities, relationships, behaviors, and preferences about how the team should work (Kozlowski & Ilgen, 2006; Mohammed et al., 2010). Most TMM research has studied military tank or airplane crews, civilian airplane cockpit crews, or nuclear power plant teams, whose tasks often occur in episodes that are *mission critical*: consequences of error can be very serious. Some research has used sophisticated task simulations in laboratory settings but existing teams have also been studied as they work.

Teams with members similar in education or organizational level and experienced in group work have stronger TMMs (Mohammed et al., 2010). In addition, leadership and appropriate training are both important (Kozlowski & Ilgen, 2006). For example, the leader can guide a team to learn continually from its work by using a *pre-brief* focusing on goals, strategies, and learning opportunities. During work the leader monitors performance (intervening when necessary), and afterwards guides a debriefing that identifies any deficiencies or strengths and uses them to guide planning future work. In self-managing teams without a designated leader, the team can develop its own method for pre-briefing, monitoring and feedback, and debriefing to improve task and teamwork. This process emphasizes overcoming problems and improving teamwork, not assigning responsibility or accountability for problems.

Effective team training emphasizes communication among members, especially on new tasks. It may also involve *cross-training* in which members learn to do one another's jobs so they can better coordinate and provide back up when necessary. *Self-correction training* strengthens TMMs and subsequent performance by building skills in reviewing task episodes, identifying errors, feeding back information to team members, and planning for subsequent work (Kozlowski & Ilgen, 2006). Team development focusing on team interaction and coordination is also effective (Mohammed et al., 2010). Teams learn best by *doing* and then *analyzing* their work. The best training focuses squarely on the team's work by improving relevant patterns of interaction based on analysis of requirements for that task.

Such empirically guided team training is sometimes included in the category of "team building" (discussed in Chapter 14), along with activities and experiences that supposedly improve work group functioning. Kozlowski and Ilgen (2006) reported that evidence of effectiveness of team building in developing existing teams was "mixed at best" (p. 113), but subsequent meta-analyses have reached more optimistic conclusions (e.g., Klein et al., 2009). Team training and development activities should be based on behaviors, knowledge, or group processes that have or are likely to present problems for the team. The Steiner Model can help identify training needs of a particular team.

Resources

A team's success obviously depends upon whether it has the resources needed to accomplish its work. However, *distribution* of resources among members is also important and often related to internal diversity. People from different functional areas or educational backgrounds are likely to have non-overlapping information and different skill sets. Women and men of different ages, racio-ethnicities, family situations, organizational levels or areas can offer different perspectives and suggest how other constituencies (e.g., customers, other employees) might react to various proposals. On some tasks, such resource differences can help a team perform a complex task better. For example, one person may have needed technical knowledge while others have skills in organizing, writing, public speaking, or managing budgets. Compare this with a team whose members have similar skills and information, with no one person having all needed resources. If team process allows different information bases and skills to be expressed where they are most effective, the team is more likely to succeed.

Resources: Barriers and Solutions

Sometimes teams do not make use of information or skills available to them, as in *information sampling bias (collective information sampling;* Stasser & Titus, 1985). Teams tend to focus on information that members hold in common. With information sampling bias, information held by only one member is unlikely to be shared and benefits of a diverse group are undermined (see Argote, Gruenfeld, & Naquin, 2000, for a review). Another problem stems from status differences or conformity pressures. Critical information may never be shared if it is known only by members with lower status, lack of confidence, or unwillingness to deviate from an emerging consensus. The *Groupthink* process (Janis, 1972, 1982) discussed later illustrates this problem.

Several strategies can help teams make best use of information resources. The group or its leader can specifically ask for any aspect or information not yet considered. A *devil's advocate* can be assigned to argue against an emerging decision by identifying any flaws or shortcomings. Round-robin rules can encourage members to mention unduplicated information (without necessarily revealing their preferences). Team members can be assigned to investigate aspects of a decision situation and report to the group before discussion. Although these strategies do not assure a high-quality decision, they can assure that all available information is considered (Greitemeyer, Schulz-Hardt, Brodbeck, & Frey, 2006).

Resources: Transactive Memory

Transactive memory (TM; Wegner, 1986) is knowledge among members about task-relevant information and how it is distributed and will be used (Hollingshead, Gupta, Yoon, & Brandon, 2012). TM is stronger when members have more task-relevant knowledge individually and collectively, their knowledge is accurate, and they agree about how this knowledge is distributed and who are the experts in various areas. Stronger team TM systems are related to better group performance in continuing work teams as well as in *ad hoc* laboratory groups (Austin, 2003). Good TM seems especially important for diverse teams whose members may not be previously acquainted and may have inaccurate understandings of other members' expertise.

Motivation

Motivational processes concern members' interest in the task, others in the team, or working on *this* task with *this* particular team. Attraction to a team is often related to feelings of commitment and interest toward the work or to positive or negative feelings about other members. Attraction may also be based on positive or negative consequences the member expects from participation, e.g., skill development; prestige or status; opportunities for networking, learning, or career advancement; time involved; or opportunities foregone due to participation. Members may believe that membership will have positive or negative consequences for other constituencies, such as departmental colleagues.

A team is *cohesive* when its members are strongly attracted to the team and its members. Cohesive teams only sometimes perform better (Levi, 2017). Cohesion is most likely to be associated with good communication and performance when based on commitment to task and when team norms support high-quality work. However, cohesiveness can also bring strong conformity norms that impair good problem analysis and decision-making. Cohesiveness can also become a problem if team members focus time and energy excessively on non-task activities.

Team diversity can affect cohesiveness. One early study found age, sex, or race differences within a unit were associated with lower attachment to the organization (Tsui, Egan, & O'Reilly, 1992). Organizational commitment was lower for Whites when more racial minorities were in their unit, and for men in units with more women. However, commitment of racial minority individuals was unaffected by the presence of Whites, and women were actually more committed when there were more men. Said another way, members of the dominant group (Whites or males) were less committed when more racial minorities or women were present. Presence of lower status individuals may have lowered unit prestige for Whites and males.

Later studies of tenure or demographic diversity indicate that effects of diversity *per se* are strongly influenced by other factors such as inclusive behavior of leaders (e.g., Nishii & Mayer, 2009) and diversity climate in the organization (e.g., McKay et al., 2007). Such research reinforces the importance of good diversity management in maintaining motivation of employees to work effectively in their organizations and work units.

Motivation: Conflict

Conflict can reduce members' motivation, particularly if it is *relationship conflict* resulting from differences in values, preferences, personality, or less-than-positive past interactions (de Wit, Greer, & Jehn, 2012). Relationship conflict may arise in a diverse team as a result of unfamiliarity or anxiety about interacting with different others or from stereotypes or prejudices about demographic groups. Most researchers have concluded that relationship conflict is generally harmful to team productivity and satisfaction.

However, *task conflict* about the nature or importance of the work or its outcomes has been found to have both positive and negative effects (De Dreu & Weingart, 2003; de Wit et al., 2012). A third type, *process conflict*, concerns differences about procedures, leadership, or allocation of roles and responsibilities (Jehn & Bendersky, 2003). Task or process conflict can be helpful if they lead a team to a better strategy, more careful work and fewer errors, wider consideration of information, or more innovative decisions.

Effects of conflict are complex because positive or negative effects may occur on different outcomes (e.g., short-term vs. longer term, satisfaction of members vs. quality of product) or with timing of conflict in the task cycle (Jehn & Bendersky, 2003). Meta-analysis of 116 studies concluded that relationship and process conflict were generally but not always associated with lower outcomes (de Wit et al., 2012).

Diversity professionals should recognize that relationship-based conflict is most likely to impair team functioning and should be considered when forming teams and managing their process. On the other hand, conflict about task and how it should be done can sometimes lead to better outcomes, especially if mild (Todorova, Bear, & Weingart, 2014) and occurring in a context of psychological safety (Bradley, Postlethwaite, Klotz, Hamdani, & Brown, 2012). Early discussion of groundrules for management of conflict before it develops can sometimes be helpful.

Motivation: Social Loafing, Free-riding, and Social Facilitation

Motivational process losses can occur when some individuals do not contribute at the same level as others. Students who have participated in group projects on which everyone earns the same grade have likely experienced this phenomenon. *Social loafing* occurs when a member reduces effort on a team task and does not share equitably in work. It is most likely to occur when contributions of individual members are not separately identifiable, and when people and their work are not evaluated individually (Baron & Kerr, 2003). Social loafing is reduced or eliminated if the task is involving, attractive, or interesting; the team is highly cohesive and regard of teammates is important to members; and the team's goals for performance are high. *Free-riding* is a similar concept, but also implies that reduced effort occurs because a team member believes the group will be successful even without his or her contributions. Often the two processes cannot be distinguished.

When teammates are aware that someone is not contributing, serious problems can result even if overall performance or product quality is not affected. Those who have worked hard are likely to resent the social loafer and over time this may affect team cohesion and produce turnover. However, what appears to be social loafing may actually be a response to dominant or exclusionary behavior by some team members or inability to contribute due to other demands of family or work life, ill health, or other factors. If power or status differences occur within a diverse team, less influential members may be reluctant to contribute or may expect that their participation will not be valued. Some strategies for avoiding free-riding or social loafing are:

1. Team size no larger than necessary for the work;
2. Ground rules for participation and goal accomplishment set by consensus when the team is formed;
3. Open discussion of expectations for member contributions;

4. Matching member roles to areas of strength as much as possible;
5. Peer feedback process that identifies and evaluates individual contributions;
6. Direct attention to lack of participation to identify why it is occurring.
7. To the extent possible, making the task interesting and attractive and the team cohesive.

In contrast, *social facilitation* refers to *increased* motivation when work is done by people working together or in the presence of others (Zajonc, 1965). (Note: The GPM does not mention *process gains— only losses.*) Facilitation is most likely when behavior is easy or well-learned and increased arousal from others' presence has positive effects. However, if behavior is difficult or novel, increased arousal is likely to have negative performance effects. Thus social facilitation research suggests that people work alone to master new tasks, but together when they are experienced. Implications for diverse teams are unclear but presence of diverse others can produce increased arousal.

Motivation: Groupthink

Although this phenomenon involves faulty use of informational resources, its basis is actually a motivational change that sometimes occurs in decision-making teams when cohesiveness and conformity pressures are strong. Analysis of several well-known decision-making fiascoes led Janis (1972, 1982) to develop the concept of Groupthink, which he believed was a problem for cohesive teams with directive leaders and functioning in relative isolation from other perspectives. When Groupthink occurs, the team overestimates its correctness and morality, resists contradictory information, and develops strong conformity norms. As a result the team fails to engage in thorough examination of its preferred decision and alternatives, overlooks warning signs, and may make a faulty decision, sometimes with major negative consequences. In terms of the GPM, Groupthink is a process loss due to motivation. The shaded box presents eight symptoms of Groupthink identified by Janis (1982) and some recommendations for avoiding it.

Recognizing and Controlling Groupthink

Several disastrous decisions by high-level public sector teams or agencies were analyzed by Irving Janis (1972, 1982). These included the Pearl Harbor attack, management of the Viet Nam War, the Bay of Pigs invasion, and the Challenger explosion. The Groupthink concept has also been applied to recent disasters such as the 2010 explosion at BP's Deepwater Horizon well in the Gulf of Mexico (Corrigan, 2010). Symptoms of Groupthink identified by Janis (1972, 1982) include:

1. Illusion of invulnerability: mistaken sense of optimism and risk-taking;
2. Group rationalization: discounting of contrary information, failure to examine assumptions;
3. Belief in group morality: assuming that the group is right and moral, leading the group to ignore ethical and moral concerns;
4. Stereotyped views of opponent: derogatory ideas that underestimate out-groups;
5. Direct pressure: on dissenters, to maintain group unity;
6. Illusion of unanimity: underestimation of existing team disagreement;
7. Self-censorship: believing the team is in agreement, not sharing doubts;
8. *Mindguards*: members who enforce agreement and protect the team from contradictory information.

Several tactics have been suggested for preventing or overcoming Groupthink in decision-making groups. The leader can refrain from stating a preference. Each member can be advised to think critically about alternatives and voice any concerns or objections. A "devil's advocate" can be assigned to argue against proposals moving toward acceptance. Outside experts can be invited to meetings and invited to challenge proposals. The leader can guide a directed search for contradictory information or alternatives that have not been considered.

Do you recall decisions in your experience that showed symptoms of Groupthink? How did they turn out?

Groupthink provides a compelling narrative about how teams can fall into faulty decisions. Like most concepts, Groupthink has its critics and support from empirical research is mixed (e.g., Tetlock, Peterson, McGuire, Chang, & Feld, 1992; Aldag & Fuller, 1993; Paulus, 1998). A journal special issue devoted to evaluation of 25 years of Groupthink research (Turner & Pratkanis, 1998) was itself a case study in the popularity of this concept and ironically suggested that wide support for Groupthink may actually be a result of a Groupthink process! A related concept, *The Abilene Paradox* (Harvey, 1988), applies when a team moves in a particular direction despite unexpressed private disagreement of members. In both Groupthink and the Abilene Paradox, members' motivation to conform undercuts a team's ability to use its resources optimally. In diverse teams, those from underrepresented groups may be unlikely to contradict others.

Coordination

A team may have all resources needed for the task and be motivated to perform well, but if resources are not coordinated, results will be disappointing. Process may be chaotic, unnecessarily duplicative, unpleasant, or wasteful of time or contributions of members. Benefits of team diversity may be lost if people and subtasks are not well matched or if process prevents productive use of resources.

Coordination: Roles

As teams develop, *roles* evolve. These are collections of behaviors expected of people in certain positions. Sometimes roles are formal and publicly acknowledged (e.g., note taker, president). In other cases, roles develop informally as behavior patterns emerge during interaction. Early group dynamics research identified two types of roles: task and socio-emotional (Bales, 1950). In most groups, both were performed, but usually by two different people, called *task leaders* and *socio-emotional leaders*. A key factor in team coordination is matching people with roles in which they can be most effective. In demographically diverse teams, roles should not fall to people based on stereotypic assumptions (e.g., women make good secretaries), but rather on capability. Have you worked with someone in a role for which he or she was not well suited? What were the consequences?

Coordination: Leadership

Task and relationship dimensions identified years ago continue to be useful in understanding team process, particularly leadership. Team coordination usually includes things like managing internal communication and information flow, assigning and changing team member responsibilities, monitoring task progress and making adjustments when necessary, and communicating with constituencies outside the team. Leadership is a broader and overarching concept including not only coordination, but also other points in the Steiner GPM: obtaining and managing *resources*, defining and structuring the *task*, and attending to *motivation* of members so they will function productively and remain with the team. When the team is internally diverse, leadership is important for effective use of member resources and management of communication and conflict issues arising in heterogeneous teams.

Leadership in Internally Diverse Teams

Leadership has been viewed as a trait of individuals, a function carried out by more than one person in a team, or a set of behaviors that characterize the style of individual leaders. Comprehensive discussions of leadership theories and their empirical support are presented by Chemers (1997), Jex and Britt (2014), and Yukl (2012). Major theories are briefly summarized in Table 8.1. Because space does not permit complete discussion here, we focus on implications for successful management of diversity in teams. Leaders' role in moving organizations toward diversity competence is discussed in Chapter 14.

How does leadership relate to D&I? Theories in Table 8.1 were developed by White men studying other White men, in general without considering diversity (Chin, 2010). With the exception of Leader-Member Exchange (LMX, e.g., Nishii & Mayer, 2009), Transformational Leadership

Table 8.1 Leadership Theories

Trait Approach: Personal attributes distinguishing leaders from non-leaders.
• Considered leadership *role*, not leadership *success*.
• Considered those in leadership roles, not functional leaders.
• Inconsistent results; dominance, intelligence often found.
• Stogdill (1948).

Leader Behavior Approach: What successful leaders actually do.
• Considered behaviors and outcomes (e.g., job satisfaction, turnover).
• Bales (1950): Task, socio-emotional behaviors.
• Ohio State Research (Fleishman, Harris, & Burtt, 1955): Consideration, initiating structure.
• University of Michigan (Likert, 1961): Employee-centered, job-centered behaviors.
• Most leaders emphasize one more than the other.
• Methodological and measurement issues, inconsistent results. Specific behaviors do not predict outcomes in all situations (Jex & Britt, 2014).

Contingency Theories (Leadership Style): The most effective behavior is contingent upon situation.
• Fiedler (1967): Contingency or LPC (Least Preferred Co-worker) Theory. Three situational dimensions: (a) task structure, clarity; (b) leader-member relations; (c) leader position power. Task focus (low LPC) best with very favorable or very unfavorable situations. Person orientation (high LPC) best in intermediate situations.
  o Leaders can be trained to diagnose situation, modify approach or change situation.
  o Methodological and measurement critiques, e.g., what does LPC actually measure?
• House (1971, 1996): Path-Goal Theory. Effective leaders help workers understand goals and paths to them.
  o Four leadership styles: (a) directive; (b) supportive; (c) achievement-oriented (coaching or goal-setting); (d) participative.
  o Most effective style dependent on work environment (norms, task structure) and subordinates (ability and performance).

Leader-Member Exchange (LMX) Theory: Focus on quality of relationship between leader and each member (Graen, 1976).
• Leader-member relationship quality varies for different members.
• "In-group" (high LMX) characterized by trust, information, responsibility, discretion over work.
• "Out-group" (low LMX) characterized by more formal relationship, possibly less liking, trust, or capability.
• High LMX associated with job performance and satisfaction, organizational commitment, lower stress and turnover.

(continued)

Table 8.1 Leadership Theories *(continued)*

Cognitive Theories: Emphasis on how followers *think* of leaders and leadership.
- Attributional theories: What underlies attribution of leadership?
- Implicit Leadership Theory (Lord & Maher, 1991): Individual personal "theories" or prototypes of effective leadership affecting perception, memory, evaluation of leaders.
- Social Identity Theory of Leadership (Hogg, 2001): Leaders identified based on social categorization, development of depersonalized prototypes based on social identity, attribution of charisma to the leader.

Transformational/Charismatic Leadership: Emphasis on personal qualities and behavior of leaders who inspire and motivate others toward leader's vision.
- Distinguished from "transactional" leadership (rewarding others for behaving according to organizational rules and expectations).
- House (1977): personal characteristics (e.g., self-confidence and dominance), behaviors (e.g., modeling commitment, articulating goals), situational factors (e.g., stressful, non-routine situations).
- Bass (1985): four transformational factors: charisma, inspirational motivation, intellectual stimulation, individualized consideration. Two transactional factors: contingent reward, management by exception (leader acts only when something goes wrong).
- Conger and Kanungo (1987): four factors leading to attribution of charisma: difference between current status and leader's vision; innovative means of achieving change; leader's success in evaluating environmental resources and constraints; leader's impression management.

(e.g., Kearney & Gebert, 2009), and the Social Identity Theory of Leadership (Hogg, 2001; Hogg et al., 2005), they have not generally been applied to leadership in diverse work environments. This chapter reviews selected work and suggests possible applications.

Questions about leadership in diverse contexts have taken two forms. First, are there special requirements for successful diversity leadership in teams or organizations that include members from varied backgrounds? The second question, whether persons from different backgrounds face special challenges when aspiring to or finding themselves in leadership positions, is addressed in Chapter 13.

Implications from Earlier Theories

First, trait research showed that attributes of those in *leadership roles* differ from those of *successful leaders*. People come to leadership roles in many ways and only some of them are effective leaders. Furthermore, personal qualities alone do not predict success, and they describe only those who have attained leadership roles. Second, it is useful to study successful leaders' *behavior*, which to a great extent can be widely learned. Important leadership behaviors fall into two major categories, with focus on task or on interpersonal climate and relationships. Team diversity affects the range of resources brought by diverse members as well as patterns of attraction, respect, cooperation, or conflict among them. Third, successful behaviors are *contingent upon* (depend upon) aspects of a situation. Besides those identified by Fiedler (1967) and House (1971, 1996), other contingencies include mix of identity groups (e.g., gender, ethnicity) and diversity climate in team and organization. Fourth, it is important to consider the leader's relationship with individuals as well as the team as a whole. LMX research shows that even in relatively homogeneous teams, quality of leader-member relationships can be quite variable. In diverse teams, this is especially problematic if LMX quality is higher for those sharing the leader's identity group than for those with different backgrounds. Fifth, cognitive theories imply that leaders are identified and evaluated based on expectations and stereotypes of others as much as by their actual attributes, behavior, and accomplishments. Sixth, leadership involves exchanges or transactions between leaders and team members, but also an emotional connection that attracts and motivates followers. Development of transactional and transformational components may be affected by diverse backgrounds and expectations of team members.

Leadership in Diverse Social Contexts

Leadership can be understood as a property of relationships rather than an attribute of a person. This section draws heavily from a review by Chrobot-Mason, Ruderman, and Nishii (2013), who considered diversity leadership from perspectives of (a) leading self; (b) leading others; and (c) leading the organization. First, leading oneself implies continual development of understanding and claiming one's own social identity as well as identity as a leader. This involves understanding how diverse others will respond to the leader and how their reaction may be affected by their own social identities. In most work settings the leader prototype based in organizational culture and power structure is White (Rosette, Leonardelli, & Phillips, 2008) and male (e.g., Schein, 1973, 1975). Leader prototypicality is a challenge for anyone of non-dominant status: "claiming and being granted a leadership identity is much tougher for someone who is not of the dominant leader prototype" (Chrobot-Mason et al., 2013, p. 319).

Second, leading others becomes more challenging in a diverse team whose members may not share a common vision, value system, experience base, or language, and where influence and coordination are more difficult. Chrobot-Mason et al. (2013) suggested that as workplaces become more heterogeneous, demographic bases of social identity become intersected by other identities and commonalities with team members. Norms may change and nontraditional leaders may emerge as prototypical. High-quality LMX is more likely to develop when leader/subordinate dyads are demographically similar (e.g., Scandura & Lankau, 1996; Varma & Stroh, 2001). Recent empirical work has suggested that this selectivity may have negative consequences and that leaders should attempt to develop high-quality relationships with each member (Chrobot-Mason et al., 2013). Though difficult, this is consistent with the goal of workplace inclusion.

Third, leading the organization includes understanding costs of ignoring or mismanaging diversity, and communicating the importance of D&I based not only on external pressures but also on the leader's internal belief in its value. Active management of diversity-related tensions, including recognizing and apologizing for errors, is superior to hands-off or directive approaches in fostering a culture of inclusion. Leaders must effectively manage organizational faultlines, deal with diversity-related crises, put in place D&I-conscious HR policies, and promote a culture of learning from diversity.

Skills for Diversity Leadership

Two skill sets are (a) working with heterogeneous individuals and (b) working with the team as a whole (Chrobot-Mason et al., 2013). Working with others requires sensitivity to salient aspects of own and others' identities, communication of respect and confidence, and development of an inspiring vision. The leader must also build respectful relationships with individuals by acknowledging unique ways in which each can contribute. Leaders should provide intellectual challenge by encouraging consideration of better alternatives to usual procedures. Focus on individuals rather than categories is also important (Greer, Homan, De Hoogh, & Den Hartog, 2012).

Working with the group as a whole is illustrated by fostering collective goals. Also important are reducing negative attitudes and managing conflict across subgroups, encouraging positive attitudes toward members of other subgroups, and doing so while respecting identity differences among subgroups. Some suggestions are listed in the shaded box.

Leading across Differences

Social identity-based conflict should be expected in demographically variable teams. Anticipating this, leaders in diverse environments should develop strategies for dealing with it for the benefit of team and organization. According to Ruderman, Glover, Chrobot-Mason, and Ernst (2010), employees expect leaders to handle such situations but many times they do not, perhaps because they feel unprepared to respond effectively or are concerned about making matters worse. Suggestions for leaders include:

- Proactively study team and organizational situations to understand how social identity conflict may be expressed and the leader's role.
- Consistent with leader's values and organization's culture and mission, develop a clear message for those involved in conflict as well as the larger group.
- Develop and evaluate options for handling conflict in terms of required resources, liability, other concerns.
- Respond appropriately, monitor situation and respond further if needed.
- Learn from conflict situations; consider how they apply to future cases.
- Create norms and expectations to guide others' behavior in leader's absence.

Effective diversity leadership also requires *multicultural competence*, the knowledge and skill to diagnose diversity-based issues and manage them to a resolution satisfactory to those involved (Chrobot-Mason & Ruderman, 2004). Diversity leaders must understand relevant cultural differences and be self-aware in terms of their own biases and assumptions. In addition, they should possess four important skills: conflict management, interpersonal communication, feedback-seeking behavior, and role modeling.

Teams are all around us, not only in work organizations. In addition to athletic teams, boards of directors, committees for community organizations, and others, musical performing groups have been studied as a context for effective group and organizational processes. Some examples are discussed in the shaded box.

A Musical Model for Diversity Management

Musical ensembles combine diverse individual vocal or instrumental skills into a pleasing performance. Improvisational aspects of jazz as a metaphor for organizing were discussed in a special issue of the journal *Organization Science* (Meyer, Frost, & Weick, 1998). The Orpheus Chamber Orchestra, a famous 26-person conductorless and self-governing organization in New York City, was a model for effective self-managing teams (Lehman & Hackman, 2001; Hackman, 2002). Organizational psychologists Jex and Britt have written about the rock band Van Halen as illustration of the importance of managing organizational transitions as key members leave and are replaced (2008).

Diversity management in ensemble performance occurs in chamber ensembles. Chamber music is classical music written to be played in a small space such as a palace chamber or room. These ensembles include four to six performers with one instrumentalist for each musical part and no conductor. Typically the audience has a good view of each performer.

Musicians generally sit in a semicircle to project sound toward the audience and allow musicians to see and hear each other better. Without a conductor, musicians rely on knowledge of the music, extensive practice, and mutual interaction to assure that playing is well coordinated. Without any one of these, excellent performance would be impossible. Process losses, such as social loafing or poor communication, have immediate, obvious, and deleterious effects. When the group is really "on," the interplay of musicianship and emotional expression leads to a *fifth presence:* "one feels something beyond four individuals; the whole becomes more than the sum of the parts" (Blum, 1986, p. 168).

Advice from String Quartets

What can we learn about management of diversity from successful string quartets? These ideas are based on observation and reading about string quartets and interviews with musicians including the award-winning Miami String Quartet (Hays-Thomas, 2000).

Musicians report a passion for playing repertoire for four instruments, requiring that members truly work *together.* This is a team task, a superordinate goal, leading to the first point:

* *Care about something bigger than you.*

Second, musicianship is of the highest caliber. Individual members must be excellent at their separate parts. At work, diversity may be seen as an explanation for lack of success which is actually due to skill deficits on the part of individual members, suggesting:

* *Be very good at what you do.*

String players performing at very high levels are personally devoted to their work. Most train for many years before attaining success in a recognized ensemble. Generally they travel widely to perform and, unless they hold an academic appointment or other sponsorship, experience financial uncertainty. Constant practice and mastery of new music are required for success. Individual motivation must be very high, implying:

* *Love what you do.*

In the past, most string quartets consisted of four White men. Today it is more common for ensembles to include men and women and different ethnicities (most often, European or Asian ancestry). They use different instruments and play different parts, but in terms of musicality, motivation, and preparation they must be similar for the group to succeed. This suggests another point:

* *Be similar, yet different. Collaborate, don't assimilate.*

Effective communication is essential. Musicians must agree on what is to be played, interpretation, scheduling practice and performance, style of dress, and other critical things. During performance, cueing by one member (usually the first violin) is important. Excellent listening and continuous attention to each other's hands and fingers are critical. Performers know each other's playing so well that they can react spontaneously to their colleagues. However, long-standing ensembles also maintain a zone of individuality and separateness in areas outside their musical interactions. Sometimes they travel separately. An important point is:

* *Communicate well, but not too much. Some things are best left unsaid.*

For effective performance, musicians must agree on musical selections and interpretation of passages. The musical score guides performance, but many other decisions must be made, e.g., selecting an agent, deciding on rehearsal schedules and performance engagements, making travel arrangements, managing finances and taxes. In a four-member group, voting may sometimes lead to a tie. Processes are needed to make decisions and resolve disagreements yet protect everyone's interests. Another conclusion is:

- *Make a few good rules and follow them.*

Often in a quartet, the first violin opens and cues the others because of how the score is written; the audience may perceive that musician to be the "leader." The second violin is sometimes thought of as the *other violin* and less prestigious. However, like other parts, its role is critical to an excellent performance. Successful quartets, like successful teams, respect colleagues' opinions, habits, and skills. They recognize that at times someone must take the lead, but that leadership is sometimes shared among members. Thus another recommendation is:

- *Develop democratic flexibility.*

Compared to symphony players, ensemble musicians can be more creative and exert more influence over musical selections and performance. They can hear themselves play. Compared to solo performance, they alternate between first and supporting roles and have the group to back them up. Collectively, the quartet must manage not only internal relationships but also connect with audiences, representatives, and the larger musical world. A final suggestion for teams is:

- *See both inside and outside.*

Leading Effective Teams

Organizational psychologist and business consultant J. Richard Hackman studied groups as varied as athletic teams, airplane cockpit crews, manufacturing and top management teams, and musical groups. Comparison of symphony orchestras with conductors and the self-managing Orpheus Chamber Orchestra (e.g., Hackman & Oldham, 1980; Hackman, 1990) provided clues about the leader's (i.e., the conductor's) effects. Hackman developed a framework for how leaders can help teams perform their best: "work teams perform poorly when leaders have focused on the wrong things in designing and supporting them . . . when leaders focus on creating and sustaining (five conditions), teams really can perform superbly" (2002, p. ix).

According to Hackman (2002), effective teams must (a) meet or exceed client expectations for quality, quantity, and timeliness of output; (b) become more capable over time as members learn about others' capabilities and develop successful ways of working together; and (c) provide experience of learning and personal well-being for members. Five characteristics enable team effects, three of which are *core conditions* summarized in Figure 8.3.

What does this imply for managing diversity within teams? First, a *real team* should be more productive if its diversity is managed well. Members should grow in ability to work successfully with others who are different, and from others learn information and skill as well as effective ways of managing interpersonal relationships within the team. Contact with others who are different can be powerful in reducing prejudice if characterized by equal status contact, superordinate goals, cooperative relations, friendship potential, and support from norms or those in authority. In a

Characteristics of Effective Teams   Productive output
Growth as a team
Learning and fulfillment of team members

Conditions for Effectiveness
*A *real* team: team task, bounded membership, specified authority, stable membership
*Compelling direction: energizing, orienting, engaging
*Enabling Structure: design, core norms, appropriate composition
Supportive context: reward, information, and education structures; material resources
Expert coaching in teamwork: effort level, performance strategies, task knowledge and skill

*Core conditions for effectiveness

Figure 8.3 The Hackman Model of Effective Teams

diverse team, faultlines may threaten team cohesiveness and membership stability. Feeling lack of inclusion, those who are different may leave the team or reduce their participation.

Concerning the second enabling condition of *compelling direction*, the successful diversity leader is sensitive to how team diversity may affect member motivation and will work to make it a positive factor. Regarding *enabling structure*, team norms and composition (particularly mix of interpersonal and task skills) should be managed carefully and aligned with the task for the team to be effective.

Supportiveness may be experienced in various ways by different members depending on the level of information, education, or skill, all of which should be supplemented when needed. Consultation about managing interpersonal relations should be provided when appropriate. Finally, if membership on a diverse team is a new experience for team members, *expert coaching* may be needed at the beginning (to stimulate motivation) and midpoint (to examine and improve strategies for performance). The end of the task cycle provides an opportunity for the leader and members to experience diversity learning as they examine ways in which D&I were well or not well managed.

In Conclusion

This chapter has reviewed selected findings in group dynamics with implications for functioning of diverse teams. Subsequent chapters address issues relevant for management of D&I in various identity groups.

References

Aldag, R. J., & Fuller, S. R. (1993). Beyond fiasco: A reappraisal of the Groupthink phenomenon and a new model of group decision processes. *Psychological Bulletin, 113*, 533–552.

*Argote, L., Gruenfeld, D. H., & Naquin, C. (2000). Group learning in organizations. In M. E. Turner (Ed.), *Groups at work: Advances in theory and research* (pp. 369–412). Hillsdale, NJ: Erlbaum.

Austin, J. R. (2003). Transactive memory in organizational groups: The effects of content, consensus, specialization, and accuracy on group performance. *Journal of Applied Psychology, 88*, 866–878.

Bales, R. F. (1950). *Interaction process analysis: A method for the study of small groups.* Cambridge, MA: Addison-Wesley.

Baron, R. S., & Kerr, N. L. (2003). *Group process, group decision, group action.* Philadelphia, PA: Open University Press.

Bass, B. M. (1985). *Leadership and performance beyond expectations.* New York: Free Press.

*Bell, S. R., Villado, A. J., Lukasik, M. A., Belau, L., & Briggs, A. L. (2011). Getting specific about demographic diversity variable and team performance relationships: A meta-analysis. *Journal of Management, 37*, 709–743.

Blum, D. (1986). *The art of quartet playing: The Guarneri Quartet in conversation with David Blum.* New York: Alfred A. Knopf.

Bradley, B. H., Postlethwaite, B. E., Klotz, A. C., Hamdani, M. R., & Brown, K. G. (2012). Reaping the benefits of task conflict in teams: The critical role of team psychological safety climate. *Journal of Applied Psychology, 97,* 151–158.

Cannon-Bowers, J. A., & Salas, E. (1990). *Cognitive psychology and team training: Shared models in complex systems.* Paper presented at the annual meeting of the Society for Industrial and Organizational Psychology, Miami, FL.

Cantrill, J. A., Sibbald, B., & Buetow, S. (1996). The Delphi and nominal group techniques in health services research. *The International Journal of Pharmacy Practice, 4,* 67–74.

Chemers, M. M. (1997). *An integrative theory of leadership.* Mahwah, NJ: Lawrence Erlbaum Associates.

Chin, J. L. (2010). Introduction to the special issue on diversity and leadership. *American Psychologist, 65,* 150–156.

Chrobot-Mason, D., & Ruderman, M. N. (2004). Leadership in a diverse workplace. In M. S. Stockdale & F. J. Crosby (Eds.), *The psychology and management of workplace diversity* (pp. 100–121). Malden, MA: Blackwell Publishing Ltd.

*Chrobot-Mason, D., Ruderman, M. N., & Nishii, L. H. (2013). Leadership in a diverse workplace. In Q. M. Roberson (Ed.), *The Oxford handbook of diversity and work* (pp. 315–340). New York, NY: Oxford University Press.

Conger, J. A., & Kanungo, R. A. (1987). Towards a behavioral theory of charismatic leadership in organizational settings. *Academy of Management Review, 12,* 637–647.

Corrigan, T. (2010, August 27). So many warnings, so little action ahead of BP's Deepwater disaster. *The Telegraph.* Retrieved from www.telegraph.co.uk/finance/comment/tracycorrigan/7966587/So-many-warnings-so-little-action-ahead-of-BPs-Deepwater-disaster.html

De Dreu, C. K. W., & Weingart, L. R. (2003). Task versus relationship conflict. *Journal of Applied Psychology, 88,* 741–749.

de Wit, C. K., Greer, L. J., & Jehn, K. (2012). The paradox of intragroup conflict: A meta-analysis. *Journal of Applied Psychology, 97,* 360–390.

Diehl, M., & Stroebe, W. (1987). Productivity loss in brainstorming groups: Toward the solution of a riddle. *Journal of Personality and Social Psychology, 53,* 497–509.

Fiedler, F. E. (1967). *A theory of leadership effectiveness.* New York: McGraw-Hill.

Fleishman, E., Harris, E. F., & Burtt, H. E. (1955). *Leadership and supervision in industry.* Columbus, OH: Bureau of Educational Research, Ohio State University.

Graen, G. (1976). Role making processes within complex organizations. In M. D. Dunnette (Ed.), *Handbook of industrial and organizational psychology* (pp. 1202–1245). Chicago, IL: Rand McNally.

Greer, L. J., Homan, A. C., De Hoogh, A. H. B, & Den Hartog, D. N. (2012). Tainted visions: The effect of visionary leader behaviors and leader categorization tendencies on the financial performance of ethnically diverse teams. *Journal of Applied Psychology, 97,* 203–213.

Greitemeyer, T., Schulz-Hardt, S., Brodbeck, F. C., & Frey, D. (2006). Information sampling and group decision-making: The effects of an advocacy decision procedure and task experience. *Journal of Experimental Psychology: Applied, 12,* 31–42.

Hackman, J. R. (1987). The design of work teams. In J. W. Lorsch (Ed.), *Handbook of organizational behavior* (pp. 315–342). Englewood Cliffs, NJ: Prentice-Hall.

*Hackman, J. R. (Ed.) (1990). *Groups that work (and those that don't): Creating conditions for effective teamwork.* San Francisco, CA: Jossey-Bass Publishers.

*Hackman, J. R. (2002). *Leading teams: Setting the stage for great performances.* Boston, MA: Harvard Business School Press.

Hackman, J. R., & Oldham, G. R. (1980). *Work redesign.* Reading, MA: Addison-Wesley.

Harrison, D. A., Price, K. H., & Bell, M. P. (1998). Beyond relational demography: Time and the effects of surface- and deep-level diversity on work group cohesion. *Academy of Management Journal, 41,* 96–107.

Harrison, D. A., Price, K. H., Gavin, J. H., & Florey, A. T. (2002). Time, teams, and task performance: Changing effects of surface- and deep-level diversity on group functioning. *Academy of Management Journal, 45,* 1029–1045.

Harvey, J. B. (1988). The Abilene Paradox: The management of agreement. *Organizational Dynamics, 17*(1), 17–43.

Hays-Thomas, R. (2000). *The fifth voice: Lessons learned from the string quartet about the self-management of diversity.* Unpublished manuscript.

Hill, G. W. (1982). Group versus individual performance: Are N + 1 heads better than one? *Psychological Bulletin, 91,* 517–539.

*Hogg, M. A. (2001). A social identity theory of leadership. *Personality and Social Psychology Review, 5,* 184–200.

Hogg, M. A., Martin, R., Epitropaki, O., Mankad, A., Svensson, A., & Weeden, K. (2005). Effective leadership in salient groups: Revisiting Leader-Member Exchange Theory from the perspective of the Social Identity Theory of Leadership. *Personality and Social Psychology Bulletin, 31,* 991–1004.

Hollingshead, A. B., Gupta, N., Yoon, K., & Brandon, D. P. (2012). Transactive memory theory and teams: Past, present, and future. In E. Salas, S. M. Fiore, & M. P. Letsky (Eds.), *Theories of team cognition: Cross-disciplinary perspectives* (pp. 421–455). New York, NY: Routledge/Taylor & Francis Group.

Horwitz, S. K., & Horwitz, I. B. (2007). The effects of team diversity on team outcomes: A meta-analytic review of team demography. *Journal of Management, 33,* 987–1015.

House, R. J. (1971). A path-goal theory of leadership effectiveness. *Administrative Science Quarterly, 16,* 321–339.

House, R. J. (1977). A 1976 theory of charismatic leadership. In J. G. Hunt & L. L. Larson (Eds.), *Leadership: The cutting edge.* Carbondale, IL: Southern Illinois University Press.

House, R. J. (1996). Path-goal theory of leadership: Lessons, legacy, and a reformulated theory. *Leadership Quarterly, 7,* 323–352.

Ilgen, D. R., Hollenbeck, J. F., Johnson, M., & Jundt, D. (2005). Teams in organizations: From input-process-output models to IMOI models. *Annual Review of Psychology, 56,* 517–543.

Janis, I. L. (1972). *Victims of Groupthink.* New York: Houghton Mifflin.

*Janis, I. L. (1982). *Groupthink: Psychological studies of policy decisions and fiascoes.* New York: Houghton-Mifflin.

Jehn, K., A., & Bendersky, C. (2003). Intragroup conflict in organizations: A contingency perspective on the conflict-outcome relationship. *Research in Organizational Behavior, 25,* 187–242.

*Jex, S. M., & Britt, T. W. (2008, 2014). *Organizational psychology: A scientist-practitioner approach.* Hoboken, NJ: John Wiley & Sons, Inc.

Kearney, E., & Gebert, D. (2009). Managing diversity and enhancing team outcomes: The promise of transformational leadership. *Journal of Applied Psychology, 94,* 77–89.

Klein, C., DiazGranados, D., Salas, E., Le, H., Burke, C. S., Lyons, R., & Goodwin, G. F. (2009). Does team building work? *Small Group Research, 40,* 181–122.

*Kozlowski, S. W. J., & Ilgen, D. R. (2006). Enhancing the effectiveness of work groups and teams. *Psychological Science in the Public Interest, 7,* 77–124.

Laszlo, A., & Krippner, S. (1998). Systems theories: Their origins, foundations, and development. In J. S. Jordan (Ed.), *Systems theories and a priori aspects of perception* (pp. 47–74). Amsterdam: Elsevier.

Lehman, E. V., & Hackman, J. R. (2001). *The Orpheus Chamber Orchestra: Case and video.* Boston, MA: Kennedy School of Government, Harvard University.

*Levi, D. (2017). *Group dynamics for teams* (5th ed.). Los Angeles, CA: SAGE Publications.

Levine, J. M., & Moreland, R. L. (1990). Progress in small group research. *Annual Review of Psychology, 41,* 585–634.

Likert, R. (1961). *New patterns of management.* New York: McGraw-Hill.

Lord, R. G., & Maher, K. J. (1991). *Leadership and information processing: Linking perceptions and performance.* Boston, MA: Unwin-Hyman.

*Mannix, E., & Neale, M. A. (2005). What differences make a difference? The promise and reality of diverse teams in organizations. *Psychological Science in the Public Interest, 6,* 32–55.

McGrath, J. E. (1964). *Social psychology: A brief introduction.* New York: Holt.

McKay, P. F., Avery, D. R., Tonidandel, S., Morris, M. A., Hernandez, M., & Hebl, M. R. (2007). Racial differences in employee retention: Are diversity climate perceptions the key? *Personnel Psychology, 60,* 35–62.

Meyer, A., Frost, P. J., & Weick, K. E. (1998). The *Organization Science* jazz festival: Improvisation as a metaphor for organizing. *Organization Science, 9* (Special issue).

Mohammed, S., Ferzandi, L., & Hamilton, K. (2010). Metaphor no more: A 15-year review of the team mental model construct. *Journal of Management, 36,* 876–910.

Mullen, B., Johnson, C., & Salas, E. (1991). Productivity loss in brainstorming groups: A meta-analytic integration. *Basic and Applied Social Psychology, 12,* 3–23.

Nishii, L. H., & Mayer, D. M. (2009). Do inclusive leaders help to reduce turnover in diverse groups? The moderating role of leader-member exchange in the diversity to turnover relationship. *Journal of Applied Psychology, 94,* 1412–1426.

Osborn, A. F. (1957). *Applied imagination: Principles and procedures of creative problem-solving.* New York: Scribner.

Paulus, P. B. (1998). Developing consensus about Groupthink after all these years. *Organizational Behavior and Human Decision Processes, 73,* 362–374.

Rosette, A. S., Leonardelli, G. J., & Phillips, K. W. (2008). The White standard: Racial bias in leader categorization. *Journal of Applied Psychology, 93,* 758–777.

Ruderman, M. N., Glover, S., Chrobot-Mason, D., & Ernst, C. (2010). Leadership practices across social identity groups. In K. Hannum, B. B. McFeeters, & L. Booysen (Eds.), *Leading across differences* (pp. 95–114). San Francisco, CA: Pfieffer.

Scandura, T. A., & Lankau, M. J. (1996). Developing diverse leaders: A leader-member exchange approach. *Leadership Quarterly, 7*(2), 243–263.

Schein, V. E. (1973). The relationship between sex role stereotypes and requisite management characteristics. *Journal of Applied Psychology, 57,* 95–100.

Schein, V. E. (1975). The relationship between sex role stereotypes and requisite management characteristics among female managers. *Journal of Applied Psychology, 60,* 340–341.

Stasser, G., & Titus, W. (1985). Pooling of unshared information in group decision making: Biased information sampling during discussion. *Journal of Personality and Social Psychology, 48,* 1467–1478.

Steiner, I. D. (1972). *Group process and productivity.* New York, NY: Academic Press.

Stogdill, R. M. (1948). Personal factors associated with leadership: A survey of the literature. *Journal of Psychology, 25,* 35–71.

Tannenbaum, S. I., Mathieu, J. E., Salas, E., & Cohen, D. (2012). Teams are changing: Are research and practice evolving fast enough? *Industrial and Organizational Psychology, 5*(1), 2–24.

Taylor, D. W., Berry, P. C., & Block, C. H. (1958). Does group participation when using brainstorming facilitate or inhibit creative thinking? *Administrative Science Quarterly, 3,* 23–47.

Tetlock, P. E., Peterson, R. S., McGuire, C., Chang, S., & Feld, P. (1992). Assessing political group dynamics: A test of the Groupthink model. *Journal of Personality and Social Psychology, 63,* 403–425.

Thomas, D., & Ely, R. (1996). Making differences matter: A new paradigm for managing diversity. *Harvard Business Review, 74*(5), 79–90.

Thompson, J. D. (1967). *Organizations in action: Social science bases of administrative theory.* New York, NY: McGraw-Hill.

Todorova, G., Bear, J. B., & Weingart, L. R. (2014). Can conflict be energizing? A study of task conflict, positive emotions, and job satisfaction. *Journal of Applied Psychology, 99,* 451–467.

Tsui, A. S., Egan, T. D., & O'Reilly, C. A. III. (1992). Being different: Relational demography and organizational attachment. *Administrative Science Quarterly, 37,* 549–579.

*Turner, M. E., & Pratkanis, A. R. (Eds.) (1998). Special issue on Groupthink. *Organizational Behavior and Human Decision Processes, 73*(2–3).

Van de Ven, A., & Delbecq, A. L. (1971). Nominal versus interacting group process for committee decision-making effectiveness. *Academy of Management Journal, 14,* 203–212.

Van der Vegt, G. S., & Bunderson, J. S. (2005). Learning and performance in multidisciplinary teams: The importance of collective team identification. *Academy of Management Journal, 48,* 532–547.

Varma, A., & Stroh, L. K. (2001). The impact of same-sex LMX dyads on performance evaluations. *Human Resource Management, 40,* 309–320.

Wegner, D. M. (1986). Transactive memory: A contemporary analysis of the group mind. In B. Mullen & G. R. Goethals (Eds.), *Theories of group behavior* (pp. 185–205). New York: Springer-Verlag.

West, M. A., & Lyubovnikova, J. (2012). Real teams or pseudo teams? The changing landscape needs a better map. *Industrial and Organizational Psychology, 5*(2), 25–28.

Yukl, G. A. (2012). *Leadership in organizations.* Upper Saddle River, NJ: Prentice-Hall.

Zajonc, R. B. (1965). Social facilitation. *Science, 149,* 269–274.

* Recommended for advanced reading.

Chapter 9

Sex, Gender, and Work

In this text, the term "sex" refers to categories of people who are men or women. "Gender" refers to sociocultural meanings ascribed to these biological categories. *Roles* are expectations for behavior resulting from one's position in a society; they vary in clarity, breadth, and strength and are usually associated with *sanctions* or consequences that apply when someone follows or violates that role. Sanctions include acceptance, inclusion, and smooth interactions; or ostracism, rejection, avoidance, teasing or bullying, or just being considered odd. *Gender roles* are behaviors expected of women and men in a society, organization, or social unit such as a group or family. In some work organizations, both clear and subtle role expectations are associated with being male or female. Have you encountered someone whose sex was ambiguous based on appearance and behavior? If you felt anxious and wondered about the person, it was probably in part because you were unsure how to interact with them. Men are expected to be breadwinners and spend much time away from their families; women are expected to be primary caretakers for children or dependent parents and put family needs first. Women who act like men or men who act like women often elicit surprise, pity, pressure from others, or even the pressure from oneself that we call guilt.

Gender stereotypes are sets of characteristics thought to be typical for gender categories. Studies in the US show that males are generally considered *strong, aggressive*, and *good at math and science*; females are supposedly *emotional, weak*, and *good at reading and writing*. Many women and men do not correspond to these stereotypes. Sometimes there are no sanctions, but many issues in this chapter reflect stress, adaptation, confusion, or other reactions to changes in gender roles and stereotypes.

Historical Context

Employment patterns of women and men have been greatly influenced by the intersectionality of gender, social class, and ethnicity. What is often imagined today to be "traditional" actually represents only a small slice of middle- and upper-class White families in Western countries in the 19th and early 20th century. During and after the Industrial Revolution, the *ideology of separate spheres* developed among the English upper classes to justify roles that applied to wealthy women. As industrialization spread, work moved out of the home into factories and offices, men worked apart from their families, and it seemed wives should take over responsibilities at home and provide a domestic haven for their husbands. For a respectable married woman, employment was shameful because it implied the husband had failed at supporting the family (Padavic & Reskin, 2002). This ideology of course did not apply to women who were poor, immigrant, or former slaves.

Although paid work, laws, technology, and customs have changed dramatically in the last century, remnants of this view still linger in the contemporary social construction of gender and work. The belief that women's employment is secondary to that of their male partner reinforces the persistent gender gap in earnings and underlies devaluation of work done predominantly by women (e.g., teaching, child care), lack of employment benefits for part-time (PT) workers, belief that quality day care and other family supports are the responsibility of parents rather than employers or the government, and the structure of benefits paid to retirees under the Social Security system.

Two World Wars and other 20th-century events brought many changes to the labor force participation (LFP) of men and women. Women's employment pattern in the US changed in phases. Before 1920, employment of single women increased; many women left the labor force at marriage and did not return (Goldin, 1990, p. 16). After 1920, employment of married women grew, especially after World War II. Rosie the Riveter became a national icon as women were recruited into wartime manufacturing and other work to replace men (and some women) who were drawn into the military. The US government and employers such as Kaiser provided free or subsidized day care so that women could work in the war effort (National Park Service, n.d.; A. Parks, 2006; Oregon State Archives, 2008). With the War's end and the return of many servicemen, it was common for women to marry and withdraw (or be released) from paid employment. Some women were employed while single, left the labor force, and returned to paid employment as their children became older or as older women. However, others had experienced the economic and personal satisfactions of working outside the home and many of them, even married women, stayed in the workforce (Goldin, 1990, p. 13). Later in the 20th century, even married women with children were likely to be employed; in 1972, the proportion of women who were employed while their children were of school age first became larger than the proportion not employed (Bernard, 1974).

Labor Force Participation and Education

After 1900, women's LFP rate (percentage employed or looking for work) steadily increased to about 60% in 1999. In contrast, men's LFP rate has fluctuated around 70% to 80% since 1900 (Powell & Graves, 2003; US Bureau of Labor Statistics; USBLS, 2014). For both sexes, LFP fell during the 2008 recession. US Census Bureau (USCB) data show that in 1970, the US workforce was 62% male and only 38% female. This ratio changed steadily so that women were almost half (47%) of people employed or seeking employment in 2010 (USCB, n.d.). Patterns of occupational segregation reviewed in Chapter 4 show wide disparities in occupations, settings, and organizational levels for men and women (USCB, 2012).

Educational attainment, an important preparation for employment, also changed dramatically and differently over time for the two sexes. After World War II, many men returned to higher education, some earning advanced degrees through the GI Bill; undergraduate men outnumbered women by 2.3 to 1 (Francis, 2013). Since 1970, the number of bachelor's, masters, and doctoral degrees has increased dramatically for both sexes. For women, degree completion at all levels increased steadily over this 40-year period, but men's degree completion declined from the late 1970s until around 1990 (for doctorates, until 2005). Currently women complete more degrees at all levels than men. Women first earned the majority of bachelor's degrees in the early 1980s, master's degrees in the late 1980s, and doctoral degrees around 2005.

Factors accounting for these trends include increased financial return to education for women who moved beyond "traditional" women's careers; availability of reliable contraception; and behavioral/developmental factors related to men's lower high school completion rates and higher self-reported rates of arrests and school suspensions (Heckman & LaFontaine, 2010; National Center for Education Statistics, 2012; DiPrete & Buchmann, 2013; Francis, 2013). Laws (e.g., Civil Rights Act of 1964, Title IX of the Education Amendments of 1972) also increased women's access and aspirations.

Themes in the Study of Gender and Work

The literature on gender and work is very extensive, crosses several fields of study (e.g., psychology, sociology, economics, history, women's studies), and can only be sampled here as we try to understand gender as a dimension of D&I at work. Benschop (2006) identified several common themes in empirical research on gender and work, which appear in this chapter and Chapter 4. Two basic conceptual distinctions are (a) whether sexes should be seen as fundamentally different or the same in work-related attributes; and (b) separation of public (work) and private (home and non-work life) activities and concerns. Empirically, three major lines of research are (a) how women's choices are made and affect their work outcomes (men's choices are seldom studied); (b) how organizations are "gendered" by structures, formal policies, and informal procedures; and (c) how the labor market functions at the macro level to create and maintain sex segregation and differences in outcomes.

A gender frame illuminates how seemingly neutral processes actually create sex discrimination. For example, women's work became invisible when labor markets began placing higher value on activities performed outside the home. Labor of farm wives and those who kept boarding houses was not included in census calculations of LFP for adult married women in 1890, which led to underestimating women's economic contributions by about 10% (Goldin, 1990). Even today, the value of uncompensated work in the home is not included in calculations of Gross National Product or Social Security benefits. A married woman (or man) who spent adult working life tending home and family draws retirement benefits based on status as a dependent spouse, not as a working person. Skills and experience in home management and family care are generally not considered legitimate resumé-building activity.

Sex Similarities and Differences

For years, researchers have tried to separate gender stereotypes from objectively-verifiable differences relevant to work. This distinction is surprisingly difficult, partly because the measures themselves are easily affected by gendered expectations. For example, observers' evaluations of infants' behavior and attributes are affected more by what they are *told* is the infant's sex than by the *actual* sex. How "tall" is a woman who is 5'9?

In the 1980s psychologists began using *meta-analysis* to draw overall conclusions from the large body of sex-difference research. Social psychologist Alice Eagly conducted several meta-analyses of social behaviors and personality traits for which sex differences had been asserted and sufficient studies could be found. Her 1987 book explained these differences in terms of expectations resulting from different family and occupational roles held by men and women. For example, overall comparisons of altruistic behavior find men to be more "helpful" than women—but only when altruism or helping is defined and measured in terms of public interventions in potentially dangerous situations involving strangers, where societal expectations about men's assertiveness and bravery are relevant. When "helping" is measured with less public behaviors assisting family and friends, this apparent sex difference is reversed. In effect, the social construction of "altruism" in psychological research has been in terms of public heroics, not interpersonal generosity and support. Gender roles similarly affect conceptualization of work-related attributes such as leadership or supervision.

Social psychologist Janet Hyde also conducted meta-analyses of sex differences in cognitive variables such as mathematics and verbal abilities (e.g., Hyde, Fennema, & Lamon, 1990). Unlike the social and personality behaviors studied by Eagly, these abilities are often assessed in hiring and promotion and are not easily altered by applicants. Reliable sex differences would raise issues of adverse impact and discrimination. Hyde and Plant (1995) summarized results of many meta-analyses of sex differences and reported that one-quarter found no sex difference and another 35% found differences that were small. Only 13% of meta-analyses found large or very large sex differences. Overall, results showed that meta-analytic comparisons of sex differences yield small or no differences more often than are found in other areas of psychology (e.g., comparisons of various treatments with non-treated controls). What does this imply for diversity professionals?

First, in an employment setting the behavior and ability of an *individual* should be considered, not stereotypic expectations based on sex. Even in areas where reliable sex differences are found, this simply means that the *average* for males and females is different. In most cases data show much score overlap between distributions for females and males. Therefore, even knowing that men in general score higher on a particular ability tells us very little about how a particular man or woman will score.

Second, in hiring decisions one should avoid using predictors known to produce significant differences between sexes because this could be interpreted as adverse impact. In general, predictors should only be used if shown to be valid for the job in question; validity information is *essential* for measures that show adverse impact. When in doubt, seek other measures that do not have adverse impact.

Much Ado about Sex Differences

Legal restrictions on physical requirements, hours of work, and other aspects of work for women and children, called "protective laws," were enacted in response to abuses of workers during the Industrial Revolution. One effect was to exclude women from some desirable jobs and eligibility for overtime work. In the late 1960s, these protective laws were found unconstitutional in some places (Gutman, Koppes, & Vodanovich, 2011).

Minimum height and weight requirements often have adverse impact on women (and Hispanic or Asian men). The US Supreme Court in 1977 held that minimum height and weight requirements, if used *as a surrogate* for another job requirement such as strength, were not permissible because they excluded significantly more women than men (Southern Poverty Law Center, 2013). Height or weight requirements may be held illegal under federal law unless the employer can show how they are related to the job (EEOC, n.d.-e). Physical ability and personality tests pose a different dilemma. Reliable sex differences exist on many of these (Costa, Terracciano, & McCrae, 2001), and they are usually interpreted using gender-specific norms (Jones & Arnold, 2008).

Personality tests are sometimes included with other measures to reduce adverse impact of the composite score. Physical ability measures are probably valid for positions involving physical labor but may screen out many women, including those otherwise suited for particular jobs (Courtright, McCormick, Postlethwaite, Reeves, & Mount, 2013).

Are there sex differences in leadership? A simple question, but a complicated answer! First, meta-analysis (Eagly & Johnson, 1990) found that across studies (lab experiments, assessment studies, and field research in organizations), women led more democratically or participatively than men. Sexes did not differ in interpersonal vs. task-oriented styles in field research; in lab and assessment studies, women tended to be more interpersonally oriented. A second meta-analysis concluded that men were more likely to *emerge* as leaders of groups in both lab and field research, especially in short-term groups and those with tasks not requiring complicated interaction. Women were slightly more likely to emerge as socio-emotional leaders (Eagly & Karau, 1991). In a third meta-analysis of lab experiments, females' evaluations were somewhat lower than males', but especially so when the leadership style was a "masculine" one (e.g., directive), when the leader held a male-dominated role, or when evaluators were male (Eagly, Makhijani, & Klonsky, 1992). Males and females were equally effective as leaders (Eagly, Karau, & Makhijani, 1995). However, males were more effective in masculine roles, and when most leaders and followers were male. Females were more effective in less masculine situations. A final meta-analysis found small tendencies for women to lead in more transformational or charismatic styles whereas men led in transactional styles, responding to specific good behaviors or mistakes. Men also more often demonstrated *laissez faire* leadership, essentially non-leadership (Eagly, Johannesen-Schmidt, & van Engen, 2003). So, are there sex differences in leadership, due to sex, gender, situations, other people's behavior, the method of evaluating leadership? Probably the answer is "yes"!

One final point about the study of sex differences with respect to employment: even empirically reliable sex differences seem small in comparison with differences in occupations, pay and benefits, employment settings (nonprofit or government vs. private sector), positions in upper and top management, and election to public office. The wage gap still hovers around 25%, and women constitute:

- Only four Supreme Court justices in US history, three currently;
- Only 20% of US Senate;
- Only 19.3% of US House of Representatives;
- Only 4% of CEOs of 500 largest US companies (Center for American Women and Politics, 2016; Catalyst, 2016).

It seems unlikely that differences in these tangible employment outcomes can be justified by measurable differences in abilities between the sexes. Other factors must be important as well.

Sex Discrimination and Sexism

Sex discrimination is differential treatment based on sex, whether intentional or not. In a work environment, the term "sex discrimination" usually applies to employment decisions with negative consequences for the target, e.g., unfair denial of employment, lower pay, segregated job assignments, or lack of access to training or promotions. ("Sex" is used instead of "gender" because it appears in wording of Title VII.)

Ridgeway and England (2007) listed several causes of sex discrimination in employment. Primary causes are based in culturally-influenced behavior of *individuals* including stereotypes and beliefs about the status of women and men as well as in-group bias occurring in the context of gender segregation. Secondary causes are rooted in *institutional factors*: structures and practices of organizations. Three contextual changes were suggested to reduce gender-based inequity: holding people accountable for monitoring practices and explaining their decisions, using formal personnel procedures that limit subjectivity, and making gender less salient in the workplace by avoiding gender-typed work assignments and creating mixed-sex groups of peers. Similar changes should also reduce discrimination based on other factors such as racio-ethnicity.

Because of the gendered nature of organizations and common assumptions and habits relevant to gender roles, people often disagree about whether a particular action or decision constitutes inappropriate sex discrimination. The reason for differential treatment is not always clear, especially when there are many possible explanations in addition to sex. Unlike other forms of discrimination such as those based on ethnicity, disability, or sexual orientation, sex discrimination does not stem from lack of contact or information about out-group members. Cross-gender interactions occur frequently in family, social, and work environments, but in a different gender role context.

"Seeing" Discrimination

Discrimination is often difficult to recognize. There may be only one job opening or promotion, or limitations on salary allocations. Applicants have little comparative information about other candidates and often pay information is difficult to obtain and understand. Managers may be unaware of their own biases and are unlikely to explain them in ways that confirm intent to discriminate. Almost 50 years after Title VII, "smoking gun" memoranda, emails, or other documents showing discriminatory intent are extremely rare.

Potentially discriminatory decisions are usually made one at a time when someone is hired, evaluated, or promoted. Each unfavorable decision can be explained away by a nondiscriminatory reason. Faye Crosby and her colleagues showed the difficulty of detecting systematic discrimination with information presented on a case-by-case basis; aggregated data are much more persuasive (Crosby, Clayton, Alksnis, & Hemker, 1986; Twiss, Tabb, & Crosby, 1989). When systematic salary discrimination against women was embedded in information about a fictitious company, those viewing information one department at a time were less likely to detect discriminatory patterns than when data for all departments were presented in a table.

Salary inequity is particularly likely to go undetected when members of one group are underpaid relative to their qualifications (Rutte, Diekmann, Polzer, Crosby, & Messick, 1994). For example, participants readily identified cases in which one sex was paid more but had lower qualifications. However, discrimination was less noticeable when one sex was much better qualified but only slightly better paid. Discrimination is also difficult to detect when it favors a privileged group and the other group receives ordinary and appropriate treatment. Effects of subtle favoritism accumulate over time to create unfair advantage (Krieger, 2007).

A victim of discrimination might not see or label it as such due to *denial of personal discrimination* (Crosby, 1984), i.e., recognizing systematic discrimination against her *group*, but not against *herself*. People do not want to see themselves as victims and may believe in the *just world* (that the world is fair). Identifying personal discrimination seems to require judgment of who is to blame in a way that group discrimination does not, and blaming someone disrupts interpersonal relationships. Claiming one has been unfairly treated involves social costs such as avoidance by others (Kaiser & Miller, 2001). Finally, deciding that you have been unfairly treated implies you should do something about it!

Crosby concluded organizations should not rely on individuals to come forward with discrimination claims. Instead they should monitor personnel decisions for suspicious patterns and take corrective action if appropriate. Administrators should also scrutinize how qualifications and performance are measured. Are measures valid, or are they subject to bias and stereotypic assumptions? Crosby advised individuals to "complain, compare, and question" (1984, p. 383). Calmly pointing out apparently unfair circumstances may lead to corrective action that would not occur otherwise. Women (and others) can look for patterns, not explaining away results in individual cases; decision-makers should explain the basis for decisions that seem unfair.

Sexism refers to prejudicial attitudes based on sex, in a context of power and advantage privileging men (Cyrus, 1997, p. 239; Rothenberg, 2007, p.118). Thus sexism rests on an underlying assumption that women's status is inferior to men's. Sexist attitudes can be directed at men or at women. However, given the male-oriented power imbalance in most organizations, sexism directed at women is probably more common and more likely to cause distress. People who have not been the target of serious gender-based disadvantage may say or do things they think are funny or even polite; these may be interpreted differently by a woman who has personally experienced disparaging treatment or discrimination.

Sheryl Sandberg, now Chief Operating Officer of Facebook, described incidents in her early career that illustrate sexist remarks. When a manager wanted to speak with a male associate, he walked over to their desks. But to talk with Ms. Sandberg, he would shout at her "Sandberg, get over here!" (2013, p. 75). One client kept trying to fix Sandberg up with his son, mentioning this in front of other clients. Though intended as a compliment, this undermined her professionalism. He did not stop, despite her requests, until a senior manager told him to do so.

These verbal behaviors targeted a woman in a business setting in which the speaker seems to believe that the woman's sex justifies unprofessional treatment. An environment heavily laden with such sexist comments (each by itself seeming trivial), may be interpreted as a hostile environment and actually lead to serious sex discrimination. Thus in addition to the possible negative effects of such an environment on inclusion and performance of employees, the bottom-line reason for diversity professionals to be alert to sexism is organizational liability.

Klonoff and Landrine (1995) measured the occurrence of sexism in women's lives with their Schedule of Sexist Events. Sexism in the workplace was one of four types of events identified, in addition to sexism in distant relationships (e.g., salespeople), close relationships (e.g., family or partner), and sexist degradation (jokes, name-calling, unwanted sexual advances). Frequency of reported sexist events did not vary with women's education or social class. Sexist discrimination is associated with women's reports of physical and psychiatric symptoms over and above the effects of other stressors (Landrine, Klonoff, Gibbs, Manning, & Lund, 1995).

Ambivalent Sexism

If sexist attitudes about women were always negative, they might be easy to identify. However, sexism is complex and often involves both hostility and benevolence toward women. Glick and Fiske (1996) developed The Ambivalent Sexism Inventory (ASI) containing two separate but correlated subscales. *Hostile sexism* involves expression of negative beliefs and feelings toward women, who are perceived as trying to control men, e.g., by seeking favoritism. *Benevolent sexism*, in contrast, seems subjectively positive (for the speaker) but reflects stereotypic, subordinate, and restricted roles for women, e.g., by being cherished.

Glick and Fiske (2001) reviewed ASI research conducted in 19 countries and found a significant relationship between men's scores on hostile sexism and indexes of gender inequality (economic and political participation). Women rejected hostile sexism but often agreed with benevolent sexism, especially in cultures with higher gender inequality. (Similar results were found across 16 nations with the Ambivalence Toward Men Inventory; Glick & Fiske, 1999.) Both hostile and benevolent sexist ideologies support continued gender inequality in a society because the former punishes women who challenge existing norms and the latter rewards those who accept traditional roles and power relations (Glick & Fiske, 2001, 2007). Benevolent sexism is particularly destructive of gender equality because men do not experience it as prejudice and women may have difficulty objecting to being cared for and protected. Is a man just being polite when he compliments a female associate on her appearance, or helps her with a task she can do independently? Would he offer to help a man in the same situation? If she declines help, will she seem rude? Will he be offended?

Sexism, Old-fashioned and Modern

This framework assumes that expressions of prejudice have become more subtle over the last century and therefore scales used in older research would not effectively capture contemporary racism or sexism. Modern and Old-fashioned Sexism Scales were developed to measure this distinction (Swim, Aiken, Hall, & Hunter, 1995) by adapting items from the Modern Racism Scale (McConahay, 1986; see Chapter 10). Old-fashioned Sexism consists of agreement with traditional gender roles, stereotypes that women are less competent, and different treatment of the two sexes. Modern Sexism, in contrast, denies the continued existence of sex discrimination, reacts negatively to women's demands for equality, and rejects policies to improve women's opportunities and status.

Diversity professionals should attend to sexism because in subtle and overt forms it often affects working relationships. Persistent sexism may develop into a hostile environment or sex discrimination, a formal complaint or even a lawsuit. Intervention by someone in authority may be needed to explain why a particular behavior is unacceptable and must stop.

Younger people may not realize the magnitude of change in gender roles older co-workers have experienced and the ambiguity and anxiety that can result. Apparent personal animosity may actually reflect difficulty in adapting to a man or woman in an unfamiliar role, especially supervision. Leadership styles that work well for men may seem too directive or autocratic in women. In gender-typed cultures (e.g., some military environments, day care centers) this may be more obvious.

Often patterns of gender relations appropriate or accepted in family, romantic, or other social situations spill over into work environments. Employees may receive special assignments (e.g., planning parties, making coffee, organizing events) that are gender-role-consistent but not actually part of their jobs. Objections to such gendered assignments should be honored whenever possible without implying that an employee is overreacting or "too sensitive." Often subtle sexism is not intended to be offensive, but others may perceive their actions and comments as sexist. A third party may be able to defuse a situation tactfully if the parties are not able to do so.

The first person entering an occupation or job that is gender-typed for the other sex often meets with strong reactions. Women entering "men's" jobs have experienced discrimination, threats, harassment, or even sexual assault. Reports of sexual assault in the US military have risen dramatically at a time when women's roles in the armed services are expanding, even into combat. For another example of the military's adaptation to women in its ranks, see the shaded box.

Women in Combat

Women were banned from serving in thousands of combat and combat-related roles in the US military in 1994 (Carroll, 2013), but the nature of battle changed dramatically in later years. After 2001 over 280,000 women deployed to Iraq and Afghanistan, where battle lines were ill defined, no "front line" existed, and even those not in combat roles risked injury and death. In fact, over 150 women were killed and more than 800 wounded in these wars (Alemany, 2013; Myre, 2013). In December 2015 Secretary of Defense Carter announced that all combat jobs would be opened to women (Baldor, 2016).

In September 2012, female soldiers at Fort Campbell, KY, demonstrated new features of body armor especially designed for women's smaller and differently shaped torsos. Three years earlier, female soldiers had reported difficulty bending over, entering and exiting tight spaces, or placing rifles correctly ... "long plates inside the vests would rub against their hips and cut into their thighs when they sat down" (Hall, 2012). Protective vests that are too long prevent soldiers from picking up rifles from the ground and restrict mobility because plates dig into their sides. New properly sized body armor increases efficiency and performance as well as safety.

In many cases, apparent job requirements are actually due to equipment design. Very tall men in small automobiles and women who struggle to see above the steering wheel immediately understand this. Work environments and equipment for jobs that have always been held by men are designed for their typical sizes. In many cases, human factors scientists can redesign equipment for safe and efficient operation by people of different statures, which removes one barrier keeping women out of jobs they can do well.

Violations of the Law: Sex Discrimination and Harassment

Major federal laws addressing sex discrimination are the Equal Pay Act and Title VII of the Civil Rights Act of 1964. Also relevant is the Pregnancy Discrimination Act (PDA), a Title VII amendment clarifying that discrimination based on "pregnancy, childbirth, and related medical conditions" is a form of sex discrimination. Sexual harassment (SH) has also been interpreted by the Supreme Court as a type of sex discrimination actionable under Title VII (Gutman, Koppes, & Vodanovich, 2011). About one-third of EEOC charges each year allege sex discrimination of some type (n.d.-a); over 26,000 charges concerned sex discrimination in 2015 (n.d.-f). Finally, the Family and Medical Leave Act (FMLA) applies to situations involving gender roles and work.

Although laws and regulations have been effective in some cases in addressing sex discrimination, gender inequities remain in part due to limitations in current laws and enforcement strategies. These include (a) restriction in scope of some statutes such as EPA and FMLA; (b) differences between organizational policies and actual practices; and (c) cost of enforcing legal rights and difficulties in obtaining evidence that will satisfy the court (Rhode & Williams, 2007). In addition, because anti-discrimination laws and regulations are enforced by federal agencies, their impact has varied greatly as a function of the political climate (see Krieger, 2007, pp. 302–306).

Pay Discrimination

Often these charges are filed under both Title VII and the EPA because of different legal rules and penalties. The EEOC reported about 1,000 complaints annually (1997–2015) of sex discrimination under EPA (n.d.-d). Title VII wage discrimination complaints 2010–2015 numbered about 4,600–6,000 annually, only some of which involved sex discrimination (n.d.-h). Very few led to lawsuits; in 2015, EEOC reported only seven suits under EPA and 83 with Title VII claims (not all of which were based on sex or involved pay; n.d.-c). Each year, 50–60% of complaints were found to have "no reasonable cause" and about 10% were settled (n.d.-f).

In January 2010, the EEOC established an Equal Pay Enforcement Task Force and, in just over three years, secured more than $78 million on behalf of victims of sex-based wage discrimination. During this time, approximately 20,000 wage discrimination charges were filed of which 45% alleged sex-based discrimination (2013, June 10). Sample results were:

- 2014 settlement with Extended Stay Hotels, owner/operator of almost 700 US and Canadian hotels; alleged violations of EPA and Title VII included paying women less than men for equal work (EEOC, 2014); agreement to pay plaintiffs over $75,000, post notice of settlement, provide annual anti-discrimination training, report to EEOC on other wage discrimination claims.
- Amtrak Title VII settlement for $171,483 in suit alleging pay discrimination against a female *human resources regional director* (EEOC, 2011, November 10)!

Despite successes of EPA and Title VII in addressing some cases of sex discrimination in wages, their effect is limited by the requirement that sex-based differences can only be challenged when jobs in question are *the same or substantially equal* in content. A new law or a new interpretation of Title VII would be required to address pay inequity based on jobs of "comparable worth" but different content; this is a major factor in the continuing gender-based wage gap (Rhode & Williams, 2007). In addition, EPA has been interpreted by courts as applying only to blue-collar jobs which deal with "commodity-like" work and not to white-collar occupations (James, 2004; Rhode & Williams, 2007) although there is no such exemption in the Act itself. Beyond shortcomings in laws, other reasons for the gender wage gap for comparable work are discussed in Chapter 4. Two further illustrations related to gender roles are negotiation of initial salary and allocation of pay raises.

A meta-analysis by Stuhlmacher and Walters (1999) is often cited as showing that women are less successful pay negotiators than men. However, the authors found the overall difference favoring male negotiators was small by meta-analysis standards, and not all studies involved salary negotiations. They expressed concern "that conclusions regarding gender differences in negotiation are based on a small amount of contradictory evidence" (p. 654). Could the stereotype of women as less successful negotiators be stronger than the empirical results?

An extensive review documented complex ways in which gender stereotypes affect negotiating behavior and outcomes in different contexts (Kray & Thompson, 2005). Female negotiators' disadvantage depends on things like sex of negotiating partner, ethical concerns, whether the relationship will continue after negotiation ends, anticipated backlash against self-promoting and competitive behavior by women, and stereotype threat. Notably, when advocating for others' interests (advocacy negotiation), women achieve *equivalent or better* outcomes than men (Bowles, Babcock, & McGinn, 2005, Study 3; Amanatullah & Morris, 2010).

In every negotiation, there are at least two parties, and these results suggest that instead of "fixing the woman" we should consider the entire context, including how the other person behaves when negotiating with a woman. Women may negotiate in settings with lower pay scales or where negotiating latitude by the hiring authority is limited (e.g., public sector organizations with fixed pay scales). Gender differences are smaller when boundaries are clear and information about negotiating range is adequate (Bowles et al., 2005). Often salary negotiations are based on prior salary and, given the gender wage gap, women are often disadvantaged by lower prior salaries. Furthermore, women may set their target values too low if they use salaries of other women as their standard. Restricting job search to particular geographic areas, common for partners in dual-career relationships, also limits ability and willingness to negotiate; this probably affects women than men. For another popular view on women's salary negotiation, see the shaded box.

Negotiation

Management professor Linda Babcock discovered that male graduate students received some perks that seemed unavailable to female students. Upon investigation, she was told that "women just don't ask" (Babcock & Laschever, 2003, p. 1). This led to a research program and three books with Sara Laschever to help women learn to negotiate more effectively. Among their masters graduates, males' starting salaries were almost $4,000 or 7.6% higher on average than salaries of females. Among men, 57% had negotiated for more money but only 7% of women had done so, instead accepting the salary offered. Similar patterns appeared in a lab experiment, an online survey about negotiation experiences, and interviews. The authors concluded that many women overlook opportunities to improve offers by asking for what they want, resulting from socialization to focus on needs of others rather than themselves. Furthermore, gender role expectations lead others to offer and concede less to women. Small discrepancies in initial outcomes snowball over time in an *accumulation of disadvantage* when raises are awarded as percentage of current salary, and bonuses, stock options, pensions, and severance pay depend on salary.

Their second book, *Ask For It* (2008), describes a four-phase program of becoming a better negotiator, illustrated with examples from interviews. Phases include gathering background information, learning negotiation basics, developing strategies and plans, and role-playing. Appendix worksheets and a website provide helpful information and materials (Women don't ask, n.d.). Over a three-year period when students learned this material and read *Women Don't Ask*, Babcock found that similar percentages of men and women negotiated first job offers and starting salaries increased 14–16%. Students saw more opportunities for negotiation, both at work and at home.

A study of athletes showed that women did not differ from men on seeing opportunities to negotiate or sense of entitlement, but reported more apprehension about negotiation (Guthrie, Magyar, Eggert, & Kahn, 2009). This apprehension seems well founded based on experiments in which participants viewed salary negotiation scenarios or videos. Female candidates were penalized more than males in ratings of niceness and demandingness for attempting to negotiate, especially by male evaluators. When role-playing candidates in scenarios, females initiated negotiations less often than males, especially when negotiation was with a man (Bowles, Babcock, & Lai, 2006). Sandberg commented, "instead of blaming women for not negotiating more . . . recognize that women often have good cause to be reluctant to advocate for their own interests because doing so can easily backfire" (2013, p. 46).

Belliveau (2012) found that managers' gender stereotypes led them to pay women less than men, especially when they could explain in terms of the company's financial situation. Managers assumed women were relationship-oriented and placed a higher value on explanations as a substitute for pay in comparison to agentic men. Experienced decision-makers also believed that an explanation and apology for not providing a raise would be more persuasive with women.

D&I professionals should understand how gender bias can affect hiring authorities' decisions about salary offers and provide this information to those negotiating with new hires. Benefits to employers who save money by hiring women at lower rates than men must be balanced against unpleasant consequences when this inequity is discovered later. Cost in lower morale, loss of good employees, complaints and even litigation must be considered as well as any short-term savings.

Discrimination in Hiring and Promotion

Across all protected categories, in 2015 the EEOC reported over 3,000 Title VII charges of discriminatory assignments, more than 3,200 involving hiring, and over 4,300 dealing with promotion (n.d.-h). Thousands of other charges were filed (e.g., job classification, segregated facilities, seniority or severance pay, access to training). Many alleged sex discrimination.

In 2011 the EEOC settled a lawsuit brought against a Mississippi subsidiary of Forrest City Grocery Company, which was alleged to have denied sales positions to a female employee who was told the job was "too dangerous for a woman" and that she "would not be a good mother if she were on the road meeting customers." The EEOC also alleged she was paid less than men doing the same work. The EEOC tried unsuccessfully to reach settlement through conciliation. The company paid $125,000 to settle and agreed to EEOC monitoring, dissemination of employment policies to workers, and management training on sex discrimination (EEOC, 2011, August 24).

Although most sex discrimination complaints come from women, Title VII also protects men. Hooters restaurant and entertainment chain has been sued by men denied employment as waitstaff;

the restaurant claimed that being female is a *bona fide occupational qualification* (BFOQ) for hiring as a "Hooters Girl." A Chicago case was settled for $3.75 million when the chain agreed to add positions of bartender and host for which men would be eligible (Groos, 2009). In Corpus Christi, Nikolai Grushevski was told the restaurant would not hire men as waitstaff. In *Grushevski v. Texas Wings and Hooter's* it was noted that because Hooters prevented males from applying, there would be no record of failure to hire male applicants (McKenzie, 2015). A confidential settlement closed this case in 2009 (Brown, n.d.).

Males seldom allege sex discrimination in pay or in access to jobs. Why might this be? What reaction do you think men receive if they sue for access to a job such as a Hooter's server?

Pregnancy Discrimination

EEOC charge statistics show 250–300 Title VII charges each year involving maternity, and 10–20 in which the alleged discrimination involves paternity (EEOC, n.d.-h). The PDA requires pregnancy, childbirth, and related medical incapacitation be treated as other temporary disabling conditions (Society for Human Resource Management; SHRM, 2012b). Adverse employment actions based on pregnancy are considered sex discrimination. Major issues concern hiring, pregnancy and maternity leave, health insurance and fringe benefits (EEOC, 2008).

EEOC cases have been based on changed treatment on the job after the employee became pregnant. For example, Landau Uniform Company settled a suit which alleged frequent reprimands, multiple extensions of probationary period, unfair performance evaluations, instructions to others not to answer the pregnant employee's questions, and eventual termination after the employee complained to the supervisor's boss (Greenwald, 2013). In another case, an employee and her husband were terminated after they alleged Title VII pregnancy discrimination and ADA disability discrimination. The plaintiff's request for her workstation to be closer to the restroom was denied. Later, while she was on pregnancy leave, her job description was changed and she was terminated. The new father was subsequently terminated for complaining about his wife's treatment and for taking part in the EEOC's investigation. In the settlement, Engineering Documentation Systems agreed to hire an EEO consultant, conduct EEO training, implement systems and policies to deter and monitor complaints, pay $70,000 to the couple and remove any negative references from their employment records (EEOC, 2013, April 15). Other pregnancy discrimination complaints have been based on policies of laying off women after three months of pregnancy or demotions and schedule changes after notification of pregnancy.

Lactation Discrimination

The rate of breastfeeding in the US has risen to 77% and in 2010 almost 50% of children were still being breastfed by six months of age (Centers for Disease Control, 2013). By this time many new mothers will have returned to employment, making lactation a relevant workplace concern. The Court has determined that lactation discrimination violates the PDA (EEOC, 2013, May 31). A new mother alleged that her employer had fired her after she inquired about being able to pump breast milk after maternity leave. Eventually the *EEOC v. Houston Funding II LLC* case was settled with financial restitution to the mother (Barnes, 2014).

Under the Patient Protection and Affordable Care Act ("Obamacare"), employers of more than 50 persons must provide periodic breaks and a private environment for nursing mothers who express milk for one year after childbirth. Employers are not required to pay hourly employers for these break periods. Best practices relevant to lactation areas are described in the shaded box.

Employer Best Practices for Lactation Arrangements

Best practices for accommodating nursing mothers include two or three breaks of 15–20 minutes during a typical eight-hour day to express milk (Miller, 2012). Other recommendations include an advisory group to develop a plan to respond to employee needs, supervisor training, and an appropriate lactation room. This should be private (preferably with a lock), comfortable and relaxing (not a bathroom), with chair and a flat surface for the pump. Electrical outlet, sink, antiseptic wipes, and a small refrigerator should be provided. Temperature should be comfortable and a mirror, clock, and telephone are desirable. A US Office of Personnel Management (2013) brochure describes best practices for lactation programs in several federal agencies.

Breastfeeding mothers must express milk periodically to avoid discomfort and leaking unless the baby nurses at work. Typically a breast pump is used and milk is stored in small bags or bottles, refrigerated, and fed to the infant later. Expression of breast milk also permits the baby to be fed by someone else when mother is away.

Because breastfed babies are often more resistant to illness, lactation programs are associated with 77% reduction in mother's absence from work due to infant illness, and nursing mothers have half the one-day absences of non-nursing mothers. Thus, lactation programs are not just a way to be inclusive of new mothers—they are good for the bottom line as well!

Sexual Harassment

Reported experiences of SH include sexist comments, unwanted and persistent pressure for dates, vulgar comments and jokes, inappropriate touching and groping of body parts, discussions about sexual preferences, posting of sexually offensive pictures, equipment sabotage, leaving used condoms in a victim's locker, or pressure for sexual behavior, sometimes under threat of demotion or termination. Some could be misinterpreted, but others are clearly SH. For example, a church on Long Island, NY, agreed to pay over $190,000 to settle a SH and retaliation lawsuit in which two employees claimed the interim rector had subjected them to unwelcome advances, sexual remarks, touching, and kissing. One was fired after refusing sexual advances (EEOC, 2013, May 22).

SH, like sexism, can be patronizing or hostile. SH is more likely to occur in environments where gender balance is skewed and/or where the climate is highly sexualized or lacks professionalism (Cleveland, Stockdale, & Murphy, 2000). It may target men or women seen as "gender-deviant," for example women in traditionally male jobs or men who are physically small or seen as effeminate (Glick & Fiske, 2007). Victims of SH are most commonly young women, but women and men of differing age, marital status, and sexual orientation have also been victims. Perpetrators are more often men (Cleveland et al., 2000).

Employees have their own ideas about appropriate sexual, romantic, and flirtatious behavior, perhaps differing with generation, gender, or personal experiences. Expectations and norms about what is acceptable in non-work relationships can spill over into the work environment. Strict separation between work and social domains is no longer reasonable given changes in societal gender roles and the nature of contemporary work and careers. A survey of more than 7,000 full-time private sector employees by a professional polling firm found that nearly one-third reported marrying a co-worker and many had dated someone at a higher level in the organization, often their boss (CareerBuilder, 2012).

Men and women often interpret friendly interactions in different ways. Numerous studies show that men see women's friendly behavior as more "sexual" than women do, overestimate women's sexual interest, and are more accepting of sexual interactions in the workplace (reviewed by Cleveland et al., 2000, p. 53). In an environment of sexual "static," victims may be confused about the harasser's intent, not want to "make trouble," wonder what they may have done to elicit the behavior, or be unsure how to respond.

In the typical hierarchy men are likely to hold power and authority as a result of higher positions and roles supervising and evaluating others. Young inexperienced workers or those in vulnerable positions may find sexually-toned interactions especially problematic. They may not understand their rights as employees, that SH is inappropriate and illegal, and how to handle such situations. In the EEOC's *Youth@Work* initiative established in 2004, information about SH is prominent. This program provides online resources (case examples, videos, classroom guides) and sponsors events to educate young people about their rights and responsibilities (EEOC, 2012, September 19).

How common is SH? In a survey of over 460 SHRM members, more than one-third of respondents reported a SH claim in their organization within the last two years (SHRM, 2010). The EEOC reported about 7,000 SH charges filed each year since 2010, and including charges filed by state Fair Employment Practice Agencies, the total is over 11,000 yearly from 1997–2011 (EEOC, n.d.-b, n.d.-g). Although this total has dropped in the years since its high of 15,889 in fiscal year 1997, the number of complaints remains high. Women file about 85% of claims, but the percentage filed by men increased yearly from 1997 to 2012 (Cardinale, 2013; EEOC, n.d.-b, n.d.-g). This may be due to greater awareness of male victimization following the 1998 *Oncale v. Sundowner* and other decisions, reduced supervisory training, more acceptance of complaints from men who might formerly have resigned, and possible increases in SH of men (Rashby & Hutchinson, 2013).

SH in service industries (employing many women and young people) often occurs from customers or clients. Supervisors and the target of harassment may go along with the harassing behavior or respond passively out of fear of lost business. However, employers are required to protect employees from harassment by a third party. Gettman and Gelfand (2007) developed a tool for measuring Customer Sexual Harassment (CSH) and demonstrated that those who experienced it reported reduced job satisfaction. Given the frequency of CSH, this topic should receive further attention from managers and supervisors as well as researchers.

Victims experience harassment in various ways and their response does not reliably indicate the extent of harassment experienced. Stockdale (1996) suggested that victims' response depends on seriousness of harassment and on likelihood that various responses will lead to outcomes desired or feared by the victim (e.g., reduction in stress, stopping harassment, or punishment of harasser; or victim's fears of ostracism, job transfer or loss). Victim responses vary in activity and assertiveness. Some responses are *internally-focused* (e.g., trying to handle emotions and thoughts by ignoring, denying or reinterpreting, blaming oneself, or mentally detaching from the situation). Others are *externally-focused* (e.g., the most common response of avoiding the harasser, appeasing or deflecting with jokes or excuses, seeking social support, or assertive responses). The most common assertive response is directly communicating that the behavior is unwelcome and should stop. Infrequently, victims may also threaten to expose the harasser or attack him/her verbally or physically. The least common assertive response is using organizational policies or taking legal recourse with complaint or lawsuit (Fitzgerald, Swan, & Fischer, 1995).

Reviews of literature on consequences of SH (e.g., Hanisch, 1996; Cleveland et al., 2000) describe negative effects on both victim and organization. Individuals may experience difficulties with mental and physical health (e.g., depression, stress responses); worsened working conditions; poor concentration; and feelings about work leading to lower job effectiveness, job reassignment, resignation, termination (and costs of finding another job), or retirement. Costs to organizations include absenteeism, time and resources to deal with complaints and resolutions, legal and medical expenses, turnover, and lost productivity. The US Merit Systems Protection Board studies (1995) estimated the cost of SH to taxpayers in the millions of dollars over a two-year period.

Diversity professionals should be well informed about SH and the range of possible responses by victims and organizations. Employers should have a comprehensive policy concerning SH and handling of complaints. The shaded box includes suggestions for individuals and best practices for organizations on this topic.

Sexual Harassment—Recommendations

Dealing with SH is challenging because interests of three parties are involved: victim, alleged perpetrator, and employing organization. Conflict may exist between doing what is required to protect the organization and what seems in the interest of individual employees. SHRM has developed a sample policy covering prevention and management of SH complaints (SHRM, 2014). No policy exists that all workplaces must follow.

Recommendations based on concern for organizational liability include:

- Communicate clear written policy describing what constitutes SH, stating it is unacceptable and outlining procedures to follow when a SH allegation is made.
- Identify more than one route for complaints to provide for situations in which the harasser is the supervisor.
- Include warnings against retaliation and statements of limits of confidentiality.
- Promptly investigate and take timely corrective action (Beiner & O'Connor, 2007).
- Train employees on policy and how to respond if they are victim or observer of SH or the person to whom it is reported.

If questionable behavior (e.g., inappropriate joking) occurs, a manager or diversity professional should speak with employees privately or in a group to clarify why this can be offensive and should be avoided. This may reduce ambiguity and defuse borderline situations. Continuing problematic behaviors should be handled by organizational policies.

A manager receiving a report of SH must relay this information according to policy because allegations, if true, may be legal violations. Because complaints must be investigated, information cannot be kept completely confidential (which victims often request) but should be shared only on a "need to know" basis. Care must be taken to protect reputations and satisfactory working conditions for both complainant and person accused. Transferring the victim to another position may be perceived as punishment and should be avoided. Some victims say they just want the offending behavior to stop and do not want to "get anyone in trouble." One attorney suggested thinking how the person (and the manager) would respond if the reported misconduct were stealing rather than SH (Wilkie, 2013).

Training should include live or video scenarios based on real SH incidents (especially showing actual words and behavior); video of a harassment lawsuit deposition is recommended (Wilkie, 2013) to stress importance of rapid response to complaints. For the organization's protection, trainees should be required to sign a statement (kept in their personnel file) that they have received training and understand organizational SH policy. Surveys of HR professionals have shown that most organizations have policies in place and require training for employees, especially managers and supervisors (SHRM, 2010). Little is known about the quality or effectiveness of this training, which often stresses legal concerns. Unfortunately some employees may not take it seriously (Rashby & Hutchinson, 2013), perhaps because of awkwardness of public discussions of the topic.

If one is told that something said or done is offensive and is asked to stop, the person should stop and consider apologizing. Advice to victims and observers is more complex. Many employees are uncertain about boundaries between what is acceptable and SH. For example, off-color jokes could be considered harassment if the recipient tells the joke-teller they are unwanted and inappropriate and the jokes continue. However, if the recipient thinks the jokes are funny, laughs, and also behaves similarly, this situation would likely not be considered harassment. In fact, responding this way could be held against an employee who later complained. Therefore, employees are often advised to speak out when they find something offensive. A statement like "I am offended by jokes like that, and I would like you to stop telling them at work" can be helpful in stopping the behavior.

When offending behavior is more serious (e.g., physical contact, requests or demands for sexual favors), the target of harassment should make it clear the behavior is unwelcome. If it continues, the victim should follow organizational policy and report the problem promptly to the appropriate person. Failure to follow policy will weaken any later complaint or suit. However, often there are valid reasons why a victim is reluctant to do this: concern about retaliation by the person accused, damage to working relationships, ostracism by other employees, job transfer or demotion, loss of income and benefits, stress of involvement in a lengthy and contentious dispute, or damage to reputation. However, reporting sometimes leads to discovery that the harasser has targeted others as well. Victims should keep a contemporaneous dated written record of events and share events with a trusted confidante who can later verify the victim's statement if needed. Even when a victim decides not to report, this information may be important to support any later complaints by others. Employees should consult the EEOC as early as possible because of deadlines for filing a grievance if one later decides to take legal action (Beiner & O'Connor, 2007). In some cases, the SH target may find the best solution is to transfer jobs or resign. The organization loses due to costs of employee turnover, likelihood the problem may continue, and damage to employee morale.

Some assert that SH complaints are made by problem employees to "get back at" a manager or progress in one's career. Although this may happen occasionally, it is unlikely given emotional and other costs to the victim when a complaint is filed. To the contrary, most experts agree that complaints are filed in only a small percentage of cases and only a tiny percentage lead to legal action (Fitzgerald, Swan, & Fischer, 1995).

Good sources about SH are based on scholarly research and experience (Rowe, 1996; Beiner & O'Connor, 2007) as well as advice to individuals from advocacy or professional organizations (e.g., National Women's Law Center, 2000; SHRM, 2014) or employment law firms specializing in harassment and discrimination.

Reactions to Sexism and Discrimination

Employers should learn how to *prevent* discrimination and avoid lost productivity, turnover, and grievances or complaints that may lead to lawsuits. However, for diversity professionals it is also important to consider effects on victims of discrimination and harassment that contradict inclusion and positive working conditions and may lead to performance or attendance problems. Documented reactions to gender discrimination and harassment include anxiety, depression, anger, rumination and counterfactual thinking, sleep disturbance, and a variety of physical symptoms (e.g., headaches, gastrointestinal disorders, high blood pressure; Fitzgerald, 1993; Landrine et al., 1995; Klonoff, Landrine, & Campbell, 2000). Supervisors and managers should be aware of the link between negative treatment and reactions when considering how to deal with problems in an employee's work performance.

The *lack of fit* model (Heilman, 1983, 1995) predicts that gender discrimination will be most likely when incumbent sex does not fit the job stereotype based on sex of most incumbents and nature of job tasks. Women may be targets of such prejudice more often than men because men less often seek stereotypically female jobs due to their lower pay and status. Women (and others) who are *tokens*, i.e., in a tiny minority in a work setting, are more noticeable. Kanter (1977) identified three characteristics of tokens: (a) visibility, leading to pressures to perform well; (b) isolation, leading to stereotyped exaggeration of differences from majority group members; and (c) encapsulation or assignment to stereotyped roles. Kanter believed the solution was more women; some have suggested a "tipping point" or critical mass of about 15% representation. However, token men do not experience the same negative consequences, and increasing numbers alone may be insufficient because minorities' increased presence is likely to elicit backlash from the dominant group (Yoder, 1991). Research has shown that increasing the number of women scientists may still leave them isolated by differing responsibilities, lab locations, nationalities, or a toxic culture restricting their association (Etzkowitz, Kemelgor, & Uzzi, 2000). Complaints and grievances may also grow in response to backlash or because they feel empowered to try to correct mistreatment. Organizational culture and processes must also change to support all employees, regardless of demographic difference.

Coping in response to discrimination and harassment can be *appraisal-focused, emotion-focused,* or *problem-focused* (Cleveland et al., 2000, p. 345). Coping through appraisal involves redefining the situation ("It's a challenge that will make me stronger") or avoiding thoughts of the situation and directing energies elsewhere. Emotion-focused coping may involve controlling one's feelings, withdrawing emotionally and accepting the situation, sharing emotions with supportive others, or actively expressing anger and other feelings. Problem-focused coping includes seeking out further information, avoiding the source of discrimination, using organizational policies to address the problem, developing a plan to get out of the situation, or filing a formal grievance or lawsuit.

Self-silencing is reacting to sexist events by not speaking out or reacting in other overt ways (Swim, Eyssell, Murdoch, & Ferguson, 2010), consistent with prescriptive gender roles for women including conflict avoidance and prioritizing other's needs before one's own. Self-silencing can be understood in terms of a simple model of "ask, answer, announce" involving (a) noticing an event and recognizing it might be sexist; (b) deciding whether the event actually is sexist; and (c) deciding to confront the behavior. This general framework also applies to understanding reactions to other discriminatory events.

Situations differ greatly in terms of seriousness and pervasiveness of discrimination, e.g., whether it is potentially illegal, organization policies, victim resources and his or her vulnerability, and available alternatives. General recommendations cannot be made about the best strategy in a particular instance.

Other Challenging Issues

Romance, Dating, Marriage, and Nepotism

Views on romantic and other close relationships at work differ widely but overall are probably more liberal now than many years ago. Effects of these policies should be monitored to assure that a pattern of institutional discrimination does not develop in which job assignments and career progression of female (or male) employees are systematically harmed.

Organizations vary greatly in restricting, allowing, or encouraging employment of friends or relatives. *Anti-nepotism* policies restrict employment of members of the same family, including spouses, in order to reduce conflicts of interest and the appearance or reality of favoritism. In a "focused conflict of interest policy" (Howard, 2008), spouses or other family members may be employed but with restrictions (e.g., one cannot supervise another). Many organizations have employee referral programs in which employees receive incentives for referring new hires or require that applicants be "sponsored" by a current employee. Diversity professionals should consider implications of such practices for D&I and discrimination against members of a protected category (Gutman, 2012). Strict anti-nepotism policies more often restrict opportunities of women than men, and employees are most likely to refer others of the same ethnicity.

In employee surveys, between one-third and two-thirds reported that they have dated a work colleague (SHRM, 2011; CareerBuilder, 2012). Nevertheless, two-thirds of HR professionals surveyed by SHRM believed that office romances should be discouraged because they may result in SH claims, or in disrupted working relationships or retaliation in case of a breakup. The majority of HR staff and employees believed that relationships should not occur between supervisor and subordinate (M. Parks, 2006). Despite advice to employers to have a clear, reasonable policy in place to forestall problems (Tyler, 2008), over 70% of HR professionals reported that their organizations did not have such policies (M. Parks, 2006). Many romantic relationships continue or resolve amicably, but some create lowered morale or productivity, or perceptions of un-professionalism or of favoritism if one party is at a higher level. Retaliation, stalking, or SH claims may result if one party does not wish the relationship to end (Neal, 2008). In a widely cited case in California (*Miller v. Department of Corrections*, 2005) a warden was conducting sexual affairs with three different women under his supervision. Another correctional officer not involved in the relationships filed a successful claim of SH (Segal, 2006). The shaded box presents suggestions about organizational policies, including so-called "Love Contracts."

Policies on Consensual Relationships at Work

Should office romances be permitted, and if so, under what circumstances? In the past, organizations often had nepotism policies restricting employment by relatives or "no fraternization" policies prohibiting romantic relationships between employees. Depending upon state law, some such policies may be found to violate rights of privacy or assembly, and public opinion has shifted so that these relationships are more common and accepted.

Alternative policies were described by employment lawyer Barbara Neal (2008). First, an organization can prohibit workplace romances if this is legally permissible. This would probably be difficult to enforce and could encourage secrecy rather than prevent romances. Terminating employees for romantic relationships is undesirable for legal and morale reasons.

Second, employers could prohibit certain types of romantic relationships (e.g., when one party has supervisory authority over the other, the most common source of problems). Most feasible in large organizations where suitable job transfer for one party may be found, sometimes this creates hardship or difficulty in career progression or may lead to sex discrimination claims if the policy adversely affects mostly women.

Third, a Consensual Relationship Agreement, informally called a "Love Contract," could be used to avoid legal claims. However, this may seem overly intrusive to employees; those in the most troubling relationships (e.g., employees married to others) would be unlikely to come forward and sign an agreement. Any such contracts should be included in the employee handbook, widely communicated, and included in any training about SH.

If an organization decides to use these agreements, Neal advises including:

- Reference to SH policy and indication that employees understand it;
- Agreement that both people freely agree to the relationship and that neither will later allege that SH occurred before signing the agreement;

- Agreement that neither will seek or accept a supervisory position over the other, and that if this situation already exists, the supervisor will relinquish decision-making over the partner;
- Agreement that both parties concede the other can end the relationship at any time, and a statement that the organization will not retaliate against either person for doing so;
- Agreement that any disputes about the contract will be resolved through mediation, arbitration, or other internal dispute resolution procedures;
- A statement that professional behavior is expected at work and displays of affection are discouraged;
- Advice to consult an attorney before signing the contract.

Finally, an employer could use a less formal "Open Disclosure, No Stigma" policy. This alternative recognizes that workplace relationships are likely and should be treated like any other employee situation that could potentially cause difficulty at work. Employees are expected to inform supervisor or HR of a workplace romantic relationship and should be assured of confidentiality for doing so. This provides an opportunity for informal discussions about managing the relationship in the culture of that organization, workplace expressions of affection, restriction of personal communications at work (e.g., only directly and in person and not through company email). Employees should also understand there will be no reprisals for their choice to date a co-worker.

Three factors affect the likelihood of workplace romance: organization culture, individuals' attitudes about these relationships, and degree of job autonomy, with greater autonomy providing more opportunity for relationships. Types of workplace romances have been studied in addition to the impact of these relationships on participants, co-workers, and the organization (Cleveland et al., 2000, chapter 4).

Dual Careers and Dual Earners

During the 1970s and 1980s, as more women continued employment after marriage, researchers studied strategies for dual job-seeking and how couples with two demanding jobs managed family responsibilities (Rapoport & Rapoport, 1971; Bryson & Bryson, 1978). *Dual-earner* couples (both partners employed) were distinguished from *dual-career couples.* In these, both feel long-term commitment to full-time employment, with specialized professional preparation, continuity, progression over time, and neither partner considering one career automatically subordinate to the other. This gender-relevant distinction carries implications for families and organizations and represents one aspect of diversity among employees' families.

Job design, benefit structure, and institutionalized assumptions of many contemporary organizations assume a different family structure. This hypothetical family includes a primary breadwinner who is the *ideal worker*, available on-call 24/7 to respond to work demands and committed primarily to employer needs (Rhode & Williams, 2007). An "at-home" spouse or partner is primarily responsible for care of home, children, and other dependents, and if employed, accommodates those commitments to the other's primary work.

In heterosexual couples, this secondary partner is often the woman who, if employed, has a "job" instead of a career, follows her partner geographically if his job requires relocation, schedules work to accommodate family responsibilities, and/or works part-time instead of full-time. This pattern affects household dynamics and leads to reduced income and increased financial dependency for the woman due to employment discontinuities and jobs with lower pay. It may lead to greater financial insecurity in case of the partner's job loss, illness, disability, or death, or if divorce or separation occur (Rhode & Williams, 2007). In media and research, accommodation to the breadwinner's employment is usually cast as the woman's "choice," implying that women create their own disadvantage in terms of employment quality and compensation. However, economists Rose and Hartmann, expert analysts of the US gender wage gap, ask "when women 'choose' to spend more time out of the labor market taking care of children than their husbands do, how much of that choice is constrained by lack of affordable, good quality alternative care, women's lower pay or inferior working conditions on the job, their expectations that they won't be promoted anyway, or social norms in their kinship network, religious group, or community?" (2004, p. 2). Ways in which choices of men (partners/spouses, supervisors, managers) influence these patterns are seldom examined (Benschop, 2006).

Facebook's Sandberg (2013) described a young woman who asked advice about balancing work and family though she had no partner and no imminent plans for motherhood! Sandberg noted that many young women make self-limiting early career choices and accommodations based on a hypothetical future including family commitments. Do young men make initial career choices taking spouse and family into consideration, even before they exist?

The "ideal worker" also contradicts the reality of single or never-married adults caring for children. According to Census data analyzed by Catalyst (2012), of the 11–12 million households of single parents with children, over 85% are maintained by women, most employed. About 65% of single mothers with children under 18 and half of single mothers with children under three are employed. For fathers, about 75% of those with children under 18 and 80% of those with children under three are employed. These parents combine work with family but without support of an adult partner at home, and most live on one income.

In the hypothetical family of the "ideal worker," the breadwinner provides income sufficient for the household and any second earner's income is for "extras." However, providing for a family today often requires two incomes. Many stresses of contemporary employment can be seen as results of organizations' failure to change as rapidly as the structure and needs of employees' families. Some organizations and employment laws are changing to adapt to this new reality. Diversity professionals may be involved in administration of *family-friendly* programs aimed at the interface between demands of work, family, and other non-work commitments.

Part-time and Contingent Employment

Government agencies usually consider PT employment to be fewer than 35 hours per week. Over two-thirds (70%) of part-timers are women (Rose & Hartmann, 2004), who are also less likely to work year-round. In 2007, 88% said their reason was "noneconomic" or voluntary; about 25% listed child care/other family or personal obligations, and 30% were in school or training (Shaefer, 2009).

Contingent work refers to arrangements that are temporary, on-call and unpredictable, contracted, or for other reasons not part of the employer's core workforce; sometimes PT workers are considered contingent workers. Numerical estimates vary with definition, but some sources say this category includes up to 30–40% of the US workforce (Wilbanks, 2013). About 49% are women (slightly higher than their representation in the workforce). Over two-thirds of independent contractors and workers from contract companies are men, but 53% of temporary help agency workers are women. Some independent contractors are highly paid, e.g., in information technology, but in general PT and other contingent employees do not fare well in wages and benefits (USBLS, 2005).

Part-timers are seldom eligible for unemployment insurance (Lovell & Hill, 2001). The exclusion of PT employees from other benefits continues not due to legal restrictions but as an employer decision. Benefits can be pro-rated to time worked or in other ways made available to part-timers.

For example, in the Netherlands parental leave is available after 12 months, and pensions are provided for PT and temporary workers (United Nations, 2000).

Some employers, such as restaurants and fast food outlets, hire mostly contingent workers. Others use them on a large or small scale to respond to intermittent fluctuations in work (e.g., seasonal work such as agriculture or retail sales at holidays). Most universities have adjunct faculty who may be as qualified as longer-term and full-time faculty but are hired to teach by the course at dramatically lower rates of pay, usually without benefits. Typically men predominate in core faculty and women are overrepresented in contingent positions (non-tenure-earning, time-limited, and adjunct appointments).

How is this relevant to diversity? First, often large differences exist between contingent and core workers in compensation and benefits, access to company resources (e.g., parking, office space, recreation facilities), inclusion in communications and non-work events, and status. Diversity professionals should consider ways in which an appropriately inclusive environment for contingent employees can be maintained. Second, members of ethnic minorities and women are often overrepresented in contingent work categories. This may be due to employee qualifications or preferences, but in other situations demographic faultlines and employment status coincide to a degree that suggests unfair discrimination.

Domestic Violence (DV)

Among HR professionals, 19% reported that a DV situation had occurred in their organization within the past year (SHRM, 2013). Similar percentages of men and women experience intimate partner violence (IPV) but women report more violent and more frequent abuse (O'Leary-Kelly, Lean, Reeves, & Randel, 2008). In contrast, most victims of workplace IPV are women. Of the more than 18,000 IPV victims at work each year, approximately 13,000 acts are aimed at women and 70% of those who report being harassed at work by abusers are women (Swanberg & Logan, 2005, 2007). Homicide is the second leading cause of death for women at work, and 15–20% of these are committed by a current or former spouse/partner (Swanberg, Logan, & Macke, 2005). Employment gives a victim some sense of physical safety, autonomy, and normalcy, as well as financial resources that may be needed to leave the relationship; for the abuser, work-related attacks on a spouse/partner are a way of exerting power and control. Both may work in the same setting but in other cases the abuser knows where and when the victim can be found at work.

Two main types of work-related abuse are (a) disrupting or preventing work (e.g., hiding or destroying clothing, alarm clocks, or car keys, or cutting off the victim's hair); and (b) stalking (O'Leary-Kelly et al., 2008). Swanberg and Logan (2005) found that more than half of female victims did not disclose at work that they were victims of IPV due to shame, fear of losing employment, or the sense they could handle it themselves. Others had informed supervisors or managers (46%) or a co-worker (42%) for safety reasons (change of work location, help with screening calls) or because they believed people would learn about it from their behavior or if the abuser came to the workplace.

Costs of IPV to employers include abusers' use of company resources (vehicles, email, phone) to threaten or abuse, errors or accidents due to lack of concentration, lateness, or paid time off from work for arrests or court appearances (O'Leary-Kelly et al., 2008). Over 90% of victims reported inability to concentrate on work or perform job duties, and more than two-thirds reported lateness or job loss through termination or resignation ("Workplaces Respond," n.d.). Many victims lose all or part of their income and co-workers report being obligated to cover for victims by giving excuses for their absence, performing work that victims should have done, or feeling concern for their own safety at work (Corporate Alliance to End Partner Violence, CAEPV, 2002–2016).

IPV concerns D&I professionals because it disrupts work performance and inclusion, carries employer costs, and disproportionately affects female employees. When an otherwise satisfactory worker shows unusual absenteeism, tardiness, poor concentration, injuries, signs of emotional distress, or unwelcome contacts at work from a present or former partner, domestic abuse should be suspected. Employers should develop policies about handling IPV and should be aware that some state laws protect workplace rights of targets of domestic or sexual violence (SHRM, 2012a). Nevertheless, among 700 SHRM members surveyed, only about one-third of organizations reported policies on IPV and/or stalking. The larger the organization, the more likely such a policy existed, with 58% of very large organizations (over 25,000 employees) having such policies. Recommended policies are discussed in the shaded box.

Responding to Domestic Violence

Women's clothing firm Liz Claiborne Inc. (LCI) became a leader in the area of corporate responsibility for addressing IPV in the 1990s (O'Leary-Kelly, Lean, Reeves, & Randel, 2008). After an employee reported that she was a victim, executives realized that IPV had serious implications for the company and its predominantly female employees. Management formed a multidisciplinary team (executives from HR, corporate security, and legal counsel) and sought consultation from outside experts on DV. The approach had four important aspects: first, recognition that a multidisciplinary team was needed; second, extensive outreach to IPV experts; third, understanding what the company could and could not do. (For example, a major support for employees was referral to external resources for counseling.) The fourth aspect was investment in training throughout the organization so managers could better recognize and handle possible IPV incidents and employees would see their employer as a potential support in helping them deal with IPV. These initiatives are now seen as critical to core firm performance issues of employee well-being and retention (O'Leary-Kelly et al., 2008; SHRM, 2013).

CAEPV is a consortium of large corporations that have come together around IPV prevention and the role employers might play. Their "best practice" steps mirror LCI's work: forming a multidisciplinary team, developing company policy, training throughout the organization ("recognize, respond, refer"), and communicating extensively to build awareness (O'Leary-Kelly et al., 2008).

Recommendations from SHRM (2012a) include the following:

- Assure that managers learn to recognize signs of domestic abuse.
- Encourage use of company's Employee Assistance Program or community resources rather than attempt to counsel the employee.
- Consider obtaining a restraining order against the abuser if legal under state law.
- Provide abuser photos to security personnel and the employee's manager and limit or prohibit the person's access to premises.
- Consider additional security such as providing nearby parking and/or escort to transportation, screening calls, changing employee contact information, moving the work location, and using flexible or varied work hours.

An employer should not simply copy another organization's approach but instead should decide what is most appropriate for its workplace. No specific policies and procedures will work best in every setting (O'Leary-Kelly et al., 2008; CAEPV, 2009).

Mothers and Fathers

Parenthood is an important element of diversity and has different effects on employed men and women, beyond obvious physical changes accompanying pregnancy and childbirth. The concept of a "good father" does not conflict with that of the "ideal worker"; although fathers are away from children while at work, being a good provider is part of the father's role. Studies generally show that fathers are more successful at work than non-fathers (Correll, Benard, & Paik, 2007, Study 2; Wilde, Batchelder, & Ellwood, 2010). In fact, labor economists have identified a "marriage premium" for men's wages, with married men earning more than unmarried men.

In contrast, considerable evidence shows that motherhood has deleterious effects on women's employment and income (Sonfield, Hasstedt, Kavanaugh, & Anderson, 2013). Control of pregnancy is key to employment outcomes for women (see shaded box.) Women usually face a "family gap": lower wages for women with children. Correll et al. (2007) conducted laboratory and field experiments in which equivalent applications to an actual job advertisement differed only in applicant sex and parental status. In both studies, women without children were more favorably treated than mothers. In the field research, non-mothers received follow-up contacts from employers 2.1 times more frequently than mothers. In the laboratory experiment, women with children were perceived as less competent and committed than fathers; held to higher standards of performance and attendance; and rated as less promotable, less likely to be recommended for management, and less likely to receive a job offer (47% vs. 84%). Recommended starting salary if a job were offered was 7.4% lower for mothers! Although one explanation for gender and parental salary differences lies in different employment patterns for mothers who adjust their work to family needs, this research shows an additional factor: perceptions and expectations about mothers.

Women's Employment and Control of Pregnancy

Employment outcomes for women and their families are related to ability to control timing and number of pregnancies. An extensive review by the Guttmacher Institute found a clear relationship between women's employment patterns and availability of contraceptive methods (Sonfield, Hasstedt, Kavanaugh, & Anderson, 2013).

Women's employment, educational levels, and income increased following development of oral contraceptives and intrauterine devices in the 1960s and confirmation of married women's legal access to contraception in 1965 in *Griswold v. Connecticut*. Subsequently US women had fewer children before age 21 and labor force participation and hours worked per year increased significantly (Bailey, 2006). The typical dip in women's employment during their 20s relative to men shrunk dramatically and women's share of professional and managerial jobs grew to almost the level of men's (Bailey, Hershbein, & Miller, 2012). Young women also invested in more education which increased access to better-paying jobs. Labor force participation between 1979 and 2006 was higher for women who were older at the time of their first child and whose children were more widely spaced (Miller & Xiao, 1999). Number of children and amount of time children are present in the home were also important. Women who were primary caretakers spent fewer years in paid employment, with more years of reduced employment hours and lower annual compensation when employed (Rose & Hartmann, 2004). The gender wage gap began shrinking as well. About 40 cents per dollar in the 1960s, it fell to about 25 cents around 2000 and continues around that level (Hartmann, Hegewisch, Liepmann, & Williams, 2010). Bailey et al. (2012) estimated that early access to oral contraception accounted for about 10% of this drop in the gender gap during the 1980s and 30% in the 1990s. Ability to control childbearing is clearly critical to gender equity in employment.

The Stereotype Content Model (Fiske, Xu, Cuddy, & Glick, 1999) proposed that stereotypes can be understood in terms of two dimensions of *competence* and *warmth*. Groups seen as low competence and low warmth usually elicit reactions of antipathy and dislike, and those perceived as high on both dimensions are the object of pride and admiration. *Female professionals* are rated as high competence but low warmth, leading to dislike and envy (Fiske, Cuddy, Glick, & Xu, 2002). When college undergraduates evaluated possible consultants, ratings varied with sex and parental status of consultants. The study concluded that women consultants with children were seen as less competent but warmer than childless women. In contrast, men were seen as competent regardless of parental status, but fathers seemed warmer. Because recommendations to hire, promote, or train were related to competence judgments (not warmth), consultant-mothers were least preferred (Cuddy, Fiske, & Glick, 2004).

In actual work settings part of the gender gap is a wage penalty against mothers. Rhode and Williams (2007) reviewed empirical studies, most using Census and other publicly available data sets with large sample sizes and detailed information about men, women, and employment. They found a *motherhood penalty* (non-mothers vs. women with at least one child at home) of 4–7% per child in the US; this had not declined from the mid-1970s to the late 1990s. Cross-country studies show this penalty is largest in Korea and Japan, and very small in Italy and Spain (Organisation for Economic Co-operation and Development, 2012). Seniority and job experience (including PT work) explain only one-third of the difference between mothers and other women and job characteristics explain very little (Budig & England, 2001). Researchers speculate that most of the motherhood penalty is due to employer discrimination against mothers based on bias or expectations about work behavior, or to "reduced productivity" (from distraction or exhaustion at work, or sick leave taken to deal with children's illnesses).

Caretaking and Employment

Part of the motherhood penalty seems related only indirectly to sex. For example, low status accrues to caretaking roles in our society (Ridgeway & Correll, 2004). Those paid to care for others such as children or the elderly, or those who perform the most personal and direct caretaking in hospitals are generally poorly paid whether male or female. In job evaluations, nurturance requirements are associated with lower job worth points and wages (England, 1992). Nurturing jobs are often filled by women.

In our culture a "good mother" puts her children first and is always available to them; this contradicts the ideal worker's responsibility to employers first, 24/7. This contradiction underlies the common belief that a woman cannot be both an outstanding employee and a good mother (Rhode & Williams, 2007) and implies that employed mothers will be unreliable in performance or attendance; many workplaces make little allowance for employees to provide care to children or elderly relatives. Social class bias is embedded in this assumption; the "good mother" idea seems to apply only to women of middle and upper socioeconomic status. Federal law requires mothers receiving public assistance to be employed or in school/training, whether or not affordable day care is available.

Part of the motherhood penalty is probably a "flexibility stigma" against those who use workplace flexibility arrangements (e.g., flexible hours, compressed work weeks, job sharing, PT work). These are available in many workplaces but often not widely used due to fear of repercussions or the view that "face time" at work is important for career success. Use of such accommodations is often associated with wage penalties, marginalization, assignment to less desirable work, reduced performance evaluations, and fewer promotions (Williams, Blair-Loy, & Berdahl, 2013) and is sometimes a factor in women's decisions to suspend their careers (Stone & Hernandez, 2013).

A recent development in employment law is "family responsibility discrimination" (FRD) or discrimination against those with responsibilities for family caregiving (Center for WorkLife

Law, n.d.). This legal theory seeks to apply federal and state anti-discrimination law in defining caregiver discrimination as a form of sex discrimination based on gender stereotypes, applicable to both men and women. Three trends have been identified in these claims: changes instituted by new supervisors (e.g., withdrawing prior flexible work arrangements); discrimination occurring with a second child; and situations involving elder care (Ludden, 2010). Such complaints increased almost 400% in the decade before 2008, and about two-thirds of these cases were successful (Williams & Cuddy, 2012). The average verdict was $570,000 with over 20 awards above $1 million. The EEOC has developed guidance on discriminatory treatment of workers with responsibilities for caregiving (2007a, 2007b).

In Sum

Many organizations recognize diversity in family structures and some accommodate needs of families. Concerns of the single adult with no dependents should not be overlooked. Diversity professionals should work toward equitable employment arrangements supporting effective participation by all employees. If women and other demographic minorities are disproportionately represented in contingent positions, this pattern should be questioned. Consideration should be given to pro-rated or proportional benefits for PT workers.

Work, Family, and Non-Work Life

The major federal legislation dealing with work and family obligations is the FMLA, which is limited in coverage and benefits. Those not covered include: (a) employees of small businesses (below 50 employees); (b) those employed less than 12 months; (c) seasonal or temporary workers; and (d) PT employees working fewer than 1,250 hours in 12 months. The 12 weeks leave available to covered employees is *unpaid*. Required family leave is not available to care for parents-in-law or unmarried domestic partners. In 2014 only three states (CA, NJ, RI) offered paid family and medical leave financed through a payroll tax (National Conference of State Legislatures, 2014).

Conflict and Facilitation

Most employees recognize the feeling of *work-life conflict (WLC, also Work-Family or WFC)*, the stress experienced from trying to handle responsibilities at home and at work. Higher conflict levels are associated with lower satisfaction with work, life, or both (Kossek & Ozeki, 1998). Three types of WLC have been identified: (a) *time-based* from limited time or schedule conflicts; (b) *strain-based*, when work stresses carry over into home or vice versa; and (c) *behavior-based*, when behaviors needed in one domain contradict roles in the other (Greenhaus & Beutell, 1985). For example, a manager may be directive or emotionally controlled at work and have difficulty being more egalitarian, open, or emotionally communicative with family members. Most programs developed to address WLC focus on either time- or strain-based conflict.

Sometimes one role provides resources, contacts, experiences, or skills that actually *improve* role performance in other areas. Managerial skills may be applied to family or community settings. Time management or prioritizing skills developed at home may be useful at work. These illustrate *work-family* or *work-life facilitation* (also *work-life enhancement* or *enrichment*).

Four processes occur in conflict and facilitation (Konrad, 2013). *Spillover* occurs when feelings or behavior from one area extend into the other domain, and *segmentation* refers to compartmentalization by actively separating the two domains. In *compensation*, one domain makes up for what may be lacking in the other. Finally, *resource drain* describes negative effects of moving energy, time, or other resources from one area to invest them in another. Studies of conflict have generally found support for the resource drain model and facilitation studies frequently find positive spillover, although the other processes cannot be ruled out.

WLC research relies on participants' ratings of conflict or facilitation levels and outcomes (e.g., satisfaction with life, work, family concerns). Because research is correlational, cause and effect cannot be inferred. Predominant patterns and explanations for the sample as a whole may not apply equally well to individual cases. Researchers are better informed about what produces WLC than about how employees cope or effects of various workplace policies on employee well-being (Eby, Casper, Lockwood, Bordeaux, & Brinley, 2005). See the shaded box.

The Practical Side of Work-Family Conflict

How can conflict involving work and non-work roles be managed? Research shows:

- Three major patterns of reported coping: (a) emotional, by increasing resources; (b) cognitive, by prioritizing home and work responsibilities; and (c) behavioral by withdrawing from social interactions to manage time (Neale & Hammer, 2009). Emotional coping (e.g., reaching out to others for moral support) and cognitive coping (e.g., scheduling) were associated with measures of well-being. Withdrawing from others freed up time but affected well-being negatively.

- External strategies (e.g., acting to deal with source of stress) were helpful, while internal strategies (e.g., trying to control emotions or change expectations), were likely to increase distress or have little effect. Withdrawal from others was generally unhelpful (Morganson, Culbertson, & Matthews, 2013). Long- and short-term effects may differ and people often choose multiple strategies.

- Employees are better able to deal with WFC when they have a family-supportive supervisor and work culture. Work-Life Job Analysis (WL JA; Morganson, Major, & Bauer, 2009) can help determine factors that help or hinder fulfillment of non-work roles. Results can identify specific aspects of jobs that students, trainees, or applicants might wish to seek or avoid. Job coaches or mentors could help employees develop ways to reduce WFC, and organizations could modify jobs or develop work-life benefits best suited to particular job characteristics.

Research has focused on what individuals and organizations can do to manage the work/life interface. Social policy, a third focus for action, reminds us that other countries approach these experiences in varied ways.

What Organizations Can Do

Work-Family (W-F) benefits can improve inclusion of employees with diverse family structures. These include flexible work hours or compressed work weeks, flexplace or telecommuting, leaves (especially paid leaves) for maternity/paternity or family needs, health insurance coverage, temporary reductions in hours, job sharing, and referrals about or access to child or elder care services. In addition, culture and/or behavior of supervisors can support informal adjustments for family responsibilities, even in the absence of formal organizational policies. W-F benefits are discussed in more detail in Chapter 13.

Families, Gender, and D&I

Gender and work/life/family issues are strongly linked. Furthermore, families are diverse, with many employees responsible for elderly, disabled, or chronically ill family members. Some employees are partnered and some are not. Children may have one parent or two, and some have same-sex parents. Leslie and Manchester (2011) have suggested that work/life policies should be administered by organizational effectiveness departments to convey that these policies are a response to family needs and aimed at everyone, regardless of sex, in the interest of reduced conflict and enhanced work performance. Regardless of where these programs are administered, work/life policies are part of managing diversity and improving inclusion.

References

Alemany, J. (2013, June 28). *Military readies to integrate women into combat.* Retrieved from www.cbsnews.com/8301-201_162-57591624/military-readies-to-integrate-women-into-combat/

Amanatullah, E. T., & Morris, M. W. (2010). Negotiating gender roles: Gender differences in assertive negotiating are mediated by women's fear of backlash and attenuated when negotiating on behalf of others. *Journal of Personality and Social Psychology, 98,* 256–267.

Babcock, L., & Laschever, S. (2003). *Women don't ask: Negotiation and the gender divide.* Princeton, NJ: Princeton University Press.

Babcock, L., & Laschever, S. (2008). *Ask for it: How women can use the power of negotiation to get what they really want.* New York, NY: Bantam Books.

Bailey, J. M. (2006). More power to the pill: The impact of contraceptive freedom on women's life cycle labor supply. *Quarterly Journal of Economics, 121,* 289–320.

Bailey, M. J., Hershbein, B., & Miller, A. R. (2012). The opt-in revolution? Contraception and the gender gap in wages. *American Economic Journal: Applied Economics, 4,* 225–254.

Baldor, L. C. (2016, March 4). Military beginning to recruit women for combat jobs. *PBS Newshour.* Retrieved from www.pbs.org/newshour/rundown/military-beginning-to-recruit-women-for-combat-jobs/

Barnes, P. (2014, May 13). *Settlement is Mother's Day gift to working mothers.* Retrieved from http://abusergoestowork.com/tag/eeoc-v-houston-funding-ii/

Beiner, T. M., & O'Connor, M. (2007). When an individual is the victim of discrimination. In F. J. Crosby, M. S. Stockdale, & S. A. Ropp (Eds.), *Sex discrimination in the workplace* (pp. 19–56). Malden, MA: Blackwell.

Belliveau, M. A. (2012). Engendering inequity? How social accounts create vs. merely explain unfavorable pay outcomes for women. *Organization Science, 23,* 1154–1174.

*Benschop, Y. (2006). Of small steps and the longing for giant leaps: Research on the intersection of sex and gender within work and organizations. In A. M. Konrad, P. Prasad, & J. K. Pringle (Eds.), *Handbook of workplace diversity* (pp. 273–298). Thousand Oaks, CA: SAGE Publications.

Bernard, J. (1974). Introduction. In M. L. Carden (Ed.), *The new feminist movement* (pp. ix–xv). New York, NY: Russell Sage Foundation.

Bowles, H. R., Babcock, L., & Lai, L. (2006). Social incentives for gender differences to initiate negotiations: Sometimes it does hurt to ask. *Organizational Behavior and Human Decision Processes, 103,* 84–103.

Bowles, H. R., Babcock, L., & McGinn, K. L. (2005). Constraints and triggers: Situational mechanics of gender in negotiation. *Journal of Personality and Social Psychology, 89,* 951–965.

Brown, D. (n.d.) *Can gender discriminate or provocative dress requirements ever be appropriate for your employees?* Retrieved from http://hotelexecutive.com/business_review/2014/can-gender-discriminate-or-provocative-dress-requirements-ever-be-appropriate-for-your-employees

Bryson, J. B., & Bryson, R. (Eds.) (1978). Dual-career couples. *Psychology of Women Quarterly, 3.* (Special issue.)

Budig, M. J., & England, P. (2001). The wage penalty for motherhood. *American Sociological Review, 66,* 204–225.

Cardinale, J. (2013, April 29). *Sexual harassment complaints by males on the rise: 2012 EEOC enforcement and litigation statistics.* Retrieved from www.employmentlawblog.info/2013/04/sexual-harassment-complaints-by-males-on-the-rise-2012-eeoc-enforcement-and-litigation-statistics.shtml

CareerBuilder. (2012). *Nearly one-third of workers who had office romances married their co-worker, finds annual CareerBuilder Valentine's Day survey.* Retrieved from www.careerbuilder.com/share/aboutus/pressreleasesdetail.aspx?id=pr678&sd=2%2F9%2F2012&ed=12%2F31%2F2012

Carroll, C. (2013, June 18). *Supporters, critics open fire on women in combat.* Retrieved from www.stripes.com/news/supporters-critics-open-fire-on-women-in-combat-1.226563

Catalyst. (2012, May 31). *Working parents.* Retrieved from www.catalyst.org/knowledge/working-parents

Catalyst. (2016, February 3). *Women CEOs of the S&P 500.* Retrieved from www.catalyst.org/knowledge/women-ceos-sp-500

Center for American Women and Politics. (2016). *Women in the U.S. Congress 2015.* Retrieved from www.cawp.rutgers.edu/women-us-congress-2015

Center for WorkLife Law. (n. d.). *Fact sheet: Family responsibilities discrimination.* San Francisco, CA: UC Hastings College of the Law. Retrieved from http://worklifelaw.org/pubs/FRD_Fact_Sheet.pdf

Centers for Disease Control. (2013, July). *Breastfeeding report card.* Retrieved from www.cdc.gov/breastfeeding/pdf/2013BreastfeedingReportCard.pdf

Cleveland, J. N., Stockdale, M., & Murphy, K. R. (2000). *Women and men in organizations: Sex and gender issues at work.* Mahwah, NJ: Lawrence Erlbaum Associates.

Corporate Alliance to End Partner Violence. (2009). *Sample policy for workplace threats and violence.* Retrieved from www.caepv.org/membercenter/files/sample_policy_may_2009.pdf

Corporate Alliance to End Partner Violence. (2002–2016). *Workplace statistics.* Retrieved from www.caepv.org/getinfo/facts_stats.php?factsec=3

Correll, S. J., Benard, S., & Paik, I. (2007). Getting a job: Is there a motherhood penalty? *American Journal of Sociology, 112,* 1297–1338.

Costa, P. T., Jr., Terracciano, A., & McCrae, R. R. (2001). Gender differences in personality traits across cultures: Robust and surprising findings. *Journal of Personality and Social Psychology, 81,* 322–331.

Courtright, S. H., McCormick, B. W., Postlethwaite, B. E., Reeves, C. J., & Mount, M. K. (2013). A meta-analysis of sex differences in physical ability: Revised estimates and strategies for reducing differences in selection contexts. *Journal of Applied Psychology, 98,* 623–641.

Crosby, F. (1984). The denial of personal discrimination. *American Behavioral Scientist, 27,* 371–386.

Crosby, F. J., Clayton, S., Alksnis, O., & Hemker, K. (1986). Cognitive biases in the perception of discrimination: The importance of format. *Sex Roles, 14,* 637–646.

Cuddy, A. J., Fiske, S. T., & Glick, P. (2004). When professionals become mothers, warmth doesn't cut the ice. *Journal of Social Issues, 60,* 701–718.

Cyrus, V. (1997). Power, sexism, and heterosexism. In V. Cyrus (Ed.), *Experiencing race, class, and gender in the United States* (2nd ed.) (pp. 238–241). Mountain View, CA: Mayfield Publishing Company.

DiPrete, T. A., & Buchmann, C. (2013). *The rise of women: The growing gender gap in education and what it means for American Schools.* Retrieved from www.russellsage.org/sites/all/files/riseofwomen_brief_04082013_web.pdf

Eagly, A. H. (1987). *Sex differences in social behavior: A social-role interpretation.* Hillsdale, NJ: Erlbaum.

Eagly, A. H., Johannesen-Schmidt, M. C., & van Engen, M. L. (2003). Transformational, transactional, and laissez-faire leadership styles: A meta-analysis comparing women and men. *Psychological Bulletin, 129,* 569–591.

Eagly, A. H., & Johnson, B. T. (1990). Gender and leadership style: A meta-analysis. *Psychological Bulletin, 108,* 233–256.

Eagly, A. H., & Karau, S. J. (1991). Gender and the emergence of leaders. *Journal of Personality and Social Psychology, 60,* 685–710.

Eagly, A. H., Karau, S. J., & Makhijani, M. G. (1995). Gender and the effectiveness of leaders: A meta-analysis. *Psychological Bulletin, 117,* 125–145.

Eagly, A. H., Makhijani, M. G., & Klonsky, B. G. (1992). Gender and the evaluation of leaders: A meta-analysis. *Psychological Bulletin, 111,* 3–22.

Eby, L. T., Casper, W. J., Lockwood, A., Bordeaux, C., & Brinley, A. (2005). Work and family research in IOOB: Content analysis and review of the literature (1980–2002). *Journal of Vocational Behavior, 66,* 124–197.

EEOC. (n.d.-a). *Charge statistics: FY 1997 through FY 2015.* Retrieved from www1.eeoc.gov//eeoc/statistics/enforcement/charges.cfm

EEOC. (n.d.-b) *Charges alleging sexual harassment: FY 2010–FY 2015.* Retrieved from www1.eeoc.gov/eeoc/statistics/enforcement/sexual_harassment_new.cfm

EEOC. (n.d.-c). *EEOC litigation statistics, FY 1997 through FY 2015.* Retrieved from www.eeoc.gov/eeoc/statistics/enforcement/litigation.cfm

EEOC. (n.d.-d). *Equal Pay Act charges (includes concurrent charges with Title VII, ADEA, and ADA): FY 1997–FY 2015.* Retrieved from www1.eeoc.gov/eeoc/statistics/enforcement/epa.cfm

EEOC. (n.d.-e). *Pre-employment inquiries and height & weight.* Retrieved from www.eeoc.gov/laws/practices/inquiries_height_weight.cfm

EEOC. (n.d.-f). *Sex-Based charges: FY 1997—FY 2015*. Retrieved from www1.eeoc.gov//eeoc/statistics/enforcement/sex.cfm

EEOC. (n.d.-g). *Sexual harassment charges: EEOC & FEPAs combined: FY 1997—FY 2011*. Retrieved from www.eeoc.gov/eeoc/statistics/enforcement/sexual_harassment.cfm

EEOC. (n.d.-h). *Statutes by issue: FY 2010–FY 2015*. Retrieved from www1.eeoc.gov/eeoc/statistics/enforcement/statutes_by_issue.cfm

EEOC. (2007a). *Enforcement guidance: Unlawful disparate treatment of workers with caregiving responsibilities*. Retrieved from www.eeoc.gov/policy/docs/caregiving.html

EEOC. (2007b). *Questions and answers about EEOC's enforcement guidance on Unlawful disparate treatment of workers with caregiving responsibilities*. Retrieved from www.eeoc.gov/policy/docs/qanda_caregiving.html

EEOC. (2008, September 8). *Facts about pregnancy discrimination*. Retrieved from www.eeoc.gov/facts/fs-preg.html

EEOC. (2011, August 24). *Forrest City Grocery Company to pay $125,000 to settle EEOC sex discrimination suit*. Retrieved from www.eeoc.gov/eeoc/newsroom/release/8-24-11.cfm

EEOC. (2011, November 10). *Amtrak to pay $171,483 to settle EEOC sex/wage discrimination suit*. Retrieved from www.eeoc.gov/eeoc/newsroom/release/11-10-11a.cfm

EEOC. (2012, September 19). *EEOC releases tools to educate young workers about workplace discrimination*. Retrieved from www1.eeoc.gov/eeoc/newsroom/release/9-19-12.cfm

EEOC. (2013, April 15). *EDSI to pay $70,000 to settle EEOC pregnancy & disability discrimination suit*. Retrieved from www1.eeoc.gov/eeoc/newsroom/release/4-15-13.cfm

EEOC. (2013, May 22). *EEOC settles sex harassment and retaliation suit against Grace Church and Episcopal Diocese of L.I.* Retrieved from www.eeoc.gov/eeoc/newsroom/release/5-22-13.cfm

EEOC. (2013, May 31). *Fifth Circuit holds lactation discrimination is unlawful sex discrimination*. Retrieved from www1.eeoc.gov/eeoc/newsroom/release/5-31-13a.cfm

EEOC. (2013, June 10). *Equal Pay Act signed 50 years ago today*. Retrieved from www.eeoc.gov/eeoc/newsroom/release/6-10-13.cfm

EEOC. (2014, February 19). *Extended Stay Hotels will pay $75,800 to settle EEOC pay discrimination lawsuit*. Retrieved from www.eeoc.gov/eeoc/newsroom/release/2-19-14.cfm

England, P. (1992). *Comparable worth: Theories and evidence*. New York, NY: Aldine.

Etzkowitz, H., Kemelgor, C., & Uzzi, B. (2000). *Athena unbound: The advancement of women in society and technology*. New York, NY: Cambridge University Press.

Fiske, S. T., Cuddy, A. J., Glick, P., & Xu, T. (2002). A model of (often mixed) stereotype content: Competence and warmth respectively follow from perceived status and competition. *Journal of Personality and Social Psychology, 82,* 878–902.

Fiske, S. T., Xu, T., Cuddy, A. J., & Glick, P. (1999). (Dis)respecting versus (dis)liking: Status and interdependence predict ambivalent stereotypes of competence and warmth. *Journal of Social Issues, 55,* 473–489.

Fitzgerald, L. F. (1993). Sexual harassment: Violence against women in the workplace. *American Psychologist, 48,* 1070–1076.

Fitzgerald, L. F., Swan, S., & Fischer, C. (1995). Why didn't she just report him? The psychological and legal implications of women's responses to sexual harassment. *Journal of Social Issues, 51,* 117–138.

Francis, D. R. (2013). *Why do women outnumber men in college?* Retrieved from www.nber.org/digest/jan07/w12139.html

Gettman, H. J., & Gelfand, M. J. (2007). When the customer shouldn't be king: Antecedents and consequences of sexual harassment by clients and customers. *Journal of Applied Psychology, 92,* 757–770.

Glick, P., & Fiske, S. T. (1996). The Ambivalent Sexism Inventory: Differentiating hostile and benevolent sexism. *Journal of Personality and Social Psychology, 70,* 491–512.

Glick, P., & Fiske, S. T. (1999). The Ambivalence Toward Men Inventory. *Psychology of Women Quarterly, 23,* 519–536.

Glick, P., & Fiske, S. T. (2001). An ambivalent alliance: Hostile and benevolent sexism as complementary justifications for gender inequality. *American Psychologist, 56,* 109–118.

Glick, P., & Fiske, S. T. (2007). Sex discrimination: The psychological approach. In F. J. Crosby, M. S. Stockdale, & S. A. Ropp (Eds.), *Sex discrimination in the workplace* (pp. 155–187). Malden, MA: Blackwell.

Goldin, C. (1990). *Understanding the gender gap: An economic history of American women*. New York, NY: Oxford University Press.

Greenhaus, J. H., & Beutell, N. J. (1985). Sources of conflict between work and family roles. *Academy of Management Review, 10,* 76–88.

Greenwald, J. (2013). *Uniform company settles EEOC pregnancy bias suit for $80,000.* Retrieved from www.businessinsurance.com/article/20130408/NEWS07/130409855?template=printart

Groos, C. (2009, April 17). *Can men be Hooters Girls? When can businesses hire only women?* Retrieved from http://blogs.findlaw.com/free_enterprise/2009/04/can-men-be-hooters-girls-when-can-businesses-hire-only-women.html

Guthrie, S. R., Magyar, T. M., Eggert, S., & Kahn, C. (2009). Female athletes do ask! An exploratory study of gender differences in the propensity to initiate negotiation among athletes. *Women in Sport and Physical Activity Journal, 18,* 90–101.

Gutman, A. (2012). Nepotism and employment law. In R. G. Jones (Ed.), *Nepotism in organizations* (pp. 11–41). New York, NY: Taylor & Francis.

Gutman, A., Koppes, L. L., & Vodanovich, S. J. (2011). *EEO law and personnel practices* (3rd ed.). New York: Psychology Press.

Hall, K. M. (2012, September 23). Army testing body armor for women. *Pensacola News-Journal* (p. 2B).

Hanisch, K. A. (1996). An integrated framework for studying the outcome of sexual harassment consequences for individuals and organizations. In M. S. Stockdale (Ed.), *Sexual harassment in the workplace: Responses, frontiers, and response strategies* (pp. 174–198). Thousand Oaks, CA: SAGE Publications, Inc.

Hartmann, H., Hegewisch, A., Liepmann, H., & Williams, C. (2010). *The gender wage gap: 2009.* (IWPR Working Paper #C350). Washington, DC: Institute for Women's Policy Research.

Heckman, J. J., & LaFontaine, P. A. (2010). The American high school graduation rate: Trends and levels. *Review of Economics and Statistics, 92,* 244–262.

Heilman, M. (1983). Sex bias in work settings: The lack of fit model. In B. Staw & L. Cummings (Eds.), *Research in Organizational Behavior* (Vol. 5). Greenwich, CT: JAI.

Heilman, M. (1995). Sex stereotypes and their effects in the workplace: What we know and what we don't know. *Journal of Social Behavior and Personality, 10,* 3–26.

Howard, J. L. (2008). Balancing conflicts of interest when employing spouses. *Employee Rights and Responsibilities Journal, 20,* 29–43.

Hyde, J. S., Fennema, E., & Lamon, S., J. (1990). Gender differences in mathematics performance: A meta-analysis. *Psychological Bulletin, 107,* 139–155.

Hyde, J. S., & Plant, E. A. (1995). Magnitude of psychological gender differences: Another side to the story. *American Psychologist, 50,* 159–161.

James, J. (2004). The equal pay act in the courts: A *de facto* white-collar exemption. *New York University Law Review, 79,* 1873–1901.

Jones, J. W., & Arnold, D. W. (2008). Protecting the legal and appropriate use of personality testing: A practitioner perspective. *Industrial and Organizational Psychology, 1,* 296–298.

Kaiser, C. R., & Miller, C. T. (2001). Stop complaining! The social costs of making attributions of discrimination. *Personality and Social Psychology Bulletin, 27,* 254–263.

Kanter, R. M. (1977). *Men and women of the corporation.* New York, NY: Basic Books.

Klonoff, E. A., & Landrine, H. (1995). The Schedule of Sexist Events: A measure of lifetime and recent sexist discrimination in women's lives. *Psychology of Women Quarterly, 19,* 439–470.

Klonoff, E. A., Landrine, H., & Campbell, R. (2000). Sexist discrimination may account for well-known gender differences in psychiatric symptoms. *Psychology of Women Quarterly, 24,* 93–99.

Konrad, A. M. (2013). Work-life interface and flexibility: Impacts on women, men, families, and employers. In Q. M. Roberson (Ed.), *The Oxford handbook of diversity and work* (pp. 366–390). New York: Oxford University Press.

Kossek, E. E., & Ozeki, C. (1998). Work-family conflict, policies, and the job-life satisfaction relationship: A review and directions for organizational behavior-human resources research. *Journal of Applied Psychology, 83,* 139–149.

Kray, L. J., & Thompson, L. (2005). Gender stereotypes and negotiation performance: A review of theory and research. In B. Staw & R. Kramer (Eds.), *Research in organizational behavior: An annual series of analytical essays and critical reviews* (Vol. 26) (pp. 103–182). Oxford, England: Elsevier.

Krieger, L. H. (2007). The watched variable improves: On eliminating sex discrimination in employment. In F. J. Crosby, M. S. Stockdale, & S. A. Ropp (Eds.), *Sex discrimination in the workplace* (pp. 295–329). Malden, MA: Blackwell.

*Kunin, M. M. (2012). *The new feminist agenda: Defining the next revolution for women, work, and family.* White River Junction, VT: Chelsea Green Publishing.

Landrine, H., Klonoff, E. A., Gibbs, J., Manning, V., & Lund, M. (1995). Physical and psychiatric correlates of gender discrimination: An application of the Schedule of Sexist Events. *Psychology of Women Quarterly, 19,* 473–492.

Leslie, L. M., & Manchester, C. F. (2011). Work-family conflict is a social issue not a women's issue. *Industrial and Organizational Psychology, 4,* 414–417.

Lovell, V., & Hill, C. (2001, May). *Today's women workers: Shut out of yesterday's unemployment insurance system.* (IWPR Publication #A127.) Retrieved from www.iwpr.org/publications/pubs/today2019s-women-workers-shut-out-of-yesterday2019s-unemployment-insurance-system-1

Ludden, J. (2010, June 10). *More workers alleging bias against caregivers.* National Public Radio. Retrieved from www.npr.org/templates/story/story.php?storyId=127531355

McConahay, J. B. (1986). Modern racism, ambivalence, and the Modern Racism Scale. In J. F. Dovidio & S. L. Gaertner (Eds.), *Prejudice, discrimination, and racism* (pp. 91–125). Orlando, FL: Academic Press.

McKenzie, L. (2015). *Man hits Hooters with new sex discrimination suit.* Retrieved from www.law360.com/articles/82868/man-hits-hooters-with-new-sex-discrimination-suit

Miller v. Department of Corrections, 115 P. 3d 77 – Cal: Supreme Court (2005).

Miller, S. (2012). *Ensure compliance with reform law's lactation room requirements.* Retrieved from www.shrm.org/hrdisciplines/benefits/articles/pages/lactationroom.aspx

Miller, C. F., & Xiao, J. (1999). Effects of birth spacing and timing on mothers' labor force participation. *Atlantic Economic Journal, 27,* 410–421.

Morganson, V. J., Culbertson, S. S., & Matthews, R. A. (2013). Individual strategies for navigating the work-life interface. In D. A. Major & R. Burke (Eds.), *Handbook of work-life integration among professionals* (pp. 205–224). Northampton, MA: Edward Elgar.

Morganson, V. J., Major, D. A., & Bauer, K. (2009). Work-Life Job Analysis: Applying a classic tool to address a contemporary issue. *The Psychologist-Manager Journal, 12,* 252–274.

Myre, G. (2013, January 24). *Women in combat: 5 key questions.* Retrieved from www.npr.org/blogs/thetwo-way/2013/01/24/170161752/women-in-combat-five-key-questions

National Center for Education Statistics. (2012). *Digest of education statistics: Table 310.* Retrieved from http://nces.ed.gov/programs/digest/d12/tables/dt12_310.asp

National Conference of State Legislatures. (2014, December 31). *State family and medical leave laws.* Retrieved from www.ncsl.org/research/labor-and-employment/state-family-and-medical-leave-laws.aspx

National Park Service. (n.d.). *Rosie the Riveter—World War II Home Front National Historical Park.* Retrieved from www.nps.gov/nr/travel/wwiibayarea/ros.htm

National Women's Law Center. (2000). *Frequently asked questions about sexual harassment in the workplace.* Retrieved from www.nwlc.org/resource/frequently-asked-questions-about-sexual-harassment-workplace

Neal, B. R. (2008). *August 2008: Love contracts get the double take.* Retrieved from www.shrm.org/legalissues/legalreport/pages/lovecontractsgetthedoubletake.aspx

Neale, M. B., & Hammer, L. B. (2009). Dual-earner couples in the sandwiched generation: Effects of coping strategies over time. *The Psychologist-Manager Journal, 12,* 205–234.

O'Leary-Kelly, A., Lean, E., Reeves, C., & Randel, J. (2008). Coming into the light: Intimate partner violence and its effects at work. *Academy of Management Perspectives, 5,* 57–72.

Oregon State Archives. (2008). *With mothers at the factory . . . Oregon's child care challenges.* Retrieved from http://arcweb.sos.state.or.us/pages/exhibits/ww2/services/child.htm

Organisation for Economic Co-operation and Development. (2012*). Lack of support for motherhood hurting women's career prospects, despite gains in education and employment, says OECD.* Retrieved from www.oecd.org/newsroom/lackofsupportformotherhoodhurtingwomenscareerprospectsdespitegainsineducationandemploymentsaysoecd.htm

Padavic, I., & Reskin, P. (2002). *Women and men at work* (2nd ed.). Thousand Oaks, CA: Pine Forge Press.

Parks, A. (2006). *Child care during World War II.* Retrieved from www.forgeofinnovation.org/springfield_armory_1892-1945/Themes/People/Women/World_War_II/Child_Care/index.html

Parks, M. (2006). *2006 Workplace Romance.* Retrieved from www.shrm.org/research/surveyfindings/articles/documents/06-workplaceromancepollfindings%20(2).pdf

Powell, G. N., & Graves, L. M. (2003). *Women and men in management* (3rd ed.). Thousand Oaks, CA: SAGE Publications, Inc.

Rapoport, R., & Rapoport, R. (1971). *Dual-career families*. Baltimore, MD: Penguin Books.

Rashby, C., & Hutchinson, M. R. (2013, January 21). Male sexual harassment claims: Training is the best prevention. *SHRM Legal Report* (1–4). Retrieved from www.shrm.org/legalissues/legalreport/pages/male-sexual-harassment-claims.aspx

Rhode, D. L., & Williams, J. C. (2007). Legal perspectives on employment discrimination. In F. J. Crosby, M. S. Stockdale, & S. A. Ropp (Eds.), *Sex discrimination in the workplace* (pp. 235–270). Malden, MA: Blackwell.

Ridgeway, C. L., & Correll, S. J. (2004). Motherhood as a status characteristic. *Journal of Social Issues, 60,* 683–700.

Ridgeway, C. L., & England, P. (2007). Sociological approaches to sex discrimination. In F. J. Crosby, M. S. Stockdale, & S. A. Ropp (Eds.), *Sex discrimination in the workplace* (pp. 189–211). Malden, MA: Blackwell.

Rose, S. J., & Hartmann, H. I. (2004). *Still a man's labor market: The long-term earnings gap.* Washington, DC: Institute for Women's Policy Research.

Rothenberg, P. S. (2007). Understanding racism, sexism, heterosexism, and class privilege. In P. S. Rothenberg (Ed.), *Race, class, and gender in the United States: An integrated study* (7th ed.) (pp. 117–121). New York, NY: Worth Publishers.

Rowe, M. P. (1996). Dealing with harassment: A systems approach. In M. S. Stockdale (Ed.), *Sexual harassment in the workplace: Responses, frontiers, and response strategies* (pp. 241–271). Thousand Oaks, CA: SAGE Publications, Inc.

Rutte, C. G., Diekmann, K. A., Polzer, J. T., Crosby, F. J., & Messick, D. M. (1994). Organization of information and the detection of gender discrimination. *Psychological Science, 5,* 226–231.

Sandberg, S. (with N. Scovell). (2013). *Lean in: Women, work, and the will to lead.* New York, NY: Alfred A. Knopf.

Segal, J. (2006). *Be aware of a new danger in office romances.* Retrieved from www.shrm.org/publications/managingsmart/winter06/documents/story7.doc

Shaefer, H. L. (2009). Part-time workers: Some key differences between primary and secondary earners. *Monthly Labor Review,* Oct. (pp. 3–15).

Society for Human Resource Management. (2010). *SHRM poll: Is workplace sexual harassment on the rise?* Retrieved from www.shrm.org/research/surveyfindings/articles/pages/sexualharassmentontherise.aspx

Society for Human Resource Management. (2011). *Every day is Valentine's Day for some workers.* Retrieved from www.shrm.org/publications/hrnews/pages/valentinesday.aspx

Society for Human Resource Management. (2012a, August 7). *Domestic violence at work.* Retrieved from www.shrm.org/templatestools/hrqa/pages/workplaceviolencedomesticdomesticviolenceatwork.aspx

Society for Human Resource Management. (2012b, May 3). *Leave benefits: Maternity/paternity: What are some of the issues an employer should consider when developing a maternity and/or paternity leave benefits policy?* Retrieved from www.shrm.org/templatestools/hrqa/pages/maternitypaternitywhataresomeoftheissuesanemployershouldconsiderwhendevelopingamaternityandorpaternityleaveben.aspx

Society for Human Resource Management. (2013). *The Workplace Impact of Domestic and Sexual Violence and Stalking.* Retrieved from www.shrm.org/research/surveyfindings/articles/pages/shrm-workplace-impact-domestic-sexual-violence-stalking.aspx

Society for Human Resource Management. (2014, May 23). *Harassment: Anti-harassment policy and complaint procedure (includes Dating/Consensual Relationship Policy).* Retrieved from www.shrm.org/templatestools/samples/policies/pages/cms_000534.aspx

Sonfield, A., Hasstedt, K., Kavanaugh, M. L., & Anderson, R. (2013). *The social and economic benefits of women's ability to determine whether and when to have children.* New York, NY: Guttmacher Institute.

Southern Poverty Law Center. (2013). *Dothard v. Rawlinson.* Retrieved from www.splcenter.org/get-informed/case-docket/dothard-v-rawlinson

Stockdale, M. S. (1996). What we know and what we need to learn about sexual harassment. In M. S. Stockdale (Ed.), *Sexual harassment in the workplace: Responses, frontiers, and response strategies* (pp. 3–25). Thousand Oaks, CA: SAGE Publications, Inc.

Stone, P., & Hernandez, L. A. (2013). The all-or-nothing workplace: Flexibility stigma and "opting out" among professional-managerial women. *Journal of Social Issues, 69,* 235–256.

Stuhlmacher, A. F., & Walters, A. E. (1999). Gender differences in negotiation outcome: A meta-analysis. *Personnel Psychology, 52,* 653–677.

Swanberg, J. E., & Logan, T. K. (2005). Domestic violence and employment: A qualitative study. *Journal of Occupational Health Psychology, 10,* 3–17.

Swanberg, J., & Logan, T. K. (2007). Intimate partner violence, employment and the workplace: An interdisciplinary perspective. *Journal of Interpersonal Violence, 22,* 263–267.

Swanberg, J. E., Logan, T. K., & Macke, C. (2005). Intimate partner violence, employment, and the workplace: Consequences and future directions. *Trauma, Violence, & Abuse, 6,* 286–312.

Swim, J. K., Aikin, K. J., Hall, W. S., & Hunter, B. A. (1995). Sexism and racism: Old-fashioned and modern prejudices. *Journal of Personality and Social Psychology, 68,* 199–214.

Swim, J. K., Eyssell, K. M., Murdoch, E. Q., & Ferguson, M. J. (2010). Self-silencing to sexism. *Journal of Social Issues, 66,* 493–507.

Twiss, C., Tabb, S., & Crosby, F. J. (1989). Affirmative action and aggregate data: The importance of patterns in the perception of discrimination. In F. A. Blanchard & F. J. Crosby (Eds.), *Affirmative action in perspective* (pp. 159–167). New York, NY: Springer-Verlag.

Tyler, K. (2008). Sign in the name of love. *HR Magazine, 53*(2). Retrieved from www.shrm.org/publications/hrmagazine/editorialcontent/pages/2tyler-love%20contracts.aspx

United Nations Department of Economic and Social Affairs. (2000). *Families and the world of work: Four country profiles of family-sensitive policies.* New York, NY: United Nations. Retrieved from www.un.org/esa/socdev/family/Publications/WorkandFamily1s.PDF

US Bureau of Labor Statistics. (2005, July 27). *Contingent and alternative employment arrangements: February 2005.* Retrieved from www.bls.gov/news.release/pdf/conemp.pdf

US Bureau of Labor Statistics. (2014, December). *Women in the labor force: A databook.* Retrieved from www.bls.gov/opub/reports/womens-databook/archive/women-in-the-labor-force-a-databook-2014.pdf

US Census Bureau. (n.d.) *How do we know? America's changing labor force.* Retrieved from www.census.gov/how/pdf/EEO_infographic.pdf

US Census Bureau. (2012). *Statistical abstract of the United States: 2012: Table 616. Employed civilians by occupation, sex, race, and Hispanic origin.* Retrieved from www.census.gov/history/pdf/musician_employment.pdf?cssp=SERP

US Merit Systems Protection Board. (1995). *Sexual harassment in the federal workplace: Trends, progress, and continuing challenges.* Washington, DC: US Government Printing Office.

US Office of Personnel Management. (2013). *Guide for establishing a federal nursing mother's program.* Retrieved from www.opm.gov/policy-data-oversight/worklife/reference-materials/nursing-mother-guide.pdf

Wilbanks, C. (2013, March 7). *Temp work raises long-term questions for economy.* Retrieved from www.cbsnews.com/8301-505143_162-57573141/temp-work-raises-long-term-questions-for-economy/

Wilde, E. T., Batchelder, L., & Ellwood, D. (2010). *The mommy track divides: The impact of childbearing on wages of women of differing skill levels* (NBER Working Paper 16582). Retrieved from www.nber.org/papers/w16582

Wilkie, D. (2013, July 16). *Anti-harassment training following the Supreme Court's* Vance *ruling.* Retrieved from www.shrm.org/hrdisciplines/employeerelations/articles/pages/anti-harassment-training-following-supremecourt-vance-ruling.aspx

Williams, J. C., Blair-Loy, M., & Berdahl, J. L. (2013). Cultural schemas, social class, and the flexibility stigma. *Journal of Social Issues, 69,* 209–234.

Williams, J. C., & Cuddy, A. J. C. (2012). Will working mothers take your company to court? *Harvard Business Review, 90*(9), 94–100.

Women don't ask: Negotiation and the gender divide. (n.d.) Retrieved from www.womendontask.com

Workplaces Respond to Domestic & Sexual Violence: A National Resource Center. (n.d.). *The facts on the workplace and domestic violence.* Retrieved from www.workplacesrespond.org/learn/the-facts/the-facts-on-the-workplace-and-domestic-violence

Yoder, J. (1991). Rethinking tokenism. *Gender and Society, 5,* 167–192.

* Recommended for advanced reading.

Chapter 10

Race, Ethnicity, and Work

Race distinctions categorize people in terms of how others respond to them, socially constructed and with meaning changing over time and place. Usually they are a means of allocating status and privilege in a society; categories are arbitrary and not consistently related to underlying biological variables, but resulting social classifications are useful in understanding outcomes for groups of people. Ethnicity is a socially constructed way of sorting people into groups in terms of shared culture, heritage, language, and/or religion. Proudford and Nkomo (2006) refer to the English, Scots, and Welsh, living on the same island and sharing race but not ethnicity. The term "racio-ethnicity" has also been used to refer to groups identified by a combination of presumed biology and culture (Cox, 1990/2004).

This chapter avoids the term "minority" except to designate numerical representation in a particular environment, for three reasons. First, this avoids confusion with another meaning in social science and common language: a group that is identifiable, lower in power, treated differently and unfavorably, and whose members are aware of themselves as a group (Dworkin & Dworkin, 1999). In this sense, White Americans are not a minority even when in the numerical minority—as they are predicted to be in the US around the year 2043 (Yen, 2013). Women are often considered a minority although females outnumber males in the US. Second, numerical minority status is not fixed as an essential characteristic. Groups in the minority in one community may be in the numerical majority elsewhere (e.g., certain US cities, other countries). In fact, those considered minorities in the US are actually the majority of the people in the world (Tatum, 1997). Third, some find the term offensive as a reference to lower status. Therefore, this chapter refers to "people of color" (not itself a perfect term) and to various racio-ethnic groups in their preferred terminology.

Terminology

As a general rule, it is courteous to use the label preferred by members of another group. Surveys of US Blacks have generally found no clear preference for "Black" vs. "African American" (Jones, 2013a). However, not all US Blacks are African American. For example, Affirmative Action (AA) or EEO-1 reports commonly consider natives of sub-Saharan Africa to be Black although they do not share the cultural history of American descendants of former slaves and probably do not consider themselves African American. Although "colored people," "colored," and "Negro" were used in the past, these terms are seldom heard today in the US except in organization names (e.g., National Association for the Advancement of Colored People) or historical contexts. Colloquial euphemisms (e.g., the "N" word) date from slavery days and are now considered derogatory and insulting racial slurs when used by non-Blacks, but have a different connotation when used by Blacks. Have you ever discussed this in an interracial context?

Since 1980, Gallup polls have asked about "Hispanic" and "Latino." Currently, 70% of respondents from this group express no preference, with others generally preferring "Hispanic" (Jones, 2013a). "Mestizo" is a person of mixed descent, generally Hispanic and American Indian;

"Chicano/a" properly refers only to Hispanics of Mexican descent. "Native American" or "American Indian" are appropriate terms today, but tribal affiliation is also useful if it is known. In Canada, the term "First Nations people" is used. Today's term "people of color" refers collectively to Blacks, Latinos, Native Americans, Asian Americans, and other racio-ethnic groups other than Euro-Americans. For a helpful chart including a wider range of terms, see Vogeler (2013).

Racio-ethnicity and Work

Colorblindness vs. Multiculturalism

At what point in a face-to-face conversation do you realize that you are speaking to an African American, Asian American, or White person? Do you notice accents or pronunciations suggesting someone is Latino, African Black, or African American from the Southern US? Are you surprised when a Black person speaks with a British acent? Have you wondered about the racio-ethnic background of someone of racially ambiguous appearance? Racial distinctions are so engrained in our culture that it is impossible not to notice them. According to Thomas and Chrobot-Mason, "Colorblindness is a myth" (2005, p. 82).

Law and fairness imply that decisions in work environments should be made without attention to race, as if it did not exist. Yet to determine whether race has made a difference, we must attend to it. This paradox underlies recent research on consequences of a *color-blind* (CB) ideology vs. a *multicultural* (MC) view that explicitly recognizes and values racio-ethnic differences. Is it "fair" to ignore race in today's workplace decisions, when the standing and accomplishments of people of color have long been suppressed as a result of race?

Someone with CB racial attitudes believes "that race should not and does not matter" (Neville, Lilly, Duran, Lee, & Browne, 2000, p. 60). Although this ideal is commendable, social science research indicates it has not yet been attained (Neville, Awad, Brooks, Flores, & Bluemel, 2013). Neville et al. (2000) developed a *Color-Blind Racial Attitudes Scale (CoBRAS)* and explored its correlates in a series of studies. They identified three factors on the CoBRAS: (a) unawareness of blatant racial issues; (b) denial of White privilege; and (c) denial of institutional racism and need to correct it. The first factor is *color evasion* or denial of differences related to color. The second and third factors are forms of *power evasion* or denial of power differences, in which lower outcomes are seen as due to deficiencies in people of color rather than behavior of the dominant majority.

What are the consequences of adopting the CB ideology vs. the pluralistic MC viewpoint? In one study, CB-primed students were less likely to identify clear instances of racial bias and describe them in a way that would lead a responsible adult to intervene (Apfelbaum, Pauker, Sommers, & Ambady, 2010). Thus, colorblindness led to bias-blindness as well. CB ideology can also impair perceptions of racial discourse and climate (Zou & Dickter, 2013). College students read conversations between two friends in which one's ambiguous remark was perceived as prejudiced and offensive by the other, who then verbally confronted the speaker. Participants with higher CB attitudes rated the confronter more negatively and her remark as less appropriate than other participants. Unless the comment was blatantly racist, CB participants thought the offended friend overreacted and rated her less highly.

When someone actively tries to avoid mentioning race or acknowledging relevant racial differences, communication with a person of color is less effective and in fact may seem more prejudiced (Norton, Sommers, Apfelbaum, Pura, & Ariely, 2006; Apfelbaum, Norton, & Sommers, 2012). In units of a health care organization where Whites responded in a CB manner, work engagement was lower for people of color; their engagement was higher when Whites endorsed a MC perspective (Plaut, Thomas, & Goren, 2009). Relevant to D&I, people of color often experience the work environment as one in which race *does* matter. A White person who appears to overlook or actively ignore race seems inauthentic and insensitive and creates psychological distance. Studies show that people quickly and automatically notice race (Apfelbaum et al., 2012) although they may think they do not (Norton et al., 2006) and may try to prevent it from influencing their behavior.

> "I had always thought that not acknowledging a difference was a good way to manage diversity with regard to race and ethnicity, when in reality that can be perceived as just as discriminatory as saying inappropriate things . . ."
>
> Undergraduate student, 2010

The Ethnicity Paradigm

Assumptions and policy about racio-ethnic groups are affected by what Nkomo (1992) called *The Ethnicity Paradigm:* a set of assumptions about people of color based in sociological study of immigrant groups in the 1920s. Largely urban European ethnics, they were thought to be inferior in intelligence and motivation. With "contact, competition, accommodation, and eventual assimilation" (Nkomo, 1992, p. 491; quoting Park, 1950/1939, p. 150) they would be absorbed into American society's great melting pot, and assimilation would lead to racism's disappearance. Racial groupings were seen as temporary and resulting from characteristics of immigrants themselves such as personality, lack of education, poor language skills, and poverty. Nkomo identified three problems with this view: (a) accepting inequality as natural and inevitable; (b) ignoring institutional structures that perpetuate inequality; and (c) "blaming the victim" for being different and inferior.

By the mid-20th century, other groups (African Americans, Latinos, Native Americans, Asian Americans) were also seen from this framework. Assimilation and integration were assumed as goals, and the Civil Rights Act of 1964 was understood as a means of removing barriers to this process. This viewpoint assumed that racial groupings would become less important, racism and discrimination resulted from economic and psychological factors, and over time, these racial groups would repeat the assimilation pattern of European White immigrants before them. However, this paradigm overlooks implications of differences in physical appearance as well as cultural barriers to intermarriage and assimilation across racial and ethnic divides.

To some extent, the Ethnicity Paradigm still underlies expectations in work organizations about racio-ethnic groups. Tensions arise around the extent to which inequality will or should continue as a natural feature of organizations, the role of individual characteristics vs. institutional structures in intergroup stresses, whether racio-ethnic groupings will or should continue to exist over time, and the role of economic and psychological factors.

The Back-handed Compliment: Asian Americans as "Model Minority"

Among US racial groups, those of Asian descent face an unusual stereotype, seemingly positive but with several potentially negative consequences (Lai, 2013). The term "Model Minority" began to be applied to Asian Americans in the 1960s. Articles in the popular press described in positive terms the socioeconomic and educational achievement of Japanese Americans and Chinese Americans, despite severe discrimination faced in this country as immigrants and around the time of World War II. This stereotype was soon applied to Asian Americans in general and now extends to include personality traits such as motivation, politeness and compliance, and cognitive skills such as talent for math, science, and technology. The stereotype implies that more than some other racial minorities, Asian Americans have worked hard to conform to American cultural ideals of meritocracy, hard work, self-sufficiency, respect for family, and low delinquency. In essence, they conform to the Ethnicity Paradigm.

Some facts about this racio-ethnic group appear to confirm this rosy picture. In his critique, Lai (2013) acknowledged that Asian Americans as a group are more highly educated than other ethnicities, proportionally overrepresented among professionals, and apparently financially secure and successful. However, this overlooks diversity among those of Asian descent in national heritage as well as levels of educational, professional, and financial success. Furthermore, US immigration policies have favored those Asians prepared for professional careers by good educations in their native countries or from affluent families who have supported their education abroad. Thus high levels of accomplishment may be as much a result of selective immigration policy as presumed Asian cultural values, personality, and ability (Lai, 2013; Tatum, 1997).

Household income is high relative to other racio-ethnic groups. However, *per capita* income of Asian Americans is actually lower than that of other people of color in the US because more household members are employed. Furthermore, although many Asian American households succeed by educational, financial, and status indicators, many others of very modest means live at or below the poverty level (Lai, 2013).

Negative consequences result from this Model Minority stereotype, both for individual Asian Americans and for their group as a whole (Lai, 2013). First, the stereotype masks the glass ceiling for Asians in the US. Among people of color, Asian Americans are least likely to be promoted to managerial positions. Second, the stereotype reinforces the "differentness" of Asian Americans and is likely to be a barrier to inclusion. Third, it creates tensions with other groups. Blacks, Latinos, and Native Americans may hear "Why can't you succeed like Asian Americans?" and Whites may resent their apparent success (Tatum, 1997). Fourth, the stereotype distracts us from other negative reactions such as the perception that Asian Americans lack social skills (Lai & Babcock, 2012), discrimination based on accent (Hosoda, Stone-Romero, & Walter, 2007), and the *perpetual foreigner syndrome* (Cheryan & Monin, 2005). Although superficially the stereotype may appear complimentary, like other stereotypes it causes us to overlook important differences among individuals and make assumptions about others that may be very inaccurate. In the 1998 Winter Olympics, champion US figure skater Michelle Kwan was edged out of the Gold Medal by Tara Lipinski. MSNBC ran the headline "American beats out Kwan," implying that Kwan, who was born in California, was not an American. MSNBC apologized for the "headline error" (Sorensen, 1998). "*No, really, where are you from?*" (NPR, 2013, November 11).

Themes in the Study of Racio-ethnicity and Work

Three themes appear in research on racio-ethnicity:

- Until recently, research about racio-ethnicity and employment was relatively infrequent and largely driven by political, legal, and socioeconomic factors (Cox & Nkomo, 1990; Proudford & Nkomo, 2006).
- Contemporary employment research is broader, more representative, and more useful to diversity professionals. Latinos are studied more than Asian Americans, with Native Americans/ Alaska Natives the least studied (Bell, 2012). New topics are "Whiteness" (Grimes, 2001), experiences of mixed race persons (Winters & DeBose, 2003; Shih & Sanchez, 2009), and interactions between racio-ethnicity and sex (Proudford & Nkomo, 2006).
- Focus has increased on conceptual explanations aimed at understanding rather than simple description. Examples include general processes like leadership and mentoring as well as race-relevant processes (e.g., implicit bias and modern/aversive racism), and theories such as Social Identity Theory and Social Dominance Theory.

This increased attention to process is illustrated by Ilgen and Youtz (1986), who discussed several mechanisms that could produce race differences in *evaluations* of job performance. Consider your own experiences with feedback on your job or school performance. How would you respond to a low evaluation? Accept it as valid? Work harder, seek out help, or just give up? Wonder whether judgments were affected by your age, race, sex, or other demographic characteristics? The next section extends this framework to contexts beyond performance evaluation.

A Framework for Understanding Discriminatory Processes

Diversity professionals can use this framework to identify potentially discriminatory processes. *Access discrimination* occurs in recruiting, hiring, and placement and limits incorporation of underrepresented group members. After hiring, *treatment discrimination* occurs through such things as ineffective or inaccurate feedback, limited training or mentoring opportunities, or lower rates of promotions or raises. These processes often interact, for example when differential treatment reduces access to advancement. Advocacy for D&I means bringing qualified underrepresented people into the organization, and also making systems operate as well for them as those systems do for others.

How can access and treatment discrimination disadvantage people of color? Access discrimination may involve:

- Biased judgments underestimating actual ability or performance; stereotypic expectations producing inaccurate evaluation of ability or work quality and less frequent selection.
- Inaccurate initial evaluations depressing motivation and leading to lower performance levels and future outcome cycles.
- Evaluator leniency when judging others similar to themselves (*similar-to-me* effect).
- Supervisors of different races producing different rating patterns depending upon ratee race (Stauffer & Buckley, 2005). Because Whites probably more likely to serve as evaluators, rater-ratee effect implies lower performance evaluations for non-Whites.

Illustrations of treatment discrimination include:

- Self-fulfilling prophecies as people of color are *treated* differently in ways that produce lower performance, later reflected accurately in evaluations.
- Performance evaluation errors involving attributions for performance: attributing unexpected success to luck or external circumstances rather than ability and motivation. *Raises* are often awarded for high performance due to ability or motivation, but *promotion* only when high performance is believed due to ability (Heilman & Guzzo, 1978). More punitive reactions to poor performance when attributed to low motivation rather than low ability or task difficulty (Pence, Pendleton, Dobbins, & Sgro, 1982).
- Selectively using information or relying on different kinds of information when evaluating people of color; e.g., supervisor believing Black employee hired due to AA might scrutinize employee's behavior more closely—or be reluctant to make note of actual shortcomings, so employee receives inaccurate evaluations.
- *Lost opportunities* if people of color receive less mentoring or sponsorship, perhaps because experienced employees are drawn to similar others. Individual excluded or identified as poor performer receives fewer opportunities than majority-race person of similar ability.
- Less *in-group status* experienced by people of color, thus less attention, assistance, and interesting or challenging work; interactions with out-group members less extensive and more transactional (Dansereau, Graen, & Haga, 1975).

- *Tokenism* because people of color are few and visually recognizable: increased performance pressure, isolation, and assignment to roles seen as race-appropriate.
- *Self-limiting behaviors* as self-confidence and motivation are affected, with actual ability dropping relative to other employees after developmental opportunities are foregone and more complex tasks unlearned.

We cannot say how often such destructive processes actually occur in typical work organizations; they can be very subtle and not easily detected. Through *accumulation of advantage and disadvantage* (Merton, 1968; Valian, 2000), effects of early positive or negative treatment, even small ones, can snowball over time and lead to further opportunity and development or lack thereof. Managers and diversity professionals should be alert to these sources of bias and try to prevent and correct them through organizational procedures and systems.

Racio-ethnic Differences

Employers should use fair selection processes and, if challenged, be able to defend against charges of discrimination in hiring. Best practice is to use valid predictors; however, persistent evidence of race differences on many of these measures makes them potentially discriminatory. For historical and sociocultural reasons, increased hiring of women has focused on institutional, societal, and personal factors reviewed in Chapter 9. In contrast, increased hiring of people of color has placed more emphasis on the measurement of potential and actual performance. Therefore, this topic is covered in some detail in this chapter though it is also relevant to other dimensions of diversity.

Research on race differences in job attributes is largely conducted in large-scale employment settings (e.g., major corporations, the military, civil service environments including public safety) where large numbers of applicants or incumbents are measured with carefully developed standardized cognitive ability or personality tests, work samples, situational judgment tests, assessment centers, or structured and scored interviews. Usually these jobs have compensation well above minimum wage, some stability, good employment benefits, and opportunities for advancement. (Because these jobs are desirable and numerous, and because large employers are perceived to have "deep pockets," these are also the settings in which legal challenges are most likely.) In these settings, several predictor scores are often combined in a formula identifying people whose job performance is likely to be highest. Usually there are a limited number of job openings and, if top-down selection is used, there will be many capable people whose scores are not close enough to the top to be considered. The literature on selection methods comes from situations like these.

Box 10.1   What Are Those Tests?

Tests of cognitive ability measure thought, job knowledge, and intelligence. Personality tests for employment assess traits by asking about preferences or choices among behaviors. Standardized procedures for presentation and scoring are used for both. In biodata, weights are assigned to application blank items based on how strongly each life experience relates to job performance. Work samples include mini-versions or analogs of actual job tasks. Situational Judgment Tests (SJTs) describe a situation and the applicant chooses from among previously scored answers. Assessment Centers include standardized tests, leaderless group discussions, in-basket simulations, and other exercises and are scored by observers. In structured interviews, the same questions are asked of all candidates and a pre-developed scoring key is used.

Have your hiring experiences involved this level of complexity and precision? Many smaller organizations, unlikely to be challenged legally, do not use rigorously developed selection processes and rely on application blanks, brief unstructured and unscored interviews, drug and background checks, recommendations from current employees or friends of the manager. McKay and Davis (2008) cite studies showing that only a minority of firms report using validated selection techniques, with the most common method being the (unreliable and invalid) unstructured interview! In these settings, technical arguments about test bias, combination formulas, and cutoff scores are irrelevant and ordinary subjective judgmental bias is the major threat to fair hiring. Diversity professionals should be knowledgeable about both areas and prepared to work in either environment.

Technical Considerations

No test is perfect. The word "test" is used broadly to refer to any experience used to measure knowledge or skill, including interviews and work samples, typical standardized tests and other methods. Professionally developed tests are designed to assess a theoretical construct (such as *Diversity competence*; DComp). A well-developed test includes questions or tasks measuring different aspects of that construct, but because measurement is imperfect it will also measure other related constructs (in DComp, perhaps shyness or experience interacting with diverse people).

A test should be *reliable* or consistent: does it give the same results every time (if circumstances have not changed)? Or is it greatly affected by *extraneous factors* that are not controlled, such as weather, sneezes, or broken pencils, number of people taking the test, or the test administrator's demographic characteristics? Extraneous factors lead to *random error* in measurement and can never be completely prevented. Therefore, small differences among candidate scores resulting from measurement error actually indicate equivalent ability. A test should also be *valid*: it should measure what it claims to measure and very little else. Determining validity is a complex and challenging task and usually requires much data collection. In the example of DComp, we would seek evidence that our test actually measured DComp and not other things such as shyness or interaction experience.

In an employment context, cognitive ability and other tests should be used because of evidence they are correlated with measures of job performance. The test possesses *criterion-related validity* because it successfully estimates the criterion of how well an applicant does on the job. Measures of job performance (criteria) are themselves not perfectly reliable and valid. For example, even simple performance criteria such as number of items produced will vary with environmental distractions, age of equipment, or humidity. Tardiness is affected by unpredictable problems with public transportation or traffic. Supervisor ratings are affected by how much the supervisor actually knows about what the employee is doing, interpersonal preferences, demographic similarity, prejudice, and other subjective factors.

Tests can be very useful in evaluating candidates when there is little other information available about them. However, once employees are in the system, test scores themselves are much less informative than how the person actually functions on the job. Job performance is determined by many different things, only a few of which can be captured by test scores at the time of entry.

Racio-ethnic Differences in Selection Measures

The extensive technical literature on racial differences in selection measures comes predominantly from large employment databases using professionally developed tests. Most studies compare samples of Blacks and Whites; because meta-analysis requires a large number of studies, fewer overall comparisons involve other racio-ethnic groups. The small number of Hispanic–White comparisons is especially surprising because the growing Latino workforce is comparable in size to that of Blacks (Roth, Bevier, Bobko, Switzer, & Tyler, 2001). The few comments about Asian–White differences in the employment literature (Hough, Oswald, & Ployhart, 2001; Ployhart & Holtz, 2008) are based on data collected some time ago and suggest that Asians score higher than Whites on general intelligence. According to Roth et al. (2001), Asian–White differences tend to be smaller and usually do not exclude Asians from employment or educational opportunities; this may explain why this comparison receives less attention in employment research.

In meta-analysis, comparisons of test scores produce *effect sizes* indicating the size of the difference between the means (averages) of two groups across many individual studies. Meta-analysis computes the average of the differences, adjusted for characteristics of each study's statistical results. Generally these effects (*d* scores) are classified as large, medium, or small. Even with a large *d* score, there is considerable overlap in score distributions for Blacks and Whites with many individuals from one group scoring above (or below) the average of the other group. However, when Whites score higher and *d* is large, there will be few Blacks among those with the very highest scores who are most likely to be hired, and adverse impact is likely to result. When there are only a few job openings and top-down selection is used, all those selected may be White even when the pool is racially varied. From the perspective of diversity, this is a problem, especially because tests are imperfect and we do not understand all factors accounting for group differences. Adverse impact is also an issue of liability for the organization. Bobko and Roth (2013) have reviewed evidence on predictor differences as a function of race. Their findings are summarized in Table 10.1.

In summary, most commonly used predictor measures show mean differences between groups of applicants with Whites scoring higher as a group. Measures emphasizing cognitive abilities generally show the largest difference, with interpersonal abilities, working together with others, personality and background data often showing smaller or no difference. Few such comparisons are available for racio-ethnic groups other than Blacks, although existing data suggest that Hispanics score lower than Whites on cognitively loaded measures. Experts agree that there are many reasons for the differences that are usually obtained, most of which are beyond the ability of industrial-organizational psychologists to correct.

Diversity professionals should understand that cognitive ability tests, while often valid, are likely to show adverse impact. Other predictors such as structured interviews, work samples, or evaluations from probationary appointments may reduce adverse impact and increase selection of qualified persons from underrepresented groups when their use can be justified on technical grounds.

Table 10.1 Summary of Meta-Analytic Results: Race Comparisons in Selection Measures

Selection Measure	Summary of Comparisons
Cognitive ability	White>Black differences. Large effect size but smaller for complex jobs, industrial samples, and specific abilities (verbal and math).
Work samples	W>B differences. Large to medium effect sizes. Larger when cognitively loaded, smaller for oral communication, interpersonal skills, leadership and persuasion.
Situational judgment tests	W>B effect sizes moderate to small. W>Hispanic and Asian effect sizes smaller.
Biodata	Small effect sizes but few studies.
Assessment centers	W>B effects medium to small. W>H effects smaller.
Personality	Small effects.
Structured interviews	Medium to small effects.

Sources: Bobko and Roth (2013); Dean, Roth, and Bobko (2008); Roth, Bobko, McFarland, and Buster (2008); Roth et al. (2001); Whetzel, McDaniel, and Nguyen (2008).

Racio-ethnic Differences in Measures of Job Performance

Research shows that differences in performance measures favor Whites, but these differences are considerably smaller than differences in selection measures. Typical hiring plans often eliminate people of color who, if hired, would likely succeed. Comparisons of job performance come from many different jobs and physical and social environments. These studies gather data about job incumbents, meaning that those included are performing at satisfactory levels, high enough for them to retain their jobs. Very poor performers generally do not appear in these samples, nor do those who score low on selection tests and thus are not hired in the first place.

Perhaps the most widely used measure of job performance is supervisor ratings. Landy (2010) reviewed studies and meta-analyses from 1997 to 2007 and concluded that statistically significant Black–White differences (favoring Whites) often occurred, but these were small and much smaller than the typical race difference in predictors such as cognitive ability. Although in individual cases performance ratings could easily be biased on the basis of race (or other factors), Landy found no persistent pattern to suggest that people of color frequently or typically received ratings contaminated by racial bias. On the other hand, Stauffer and Buckley (2005) found lower ratings for Blacks, but larger differences when those employees were rated by Whites than by other Blacks. They concluded that supervisor's race did not affect performance ratings for Whites, but a Black worker's evaluation was likely to be lower if the supervisor was White.

Meta-analysis of Black–White differences on other measures of work performance (McKay & McDaniel, 2006) found higher scores for Whites. Differences were small on non-cognitive criteria (e.g., absenteeism, accidents, interactions with others, on-the-job training) and larger on criteria emphasizing cognitive factors (e.g., job knowledge tests, work samples, overall job performance). McKay (2010) found only one meta-analysis comparing job performance of Hispanics and Whites (Roth, Huffcutt, & Bobko, 2003). Overall a very small performance difference favored Whites, but the difference was larger when jobs were more complex or criteria were cognitively loaded. The number of studies for meta-analysis was small and some participants may not have been fluent in English language.

To conduct meta-analysis, researchers need a large number of people in each racio-ethnic group whose performance has been measured in the same way, usually from *the same job or job category*. Given significant occupational segregation by racio-ethnicity and the relatively few people of color at managerial and higher levels in organizations, it is difficult or impossible to conduct these studies for some jobs (Mintz & Krymkowski, 2010; Hamilton, Austin, & Darity, 2011).

Racio-ethnic Differences in Validity and Prediction

A different topic is whether predictor and criterion are related in the same way for different racio-ethnic groups. For example, a selection measure might predict performance well for Whites, but not for other ethnic groups. This topic is statistically complex and controversial, with legal implications for use of particular predictors or criteria. It is beyond the scope of responsibilities for most diversity professionals, who nevertheless should understand that this may be a selection problem in some large organizations. In a detailed explanation by Berry, Clark, and McClure (2011), meta-analyses of validities for cognitive ability test scores found that validity (not scores, but prediction) was higher for Whites and Asian samples than for Black and Hispanic groups. (See also Cascio & Aguinis, 2005; Sackett, Borneman, & Connelly, 2008; Berry, Cullen, & Meyer, 2013.)

What's To Be Done About This?

To summarize, racio-ethnic group differences exist on most measures used to select employees and measure job performance. Cognitively loaded measures show the largest differences. Whites generally score higher but the difference varies from small to substantial, depending on the measure.

(In some cases, Asians score higher than Whites. See Outtz & Newman, 2010, Figure 3.3.) Racio-ethnic differences in *selection* tend to be higher than differences in *actual job performance* for those who are hired. That is, these assessments make it harder for people of color to be hired; however, if hired, their performance is likely to be closer to that of Whites than it was on predictors at the time of hire. Nothing in these studies tells us *why* these differences are found. In the context of employee selection, illegal discrimination is suggested by a significant difference (adverse impact) in scores between Whites and people of color. Therefore, employers often experience conflicts among validity, fairness, and support for diversity. What's an employer to do? Some possible answers appear in the shaded box.

The Diversity-Validity Dilemma: Suggestions for Balance

In complicated situations, often no "right answers" exist—just alternatives with positive and negative aspects. An example is the *Diversity-Validity (D-V) Dilemma*. Large employers, trying to use best practices in hiring and in diversity, often find both these goals cannot be accomplished at the same time. The D-V Dilemma refers to contradictions between increasing diversity and the realities of employment anti-discrimination law, given existing racio-ethnic and sex differences on many valid selection procedures (Pyburn, Ployhart, & Kravitz, 2008). Organizations seem to respond in one or both of two major ways to this dilemma: revise selection procedures (Ployhart & Holtz, 2008) and/or increase diversity through affirmative action (Kravitz, 2008).

Pyburn et al. (2008) outlined the legal context. In very limited circumstances an employer might legitimately use race or sex preferences in hiring or promotion to increase numbers of successful candidates from targeted groups. Courts have clearly stated that such preferences are only acceptable when there is a history of prior discrimination against the target group. Preferences must also be narrow and time-limited. In some public sector cases, a showing of "compelling public interest" has also been required. An example might be hiring police officers to work in neighborhoods where race would affect officers' ability to police effectively and safely. Whether even this situation would survive a Supreme Court challenge at this time is unclear. The crux of the D-V issue is that the most valid measures for predicting job success generally show adverse impact by sex and race, leaving employers vulnerable to discrimination lawsuits from those in the excluded group.

With respect to the first response of revising selection procedures, Ployhart and Holtz (2008) reviewed 16 selection strategies used to balance diversity and validity. Strategies fall into five categories. First, use predictors with smaller between-group differences (e.g., work samples or assessment centers, educational attainment or GPA, measures of *specific* cognitive abilities). Second, combine scores in ways that reduce subgroup differences while maintaining acceptable validity. For example, employers could broaden their selection measures beyond cognitive ability to address the full range of knowledge, skill, or ability a job requires. They could weight predictors or performance criteria differently to minimize adverse impact. Another possibility is selecting within "bands" of applicants with scores so similar they are considered equivalent, expecting that applicants of color could be reached in this way. However, unless legally problematic racial preferences are used within bands, this is unlikely to reduce adverse impact.

A third category includes strategies for reducing score differences by trying *not* to measure things unrelated to performance. These include removing or extending time limits on tests, eliminating potentially biased test items showing large subgroup differences, or writing test items that are "culture-free" as much as possible. Sensitivity review panels can review items for inappropriateness or offensiveness to various subgroups. To the extent justified, cognitive ability can be de-emphasized relative to other relevant measures.

Category four involves allowing practice before testing by conducting orientations with similar materials or allowing people to re-apply and be tested a second time. The fifth category focuses on leaving applicants with a favorable impression of the selection process, which might be beneficial in the future. For example, companies might include targeted recruiting to increase diversity among applicants. Reactions are generally more favorable to procedures that are "face valid" and seem job-related (e.g., interviews, work samples), clear and satisfactory explanations and courteous treatment.

Ployhart and Holtz (2008) discussed the likely success of these strategies in reducing adverse impact and extent to which each reduces validity in attempting to increase diversity. They also evaluated alternatives to cognitive ability tests, such as open-ended rather than multiple-choice items. This allows the applicant to answer questions in his or her own words rather than by reading and choosing from several alternatives. Use of "constructed response options" has reduced Black–White adverse impact substantially on promotional exams for firefighters (Arthur, Edwards, & Barrett, 2002).

The second major response to the D-V Dilemma is to increase diversity through AA. Kravitz (2008) reviewed the legal basis for AA and literature on attitudes about AA, which vary with details of the AA plan and characteristics of the perceiver. For example, racial differences exist in reactions to stronger forms of AA (which are also subject to severe legal restrictions), and women are generally more favorable toward AA than men. Those scoring higher on measures of racism and sexism and on Social Dominance Orientation are more opposed to AA (especially its stronger forms), and those who believe discrimination still exists are more positive.

Kravitz presented evidence that discrimination still exists, suggesting AA or another remedial approach is still needed. On a large-scale basis, AA has had positive effects on employment of women, Blacks, and Hispanics although that is not the case for all jobs, places, occasions, and individuals. The few studies of AA effects on productivity indicate no substantial effect, positive or negative, on organizational performance.

One alleged negative impact of AA is that it leads to questioning the competence of someone perceived as an "AA hire." Kravitz's review showed that stigmatization does not occur or is much reduced when others have clear knowledge of the target person's competence and successful job performance, and when it is known that the AA does not involve specific group preferences. Self-stigmatization or "AA guilt" may occur for candidates who believe they were given preference due to sex. This has been found with female undergraduate students when they were not provided evidence of their performance or relevant qualifications, and when their personal self-confidence was low (Heilman, Rivero, & Brett, 1991; Heilman, Battle, Keller, & Lee, 1998). However, it was absent or much weaker when participants had clear evidence of their competence, and when *White males* believed they were selected on the basis of sex (Heilman, Simon, & Repper, 1987; Heilman et al., 1991, 1998).

Kravitz (2008) recommends that firms seldom if ever use forms of AA with specific sex or racial preferences. Instead, employers should strive to eliminate obvious and covert discrimination and to increase the numbers of well-qualified target group members who are recruited, considered, hired, and retained as successful employees.

Outtz and Newman (2010) made several suggestions, focusing on the substantial variation in cognitive ability scores that is *not* related to job performance criteria. That variation comes from many factors including random error in testing. The typical way of using validated tests for selection they called the "first generation adverse impact model." It is color-blind and does not explicitly consider racio-ethnicity. It is also a "mechanical" or "cookbook" model based on statistical relationships among scores but without attention to why those scores or relationships occur, and relies on validated predictors to select applicants most likely to succeed. Adverse impact is seen as a problem to be solved by improving the test or adding other less discriminatory predictors to prevent elimination of Blacks (or others) from consideration. The employer must maintain evidence that selection devices are valid in case of legal challenge. This model tries to treat everyone in the same way, value-free with respect to race.

Contrasted with this is Outtz and Newman's "second generation adverse impact model" that attempts to understand *why* adverse impact occurs by adding additional factors (see Box 10.2). These could produce adverse impact for people of color on cognitive ability tests, despite scores that indicate ability to do the job.

According to Outtz and Newman, "Adverse impact is a major social problem . . . (which) systematically excludes African Americans from many occupations. To make things worse, a huge majority of this exclusion is completely unjustified by the corresponding improvement in job performance" (from using these tests) (2010, p. 83). What can be done? Outtz and Newman suggested long-, medium-, and short-term strategies. Long-term strategies include public policy interventions (e.g., addressing poverty, education, child care, health status). Another is overturning the prohibition of subgroup norming in the 1991 Civil Rights Act, politically difficult but allowing compromise between including more Blacks and efficient, valid selection.

Medium-term strategies involve development of better predictors, because cognitive ability test scores "predict race far better than they predict performance" (p. 84). Instead of trying to improve cognitive ability tests, psychologists should develop other measures that are better at estimating job performance. For example, *contextual performance* refers to a combination of persistence and enthusiasm (volunteering for tasks beyond one's own job, helping and cooperating, following rules and procedures), non-cognitive aspects of actual work (Borman & Motowidlo, 1997).

Short-term strategies include weighting of predictors or criteria and targeted recruiting. *Weighting* involves selecting new hires on the basis of a composite score that gives different weights to various parts of the composite based on amount of adverse impact. This statistical remedy is usually only partly successful and requires considerable technical expertise. In *targeted recruiting*, the organization actively works to broaden the applicant pool to include people of color who are strong applicants and likely to be hired. This involves thoughtful advertising and outreach, but not preferential hiring. Relying on word-of-mouth and referrals from current employees is likely to yield applicants similar to current employees; so will internal recruiting (advertising job openings within the organization first). In contrast, more diverse applicant pools can be reached through contacts

---

Box 10.2 Second Generation Adverse Impact Factors

Environmental effects on cognitive ability: Effects of social class, prenatal and child care including nutrition and health, educational opportunity, teacher attitudes and expectations.

Test content: Exposure to and practice with content and format of items, similarity of content to actual job requirements.

Patterns of reward at work: Level of job performance and supervisor reactions to it, evaluator bias, out-group membership relative to leader.

Racio-ethnicity: Physical appearance, genetic makeup, racio-ethnic identity.

with high schools, colleges, churches, or other locations with high percentages of people of color, and by advertising in media sources likely to reach underrepresented groups. In addition, many ads state that an organization is an "Affirmative Action employer" or mention its EEO policy. Employers may also use recruiters who are women or people of color, or develop brochures or websites that imply or describe diversity-friendly policies. In one survey of HR professionals, 79% reported that their organizations relied on targeted recruiting strategies designed to increase diversity (SHRM, 2010).

How well do such practices work to attract candidates from underrepresented groups? Kulik and Roberson (2008) summarized research on effectiveness of three major recruiting practices in increasing diversity: (a) photos or information highlighting workforce diversity; (b) statements of EEO or AA policy; and (c) recruiters who are female or people of color. In general, individuals of color are more attracted to an organization when photos or text show people from their demographic group, especially in higher statuses, but attraction of Whites is not affected (e.g.,Walker, Feild, Bernerth, & Becton, 2012). In one experiment, participants were more attracted to an organization whose website included testimonials. Blacks responded more favorably and Whites less favorably as the proportion of testimonials by people of color increased. However, this difference was minimal when informationally rich audio-visual testimonials were presented vs. those with only photo and text (Walker, Feild, Giles, Armenakis, & Bernerth, 2009).

Attraction also seems to depend on perceiving the depicted representative as similar to the job-seeker (Avery, Hernandez, & Hebl, 2004). Applicants with attitudes supportive of diversity, regardless of race, were attracted to organizations that appeared to have positive diversity climates (Avery et al., 2013). However, if information is later found to be inaccurate or misleading, backlash may occur (McKay & Avery, 2005). In some cases, university recruiting brochures or websites have been digitally altered to include faces of minority individuals (Durhams, 2000; Mikkelson, 2014). Applicants generally react negatively to discovering that recruiting materials were deceptive (Knouse, 2009). See the *phantom diversity* example in Chapter 5.

Kulik and Roberson's review (2008) classified EEO policy "identity blind" if it described equal opportunity regardless of applicant demographic characteristics. AA policies were considered "identity conscious" because they imply attention to race or sex. They found that Whites and people of color reacted more favorably to EEO policies than to identity conscious ones. Generally those from underrepresented groups found organizations more attractive when diversity statements and policies appeared in recruiting materials. Those with stronger ethnic identities were more attracted when diversity initiatives were described (Kim & Gelfand, 2003).

Research on recruiters who are female or people of color has yielded inconsistent results. Demographic similarity to a recruiter probably does lead to liking, but other aspects of the recruiting and application process are probably more important. A recruiter who is warm, friendly, forthcoming, well informed, and apparently honest is likely to elicit a positive response even when demographically different from the applicant (Thomas, 2005, p. 29). Finally, Kulik and Roberson (2008) cautioned that much recruiting research has relied on samples of students, not actual applicants, and on measures of self-reported attraction rather than actual acceptance of job offers.

Recruitment contexts are rarely as simple as those used in these experiments. Applicants have access to much information about employing organizations so the effect of any one factor may be reduced. In addition, in actual organizations different people often control recruiting and decisions to make job offers. A glaring real-world example of the disjunction between recruitment and hiring in elite professional firms is described in the shaded box. Finally, even if diversity recruiting improves attraction and acceptance of job offers, employee *retention* depends on other factors.

The Slip between Diversity Cup and Lip

Sociologist and management professor Lauren Rivera (2012) studied recruitment and hiring processes in prestigious professional firms in law, investment banking, and management consulting. These firms tend to hire a set of new employees as a cohort, invest in their training and professional socialization, and promote from within. Thus the key to diversifying employment in these settings is to recruit and hire people from underrepresented groups shortly after graduation and successfully retain them. Rivera conducted 120 interviews with those who hired new graduates each year and served as an unpaid intern in return for permission to study recruitment and hiring in one elite firm. She attended recruitment activities, observed candidate evaluation meetings, and interacted with candidates before and after interviews. She also attended diversity job fairs and other public recruitment events, presenting herself as a graduate student seeking summer opportunities.

On paper, these firms' plans and processes were exactly what is recommended for diversity recruitment, yet their efforts were largely unsuccessful in increasing diversity among new employees. Most firms were federal contractors and thus subject to OFCCP's AA requirements. Generally they used targeted diversity recruitment, developed diversity hiring goals, kept records of diversity-relevant activities, and had full- or part-time staff responsible for diversity. Firms tended to hire both women and men (although investment banks were least gender diverse), but racial diversity was lacking among new-hire cohorts. What accounted for this discrepancy between what was "planned" and what was enacted? Rivera's research showed how this happens.

The Pipeline Problem

Professionals in these firms generally believed their hiring procedures were gender- and race-neutral and that the problem was lack of qualified persons from underrepresented groups. However, they defined the pipeline narrowly, recruiting only from the top five to 15 "core" or "elite" schools in the field. They believed this was efficient and "prestige of one's educational credentials is a crucial indicator of an individual's intellectual, social, and moral worth" (p. 77). Rivera noted that two investment banks included Spelman and Morehouse, two prestigious historically Black universities, in their recruiting; one law firm offered an interview to the top graduate from any law school regardless of institutional prestige. However, these firms were the exception. Employers perceived that eligible Blacks at elite schools were uninterested in careers with firms like theirs, and that those interested were not "qualified." Loosening the criterion of institutional prestige was perceived as "lowering the bar" (p. 78) or hiring substandard professionals. Diversity job fairs were perceived as occasions for publicizing their firms, marketing, or community service rather than opportunities for serious recruiting. One savvy recruiting manager said that hiring committees were focused on competing for the same small slice of the pie rather than figuring out how to make the pie slice larger—but that she had no influence in bringing this about.

The Great Divide

A gap in priorities, power, and decision-making authority existed between HR/Diversity staff recruiting applicants and revenue-generating professionals (RGPs) making hiring decisions. Evaluators often thought Black and Latino candidates were lacking in "polish" or interpersonal skills required to interact with clients. However, this crucial attribute was based on "evaluators' gut reactions and feelings of comfort" (p. 85) rather than any standard and systematic judgments about behaviors, such as those from mock client interviews or other exercises. Evaluators in one firm seemed unable to recognize or correct their own obvious bias even when the firm was being investigated for their small number of ethnically diverse hires, and in fact erased and altered candidate scores to match and justify their hiring decisions!

Rivera made useful recommendations for elite professional service and other firms that are truly committed to hiring people from underrepresented demographic groups. First, serious recruiting efforts should be directed at graduates of a wider range of institutions, perhaps giving more weight to students' grades or other activities while in school. Second, power and decision-making authority of diversity recruiting managers should be increased. Rivera found that RGPs did not believe that HR and diversity staff could understand and evaluate candidates' merit. In a few cases, someone with previous experience as RGP who had moved into the HR function was fully included in hiring decisions. Rivera recommended assigning an RGP to this role or seeking individuals who have worked in both roles. Third, firms should improve procedures for assessing "merit," for example by developing more objective rating procedures or evaluating role-plays of client interviews or other behavioral activities.

The late Thurgood Marshall grew up in Baltimore, MD, and attended a segregated high school. Graduating with honors from Lincoln University in Pennsylvania, a historically Black college, he was rejected by the University of Maryland Law School because of race. Marshall attended Howard University, another historically Black institution, but could not attract important cases as a Black attorney with little experience. After joining the National Association for the Advancement of Colored People (NAACP), he fought several cases undermining racial segregation beginning with *Murray v. Pearson,* a racial bias suit against the University of Maryland Law School. Marshall successfully led the NAACP's challenge to racially segregated schools in the 1954 *Brown v. Board of Education of Topeka* suit. This case, a landmark in the Civil Rights movement and one of the most significant in the history of the Supreme Court, marked Thurgood Marshall as one of the most famous and successful lawyers in the US. Marshall was appointed to the Second Circuit Court of Appeals and later as Solicitor General was the US government's attorney in Supreme Court cases. In 1967 President Johnson appointed Marshall to the US Supreme Court, where he served for 24 years as the first African American justice of the nation's highest court. Today, Baltimore/Washington International Thurgood Marshall Airport (BWI) houses a small museum honoring this important American jurist and Civil Rights advocate (Thurgood Marshall, 2013).

Would law firms studied by Professor Rivera have interviewed the young Thurgood Marshall if he had applied for a position?

Race Discrimination and Racism

In legal contexts, *race discrimination* is differential treatment based on race or ethnicity (including national origin or color) rather than job-related skills and abilities, especially when behavior or employment decisions negatively impact the target of discrimination. Race discrimination includes unfair denials of employment or promotion, segregation of job assignments, lower pay, or exclusion from information or developmental opportunities such as mentoring or training. It also includes discrimination based on language or personal appearance related to racio-ethnicity. *Racism* is a negative explicit or implicit attitude based on racio-ethnicity. From this perspective, members of any racial group can be racist. Because much recent psychological research on racism considers it to be a negative prejudicial attitude based on race, we use the term racism in that sense.

Box 10.3 Institutional Racism

"Limiting our understanding of racism to prejudice (is not) a sufficient explanation for (its) persistence … racism, like other forms of oppression, is not only a personal ideology based on racial prejudice, but a *system* involving cultural messages and institutional policies and practices as well as the beliefs and actions of individuals." (Tatum, 1997, p. 7)

However, others define racism as a comprehensive system of advantage based on race, including subordination and oppression of others based on their origins and physical characteristics (Tatum, 1997; Rothenberg, 2007). From this perspective, the term "racist" is applied only to those who benefit from the system, without regard for their individual opinions; in the US this would be Whites. The term *institutional racism* denotes this system or structure of assumptions, procedures, norms, and regulations that disadvantages a group based on color, race, or ethnicity. Racial disadvantage is embedded in institutions of the organization rather than conscious intentions of individuals. Nevertheless, individuals holding racist attitudes would have difficulty maintaining those attitudes without support from the culture and social environment.

Diversity professionals should understand these two definitions of racism. If an employee holds racist attitudes toward others that are expressed in hurtful speech or harmful behavior, the appropriate response is to deal with this as an unacceptable workplace behavior. Employer policies for progressive discipline should be applied and offensive behavior or speech should not be allowed to continue. However, racism can be embedded in an organization's culture even though individuals profess no prejudicial attitudes and in fact would be shocked and offended at an accusation of racism. In this situation the diversity professional should document consequences of policies and procedures for those of different racio-ethnicities and work to change any which may lead to discriminatory results.

Modern, Symbolic, and Aversive Racism

These forms of contemporary racism are very different from earlier blatant race prejudice that is unacceptable by today's standards. "Old-fashioned" race prejudice prior to World War II had three characteristics: (a) the firm belief that Whites were inherently superior to other racial groups; (b) widespread acceptance of the rightness of racial segregation; and (c) support for government's role in maintaining segregation and denying equality of rights to people of color (Sears, Hetts, Sidanius, & Bobo, 2000; Whitley & Kite, 2006). When targeted at Blacks, this was called *Jim Crow racism* after the oppressive system of laws in the US at that time.

Jim Crow and his Laws

"Jim Crow" referred to a black-face minstrel routine ("Jump Jim Crow") first performed in 1828. This derogatory term referred to the system of laws maintaining legal segregation (Jim Crow Law, n.d.). These laws existed in many states, especially across the Southern US, reinforcing racial segregation after Reconstruction around 1880 until the modern Civil Rights Movement in the 1950s and 1960s (National Park Service, 2015). This period was repressive and dangerous for Blacks, particularly in the Southern states, where a rigid system of legally supported forceful subordination denied basic rights and often led to violence and lynching.

Jim Crow laws required racial separation in education, hospitals and clinics, transportation, restaurants, cemeteries, parks and swimming pools, and other public settings. Legal segregation was illustrated by the iconic and widely photographed "Colored Only" water fountains. This system of separate facilities, usually of lower quality, created danger and inconvenience for Blacks. For example, they could not use White-designated restrooms, dining, or hotel facilities when traveling. Interracial marriage was a crime leading to incarceration and was finally legalized by the famous *Loving v. Virginia* (1967) Supreme Court case. *Brown v. Board of Education* (1954) and the Civil Rights Act of 1964 marked the end of legal segregation but its consequences continue to the present day.

Contemporary racism is usually more subtle than the earlier blatant racial prejudice that still exists but is now generally considered unacceptable, at least openly. Whitley and Kite (2006) list three points about today's racism: (a) America's norms have actually changed since the 1950s toward accepting equal treatment for everyone; (b) however, people differ in how much they agree with and accept this change; and (c) even people who do not fully agree with this change usually try to act in ways that others will think are non-prejudiced. They are reluctant to be seen as racist and believe that others would disapprove of clearly discriminatory behavior. Signs of this contemporary form of prejudice are behavior, attitudes, and beliefs that are *ambiguous* and can be justified as non-prejudiced in light of other accepted principles.

One form of contemporary race prejudice is *Modern* or *Symbolic Racism* (M/SR). This view supports denigration of Blacks as a group because they supposedly do not follow traditional American values such as hard work, self-sufficiency, and determination of outcomes based on merit (Sears & McConahay, 1973). Although this form of prejudice no doubt occurs with respect to other out-groups (e.g., Latinos, poor people), the concepts originally pertained to anti-Black prejudice and most research has concerned beliefs and behaviors towards Blacks.

M/SR is usually clothed in political views (e.g., opposition to Black candidates or to measures designed to reduce segregation, such as AA). M/SR and conservative political views are not the same thing. However, some who hold contemporary racist views express them in support of "traditional values" and conservative socio-political views. According to Whitley and Kite (2006), M/SR share several beliefs:

1. Racial prejudice and discrimination no longer exist or are very rare.
2. Black–White differences in economic outcomes result from Blacks' lack of ability or motivation to work hard.
3. Because Blacks are not willing to work for what they want, they should not be angry over continuing inequality.
4. Instead of working hard, Blacks ask for special treatment and handouts.
5. For this reason, Blacks have been getting more than their share in comparison to Whites.

The belief structure underlying M/SR also includes five aspects: (a) somewhat negative attitudes towards Blacks despite; (b) little direct and personal knowledge about them; (c) belief in traditional values such as self-reliance, hard work, individualism, and self-control; (d) belief in equality of opportunity, but not equality of outcomes; and (e) sensitivity to threats against interests of one's own group.

Aversive racism is somewhat different in origin and substance but also underlies behaviors that subtly disadvantage Blacks. The term denotes prejudice characterizing those who find the notion of racism "aversive" or offensive. According to Gaertner and Dovidio (1986), growing up White in the US with its history of institutional and cultural racism *without* developing some negative ideas and feelings about Blacks is nearly impossible. Aversive racists consider themselves non-prejudiced and strongly egalitarian, probably adopt liberal political views, and actively try to avoid discriminating. Their behavior is motivated by pro-White rather than anti-Black feelings and may be based in discomfort, uneasiness, anxiety, and perhaps fear, and likely includes avoidance rather than active negative behavior. When a non-racial rationale for behaving differently toward members of the two groups exists, aversive racists may show favoritism towards Whites.

In a typical US work setting, the diversity professional will likely encounter employees fitting the description of Modern, Symbolic, or Aversive Racists. In many business settings it is rare for employees openly to espouse negative beliefs or feelings toward people of color. However, events such as these might be observed:

- Hiring an Asian American applicant rather than a Black based not on qualifications and experience but instead on how the manager thinks co-workers or customers might react.
- Not providing appropriate corrective feedback to Black supervisees and instead giving inflated performance evaluations, which does not happen with White employees.
- Saying "Don't mention this to (the Black person) because she/he might think I am prejudiced."
- Asking Black participants in a meeting for their ideas, suggesting that they could give "the Black point of view."

Such situations probably will not lead to grievances or lawsuits, but are likely to lower inclusion and engagement experienced by people of color and the degree to which they feel comfortable contributing to the work environment on the same basis as others. What can a diversity professional do to overcome subtle but negative effects of these contemporary forms of race prejudice? Gaertner et al. (2003) suggest applying the Common Ingroup Identity Model by emphasizing identities shared by everyone in the group (e.g., our department or team) without calling attention to faultlines separating members of the group. Shared identity can be accomplished through small things like birthday cakes or items (hats, pens, or notepads) with a group logo, or larger things like public service projects completed off-site as a group where everyone has the same t-shirt and interaction is equal status and friendship-based. However, to avoid creating the illusion of colorblindness, this should be done while continuing to value the multiple social identities within the group (Thomas & Chrobot-Mason, 2005).

Implicit Bias

Forms of racism described above are generally considered explicit in that they are measured directly; the person is aware of his or her reactions and presumably can change or control them—although the person may not realize others consider them racist. A different form of prejudice is called *implicit bias*, a nonconscious and automatic response based on previous experience and implying favorable or unfavorable emotional, cognitive, or behavioral reactions toward an attitude object (Greenwald & Banaji, 1995). Implicit bias is thought to underlie subtle nonverbal behaviors that are difficult for a person to control but may be interpreted as prejudice by others. It may also affect decisions experienced as rational but in fact reflecting bias of which the person is unaware, such as racially biased actions by law enforcement or others in the legal system (Staats, Capatosto, Wright, & Contractor, 2015). Implicit bias is usually measured indirectly by assessing how quickly a person reacts to associations of the attitude object with positive or negative words. The Implicit Association Test (IAT) is widely used as a measure of automatic preferences that an individual is thought to be unable or unwilling to recognize or report (Greenwald, McGhee, & Schwartz, 1998). A meta-analysis of IAT predictive validity studies found that this indirect measure was a better predictor of Black–White interracial behavior than were explicit self-report measures of attitude (Greenwald, Poehlman, Uhlmann, & Banaji, 2009). The IAT is frequently used to

---

Box 10.4 More About Implicit Bias . . .

Banaji and Greenwald have developed Project Implicit, a research and demonstration site. Visitors can try out the IAT at http://implicit.harvard.edu/implicit. Everyday implications of their work are described in a recent popular book, *The Blind Spot* (Banaji & Greenwald, 2013).

---

investigate racial attitudes. However, versions have also been developed to study implicit bias using stimulus words or faces depicting categories of age, sex, race, and other dimensions that are often the basis for prejudice.

Critiques of the IAT's empirical and conceptual basis have argued that scores can be affected by familiarity with stimulus faces or words, fear of appearing racist, or cognitive skill of the person taking the IAT (Blanton, Jaccard, Klick, Mellers, Mitchell, & Tetlock, 2009). People do have biases of which they may be only dimly aware, and these biases may affect their decisions and other behavior. However, the specific way in which these biases develop, their extent, their measurement, and how they change remain a topic of some disagreement among researchers. The idea of *dual attitudes* has also been suggested (Wilson, Lindsey, & Schooler, 2000), referring to the existence of implicit and explicit evaluative responses to the same attitude object. The implicit attitude is activated automatically, influences subtle responses, and changes very slowly. The explicit attitude is retrieved from memory, under conscious control, likely to influence the person's report of feelings, and more easily changeable.

Violations of the Law: Race Discrimination and Harassment

Legal Bases

Title VII of the Civil Rights Act (CRA) of 1964 prohibits discrimination or segregation on the basis of race, color, or nationality (as well as sex and religion). The CRA of 1991 later clarified how Title VII adverse impact cases should be interpreted. It also prohibited subgroup norming, extended Title VII to subsidiaries of American companies in other countries, and included jury trials and additional remedies in Title VII (and ADA) cases (Gutman et al., 2011). The Immigration Control and Reform Act (IRCA) is not generally considered an anti-discrimination statute because its main purpose concerns employment of immigrants. However, IRCA also prohibits discrimination on the basis of national origin so that an employer cannot simply decide not to hire Latinos, for example.

Under Title VII, discrimination can be obvious or it can be difficult to recognize when embedded in a seemingly normal system. Race discrimination may take the form of racial or ethnic harassment, which can be disparate treatment. Race harassment refers to creation of a work environment imbued with slurs, graffiti, threats, incivility, or exclusionary behavior based on racio-ethnicity. It is associated with reduced organizational commitment and job satisfaction as well as increased anxiety and depression, physical symptoms, and intention to leave, and is more often targeted at people of color than at Whites (Raver & Nishii, 2010). Title VII race-based claims proceed in the same way as for sex, religion, or national origin, except that by law race or color cannot be considered a *bona fide occupational qualification*.

Plaintiffs often make Title VII and/or Constitutional claims for the same offense because of differences in timelines and relevant case law as well as remedies (e.g., monetary damages) if the plaintiff is victorious. Also, in some situations Title VII does not apply but Constitutional claims are valid, for example, in claims against small private employers (Gutman, Koppes, & Vodanovich, 2011). A 1987 Supreme Court ruling determined that the meaning of "race" included ethnicity, thus clarifying that Constitutional claims could be brought by Arabs or others who might be considered White. Further detail about these provisions is provided by Cascio and Aguinis (2005) and Gutman et al. (2011).

Overall Frequency

How common is racio-ethnic discrimination? In a population survey, Blacks most frequently reported that they had experienced discrimination (about 35–40%), followed by Hispanics and Asians (about 20%). Whites reported experiences of discrimination infrequently (about 10%). However, survey questions did not distinguish workplace discrimination from that in other contexts (Pew Research Center, 2013a, 2013b). Data from a large national phone survey conducted in 2005 by the Gallup organization found that in comparison to Whites, Blacks were four times as likely and Hispanics were over three times as likely to have perceived racio-ethnic discrimination within the preceding year. In this survey, the likelihood of perceived discrimination was significantly lower for those with supervisors of the same racio-ethnicity (Avery, McKay, & Wilson, 2008). Another Gallup survey (Jones, 2013b) reported that 60% of Black Americans felt that Whites had better chances at jobs for which they were qualified. This is consistent with persistently higher unemployment rates for Blacks and Latinos than for Whites (USBLS, 2016).

The number of EEOC charges filed each year is considered a conservative indicator because most experiences of discrimination do not lead to formal charges. Generally more than one-third of charges in a single year deal with race discrimination. In 2015, there were 31,027 such charges, 35% of the year's total. National origin discrimination charges were 9,438 or 11%, and color discrimination charges were 2,853 or 3% of the total. (Some charges alleged more than one type of discrimination.) In the same year, there were 9,286 charges of race harassment (EEOC, n.d.-a, c).

Segregation

Other estimates of the extent of racio-ethnic discrimination come from statistics about distribution of people of color in the labor market. Chapter 4 discussed occupational and job segregation, the unequal sorting of people into occupations or jobs on the basis of sex or race. Most studies of racio-ethnic segregation at work concern comparisons of Whites with Blacks or Hispanics (Tomaskovic-Devey, Zimmer, Stainback, Robinson, Taylor, & McTague, 2006). In 2003, between 30 and 40% of women, Blacks, or Hispanics would have had to change jobs in order for people to be sorted proportionally by sex or ethnicity. However, one-sex or one-race workplaces declined dramatically so that almost none existed in 2003. Segregation by job and occupation *within* workplaces continued, however. Mintz and Krymkowski (2010) reported historical patterns of sex and race segregation and pointed out that this pattern negatively affects wages and promotion of persons who are not White and male. Sex segregation also varies within the different racio-ethnic groups, according to the Institute for Women's Policy Research researchers who analyzed data from the Department of Labor (USDoL) (Hegewisch, Liepmann, Hayes, & Hartmann, 2010). In 2009, Asian Americans were least segregated by sex and Hispanics most sex-segregated. Intermediate levels of sex segregation occurred for Whites and African Americans.

Both discriminatory and legitimate reasons produce these patterns. Occupational segregation sometimes occurs due to employee preferences or credentials, but it also results from obvious or subtle processes channeling men or women of different racio-ethnicities into different kinds of employment or excluding them from others. In addition to socialization patterns, these processes include deliberate or implicit discrimination; gender or racial stereotypes or bias; selective recruitment strategies; location of work facilities with respect to residence patterns and modes of transportation; requirements for employment such as licensure or certification; restricted access to apprenticeships, internships, specific educational or other training programs; and even educational and career counseling.

Sociologists Tomaskovic-Devey and Stainback (2007) have described three processes underlying segregation patterns. *Prejudice and cognitive bias* refers to individual-level processes discussed in Chapter 6. *Statistical discrimination* refers to employers' reliance on what they believe are factual differences among demographic groups to make decisions about individuals from those groups. Although this seems logical and fact-based, it is illegal since the person is affected by decisions based on membership in a particular group and not on test scores or other personal job-relevant information. *Social closure* refers to including members of one's own group in opportunities that are closed to out-group members. Networking, referrals, informal recruiting, employment in family businesses, and other sorts of help provided to friends and relatives are examples of social closure.

Hellerstein and Neumark (2008) examined occupational segregation by education, race, and ethnicity, finding that Whites were sorted into jobs according to level of education. Segregation of Hispanics from Whites was related to English language proficiency, not education. Notably, English proficiency was not an important factor for *non-Hispanics with limited English skills.* For Blacks, the pattern was related to race but neither educational or language differences.

Statistics on people of color in upper-level jobs are also informative. For example, EEO-1 reports from federal contractors in private industry show that 88% of executive or senior level officials and managers are White. Of people of color, almost 3% are Black, 3.6% are Hispanic, 4% are Asian, and less than 1% each are American Indian, Hawai'ian or more than one race (EEOC, 2012). Thus, Whites are overrepresented at higher levels given their numbers in the workforce. Similar patterns are found in the public sector, where barriers to entry are weaker for people of color (EEOC, 2010), and in monthly household surveys by the Census Bureau for both private and public sector employment (USCB, 2012).

Wages

Where there is occupational segregation and crowding into limited occupations, a wage gap is also likely. A significant wage penalty for Blacks was found in 1990 Census data (Huffman & Cohen, 2004) with Blacks excluded from jobs with higher skill requirements, and paid less than comparably skilled Whites in similar jobs. Other Census Bureau data from 2005–2007 showed Black men to be proportionately represented in only 13% of occupations; average annual wage in occupations with more Blacks than would be expected was over $13,000 less than in occupations where they were underrepresented (Hamilton, Austin, & Darity, 2011). This could not be accounted for by levels of education, "soft skills," or occupational interests, suggesting labor market discrimination was a plausible explanation.

Similar processes affect employment of low-skill Latino immigrants (Catanzarite, 2002). Los Angeles census data showed that certain low-skill and low wage occupations became "brown-collar occupations" as new immigrants entered occupations already dominated by native and earlier legalized immigrant Latinos. Crowding of low-status Latinos into low wage work led to further work devaluation and wage degradation over time, both for immigrants and for native Latinos.

Census data also show racio-ethnic differences in earnings, with Asians and Whites reporting higher weekly earnings than Hispanic and Black men and women. Median usual weekly earnings in 2014 for Asians were $1,080 (men) and $841 (women) and $897 (men) and $734 (women) for Whites; this contrasted with $680 and $611 for Black men and women, $616 and $548 for Hispanic men and women (USDoL, 2015).

Hiring

An indication of frequency of racio-ethnic discrimination in hiring comes from field experiments called *audit studies* or *paired comparison testing* (Bendick & Nunes, 2012). In these experiments matched pairs of individuals apply for actual jobs after selection and training to be equivalent in all relevant ways other than racio-ethnicity. Audit studies in New York City and Milwaukee were conducted with young male testers, selected and trained to be as similar as possible except for racio-ethnicity (Black, White, Latino). They were given fictitious resumés equivalent on work experience, education, and residence neighborhood. When applying for advertised entry-level jobs for which they were qualified, White applicants were twice as likely to receive a callback or a job offer as equivalent Blacks (34% vs. 14% in Milwaukee and 31% vs. 15% in New York City). Latino testers, used only in New York City, received an intermediate number of positive responses (25%; Pager & Western, 2012). Another field experiment used Black or White male testers with or without criminal records. Whites were two to three times more likely to receive a callback. In fact, a White with a criminal record was slightly *more likely* (17%) to be called back than a Black *without a criminal record* (14%); effect of criminal record was stronger for Black applicants than for White applicants. This is especially noteworthy given higher incarceration rates for Blacks and the significant barrier that a criminal record poses for employment (Pager, 2003).

Another version of this design uses resumés or applications equivalent except for an indicator of racio-ethnicity, such as name or educational institution; these are called *correspondence studies* (Pager & Western, 2012). In one widely-cited study, Bertrand and Mullainathan (2004) mailed or faxed matched resumés in response to more than 1,300 advertised openings in sales, administrative support, clerical, and customer service positions in Chicago and Boston. Resumés were prepared to be appropriate for advertised positions and differed only in use of "White-sounding" vs. "Black-sounding" names (e.g., Emily or Greg vs. Lakisha or Jamal). Employers responded significantly more positively to White-sounding names (9.7% vs. 6.5% callbacks). For higher quality resumés, "White" callback rate increased but callback to "Blacks" did not. More information about audit studies, including a methodological critique, additional results, and ideas for how this technique can be used to clarify mechanisms of discrimination is found in Pager (2007) and Bendick and Nunes (2012).

Language

Language restrictions are an issue for some ethnic groups. Companies hiring non-native English speakers may feel an "English-only" policy is appropriate, sometimes concerned about workers communicating in a language their supervisors or managers cannot understand. Safety or quality control problems may occur if employees with limited English skills avoid acknowledging they do not understand instructions or policies. In general, employers should not restrict use of other languages for informal communications or during break times without a job-related reason. In contrast, in some settings (e.g., hospitals, public safety agencies, restaurants, hotels, retail) ability to speak a language other than English is very important in performing a job. Bilingual employees may be repeatedly required to help monolingual workers and as a result fall behind in their own work. Employers should consider additional compensation for skills in non-English languages that are important for the organization. Finally, language is an important aspect of social identity and restrictions based on its use may be experienced as unfairly exclusionary.

Some organizations behave inclusively by offering English-language courses (Zeidner, 2009), encouraging managers and supervisors to learn employees' languages or publishing communications in non-English versions. In fact, some workplace regulations *must* be posted in non-English languages in which a significant number of employees are literate (Lau, 2013).

Illustrations

The EEOC case list for its E-Race initiative, *Eradicating Racism and Colorism from Employment* (EEOC, n.d.-b), is organized by major type of alleged discrimination and shows the reality of race discrimination and harassment in contemporary workplaces.

- Alleged race discrimination and retaliation by New York cleaning company that prevented White supervisor from hiring Black cleaners for particular client; supervisor fired after disregarding illegal instructions. Blacks required to sit in back of cafeteria, later excluded entirely. Entire Black crew terminated and non-Blacks hired instead. Legal settlement in 2012 included $450,000 paid to 15 former employees, manager/supervisor training, report describing measures taken to prevent future discrimination.
- Settlement of 2012 EEOC lawsuit by Tennessee marine construction and transportation company with $75,000 paid to qualified but rejected Black applicant for deckhand position. Agreement to try to hire African Americans for up to 25% of openings in three years, keep records of discrimination complaints, submit EEOC reports each year, and post notice about lawsuit containing EEOC contact information. Case illustrates remedial use of court-ordered quota designed to reach level of integration that would exist in absence of blatant discrimination.
- Wal-Mart Stores settlement of $17.5 million class action suit by applicant for over-the-road truck driving for Southeast US distribution centers. Applicant required to have good credit rating (allegedly to favor Whites) despite commercial driver's license, good work history. HR staffer said he would be hired as laborer instead because of "gut feeling" that driving and credit records were falsified. Settlement included agreements to set hiring goals for representative workforce, select diversity recruiter, broaden recruiting, advertise to African Americans. Wal-Mart denied race discrimination (Wal-Mart Settles, 2009).

Selection on the basis of credit records is difficult to justify unless directly related to job requirements because of likely adverse impact against people of color. Customer preference is not an acceptable reason for race discrimination. Other examples are provided in the shaded box.

Not Managing for Diversity and Inclusion

- Color harassment: Darker-skinned African American Family Dollar Store employees allegedly berated by lighter-skinned Black manager who addressed them with terms like "Charcoal" until one employee quit.
- Same-race discrimination: Shuttle service discriminated against African Americans, favored native African drivers. African Americans denied more profitable routes, sent to places without riders to pick up, saw their tips awarded to African drivers.
- Race and national origin discrimination: Restaurant manager and waiter from Morocco and Tunisia, both Arabs, subjected to customer comments such as "I fought two wars to get rid of people like you!" and "Why don't you go back to your country!" Manager objecting to this harassment was terminated.
- Race and sex discrimination: Temporary employment agency placed employees based on clients' requests for race, sex, age, and national origin, allegedly using code words to avoid detection. For example, "chocolate cupcake" referred to young Black women, and "small hands" denoted females. (A temp agency should respond to illegal requests with "We cannot comply with your request because it is a violation of federal law.")
- National origin hostile work environment, language policy: Racist name calling and slurs toward immigrant Mexican workers in large Utah moving and storage company. Restrictive English-only language policy prevented Mexican and Polynesian employees from using native languages at work.

In retaliation for complaints, workers' hours reduced and one terminated. Settlement for $450,000 the largest achieved by EEOC in Utah (EEOC, 2013b).

• Racial harassment and retaliation: U-Haul moving supply company settled with EEOC for $750,000 after being charged with racial slurs and racially offensive comments toward African American employees; employee fired after complaining to offending supervisor and company president (EEOC, 2013a).

Source, unless otherwise noted: EEOC (n.d.- b)

A "Reverse Discrimination" Quandary

An important Supreme Court race discrimination case illustrates the complexity of legal, measurement, and fairness issues, as well as the concept of *reverse discrimination*. The *Ricci v. DeStefano* case concerned assessment of firefighters for promotion in New Haven, CT.

"Reverse discrimination" refers to a situation in which the White majority is harmed by a procedure put in place to prevent or correct unfair consequences to members of a traditionally underrepresented group, usually people of color or women. The term is misleading because it implies that discrimination can occur only to members of oppressed groups when in fact it can occur to any protected group. In addition, the term suggests a sense of entitlement on the part of the privileged group and may imply that the person of color or woman was less qualified than the person(s) whose opportunity was taken "unfairly."

The New Haven Civil Service Board (CSB) administered an examination to fill vacancies for 16 Fire Department officer positions. Following terms of a union collective bargaining agreement (CBA), the CSB based selection on an oral exam of leadership ability (40%) and written exams (60%). The City Charter required that each hire be made from among the top three scorers, so once tests were scored, the CSB had little discretion about whom to select. For each rank, there were twice as many White applicants as there were Blacks and Hispanics combined. Among top scorers were 17 Whites, 2 Hispanics, and no Blacks (Dunleavy & Gutman, 2009).

Recognizing that the result would be adverse impact toward Black candidates and fearing a lawsuit, the CSB decided not to certify test results and to test again. White candidates who would have been promoted then filed suit, alleging they had been denied promotion through a race-based process of disparate treatment.

The trial court decided in favor of the City of New Haven and the appeals court agreed. However, when the case was appealed to the Supreme Court, justices ruled in a 5–4 decision that the City had erred in discarding the test after results were known. In retrospect, the CSB should have anticipated that use of a cognitively loaded written exam would produce adverse impact against Black firefighters. The CSB could have used an alternative examination procedure, an assessment center, commonly used for firefighter selection and generally with less adverse impact than written exams. However, this would have required that the CSB challenge requirements of the CBA, claimed to require the CSB to discriminate unfairly.

This case is controversial for many reasons. Is it "fair" to White firefighters to be denied promotion after passing the test? Is it "fair" to Black firefighters, already in the minority, to be denied promotion by a test that seemed not to provide opportunity to demonstrate mastery of KSAs needed for promotion? Do jobs of lieutenant or captain require good interviewing skills and ability to score highly on a written exam, or demonstrated ability to perform various firefighting tasks? Is a more diverse authority structure important in this urban Fire Department? Should the union determine that written tests be used although this may not be best for assessing candidates given the legal and psychometric context? Case transcripts and the split legal decisions show that answers are far from clear. What would you do in this situation?

References

*Apfelbaum, E. P., Norton, M. I., & Sommers, S. (2012). Racial color blindness: Emergence, practice, and implications. *Current Directions in Psychological Science, 21*, 205–209.

Apfelbaum, E. P., Pauker, K., Sommers, S. R., & Ambady, N. (2010). In blind pursuit of racial equality. *Psychological Science, 21*, 1587–1592.

Arthur, W., Edwards, B. D., & Barrett, G. V. (2002). Multiple-choice and constructed response tests of ability: Race-based subgroup performance differences on alternative paper-and-pencil test formats. *Personnel Psychology, 55*, 985–1008.

Avery, D. R., Hernandez, M., & Hebl, M. (2004). Who's watching the race? Racial salience in recruitment advertising. *Journal of Applied Social Psychology, 34*, 146–161.

Avery, D. R., McKay, P. F., & Wilson, D. C. (2008). What are the odds? How demographic similarity affects the prevalence of perceived employment discrimination. *Journal of Applied Psychology, 93*, 235–249.

Avery, D. R., Volpone, S. D., Stewart, R. W., Luksyte, A., Hernandez, M., McKay, P. F., & Hebl, M. (2013). Examining the draw of diversity: How diversity climate perceptions affect job-pursuit intentions. *Human Resource Management, 62*, 175–194.

*Banaji, M., & Greenwald, A. G. (2013). *The Blind Spot*. New York, NY: Delacorte Press.

Bell, M. P. (2012). *Diversity in Organizations* (2nd ed.). Mason, OH: South-Western.

Bendick, M., Jr., & Nunes, A. P. (2012). Developing the research basis for controlling bias in hiring. *Journal of Social Issues, 68*, 238–262.

Berry, C. M., Clark, M. A., & McClure, T. K. (2011). Racial/ethnic differences in the criterion-related validity of cognitive ability tests: A qualitative and quantitative review. *Journal of Applied Psychology, 96*, 881–906.

Berry, C. M., Cullen, M. J., & Meyer, J. M. (2013). Racial/ethnic subgroup differences in cognitive ability test range restriction: Implications for differential validity. *Journal of Applied Psychology, 99*, 21–37.

Bertrand, M., & Mullainathan, S. (2004). Are Emily and Greg more employable than Lakisha and Jamal? A field experiment on labor market discrimination. *The American Economic Review, 94*, 991–1013.

Blanton, H., Jaccard, J., Klick, J., Mellers, B., Mitchell, G., & Tetlock, P. E. (2009). Strong claims and weak evidence: Reassessing the predictive validity of the IAT. *Journal of Applied Psychology, 94*, 567–582.

*Bobko, P., & Roth, P. L. (2013). Reviewing, categorizing, and analyzing the literature on Black-White mean differences for predictors of job performance: Verifying some perceptions and updating/correcting others. *Personnel Psychology, 66*, 91–126.

Borman, W. C., & Motowidlo, S. J. (1997). Task performance and contextual performance: The meaning for personnel selection research. *Human Performance, 10*, 99–109.

Brown v. Board of Education of Topeka, 347 U.S. 483 (1954).

Cascio, W. F., & Aguinis, H. (2005). *Applied psychology in human resource management* (6th ed.). Upper Saddle River, NJ: Pearson Prentice Hall.

Catanzarite, L. (2002). Dynamics of segregation and earnings in brown-collar occupations. *Work and Occupations, 29*, 300–345.

Cheryan, S., & Monin, B. (2005). "Where are you *really* from?": Asian Americans and identity denial. *Journal of Personality and Social Psychology, 89*, 717–730.

Cox., T., Jr. (2004). Problems with research by organizational scholars on issues of race and ethnicity. *The Journal of Applied Behavioral Science, 40*, 124–145. (Original work published 1990.)

Cox, T., Jr., & Nkomo, S. M. (1990). Invisible men and women: A status report on race as a variable in organization behavior research. *Journal of Organizational Behavior, 11*, 419–431.

Dansereau, F., Graen, G., & Haga, W. (1975). A vertical dyad approach to leadership within formal organizations. *Organizational Behavior and Human Performance, 13*, 46–78.

Dean, M. A., Roth, P. L., & Bobko, P. (2008). Ethnic and gender subgroup differences in assessment center ratings: A meta-analysis. *Journal of Applied Psychology, 93*, 685–691.

*Dunleavy, E., & Gutman, A. (2009). Fasten your seatbelts: Supreme Court to hear *Ricci v. Destefano*. *The Industrial-Organizational Psychologist, 46*(4), 31–43.

Durhams, S. (2000, September 21). Altered photo forces UW-Madison to reprint 1,000,000 brochures. *The Milwaukee Journal Sentinel*, p. A2.

Dworkin, A. G., & Dworkin, R. J. (1999). *The minority report: An introduction to racial, ethnic, and gender relations* (3rd ed.). New York, NY: Harcourt Brace College Publishers.

Equal Employment Opportunity Commission. (n.d.-a). *Charge statistics: FY 1997 through FY 2015*. Retrieved from www1.eeoc.gov//eeoc/statistics/enforcement/charges.cfm

Equal Employment Opportunity Commission. (n.d.-b). *E-RACE: Significant EEOC race/color cases (covering private and federal sectors)*. Retrieved from www1.eeoc.gov//eeoc/initiatives/e-race/caselist.cfm

Equal Employment Opportunity Commission. (n.d.-c). *Charges alleging race and harassment FY 1997–FY 2015*. Retrieved from www1.eeoc.gov//eeoc/statistics/enforcement/race_harassment.cfm

Equal Employment Opportunity Commission. (2010). *Annual report on the federal work force Part II: Work force statistics: Fiscal Year 2010*. (Tables 3 and A-2.) Retrieved from www1.eeoc.gov//federal/reports/fsp2010_2/index.cfm

Equal Employment Opportunity Commission. (2012). *2012 job patterns for minorities and women in private industry (EEO-1)*. Retrieved from www1.eeoc.gov/eeoc/statistics/employment/jobpat-eeo1/2012/index.cfm

Equal Employment Opportunity Commission. (2013a, September 24). *U-Haul to pay $750,000 to settle EEOC racial harassment & retaliation suit*. Retrieved from www1.eeoc.gov//eeoc/newsroom/release/9-24-13a.cfm

Equal Employment Opportunity Commission. (2013b, September 30). *Mesa Systems to pay $450,000 to settle EEOC national origin discrimination lawsuit*. Retrieved from www1.eeoc.gov//eeoc/newsroom/release/9-30-13a.cfm

Gaertner, S. L., & Dovidio, J. F. (1986). The aversive form of racism. In J. F. Dovidio and S. L. Gaertner (Eds.), *Prejudice, discrimination, and racism* (pp. 61–89). Orlando, FL: Academic Press.

Gaertner, S. L., Dovidio, J. F., Banker, B. S., Rust, M. C., Nier, J. A., Mottola, G. R., & Ward, C. M. (2003). The challenge of Aversive Racism: Combating pro-White bias. In S. Plous (Ed.), *Understanding prejudice and discrimination*. Boston, MA: McGraw Hill.

Greenwald, A. G., & Banaji, M. (1995). Implicit social cognition: Attitudes, self-esteem, and stereotypes. *Psychological Review, 102*, 4–27.

Greenwald, A. G., McGhee, D. E., & Schwartz, J. L. K. (1998). Measuring individual differences in Implicit Cognition: The Implicit Attitude Test. *Journal of Personality and Social Psychology, 74*, 1464–1480.

Greenwald, A. G., Poehlman, T. A., Uhlmann, E. L., & Banaji, M. R. (2009). Understanding and using the Implicit Association Test: III. Meta-analysis of predictive validity. *Journal of Personality and Social Psychology, 97*, 17–41.

Grimes, D. (2001). Putting our own house in order: Whiteness, change and organization studies. *Journal of Organizational Change Management, 14*, 132–149.

Gutman, A., Koppes, L. L., & Vodanovich, S. J. (2011). *EEO law and personnel practices* (3rd ed.). New York, NY: Routledge.

Hamilton, D., Austin, A., & Darity, W., Jr. (2011, February 28). *Whiter jobs, higher wages: Occupational segregation and the lower wages of Black men*. Economic Policy Institute Briefing Paper #288. Washington, DC: Economic Policy Institute. Retrieved from www.epi.org/files/page/-/BriefingPaper288.pdf

Hegewisch, A., Liepmann, H., Hayes, J., & Hartmann, H. (2010, September). *Separate and not equal? Gender segregation in the labor market and the gender wage gap* (Report No. IWPR C377). Washington, DC: Institute for Women's Policy Research.

Heilman, M. E., Battle, W. S., Keller, C. E., & Lee, R. A. (1998). Type of affirmative action policy: A determinant of reactions to sex-based preferential selection? *Journal of Applied Psychology, 83*, 190–205.

Heilman, M. E., & Guzzo, R. A. (1978). The perceived cause of work success as a mediator of sex discrimination in organizations. *Organizational Behavior and Human Performance, 23*, 429–458.

Heilman, M. E., Rivero, J. C., & Brett, J. F. (1991). Skirting the competence issue: Effects of sex-based preferential selection on task choices of women and men. *Journal of Applied Psychology, 76*, 99–105.

Heilman, M. E., Simon, M. C., & Repper, D. P. (1987). Intentionally favored, unintentionally harmed? Impact of sex-based preferential selection on self-perceptions and self-evaluations. *Journal of Applied Psychology, 72*, 62–68.

Hellerstein, J. K., & Neumark, D. (2008). Workplace segregation in the United States: Race, ethnicity, and skill. *The Review of Economics and Statistics, 90*, 459–477.

Hosoda, M., Stone-Romero, E. G., & Walter, J. N. (2007). Listeners' cognitive and affective reactions to English speakers with standard American English and Asian accents. *Perceptual and Motor Skills, 104*, 307–326.

Hough, L., Oswald, F., & Ployhart, R. (2001). Determinants, detection, and amelioration of adverse impact in personnel selection procedures: Issues, evidence and lessons learned. *International Journal of Selection and Assessment, 9*, 152–194.

Huffman, M. L., & Cohen, P. N. (2004). Racial wage inequality: Job segregation and devaluation across U.S. labor markets. *American Journal of Sociology, 109*, 902–936.

Ilgen, D. R., & Youtz, M. A. (1986). Factors affecting the evaluation and development of minorities in organizations. In K. M. Rowland and G. R. Ferris (Eds.), *Research in personnel and human resources management*, Vol. 4 (pp. 307–335). Greenwich, CT: JAI Press.

Jim Crow law. In *Encyclopedia Britannica*. (n. d.). Retrieved from www.britannica.com/EBchecked/topic/303897/Jim-Crow-law

Jones, J. M. (2013a, July 26). *U.S. Blacks, Hispanics have no preferences on group labels*. Retrieved from www.gallup.com/poll/163706/blacks-hispanics-no-preferences-group-labels.aspx?

Jones, J. M. (2013b, August 28). *As in 1963, Blacks still feel disadvantaged in getting jobs*. Retrieved from www.gallup.com/poll/164153/1963-blacks-feel-disadvantaged-getting-jobs.aspx

Kim, S. S., & Gelfand, M. J. (2003). The influence of ethnic identity on perceptions of organizational recruitment. *Journal of Vocational Behavior, 63*, 396–416.

Knouse, S. B. (2009). Targeted recruitment for diversity: Strategy, impression management, realistic expectations, and diversity climate. *International Journal of Management, 26*, 347–353.

*Kravitz, D. A. (2008). The diversity-validity dilemma: Beyond selection—The role of affirmative action. *Personnel Psychology, 61*, 173–193.

Kulik, C. T., & Roberson, L. (2008). Diversity initiative effectiveness: What organizations can (and cannot) expect from diversity recruitment, diversity training, and formal mentoring programs. In A. P. Brief (Ed.), *Diversity at work* (pp. 265–317). New York, NY: Cambridge University Press.

Lai, L. (2013). The Model Minority thesis and workplace discrimination of Asian Americans. *Industrial and Organizational Psychology: Perspectives on Science and Practice, 6*(1), 93–96.

Lai, L., & Babcock, L. C. (2012). Asian Americans and workplace discrimination: The interplay between sex of evaluators and the perception of social skills. *Journal of Organizational Behavior, 34*, 310–326.

Landy, F. (2010). Performance ratings: Then and now. In J. L. Outtz (Ed.), *Adverse impact: Implications for organizational staffing and high stakes selection* (pp. 227–248). New York, NY: Routledge.

Lau, S. (2013, September). Must employers provide labor law posters in languages other than English? *HR Magazine*, p. 22.

Loving v. Virginia. 388 U.S. 1 (1967).

McKay, P. F. (2010). Perspectives on adverse impact in work performance: What we know and what we could learn more about. In J. L. Outtz (Ed.), *Adverse impact: Implications for organizational staffing and high stakes selection* (pp. 249–270). New York, NY: Routledge.

McKay, P. F., & Avery, D. R. (2005). Warning! Diversity recruitment could backfire. *Journal of Management Inquiry, 14*, 330–336.

McKay, P. F., & Davis, J. (2008). Traditional selection methods as resistance to diversity in organizations. In K. M. Thomas (Ed.), *Diversity resistance in organizations*, (pp. 151–174). New York, NY: Lawrence Erlbaum Associates.

McKay, P. F., & McDaniel, M. A. (2006). A reexamination of Black-White mean differences in work performance: More data, more moderators. *Journal of Applied Psychology, 91*, 538–554.

Merton, R. K. (1968). The Matthew effect in science. *Science, 159*, 56–63.

Mikkelson, D. (2014). *Photo finish*. Retrieved from www.snopes.com/college/admin/uwmadison.asp

Mintz, B., & Krymkowski, D. H. (2010). The intersection of race/ethnicity and gender in occupational segregation: Changes over time in the contemporary United States. *International Journal of Sociology, 40*, 31–58.

National Park Service. (2015, December 20). *Jim Crow laws*. Retrieved from www.nps.gov/malu/learn/education/jim_crow_laws.htm

Neville, H. A., Awad, G. H., Brooks, J. E., Flores, M. P., & Bluemel, J. (2013). Color-blind racial ideology. *American Psychologist, 68*, 455–466.

Neville, H. A., Lilly, R. L., Duran, G., Lee, R. M., & Browne, L. (2000). Construction and initial validation of the Color-Blind Racial Attitudes Scale (CoBRAS). *Journal of Counseling Psychology, 47*, 59–70.

*Nkomo, S. M. (1992). The emperor has no clothes: Rewriting "race in organizations." *Academy of Management Journal, 17*, 487–513.

Norton, M. I., Sommers, S. R., Apfelbaum, E. P., Pura, N., & Ariely, D. (2006). Color blindness and interracial interaction. *Psychological Science, 17*, 949–953.

NPR. (2013, November 11). *Seeing opportunity in a question: "Where are you really from?"* Retrieved from www.npr.org/2013/11/11/242357164/seeing-opportunity-in-a-question-where-are-you-really-from

Outtz, J. L., & Newman, D. A. (2010). A theory of adverse impact. In J. L. Outtz (Ed.), *Adverse impact: Implications for organizational staffing and high stakes selection* (pp. 53–94). New York, NY: Routledge.

Pager, D. (2003). The mark of a criminal record. *American Journal of Sociology, 108*, 937–975.

Pager, D. (2007). The use of field experiments for studies of employment discrimination: Contributions, critiques, and directions for the future. *Annals, Academy of Political and Social Science, 609*, 104–133.

*Pager, D., & Western, B. (2012). Identifying discrimination at work: The use of field experiments. *Journal of Social Issues, 68*, 221–237.

Park, R. E. (1950). *Race and culture.* Glencoe, IL: Free Press. (Originally published in 1939.)

Pence, E. C., Pendleton, W. D., Dobbins, G. H., & Sgro, J. A. (1982). Effects of causal explanations and sex variables on recommendations for corrective actions following employee failure. *Organizational Behavior and Human Performance, 29*, 227–240.

Pew Research Center. (2013a, April 4). *The rise of Asian Americans.* Washington, DC.

Pew Research Center. (2013b, August 22). *King's dream remains an elusive goal; Many Americans see racial disparities.* Washington, DC.

Plaut, V. C., Thomas, K. M., & Goren, M. J. (2009). Is multiculturalism or color blindness better for minorities? *Psychological Science, 20*, 444–446.

*Plaut, V. C., Thomas, K. M., & Hebl, M. R. (2014). Special section: Race and ethnicity in the workplace. *Cultural Diversity and Ethnic Minority Psychology, 20*(4), 479–560.

*Ployhart, R. E., & Holtz, B. C. (2008). The diversity-validity dilemma: Strategies for reducing racio-ethnic and sex subgroup differences and adverse impact in selection. *Personnel Psychology, 61*, 153–172.

Proudford, K. L., & Nkomo, S. (2006). Race and ethnicity in organizations. In A. M. Konrad, P. Prasad, & J. K. Pringle (Eds.), *Handbook of workplace diversity* (pp. 323–344). Thousand Oaks, CA: SAGE Publishing Co.

*Pyburn, K. M., Jr., Ployhart, R. E., & Kravitz, D. A. (2008). The diversity-validity dilemma: Overview and legal context. *Personnel Psychology, 61*, 143–151.

Raver, J. L., & Nishii, L. H. (2010). Once, twice, or three times as harmful? Ethnic harassment, gender harassment, and generalized workplace harassment. *Journal of Applied Psychology, 95*, 236–254.

Rivera, L. A. (2012). Diversity within reach: Recruitment versus hiring in elite firms. *Annals, American Academy of Political and Social Science, 639*, 71–90.

Roth, P. R., Bevier, C. A., Bobko, P., Switzer, F. S., III, & Tyler, P. (2001). Ethnic group differences in cognitive ability in employment and educational settings: A meta-analysis. *Personnel Psychology, 54*, 297–330.

Roth, P., Bobko, P., McFarland, L., & Buster, M. (2008). Work sample tests in personnel selection: A meta-analysis of Black–White differences in overall and exercise scores. *Personnel Psychology, 61*, 637–662.

Roth, P. R., Huffcutt, A. I., & Bobko, P. (2003). Ethnic group differences in measures of job performance. *Journal of Applied Psychology, 88*, 694–706.

Rothenberg, P. S. (Ed.) (2007). *Race, class, and gender in the United States* (7th ed.). New York, NY: Worth Publishers.

*Sackett, P. R., Borneman, M. J., & Connelly, B. S. (2008). High-stakes testing in higher education and employment: Appraising the evidence for validity and fairness. *American Psychologist, 63*, 215–227.

Sears, D. O., Hetts, J. J., Sidanius, J., & Bobo, L. (2000). Race in American politics: Framing the debates. In D. O. Sears, J. Sidanius, & L. Bobo (Eds.), *Racialized politics: The debate about racism in America* (pp. 1–43). Chicago, IL: University of Chicago Press.

Sears, D. O., & McConahay, J. B. (1973). *The politics of violence: The new urban Blacks and the Watts riot.* Boston, MA: Houghton-Mifflin.

*Shih, M., & Sanchez, D. T. (Eds.) (2009). The landscape of multiracial experiences. *Journal of Social Issues, 65*(1). (Whole issue.)

Society for Human Resource Management (2010). Workplace diversity practices: How has diversity and inclusion changed over time? Retrieved from www.shrm.org/research/surveyfindings/articles/pages/workplacediversitypractices.aspx

Sorensen, E. (1998, June 21). Asian groups attack MSNBC headline referring to Kwan—News website apologizes for controversial wording. *Seattle Times.* Retrieved from http://community.seattletimes.nwsource.com/archive/?date=19980303&slug=2737594

Staats, C., Capatosto, K., Wright, R. A., & Contractor, D. (2015). *State of the science: Implicit Bias review 2015.* Retrieved from http://kirwaninstitute.osu.edu/wp-content/uploads/2015/05/2015-kirwan-implicit-bias.pdf

*Stauffer, J. M., & Buckley, M. R. (2005). The existence and nature of racial bias in supervisory ratings. *Journal of Applied Psychology, 90*, 586–591.

*Tatum, B. D. (1997). *Why are all the Black kids sitting together in the cafeteria? And other conversations about race.* New York, NY: Basic Books.

Thomas, K. M. (2005). *Diversity dynamics in the Workplace.* Belmont, CA: Thomson Wadsworth.

Thomas, K. M., & Chrobot-Mason, D. (2005). Group-level explanations of workplace discrimination. In R. L. Dipboye & A. Colella (Eds.), *Discrimination at work: The psychological and organizational bases,* (pp. 63–88). Mahwah, NJ: Lawrence Erlbaum Associates, Inc.

Thurgood Marshall. (2013). *The Biography Channel website.* Retrieved from www.biography.com/people/thurgood-marshall-9400241

Tomaskovic-Devey, D., & Stainback, K. (2007). Discrimination and desegregation: Equal opportunity progress in U.S. private sector workplaces since the Civil Rights Act. *Annals of the American Academy of Political and Social Science, 609,* 49–84.

Tomaskovic-Devey, D., Zimmer, C., Stainback, K., Robinson, C., Taylor, T., & McTague, T. (2006). Documenting desegregation: Segregation in American workplaces by race, ethnicity, and sex, 1966–2003. *American Sociological Review, 71,* 565–588.

US Bureau of Labor Statistics. (2016, June 3). *Economic news release: Employment Situation News Release.* Retrieved from http://data.bls.gov/cgi-bin/print.pl/news.release/empsit.htm

US Census Bureau. (2012) *Statistical abstract of the United States: Table 616, Employed civilians by occupation, sex, race, and Hispanic origin.* Retrieved from www.census.gov/history/pdf/musician_employment.pdf

US Department of Labor. (2015, November). *Highlights of women's earnings in 2014.* (Report 1058). Retrieved from www.bls.gov/opub/reports/cps/highlights-of-womens-earnings-in-2014.pdf

*Valian, V. (2000). *Why so slow? The advancement of women.* Cambridge, MA: MIT Press.

Vogeler, I. (2013). *U.S. racial groups: General & specific terms.* Retrieved from http://people.uwec.edu/ivogeler/w188/4terms.htm

Walker, H. J., Feild, H. S., Bernerth, J. B., & Becton, J. B. (2012). Diversity cues on recruitment websites: Investigating the effects on job seekers' information processing. *Journal of Applied Psychology, 97,* 214–224.

Walker, H. J., Feild, H. S., Giles, W. F., Armenakis, A. A., & Bernerth, J. B. (2009). Displaying employee testimonials on recruitment web sites: Effects of communication media, employee race, and job seeker race on organizational attraction and information credibility. *Journal of Applied Psychology, 94,* 1354–1364.

Wal-Mart settles lawsuit on hiring. (2009, February 20). *The New York Times.* Retrieved from http://nytimes.com/2009/02/21/business/21walmart.html

Whetzel, D. L., McDaniel, M. A., & Nguyen, N. T. (2008). Subgroup differences in Situational Judgment Test performance: A meta-analysis. *Human Performance, 21,* 291–309.

*Whitley, B. E., Jr., & Kite, M. E. (2006). *The psychology of prejudice and discrimination.* Belmont, CA: Thomson Wadsworth.

Wilson, T. D., Lindsey, S., & Schooler, T. Y. (2000). A model of dual attitudes. *Psychological Review, 107,* 101–126.

Winters, L. I., & DeBose, H. L. (2003). *New faces in a changing America: Multiracial identity in the 21st century.* Thousand Oaks, CA: SAGE Publications.

Yen, H. (2013, March 18). White American heads for minority status. *Pensacola News-Journal,* 5A.

Zeidner, R. (2009, January). One workforce—Many languages. *HR Magazine,* pp. 33–37.

Zou, L. X., & Dickter, C. L. (2013). Perceptions of racial confrontation: The role of color blindness and comment ambiguity. *Cultural Diversity and Ethnic Minority Psychology, 19,* 92–96.

* Recommended for advanced reading.

Chapter 11

Sexual Orientation and Work

Susan E. Walch and Rosemary Hays-Thomas

Gender roles are key to understanding sex and gender in organizations; one aspect of gender roles concerns expectations for social and sexual relationships. Those who are romantically and sexually attracted to others of the same sex may be subjected to isolation, harassment, or discrimination if their status is perceived to violate important norms. This chapter considers sexual orientation as one aspect of D&I in work organizations.

Defining Terms

Sex refers to the biological assignment of a person as male or female on the basis of chromosomes and associated primary and secondary sex characteristics. Society generally classifies people as male or female on this basis. In contrast, *gender* concerns social expectations and roles associated with membership in one binary sex category. (For a counterexample, see the shaded box about the Native American concept of Two Spirits.)

More than Two Genders?

Our Eurocentric Western society generally dichotomizes sex (and gender) into two categories: male and female. It is considered problematic when a person feels like one sex but has the biological characteristics of the other sex.

However, in many Native American and other cultures there have been gender roles for individuals considered neither (or both) male nor female. These persons could be biologically either male or female, but were considered to be a separate gender category called *berdaches* (in English, derived from Spanish). Because of negative connotations of that word, in the late 20th century they began to be referred to as "Two Spirit" people because they were thought to possess the spirit of both man and woman.

Most Western observers described Two Spirits as homosexual, transsexual, or some other category of stigmatized identity. However, Schnarch (1992) made a compelling argument that this categorization was a result of the inflexible dual-gender constructions of the observers and not an accurate understanding of the function of these individuals within their native cultures. Two Spirits generally wore at least some clothing typical of the other gender but sometimes wore combinations or non-gendered attire. They usually assumed work roles typical of the other biological sex and engaged in sexual relations with men or women but not with other Two Spirit people. Held in high esteem for their spiritual and ceremonial roles, they were often mediators in disputes between men and women. There is no evidence that they or others were confused about their gender identity: they were/are a third and fourth gender!

Sexual orientation concerns attraction to male and/or female people as romantic and sexual partners. For heterosexual persons, chromosomal makeup, anatomy, and overall appearance are generally consistent with one sex and the person is attracted romantically or sexually to people of the other sex. Gay men and lesbian women are attracted to people of the same sex, and bisexuals are attracted to both males and females as sexual partners. (The shaded box presents more information about sexual orientation and identity.)

Defining Terms: Sexual Orientation

Sexual orientation is complex and multidimensional: it includes elements of sexual and emotional attraction, fantasy, and behavior as well as identity (Klein, Sepekoff, & Wolf, 1985; Worthington & Reynolds, 2009). We distinguish between *sexual orientation* (a person's predispositions toward others as the object of sexual attraction, fantasy, and behavior) and *sexual orientation identity* (defined by awareness, recognition, and labeling of oneself as a sexual being with this orientation as part of one's identity). Some individuals engage in sexual behavior with same-sex others but do not consider themselves to be homosexually-oriented. The term *"men who have sex with men" (MSM)* is used by researchers as an inclusive term based on behavior rather than identity or inferred causes.

Typically, *sexual orientation* is considered to be *heterosexual* (indicating sexual and romantic attraction to persons of the other sex), *homosexual* (indicating sexual and romantic attraction to persons of the same sex), or *bisexual* (indicating attraction to both same-sex and other-sex persons). Labels for various sexual orientation identities include *gay* (usually referring to homosexually-oriented men but sometimes also to women with homosexual orientation), *lesbian* (referring to women with homosexual orientation), and *bisexual* (referring to attraction toward both sexes). Although sexual orientation is often considered to have only three categories, much evidence suggests that this does not capture its multidimensional nature (Weinrich & Klein, 2002; Savin-Williams, 2016). Variations exist in attraction, fantasy, behavior, and identity and it has recently been suggested that actually several types of gay and bisexual men and heterosexual and bisexual women exist; heterosexual men and lesbian women may actually represent single types (Worthington & Reynolds, 2009).

Recently, additional *sexual orientation identity labels* have been used in the scholarly and lay communities, including such terms as *queer*, *heteroflexible*, and *bicurious*, to reflect great variation in sexual orientation identity. Furthermore, sexual orientation identity, like other dimensions of identity, is a developmental process shaped by internal factors such as one's sexual orientation as a predisposition and external factors such as social and cultural acceptance or rejection (Cass, 1979; Troiden, 1989; Cox & Gallois, 1996; McCarn & Fassinger, 1996). Increasing evidence shows that sexual orientation identity can change and develop over the course of the lifespan (Klein et al., 1985; Diamond, 2008).

Gender identity is *not* the same thing as sexual orientation or sex. Gender identity is the person's psychological sense of self as a man (or boy) or woman (or girl). Most biological males feel like men (or boys), and most biological females perceive themselves as women (or girls). Concordance between biological sex and gender identity is experienced by a large majority of people (an estimated 99.7% according to Gates, 2011) and is designated by the term *cisgender*. However, in some cases a person has biological attributes of one sex but a strong psychological feeling of being in the "wrong body." It's not clear why this happens but it can be very stressful for these *transgender* individuals. (The shaded box presents more information about gender identity.)

Defining Terms: Gender Identity

Agreement between gender identity and biological or anatomical sex is typical for the vast majority (more than 99%) of heterosexual, homosexual, and bisexual persons. Most gay men have male gender identity and most lesbian women have female gender identity. Most bisexual and heterosexual individuals are also *cisgender* and have gender identity consistent with biological sex.

However, not everyone experiences this. *Transsexual* persons experience difference between biological sex and gender identity (psychological sense of oneself as a man/boy or a woman/girl) along with desire for gender expression (expression of oneself as a man/boy or woman/girl in behavior, manner, and/or dress). Why this happens is unclear, and it can be associated with great distress for the individual, which in extreme cases may be considered as a psychological condition known as Gender Dysphoria. Sometimes transsexual persons decide to change their bodies to become consistent with their gender identity through hormonal treatments and/or sex reassignment surgery. Often this leads to improvement in the person's adjustment (Cohen-Ketteinis & van Goozen, 1997; Pimenoff & Pfäfflin, 2011) although it may present major challenges for family, friends, or co-workers.

A broader category consists of those who are *transgender* persons. "Transgendered people include pre-operative, post-operative, and non-operative transsexuals who feel that they were born into the wrong physical sex as well as those who cross-dress to express an inner cross-gender identity" (Walch, Ngamake, Francisco, Stitt, & Shingler, 2012, p. 1286). Some persons cross-dress for reasons other than expression of a cross-gender identity. For example, male "drag queens" and female "drag kings" perform on stage dressed as the other sex, and transvestites engage in cross-dressing almost exclusively for sexual pleasure. In these cases the person generally experiences him or herself as the sex consistent with biological body.

The expression "LGBT" (or GLBT) is quite common in everyday language. This refers to Lesbian/Gay/Bisexual/Transgender. Sometimes the letter "Q" is included to mean *questioning*, that is, someone who is considering the idea that he or she may be gay, lesbian, bisexual, or transgender. Individuals with a homosexual sexual orientation identity are probably the largest group within the LGBT community (although the size of the bisexual population is largely unknown and varies widely depending on how bisexual is defined) and have received most consideration in scholarly literature and public discourse. This chapter emphasizes sexual orientation. Additional challenges exist for transgender individuals at work (e.g., change in name and physical appearance, health insurance coverage) but these have been less studied and are not discussed as fully here. We follow conventional usage of the abbreviation LGB to indicate homosexually or bisexually oriented persons of both sexes.

LGBT History in the US during the 20th and 21st Centuries

In the early 1900s, homosexuality was pathologized and often criminalized in the US, much of Europe, and many other places (Drescher, 2010). Those who engaged in same-sex sexual behavior were viewed as sexual deviants or perverts. Police raided gay social settings (often underground or covert gathering places) and gay people were charged and often convicted of violating sodomy laws that banned "unnatural" sexual acts. These same acts were also engaged in by heterosexual couples, but laws were applied nearly exclusively to same-sex couples throughout US history.

During the early 20th century, Hirschfeld and Ellis conducted groundbreaking research challenging these early assumptions of pathology and deviance. Use of the term *homosexuality* emerged around this time. Not until the late 1930s did the term *gay* come into existence as a reference to homosexuality.

During the 1930s and early 1940s, gay and lesbian people were victims of concentration camp internment and extermination under Nazi rule. Although exact figures are uncertain, tens of thousands of homosexual and suspected homosexual persons were arrested. Many were imprisoned and thousands were exterminated. As with Jews who were marked with a yellow star, homosexual men were marked with an inverted pink triangle along with sex offenders. Lesbian women wore an inverted black triangle, as did other "asocials" such as drug addicts, prostitutes, and the mentally ill. Later, LGBT organizations modified these symbols of shame as a way to reclaim their pride. The pink triangle (uninverted) now represents a visible symbol of gay pride.

During the 1940s, a small number of military psychologists and psychiatrists shifted the conceptualization of homosexuality from sexual deviance, perversion, and criminality to one of mental illness or psychiatric disturbance. Although this was later viewed as flawed, it was a more humane approach suggesting that treatment rather than punishment was indicated. With the initial edition of the Diagnostic and Statistical Manual of Mental Disorders (DSM) by the American Psychiatric Association in 1952, homosexuality was included as a psychiatric disorder.

In the 1950s, research of Dr. Evelyn Hooker challenged the notion that homosexual persons are more psychologically maladjusted than heterosexual persons and Dr. Alfred Kinsey's research dispelled the idea that same-sex sexual behavior is radically atypical. The Kinsey Scale of sexual orientation classified behavior on a seven-point continuum from exclusively heterosexual (0) to exclusively homosexual (6), with gradations in between.

The New York Stonewall Riots in 1969 are widely credited as marking the beginning of the gay rights movement in the US. After decades of police raids on bars that catered to or permitted gay clientele, LGBT patrons of the Stonewall Inn in the Greenwich Village section of New York City finally protested. This led to a series of riots lasting for several days and sparked an advocacy movement to advance civil rights.

In 1973, largely in response to advocacy efforts of the LGBT community, the American Psychiatric Association removed homosexuality as a psychiatric diagnosis from the seventh and final printing of the second edition of the DSM in 1974. The third edition published in 1980 included a diagnosis for homosexuality that causes the individual conflict or anxiety, but this diagnosis was removed with the publication of the revised version third edition, or DSM III-R, in 1987 (Drescher, 2010).

Since the 1970s, the discipline of psychology has regarded homosexuality as a normal and natural variation in human behavior and experience, and the American Psychological Association has taken a firm public stand in support of LGBT civil rights (Drescher, 2010). Public opinion is changing rapidly but public policy has not kept pace. Stereotypes and prejudice linger today among a substantial proportion of the general public and discriminatory policies have remained in effect into the 21st century. Federal anti-discrimination protection is still lacking although with the 2012 invalidation of parts of the Defense of Marriage Act, federal benefits are now available to legally married couples whether same- or other-sex. In 2015 the Supreme Court supported constitutionality of same-sex marriage, an issue that is relevant for administration of health and other benefits in organizations as well as other legal rights. The LGBT movement has been called the civil rights issue of the 21st century.

Sexual Orientation and Gender Identity as a Dimension of Diversity

With most dimensions of difference, the attribute has job-related implications that could justify or require special consideration. For example, workers' ethnicity might be related to language issues, customs, or holidays that could affect their ability to carry out a particular job. Religious beliefs might require practices such as daily prayer or special attire that could affect assignment of critical job responsibilities. Age-related differences in physical capacity, knowledge of technology or processes, or speed and flexibility of learning could have implications for safety, training, scheduling, or job rotation. Sex might be related to occupational choice, job experience, size or physical skill and could be a *bona fide occupational qualification* (BFOQ) for some jobs such as lingerie model. Physical ability or weight might affect ability to perform essential job functions or could require reasonable accommodation. Social class might be related to customs and norms, education, language and communication.

In contrast, it is difficult to think of a situation in which one's sexual orientation or gender identity alone would have legitimate job-related implications. Unlike other diversity dimensions, management of diversity in sexual orientation or gender identity generally focuses on workplace customs or procedures that are not directly job-related, such as benefit packages, or on attitudes and behaviors of other workers—not on the work of the person who is different.

What is "Different" about Sexual Orientation?

First, unlike most other dimensions of difference, at the federal level there is currently no legal protection against workplace discrimination based on sexual orientation. At this time, approximately 21 states (American Civil Liberties Union, 2015) and some cities and counties have laws prohibiting discrimination on the basis of sexual orientation and/or gender identity. But until there is federal protection, there will continue to be many workplaces in which it is completely legal to inquire about sexual orientation; make an explicit decision about hiring, promotion, termination, and other terms and conditions of employment taking apparent sexual orientation into account; or administer employee benefits differently for those who are LGB.

Second, sexual orientation is invisible unless one chooses to "come out" and disclose it or to risk being discovered. For this reason, estimates of sexual orientation frequency are difficult to verify. Prevalence estimates vary depending on how the population is defined, with estimates as high as 11% of the adult population reporting any lifetime same-sex sexual attraction, 8.2% reporting lifetime same-sex sexual behavior, and only 3.5% identifying as LGB (Gates, 2011). Researchers have estimated men who have sex with men (MSM) represent 6.4% of adult men in the US, with percentages varying widely from state to state from as low as 3.3% in South Dakota to as high as 13.2% in Washington, DC (Lieb et al., 2011). This geographic variability likely reflects local and regional levels of tolerance for homosexuality as well as migration to more tolerant locales. To put this in perspective, consider that about 12% of the US population is classified as Black and 13–14% as Hispanic in the 2010 census. There may be almost as many LGB persons in the workforce as there are either Blacks or Hispanics. Because many LGB workers do not disclose sexual orientation at work, it is impossible to have an accurate count.

Third, LGB persons may experience *hostile environment* discrimination or harassment even when they are not "out." People around them may feel free to express anti-gay attitudes in situations where they would never speak ill of other minorities, not realizing that the person next to them may be gay or lesbian. In this situation it would be difficult for that person to object without risking disclosing his or her orientation. This may create fear of disclosure, which has been found to be related to negative work experiences (Ragins, Singh, & Cornwell, 2007).

Fourth, our stereotypes of gay people are based on people who are out, media portrayals, and sometimes people identified in error. The openly gay are only a subset of homosexually-oriented persons, and it's not known how large a subset this is. One survey of a sample of members of national gay rights organizations found that 11.7% reported being out to *no one* at work. Many were out to *some* people (37%) or *most* people at work (25%) but only about one-quarter (27%) were out to *everyone* (Ragins et al., 2007). These respondents were not a random sample of LGB people. They were members of gay rights organizations; some were likely employed in workplaces with a large number of other LGB employees, so these percentages may overestimate the frequency of coming out at work.

Someone fearing disclosure may be unlikely to come out and thus produce helpful information that could serve to counteract stereotypes. Compelling evidence shows that meaningful interpersonal contact with others who are "different" can serve to reduce the perception of differences between "us" and "them," dispel stereotypes, and reduce prejudice (Pettigrew & Tropp, 2000). Studies have repeatedly found that knowing someone who is gay or lesbian is strongly associated with greater tolerance and lower homophobia (e.g., Herek & Capitanio, 1996; Walch, Orlosky, Sinkkanen, & Stevens, 2010). The shaded box discusses homophobia.

Homophobia

When heterosexuality is deemed normal and natural, non-heterosexuality is devalued and stigmatized by comparison. When this stigma is internalized into the personal value system of a heterosexual individual, it is called *homophobia*. This should probably be called *homonegativity* because homo*phobia* implies a reaction of intense fear that does not fit the range of negative reactions usually found. However, in general usage homophobia denotes a set of negative beliefs and emotional responses to homosexuality. The term *transphobia* has been used to describe internalization of cultural stigma against transgender individuals (Carroll & Gilroy, 2002; Hill & Willoughby, 2005).

Levels of homophobia may be decreasing in the US, with recent polls indicating that a majority of people endorse equal civil rights for LGB persons (Savin-Williams, 2008). However, homophobic attitudes are still endorsed by a substantial minority of heterosexual adults (Herek, Capitanio, & Widaman, 2002; Walch et al., 2010). Although much less is known about transphobia, some studies found it is prevalent in North America (Hill & Willoughby, 2005; Nagoshi et al., 2008).

Although it is good news that over half the population expresses tolerance for diversity in sexual orientation, this majority is slim and only recently exceeded 50%. Imagine that nearly half the people you meet react negatively before getting to know you, solely on the basis of your sexual orientation, or that nearly one in four people would judge you quite harshly for the same reason. Although expressing overtly racist sentiments is frowned upon and most people refrain from doing so in public, homophobic attitudes are still freely expressed in the form of condemnation and slurs as well as discriminatory actions and violence. Despite much research, it is unclear why many people maintain homophobic attitudes.

Sex and gender role beliefs have both been found to predict levels of homophobia and emerging evidence suggests a similar pattern for transphobia. Men endorse significantly more homophobic attitudes and beliefs than women (Kite, 1984; Kite & Whitley, 1996) and transphobia has also been found to be greater in men (Hill & Willoughby, 2005; Nagoshi et al., 2008). Those who endorse traditional gender role beliefs are likely to report higher homophobia levels (Whitley, 2001) and at least one study suggests that gender role beliefs also predict transphobia (Penor Ceglian & Lyons, 2004).

Although there is less research on this point, those with conservative religious and/or political beliefs tend to endorse greater homophobia (Morrison & Morrison, 2002; Schwartz & Lindley, 2005), as do those with lower levels of education (Lemelle & Battle, 2004; Ohlander, Batalova, & Treas, 2005). Research findings are mixed for other demographic variables, including age (Wills & Crawford, 2000; Lambert, Ventura, Hall, & Cluse-Tolar, 2006) and race/ethnicity (Lewis, 2003; Negy & Eisenman, 2005).

One important factor is knowing someone who is gay or lesbian. Heterosexual individuals who have known gay or lesbian individuals are significantly less homophobic than those who say they do not know any gay or lesbian persons (Herek & Capitanio, 1996). In fact, evidence suggests that higher levels of homophobia found among conservative groups and those with lower levels of education might be related to lower familiarity with gay and lesbian persons. When interpersonal contact is taken into account, the effect of education and conservative group membership is no longer significant (Walch et al., 2010). These findings suggest that greater interaction between heterosexual and LGBT communities is an important step in reducing homophobia.

Given that LGB persons represent between one in six to one in 20 adults in the US population, it is difficult to imagine that there are any adults who have never met someone who is LGB. Nevertheless, heterosexual adults often report they do not personally know any gay or lesbian people; Walch et al. (2010) found that nearly half of participants in a community sample reported this. It is statistically likely that every reader of this text has had interactions with people who are gay or lesbian but give no hint of this in their behavior or appearance.

Fifth, the victims of race, sex, disability, and other discrimination at work often have a supportive network of family and friends who can provide some relief, counsel, and emotional support. A woman or member of an ethnic minority can go home and talk with family or friends about unfair treatment. However, the LGB employee may not have come out to family, or may have met with rejection and hostility when doing so. In these cases, the employee lacks the support and buffering influence that friends and family often can provide.

Sixth, otherwise tolerant and nondiscriminatory individuals may have a religious or moral basis for negative feelings towards LGB persons. Some consider that requiring equal treatment of LGB employees at work infringes upon their religious beliefs. As discussed in Chapter 12, in this country law and expectation is that in most organizations, one's religion should not be a basis for discrimination nor is it an acceptable basis for violation of laws protecting the rights of others. But as mentioned earlier, in most states there are no laws protecting the rights of lesbians and gay men. Since 2013, 104 bills have been introduced in multiple state legislatures proposing religious exemptions (often called religious freedom restoration acts or First Amendment protection bills) to protect individuals, organizations, and businesses against legal consequences of refusal to serve LGBT people on the grounds of religion. As of June 2016, religious exemptions have become law in three states (Nevada, Mississippi, and Arkansas; Mason, Williams, & Elliot, 2016).

Seventh, for most people sex and ethnicity are apparent at birth and do not change throughout life. On some other diversity dimensions, people may vary over the course of their work life (e.g., in age, ability, religion). The consensus of scientific opinion is that individuals possess a strong predisposition for a particular sexual orientation at birth and sexual orientation generally solidifies during adolescence or early adulthood. Studies of twins have shown that sexual orientation, like other complex human behaviors, is substantially influenced by genetic and prenatal factors (Mustanski & Bailey, 2003) and recent reviews suggest that approximately one-third of the variance in sexual orientation is attributable to genetic heritability with a substantial portion of the variance attributable to nonsocial environmental causes (e.g., prenatal environment). Little, if any, of the variance is explained by social environment (Bailey et al., 2016). Put another way, scientific evidence supports the notion that LGBT people (and heterosexual people) are "born this way" rather than "choosing" to be this way.

Do heterosexuals feel that their sexual orientation has been deliberately chosen? Or does it feel like something that developed automatically and without much thoughtful consideration of alternatives? (To consider this further, see the questionnaire in the shaded box.)

Thinking about Sexual Orientation

How would you answer the following questions? What assumptions underlie your answers?

1. When and how did you first decide you were heterosexual? Is this a phase you will outgrow?
2. Could your heterosexuality result from a neurotic fear of others of your sex?
3. Most child molesters are heterosexual men. Is it safe to expose children to heterosexual male teachers, pediatricians, priests, or scoutmasters?
4. Why are heterosexuals so promiscuous?
5. Why are heterosexual relationships so short-lived and unstable?

Adapted from Rochlin (2003)

Many environmental factors that affect complex behaviors are far beyond the individual's control and often have their greatest influence in early development. Experts consider homosexual or bisexual orientation to be no more of a choice than is heterosexual orientation. For many people, recognition of homosexual or bisexual orientation may develop slowly over time, sometimes after years of employment, marriage, or even parenthood (Ragins, 2004). For others, awareness and recognition occurs early in life but acceptance may occur much later. In the workplace, this means that established working relationships may change or even end if one begins to enact LGB identity. Those who have interacted with or even married someone thinking he/she is heterosexual may feel deceived, hurt, offended, or simply surprised and unsure how to treat this person when LGB identity has been realized and revealed.

Finally, in the US many people's stereotypes and attitudes about gay men in particular are based on the connection they see between homosexuality and HIV/AIDS. Although it is known that this disease can be contracted through intravenous drug use, blood transfusions, or heterosexual sex with an infected partner, many people in the US still think of it as a "gay disease" because in this country it was first recognized in the gay community (and despite the reality that the major route of transmission of HIV worldwide is through heterosexual sexual contact). Fears of HIV/AIDS may generalize to fears of gay persons; a strong correlation has been found between fear of AIDS and homophobia/negative attitudes toward homosexuality and homosexual persons (Walch et al., 2010).

Workplace Issues

Imagine that you work for an employer who is equally accepting of both homosexual and heterosexual persons, but who, in order to prevent discrimination, requires that *no one* can say or do anything at work that indicates their own sexual orientation. Violation of this rule is grounds for immediate termination!

In effect, no one could "come out" about sexual orientation at work. What impact would this have on heterosexual individuals? What could employees not do, or not discuss, in order to comply? Put family photos on their desks? Talk about social plans for the weekend? Think about the typical workplace and its widespread indicators that heterosexuality is the norm, perhaps with a climate of negative attitudes towards gay men and lesbians (Ragins, 2004; Ragins & Weithoff, 2005). In such an environmental context, LGB persons are the *other*.

Belle Ragins (2004) has identified several workplace issues pertinent to the diversity dimension of sexual orientation. These include discrimination and its outcomes, the disclosure process, and special challenges due to (a) the invisibility of sexual orientation, (b) negative reactions of co-workers, and (c) the lack of social support, especially related to development of identity. Finally, there are special career challenges for LGB individuals. To set the stage for this discussion, which draws substantially on the review by Ragins, we examine the legal context for sexual orientation issues at work.

Legal Provisions

At this time there is no federal protection from discrimination based on sexual orientation. A 1998 Executive Order signed by President Clinton prohibits sexual orientation discrimination for most civilians who are federal employees. The *Don't Ask Don't Tell* law (DADT) enacted in 1993 permitted LGB service members to serve as long as they were not open about their sexual orientation. The law required the Armed Forces to discharge service members on the basis of sexual orientation; it was the only law that *required* an employer to discriminate on this basis (Law & Hrabal, 2010). In December 2010, Congress voted to repeal DADT, effective September 2011 (US Department of Defense, n.d.). Burks (2011) has written persuasively about the harmful effects of this policy on difficulties experienced by LGB service members and its damaging effects on the quality of research about this important group. See the shaded box for more on this topic.

Unintended (Negative) Research Consequences of "DADT"

Researcher Derek Burks has argued convincingly that the "Don't Ask Don't Tell" (DADT) policy, originally thought to be more "benign and liberal" (2011, p. 605) than the previous prohibition against gay people in the military, actually increased the victimization of LGB individuals and damaged the quality of research data on this issue. The already difficult task of identifying research samples of gay men and lesbians in the military was magnified under this policy because participants would risk disclosure and likely expulsion. In a RAND Corporation study (2010), large percentages of LGB respondents reported they were at risk for blackmail, manipulation, and negative effects on personal and unit relationships. The majority also reported feeling anxiety and stress.

What research has been conducted is largely in the form of technical and executive reports and not in public peer-reviewed literature. Thus it is difficult to access by those who might want to improve policy, clinical service, and data collection. Victims of sexual assault, already reluctant to file complaints or request clinical services, may be even less likely to do so if this might lead to their outing. According to Burks, "Because of DADT, military research linking sexual orientation with … (trauma from harassment or assault) cannot be conducted easily, if at all. And without scientific evidence, the extent of victimization cannot be adequately be monitored, treatment efforts cannot be fully implemented, and policy initiatives cannot adequately address sexually based crimes" (2011, p. 612).

With repeal of DADT, it would be interesting to see if this continues to be true. On June 26, 2012, the Pentagon held its first-ever gay pride event to acknowledge service of LGB troops. A Marine CPT is quoted as saying that in one year he had gone from being a closeted gay man, afraid of discharge, to an invitee at the White House reception—drinking champagne with the Commander in Chief ("Pentagon holds," 2012)!

To date, attempts to pass a general anti-discrimination law at the federal level have been unsuccessful. Employment discrimination based on sexual orientation is common, with 16–68% of LGB adults reporting employment discrimination during their lifetime (Badgett, Holning, Sears, & Ho, 2007). After many attempts to pass the Employment Nondiscrimination Act (ENDA), LGBT advocates now support a broader Equality Act (Human Rights Campaign; HRC, 2015). This legislation would prohibit discrimination based on sexual orientation or gender identity in employment and other areas (e.g., housing, education, credit).

Some federal laws are relevant. For example, in 2013 the US Supreme Court determined that parts of the federal Defense of Marriage Act (DOMA), a law that defined marriage as the union of one man and one woman, were unconstitutional (Barnes, 2013). One effect of this decision was that legally married gay couples must now receive the same federal benefits as heterosexual married couples. With the 2015 Supreme Court ruling legalizing same-sex marriage at the federal level, these benefits provisions are now available in all states of the US. As a result, the Department of Labor (DoL) has redefined the term "spouse" in the Family and Medical Leave Act (FMLA) to apply to partners in any legally enacted marriage, gay or straight (USDoL, n.d.). Under FMLA, an employee is entitled to 12 weeks of unpaid leave to care for a family member who is ill.

Discrimination and its Outcomes

The level of discrimination against LGB employees is difficult to assess accurately for several reasons. The usual EEO statistics (e.g., discrimination charges) do not exist because federal law and reporting requirements do not address this type of discrimination. Self-reports of discrimination are difficult to interpret because of the invisibility of sexual orientation, variations in open acknowledgment of LGB identity, challenges in locating and surveying LGB persons, and other factors. Ragins (2004) described results of a national sample of more than 500 members of gay and lesbian organizations in which 37% reported discrimination because co-workers believed they were gay, 12% had left a previous job due to discrimination, and over a third had experienced sexual orientation harassment in a previous job. A study by Hebl, Foster, Mannix, and Dovidio (2002) examined both *access and treatment* discrimination and found that openly gay job applicants in retail establishments did not experience more formal discrimination than other applicants (e.g., information about job availability, job callback, or permission to use the bathroom). However, interactions between them and hiring managers gave more evidence of interpersonal discrimination; interactions were shorter, more negative, and involved less conversation. In this study, applicants' apparent sexual orientations were manipulated by hats they wore saying "Gay and Proud" or "Texan and Proud," which suggests that interpersonal discrimination could have resulted from the "out and proud" impression of their clothing rather than their orientation *per se*.

A more subtle manipulation was used in a study in which "applicants" responded to actual job advertisements (Tilcsik, 2011). The researcher sent two equivalent resumes to more than 1,700 actual online listings of entry-level white collar jobs in five similar fields (such as sales representatives and customer service representatives) that matched the pseudo-applicants' qualifications closely. The websites, aimed at new college graduates, covered seven states in the Northeast, West, Midwest, and South. The two resumés identified the applicant as someone who had managed the finances of a student organization for several semesters as its elected treasurer, and emphasized tasks and accomplishment in that role. The organization was randomly assigned the title of the *Gay and Lesbian Alliance* or the *Progressive and Socialist Alliance*, both of which might seem to be politically left or liberal groups.

Apparently-gay applicants received significantly fewer callbacks (7.2% fewer) than those who seemed to be heterosexual. However, this rate varied considerably in different states. There was no statistically significant difference in California, which has a state law prohibiting employment discrimination on the basis of sexual orientation. In Texas, Florida, and Ohio, where there was no such law, the difference in callback rates was statistically significant. We cannot say that existence of protective legislation alone is responsible for this difference among locales. Attitudes of the general public, the political and economic environment, and other variables probably play a role. However, this study does give us a persuasive estimate of the magnitude of *access discrimination* against men who are perceived to be gay, even when they are well-qualified for a position.

Several indicators of *treatment discrimination* against LGB persons concern differences, if any, in personal and organizational outcomes. One obvious indicator of treatment discrimination is a salary differential. Most published studies show salary levels lower for gay men and higher for lesbians than those of comparably employed heterosexuals of the same sex (see McGarrity, 2014). However, some cautions are needed in drawing these comparisons. First, salary data on a representative group of LGB employees are difficult to identify and capture. Contemporary government data do not answer this question clearly, and voluntary samples are likely to be affected by the methodology used to find the participants. Secondly, as a group, gay people are likely to attain higher levels of education than heterosexuals, and education is generally correlated with income level (Black, Makar, Sanders, & Taylor, 2003). Gay male households may be less likely to include children, thus avoiding the "parenthood penalty" discussed in Chapter 9. In lesbian households if both individuals are in the workforce, they may be employed in "women's jobs" and subject to the same gender bias in income that affects most women. However, if working in "men's fields," they may actually earn *more* than other women. What do studies show?

Blandford (2003) examined responses between 1989 and 1966 on the General Social Survey (GSS), a large sample designed to be representative of the US population. Openly gay or bisexual men suffered a wage penalty of about 32% compared to heterosexual men. On the other hand, lesbians or bisexual women earned 23% *more* than heterosexual female counterparts. This was partly due to occupation because the wage premium dropped to 18% when effect of working in male-dominated fields was statistically controlled. This pattern of gay male disadvantage/lesbian advantage was also found by Clain and Leppel (2001) using data from the 1990 Census.

Another study of GSS data from 1989–1996 estimated the wage penalty for gay men to be 14–16%, and the wage advantage to lesbian women to be 20–34%, depending on how sexual orientation was defined in the GSS (Black et al., 2003). Marital status also seems important: in 1990 Census data, Allegretto and Arthur (2001) found that partnered gay men reported a wage penalty of 15.6% below married heterosexual men. However, the gap between partnered gay men and similarly qualified partnered but unmarried heterosexual men was only 2.4%. Overall these authors estimated the gap to fall between 3% and 16%.

A later project examined data based on the 2000 Census for men and women living with either spouses or partners of the same or other sex (Antecol, Jong, & Steinberger, 2008). In these comparisons, gay men earned about 4.5% *less* than married men, but 28% *more* than cohabiting heterosexual men. Lesbian women, however, had a wage advantage, earning 31.6% *more* than cohabiting women and 20% *more* than married women. These authors attributed the wage advantage for lesbian women and for cohabiting gay men to higher levels of education, with a small influence of occupation. However, neither human capital nor occupation seemed to be responsible for the disadvantage of partnered gay men compared to married heterosexual men, suggesting it probably resulted from variables not measured in the study, such as discrimination.

King and Cortina (2010) cited other studies showing wage gaps varying between 10% and 32% for gay men compared with heterosexual men in comparable jobs. In summary, it seems that married heterosexual men are the highest earners, followed by partnered men and men living alone. Lesbians seem to have a wage advantage over heterosexual women. For men, homosexuality does seem to carry a wage penalty, and for both sexes income is also affected by factors such as marital status, occupation, and level of education.

The Process of Disclosure: Coming Out at Work

Most LGB employees face a decision when joining an organization: should they keep sexual orientation strictly private or concealed, fearing others would avoid or discriminate against them on this basis or their career opportunities would be negatively affected? Or should they treat sexual orientation like any other aspect of their identity and discuss it freely if it comes up in conversation? This significant decision is probably affected by the work and legal environment. For example, 161 LGB persons recruited electronically from universities and communities participated in an online survey (Legate, Ryan, & Weinstein, 2012). They were asked about coming out, reactions to various environments, and psychological well-being. About half of respondents said they had disclosed to co-workers. This proportion was lower than for family and friends, but higher than for school and religious settings. Respondents were more likely to disclose in settings high in *Autonomy Support*, meaning that the environment was one of interpersonal acceptance and support for authenticity in personal expression. Disclosure in such environments was associated with lower levels of anger and depression and higher self-esteem, but because this was a correlational design, we cannot say that disclosure caused these results. Deciding to come out is also related to individual factors such as comfort level with having LGB identity known to others, and experiences with past discrimination on the basis of sexual orientation (Ragins, Singh, & Cornwell, 2007).

Following the work of Woods (1993), most studies of disclosure have focused on three main strategies that LGB persons follow: *counterfeiting*, which means making up a heterosexual identity in order to appear heterosexual; *avoidance*, when the person tries control conversation and behavior so the issue does not come up; and *integration*, when the person freely discloses sexual orientation. Though there do seem to be three basic responses, a person may use different strategies at different times, or in different work or work-related contexts. Many LGB employees are out to some work colleagues, family members, or friends, but not to everyone. Some have begun using the integration strategy in their work lives after trying to counterfeit or avoid in the past, or in a different setting.

Each strategy carries consequences. Counterfeiting and avoidance can be stressful and require much concentration and energy to maintain the façade. They also may isolate the LGB person from other co-workers, including other LGB employees and potentially supportive colleagues, and are a barrier to development of comfortable and trusting relations with others who may find the person socially reserved or awkward. The LGB person constantly carries the burden of wondering what will happen if others find out his or her true identity (Woods, 1993). On the other hand, an open and integrative strategy makes the person vulnerable to prejudices and discriminatory behaviors of those who are anti-gay. The LGB employee may often wonder whether unfavorable employment decisions or personal slights result from such prejudices, or from nondiscriminatory factors that apply to most people at work. See the shaded box for another example.

"Courtesy" Stigma

Stigmas are social "markings" that indicate someone's deviant and devalued status, usually based on a characteristic like racioethnicity, unusual physical conditions, or behavior patterns such as criminal activity or mental illness (Goffman, 1963; Stone-Romero, 2005). Sociologist Erving Goffman used the term *courtesy stigma* for the process by which others avoid the "courtesy" of associating with a stigmatized person because they fear the stigma might extend to them. One illustration of this extension of stigma is an offensive term (*n-lover*) commonly used in the past to designate a White person who associated on an equal or friendly basis with African Americans. Today, the concept of courtesy stigma is understood to apply to those who may avoid associating with someone they believe to be homosexual in order to prevent others from thinking *they* are gay as well. Even other LGBT men or women who have not disclosed their identities may also avoid associating with other LGBT persons to prevent their own discovery (Ragins, 2004). This process of avoidance increases the sense of isolation that some LGBT employees feel at work.

Ragins and Cornwell (2001) randomly surveyed membership of three national gay rights organizations in a study of perceived discrimination. Although these were members of gay rights organizations and almost 70% worked in places with legal protections, some still hid their sexual orientations at least in part. About 12% reported being out to no one at work, 37% were open with some, 25% were out to most people, but only about one-quarter (27%) were out to everyone. Employees were more likely to disclose when their organizations had gay-supportive policies (forbidding sexual orientation discrimination, defining diversity to include sexual orientation, offering same-sex partner benefits, and especially welcoming partners at company events). Disclosure was also more likely when local laws addressed sexual orientation discrimination, and when the person reported having gay co-workers.

Over 500 gay or lesbian employees were identified through a "snowball sampling" procedure by Button (2001). LGB contact people in many organizations were identified through a national gay rights organization and were asked to invite other gay people in their organizations to participate. Like the Ragins and Cornwell (2001) research, this study also found that organizational policies were important in perception of discrimination and management of identity. In organizations with more supportive policies (e.g., unofficial or official networks of LGB employees, diversity training including issues of sexual orientation, leave policies applicable to domestic partnerships), respondents reported lower levels of perceived discrimination. In this case, they were more likely to report an integration strategy for managing identity. Employees who perceived higher levels of discrimination were more likely to report using counterfeiting and/or avoidance strategies as well as lower levels of job satisfaction and organizational commitment. In this study, higher levels of sexual orientation identity development were associated with decreased use of counterfeiting and avoidance and more disclosure through the integration strategy.

Clearly the process of coming out at work is for many people a stressful, complex, and developmental one. Consequences of coming out may be positive, negative, or both. Reviews (Ragins, 2004; Ragins & Weithoff, 2005) show effects on work attitudes, salary levels, and anxiety or depression, but results are inconsistent, indicating the complexity of this issue. These authors suggest that *fear* of negative consequences may be more important than the act of disclosure itself. Organizations like Lambda Legal, a national advocacy organization for civil rights for LGBTs through education, litigation, and policy development, have produced easily-accessible documents (Lambda Legal, n.d.) useful for LGBT employees or their supporters in understanding this transition and how to deal with it.

Three Challenges: Invisibility, Negative Reactions from Co-workers, and Lack of Social Support

According to Ragins (2004), special stresses occur for LGB persons because sexual orientation is not visible unless disclosed. LGB employees may feel that disclosure is not entirely under their control; they may experience *sexual identity conflict* or stress related to inconsistency of disclosure in some contexts and not others. This differs from the stress experienced by those whose membership in a stigmatized group is visible. Another form of identity conflict may occur for LGB persons who are people of color, persons with disabilities, or members of other minorities, exemplifying the concept of intersectionality (see Chapter 5).

In many employment settings, LGB employees who have not disclosed will be assumed to be heterosexual. This assumption may have two consequences: *indirect discrimination* and *disclosure backlash*. Indirect discrimination occurs when a LGB employee becomes aware of co-workers' prejudices or discriminatory behavior toward others who are known to be LGB. Disclosure backlash occurs when others react negatively or withdraw when they learn that a person assumed to be heterosexual is actually not.

Negative co-worker reactions experienced by openly gay employees may include direct discrimination or avoidance in work or social settings. Maltreatment may be worse from employees who view sexual orientation as a choice, especially one they consider morally objectionable. Co-workers may assume the LGB employee could avoid negative consequences simply by choosing to be heterosexual. Other emotional reactions may be based in fear or threat of homosexuality or of LGB persons, either directly (e.g., worries about health or safety) or symbolically (e.g., dissonance with one's religious or political views). For example, some believe that LGB persons will try to influence or recruit others, particularly children, or that same-sex partnerships are a threat to "traditional marriage." Some feel that their own sexual identity is challenged by the presence of an openly gay person at work.

Lack of social support presents concerns for the LGB employee, particularly if identity as a gay man or lesbian develops during the course of employment. Heterosexual peers may understand the course of their own development but react with puzzlement or aversion to the evolution of a co-worker's sense of being gay. Support at home and at work may vary and present special stresses. Heterosexual colleagues who never consider that they might be the victim of hate crimes, discrimination, or social isolation may think their LGB co-worker is overly cautious or fearful. Some gay men and lesbians seek out LGBT organizations or communities, and in some cases may change careers, employers, or geographic locations as they seek more comfortable environments.

Career Choice and Development

Ragins (2004) argued persuasively that existing career theories simply do not apply to development of work history over time for persons who are LGB. For example, these theories do not consider continuous development of identity through adulthood, which characterizes many gay men and lesbians; furthermore, they do not incorporate effects of discrimination on career choice and change. Ragins suggested that LGB persons may seek out *safe havens*, which are occupations or work organizations that protect against discrimination and support the development of a gay identity. Also important are *identity supporters*, those friends, family, and others who support the individual in his or her sexual orientation development.

Disclosure of LGB identity may affect the development of mentoring relationships. Even a supportive but heterosexual mentor may not be aware of special challenges faced by LGB persons at work. Disclosure may be a major disruption in the person's career; he or she may decide to change occupation or employer or move to a more gay-friendly community. On the other hand, an apparently wonderful career opportunity may lose its appeal if an openly gay employee thinks he or she will have to go back "in the closet" in the new organization.

Diversity and Inclusion for Gay People at Work: What's an Employer to Do?

As with other diversity dimensions, the employer should focus on the person and the contributions she or he can make to organizational goals, and not on the person's sexual orientation as a basis for difference. Under most circumstances the fact that an employee is or may be gay is simply not relevant to job behavior. There are at least three types of situations in which sexual orientation does become relevant and worthy of the diversity manager's attention.

One concerns social interactions that take place at work. Circumstances may arise in which other employees are offended by or intolerant of a co-worker's sexual orientation. Workplace policies should be in place to make it clear that harassment, discrimination, or other mistreatment on the bases of sexual orientation or gender identity will not be tolerated, and in company statements, diversity should be defined to include sexual orientation and gender identity. Other employees should be expected to interact with LGBT employees in the same way they would interact with anyone else. They cannot be expected or required to approve of another's sexual orientation, but they can be expected and required to behave in a respectful manner. According to the HRC (2014), about 90% of Fortune 500 companies reported workplace protections based on sexual orientation.

Heterosexual employees, perhaps without deliberate malicious intent, may speak or act in ways that offend those who are LGBT, especially if the person has not disclosed his or her sexual orientation or gender identity. Diversity training should cover invisible stigmas such as sexual minority status or some disabilities, and the possibility of giving offense without realizing it. Employees should be aware that LGBT colleagues may be out in some situations but not in others and allow the LGBT person to be in control of additional disclosure.

Another situation in which the capable diversity manager will explicitly consider sexual orientation is in the organization of workplace activities. For example, company social events (e.g., banquets, picnics) to which employees are expected to bring spouses or dates may be awkward for LGBT employees. As mentioned earlier, welcoming partners at company events is one factor associated with disclosure (Ragins & Cornwell, 2001) and presumably a sense of inclusion. Another example is the organization of an employee resource group, as discussed in the shaded box.

What are "Gayglers"?

At the worldwide Internet firm Google, there are almost 20 Employee Resource Groups (ERGs): voluntary groups of employees who share some interest or personal characteristic and get together for purposes of social interaction, support, and career development. Many are employee-initiated but receive financial support from Google. Besides the formal (funded) ERGs there are many other groups, small and large, focusing on topics like skiing, singing *a capella*, photography, or pregnancy. The company encourages formation of smaller groups to help build community and counter some of the negative aspects of working in a very large organization.

One ERG is the Gayglers, the group for gay and lesbian employees, their friends and allies (Google, n.d.; Swift, 2011). With chapters around the world, the Gayglers celebrate Pride and provide LGBT support even in countries that are less tolerant of alternative sexual orientation than the US. They also influence company policies and programs to benefit LGBT persons and others. Gayglers and other ERGs build internal community, engage in student outreach and recruiting, provide social events, and engage in social action. Gayglers have been one reason for Google's perfect score on the Corporate Equality Index of the HRC (2014).

A third situation in which sexual orientation is relevant for inclusion concerns employee benefits. Typically employer-provided health insurance plans provide a family option in which the employee can pay an additional premium for coverage of his or her spouse/partner. The most inclusive organizations offer domestic partner (health insurance) benefits to both gay and straight couples.

In addition, policies for sick leave, "personal time off," or family leave often permit employees to take time away from work to care for the needs of a spouse or other family member. These policies are most inclusive if they are available to partnered LGBT employees on the same terms as others. According to HRC (2014), 66% of the Fortune 500 employers reported offering domestic partner benefits and many have also extended other insurance, leave, and retirement benefits to LGBT employees.

Why Organizations Should Respond: Social and Economic Imperatives

Industrial-organizational psychologists Eden King and Jose Cortina (2010) have argued that work organizations have a social responsibility to act to prevent and/or correct harm to their employees (as well as other stakeholders). They also presented economic rationales consistent with the "business case" discussed in Chapter 1.

For example, unfair treatment based on sexual orientation produces negative consequences for both employees and the organization. Job satisfaction and organizational commitment are likely to be lower, and job anxiety and turnover intentions higher, when LGB employees experience a heterosexist work environment (one that is discriminatory against LGBT people). King and Cortina (2010) cite several studies showing a connection between heterosexism perceptions and negative health consequences, both physical and mental (e.g., depression and psychological distress). These may be more common for LGBT employees who have not disclosed and fear discovery. In addition, for these workers constant monitoring and regulation of speech and behavior to avoid detection can require a great deal of energy and distract cognitive resources from more productive work (Madera, 2010). Attention is divided, memory is impaired, and task performance can be affected. The employee is handicapped in his or her ability to do the best work possible for the organization.

Another economic rationale concerns the importance of using valid predictors of performance to make personnel decisions. According to King and Cortina, "There is no evidence that LGBT workers perform any less well than their straight counterparts . . . or that LGBT workers differ meaningfully from non-LGBT workers on other job-related criteria . . . we conclude that personnel decisions made on the basis of sexual orientation will be faulty, ineffective, and ultimately, costly" (2010, p. 74).

Organizations with diversity initiatives that do not consider sexual orientation in their policies and programs risk presenting a mixed message about their goals, which can have negative effects on employees, customers, and other stakeholders (Volpone & Avery, 2010). The organization's commitment to D&I may be questioned, with possible negative impacts on the effect of the entire diversity initiative. Recruitment, job satisfaction and organizational commitment, treatment of LGBT customers, and even stock price and profitability may be negatively affected.

With respect to dimensions of sexual orientation and gender identity, we suggest that the diversity manager's goal should be to create a supportive and inclusive environment in which LGBT employees feel they are as accepted and able to contribute as other employees. They should feel comfortable to disclose if they decide to do so, and others should respect this aspect of individuality as they would differences in other dimensions such as ethnicity, religion, sex, age, or disability.

References

Allegretto, S. A., & Arthur, M. M. (2001). An empirical analysis of homosexual/heterosexual male earnings differentials: Unmarried and unequal? *Industrial and Labor Relations Review, 54,* 631–646.

American Civil Liberties Union. (2015). *Non-Discrimination Laws: State-by-State Information—Map.* Retrieved from www.aclu.org/map/non-discrimination-laws-state-state-information-map

Antecol, H., Jong, A., & Steinberger, M. D. (2008). The sexual orientation wage gap: The role of occupational sorting and human capital. *Industrial and Labor Relations Review, 61,* 518–543.

Badgett, M. V. L., Holning, L., Sears, B., & Ho, D. (2007). *Bias in the workplace: Consistent evidence of sexual orientation and gender identity discrimination.* Los Angeles, CA: The Williams Institute. Retrieved from https://escholarship.org/uc/item/5h3731xr

*Bailey, J. M., Vasey, P. L., Diamond, L. M., Breedlove, S. M., Vilain, E., & Epprecht, M. (2016). Sexual orientation, controversy, and science. *Psychological Science in the Public Interest, 17*(2). (Whole issue.)

Barnes, R. (2013, June 26). *Supreme Court strikes down key part of Defense of Marriage Act.* Retrieved from www.washingtonpost.com/politics/supreme-court/2013/06/26/f0039814-d9ab-11e2-a016-92547bf094cc_story.html

Black, D. A., Makar, H. R., Sanders, S. G., & Taylor, L. J. (2003). The earnings effects of sexual orientation. *Industrial and Labor Relations Review, 56,* 449–469.

Blandford, J. M. (2003). The nexus of sexual orientation and gender in the determination of earnings. *Industrial and Labor Relations Review, 56,* 622–642.

Burks, D. J. (2011). Lesbian, gay, and bisexual victimization in the military: An unintended consequence of "Don't Ask, Don't Tell"? *American Psychologist, 66,* 604–613.

Button, S. B. (2001). Organizational efforts to affirm sexual diversity: A cross-level examination. *Journal of Applied Psychology, 86,* 17–28.

Carroll, L., & Gilroy, P. J. (2002). Transgender issues in counselor preparation. *Counselor Education & Supervision, 41,* 233–242.

Cass, V. C. (1979). Homosexual identity formation: A theoretical model. *Journal of Homosexuality, 4,* 219–235.

Clain, S. H., & Leppel, K. (2001). An investigation into sexual orientation discrimination as an explanation for wage differences. *Applied Economics, 33,* 37–47.

Cohen-Kettenis, P. T., & van Goozen, S. H. M. (1997). Sex reassignment of adolescent transsexuals: A follow-up study. *Journal of the American Academy of Child and Adolescent Psychiatry, 36,* 263–271.

Cox, S., & Gallois, C. (1996). Gay and lesbian identity development: A social identity perspective. *Journal of Homosexuality, 30,* 1–30.

Diamond, L. M. (2008). Female bisexuality from adolescence to adulthood: Results from a 10-year longitudinal study. *Developmental Psychology, 44,* 5–14.

Drescher, J. (2010). Queer diagnoses: Parallels and contrasts in the history of homosexuality, gender variance, and the Diagnostic and Statistical Manual. *Archives of Sexual Behavior, 39,* 427–460.

Gates, G. J. (2011). *How many people are lesbian, gay, bisexual, and transgender?* Los Angeles, CA: The Williams Institute, UCLA School of Law. Retrieved from https://escholarship.org/uc/item/09h684x2#page-1

Goffman, E. (1963). *Stigma: Notes on the management of spoiled identity.* New York, NY: Simon & Schuster.

Google. (n.d.). *Fostering a fair and inclusive Google.* Retrieved from www.google.com/diversity/at-google.html#tab=gayglers

Hebl, M. R., Foster, J. B., Mannix, L. M., & Dovidio, J. F. (2002). Formal and interpersonal discrimination: A field study of bias toward homosexual applicants. *Personality and Social Psychology Bulletin, 28,* 815–825.

Herek, G. M., & Capitanio, J. P. (1996). "Some of my best friends": Intergroup contact, concealable stigma, and heterosexuals' attitudes toward gay men and lesbians. *Personality and Social Psychology Bulletin, 22,* 412–424.

Herek, G. M., Capitanio, J. P., & Widaman, K. F. (2002). HIV-related stigma and knowledge in the United States: Prevalence and trends, 1991–1999. *American Journal of Public Health, 92,* 371–377.

Hill, D. B., & Willoughby, B. L. B. (2005). The development and validation of the Genderism and Transphobia Scale. *Behavioral Science, 53,* 531–544.

Human Rights Campaign. (2014). *Corporate Equality Index 2015.* Retrieved from http://hrc-assets.s3-website-us-east-1.amazonaws.com//files/documents/CEI-2015-rev.pdf

Human Rights Campaign. (2015, March 9). *Support the Equality Act.* Retrieved from www.hrc.org/campaigns/support-the-equality-act

King, E. B., & Cortina, J. M. (2010). The social and economic imperative of lesbian, gay, bisexual, and transgendered supportive organizational policies. *Industrial and Organizational Psychology: Perspectives on science and practice, 3,* 69–78.

Kite, M. E. (1984). Sex differences in attitudes toward homosexuals: A meta-analytic review. *Journal of Homosexuality, 10,* 69–81.

Kite, M. E., & Whitley, B. E., Jr. (1996). Sex differences in attitudes toward homosexual persons, behaviors, and civil rights: A meta-analysis. *Personality and Social Psychology Bulletin, 22*, 336–353.

Klein, F., Sepekoff, B., & Wolf, T. J. (1985). Sexual orientation: A multi-variable dynamic process. *Journal of Homosexuality, 11*, 35–49.

Lambda Legal. (n.d.). *Out at work: A toolkit for workplace equality.* Retrieved from www.lambdalegal.org/publications/out-at-work

Lambert, E. G., Ventura, L. A., Hall, D. E., & Cluse-Tolar, T. (2006). College students' views on gay and lesbian issues: Does education make a difference? *Journal of Homosexuality, 50*, 1–30.

Law, C. L., & Hrabal, E. A. (2010). Sexual minorities in the workplace: The status of legal and organizational protection. *The Industrial-Organizational Psychologist, 47*(4), 37–42.

Legate, N., Ryan, R. M., & Weinstein, N. (2012). Is coming out always a "good thing"? Exploring the relations of autonomy support, outness, and wellness for lesbian, gay, and bisexual individuals. *Social Psychological and Personality Science, 3*, 145–152.

Lemelle, A. J., Jr., & Battle, J. (2004). Black masculinity matters in attitudes toward gay males. *Journal of Homosexuality, 47*, 39–51.

Lewis, G. B. (2003). Black-White differences in attitudes toward homosexuality and gay rights. *Public Opinion Quarterly, 67*, 59–78.

Lieb, S., Fallon, S. J., Friedman, S. R., Thompson, D. R., Gates, G. J., Liberti, T. M., & Malow, R. M. (2011). Statewide estimation of racial/ethnic populations of men who have sex with men in the U.S. *Public Health Reports, 126*, 60–72.

Madera, J. M. (2010). The cognitive effects of hiding one's homosexuality in the workplace. *Industrial and Organizational Psychology: Perspectives on Science and Practice, 3*, 86–89.

McCarn, S. R., & Fassinger, R. E. (1996). Revisioning sexual minority identity formation: A new model of lesbian identity and its implications. *The Counseling Psychologist, 24*, 508–534.

McGarrity, L. A. (2014). Socioeconomic status as context for minority stress and health disparities among lesbian, gay, and bisexual individuals. *Psychology of Sexual Orientation and Gender Diversity, 1*, 383–397.

Mason, E., Williams, A., & Elliott, K. (2016, June 10). The dramatic rise in state efforts to limit LGBT rights. *The Washington Post.* Retrieved from www.washingtonpost.com/graphics/national/lgbt-legislation/

Morrison, M. A., & Morrison, T. G. (2002). Development and validation of a scale measuring modern prejudice toward gay men and lesbian women. *Journal of Homosexuality, 43*, 15–37.

Mustanski, B. S., & Bailey, J. M. (2003). A therapist's guide to the genetics of human sexual orientation. *Sexual and Relationship Therapy, 18*, 429–436.

Nagoshi, J. L., Adams, K. A., Terrell, H. K., Hill, E. D., Brzuzy, S., & Nagoshi, C. T. (2008). Gender differences in correlates of homophobia and transphobia. *Sex Roles, 59*, 521–531.

Negy, C., & Eisenman, R. (2005). A comparison of African American and white college students' affective and attitudinal reactions to lesbian, gay, and bisexual individuals: An exploratory study. *The Journal of Sex Research, 42*, 291–298.

Ohlander, J., Batalova, J., & Treas, J. (2005). Explaining educational influences on attitudes toward homosexual relations. *Social Science Research, 34*, 781–799.

Penor Ceglian, C. M., & Lyons, N. N. (2004). Gender type and comfort with cross-dressers. *Sex Roles, 50*, 539–545.

Pentagon holds gay pride event. *Pensacola News-Journal,* June 27, 2012, p. 4A.

Pettigrew, T. F., & Tropp, L. R. (2000). Does intergroup contact reduce prejudice? Recent meta-analytic findings. In S. Oskamp (Ed.), *Reducing prejudice and discrimination* (pp. 93–114). Mahwah, NJ: Erlbaum.

Pimenoff, V., & Pfäfflin, F. (2011). Transsexualism: Treatment outcome of compliant and noncompliant patients. *International Journal of Transgenderism, 13*, 37–44.

Ragins, B. R. (2004). Sexual orientation in the workplace: The unique work and career experiences of gay, lesbian, and bisexual workers. In J. J. Martocchio (Ed.), *Research in personnel and human resource management* (Vol. 23, pp. 35–120). London: Elsevier JAI.

Ragins, B. R., & Cornwell, J. M. (2001). Pink triangles: Antecedents and consequences of perceived workplace discrimination against gay and lesbian employees. *Journal of Applied Psychology, 86*, 1244–1261.

Ragins, B. R., Singh, R., & Cornwell, J. (2007). Making the invisible visible: Fear and disclosure of sexual orientation at work. *Journal of Applied Psychology, 92*, 1103–1118.

Ragins, B. R., & Weithoff, C. (2005). Understanding heterosexism at work: The straight problem. In R. L. Dipboye & A. Colella (Eds.), *Discrimination at work* (pp. 177–201). Mahwah, NJ: Lawrence Erlbaum Associates.

RAND National Defense Research Institute. (2010). Sexual orientation and U.S. military personnel policy: An update of RAND's 1993 study (Report No. MG-1056-OSD). Retrieved from www.rand.org/pubs/monographs/MG1056.html

Rochlin, M. (2003). The heterosexual questionnaire. In M. S. Kimmel & A. L. Ferber (Eds.), *Privilege: A reader.* Boulder, CO: Westview Press.

Savin-Williams, R. C. (2008). Then and now: Recruitment, definition, diversity, and positive attributes of same-sex populations. *Developmental Psychology, 44,* 135–138.

Savin-Williams, R. C. (2016). Sexual orientation: Categories or continuum? Commentary on Bailey et al. (2016). *Psychological Science in the Public Interest, 17,* 37–44.

Schnarch, B. (1992). Neither man nor woman: Berdache—A case for non-dichotomous gender construction. *Anthropologica, 34,* 105–121.

Schwartz, J. P., & Lindley, L. D. (2005). Religious fundamentalism and attachment: Prediction of homophobia. *The International Journal for the Psychology of Religion, 15,* 145–157.

Stone-Romero, E. F. (2005). Personality-based stigmas and unfair discrimination in work organizations. In R. L. Dipboye & A. Colella (Eds.), *Discrimination at work* (pp. 255–280). Mahwah, NJ: Lawrence Erlbaum Associates.

Swift, M. (2011). At Google, groups are key to the company's culture. *Mercury News.* Retrieved from www.mercurynews.com/top-stories/ci_18333328?nclick_check=1

Tilcsik, A. (2011). Pride and prejudice: Employment discrimination against openly gay men in the United States. *American Journal of Sociology, 117,* 586–626.

Troiden, R. R. (1989). The formation of homosexual identities. *Journal of Homosexuality, 17,* 43–73.

US Department of Defense. (n.d.). *Don't Ask, Don't Tell is repealed.* Retrieved from http://archive.defense.gov/home/features/2010/0610_dadt/

US Department of Labor (n.d.). *Family and Medical Leave Act: Final rule to revise the definition of "spouse" under the FMLA.* Retrieved from www.dol.gov/whd/fmla/spouse/

Volpone, S. D., & Avery, D. R. (2010). I'm confused: How failing to value sexual identities at work sends stakeholders mixed messages. *Industrial and Organizational Psychology: Perspectives on Science and Practice, 3,* 90–92.

Walch, S. E., Ngamake, S. T., Francisco, J., Stitt, R. L., & Shingler, K. A. (2012). The Attitudes Toward Transgendered Individuals scale: Psychometric properties. *Archives of Sexual Behavior, 41,* 1283–1291.

Walch, S. E., Orlosky, P. M., Sinkkanen, K. A., & Stevens, H. R. (2010). Demographic and social factors associated with homophobia and fear of AIDS in a community sample. *Journal of Homosexuality, 57,* 310–324.

Weinrich, J. D., & Klein, F. (2002). Bi-gay, bi-straight, and bi-bi: Three bisexual subgroups identified using cluster analysis of the Klein Sexual Orientation Grid. *Journal of Bisexuality, 2,* 109–139.

Whitley, B. E., Jr. (2001). Gender-role variables and attitudes toward homosexuality. *Sex Roles, 45,* 691–721.

Wills, G., & Crawford, R. (2000). Attitudes toward homosexuality in Shreveport-Bossier City, Louisiana. *Journal of Homosexuality, 38,* 97–116.

Woods, J. D. (with Lucas, J. H.) (1993). *The corporate closet: The professional lives of gay men in America.* New York: The Free Press.

Worthington, R. L., & Reynolds, A. L. (2009). Within-group differences in sexual orientation and identity. *Journal of Counseling Psychology, 56,* 44–55.

* Recommended for advanced reading.

Chapter 12

Religion, Age, Ability, Appearance, Weight, Social Class, and Work

These significant diversity dimensions are covered in one chapter because litigation and research literature are less extensive and complex than for other dimensions. Some of these attributes are easily changeable, others not. Age is objective, but appearance and weight judgments are highly subjective. Relationships with usual markers of privilege are complex: social class is reliably related to socioeconomic indicators (e.g., education, income), but religion, age, and disability status are not. Federal anti-discrimination law covers all categories of religious belief, only some categories of age, and the *reality* or *perception* of disability. Federal laws protecting religion, age, and disability have different provisions and histories of case law. Appearance, weight, and social class do not fall under federal anti-discrimination protection unless interpreted in terms of color/race/national origin, sex, religion, disability, or age. However, local laws or ordinances may concern appearance, weight, or social class, which are often the basis of exclusion, harassment, and discrimination and deserve serious consideration whether or not legal protections exist.

Religion

Managing religious differences at work requires balancing rights of different employees with legitimate organizational business interests. One's religion is a choice, invisible unless disclosed, and sometimes changes over time. Religious beliefs are often held with strong conviction of correctness of one's position and wrongness of others' views. Ethnic background may be conflated with religion (e.g., Muslims, Sikhs, Hindus). Feelings intensified in the US following attacks on the World Trade Center in 2001 and elsewhere, US military actions in the Middle East, and perceived connections between religion and political views.

The Facts: Distribution of Religious Belief in the US

As of 2008, about 75% of US adults surveyed said that they were Christian (Pew Forum, 2008; US Census Bureau; USCB, 2012). Of non-Christians, the largest group was unaffiliated individuals (atheist, agnostic, or other secular). Fewer than 2% were Jewish, and fewer than 1% each were Buddhist, Muslim, Hindu, or of other faiths. Among Christians, about one-third were Roman Catholic and the remainder were members of various Protestant denominations. The largest of these were Evangelical churches (about 25% of Christians), and mainline churches (e.g., Baptist, Methodist, Lutheran, Presbyterian, Episcopalian; about 18% of Christians). Very small percentages reported being Mormon, Jehovah's Witnesses, and Greek or Russian Orthodox.

Proportional trends since the 1970s show a drop in Protestants, stability for Catholics (partly due to immigration), and dramatic increase in "nones" reporting no religious affiliation (Pew Forum, 2012). In 2012 for the first time, Protestants were fewer than half the adult US population (48%). Most of these changes have occurred since the 1990s, with almost one in five (18%) now reporting no religious affiliation. Although collectively Protestants are still the largest group, the largest single reported affiliation is Catholic.

US Historical and Legal Context

Many colonists came to the New World to escape religious persecution in Europe. By the time of the Declaration of Independence, most citizens of the new nation accepted religious diversity and opposed state religion and intrusion by the State into religious belief or practice (Epps, 2011). Historical documents of Founding Fathers confirm their belief that neither Christianity nor any other religion should be government-endorsed.

Today the legal context for religious diversity at work includes the First Amendment to the US Constitution and Title VII of the Civil Rights Act of 1964. The First Amendment contains the "establishment clause" preventing Congress from making law establishing a religion, and the "free exercise clause" prohibiting limitations on free exercise of religion. The familiar term "separation of church and state" is not in the Constitution but in letters of Thomas Jefferson in 1802 and Roger Williams in 1544 (Epps, 2011) describing protections that *churches needed* from abuse and involvement by political leaders.

Title VII is the major federal basis for religious discrimination claims. Religion-based complaints usually involve allegations of failure to provide reasonable accommodation, disparate treatment discrimination, or harassment (Levin, 2007). New religious discrimination complaints increased sharply by nearly 75% after 2001, when Islamic terrorists destroyed the World Trade Center. In 2015, the EEOC reported 3,502 new such complaints. About 15% of religious discrimination cases that year were "merit resolutions" (i.e., outcome favored the plaintiff), and financial awards totaled $10.8 million (EEOC, n.d.-f).

According to Gutman, Koppes, and Vodanovich (2011), three themes relate to Title VII enforcement in this area: (a) requirement to "reasonably accommodate sincerely held religious beliefs unless doing so causes an undue hardship" (p. 100); (b) the two First Amendment clauses, which prevent favoring or restricting religious expression, respectively; and (c) religious harassment as a form of prohibited discrimination. "Sincerely held religious beliefs" include religious beliefs and practice regardless of whether the individual belongs to an organized religion or simply holds religious, ethical, or moral beliefs about right and wrong "sincerely held with the strength of traditional religious views" ("Part 1605—Guidelines on discrimination," 2013, §1605.1). Those with atheistic or agnostic beliefs are also protected. The EEOC's 2008 Compliance Manual defines terms and provisions and gives numerous examples of potentially discriminatory situations and how to deal with them (EEOC, 2011a).

Three exemptions have developed under case law pertaining to religious institutions such as churches (Gutman et al., 2011). First, religious employers may hire and discriminate in other ways *for the position of minister* but not for other positions. Second, for non-ministerial positions religious employers may discriminate *on the basis of religion*. For example, a church may refuse to hire applicants not sharing its faith. Third, for non-ministerial employees, religious employers may not discriminate on the basis of race/color/national origin, age, or ability. For secular businesses, no exemptions exist from anti-discrimination law based on the employer's religious views. For example, a public or private business may not require employees to attend faith-based activities or hold a particular religious view.

In today's workplaces, organizations must provide reasonable accommodation for employees' religious belief and practice as long as it is compatible with others' rights and does not impose undue hardship on employers' legitimate business interests (Gutman et al., 2011). The employee must request a reasonable accommodation and the two parties are expected to "flexibly interact" to find a solution. A party who refuses to cooperate in finding a workable solution will generally lose any resulting dispute.

Typical Workplace Dilemmas

Examples include employer-imposed religious requirements affecting inclusion or decisions about hiring, retention, or promotion; excessive proselytizing by an employee whose behavior offends others; dress policies that conflict with religious dress or grooming; conflicts between work scheduling and religious observation; or slurs, graffiti, or denigrations based on religious belief (EEOC, n.d.-g).

Two cases illustrate how organizations and courts have handled situations involving potential religious discrimination. In *Peterson v. Hewlett Packard* (2004), a 20-year employee objected to posters illustrating various kinds of diversity as a source of company strength. Peterson objected to homosexuality on religious grounds and hung hostile posters with Biblical passages in an area of his workspace visible to customers, co-workers, and visitors. Supervisors deemed his posters offensive to others and a violation of company policy. During repeated meetings with management, Peterson expressed his intent to be hurtful to others in order to change their behavior and refused to remove his posters unless the company removed theirs. After time off with pay to consider his actions, he reposted the materials and, after additional meetings with management, was terminated for insubordination. Peterson sued, alleging religious discrimination, failure to accommodate, and wrongful termination.

Another case, *Buonanno v. AT&T Broadband LLC* (2004), involved refusal to sign an agreement to "respect and value" behavior that contradicted Buonanno's religious beliefs, but no offensive or discriminatory behavior toward others. He agreed not to discriminate or harass anyone and asked for policy clarification, but none was provided. Management insisted that signing the agreement was a job requirement and terminated employment because he refused to sign. Buonanno sued, alleging disparate treatment discrimination and failure to accommodate his religious beliefs.

The 9th Circuit Court of Appeals determined that the only accommodations Peterson would accept would have also imposed undue hardship on Hewlett Packard by interfering with its legitimate diversity program and allowing his demeaning and harassing behavior to continue. Furthermore, management had attempted without success to find a mutually agreeable compromise. Peterson's claim was denied. In contrast, the Colorado District Court found that AT&T could have accommodated Buonanno's religious objection without undue hardship, and that management did not engage in sufficient discussion to realize that he objected to the statement's ambiguous wording and not to its intent or required conduct. Buonanno was awarded more than $146,000 in damages.

Levin (2007) provided helpful suggestions to employers for accommodating religious belief and practice and avoiding religious discrimination. First, communicate to employees a commitment to nondiscrimination and reasonable accommodation. Appropriate policies should be developed and communicated, and supervisors and others should be well trained in handling requests or complaints. Second, become knowledgeable about religious practices or observations of various world religions, asking respectful questions if necessary. For example, many supervisors may not know that Sikh men must wear their hair long and covered by a turban and carry a Kirpan or short ceremonial sword (Khalsa, n.d.). Third, before any situations arise, think about appropriate accommodations for situations such as dress, attendance, and breaks. Flexible schedules and leave might be permitted for Saturday Sabbaths or during special religious observances (e.g., Good Friday, Yom Kippur, Ramadan). A quiet place could be provided for prayer during work breaks. Dress policies should be professional yet permit religious expression that does not infringe on others' rights or the employer's legitimate business interests. The aim is to provide an environment of "respectful pluralism" (Hicks, 2002).

The Tanenbaum Center for Interreligious Understanding has published a checklist for organizations wishing to evaluate their practices and policies about managing religious diversity (2014). The EEOC also provides extensive lists of best practices for avoiding religious disparate treatment discrimination, harassment, and retaliation and providing reasonable accommodation for religious practice and belief (EEOC, 2011a). The agency has published several helpful fact sheets and Q&A documents about religious garb and grooming and about employment of Muslims, Arabs, South Asians, and Sikhs (EEOC, n.d.-e, h).

Appropriate Management of Religious Diversity

Diversity professionals and managers who are sensitive to employee needs, creative, and concerned about maintaining respectful pluralism should try to develop workable solutions to challenges involving religious difference. Illustrations from EEOC documents (EEOC, n.d,-e, h) include:

- A South Asian man wearing a Sikh turban is hired as a discount store cashier using job-based criteria for hiring qualified employees. Some employees worry that his attire may make customers uncomfortable. Management ensures that supervisors and employees understand that religion-based discrimination is illegal and will not be tolerated, and educates employees about examples of faith-based dress in certain religions.

- A temp agency places an experienced clerical worker in a front-desk position with one of its clients. The employee wears a hijab (head scarf) in accord with her Muslim faith. The client company reports that this dress conveys the "wrong image" and requests the temp agency to tell her to remove the hijab at the front desk, or send a replacement. The temp agency explains that religious accommodation requires an exception to the client's dress code and that perceived customer preferences are not an acceptable basis for rejecting religious garb. The client continues to insist, so the temp agency places the clerical employee elsewhere at the same pay level and declines to assign someone else to the client's position. If the temp agency honored the client's request, it would be equally liable for any complaint or legal charge of discrimination.

- A woman is hired as office staff at an exercise facility. Based on religious belief, she asks to wear a long white skirt rather than white tennis shorts and polo shirt worn by other employees. The exercise facility provides this accommodation, which does not present an undue hardship.

- An observant Jewish man wears a yarmulke (skull cap) and tzitzit (four knotted tassels at corners of his shirt). In a friendly way, co-workers ask about his special clothing and he explains its religious significance. This becomes a non-issue because it does not interfere with his work or present any safety or other concerns.

- Some employees of a small company do not belong to any organized religion. Most working there are Christian, one of whom asks to start a prayer group after work. Management allows this in a room not in use at that time as long as everyone is invited to attend and no questions or pressure are applied to people who do not come.

Age

On the diversity dimension of age, all employees change with continued employment. They enter the workforce at different ages, and those continuing in the workforce over a period of years will experience differential expectations and treatment as they become older.

- Young workers: career preparation; balancing employment with education; sexual harassment due to youth, inexperience, lack of information about rights.

- Twenties to forties: dual career and parenthood challenges, career advancement; women's "biological clock" of declining fertility.
- Mid-career: "sandwich generation" responsible for both aging parents and children; career changes; "up or out" policies (e.g., military, tenure track faculty) as lack of promotion leads to job loss.
- Older workers: social and financial issues of retirement; greater competition with rise through triangular structure of fewer jobs at higher levels; declining motivation and satisfaction as opportunities decrease.
- All ages: illnesses, accidents, loss of family members producing change in employment trajectories; short career ladders and plateaus with advancement requiring career change; physical and mental changes associated with getting older.

Even this description minimizes tremendous variation in careers. Some workers enter or re-enter the workforce after periods of military service, homemaking and child care, or incarceration. Many enroll in further education while employed, and some return to school at mid-career. Some become self-employed; others experience extended periods of unemployment or under-employment.

The Facts: Age Distribution in the US Workforce

US Census data show that in 2010 just over one-third of the population was 18–44, about one-quarter was 45–64, and 13% reported being 65 or over (Howden & Meyer, 2011). Approximately one-quarter of the population was younger than 18 (most in school, not core workforce). Considering those working or looking for work, longitudinal analyses of census data show that workers 16–24 have been declining since 1990 from 17.9% of the labor force and are projected to be only 11.2% in 2020. This drop is due to increased school attendance, reduced job opportunities during economic recession, and increased competition for entry-level jobs from displaced older workers (Toossi, 2012).

The workforce is also aging. From 1990 to 2010 the "prime age" cohort of workers aged 25–54 has increased in size but is a smaller percentage of the labor force (71% in 2000, projected at about 64% in 2020) because the cohort of older workers is increasing (Toossi, 2012). Over 20 years from 1990 to 2010, this older cohort doubled from 15 million (11.9%) to 30 million workers (19.5%). In 2020, older workers are projected to number 41.4 million (25.2%). Median age rose from 36.4 (1990) to 41.7 years (2010) and is projected to be 42.8 years in 2020. This increase in older workers has occurred for several reasons, including increased life expectancies, legal prohibition of age discrimination and elimination of mandatory retirement by the Age Discrimination in Employment Act (ADEA), economic uncertainty and inadequate retirement savings, increased cost of health care and insurance, and rise in eligibility age for Social Security retirement benefits.

Historical and Legal Context

Before ADEA in 1967, age discrimination at work was not prohibited. Mandatory retirement policies were common and long-term employees could be terminated just before eligibility for retirement benefits and targeted for layoffs because of their higher payroll costs. Amendments to ADEA have extended coverage to overseas employees, eliminated maximum age for ADEA coverage, dealt with pension and other benefits, and extended the period of a right to sue from 30 to 90 days (Gutman et al., 2011). An EEOC fact sheet discusses avoiding age discrimination and how ADEA is applied (EEOC, n.d.-a).

Neither ADEA nor other federal law prevents discrimination on the basis of *youth*; the ADEA protected class is workers 40 or older. However, federal and state child labor laws regulate employment of young workers. In general under the Fair Labor Standards Act (FLSA), 14 is the minimum age for paid employment and for those under 16 the number of hours worked is restricted (USDoL, n.d.-a). Youth of any age can be employed in certain types of work (e.g., newspaper delivery; radio/TV/film/theater; babysitting or other minor jobs at private residences). Hazardous work is generally prohibited before age 18 and special rules govern agricultural employment. Helpful information for teen employees (wage information, Young Worker Toolkit) is provided by the Department of Labor (USDoL, n.d.-d). The EEOC's "Youth at Work" website provides extensive information (e.g., employment discrimination, filing complaints, sample cases, fact sheets; EEOC, n.d.-i).

The ADEA (see Chapter 7) was amended by the Older Workers Benefits Protection Act of 1990 (OWPBA) in which Congress clarified that differential treatment of older and younger workers in benefits is permitted only when benefits for older workers are more costly to the employer. The EEOC Compliance Manual describes legal requirements under ADEA and other laws for management of benefits as well as other human resource activities (EEOC, 2000).

In 2015, the EEOC reported over 20,000 new age discrimination complaints. This number was about 14–18,000 before the recession of 2008, when it spiked dramatically to 22–25,000 (EEOC, n.d.-b). One possible explanation for this pattern is that companies reduced employee rolls through layoffs and downsizing, to which some employees responded with age discrimination complaints.

Typical Workforce Issues and Dilemmas: Stereotypes

Posthuma and Campion (2009) identified six main stereotypes about older workers in the research literature: (a) poor performance; (b) resistance to change; (c) lower learning ability; (d) increased likelihood of leaving; and (e) increased cost (wages and benefits); but (f) increased dependability. Empirical studies on age and performance contradict the poor performance stereotype. In fact, for most workers performance does not decline with age, often it improves due to increased experience, and declines are usually small. Differences among workers in skill level and health are more important than age alone in determining productivity. Posthuma and Campion found almost no empirical research on the stereotype about resistance to change despite widespread belief in it.

Few studies of learning ability exist and empirical results are mixed; Posthuma and Campion (2009) suggested that ability to learn may vary with the training method used. Older workers are less likely than younger workers to leave for reasons other than retirement and are less likely to quit. Because the major payoff from training is short-run, employers' investment in older workers is not lost.

Little empirical evidence was found about the relationship of age to employee cost (Posthuma & Campion, 2009). Older workers generally have higher wages but they tend to be absent less often than younger employees. Some supportive evidence was found for the last and only positive stereotype of dependability: stealing, absenteeism, and quit rates are lower for older workers. Little evidence was found about positive dimensions of citizenship behaviors at work, teamwork, or customer service. However, another meta-analytic review by Ng and Feldman (2008) of 380 empirical studies showed that more mature employees were likely to engage in better safety behavior and more organizational citizenship behaviors (e.g., helping others, following rules, not complaining about small things). Older workers also showed lower levels of counterproductive behaviors such as theft, workplace aggression, tardiness, and substance use on the job. Ng and Feldman found that age was largely unrelated to measures of core task performance and creativity and training performance at older ages declined only slightly.

Posthuma and Campion (2009) warned that even inaccurate age-related stereotypes are likely to affect decisions at work. For example, age stereotypes may affect subjective interview and performance appraisal ratings, especially when other work-related information is not available or considered. Age stereotypes are especially strong in some types of work (e.g., finance, information technology/computing) and more likely to bias ratings in jobs perceived to be appropriate for people of certain ages. This creates a *stereotype cycle* because these perceptions are largely based on restricted age ranges! Older and younger employees are equally likely to hold these general stereotypes but older workers who identify with this in-group may hold less negative views. Diversity professionals and managers should emphasize the importance of judging people as individuals based on work skills, knowledge, and results rather than on stereotypes about age—good advice, no matter what the group.

Issues and Dilemmas: Discrimination

A review by Perry and Parlamis (2006) found that laboratory experiments have consistently found bias against older applicants in recruitment and selection, sometimes affected by the nature of the job in question. In the work world, older workers generally take longer to find employment and often must take lower pay when they do. In contrast, age bias has not generally been found in performance or performance evaluations in organizations (with the exception of harsh evaluations deliberately given to provide grounds for termination for a reason "other than age"). Perhaps with little direct information about an older applicant, recruiters favor younger people, but once on the job many older workers perform as well as their younger counterparts and sometimes better.

According to Perry and Parlamis (2006), studies have found that older workers receive less career counseling and formal training, but it is unclear whether this results from worker preference or from employer discrimination. Employers may believe there will be less return on investments in training older workers, but an employee expecting to retire in five years may also expect less benefit from career counseling or training not perceived to have direct job focus. For example, when new equipment is installed employees must learn to use it safely and effectively. In contrast, older employees may see little direct benefit from training on more general issues (e.g., interpersonal skills). Some studies have found that training performance of older workers is improved by use of lecture, modeling, and active participation methods and by training in smaller groups or self-paced modes (Callahan, Kiker, & Cross, 2003).

Age discrimination complaints filed with the EEOC are relatively frequent and increased dramatically from 2007 through 2012 (EEOC, n.d.-b). During 2013, the EEOC reported almost $98 million in settlements of age discrimination complaints. For example, the restaurant chain Ruby Tuesday, Inc., agreed to pay $575,000 to settle a case (EEOC, 2013b). The EEOC alleged that at six locations in Pennsylvania and Ohio the restaurant engaged in a pattern or practice of age discrimination for positions as servers, bartenders, host/hostess, and "back of the house" jobs such as dishwasher. Employees claimed that managers were either directly or indirectly instructed not to hire older applicants (Harrington, 2009). Furthermore, the company violated ADEA and EEOC regulations by not retaining employment records that could have been useful in investigating claims. The chain agreed to review ads and hiring decisions for discrimination, set recruiting and hiring goals (*not* quotas) for older workers, provide training to those involved in hiring, and keep adequate records.

Other settlements included $90,000 paid by Western Energy Services of Durango, Inc. (EEOC, 2013a) and $3 million paid by 3M (EEOC, 2011b). In the first case, two electricians (ages 61 and 72) were referred by their union for employment with the energy company, which rejected the referrals, then hired two men in their twenties for the positions. The superintendent allegedly stated the rejections were based on age. In the 3M case, the EEOC alleged that the company had selectively laid off older and more highly paid employers to save money and reduce positions at higher levels, and had denied leadership training to older employees. The $26 million age discrimination jury award against Staples (City News Service, 2014) was the largest such award in Los Angeles. See the shaded box for more information about another age discrimination case, noteworthy because the organization has been recognized for its global diversity management work (L'Oréal, n.d.-b).

Evidence of Diversity and Inclusion at L'Oréal

The French cosmetics giant L'Oréal, maker of more than 30 lines of beauty products and supplies, employs over 77,000 persons of 156 nationalities and operates in 130 countries around the globe (L'Oreal, n.d.-a). Its products are designed to appeal to diverse beauty needs and desires worldwide, to men as well as women. In 2004 the EEOC settled an age discrimination suit with L'Oréal USA based on a claim by Joyce Head, a senior director dismissed in 2003 after about 20 years with the company ("L'Oréal settles," 2004). The suit alleged that Head was fired because of her age and because she complained about age harassment.

According to the EEOC, Head was the target of ageist comments such as "too old to move to New York," "too old for a VP sales position," and requiring a makeover because she did not "fit in with L'Oréal's youthful image." Head was allegedly denied promotion to VP of sales for a company division and subjected to age harassment by the person hired for that position. After Head complained to the company's HR office, she was terminated, leading to charges of retaliation (EEOC, 2003). An EEOC trial attorney called Ms. Head a "dynamo" with sales of $30 million in the previous year and at times as much as 70% of her department's business. Head was 58 years old at the time of the claim.

Later the French Supreme Court upheld an earlier ruling that the cosmetics company had violated French law by excluding non-White women as in-store sales representatives for Garnier Fructis, a hair product. Evidence included an internal communication which required that these representatives should be "BBR," which stands for *bleu, blanc, rouge* (blue, white, red—the colors of the French flag). This expression is commonly understood to refer to White French people whose parentage is also White (Neff, 2009; Samuel, 2009).

Issues and Dilemmas: Generational Differences

The popular press makes much of supposed differences between groups of workers born in different eras: Baby Boomers (born 1946–1964), Generation X (born 1965–1980), and Millennials (born after 1980, also called Generation Y). The generational names, which are "the handiwork of popular culture" (Pew Research Center, 2010, p. 6), refer to birth years corresponding roughly to (a) the period between the end of World War II and the era of the birth control pill; (b) the period after the availability of reliable contraception; and (c) the generation whose members entered their 20s around the turn of the 21st century. Many comparisons in the popular press are stereotypic and have not been empirically supported (Joshi, Dencker, Franz, & Martocchio, 2010; Becton, Walker, & Jones-Farmer, 2014; Costanza & Finkelstein, 2015), and some of the value differences found in empirical research are based only on cross-sectional studies. (To separate differences that are a function of generational cohort from those due to age/career stage, members of different cohorts must be studied as they age using a time-lag design.) Review of both cross-sectional and time-lag studies found that later generations consistently placed a higher value on leisure, extrinsic work values such as salary, and individualistic traits, but earlier generations were higher on work centrality and work ethic. Other differences were inconsistent (Twenge, 2010).

Despite some differences in values, little empirical support has been found for work-related differences in personality, job performance, or employment outcomes as a function of generational groups alone. Experience of economic recession, war, tragedies (e.g., 9/11 or Hurricane Katrina), technology, or political and legislative changes (e.g., Civil Rights laws) may be more significant. Joshi et al. (2010) have identified three different conceptualizations of generations in organizations:

(a) by cohort, those who have experienced a particular event within a certain period regardless of their ages; (b) by age, chronologically based; and (c) by role incumbency, those who have occupied particular organizational roles during a certain period regardless of age. In some organizations, variation in cohort or role incumbency are probably equally or more significant than differences in actual age. Diversity professionals should be sensitive to developmental groupings that may have important implications for employment outcomes and a sense of inclusion. In addition, relations among "generations" in an organization may create faultlines that are important for the successful management of D&I.

Diversity professionals should consider how inter-generational relations can be managed as an asset rather than a source of exclusion and frustration. "Age" is a complex concept going beyond chronological age and concerns about ADEA violations. Among the benefits of developmental diversity are (a) spreading over time transitions like resignation, retirement, and requests for maternity or paternity leave; (b) development of informal training or mentoring relationships and mutual assistance among workers of different ages and capacities; (c) maintenance of "institutional history" and insight into reasons for certain procedures and past attempts at change; (d) fresh perspectives and potential to improve operations by questioning long-standing routines.

Issues and Dilemmas: Retirement

Many workers entering their 50s and 60s consider when and how they might reduce or retire from paid employment. Younger workers, in contrast, often believe that retirement is so far away that it is irrelevant except as it concerns older colleagues and issues of succession. Diversity professionals should be aware of differences among employees that may appear age-related but are actually based in concerns about retirement.

Retirement is a process, not a single point in time, and an extremely variable experience (Shultz & Wang, 2011). Retirement decision-making includes three facets: (a) imagining a different future; (b) thinking about the past; and (c) acting on transition plans with focus on the present (Feldman & Beehr, 2011). Each facet involves both attractive and unpleasant aspects and is often experienced as stressful. Among other things, retirement alters daily activities, schedules, income, social interaction, status, security, and learning opportunities. Some changes are welcome, exciting, and a relief; others involve anxiety, sadness, fear, a feeling of loss, and considerable ambivalence (Shultz & Wang, 2011). Uncertainties about the future may lead to positive or negative stress, and pre-retirees may appear distracted or react differently than usual. Some co-workers are sensitive to pre-retirees' feelings but at times interactions become strained because younger and older employees experience different realities at work.

The transition varies a great deal with income and wealth, health status, family configuration, and other factors. Some look forward to retirement as an opportunity for travel, volunteer work, time with family, or development of deferred interests and hobbies. Others experience insecurity, grief, or various challenges. These stresses may have workplace effects which appear age-related but are actually due to other factors.

Surveys of US working adults consistently show serious shortfalls in retirement savings other than Social Security (SSA, 2015a, b). For example, the nonprofit National Institute for Retirement Security analyzed survey data from the US Federal Reserve and found an alarming lack of financial preparation for most working households. More than 45% had no employer-sponsored retirement or individually funded Individual Retirement Account (IRA); the median amount of retirement savings was only $3,000 and only $12,000 for those nearing retirement. Ownership of retirement accounts was correlated with level of income and accumulated wealth (Rhee, 2013), one aspect of the striking wealth gap discussed later in this chapter. To provide 85% of pre-retirement income after retirement, a family should save 8–11 times their annual income, an amount dramatically larger than most at lower income levels are able to accumulate (Harris, 2013).

Many wish to enter this phase of life by continuing employment at a reduced level. *Bridge employment* refers to leaving career employment but not the labor force (Wang, Zhan, Liu, & Shultz, 2008). Work might be part-time in one's previous job (e.g., phased retirement), self-employment, or temporary employment in the same or a different field. Some take a short break from employment, then begin working in a new setting. Wang et al. analyzed a subset of data from a large-scale longitudinal nationally representative sample of employees and found that about one-third chose bridge employment either in their own field (24%) or a different field (10%). Those choosing bridge employment were likely to be younger, with better education and health, less reported work stress, and higher job satisfaction. Financial considerations were important for some participants but were not a primary motivator.

Bridge employment looks attractive to many younger people as well. In a large-scale nationally representative survey, researchers found that 72% of those 50 or over said they wanted to keep working after retirement, and 47% of retirees said they had or planned to continue working during retirement (Merrill-Lynch, 2014). Bridge employment is a "soft landing" from sudden loss of income, status, social and professional connections, daily structure, and stimulation. Volunteer work provides a similar but nonfinancial buffer for other retirees.

Optional phased retirement programs are available to certain categories of employees. In other cases reduced commitment is informally negotiated on a case-by-case basis. A program is likely to be seen as more fair when it is available to all similarly situated employees, particularly if salary, benefits, and responsibilities are assigned on a proportional basis. Diversity professionals should consider how this benefit can be offered without threatening the sense of inclusion for those choosing phased retirement.

Health care costs create uncertainty and stress for workers of any age, but especially for older workers considering retirement. Financial experts estimate that a 65-year-old couple will require $200,000 to $250,000 to cover medical expenses during retirement even with Medicare coverage. This does not include significant costs of long-term assisted living or skilled nursing care, for which a separate form of insurance must be purchased (Hamilton, 2013).

Medicare eligibility begins at age 65 regardless of the age when a person claims Social Security (SS) benefits. Medicare covers a large portion of medical expenses for most retirees who were covered by SS, for whom there is no premium for hospital coverage (Part A). Premiums for Part B (outpatient coverage) are deducted from SS payments (USDoL, n.d.-c). Many older workers decide when to retire based in part on eligibility for Medicare because costs of health insurance coverage for older people can be substantial. Employer-sponsored health insurance may not include retirees or may rise in cost if it does.

Diversity professionals and managers should be aware of financial and medical concerns for those nearing retirement because these are major stressors of which younger workers may be unaware. For many older workers, unwillingness to retire has a sound rational basis and should not be misunderstood as a personality trait, reluctance to "move on," or need to maintain control.

Ability, Appearance, and Weight

These characteristics are considered together because *in limited situations* appearance or body size may be considered an employment disability covered by the Americans with Disabilities Act (ADA). Nevertheless, often appearance and/or weight lead to discrimination or exclusion not addressed by current law as a disability. The diversity professional should understand how ability, appearance, and weight are relevant for management of D&I whether or not legal concerns apply.

As a dimension of D&I, ability is unique in two important ways. First, rarely is it true that a person actually cannot do a job simply because of age, racio-ethnicity, sex, or religion. However, in many situations someone's disability really does prevent performance of a given job. In these cases, the organization should examine whether accommodations can be made that will enable an otherwise qualified person to succeed, or whether the disability is more properly a basis for a negative employment decision. This must be determined on a case-by-case basis because of great variation among disabilities and essential job functions.

A second difference is that disability status can change dramatically, slowly or quickly, in the direction of either greater or less ability, and is often beyond the individual's control. An abled person may become disabled as a result of disease or accident. Some disabling conditions improve temporarily or permanently and some chronic conditions cycle between better and worse over time. Some disabilities are readily apparent, but others are invisible and not obvious to co-workers and supervisors.

Weight and appearance are unusual for two reasons. First, judgments and even fundamental categorizations of weight and appearance are highly subjective in comparison to age, disability, sex, racio-ethnicity, and religion. The weight and appearance of the same person may be described quite differently by various people. Second, in most cases there is no legal basis for challenging discrimination and exclusion based on weight or appearance.

The Facts: Disability

The US Census Bureau collects information on disability status in its American Community Survey (ACS) and Survey of Income and Program Participation (SIPP). This chapter relies on SIPP because it provides a broader estimate of prevalence of disability and employment information. SIPP is a longitudinal survey of a large sample of households (over 35,000) interviewed about three times a year concerning the status of those aged 15 and over (Brault, 2012; USCB, 2014). Respondents are civilians who are not residents of institutionalized settings such as nursing homes and correctional institutions. SIPP data give a good picture of individuals with disabilities, although underestimating the number in the population as a whole because institutionalized persons are not included.

Disabilities are classified in terms of domain and severity. Three domains are: communicative (vision, hearing, speech); mental (learning, intellectual, senility or dementia, or other emotional condition); and physical (e.g., locomotion, disease, musculo-skeletal, head injury or stroke; Brault, 2012). Disabilities are classified as nonsevere or severe depending upon which and how many functions are affected. For example, "severe" disabilities include inability to see, hear, or be understood; inability to perform ordinary activities without assistance; or intellectual/developmental disability such as autism or cerebral palsy. Some persons have more than one type of disability.

In the prime working age population (21–64), 16.6% reported a disability (11.4% severe, 5.2% nonsevere). Over 41% of those with a disability were employed compared to more than 79% of those without disabilities. Among those reporting a disability, employment was more common when disabilities were nonsevere: 71% versus 27.5% for severe disabilities (Brault, 2012). Over half (55.5%) with severe disabilities reported being unable to work. Among those with nonsevere disabilities, only 7.8% reported being unable to work, and an additional one-quarter (24.1%) reported limitations in the kind or amount of work they could do. Almost three-quarters of those with only communicative disabilities were employed, contrasted to about half of those with only physical or mental disabilities.

The Facts: Weight and Appearance

Judgments about appropriate weight are extremely subjective and vary with sex, racio-ethnicity, and culture. Exclusion and discrimination occur against those perceived as too thin as well as too fat. However, most concern about weight as a basis for employment discrimination deals with overweight and obesity rather than underweight; in many cases extreme thinness is associated with illness or malnutrition that may itself prevent or limit employment. In the US, weight is often assessed with body mass index (BMI), calculated from a formula based on height and weight and generally related to amount of body fat (National Institutes of Health; NIH; 2012). Published weight standards are based on data from insurance purchasers, mainly middle class Whites, which may not apply accurately to other demographic groups (Kristen, 2002). Thus larger percentages of Black and Hispanic adults but smaller percentages of Asians are classified as overweight or obese in comparison to Whites, which may lead to adverse impact. Of every three adults in the US, one is considered obese and another one overweight. Only one in twenty is considered extremely or morbidly obese (NIH, 2012).

Evaluations of personal appearance are also highly subjective and variable. Exclusion or discrimination is sometimes based on general appearance or on more specific characteristics such as facial scarring or other disfigurement, weight, grooming (e.g., facial hair), clothing, makeup, adornments (e.g., piercings, tattoos) or general conformity to the look an employer wishes to present. Few legal constraints exist against discrimination based on appearance unless it is "perceived as a disability" (e.g., disfigurement) or related to protected categories such as racio-ethnicity or religion (e.g., hair style, facial hair, clothing or jewelry).

Historical and Legal Context: Disability

Legal protection against discrimination on the basis of disability status began with the 1973 Rehabilitation Act covering recipients of federal funds. For private employers the 1990 ADA is enforced by the EEOC, which in 2015 filed 53 new cases and resolved 61 pending cases (ADA alone) with monetary relief of $6.2 million (EEOC, n.d.-d). These numbers are much higher when based on cases filed concurrently under ADA and other statutes (e.g., Title VII): almost 27,000 charges received and total monetary benefits over $128 million (EEOC, n.d.-c). Of recent EEOC cases and settlements, many have concerned invisible disabilities (Santuzzi, Waltz, Finkelstein, & Rupp, 2014). The shaded box describes illustrative recent ADA cases.

Examples of Legal Settlements Related to Disability

During May 2014 the EEOC filed or settled 22 lawsuits for alleged illegal discrimination; almost half (10) were based on disability (Hyman, 2014). These included a settlement of more than $72,000 to an emergency medical technician with multiple sclerosis who was fired without reasonable accommodation; over $110,000 to a railway track maintenance worker with degenerative back disease who was disqualified without assessment of whether he could perform the job's essential functions; and $90,000 to an HIV-positive nurse terminated by a nursing home.

Other recent examples of settled disability lawsuits include:

- $180,000 settlement from Walgreen's to an 18-year employee who ate a $1.39 bag of chips when suddenly experiencing low blood sugar; terminated for violating "anti-grazing" policy against consuming merchandise without paying for it first (but no one was at the counter where she tried to pay); condition well known after 13 years of employer accommodations. Also agreed: anti-discrimination training, periodic EEOC reports, and posting of revised accommodation policy and notice of decree (EEOC, 2014b).
- Million or multimillion-dollar settlements with Princeton Healthcare, Interstate Distributor, Sears, Supervalu, Verizon, focusing on employee leave under federal statutes (EEOC, 2014a).

Need for understanding of and compliance with the law is underscored by a $38,500 settlement with Disability Network/Wayne County, *whose mission is to assist individuals with disabilities!* The EEOC charged the employer had unlawfully fired a deaf independent living specialist after denying his request for accommodations (e.g., video phone, text messaging) without offering alternatives (EEOC, 2014c).

The ADA protects individuals with a disability who are qualified to perform the essential functions of the job in question, as explained in Chapter 7. In some situations, certain accommodations may be required even if not directly linked to essential job functions (Duggan, 2013). Expected accommodations include making the workplace accessible, job restructuring, modifying work schedules and equipment as long as these do not place an "undue burden" on the employer. If a suitable position is vacant, the individual with a disability can also be reassigned. ADA codifies a practical approach to employing persons with disabilities, but employers should not stop at what is legally required. Even small employers not covered by the ADA sometimes negotiate flexibility and accommodation, which is a way of increasing inclusion when the workforce is increasingly diverse.

Legal Context: Weight and Appearance

Federal law does not specifically address discrimination on the basis of weight or appearance and few Title VII or ADA claims have been successful. In some locations, state law or local ordinances may apply, as in Michigan and some cities (e.g., Washington, DC; Madison, WI; San Francisco, CA; Rudd Center, 2015). Diversity professionals should be knowledgeable about relevant local laws or ordinances.

Although ample evidence exists of workplace prejudice and discrimination based on weight and appearance (Bell & McLaughlin, 2006), most discrimination against overweight employees probably could not be successfully addressed by federal law at this time. If it could be shown that weight requirements (or appearance) were applied only to women or members of particular racio-ethnic groups, this might constitute a disparate treatment claim under Title VII (Roehling, 1999). If weight or appearance standards were set differently or enforced more frequently for those in a protected class than for others, this might support a claim of disparate impact.

In *EEOC v. Resources for Human Development, Inc.* (2011), the EEOC sued a substance abuse facility that fired an employee for severe obesity although she had worked successfully for over seven years and could perform her job's essential functions. The Court-ordered settlement required the employer to provide employee training on disability law and for three years report discrimination complaints and denials of reasonable accommodation to the EEOC. The employer also dedicated a room and installed a memorial plaque in the name of the employee, who died before the settlement (EEOC, 2012). Other successes include the Rhode Island Department of Mental Health under the Rehabilitation Act (Taussig, 1994), and against Jazzercise under a San Francisco ordinance (settled; Brown, 2002).

Evidence of blatant discrimination is infrequent but subtle discrimination is common. Extreme obesity (more than 100% over the norm for one's sex and height) clearly is an impairment that can be addressed under ADA, but the morbidly obese are often unable to work or perform job duties and thus are unlikely to file a complaint. Most weight discrimination occurs against those who, despite their weight, are able to conduct everyday activities and therefore would not meet the definition of disability. Overweight people may be unaware of existing legal protections. They may be reluctant to challenge discrimination because they expect it, believe nothing can be done, or feel that they are responsible for their weight issue ("Weight Bias Laws," 2010). Strong public support exists for laws prohibiting weight discrimination on a national basis (Suh, Puhl, Liu, & Milici, 2014).

Legal protections against discrimination on the basis of appearance are very few. Some localities (Washington, DC; Madison, WI) have ordinances addressing appearance discrimination but successful challenges under federal law have relied on showing that appearance discrimination is actually a form of sex, ethnic, or religious discrimination under Title VII. In the famous *Hopkins* case (see Chapter 7), evidence included statements about Hopkins's lack of femininity in style and appearance. However, technically the outcome was based on a showing of sex discrimination, not discrimination based on appearance.

Typical Workplace Issues: Disability

Several issues lead to awkward interactions around disability, the first of which is stereotypes. The typical image of someone with a disability is someone in a wheelchair or with serious vision or hearing problems, but the wide range of conditions considered disabilities and extreme variations in severity make generalizations very difficult. Stereotypic concerns include: (a) limited ability and skill, low emotional adjustment; (b) increased demands on supervisors; (c) inequity for others when accommodations for disability are made; and (d) increased health care costs (Stone-Romero, Stone, & Lukaszewski, 2006). In fact, these consequences are highly dependent upon the nature of the disability and abilities of the particular individual. Overall, employees with disabilities have lower turnover and absenteeism rates than others, and perform at least as well as others in similar jobs. Some with cognitive disabilities may require longer training times. Health care costs do not generally rise and in fact in some cases a disability *results from* a health condition rather than the reverse. Most of us are one accident or illness away from a disability that affects employment at least temporarily.

Another issue is the importance of respectful terminology. People often say offensive things to those with disabilities; some advice appears in the shaded box.

Speaking about Disability   — #4, #5 Initiate ↓

An older man is in a wheelchair pushed by his spouse. Someone addresses the spouse as if the man could not hear, speak, or think for himself. What would he like for lunch? Is he warm enough? What medications is he taking? (Answer: *Why don't you ask him?*) This experience is common for people whose "disability" is indicated by a wheelchair. Many people apparently think if a person has one disability, senses and thought processes are also impaired.

Individuals with disabilities and their advocates recommend that we think of the PERSON first. Those disabled for some time usually know what they can do without assistance and may be embarrassed, frustrated, or even endangered by well-meaning observers' attempts at assistance. One idea is to say, "You may not need help, but please don't hesitate to ask me if you do" ("Things 'to' say," n.d.). When a new co-worker starts work and a disability is apparent, talk with that person just as you would with any other co-worker. Don't begin a work relationship by asking about the disability. Use "people first" language, such as "man with a vision impairment" or "woman with cerebral palsy" instead of terms like "disabled person," "handicapped person," "cripple," or "wheelchair-bound person" (Ulmstead, 2012; "Appropriate terms," 2014).

DiversityInc., a media and consulting organization, publishes frequent advice about how to speak—or not to speak—with members of various underrepresented groups, including those with disabilities. Among its recommendations for tactful speech are:

- Say "low vision," "hard of hearing," or "uses a wheelchair" instead of "impaired" or "disabled."
- Say "nonvisible" or "nonapparent" instead of "hidden" disabilities.
- Describe situations directly without using "hero" or "victim" language to describe the person with a disability (Golden, n.d.).

Another list of things NOT to say to people with disabilities is culled from actual examples of unfortunate conversations and listed on the DiversityInc website:

- "How do you go to the bathroom?" (Would you say that to another colleague?)
- "I don't even think of you as a person with a disability." If a colleague discloses a disability, thank the person for sharing the information and ask him or her to let you know if anything is needed.
- "Can you still have children?" (Would you say this to another co-worker?)
- "This organization is really a great place if it would hire someone like you."
- "Wow, you can drive!" For many individuals with disabilities, driving (perhaps with a specially designed vehicle) is an everyday task not requiring special comment.
- "When will you get better and not have to use a wheelchair (cane, walker, etc.)?" Sometimes adaptive equipment is a way of maintaining health; a question like this suggests instead that it is a stigma of disability.
- "It must be bad for you." Most with longer-term disabilities have learned to adapt to their situation and do not need or want sympathy or pity ("How do you," n.d.).

Individuals with disabilities are, like others, diverse in their feelings about how others speak about and think of ability and disability. In the workplace as co-workers become friendly, the topic of disability may come up. Questions like "What is the term you prefer?" (also helpful with persons from ethnic minority groups) or "May I ask about your disability?" may be appropriate. However, these are not a good way to begin a relationship with a newly hired person. In general, we should behave toward individuals with disabilities as we would to anyone else and focus on the person's ability rather than what he or she seems unable to do.

A third issue concerns costs associated with employment of those with disabilities. The Job Accommodation Network (JAN), a service of the US Department of Labor, assists employers in devising appropriate accommodations and conducts periodic employer surveys of costs and consequences of accommodations. Employers report that more than half of accommodations (58%) cost nothing and the rest typically cost about $500. One very low cost accommodation is adding wood blocks under a desk to raise it to accommodate a wheelchair. Employers have reported benefits of retaining qualified employees, whose average tenure was about seven years. Other benefits were improved morale and co-worker interactions, higher productivity, reduced costs for workers' compensation and training of new employees, and increased workforce diversity (Loy, 2015).

A fourth issue concerns reactions of co-workers and supervisors to employment and accommodation of those with disabilities. Many types of accommodations affect working conditions or resources affecting co-workers (e.g., schedule changes, task reallocation, work restructuring). Their willing cooperation is needed for smooth implementation of changes benefiting the person with a disability but perhaps imposing on others (Colella, 2001). Anticipated worker reactions may discourage an individual with a disability from requesting accommodations and may discourage supervisors from granting them. Colella suggested some factors that may influence others' judgments of fairness by affecting either how obvious or relevant the accommodation seems to others: (a) visibility of disability; (b) independence of task structure; (c) diversity climate; and (d) likely impact on co-workers. Colella suggested that these factors are associated with a belief that accommodation is not really needed, or a sense of unfairness on the part of those without disabilities. A competent, valuable, and well-known colleague who becomes disabled would probably be more likely to receive supportive reactions from others than a "difficult" employee, someone new and unknown, or someone seen as responsible for the disability.

McLaughlin, Bell, and Stringer (2004) examined reactions to scenarios about a fictitious co-worker with HIV/AIDS, cerebral palsy, or stroke, conditions differing in degree of stigma (e.g., impact of condition on performance, controllability, unattractiveness and social impact, long-term implications). Judgments were harsher when stigma was higher, as in HIV/AIDS, but only opinions about the condition's impact on performance were by themselves related to acceptance. This suggests that managers should stress ability to do the work required rather than nature of accommodation.

Managers' actual or expected reactions to accommodation requests are also important. Accommodation requires adjustment in the usual business approach to human resources management. Policies cannot be too specific, standardization is impossible, and supervisors must exercise judgment in unique individual/job combinations.

During the first decade after enactment of ADA, a state government study found reluctance to provide accommodation for two reasons: controlling costs and maintaining administrative control of work processes (Harlan & Robert, 1998). Early problems included lack of familiarity with procedures, differences in accommodation as a function of sex and job grade of individual, supervisor knowledge and flexibility, and type of accommodation. Approval was more likely when the requested accommodation was straightforward, inexpensive, a one-time expense (e.g., equipment), not time consuming, and easy to put in place. Strangely, approval did not seem to depend on the employee's need for or entitlement to an accommodation. Two-thirds of employees hesitated to request needed accommodation, fearing termination or labeling as incompetent, lazy, or a troublemaker. Many workers worked harder or longer hours, came to work sick or in pain, or compensated by using sick or vacation leave or personal time on weekends.

Since that time, information about appropriate ADA compliance is more widely available as a result of litigation and efforts of advocacy groups and professional organizations. EEOC press releases show that most cases of accommodation denial also include complaint of termination, which is the major basis for charging ADA violation. This suggests that unless they are terminated, people who request accommodation but do not receive it either resolve the situation, adapt in some way, or leave the organization voluntarily.

Several challenges arise when disability status is not obvious to others (e.g., chronic pain, recurring medical conditions, learning disabilities, mental illness; Santuzzi et al., 2014). Because ADA protections and accommodations follow only when a disability is disclosed, the individual must balance these benefits and possible negative consequences of disclosure, such as stigmatization and negative reactions from others. An employee might not disclose a disability for several reasons: (a) considering it part of normal variation rather than a disability; (b) vanity or fear of stereotypic judgments about age or ability, leading to denial or resistance to use of corrective equipment; (c) diagnostic difficulty or change in diagnosis or diagnostic categories and criteria. (Clinical diagnosis does not necessarily imply that a condition meets the legal definition of ADA disability.) On the other hand, nondisclosure is stressful and depletes cognitive resources and energy. Supervisors should not inform others of an employee's disability and accommodation needs because of ADA's confidentiality requirement; thus, others who are uninformed may misinterpret an appropriate accommodation as unfair favoritism.

Typical Workplace Issues: Weight and Appearance

Two concerns are stereotyping and discrimination. Studies usually focus on either appearance or weight, although in reality effects of weight and appearance on others' reactions are hard to disentangle.

Stereotypes about the overweight/obese are widely held. In work settings, overweight people are seen as less outgoing, less emotionally stable, less pleasant, and less conscientious than others although these beliefs are largely invalid (Roehling, Roehling, & Odland, 2008). Attractive people are often thought to have more favorable personalities and better life outcomes. Meta-analysis has shown greatest associations of attractiveness with judgments of social competence, and moderate effects on strength, adjustment, and intellectual competence (Eagly, Ashmore, Makhijani, & Longo, 1991). Another meta-analysis found similar results for social appeal, interpersonal competence, general adjustment, and especially occupational competence (Langlois, Kalakanis, Rubenstein, Larson, Hallam, & Smoot, 2000).

Second, evidence of weight and appearance discrimination is consistently found (Bell & McLaughlin, 2006), most unrelated to job-related knowledge, skill, or ability. IAT research has documented that negative reactions to weight occur quickly without conscious control and can affect judgments about likely job performance and discriminatory hiring decisions (Agerström & Rooth, 2011). Research on work outcomes and body weight has consistently found that "the thin win" when it comes to a variety of work outcomes (Judge & Cable, 2011). A comprehensive review of 29 studies conducted in field and laboratory settings between 1979 and 1998 found "sobering" evidence of discrimination across the employment cycle, including selection, placement, compensation, promotion, discipline, and termination (Roehling, 1999), with results more consistent in laboratory than field research. Roehling concluded that weight bias was stronger than sex, age, or race bias, and that stigmatization was stronger toward overweight employees than toward ex-felons or former mental patients. "Courtesy stigma" has also been found; even men merely seated near an overweight woman were rated more negatively as job applicants, regardless of whether a relationship was thought to exist between the two (Hebl & Mannix, 2003).

Meta-analytic reviews have consistently found moderate or strong negative effects of weight for work judgments of suitability, hiring, performance evaluation, and likely success (Roehling, Pichler, & Bruce, 2013; Rudolph, Wells, Weller, & Baltes, 2009). Meta-analytic evidence also found weight bias to be stronger against women than men (Roehling, et al., 2013; Vanhove & Gordon, 2014). Compared to men, women were significantly more likely to *perceive* that they had been targets of weight discrimination (Roehling, Roehling, & Pichler, 2007).

Salary levels are often related to weight, but results are complex and inconsistent (Roehling, 1999; Bell & McLaughlin, 2006). Heavier people often earn less than slimmer employees but in some studies this occurs only for overweight women, (e.g., Register & Williams, 1990; Pagan & Davila, 1997). Sometimes weight is associated with lower wages for women but a weight *premium* for men up to the point of obesity. For example, Judge and Cable (2011) reported that the highest paid women were very thin (25% below average weight) and the negative correlation of wages to weight was strongest for women of below average weight. "All else equal, a woman who is average weight earns $389,300 less across a 25-year career than a woman who is 25 lbs. below average weight" (p. 109)! In contrast, the highest paid men were of average weight or above, with this positive correlation of wages to weight continuing until very high weight levels.

Meta-analysis of workplace appearance discrimination found medium but consistent effects with more attractive people faring better at work (Hosoda, Stone-Romero, & Coats, 2003). This occurred regardless of how much job-relevant information was provided about the target persons, whether the respondents were professionals or students, men or women. The relationship with attractiveness was large for choice as a business partner and small for evaluation of employee performance. Intermediate effect sizes were found for other outcomes (e.g., hiring or promotion decisions, predictions of success or employment potential).

Narrative reviews (Bell & McLaughlin, 2006; Dipboye, 2005) also provide evidence of attractiveness discrimination in many work behaviors and outcomes, including selection, performance appraisal, and promotion. Attractiveness is also related to starting salary and annual income but in some studies, results are different for men than women. Women's attractiveness may relate positively or negatively to job outcomes, depending on job level and type. For example, attractiveness may be an advantage for women in lower level jobs and those held predominantly by women, but not in male-occupied jobs or those at higher organizational levels. Ability of very attractive women may also be underestimated or attributed to external factors (e.g., luck, the influence of others) rather than skill or competence (Bell & McLaughlin, 2006).

Intersectional analysis (Sawyer, Salter, & Thoroughgood, 2013) addressed the relationship between weight/appearance and evaluative reactions/work outcomes. Weight and appearance of men and women often elicit quite different responses, with negative impact usually greater for women. Height sometimes predicts success for men but not for women.

What does this research imply for diversity professionals and managers? First, appearance and weight bias, explicit or implicit, often occurs toward applicants and employees. Hiring should be based on job-related attributes and valid measures of job performance, not biased by irrelevant personal characteristics. For personnel decisions, sufficient information about applicant characteristics and employee performance should be available to reduce reliance on superficial attributes. Training workshops should cover bias from weight/appearance bias as well as demographic characteristics. Second, training should address how to deal with "awkward moments" in interactions involving those of different appearance, from the observer's and target's perspectives (Hebl, Tickle, & Heatherton, 2000; Dipboye, 2005). Third, although weight and appearance discrimination generally do not violate the law, they can create a culture that normalizes unfairness and exclusion and legitimizes other prejudice and discrimination, undermining attempts to provide fair and inclusive environments for all employees (Dipboye, 2005).

Social Class

Social class is a major difference among employees, reinforced by organizational structures and processes. Social class constrains opportunities for employment, advancement, and financial success in ways that are "undiscussable" (i.e., threatening or risky to discuss; Argyris, 1980, p. 205) and therefore usually described in more acceptable terms (e.g., "fit," education).

Organizations reflect the class structure of surrounding society. Class is usually understood in structural terms but can also be conceptualized in terms of style or process (Scully & Blake-Beard, 2006). In the US, classes can be described as upper or elite, middle (upper and lower middle), working class, and lower class, varying in terms of income and wealth, property ownership, type of work, authority, and power. This reflects a view of society in which family class is determined by characteristics of one adult wage-earner. It assumes consistency among levels of education, income, wealth, authority, and ownership which contradicts the complexities of contemporary US society. For example, many tradespeople (e.g., electricians, plumbers) have greater income, property ownership, and autonomy than some professional workers (e.g., teachers). Judgments of class and race are interrelated; in one study lower-class Black men (identified in photos by clothing, grooming, and supposed occupation) were perceived as "Black" whereas the same individuals dressed differently were categorized by class instead of race. This did not occur for photos of White men (Weeks & Lupfer, 2004).

Most organizations also have a "class system" with positions stratified on the basis of power, authority, autonomy and flexibility, salary, and benefits. This *structural* view portrays class as something outside the organization which workers can do little to change. It also legitimizes inequality and focuses workers' attention on moving up within their class without considering and challenging ways in which power and advantage of higher classes limits others' opportunity (Scully & Blake-Beard, 2006). In contrast, conceptualizing class as *style* directs attention to clothing, speech pattern and accent, manners, and ways of thinking—individual attributes that can be changed through coaching, modeling, or direct instruction. When and if diversity programs address class, it is probably from this approach. However, this emphasis ignores the economic basis

↳ Diversity Programs don't address class

OPEN MS

USE MS

of class distinctions, emphasizing superficial rather than fundamental differences which are harder to alter. Finally, class as *process* examines how organizational procedures reinforce existing distinctions, how class is both like and unlike other sorts of difference, and how and whether an organization addresses class as a dimension in its management of D&I. For example, in most organizations, systems operate differently for hourly/salaried, full/part-time, and management/non-managerial employees.

The Facts

Class is often defined by level of income or wealth but sometimes refers to a shared viewpoint or self-identification. The federal government uses no specific metric of how many people or households fall in each class (Elwell, 2014). One categorization divides the income distribution into fifths; upper 20% (UC); middle 60% (MC); and lower 20% (LC). By this definition, in 2012 the MC comprised approximately 73.5 million households with pre-tax incomes from $20,592 to $104,087 (but still less than half of total income). The *top 20%* earned more than half (51%) of US income and the *lowest 20%* earned only 3.2%. Another income-based definition (e.g., Reich, 2010) considers as MC those households in a band above and below median income level: $51,017 in 2012 (Elwell, 2014). Self-report is another measure of social class. The Pew Research Center (2012) found that *89%* of surveyed Americans identified themselves as MC! Of these, 15% considered themselves upper middle and 25% lower middle with the remaining 49% reporting middle. Only 2% identified as UC and 7% as LC (2% did not know).

Income and Wealth Inequality in the US

By most measures, level of *income* inequality in the US is as high as it has been since 1928 (just before the Great Depression), but level of *wealth* inequality is even higher (DeSilver, 2014). In 2012 those in the top 1% income level (above $394,000) received 22.5% of income before taxes, but the bottom 90% (almost everyone else, those earning $114,000 or less) earned only 49.6% of pre-tax income. This discrepancy is larger than in most developed countries—only Chile had a larger income disparity. The wealth gap is even more striking: the best-off 1% of households in 2010 held over one-third (35.4%) of all wealth; the small number in the top 20% held 88.9%, leaving about 11% of wealth to be divided among everyone else!

Reasons for this wealth gap include several factors affecting many jobs, such as globalization, outsourcing, and technological change. Policy choices driven by political factors have also played a role: deregulation of business, weakening of unions, privatization of some public sector work (e.g., prisons, schools), tax policies, and reductions in the welfare safety net (Reich, 2010). Wealthy households are better able to absorb costs of higher education and college loans. Job losses during the 2008 recession and widespread and longer-term unemployment have also eroded wealth of moderate-income households more than those at higher levels. Drops in housing values threatened MC households, especially those of Hispanics and Blacks, more than households whose wealth was less concentrated in home equity (Taylor, Fry, & Kochhar, 2011). Those with investments profited as the stock market rebounded faster than other aspects of the economy. Wages at the top have increased while national minimum wage has not increased since July 2009 and MC wages have stagnated (Mishel, Bivens, Gould, Shierholz, 2012).

Economists and politicians differ about the seriousness of the wealth gap but especially about what, if anything, should be done to reduce it. The wealthy have great influence on public policy, and genuine differences exist in understandings of economic factors among those in a position to affect policy choices. This controversial issue illustrates class differences in organizations as well as in society.

Historical and Legal Context

~USE

Social class is not a protected category under anti-discrimination law but some legal issues form workplace class distinctions. First, the FLSA, often called the "wage and hour law," distinguishes *exempt* and *non-exempt* employees. Minimum wage laws and overtime requirements apply to those who are non-exempt (i.e., covered). Exempt employees are identified by salary level and the nature of their work: executive, administrative, or professional work; outside sales; or certain computer-related jobs. Certain types of jobs (e.g., those paid by commission, live-in domestic service work) may be exempt from overtime pay but not from minimum wage requirements. Often, but not always, exempt employees are salaried and non-exempt employees are paid hourly. Regulations about which employers and jobs are covered, calculation of overtime, payment for tipped employees, hours "on-call," and other topics are quite detailed and specific and recently revised (USDoL, n.d.-b; 2014, 2016).

Worked both
I didn't
experience
this

Pay systems and wage levels generally differ for exempt and non-exempt employees, creating a *de facto* class system in many employment settings. Exempt employees usually work at higher levels, have more autonomy and higher salaries, and are less accountable for their time. They may—or can be expected to—work long hours and on non-work days.

Second, employee unions create another legal basis for workplace class distinctions. Major unions grew among working-class jobs in skilled trades and manufacturing but today are also found in some professions (e.g., nursing, teaching) and in public sector employment (e.g., police and fire departments), as well as in some public sector administrative work, professional sports, and some service work. For many reasons including political factors and restructuring of the domestic economy, union membership in the US has been dropping since the 1950s when about one-third of workers were unionized, and now includes about 17% of the workforce.

Management represents ownership and is not unionized. Where unions exist, terms and conditions of employment for those in the bargaining unit are determined by a *contract* or *collective bargaining agreement (CBA)* negotiated with management; a grievance system handles alleged CBA violations by individual managers or the employer. Because CBAs constrain managerial discretion and increase employee power, employers often resist unionization and expansion of employee rights under a CBA. Union presence creates a class of those covered by the CBA, and in some settings this distinction is the basis for contentious disputes, demonstrations, or strikes. In addition, managers have less discretion in making decisions and some activities or practices to enhance D&I may require management/union collaboration.

Typical Workplace Scenarios

Class is enacted in organizations in many ways, usually based on the structure of positions. Each organization is different, but most have "classes" of employees differing in terms of compensation, education and skill level, autonomy, prestige, power, and other attributes. For example:

- Large companies: "C-Suite" officers (chief officers), top and mid-level management, support staff, those who do the core work of the organization (e.g., sales, manufacturing).
- Military: officers and enlisted; differences in unit prestige.
- Universities: administration, faculty, staff (professional and others, e.g., housekeepers, campus safety).
- Faculty: tenured/tenure eligible, non-tenure earning (visiting and limited contract faculty), adjuncts.
- Hospitals: levels of administration; hierarchy of medical staff, nursing staff (supervisors, nurses, assistants), medical technicians, patient transporters.

Income levels for those at or near the top of the organization are many times greater than levels for lower-paid employees. Often compensation packages are structured differently for those at the top (e.g., deferred pay, stock options, etc.), who may also have access to financial advisors to assist in successful financial investment. Retirement funds may be different in structure and security as well as amount. Some organizations have separate parking areas, dining rooms or cafeterias, or even elevators for different "classes" of employees. Work locations and schedules may vary and striking differences may exist in quality of furnishings. "Perks" such as company cars, equipment, expense accounts, travel funding, and leave time often vary for different employee classes. In comparison to White men, fewer women or people of color hold positions at top levels of most organizations.

Some differences are required by law (e.g., FLSA requirements) or CBA, or justified by work context or commonly accepted assumptions about the relationship between job and employee characteristics (e.g., education and skill, work experience, level of work difficulty). Other differences seem larger than can be justified on these bases alone. In such cases, differential treatment of employee classes is likely to undermine a sense of inclusion and fairness. For example, attention has turned to the growing gap between the pay of Chief Executive Officers and others. According to AFL-CIO calculations from publicly available data on Fortune 500 companies, in 2013 the ratio of CEO pay to that of workers was 331:1—up from a ratio of 46:1 in 1983 (AFL/CIO, 2014; Wong, 2014). Because companies are not currently required to report these ratios, CEO pay was compared to average worker pay for production and non-supervisory employees reported by the Bureau of Labor Statistics. The shaded box describes an interesting response to the vertical wage gap.

Mind the Gap

For the third time since 2006, the president of Hampton University used his own funds to raise the bottom of the wage scale at this private university in Virginia. William R. Harvey and his wife Norma, who own a Pepsi Cola Bottling Company in Michigan, donated over $108,000 to the University to raise the wages of 121 full-time staff members with salaries below $9 per hour. Donations in 2006 and 2011 had previously raised wages to $7 and $8 per hour. This donation boosted wages through the fiscal year, after which this amount will be included in recurring funds of the University's budget. Harvey said, "A loaf of bread costs them the same thing as it costs me . . . they are a member of our team, and I appreciate them, as does my wife" (Keierleber, 2014).

At Kentucky State University, Interim President Raymond Burse requested the University's Board to cut his salary by $90,000 and allocate that money to raise the pay of hourly workers to $10.25. Before coming to KSU, Burse was employed by General Electric as a Vice President. According to Burse, "I didn't do it to be an example to anyone else . . . I did it to do right by the employees here" ("Income inequality," 2014).

Although these presidents are at the top of their campus pay scale, their salaries are significantly below average for university presidents nationally. Both have significant personal assets from other sources and have chosen to share with employees at lower wage levels. Both Hampton University and Kentucky State University are historically Black institutions (HBCUs); Hampton University is a private university and KSU is a publicly supported land grant institution.

Social class is an important factor in patterns of thought and action in organizational life (Coté, 2011). LC individuals have been found to be higher in depth of social engagement, accuracy of perceiving others' emotions, and communal versus transactional nature of helping. Coté summarized research indicating class differences in such areas as moral judgments and ethical behavior and

LOWER CLASS

warned that researchers may be developing a science of middle- and upper-class employees and overlooking important aspects of behavior.

Diversity professionals should be alert to class distinctions and the degree to which these are justified by law, best practices, or practical necessity. In some cases class distinctions may serve little purpose other than to distinguish among employees who are seen as more or less "valuable" or "important." In those cases, consideration should be given to whether distinctions obstruct engagement, inclusion, and satisfaction of employees at lower levels, and what would happen if these distinctions were reduced or eliminated.

Part III of this text has discussed types of distinctions among organization members important for management of D&I and for many aspects of organizational and individual success at work. The final part of the text considers techniques and procedures for improving how D&I are addressed in work organizations.

References

AFL/CIO. (2014). *Executive paywatch: High-paid CEOs and the low-wage economy*. Retrieved from http://edit.aflcio.org/Corporate-Watch/Paywatch-2014

Agerström, J., & Rooth, D.-O. (2011). The role of automatic obesity stereotypes in real hiring discrimination. *Journal of Applied Psychology, 96*, 790–805.

Appropriate terms to use. (2014, May 5). Retrieved from http://nda.ie/Publications/Attitudes/Appropriate-Terms-to-Use-about-Disability/

Argyris, C. (1980). Making the undiscussable and its undiscussability discussable. *Public Administration Review, 40*, 205–213.

Becton, J. B., Walker, H. J., & Jones-Farmer, A. (2014). Generational differences in workplace behavior. *Journal of Applied Social Psychology, 44*, 175–189.

*Bell, M. P., & McLaughlin, M. E. (2006). Outcomes of appearance and obesity in organizations. In A. M. Konrad, P. Prasad, & J. K. Pringle (Eds.), *Handbook of workplace diversity* (pp. 455–474). Thousand Oaks, CA: SAGE Publications.

Brault, M. W. (2012). Americans with disabilities: 2010. *Current Population Reports*, P70–131. Retrieved from www.census.gov/prod/2012pubs/p70-131.pdf

Brown, P. L. (2002, May 8). 240 pounds, persistent and Jazzercise's equal. *New York Times*. Retrieved from www.nytimes.com/2002/05/08/us/240-pounds-persistent-and-jazzercise-s-equal.html

Buonanno v. AT&T Broadband LLC, 313 F. Supp. 2d 1069 (Denver, Colorado. 2004).

Callahan, J. S., Kiker, D. S., & Cross, T. (2003). Does method matter? A meta-analysis of the effects of training method on older learner training performance. *Journal of Management, 29*, 663–680.

City News Service. (2014, February 27). 66-year-old man awarded $26 million in age discrimination lawsuit against Staples. *Los Angeles Daily News*. Retrieved from www.dailynews.com/general-news/20140227/66-year-old-man-awarded-26-million-in-age-discrimination-lawsuit-against-staples

Colella, A. (2001). Coworker distributive fairness judgments of the workplace accommodation of workers with disabilities. *Academy of Management Review, 26*, 100–116.

Costanza, D. P., & Finkelstein, L. M. (2015). Generationally based differences in the workplace: Is there a *there* there? *Industrial and Organizational Psychology, 8*, 308–323.

*Coté, S. (2011). How social class shapes thoughts and actions in organizations. *Research in Organizational Behavior, 31*, 43–71.

DeSilver, D. (2014, January 7). 5 facts about economic inequality. *Pew Research Center*. Retrieved from www.pewresearch.org/fact-tank/2014/01/07/5-facts-about-economic-inequality/

*Dipboye, R. L. (2005). Looking the part: Bias against the physically unattractive as a discrimination issue. In R. L. Dipboye & A. Colella (Eds.), *Discrimination at work: The psychological and organizational bases* (pp. 281–301). Mahwah, NJ: Lawrence Erlbaum Associates.

Duggan, S. J. (2013, October 7). No link required between job essential function and reasonable accommodation. *Fair Measures, Inc.* Retrieved from www.fairmeasures.com/enews/essential-reasonable-accommodation/

Eagly, A. H., Ashmore, R. D., Makhijani, M. G., & Longo, L. C. (1991). What is beautiful is good, but . . . : A meta-analytic review of research on the physical attractiveness stereotype. *Psychological Bulletin, 110*, 109–128.

*EEOC. (n.d.-a). *Age discrimination*. Retrieved from www.eeoc.gov/eeoc/publications/age.cfm

EEOC. (n.d.-b). *Age Discrimination in Employment Act (includes concurrent charges with Title VII, ADA and EPA): FY 1997–FY2015*. Retrieved from www1.eeoc.gov/eeoc/statistics/enforcement/adea.cfm

EEOC. (n.d.-c). *Americans with Disabilities Act of 1990 (ADA) Charges: (includes concurrent charges with Title VII, ADEA, and EPA) FY 1997–2015)*. Retrieved from www.eeoc.gov/eeoc/statistics/enforcement/ada-charges.cfm

EEOC. (n.d.-d). *EEOC Litigation Statistics, FY 1997 through 2015*. Retrieved from www.eeoc.gov/eeoc/statistics/enforcement/litigation.cfm

*EEOC. (n.d.-e). *Questions and answers about employer responsibilities concerning the employment of Muslims, Arabs, South Asians, and Sikhs*. Retrieved from www1.eeoc.gov/eeoc/publications/backlash-employer.cfm

EEOC. (n.d.-f). *Religion-based charges FY 1997–2015*. Retrieved from www1.eeoc.gov/eeoc/statistics/enforcement/religion.cfm

*EEOC. (n.d.-g). *Religious discrimination*. Retrieved from www1.eeoc.gov/laws/types/religion.cfm

*EEOC. (n.d.-h). *Religious garb and grooming in the workplace: Rights and responsibilities*. Retrieved from www.eeoc.gov/eeoc/publications/qa_religious_garb_grooming.cfm

EEOC. (n.d.-i). *Youth at work*. Retrieved from www.eeoc.gov/youth/index.html

EEOC. (2000, October 3). *EEOC Compliance Manual: Chapter 3: Employee benefits*. Number 915.003. Retrieved from www.eeoc.gov/policy/docs/benefits.html

EEOC. (2003, September 30). *EEOC sues L'Oréal for age discrimination and retaliation*. Retrieved from www.eeoc.gov/eeoc/newsroom/release/9-30-03d.cfm

*EEOC. (2009, July 15). *Understanding waivers of discrimination claims in employee severance agreements*. Retrieved from www.eeoc.gov/policy/docs/qanda_severance-agreements.html

EEOC. (2011a, February 8; 2008, July 22). *EEOC Compliance Manual: Section 12: Religious discrimination*. Number 915.003. Retrieved from www.eeoc.gov/policy/docs/religion.html

EEOC. (2011b, August 22). *3M to pay $3 million to settle EEOC age discrimination suit*. Retrieved from www1.eeoc.gov/eeoc/newsroom/release/8-22-11a.cfm

EEOC. (2012, April 10). *Resources for Human Development settles EEOC disability suit for $125,000*. Retrieved from www1.eeoc.gov/eeoc/newsroom/release/4-10-12a.cfm

EEOC. (2013a, April 8). *WESODI agrees to pay $90,000 to settle EEOC age discrimination lawsuit*. Retrieved from www.eeoc.gov/eeoc/newsroom/release/4-8-13d.cfm

EEOC. (2013b, December 9). *Ruby Tuesday will pay $575,000 to resolve EEOC class age discrimination lawsuit*. Retrieved from www1.eeoc.gov//eeoc/newsroom/release/12-9-13.cfm

EEOC. (2014a, June 30). *Princeton Healthcare pays $1.35 million to settle disability discrimination suit with EEOC*. Retrieved from http://eeoc.gov/eeoc/newsroom/release/6-30-14.cfm

EEOC. (2014b, July 2). *America's largest drug store chain to pay $180,000 to settle EEOC disability discrimination suit*. Retrieved from www.eeoc.gov/eeoc/newsroom/release/7-2-14b.cfm

EEOC. (2014c, November 26). *Disability Network*. Retrieved from www1.eeoc.gov/eeoc/newsroom/release/11-26-14.cfm

EEOC v. Resources for Human Development, Inc., F. Supp. 2d, 2011 WL 6091560 (E.D. La. Dec. 2011).

Elwell, C. K. (2014, March 10). *The distribution of household income and the middle class*. Retrieved from http://fas.org/sgp/crs/misc/RS20811.pdf

Epps, G. (2011, June 15). Constitutional myth #4: The Constitution doesn't separate church and state. *The Atlantic*. Retrieved from www.theatlantic.com/national/archive/2011/06/constitutional-myth-4-the-constitution-doesnt-separate-church-and-state/240481/

Feldman, D. C., & Beehr, T. A. (2011). A three-phase model of retirement decision making. *American Psychologist, 66*, 193–203.

*Finkelstein, L. M., Truxillo, D. M., Fraccaroli, F., & Kanfer, R. (Eds.) (2015). *Facing the challenges of a multi-age workforce*. New York: Taylor & Francis.

Golden, L. (n.d.). *Diversity leaders: 6 things NEVER to say about disabilities*. Retrieved from www.diversityinc.com/things-not-to-say/diversity-leaders-6-things-never-to-say-about-disabilities/

*Gutman, A., Koppes, L. L., & Vodanovich, S. J. (2011). *EEO law and personnel practices*. New York, NY: Routledge.

Hamilton, M. M. (2013, January/February). What health care will cost you. *AARP Bulletin*. Retrieved from www.aarp.org/health/medicare-insurance/info-12-2012/health-care-costs.html

Harlan, S. L., & Robert, P. M. (1998). The social construction of disability in organizations: Why employers resist reasonable accommodation. *Work and Occupations, 25*, 397–435.

Harrington, C. (2009, October 3). EEOC sues Ruby Tuesday. *News Sentinel*. Retrieved from www.knoxnews.com/business/eeoc-sues-ruby-tuesday-ep-409522303-359175611.html

Harris, K. K. (2013, August 7). New statistics on the American retirement crisis. *The Shriver Brief.* Retrieved from www.theshriverbrief.org/2013/08/articles/asset-opportunity/new-statistics-on-the-american-retirement-savings-crisis/print.html

Hebl, M. R., & Mannix, L. M. (2003). The weight of obesity in evaluating others: A mere proximity effect. *Personality and Social Psychology Bulletin, 29,* 28–38.

*Hebl, M. R., Tickle, J., & Heatherton, R. F. (2000). Awkward moments in interactions between nonstigmatized and stigmatized individuals. In T. F. Heatherton, R. F. Kleck, M.R. Hebl, & J. G. Hull (Eds.), *The social psychology of stigma* (pp. 275–306). New York, NY: Guilford.

Hicks, D. A. (2002). Spiritual and religious diversity in the workplace. Implications for leadership. *The Leadership Quarterly, 13,* 379–396.

*Hosoda, M., Stone-Romero, E. F., & Coats, G. (2003). The effects of physical attractiveness on job-related outcomes: A meta-analysis of experimental studies. *Personnel Psychology, 56,* 431–462.

" 'How do you go to the bathroom?' 'Can you still have children?' Things NOT to say to people with disabilities." (n.d.). *The DiversityInc.* Retrieved from www.diversityinc.com/things-not-to-say/how-do-you-go-to-the-bathroom-can-you-still-have-children-things-not-to-say-to-people-with-disabilities/

Howden, L. M., & Meyer, J. A. (2011, May). Age and sex composition: 2010. *2010 Census Brief.* Retrieved from www.census.gov/prod/cen2010/briefs/c2010br-03.pdf

Hyman, J. (2014, June 2). Employers beware: EEOC stepping up disability discrimination enforcement. *Workforce.* Retrieved from www.workforce.com/blogs/3-the-practical-employer/post/20516-employers-beware-eeoc-stepping-up-disability-discrimination-enforcement

"Income inequality: Walking the walk." (2014, August 25). *Boston Globe.* Retrieved from www.bostonglobe.com/opinion/editorials/2014/08/25/kentucky-state-president-sets-admirable-example-income-inequality/GiFdJgIixeiMTNCxVail8L/story.html

Joshi, A., Dencker, J. C., Franz, G., & Martocchio, J. J. (2010). Unpacking generational identities in organizations. *Academy of Management Review, 35,* 392–414.

*Judge, T. A., & Cable, D. M. (2011). When it comes to pay, do the thin win? The effect of weight on pay for men and women. *Journal of Applied Psychology, 96,* 95–112.

Keierleber, M. (2014, January 23). Hampton U. president helps raise its minimum wage with a personal gift. *The Chronicle of Higher Education.* Retrieved from http://chronicle.com/blogs/bottomline/hampton-u-president-helps-raise-its-minimum-wage-with-a-personal-gift/

Khalsa, S. (n.d.). *What are the five K's of Sikhism?* Retrieved from http://sikhism.about.com/od/introduction tosikhism/tp/Kakars.htm

Kristen, E. (2002). Addressing the problem of weight discrimination in employment. *California Law Review, 90,* 57–109.

Langlois, J. H., Kalakanis, L., Rubenstein, A. J., Larson, A., Hallam, M., & Smoot, M. (2000). Maxims or myths of beauty? A meta-analytic and theoretical review. *Psychological Bulletin, 126,* 390–423.

Levin, M. B. (2007). *Religious accommodations, discrimination, and harassment.* Retrieved from www.thompson.com/images/thompson/reports/hr042007_religion.pdf

*Levy, S. R., Macdonald, J. L., & Nelson, T. D. (Eds.) (2016). Ageism: Health and employment contexts. *Journal of Social Issues, 72*(1). (Whole issue.)

L'Oréal. (n.d.-a). *L'Oréal Group.* Retrieved from www.loreal.com/group

L'Oréal. (n.d.-b). *L'Oréal receives the first "Global Diversity Award."* Retrieved from www.lorealusa.com/who-we-are/awards-recognitions/loreal-receives-the-first-global-diversity-award.aspx

"L'Oréal settles discrimination case." (2004, October 5). Retrieved from www.yourlawyer.com/articles/title/loreal-settles-discrimination-case

*Loy, B. (2015, September 1). *Workplace accommodations: Low cost, high impact.* Retrieved from https://askjan.org/media/lowcosthighimpact.html

McLaughlin, M. E., Bell, M. P., & Stringer, D. Y. (2004). Stigma and acceptance of persons with disabilities: Understudied aspects of workforce diversity. *Group and Organization Management, 29,* 302–333.

Merrill-Lynch. (2014). *Work in retirement: Myths and motivations.* Retrieved from www.wealthmanagement.ml.com/publish/content/application/pdf/GWMOL/MLWM_Work-in-Retirement_2014.pdf

Mishel, L., Bivens, J., Gould, E., & Shierholz, H. (2012). *The state of working America.* Economic Policy Institute. Ithaca, NY: Cornell University Press.

National Institutes of Health. (2012, October). *Overweight and obesity statistics.* Retrieved from www.win.niddk.nih.gov/statistics

Neff, J. (2009, June 25). *L'Oréal found guilty of discrimination in France.* Retrieved from http://adage.com/article/global-news/l-oreal-guilty-french-discrimination-case/137589/

*Ng, T. W. H., & Feldman, D. C. (2008). The relationship of age to ten dimensions of job performance. *Journal of Applied Psychology, 93,* 392–423.

Pagan, J. A., & Davila, A. (1997). Obesity, occupational attainment, and earnings. *Social Science Quarterly, 78,* 756–770.

"Part 1605—Guidelines on discrimination because of religion." (2013, July 1). 29 *US Code of Federal Regulations.* Retrieved from www.gpo.gov/fdsys/pkg/CFR-2013-title29-vol4/xml/CFR-2013-title29-vol4-part1605.xml

*Perry, E. L., & Parlamis, J. D. (2006). Age and ageism in organizations: A review and consideration of national culture. In A. M. Konrad, P. Prasad, & J. K. Pringle (Eds.), *Handbook of workplace diversity* (pp. 345–370). Thousand Oaks, CA: SAGE Publications.

Peterson v. Hewlett Packard Co., 358 F. 3d 599 (2004).

Pew Forum on Religion & Public Life. (2008, February 1). *U.S. Religious Landscape Survey:Religious affiliation.* Retrieved from www.pewforum.org/2008/02/01/u-s-religious-landscape-survey-religious-affiliation/

Pew Forum on Religion & Public Life. (2012, October 9). *"Nones" on the rise: One-in-five adults have no religious affiliation.* Retrieved from www.pewforum.org/files/2012/10/NonesOnTheRise-full.pdf

Pew Research Center. (2010, February 24). *Millennials: Confident. Connected. Open to change.* Retrieved from www.pewsocialtrends.org/2010/02/24/millennials-confident-connected-open-to-change/

*Pew Research Center. (2012, August 22). *The lost decade of the middle class: Fewer, poorer, gloomier.* Retrieved from www.pewsocialtrends.org/files/2012/08/pew-social-trends-lost-decade-of-the-middle-class.pdf

*Posthuma, R. A., & Campion, M. A. (2009). Age stereotypes in the workplace: Common stereotypes, moderators, and future research directions. *Journal of Management, 35,* 158–188.

Register, C. A., & Williams, D. R. (1990). Wage effects of obesity among young workers. *Social Science Quarterly, 71,* 130–141.

*Reich, R. (2010). *Aftershock: The next economy and America's future.* New York, NY: Alfred A. Knopf.

Rhee, N. (2013, June). The retirement savings crisis: Is it worse than we think? *National Institute on Retirement Security.* Retrieved from www.nirsonline.org/storage/nirs/documents/Retirement%20Savings%20Crisis/retirementsavingscrisis_final.pdf

*Roehling, M. V. (1999). Weight-based discrimination in employment: Psychological and legal aspects. *Personnel Psychology, 52,* 969–1016.

Roehling, M. V., Pichler, S., & Bruce, T. A. (2013). Moderators of the effect of weight on job-related outcomes: A meta-analysis of experimental studies. *Journal of Applied Social Psychology, 43,* 237–252.

Roehling, M. V., Roehling, P. V., & Odland, L. M. (2008). Investigating the validity of stereotypes about overweight employees. *Group & Organization Management, 33,* 392–424.

Roehling, M. V., Roehling, P. V., & Pichler, S. (2007). The relationship between body weight and perceived weight-related employment discrimination: The role of sex and race. *Journal of Vocational Behavior, 71,* 300–318.

Rudd Center. (2015). *Legislation database.* Retrieved from www.uconnruddcenter.org/legislation-database

Rudolph, C. W., Wells, C. L., Weller, M. D., & Baltes, B. B. (2009). A meta-analysis of empirical studies of weight-based bias in the workplace. *Journal of Vocational Behavior, 74,* 1–10.

Samuel, H. (2009, June 25). L'Oréal fined for barring black and Asian women from adverts. *The Telegraph.* Retrieved from www.telegraph.co.uk/news/worldnews/europe/france/5635825/LOreal-fined-for-race-discrimination.html

*Santuzzi, A. M., Waltz, P. R., Finkelstein, L. M., & Rupp, D. E. (2014). Invisible disability: Unique challenges for employees and organizations. *Industrial and Organizational Psychology: Perspectives on Science and Practice, 7,* 204–219.

Sawyer, K., Salter, N., & Thoroughgood, C. (2013). Studying individual identities is good, but examining intersectionality is better. *Industrial and Organizational Psychology: Perspectives on Science and Practice, 6,* 80–84.

*Scully, M. A., & Blake-Beard, S. (2006). Locating class in organizational diversity work. In A. M. Konrad, P. Prasad, & J. K. Pringle (Eds.), *Handbook of workplace diversity* (pp. 431–454). Thousand Oaks, CA: SAGE.

*Shultz, K. S., & Wang, M. (2011). Psychological perspectives on the changing nature of retirement. *American Psychologist, 66,* 170–179.

*Social Security Administration. (2015a, October 13). *Social Security basic facts.* Retrieved from www.socialsecurity.gov/news/press/basicfact.html

*Social Security Administration. (2015b). *Update 2015.* Retrieved from www.socialsecurity.gov/pubs/EN-05-10003.pdf

Stone-Romero, E. F., Stone, D. L., & Lukaszewski, K. (2006). The influence of disability on role-taking in organizations. In A. M. Konrad, P. Prasad, & J. K. Pringle (Eds.), *Handbook of workplace diversity* (pp. 401–430). Thousand Oaks, CA: SAGE.

Suh, Y., Puhl, R., Liu, S., & Milici, F. F. (2014). Support for laws to prohibit weight discrimination in the United States: Public attitudes from 2011 to 2013. *Obesity, 22,* 1872–1879.

*Tanenbaum Center for Interreligious Understanding. (2014). *Religious diversity checklist.* Retrieved from https://tanenbaum.org/programs/workplace/workplace-resources/religious-diversity-checklist/

Taussig, W. C. (1994). Weighing in against obesity discrimination: *Cook v. Rhode Island, Department of Mental Health, Retardation, and Hospitals* and the recognition of obesity as a disability under the Rehabilitation Act and the Americans with Disabilities Act. *Boston College Law Review, 35,* 927–963.

Taylor, P., Fry, R., & Kochhar, R. (2011, July 26). Wealth gaps rise to record highs between Whites, Blacks, Hispanics. *Pew Research Center.* Retrieved from http://pewsocialtrends.org/2011/07/26/wealth-gaps-rise-to-record-highs-between-whites-blacks-hispanics/

"Things 'to' say to people with disabilities." (n.d.). *DiversityInc.* Retrieved from www.diversityinc.com/things-not-to-say/things-to-say-to-people-with-disabilities/

Toossi, M. (2012). Employment outlook: 2010–2020: Labor force projections to 2020: A more slowly growing workforce. *Monthly Labor Review, January,* 43–64. Retrieved from www.bls.gov/opub/mlr/2012/01/art3full.pdf

*Twenge, J. M. (2010). A review of the empirical evidence on generational differences in work attitudes. *Journal of Business and Psychology, 25,* 201–210.

Ulmstead, A. (2012). *An introductory guide to disability language and empowerment.* Retrieved from http://sudcc.syr.edu/LanguageGuide/

US Census Bureau. (2012). *Statistical abstract of the United States, Table 75.* Retrieved from www.census.gov/library/publications/2011/compendia/statab/131ed/population.html

US Census Bureau. (2014). *History: Survey of Income and Program Participation.* Retrieved from www.census.gov/history/www/programs/demographic/survey_of_income_and_program_participation.html

*US Department of Labor. (n.d.-a) *Age requirements.* Retrieved from www.dol.gov/general/topic/youthlabor/agerequirements

*US Department of Labor. (n.d.-b). *Compliance assistance—Wages and the Fair Labor Standards Act (FLSA).* Retrieved from www.dol.gov/whd/flsa/

US Department of Labor. (n.d.-c). *Retirement Toolkit.* Retrieved from www.dol.gov/ebsa/pdf/retirementtoolkit.pdf

US Department of Labor. (n.d.-d). *Youth rules! Preparing the 21st century workforce.* Retrieved from http://youthrules.dol.gov/

*US Department of Labor. (2014). *Handy reference guide to the Fair Labor Standards Act.* Retrieved from www.dol.gov/whd/regs/compliance/hrg.htm#2

US Department of Labor. (2016). *Final rule: Overtime.* Retrieved from www.dol.gov/whd/overtime/final2016/index.htm

*Vanhove, A., & Gordon, R. A. (2014). Weight discrimination in the workplace: A meta-analytic examination of the relationship between weight and work-related outcomes. *Journal of Applied Social Psychology, 44,* 12–22.

Wang, M., Zhan, Y., Liu, S., & Shultz, K. (2008). Antecedents of bridge employment: A longitudinal investigation. *Journal of Applied Psychology, 93,* 818–830.

Weeks, M., & Lupfer, M. B. (2004). Complicating race: The relationship between prejudice, race, and social class categorization. *Personality and Social Psychology Bulletin, 30,* 972–984.

"Weight bias laws: Tipping the scales against prejudice?" (2013). *Rights stuff newsletter,* summer. Retrieved from http://mn.gov/mdhr/education/articles/rs10_2weightlaws.html

Wong, V. (2014, April 18). *Top CEOs make 331 times the average worker. Does anyone care?* Retrieved from www.businessweek.com/articles/2014-04-18/top-ceos-make-331-times-the-average-worker-dot-does-anyone-care

* Recommended for advanced reading.

Part IV

Finding Solutions

Chapter 13

Building Diversity Competence for Individuals

Diversity Competence for Individuals and Organizations

How do people and organizations learn to manage D&I effectively? *Diversity competence* (DComp) is a learning process leading to "effectively respond(ing) to the challenges and opportunities posed by the presence of social-cultural diversity in a defined social system" (Cox & Beale, 1997, p. 2). At work, DComp means learning how to alter one's behavior as an employee, supervisor, or manager in an environment that is diverse, or expected to become diverse in the future. Cox and Beale described its development in phases of *awareness, understanding,* and *action*. Preceding chapters have provided background information and concepts as the cognitive foundation for DComp focused on awareness and understanding. They may also have built an affective (motivational) base for DComp, an important requirement in the action phase of competence development. This chapter focuses on processes for increasing the D&I competence of employees.

Cox and Beale (1997) believed that organizations—not just individuals—must build DComp, and that one important factor is the presence in the organization of those who are personally diversity competent. *Organizational competence* also requires an infrastructure that supports these people in their efforts to behave in diversity-competent ways; this topic is addressed in the next chapter. We begin by explaining what is required for individual DComp and discussing ways to build this capability. Diversity professionals, in addition to their own development, often are concerned with design and implementation of programmatic measures to increase DComp of others.

Getting Started on a D&I Program

Often diversity initiatives begin with *Valuing Diversity* activities designed to educate and create a positive image about an ethnic or other group (or a diversity topic) as a way of counteracting negative stereotypes. This might be a film or lecture, fair, reception or dinner featuring and celebrating food, dress, and culture of one or more ethnic groups. Other examples are pamphlets, articles, or inserts in employer communications informing about relevant topics (e.g., historical

---

Box 13.1 A Reminder . . .

The Cox and Beale model addresses *self-directed* development. Recall that Chapter 6 made the case that it is not always necessary to *persuade* people by changing knowledge or attitude first in order to produce behavior change. Sometimes environmental factors bring about change even when cognitive or affective change has not yet occurred. Sometimes beliefs or feelings change AFTER new behaviors have occurred.

information, tips for tactful communication, other companies' diversity programs). These are probably the easiest and least controversial aspects of a D&I program but should be supplemented with more challenging initiatives.

Building Individuals' Diversity Competence

When learning something new, we begin by identifying the knowledge, skills, and abilities (KSAs) comprising competence. Strangely, efforts to build DComp for individuals do not appear to follow this pattern. Despite great effort, time, and money expended to train people about diversity, very little information is available about KSAs actually needed for competence in managing D&I (Roberson, Kulik, & Tan, 2013).

A tentative listing of multicultural competencies for managers was constructed by Chrobot-Mason (2003) after reviewing literature in Counseling Psychology, organizational training, and diversity. Counseling Psychology has long been concerned with identifying and developing skills for working with clients from varied cultural backgrounds. "Multicultural competence" is seen as a combination of awareness and skill related to effective communication with various cultural groups. Chrobot-Mason identified a number of attributes and suggested that they fall in three phases. Examples of these three competence areas appear in the shaded box.

Proposed Multicultural Competencies for Managers

Donna Chrobot-Mason, known for research on workforce diversity and on training in work organizations, reviewed literature on multicultural competencies in counseling psychology (e.g., see Sue et al., 1998) and organizational psychology. Chrobot-Mason (2003) developed a framework for multicultural competence for managers in diverse work settings that describes three stages occurring in order but perhaps with some overlap: *increasing awareness, developing behavioral and coping skills,* and *action planning.* The following items illustrate these stages. Chrobot-Mason's complete listing of 20 competencies appears in her article, along with illustrations of workplace behaviors.

Stage 1: Increasing Awareness

- Is aware of possible impact of one's values, attitudes, and experiences about diversity on inter-actions in the workplace.
- Understands how institutional barriers affect behavior and outcomes at work.

Stage 2: Behavioral and Coping Skills

- Monitors own language and action so that it is racially and culturally sensitive and appropriate.
- Tries to understand situations from the perspective of employees from minority groups.

Stage 3: Continuous Development (Action Plan)

- Acts to eliminate bias and discriminatory decisions in the workplace.
- Works to develop and maintain minority representation at work.

Although these attributes can be used informally to assess one's level of multicultural competence, like other descriptions of "diversity skills" this list reflects professional opinions of researchers. Evidence of empirical validation of such lists seems lacking, as does empirical evidence that they represent a consensus of *skilled experts*. Specifically, it would be helpful to know that mastery of particular skills or information predicted success at managing D&I, or that certain diversity skills represented a consensus among those who have been successful at managing D&I.

For example, Lievens and Sackett (2012) identified skills for physician success with Belgian medical students. Two interpersonal skills ("building and maintaining relationships" and "communicating/exchanging information") were measured in a Situational Judgment Test in which applicants described how they would handle situations depicted in a video. High test scores were found to predict measures of internship performance seven years later and job performance nine years later. These results supported the validity of the test as well as the skills it was designed to measure.

Prediction of success in managing D&I is not yet this advanced. In one review of the workforce diversity skills literature, researchers were unable to find comparable empirical evidence for validity of specific skills (Hays-Thomas, Bowen, & Boudreaux, 2012). They went on to explore one straightforward empirical approach, described in the shaded box, to identifying KSAs to be included in learning experiences.

A Model of Skills for Diversity and Inclusion

One possible approach to identifying skills and information needed for successful D&I work is the Critical Incident (CI) Technique (Flanagan, 1954). This was used in a pilot demonstration project by Hays-Thomas et al. (2012) to illustrate how diversity skills might be empirically identified. Researchers identified a small number of experienced professionals familiar with work conflicts in a diverse workforce. Interviewees were asked to describe CIs in which someone else had dealt *effectively* or *ineffectively* with a work situation involving diversity-related challenges. Additional diversity-related CIs were provided by undergraduate students as part of a diversity class project. From resulting CIs, researchers derived a list of attributes shown or lacking in stories of effective or ineffective performance, and appearing frequently in the scenarios.

Researchers concluded that attributes for effectiveness (a) included not only skills but also values and knowledge; and (b) varied with the employee's organizational level. For example, for non-supervisory employees DComp seemed to include *positive outlook* (value), *understanding of power dynamics* (knowledge), and *proper use of line of authority* (skill). Middle managers with supervisory responsibility benefited from *flexibility* (value), knowledge of *techniques for managing diversity*, and *implementing corrective action* (skill). Effectiveness of executive level managers responsible for strategic decision-making seemed related to *openness to try new things* (value), knowledge of *benefits of diversity*, and *modeling diversity behaviors* (skill). For both middle managers and executives, effectiveness seemed greater with *humility* (value); and *macro viewpoint, organizational structure and policies, and relevant laws* (areas of knowledge). Across all levels, the value of *diversity*, knowledge area of *self-awareness*, and skills of *active listening* and *empathy* seemed important.

These are only a few values, knowledges, and skills derived from the CIs. Even the full listing should be considered tentative because the number of respondents was small and scenarios were based predominantly in higher education. However, the diversity professional responsible for developing learning experiences for others could easily use a modified CI technique to identify target skills for this learning. The CI technique is flexible because it can be used across different levels and jobs in different types of organizations to identify what should be included in learning experiences. CI also has the advantage of being empirically based and grounded in actual experiences of employees. For those reasons it is an *inclusive* approach to design of learning experiences and will likely guide development of learning that employees will see as engaging. When conducted within one organization, the CI approach is likely to elicit stories situated in that organization and as a result the attributes and resulting learning experiences should be highly relevant as well.

This textbook presents knowledge that should prepare someone to manage D&I effectively in work organizations. Topics were chosen because researchers and diversity professionals have investigated and written about them in the context of D&I management. Those studying and writing about diversity think this information is important although we cannot yet demonstrate that mastery of it is necessary or sufficient for success in this work. Furthermore, knowledge from text or class does not guarantee skill. Chrobot-Mason's (2003) recommendation is sound: action planning is needed to improve diversity skills.

Several strategies are commonly used to improve individuals' DComp. Some engage in self-directed diversity learning through reading, classes, interracial conversations, films, museum visits, travel, or other experiences (e.g., visiting stores, churches, or other institutions associated with ethnic or other minorities). Employees may also participate in activities offered by employers to build individual DComp. Four such activities are diversity training (DT), specialized leadership training, mentoring and networking, and affinity groups (also called employee resource groups or ERGs). In addition, Work/Family initiatives address diverse needs outside of work.

Diversity Training

Increased demographic diversity implies two things for organizational training (Ford & Fisher, 1996). First, organizations may design learning activities to prepare people to interact more effectively at work with others differing from them in important ways; this is *diversity training* and our focus here. The second implication is that training content and strategy must change as basic skills, knowledge, learning styles, and even languages of employees become more diverse. This could be called *training of diverse employees,* too complex to address here but often covered by texts on training design. Decisions about delivery of training (e.g., print, lecture, online) should be based on capabilities of learners.

The term DT is often used as if synonymous with *D&I program.* It is not. DT is one of the most common aspects of D&I programming (SHRM, 2013) but an organization that provides only training and nothing more is unlikely to become diversity competent. In some cases, training may be needed less than other processes described in this and the next chapter. Choice and design of programming for D&I, including DT, should be guided by data.

DT Characteristics

DT's focus moved from compliance (1960s–1980s) to improving worker relationships (1980s–1990s). Today's focus is likely to be on diversity's role in strategic management and business success (Anand & Winters, 2008). However, in some organizations DT is still limited to preventing and responding to harassment and discrimination, especially that which could lead to grievances or litigation.

How common is DT? Surveys have found at least two-thirds of companies provided some type of DT; it was more common in larger companies (500 or more employees) than in small companies (Esen, 2005; SHRM, 2010). In repeated SHRM surveys, training was often mandatory for top executives (60–68%) and non-executive managers (70%), more than for non-managerial employees (53–58%). DT was more likely to be required by private-sector organizations than government, and was more common when other diversity initiatives were in place (e.g., a diversity director, flextime). DT was presented by organization staff or by external consultants, and was usually offered in-house rather than off-site. It was likely to be brief (one day or less) and required only 10% or less of the training budget (SHRM, 2010). Another survey of 108 diversity trainers reported that DT was usually provided by one or two trainers to a group of 20–50 participants and varied from 4–20 hours in duration (often about 10 hours). Participants might be from the same or different organizational levels; several methods were used, such as group exercises, lectures, videotapes, or role-playing (Bendick, Egan, & Lofhjelm, 2001).

DT Goals

DT may be designed to increase *awareness, understanding, or action*, as in the Cox and Beale (1997) model of DComp described earlier. Before undertaking DT, the diversity professional should be clear on training purpose and what it is expected to accomplish. Needs assessment (discussed later in this chapter) can help determine DT goals; culture audits and organizational strategic plans (see Chapter 14) provide other information for determining goals. For example, is the goal to draw attention to importance of diversity initiatives? Describe diversity issues of organizational concern? Inform people about what the employer is doing to address D&I, and why? Explain existing or new policies addressing issues of fairness, respect, and inclusion? Clarify legal requirements or prohibitions concerning members of protected groups? Motivate people to behave in a more inclusive manner? Goal(s) of a training effort should guide selection of participants, training design, and evaluation method. In an extensive review of workplace DT, Roberson et al. (2013) identified two common models: awareness training and skills training.

One Model: Awareness Training

This model assumes that training should start by increasing awareness (and understanding) through informational and/or emotional approaches. Awareness approaches attempt to draw attention to diversity issues as a foundation for subsequent behavior change. One kind of awareness training gives information on topics such as the organization's diversity strategy and initiatives and why they are important; factual information about different identity groups; explanations of how stereotypes, prejudice, and discrimination operate (e.g., implicit bias); background on relevant laws; or demonstrations of effects of existing social norms, institutional processes, or informal behaviors on members of underrepresented groups.

A second kind of diversity awareness training informs about dynamics of in-groups and out-groups (Social Identity Theory) and social categorization processes. Although interventions based on the Common Ingroup Identity Model (Gaertner & Dovidio, 2000) and the Intergroup Contact Model (Pettigrew & Tropp, 2000) can be effective in reducing prejudice and discrimination, the brief DT typical in organizations is unlikely to cover this material effectively in a manner leading to lasting cognitive or behavioral change (Roberson et al., 2013).

A third sort of awareness-focused training aims to increase self-awareness about one's biases and attitudes and how they can affect behavior toward others. In some cases this involves confrontation and negative emotions resulting from challenges to trainees' existing ways of thinking. Increased awareness of one's biases and behaviors can be motivational and result in more positive attitudes and behavior. However, use of confrontation is controversial because it can be stressful for trainees and may backfire by eliciting anger and aggression in a situation where they cannot be processed effectively. Confrontational methods should be avoided in short-term training because they are unlikely to help participants learn skills for handling strong negative emotions and new, more constructive ways of acting (Roberson et al., 2013). Use of confrontational methods also requires considerable skill and experience on the part of the trainer to avoid harmful outcomes and assure positive learning.

A Second Model: Skills Training

The second model of DT identified by Roberson et al. (2013) is designed to help participants learn new skills for promoting D&I. One difficulty with this approach is the lack of a widely accepted and empirically supported catalog of diversity skills as mentioned earlier. However, communication, conflict resolution, and listening skills are likely to be among skills required for DComp.

The most common framework for skills training is Social Learning Theory (SLT; Bandura, 1986). Key elements include modeling of appropriate behavior, practice and feedback, positive consequences, and development of a sense of *self-efficacy*, the belief that one can learn and perform these new behaviors. Space does not permit a full description of SLT but examples of its application to DT can be found (Holmes, 2004; Combs & Luthans, 2007). Unfortunately, extensive SLT skills training is unlikely in the context of organizational DT because of the time, expense, and skill required. The most common emphasis in organizations appears to be awareness training.

Awareness and/or Skills?

Kulik and Roberson's review of effectiveness of diversity initiatives (2008b) discussed two common goals of DT: disseminating information and changing employee behavior. They concluded that training programs can effectively teach *information* about the nature of D&I and the organization's plan for managing them. With sufficient time and preparation, training can also teach specific skills. Kulik and Roberson found less support for the idea that awareness-focused DT alone increases either *personal awareness* of the operation of psychological processes or *motivation* to alter one's behavior. Awareness training alone is not likely to reduce discriminatory behavior. This is quite reasonable, given our discussion of prejudice and discrimination in Chapter 6. The most powerful factors in reducing prejudice and discrimination are likely to be in the work organization's social environment rather than the employee's internal cognitive structure.

Practical recommendations for design of DT can be derived from a meta-analysis of DT outcomes (Kalinoski et al., 2013). Analysis of 65 studies examined changes in affective (attitudinal), cognitive (informational), and behavioral outcomes with respect to several features of DT. Like Roberson et al., Kalinoski et al. found significant changes in all three areas following DT, but larger changes in cognition (information and understanding) and behavior (skill) than in attitude. When attitude change was found, it was often when training provided opportunities for social interaction among trainees, consistent with predictions from attitude literature (e.g., Contact Hypothesis) discussed in Chapter 6. Factors associated with affective and cognitive changes are shown in Boxes 13.2 and 13.3. Results were inconclusive about specific factors associated with changes in skill (behavior).

Box 13.2 Training for Change in Affect or Attitude

Affective or attitude change is more likely if training involves:

- Interdependent tasks
- Active and passive forms of learning
- Face-to-face and in-person instruction
- Sessions at least four hours long
- Sessions that are spaced out
- Highly motivated employees (e.g., those believing DT is important)
- Facilitation by managers/supervisors rather than other staff

Box 13.3 Training for Change in Cognition

Change in cognition (information or understanding) is more likely if training:

- Is active
- Is spaced out
- Involves interdependent tasks
- Includes internal staff (rather than managers) as trainers
- Is provided to groups with fewer Whites or more women
- Emphasizes a single diversity attribute (e.g., race) rather than more general topics (e.g., multicultural approaches)

Once a decision is made to provide DT, how should diversity professionals and others proceed? Fortunately the extensive literature on organizational training can guide this process.

Three Phases in Training

The *instructional design model* is a systematic approach to training in organizations that proceeds in three phases: needs assessment, design and development, and evaluation (Goldstein & Ford, 2002). The *needs assessment phase* determines three things:

- Person analysis: Who should be trained and their preparation (e.g., educational level, learning preferences) and motivation for learning;
- KSA analysis: Training content needed, based on information about work performance and attributes workers must possess to accomplish tasks; and
- Organization analysis: Whether and where in the organization support for or resistance to training exists, how training fits with organizational goals, and what resources are available in terms of funding, time, and staff.

With information from needs assessment, the second phase of *training design and development* can begin. This includes determining appropriate behavioral objectives or learning outcomes, statements of what the learner will know or be able to do at the end of training and later used as criteria for evaluating the success of the training. The second phase also includes selection of training environment and methods, schedule, and trainer(s), all chosen in light of learning outcomes. Examples of learning outcomes are shown in Box 13.4. The first three outcomes pertain to information found in earlier sections of this text. Content about the last four outcome statements not covered earlier *(microaggressions, interracial dialogues, defusing isms and active listening)* appears in the shaded box to illustrate how they could be taught.

Box 13.4 Sample Learning Outcomes: Awareness, Understanding, Skills

Examples of learning outcomes for *awareness*:

Explain why the organization has developed a program for D&I, and some of its goals.
List some consequences of creating *in-groups* and *out-groups*.

Examples of learning outcomes for *understanding*:

Explain factors in the experience of people of color that may affect their response to a *colorblind* perspective.

Give examples of sometimes unintentional insults called *microaggressions* that may be experienced by women or people of color.

List three reasons why people may experience interracial dialogues as stressful.

Examples of learning outcomes for *skills*:

Demonstrate one appropriate response when someone makes racist or sexist comments or tells a joke that is hurtful to others.

Demonstrate skill in active listening by participating in a conversation on a sensitive topic.

Examples of Diversity Training Content

Needs assessment for training in D&I can identify areas in which knowledge, understanding, or skill should be developed. Box 13.4 illustrates several learning outcomes that could be written based on results of a needs assessment. Four outcomes from that box mention concepts or situations not discussed elsewhere in this text. These outcomes appear there in italics and are briefly explained here.

Microaggressions. *Give examples of the sometimes unintentional insults called "microaggressions" that may be experienced by women or people of color.*

Microaggressions are short and common insults that derogate someone by conveying negative views or hostility based on the person's racio-ethnicity, sex, or other identity characteristic. Such comments are called "microaggressions" because they may seem trivial and are often thoughtless and not intended to be insulting. For example, in Austen's *Pride and Prejudice,* Darcy proposed marriage to Elizabeth Bennet by saying he was so ardently in love that he would overlook her inferior family background, improprieties of her relatives, and objections of his family and society. No wonder she refused him! Many women have experienced a situation in which their comment in a meeting is ignored until the same idea is conveyed by a man, when it is recognized and received positively. This effectively delegitimizes the woman and devalues her contribution.

Microaggressions based on sexual orientation, race, or gender are a frequent source of workplace stress for those experiencing these insults regularly (Sue, 2010). For example, over 75% of Asian American participants in one study reported experiencing microaggressions within a two-week study period, and bodily and emotional symptoms of stress were associated with frequency of microaggressions (Ong, Burrow, Fuller-Rowell, Ja, & Sue, 2012). Measures of microaggression experiences have been developed for people of color (Torres-Harding, Andrade, & Diaz, 2012) and for LGBT people of color (Balsam, Molina, Beadnell, Simoni, & Walters, 2011). Microaggressions are so common that a website has been constructed on which people can post examples they have experienced (Microaggressions Project, n.d.). This site gives numerous examples of the overt hostility, insults, and invalidations that people experience in everyday conversations. Diversity competence implies learning to avoid making such comments oneself and to recognize and effectively respond to microaggressions by others.

Interracial dialogues. *List three reasons why people may experience interracial dialogues as stressful.*

Many people in the US have little experience talking with persons of other racio-ethnicities about issues of race relations. Interracial conversations often occur in situations where conversation is superficial, task-focused, or strongly affected by norms and roles (e.g., nurse/patient, cashier/customer, co-workers, supervisor/employee). Talking about race can be stressful and is often avoided, particularly in work settings where employees or managers may be concerned about career consequences or legal repercussions. The result is often lack of understanding by both parties of the other person's thoughts and feelings and why the person acts in certain ways.

Anxiety about interracial dialogue may stem from several sources, particularly unfamiliarity of conversations about race. Interracial conversations are often avoided because people anticipate unpleasant consequences (Stephan & Stephan, 1985; Plant & Devine, 2003). Those of different races have been found to attribute their own reluctance to fear of rejection because of their race, but explain others' failure to initiate contact as lack of interest or an indicator of racism. These reciprocal attributions lead to misunderstanding and discomfort (Shelton & Richeson, 2005). In addition, one person's anxiety is likely to trigger anxiety in a conversation partner (West, Shelton, & Trail, 2009).

Such issues have been explored in a program of research by Derald Wing Sue and colleagues. Summarizing this work, Sue (2013) presented several conclusions about *race talk*. Often these conversations are triggered by a microaggression: one party is offended but the other party does not recognize it or understand what was offensive.

First, when the topic of race comes up in a racially mixed group, people are often reluctant to speak. For example, in classroom settings, students often talk inarticulately and in abstract terms, as if speaking but not really saying anything. Second, uncomfortable emotional reactions such as defensiveness, anger, or blame often occur. Third, students frequently interpret comments as a challenge to their own lived experience of race and become defensive. Fourth, as discussion becomes more unpleasant, participants try to withdraw, change the subject, or terminate the conversation. Fifth, students of color may experience others' comments as microaggressions, and White students may feel misunderstood and judged unfairly as racist. Finally, instructors may fear losing control of the classroom atmosphere and have difficulty turning comments into productive learning experiences, especially if inexperienced and not well-prepared in handling interracial race talk (Sue, Rivera, Capodilupo, Lin, & Torino, 2010; Sue, 2013).

Sue (2013) has identified informal norms regulating race talk, two of which seem relevant to work environments. The *politeness protocol* implies that uncomfortable or emotionally charged topics should be avoided or touched upon only lightly. The *colorblind protocol* suggests that race makes no difference. Whites may try not to see race in order to avoid being seen as racist. Yet people of color realize that race is impossible to ignore and may interpret self-professed colorblindness as an indicator of bias. Sue and others have identified four types of fears held by many White Americans about engaging in race talk: (a) fear of seeming to be racist or being misunderstood; (b) fear of confronting subtle biases that conflict with their self-concept as fair, good, and moral; (c) fear of recognizing the degree of White privilege they actually enjoy; and (d) fear of assuming personal responsibility for working to end racism. The next learning outcome deals with starting to assume this responsibility.

Confronting "isms." *Demonstrate one appropriate response when someone makes racist or sexist comments or tells a joke that is hurtful to others.*

In some cases, a comment, story, or joke is spoken thoughtlessly without realization that it could give offense to others. In other cases, comments indicate deep-seated animosities toward another person or group. Responding to these situations can be a three-step process. First, is the comment offensive to you or others? Second, should you respond to it? (Sometimes leaving the conversation and avoiding the speaker is a more prudent choice. In other cases, reporting the incident to someone in charge is appropriate.) Third, if you decide to respond, what should you say? Often we hear a comment, decide it is offensive, feel we should respond, but cannot think of what to say. It may help to practice some possible responses, such as the following:

- "Perhaps you did not intend it this way, but that sounded insulting to me."
- "When I hear a joke like that, I don't find it funny. It seems hurtful and derogatory."
- "Excuse me, what did you just say? Perhaps you did not realize that comments like that can be offensive because ..."
- "When I hear comments like that, I am offended. Please do not speak that way to me again."
- "Now, why would you say such a thing?" (Then wait until the person responds.)
- "Have you thought about how (specified people) feel when they hear such comments?"

Author's comment: Recently I had the unpleasant experience of interacting with someone who unexpectedly said, "I suppose I am a bigot, but ..." followed by some very offensive and stereotypic statements about a particular minority group. We were stunned at the sudden and virulent nature of the remarks and could not think of what to say. Fortunately the interaction came to an end. Later in a different situation the person spoke the same way. This time I was prepared and told him firmly please not to speak that way around me because it offended me. He said, "It does?" with a surprised look on his face. That ended the conversation! Apparently it had never occurred to him that others of his demographic group did not share his views.

Active listening. *Demonstrate the skill of active listening by participating in a conversation on a sensitive topic.*

Often in conversation, especially about an emotional topic, we think of how to respond instead of what the speaker is actually saying. We may be distracted by other things or upset by something that was said. Active listening is the communication skill of giving full attention to the speaker in order to understand accurately the substance and contextual meaning of the speaker's comments. When one has not accurately understood what another is trying to communicate, constructive dialogue breaks down. Often this leads to a nonproductive or stressful spiral of negative feelings and inappropriate behavior.

Some suggestions for active listening include:

- Make eye contact with the speaker and indicate by posture and facial expression that you are listening.
- Avoid being distracted by other conversations, cell phones, or other environmental events.
- Listen without planning the next comment or action. (This is very hard to do.)
- Pay attention to the speaker's verbal and nonverbal cues. Listen for feelings as well as content.
- When something is unclear, ask for clarification. "Can you explain that in another way?" "I'm not sure I understand what you mean. Can you give more information?"
- Respond by paraphrasing, summarizing, elaborating, and checking for understanding. "If I understand correctly, what you mean is ... Is that right?"
- Do not rush to fill a silence. Take a moment to think about what you will say. "What you said is complicated. Give me a moment to think about it."
- If you feel defensive in response to what is said, try not to retaliate with negative feelings and argument. Instead try to understand why the person made the comment. "It seems you are angry with what happened. Will you explain what made you feel that way so I'll be sure to understand?"

Active listening is a skill learned through practice. Numerous examples of active listening can be found in textbooks on communication skills and through a quick online search.

In the third phase, evaluation, data are gathered to determine whether training actually helped trainees accomplish the objectives or outcomes. Ideally, the evaluation phase assesses two things: (a) whether learning and other results occurred; and (b) whether results were actually due to training and not other events. Evaluation is important to determine whether training was effective and whether it should be continued, modified, or extended to other trainees. Evaluation should also consider *transfer of training*, that is, whether learning generalizes from training to actual work environment.

Four types of evaluation criteria are: (a) reaction criteria, what trainees think about training; (b) learning criteria, whether trainees learned targeted information or skills; (c) behavior criteria, whether trainees behave differently as a result of training; and (d) results criteria, whether training has effects on success of the organization itself. These are often called *Kirkpatrick's criteria* after the man who first popularized them (Kirkpatrick, 1994).

Little information is available about whether DT in organizations follows this recommended three-phase approach of needs assessment, design and development, and evaluation. Most organizational DT is not described in much detail in publicly available documents, and published articles describe training that is probably not representative of what usually happens in work organizations. Often published studies are conducted by researchers to test new methods and thus probably do not resemble typical DT provided by the organization itself. Furthermore, it appears that formal needs assessment is seldom used as a basis for training design (Hite & McDonald, 2006; Roberson et al., 2013). Without needs assessment, systematic data on people, content, and context is not available to guide development of training.

Early summaries of DT found it was seldom evaluated (Rynes & Rosen, 1995; Roberson, Kulik, & Pepper, 2001), but evaluation may now be more common (Kulik & Roberson, 2008a). However, authors of one review found that training objectives were rarely stated and often evaluation measures were not aligned with apparent training goals (Bezrukova, Jehn, & Spell, 2012). Specifically, training often seemed to emphasize awareness but measure behavior. Evaluation most commonly measured short-term change. For example, reaction criteria (trainee evaluations) were often assessed at the end of the training session itself. Measures of learning were often self-report (e.g., ratings of how much trainees liked or thought they had learned from training). Reaction criteria do not indicate what was actually learned or how employees are likely to behave. Research design was often insufficient to confirm the two important points in evaluation: that learning occurred, and that it was due to training. For example, often no pre-measure was taken of knowledge or attitude, or no control group was included against which the training group was compared. It is unclear why organizations rely on reaction criteria only and fail to use sound research design. Possible explanations include cost, lack of knowledge about how evaluation should be conducted, time constraints, or unwillingness to know if training is really effective.

Information about training effectiveness for meeting specified objectives, whether short- or long-term, is critically important. Training is a good investment only when effective; without evaluative data it is impossible to decide whether and how training should be continued, modified, or extended. Employees who do not believe that training is useful and worthwhile may react negatively not only to training but also to other aspects of the D&I program. Diversity professionals should be aware of criticisms directed against DT so that such problems can be avoided in design or presentation. Based on critiques of DT (e.g., Hite & McDonald, 2006; Anand & Winters, 2008) several recommendations include:

- Show connection between training goals and workplace behavior or results desired.
- Plan training based on needs assessment and clearly stated learning objectives.
- Evaluate based on identified learning objectives.
- Schedule sessions long enough and frequent enough to address topics adequately; schedule periodic refreshers.
- Present awareness training with information and skills learning, not as an end in itself.

- Show how issues like discrimination apply broadly instead of focusing only on certain groups; emphasize one diversity attribute at a time for greater learning.
- Avoid imposing on individuals the burden of "speaking" for their entire identity group.
- Avoid a *shame and blame* message resulting in guilt, resentment, or defensiveness.
- When introducing emotional topics, allow adequate time to process information and feelings.
- Use experienced facilitators with sufficient knowledge and skill; consider using a pair or team representing different identity groups.
- Cover legal compliance issues separately from training on proactive management of D&I through effective interpersonal and group behavior.
- Avoid superficial training of large numbers of employees—"check off the box" training designed to protect the organization from legal challenge rather than improve knowledge, attitude, or behavior.
- Recognize that D&I goals and training may conflict with existing organizational power structures and divisive policies, and that systemic cultural change may be required.

Specialized Leadership Development

Many organizations attempt to decrease turnover and increase representation of underrepresented groups in advanced positions by providing specialized learning experiences in leadership designed especially for them. These experiences are also offered by external consulting firms and nonprofit organizations aiming for advancement of women or underrepresented ethnicities. Examples include programs of the Center for Creative Leadership (2015); the Smith College Leadership Consortium for women (Smith College, n.d.); and Management Leadership for Tomorrow (MLT) programs for African Americans, Hispanics, and Native Americans (n.d.). Such programs stress information, concepts, issues, or skills thought to apply especially to women or ethnic minorities and provide a more homogeneous environment for networking, sharing experiences, and skill building.

Is specialized training more effective than leadership training available to both sexes and all racio-ethnic groups alike? Providers of specialized training believe so, but empirical evidence is scant. Specialized training might be necessary or more effective because: (a) without such programs, underrepresented groups might not have access to leadership training; (b) sensitive topics such as discrimination, stereotyping, and use of power can be discussed more openly; (c) they provide access to others in the same identity group who experience similar challenges and can provide support, networking, and mentoring.

One argument against specialized training experiences is that they suggest a "deficit" view of leadership by women and ethnic minorities. That is, training open only to them implies that something is lacking in knowledge, skills, or psychological composition of these candidates that can best be remedied by segregated training experiences; e.g., women should be taught what male peers have already learned. Another argument against specialized training is that it may provoke resentment by White males over special learning opportunities that exclude them.

Ely, Ibarra, and Kolb (2011) addressed this controversy and recommended that women's leadership development programs be theoretically grounded in the idea of *leadership identity:* coming to perceive oneself and be seen by others as a leader. A major obstacle in leadership development is *second-generation bias:* subtle but powerful barriers to advancement based in (a) cultural beliefs about gender and ethnicity of leaders; and (b) institutionalized structures, procedures, and interactions that favor White men. This differs from deliberate race or sex discrimination that is *first generation* bias. Though Ely et al. discussed only women's leadership development, a similar argument can be made for training provided to members of racial minorities.

Ely et al. (2011) noted that female role models are few, work and careers are often gendered, and women may lack access to sponsors and networks of powerful individuals. Furthermore, because of their scarcity at higher management levels, women are more visible and more critically scrutinized.

Ely et al. presented three principles for leadership programs designed for women: (a) base topics and skills in second-generation bias framework; (b) create a supportive and safe environment for experimentation and learning; and (c) develop women's identities as leaders, including sense of purpose and values.

Organizations can consider a middle ground for leadership development: provide generic training in foundational topics *along with* single-sex or race experiences addressing barriers resulting from second-generation bias. Consequences of this process as well as other topics (e.g., stereotyping, diversified mentoring) should be addressed with White men as well as women and people of color (e.g., Catalyst, 2007).

Mentoring

Frequently mentoring is included in D&I programming (Esen, 2005). In this developmental relationship between a younger person and someone more experienced, the mentor provides support, information, advice, connections, and other benefits to the younger protégé or mentee. The process is named after Mentor, trusted advisor to Odysseus in ancient Greek lore, who provided advice, support, and protection to Telemachus while his father was away at war. Mentoring relationships have been recognized as helpful or even necessary for men's career progression. Successful senior women (Ragins, Townsend, & Mattis, 1998) and women of color (Catalyst, 2002) often say that mentoring was key in their career development, and therefore these relationships are recommended as part of breaking through glass ceilings for women and ethnic minority employees. Though sufficient research now exists to answer many questions about mentoring, most has taken the perspective of protégés rather than mentors, and very little research has studied both partners in the same relationship.

Informal mentoring relationships develop spontaneously between people attracted to each other for professional and personal reasons; most often both are White men, who predominate in senior positions and upward progression. In these traditional pairings, similarity in background and interpersonal style usually leads to attraction, and both parties expect to gain something through the social exchange of the relationship. Because informal mentoring seemed beneficial, some employers started formal mentoring programs by organizing mentor-protégé pairs. Those concerned about advancement of women and people of color began to incorporate mentoring as a deliberate strategy for increasing recruitment, retention, and career advancement of protégés.

Is mentoring really helpful or necessary? Top executives often report having had mentors (e.g., Ragins et al., 1998). Ample evidence (summarized by Dawson, Thomas, & Goren, 2013) shows that informal mentoring experiences are associated with higher career and job satisfaction, compensation, and salary growth, as well as lower turnover and higher advancement. Though significantly higher salaries accrue to those who are mentored, this was significantly greater for protégés of White men (Dreher & Cox, 1996). MBA graduates mentored by White men reported annual salaries as much as $22,000 higher than unmentored respondents, and almost $17,000 more than those mentored by others! This was probably due to White male mentors' more extensive organizational and professional networks, higher positions, and greater power.

Mentors can help clarify performance expectations for protégés and provide access to informal networks and "stretch" assignments. A mentor can help women to develop a style with which men are comfortable. For both women and ethnic minorities, a mentor can assist in overcoming effects of stereotyping, dealing with direct and covert discrimination, and navigating the culture of the organization (McKeen & Bujaki, 2007).

Mentoring Processes

The two major processes in informal mentoring relationships are *career* and *psychosocial* functions (Kram, 1985, 1986). Career (or *instrumental*) functions help the protégé prepare for career progress;

they include sponsorship, exposure, coaching, delegation of challenging assignments, and protection. Psychosocial functions instead enhance identity, effectiveness, and comfort in the professional role, through role modeling, counseling, friendship, and acceptance/confirmation. A complete mentoring relationship provides some level of both career and psychosocial functions, although the amount of each may vary with phase of relationship, needs of protégé, resources and capabilities of mentor (such as power or knowledge), organizational context, and the "click" of a particular relationship (Ragins & Kram, 2007). Meta-analytic evidence shows that both functions predict outcomes, both objective (e.g., salary, promotions) and subjective (e.g., satisfaction with job, career, organization, and mentor; Allen, Eby, Poteet, Lentz, & Lima, 2004).

What D&I Professionals Should Know About Mentoring

Does mentoring occur as often for women and members of ethnic minorities? Reviews of research on mentoring as a function of gender (McKeen & Bujaki, 2007) and race (Blake-Beard, Murrell, & Thomas, 2007) summarize relevant issues. Overall, women report similar access to mentors compared to men, but also perceive more barriers to forming these relationships. African Americans may perceive more barriers and also have less access. Inconsistent results suggest that in some professions or organizations, women and/or people of color may experience more challenges developing successful informal mentoring relationships.

Does sex or racio-ethnicity make a difference in mentoring? Both male and female mentors engage in career and psychosocial functions. However, meta-analysis of gender differences found that male mentors reported giving more career support and female mentors reported providing higher psychosocial support (O'Brien, Biga, Kessler, & Allen, 2010). Males were also more likely to report having served as a mentor. Research on mentors of color is limited, in part because most mentors are White. An early study (Thomas, 1990) found that Black protégés reported receiving more psychosocial support from other Blacks, but often those were peers or employees in other departments. Black and White protégés did not differ in reported career support, later confirmed by James (2000). One study found that high-potential people of color developed two types of support networks. Relationships with Whites provided career information and support, but networking with same-race others (sometimes in other organizations) provided socio-emotional support (Ibarra, 1995).

In some cases mentors who are people of color may experience more positive outcomes than Whites in terms of improved skills in networking, recruiting, and supervision as well as increased self-confidence and commitment (Blake-Beard et al., 2007). Differential experiences for mentors of color are likely to vary with racial dynamics in particular organizations or types of work. Fewer women and members of ethnic minorities are found at higher levels of most organizations (with power, experience, and connections to be good mentors) and thus fewer are available as mentors. With more women and people of color in positions at lower levels seeking demographically similar mentors, the burden on these few potential mentors becomes high.

Cross-race and cross-sex mentoring partnerships present additional issues (Ragins, 1997; Murrell, Crosby, & Ely, 1999). For example, White male mentors may not fully understand challenges experienced by protégés who are demographically different. Though sympathetic and willing to mentor, they may be less able to provide the type of emotional support needed. They are less able to serve as role models for navigating the organization's culture as a woman or person of color. Some are reluctant to participate in cross-sex mentoring because of risk that the relationship may be seen as romantic or sexual in nature or the possibility of uncomfortable emotional entanglements. Methodological issues arising in the study of diversified mentoring relationships have also been identified (Ragins, 1999).

Nontraditional forms of mentoring can be helpful in such situations. For example, *peer mentoring* by others at the same level or *step-ahead* mentoring by those only one level higher than the protégé may be beneficial. However, some evidence exists that relationships with mentors at higher organizational levels are associated with greater job satisfaction and career success (Ensher, Thomas, & Murphy, 2001).

Do women and people of color benefit from mentoring in the same way as White men? On these topics few studies exist and results are inconsistent (Blake-Beard et al., 2007; McKeen & Bujaki, 2007). Benefits may depend in part upon the sex and racio-ethnicity of the mentor and whether they match protégé characteristics. Women and people of color are more likely to participate in cross-sex or cross-race relationships, which may limit effectiveness of role modeling and other psychosocial functions.

Formal Mentoring

Informal mentoring grows from attraction between mentor and protégé and what each wants and expects to gain from the relationship. Mentoring continues over time as long as partners wish although the relationship's nature is likely to change over time as the protégé matures professionally (Kram, 1983). Formal mentoring, in contrast, is organized by the employer or another organization, matches protégés with mentors who agree to participate, and usually lasts one year or less (Baugh & Fagenson-Eland, 2007).

Formal mentoring programs sometimes do not lead to the same quality of interaction and similar results as informal relationships (Baugh & Fagenson-Eland, 2007), but this seems to be a function of how the formal program is set up and managed. For example, quality of mentoring functions and perceptions of effectiveness are higher when mentors receive training and when protégés have input into the mentor-protégé matching process (Allen, Eby, & Lentz, 2006). Research-based recommendations for starting a formal mentoring program have been presented by Allen, Finkelstein, and Poteet (2009). Although not intended specifically for diversified relationships, these recommendations are useful for formal mentoring as part of a D&I management program.

- Plan program based on needs assessment and set up coordinating infrastructure.
- Recruit, select, and train mentors and protégés in how to manage the relationship.
- Clarify groundrules for frequency of meeting, confidentiality, and relationship duration.
- Match mentors and protégés based on relevant characteristics.
- Provide oversight; include exit mechanism for relationships that are not working.
- Monitor program and evaluate at specified times, making changes where appropriate.

Correlational research and case studies have indicated that a formal mentoring program *can* have results equal to those of good informal relationships but that simply pairing mentors and protégés is not enough. Mentoring relationships can be beneficial for inclusion and progress of women and people of color, but informal mentoring may be less available to them. Thus, in the context of a D&I program, formally organized voluntary mentoring seems a good alternative. The diversity professional should explore whether those from underrepresented groups have equal access to high-quality mentoring and consider a formal mentoring program to supplement informal mentoring where appropriate.

Effectiveness of formal mentoring has generally been judged by protégé perceptions rather than objective outcomes (e.g., salary increases), so conclusions must be tentative. However, after reviewing evidence, Kulik and Roberson (2008b) concluded that mentoring is more likely to be effective in advancement of underrepresented groups when and if it leads to changes in stereotypes that may be held by supervisors, which are sometimes an important obstacle to promotions. Because stereotype threat may limit performance of protégés who are female or people of color, Kulik and Roberson proposed that mentors will be more effective when they address this by coaching on task strategies, presenting role models that disconfirm stereotypes, and targeting improvement in protégés' knowledge and skills. According to Kulik and Roberson, research indicates that mentoring has less influence on outcomes (e.g., satisfaction, intention to quit) than do relationships with peers and supervisor. Notably, a protégé's departure from one organization to move upward in another probably marks a mentoring success rather than a failure.

The Mentoring Paradox

From the perspective of D&I, mentoring presents a contradiction. The *mentoring paradox* refers to the fact that mentoring itself is fundamentally an exclusionary process in that the relationship exists between two people and excludes others. Furthermore, this process usually aims to replicate existing culture, which usually is one that advantages White men. Paradoxically, mentoring has been adopted as a means of attempting to diversify the organization—by providing to others what an elite group of predominantly young White men has enjoyed in the past as a means to increased retention and advancement. In some work settings, mentoring programs have become group mentoring, which actually functions as a network rather than a dyadic relationship. We now turn to the deliberate use of networks as a strategy for working toward D&I.

Networking and Affinity Groups (Employee Resource Groups or ERGs)

Networking with others sharing professional interests and information is widely recommended for improving one's job performance and enhancing career development. Widest access to information and help from others is likely to result from broad and non-redundant connections with others who do not know one another, and from numerous connections, even when less intense and personal than mentoring. Affinity groups or ERGs extend the networking idea to groups of people within an organization with a common interest or characteristic, sometimes demographic. Many ERGs form around aspects of identity that are protected categories under anti-discrimination law (e.g., race, sex). Groups meet with organizational approval, usually during work hours and with space and possibly financial support provided by the employer (Segal, 2013).

ERGs are intended to provide an inclusive environment to those who might feel marginalized in the organization because of their small numbers or particular characteristics. These groups are thought to increase employee morale and retention, and evidence (summarized by Avery & Johnson, 2008) shows this occurs at least for people of color. However, like mentoring, ERGs may seem exclusionary to non-members and give mixed messages about ethnic minority employees. Avery and Johnson described a positive message of ERGs: the employer acknowledges and is willing to support diversity among employees. Simultaneously, the negative message is that ERG members' concerns are their own, not adopted by the employer.

In recent years the purpose of ERGs has expanded from employee support to activities impacting business success, such as community service, product development, or marketing; this shift is reflected in moving from the term *affinity group* to that of *Employee Resource Group*. Despite their popularity, little scholarly research exists on the formation or outcome of ERGs (Avery & Johnson, 2008; Welbourne & McLaughlin, 2013).

A survey of large employers (median size = 32,000) by a consulting firm found that among these organizations, over $7,000 was budgeted annually for support of ERGs (Mercer, 2011). On average the equivalent of one or two employees was assigned to manage, coach, and coordinate these groups, and organizations also provided technology, time, and meeting space. Membership in ERGs varied from less than 1 percent of employees to as many as 8 percent, but these numbers were difficult to verify because of the structures' informality. Groups conducted activities in three areas: business operations, talent management, and D&I activities. With respect to business operations, ERGs engaged in product development and cultural insight (e.g., marketing ideas) pertinent to the customer base as well as community service to raise company public image. In talent management, ERGs assisted with new employee recruiting and socialization as well as professional development (e.g., establishing mentoring or role modeling connections). Furthermore, high-potential employees were sometimes identified through their leadership work with ERGs. D&I work included helping to raise multicultural awareness in the organization; communicating with executives about relevant issues such as strategy development for D&I; and connecting with external organizations (e.g., diverse suppliers; publications, professional organizations, and schools appropriate for diversifying applicant pools). In about one-third of organizations, ERG leaders received performance evaluations reflecting their work in this area, and in a few organizations their work might also receive additional compensation. This survey reached only large employers who used consulting services concerning ERGs; therefore survey results may not represent typical or smaller employers.

Welbourne and McLaughlin (2013) identified two trends in use of ERGs. First, ERGs now form around a wide range of issues. Most common are gender, racio-ethnicity, and sexual orientation, but groups also focus on generational issues, disability, prior military service, status as adoptive parents or elder caregivers, and religion (single or inter-faith groups). Their research identified three categories of ERGs: those centered on social causes (e.g., literacy or environmental concerns), professionally focused groups, and those centered on demographic characteristics. A second trend was the tendency for ERGs to involve participants worldwide for those employers with global operations. Reflecting on the wide range of ERG activities, often business-related, Welbourne and McLaughlin observed that employers "are getting high-quality consulting for a much lower price than what would be paid to professional service firms" (p. 41).

Some cautions have been noted about ERGs. Interviews with female geoscientists in the oil and gas industry, a male-dominated profession and industry with relatively little focus on D&I, found that ERGs did not always receive high marks from women participants (Williams, Kilanski, & Muller, 2014). Some found them helpful for connecting with other women and an online ERG focused on ideas for work-family balance was well received. However, some women also reported that ERGs had little or no impact on career advancement or connecting with others in more powerful positions in their company. D&I programming and expertise appeared relatively undeveloped in the work culture surrounding these women. ERGs may work best when organizations are already somewhat diversified and when culture is open to diverse perspectives and identities rather than homogeneous and oriented toward assimilation.

Other cautions are based on legal factors and risk. The employer should develop a policy about conditions under which an ERG may organize and how it should operate (e.g., meetings, funding, membership criteria). Criteria for organizing should be developed and all proposals evaluated according to them in order to avoid problems such as exclusion of certain employees. For example, an ERG based on a particular religion might be proposed. Segal (2013) recommended allowing religious affinity groups but placing reasonable limits on activities as with other ERGs. Examples would be statements of who could belong to a particular group, and prohibition of proselytizing.

Provisions of the National Labor Relations Act (NLRA) restrict employer control or interference with so-called *labor organizations*, usually interpreted to mean labor unions. Employers are prohibited from providing financial or other assistance to groups that deal with the employer, such as a group organized by the employer to undercut or forestall labor union organization. To avoid this problem, organizational policy should make it clear that ERGs do not represent employees to management over terms and conditions of employment, as in collective bargaining. The ERG does not speak for all employees sharing its defining focus (such as sex) and any ideas it proposes should be understood as suggestions rather than proposals to which management is required to respond (Segal, 2013).

Another problem could develop if managers participate in an ERG in which individual employee concerns are raised. It should be clear that employee complaints must be made through the employer's formal processes rather than simply communicated in the ERG context. This includes allegations of potentially illegal behavior, e.g., sexual or racial harassment (Segal, 2013).

Overall, available information suggests that ERGs can address employee inclusion and business operations, at least in some work settings. However, the research base is very slim about how to set up and manage ERGs as well as their effects on individuals and the work organization. The Catalyst research nonprofit has published a set of six tools available to its members to help organize and nurture ERGs so that they work well over time for participants and support the organization's strategic direction (Catalyst, 2009). In their review of D&I initiatives, Kulik and Roberson (2008b) concluded that network groups such as ERGs appear to be a cost-effective means of developing peer and informal mentoring relationships and reducing turnover intentions for nontraditional employees.

Building an Employee-Supportive Organization

Life concerns outside of work are also diverse. "Work-Family" (W-F) or "Work-Life" (W-L) benefits are designed to address this diversity. About half of reporting organizations in a survey of more than 500 HR professionals (SHRM, 2013) offered flexibility in time or place of work for at least some employees. Telecommuting (58% of respondents) and flextime during core business hours (51%) were most common, with compressed workweeks (35%), shift flexibility (19%), and job sharing (only 10%) less often available. The Family and Work Institute (FWI) compared surveys from 2005 and 2012, finding that flexibility in place or time of work had increased, but flexibility in caregiving leaves, reduced time, and career flexibility (exit and re-entry or changes in workload) had decreased over that period (Matos & Galinsky, 2012).

Availability

The SHRM survey (2013) found that other "family-friendly" benefits were actually reported by only a minority of respondents. Only 20–34% reported availability of an on-site lactation room, domestic partner benefits for same- or other-sex partners, or opportunity to bring a child to work in an emergency. Smaller percentages (8–14%) reported availability of referral services for child or elder care, adoption assistance, or consultation/education services about lactation. Fewer than 5% reported benefits aimed at informing or assisting employees in areas related to child or elder care, foster care, or re-adapting to work after absence for family reasons. The most common benefit (just over 70% of respondents) was the dependent care *flexible spending account*, a mechanism for directing part of one's pay into a tax-advantaged account that is later used to pay dependent care expenses. Funds not spent during the calendar year are forfeited. This benefits employees financially but at relatively low cost, if any, to the organization; it is available to workers if their employer has adopted this plan under the tax code, but is *not* an employer contribution to child care costs.

Large-scale surveys by FWI showed that most employers provide leave for maternity, paternity, adoption or foster care, or care of a seriously ill family member (required by the Family and Medical Leave Act, FMLA; Matos & Galinsky, 2012). Data suggested that the FMLA standard is becoming the norm even for some small employers not technically required to comply; however, it also appeared that some large organizations, perhaps as many as 25%, were not in full compliance with FMLA leave requirements. Many new parents could not afford to take 12 weeks of unpaid FMLA leave and only 58% of employers reported providing *paid* maternity leave, usually funded by temporary disability insurance. Because new fathers are not "disabled" and thus ineligible for disability leave, few employers (only 14%) reported any replacement pay for fathers. With respect to assistance with dependent care, FWI's data supported SHRM's finding that tax-advantaged dependent care withholding plans are frequently offered (62%). However, only 38% reported that their organization provided information for locating dependent care, and very few employers (only 7% or fewer) provided on-site or nearby child care, backup or sick emergency care for children, or financial assistance with child care costs.

Access

The manager or supervisor typically must approve use of W-F benefits such as telecommuting or flextime and is an important gatekeeper in their use. A survey of private-sector managers found that support of these policies was often strongly influenced by their judgments about responsibility of employees, either individually or collectively (Stout, Awad, & Guzmán, 2013). This is consistent with results of a study of HR managers in 41 varied industries and government in three US regions (Kelly & Kalev, 2006), which found that most organizations had formalized policies for flexible benefits, but policies maintained managerial discretion instead of creating an employee entitlement. Discretion was sometimes based on feasibility considering characteristics of jobs, but often on judgments about employee performance. Kelly and Kalev concluded that this "formalized discretion" accounts for low use of and unequal access to flexible benefits which are often seen as a reward for excellent performance, available only to outstanding employees.

Gender bias in manager approvals was documented in an experiment by Brescoll, Glass, and Sedlovskaya (2013) in which managers were asked to judge flextime requests from men or women in lower- or higher-status jobs for either career advancement or child care obligations. Requests were most often approved for higher-status men wishing to advance their careers. Requests from women in either job status were less likely to be approved regardless of reason, and low-status men were more likely than low-status women to receive approval for child care leave. Brescoll et al. also asked participants to estimate the likelihood that their request would be approved in scenarios varying their job status and reason for request. Women were most likely to expect approval, regardless of job status and rationale, but in the first study, their requests were actually *less* likely to be approved. Men underestimated how often their requests would be approved and thus may be less likely to request it. The most likely candidate for approval of this so-called "family-friendly benefit" was actually a career-focused man!

Right to request policies have been suggested as one means of improving access to flexible work. Used in Canada, Great Britain, Germany, the Netherlands, and the State of Vermont, these policies entitle any employee to *request* a benefit—not necessarily to receive it. The manager must provide written explanation of rationale for the decision. Denial must be based on certain specified factors such as business necessity (Charlesworth & Campbell, 2005; Wilkie, 2013). In this system, flexibility is not an entitlement but is framed as a reasonable request for anyone to make, deserving of equal consideration.

W-F Culture

Beyond specific benefits, a supportive W-F culture consists of three aspects: perceived managerial support, anticipated career consequences, and time demands at work (Thompson, Beauvais, & Lyness, 1999). Evidence shows that supportive supervision and culture are more important in reducing work-family conflict (WFC) than are specific family-friendly policies themselves (Premaux, Adkins, & Mossholder, 2007). Meta-analysis of 115 separate samples (Kossek, Pichler, Bodner, & Hammer, 2011) confirmed that both general and W-F supervisor support were associated with increased perceptions of organizational support for family roles, which in turn led to lower work-to-family conflict. Perceived supervisor W-F support was also *directly* associated with reduced WFC.

Major and Lauzun (2010) offered five recommendations to management for helping employees to manage WFC: (a) develop a supportive W-F culture, with norms respecting family time and encouraging use of available policies; (b) identify ways in which work interferes with family concerns; (c) train supervisors to develop high-quality relationships with supervisees; (d) give supervisors autonomy to develop idiosyncratic but equitable arrangements in individual cases; (e) motivate supervisors to develop high-quality relationships and address W-F concerns by including this criterion in performance reviews.

Are Work-family Benefits Effective?

Konrad (2013) summarized research on W-F benefits and employee WFC. Meta-analyses showed that positive perceptions of workplace support and organizational W-F culture were both related to lower employee conflict to a small or moderate but significant degree. Higher scores on a single index of W-F benefit availability were associated with higher perceived productivity, job satisfaction, and organizational citizenship, and lower WFC, turnover intent, and burnout. Studies of individual practices such as help with dependent or elder care, parental leaves, or PT work have also found positive effects, in some cases stronger for parents than for employees without children. Effects may be confined to policies actually used by employees who need them.

Research on WFC largely reflects experiences of middle-class and professional employees, mainly Whites rather than people of color. Less is known about experiences of single parents and low-wage workers. Employees in blue-collar and service jobs often have lower income, little job autonomy, unpredictable work hours or shifts, and cannot take work home as many salaried employees at higher organizational levels do. Generally paid by the hour, they have less access to paid leave (including sick leave). Absence from work reduces take-home pay (not the case for salaried professional and managerial employees) and may result in termination. Their WFC experiences likely differ from those of salaried employees.

A survey of over 1,000 lower- and higher-level private-sector employees found that both groups reported WFC (DiRenzo, Greenhaus, & Weer, 2011). Higher-level employees reported more WFC related to work demands and hours. For lower-level employees, having an employed spouse and owning one's home (possibly reflecting higher family income) were associated with lower conflict. In contrast, for upper-level employees owning a home was related to *higher* conflict. Job autonomy and family-supportive culture and supervision were associated with lower levels of conflict for both groups, but these resources were more helpful for those at higher levels. In other studies of lower-income or lower-skill workers, researchers have documented the importance of support from children, extended family, neighbors, and community (Griggs, Casper, & Eby, 2013) and of family-supportive supervision and work culture in reducing conflict (Muse & Pichler, 2011; Griggs et al., 2013). Diversity professionals should recognize unique work-life challenges of all employees, regardless of family configuration or income level; understanding differences among employees should help shape organizational policies that suit their needs.

A "business case" can be made for W-F options in terms of benefit to employer. FWI found that for both professional and low-wage employees, more flexibility in work scheduling or location were associated with higher job satisfaction, better self-assessments of physical health, and lower intent to search for another job (Matos & Galinsky, n.d.). Low-wage employees who had access to flexibility reported that it made greater positive difference for them in handling WFC than for professional employees. Meta-analysis of 59 studies found that availability and use of family-supportive policies were associated with higher job satisfaction, emotional attachment to the organization (affective commitment), and intentions to remain. When an employee knew these options were available, whether or not they were used, the person apparently saw the employer as family-supportive and experienced lower WFC, which led to more positive work attitudes (Butts, Casper, & Yang, 2013). Costs of employee turnover and replacement can be substantial, and employees are more productive when they can focus on the job rather than the situation at home.

Work-Life Policies in Other Countries

The US stands in stark contrast to most other industrialized nations in its weak support for parents and children. Waldfogel's (2001) review of parental leave and child care policies in Canada and nine European peer countries found three parental support policies: parental leaves, child care policies, and early childhood benefits for parents of children younger than three. Peer countries offered leave that was universal, paid, and lasting at least 10 months, in contrast to FMLA leave that is unpaid, available only to about half the workforce, and limited to 12 weeks. Child care in peer countries was publicly funded, more widely available, and provided by a better-trained and better-paid workforce than in the US, which fell below all ten peer nations in child care support. Some countries have experimented with grants to families with children under three to offset costs of nonparental care for employed parents or lost wages by parents who preferred to provide care themselves. In the US a patchwork of arrangements is funded by parental payments, partial tax credits, and government-subsidized care for about 15% of eligible low-income children, and public kindergartens or pre-schools. A detailed but readable comparison of W-F policies in the US and other countries, with an astute analysis of what can be done to improve them, appears in a book by Madeleine Kunin (2012), former US ambassador and three-term Governor of Vermont.

W-F relationships have often been seen as a "women's issue" because women still carry more responsibility for child care than do men in our society. Leslie and Manchester (2011) have argued that because W-F issues are framed as a "women's issue," organizations and our society tend to underestimate the strategic importance of these policies and benefits. This perception as a women's issue is "not only inaccurate, it is also a barrier to the success of work-family initiatives" (p. 415). When other countries have experimented with "degendering" flexible hours or parental leave, they found that both men and women made use of these practices, which became used more and associated less with career penalties. For example, about one-third of Dutch men, many professionals such as engineers or surgeons, have altered their hours to work PT or take *daddy days*. This refers to a compressed work week of 5 days' work in 4 days. "Use it or lose it" provisions for family leave available only to fathers have been implemented in Norway and Sweden (Kamerman, 2000) to increase usage and decrease stigma.

This chapter focused on strategies for building DComp of individuals, such as DT, specialized leadership development, mentoring, and networking and ERGs as well as work-life initiatives. The next chapter addresses *organizational* diversity competence and how it might be developed.

References

Allen, T. D., Eby, L. T., & Lentz, E. (2006). The relationship between formal mentoring program characteristics and perceived program effectiveness. *Personnel Psychology, 59*, 125–153.

Allen, T. D., Eby, L. T., Poteet, M. L., Lentz, E., & Lima, L. (2004). Career benefits associated with mentoring for protégés: A meta-analysis. *Journal of Applied Psychology, 89*, 127–136.

*Allen, T. D., Finkelstein, L. M., & Poteet, M. L. (2009). *Designing workplace mentoring programs: An evidence-based approach*. Malden, MA: Wiley-Blackwell.

*Anand, R., & Winters, M.-F. (2008). A retrospective view of corporate diversity training from 1964 to the present. *Academy of Management Learning & Education, 7*, 356–372.

Avery, D. R., & Johnson, C. D. (2008). Now you see it, now you don't: Mixed messages regarding workforce diversity. In K. Thomas (Ed.), *Diversity resistance in organizations* (pp. 221–247). New York: Lawrence Erlbaum Associates.

Balsam, K. F., Molina, Y., Beadnell, B., Simoni, J., & Walters, K. (2011). Measuring multiple minority stress: The LGBT people of color microaggressions scale. *Cultural Diversity and Ethnic Minority Psychology, 17*, 163–174.

Bandura, A. (1986). *Social foundations of thought and action*. Englewood Cliffs, NJ: Prentice-Hall.

Baugh, S. G., & Fagenson-Eland, E. A. (2007). Formal mentoring programs. In B. R. Ragins & K. E. Kram (Eds.), *The handbook of mentoring at work: Theory, research, and practice* (pp. 249–271). Thousand Oaks, CA: Sage Publications.

Bendick, M., Jr., Egan, M. L., & Lofhjelm, S. M. (2001). Workforce diversity training: From anti-discrimination compliance to organizational development. *Human Resource Planning, 24*(2), 10–25.

Bezrukova, K., Jehn, K. A., & Spell, C. S. (2012). Reviewing diversity training: Where we have been and where we should go. *Academy of Management Learning & Education, 11*, 207–227.

Blake-Beard, S. D., Murrell, A., & Thomas, D. (2007). Unfinished business: The impact of race on understanding mentoring relationships. In B. R. Ragins & K. E. Kram (Eds.), *The handbook of mentoring at work: Theory, research, and practice* (pp. 223–247). Thousand Oaks, CA: Sage Publications.

Brescoll, V. L., Glass, J., & Sedlovskaya, A. (2013). Ask and ye shall receive? The dynamics of employer-provided flexible work options and the need for public policy. *Journal of Social Issues, 69*, 367–388.

Butts, M. M., Casper, W. J., & Yang, T. S. (2013). How important are work-family support policies? A meta-analytic investigation of their effects on employee outcomes. *Journal of Applied Psychology, 98*, 1–25.

Catalyst. (2002). Women of color in corporate management: Three years later. Retrieved from www.catalyst.org/knowledge/women-color-corporate-management-three-years-later

Catalyst. (2007). *The double-bind dilemma for women in leadership: Damned if you do, doomed if you don't.* Retrieved from www.catalyst.org/knowledge/double-bind-dilemma-women-leadership-damned-if-you-do-doomed-if-you-dont-0

Catalyst. (2009, September 30). *The Catalyst guide to employee resource groups, 1—Introduction to ERGs.* Retrieved from www.catalyst.org/knowledge/catalyst-guide-employee-resource-groups-1-introduction-ergs (Document available only to Catalyst members).

Center for Creative Leadership. (2015). *The Women's Leadership Program (WLP).* Retrieved from www.ccl.org/leadership/programs/WLPOverview.aspx

Charlesworth, S., & Campbell, I. (2005). *Right to Request regulation: A panacea for work/family imbalance?* Paper prepared for Australian Academy of Social Science Workshop: Taking care of work and family. Retrieved from www.researchgate.net/publication/237220193_Right_to_Request_Regulation_A_Panacea_for_WorkFamily_Imbalance

*Chrobot-Mason, D. (2003). Developing multicultural competence for managers: Same old leadership skills or something new? *The Psychologist-Manager Journal, 6*, 5–20.

Combs, G. M., & Luthans, F. (2007). Diversity training: Analysis of the impact of self-efficacy. *Human Resource Development Quarterly, 19*(1), 91–120.

*Cox, T., Jr., & Beale, R. L. (1997). *Developing competency to manage diversity: Readings, cases, activities.* San Francisco, CA: Berrett-Koehler.

Dawson, B. L., Thomas, K. M., & Goren, M. J. (2013). Career development. In Q. M. Roberson (Ed.), *The Oxford handbook of diversity and work* (pp. 300–314). New York, NY: Oxford University Press.

DiRenzo, M. S., Greenhaus, J. H., & Weer, C. H. (2011). Job level, demands, and resources as antecedents of work-family conflict. *Journal of Vocational Behavior, 78*, 305–314.

Dreher, G. F., & Cox, T. H. (1996). Race, gender, and opportunity: A study of compensation attainment and the establishment of mentoring relationships. *Journal of Applied Psychology, 75*, 539–546.

*Ely, R. J., Ibarra, H., & Kolb, D. M. (2011). Theory and design for women's leadership development programs. *Academy of Management Learning & Education, 10*, 474–493.

Ensher, E. A., Thomas, C., & Murphy, S. E. (2001). Comparison of traditional, step-ahead, and peer mentoring on protégés' support, satisfaction, and perceptions of career success: A social exchange perspective. *Journal of Business and Psychology, 15*, 419–438.

Esen, E. (2005, October). *2005 Workplace diversity practices: Survey report.* Alexandria, VA: Society for Human Resource Management. Retrieved from www.shrm.org/Research/SurveyFindings/Articles/Documents/05-0509WkplcDivPrcSR_FINAL_rev.pdf

Flanagan, J. C. (1954). The critical incident technique. *Psychological Bulletin, 1*, 327–355.

Ford, J. K., & Fisher, S. (1996). The role of training in a changing workplace and workforce: New perspectives and approaches. In E. E. Kossek & S. A. Lobel (Eds.), *Managing diversity: Human resource strategies for transforming the workplace* (pp. 164–193). Cambridge, MA: Blackwell.

Gaertner, S. L., & Dovidio, J. F. (2000). *Reducing intergroup bias: The Common Ingroup Identity Model.* Philadelphia, PA: Taylor & Francis Group.

Goldstein, I. L., & Ford, J. K. (2002). *Training in organizations.* Belmont, CA: Wadsworth.

Griggs, T. L., Casper, W. J., & Eby, L. T. (2013). Work, family and community support as predictors of work-family conflict: A study of low-income workers. *Journal of Vocational Behavior, 82*, 59–68.

*Hays-Thomas, R., Bowen, A., & Boudreaux, M. (2012). Skills for diversity and inclusion in organizations: A review and preliminary investigation. *The Psychologist-Manager Journal, 15*, 128–141.

Hite, L. M., & McDonald, K. S. (2006). Diversity training pitfalls and possibilities: An exploration of small and mid-size US organizations. *Human Resource Development International, 9*, 365–377.

Holmes, T. A. (2004). Designing and facilitating performance-based diversity training. *Performance Improvement, 43*(5), 13–20.

Ibarra, H. (1995). Race, opportunity, and diversity of social circles in managerial networks. *Academy of Management Journal, 38,* 673–703.

James, E. H. (2000). Race-related differences in promotions and support: Underlying effects of human and social capital. *Organizational Science, 11,* 493–508.

Kalinoski, Z. T., Steele-Johnson, D., Peyton, E. J., Leas, K. A., Steinke, J., & Bowling, N. A. (2013). A meta-analytic evaluation of diversity training outcomes. *Journal of Organizational Behavior, 34,* 1076–1104.

Kamerman, S. B. (2000). Parental leave policies: An essential ingredient in early childhood education and care policies. *Social Policy Report, 14,* 3–15.

Kelly, E. L., & Kalev, A. (2006). Managing flexible work arrangements in US organizations: Formalized discretion or a "right to ask." *Socio-Economic Review, 4,* 379–416.

Kirkpatrick, D. L. (1994). *Evaluating training programs: The four levels.* San Francisco, CA: Berrett-Koehler.

Konrad, A. M. (2013). Work-life interface and flexibility: Impacts on women, men, families, and employers. In Q. M. Roberson (Ed.), *The Oxford handbook of diversity and work* (pp. 366–390). New York, NY: Oxford University Press.

Kossek, E. E., Pichler, S., Bodner, T., & Hammer, L. B. (2011). Workplace social support and work-family conflict: A meta-analysis clarifying the influence of general and work-family-specific supervisor and organizational support. *Personnel Psychology, 64,* 289–313.

Kram, K. E. (1983). Phases of the mentoring relationship. *Academy of Management Journal, 26,* 608–625.

Kram, K. E. (1985). *Mentoring at work.* Glenview, IL: Scott, Foresman.

Kram, K. E. (1986). Mentoring in the workplace. In D. T. Hall and Associates (Eds.), *Career development in organizations.* San Francisco, CA: Jossey-Bass.

Kulik, C., & Roberson, L. (2008a). Common goals and golden opportunities: Evaluations of diversity education in academic and organizational settings. *Academy of Management Learning and Education, 7,* 309–331.

*Kulik, C. T., & Roberson, L. (2008b). Diversity initiative effectiveness: What organizations can (and cannot) expect from diversity recruitment, diversity training, and formal mentoring programs. In A. P. Brief (Ed.), *Diversity at work* (pp. 265–317). New York, NY: Cambridge University Press.

Kunin, M. M. (2012). *The new feminist agenda: Defining the next revolution for women, work, and family.* White River Junction, VT: Chelsea Green Publishing.

Leslie, L. M., & Manchester, C. F. (2011). Work-family conflict is a social issue not a women's issue. *Industrial and Organizational Psychology: Perspectives on Science and Practice, 4,* 414–417.

Lievens, F., & Sackett, P. R. (2012). The validity of interpersonal skills assessment via situational judgment tests for predicting academic success and job performance. *Journal of Applied Psychology, 97,* 460–468.

Major, D. A., & Lauzun, H. M. (2010). Equipping managers to assist employees in addressing work-family conflict: Applying the research literature toward innovative practice. *The Psychologist-Manager Journal, 13,* 69–85.

Management Leadership for Tomorrow. (n.d.). *MLT at a glance.* Retrieved from www.ml4t.org/program-overview/

Matos, K., & Galinsky, E. (n.d.). *Workplace flexibility in the United States: A status report.* New York: Families and Work Institute. Retrieved from http://familiesandwork.org/site/research/reports/www_us_workflex.pdf

Matos, K., & Galinsky, E. (2012). *2012 National Study of Employers.* New York: Families and Work Institute. Retrieved from http://familiesandwork.org/site/research/reports/NSE_2012_.pdf

McKeen, C., & Bujaki, M. (2007). Gender and mentoring: Issues, effects, and opportunities. In B. R. Ragins & K. E. Kram (Eds.), *The handbook of mentoring at work: Theory, research, and practice* (pp. 197–222). Thousand Oaks, CA: Sage Publications.

Mercer. (2011, January). *ERGs come of age: The evolution of employee resource groups.* Retrieved from www.orcnetworks.com/system/files/story/2011/5849/ergs_come_of_age_2011_study_pdf_30909.pdf

Microaggressions Project. (n.d.). *Microaggressions: Power, privilege, and everyday life.* Retrieved from www.microaggressions.com

*Murrell, A. J., Crosby, F. J., & Ely, R. J. (Eds.) (1999). *Mentoring dilemmas: Developmental relationships within multicultural organizations.* Mahwah, NJ: Lawrence Erlbaum Associates.

Muse, L. A., & Pichler, S. (2011). A comparison of types of support for lower-skill workers: Evidence for the importance of family supportive supervisors. *Journal of Vocational Behavior, 79,* 653–666.

O'Brien, K. E., Biga, A., Kessler, S. R., & Allen, T. D. (2010). A meta-analytic investigation of gender differences in mentoring. *Journal of Management, 36*, 537–554.

Ong, A. D., Burrow, A. L., Fuller-Rowell, T. E., Ja, N. M., & Sue, D. W. (2012). Racial microaggressions and daily well-being among Asian Americans. *Journal of Counseling Psychology, 60*, 188–199.

Pettigrew, T. F., & Tropp, L. R. (2000). Does intergroup contact reduce prejudice? Recent meta-analytic findings. In S. Oskamp (Ed.), *Reducing prejudice and discrimination* (pp. 93–114). Mahwah, NJ: Erlbaum.

Plant, E. A., & Devine, P. G. (2003). The antecedents and implications of interracial anxiety. *Personality and Social Psychology Bulletin, 29*, 790–801.

Premaux, S. F., Adkins, C. L., & Mossholder, K. W. (2007). Balancing work and family: A field study of multi-dimensional, multi-role work-family conflict. *Journal of Organizational Behavior, 28*, 705–727.

*Ragins, B. R. (1997). Diversified mentoring relationships in organizations: A power perspective. *Academy of Management Review, 22*, 482–521.

Ragins, B. R. (1999). Where do we go from here, and how do we get there? Methodological issues in conducting research on diversity and mentoring relationships. In A. J. Murrell, F. J. Crosby, & R. J. Ely (Eds.), *Mentoring dilemmas: Developmental relationships within multicultural organizations* (pp. 227–247). Mahwah, NJ: Lawrence Erlbaum Associates.

Ragins, B. R., & Kram, K. E. (2007). The roots and meaning of mentoring. In B. R. Ragins & K. E. Kram (Eds.), *The handbook of mentoring at work: Theory, research, and practice* (pp. 3–15). Thousand Oaks, CA: Sage Publications.

Ragins, B. R., Townsend, B., & Mattis, M. (1998). Gender gap in the executive suite: CEOS and female executives report on breaking the glass ceiling. *Academy of Management Executive, 12*, 28–42.

Roberson, L., Kulik, C. T., & Pepper, M. B. (2001). Designing effective diversity training: Influence of group composition and trainee experience. *Journal of Organizational Behavior, 22*, 871–885.

*Roberson, L., Kulik, C. T., & Tan, R. Y. (2013). Effective diversity training. In Q. M. Roberson (Ed.), *The Oxford handbook of diversity and work* (pp. 341–365). New York, NY: Oxford University Press.

Rynes, S., & Rosen, B. (1995). A field survey of factors affecting the adoption and perceived success of diversity training. *Personnel Psychology, 48*, 247–270.

Segal, J. A. (2013, September). Affinity group danger zones. *HR Magazine*, 75–80.

Shelton, J. N., & Richeson, J. A. (2005). Intergroup contact and pluralistic ignorance. *Journal of Personality and Social Psychology, 88*, 91–107.

Smith College. (n.d.). *Smith College Executive Education for Women*. Retrieved from www.smith.edu/execed/?q=programs/smith-college-leadership-consortium

Society for Human Resource Management. (2010, October 12). *Workplace diversity practices: How has diversity and inclusion changed over time? A comparative examination: 2010 and 2005*. Retrieved from www.shrm.org/research/surveyfindings/articles/pages/workplacediversitypractices.aspx

Society for Human Resource Management. (2013). *2013 employee benefits: An overview of employee benefits offerings in the U.S.* Washington, DC: SHRM. Retrieved from www.shrm.org/research/surveyfindings/articles/documents/13-0245%202013_empbenefits_fnl.pdf

*Stephan, W. G., & Stephan, C. W. (1985). Intergroup anxiety. *Journal of Social Issues, 41*, 157–175.

Stout, M. S., Awad, G., & Guzmán, M. (2013). Exploring managers' attitudes toward work/family programs in the private sector. *The Psychologist-Manager Journal, 16*, 176–195.

Sue, D. W. (2010). *Microaggressions in everyday life: Race, gender, and sexual orientation.* Hoboken, NJ: John Wiley & Sons, Inc.

*Sue, D. W. (2013). Race talk: The psychology of racial dialogues. *American Psychologist, 68*, 663–672.

Sue, D. W., Carter, R. T., Casas, J. M., Fouad, N. A., Ivey, A. E., Jensen, M., . . . Vazquez-Nutall, E. (1998). *Multicultural counseling competencies: Individual and organizational development.* Thousand Oaks, CA: SAGE.

Sue, D. W., Rivera, D. P., Capodilupo, C. M., Lin, A. I., & Torino, G. C. (2010). Racial dialogues and White trainee fears: Implications for education and training. *Cultural Diversity and Ethnic Minority Psychology, 16*, 206–214.

Thomas, D. A. (1990). The impact of race on managers' experiences of developmental relationships. *Journal of Organizational Behavior, 11*, 479–492.

Thompson, C. A., Beauvais, L. L., & Lyness, K. S. (1999). When work-family benefits are not enough: The influence of work-family culture on benefit utilization, organizational attachment, and work-family conflict. *Journal of Vocational Behavior, 54*, 392–415.

Torres-Harding, S. R., Andrade, A. L., Jr., & Diaz, C. E. R. (2012). The Racial Microaggressions Scale (RMAS): A new scale to measure experiences of racial microaggression in people of color. *Cultural Diversity and Ethnic Minority Psychology, 18*, 153–164.

Waldfogel, J. (2001). International policies toward parental leave and child care. *The Future of Children, 11*(1), 98–111.

Welbourne, T. M., & McLaughlin, L. L. (2013). Making the business case for employee resource groups. *Employment Relations Today, 40*(2), 35–44.

West, T. V., Shelton, J. N., & Trail, T. E. (2009). Relational anxiety in interracial interactions. *Psychological Science, 20*, 289–292.

Wilkie, D. (2013, August 22). Managers distrust women who ask for flextime more than men. Retrieved from www.shrm.org/hrdisciplines/Diversity/Articles/Pages/Managers-Distrust-Women-Flextime.aspx

Williams, C. L., Kilanski, K., & Muller, C. (2014). Corporate diversity programs and gender inequality in the oil and gas industry. *Work and Occupations, 41*, 440–476.

* Recommended for advanced reading.

Chapter 14

Building Organizational Diversity Competence through Organizational Development

The previous chapter described building diversity competence of individuals. Though important, alone this is insufficient. For most organizations, moving toward better management of D&I requires significant alterations in structure and process. We can think of development of organizational diversity competency as following the steps of *awareness, understanding, and action* (Cox and Beale, 1997). The shaded box applies this view to a contemporary issue.

Finding "Qualified" People of Color and Women in High Tech

One important contemporary diversity issue is representation of women and ethnic minorities (especially Latinos and Blacks) in high tech industries (Frank, 2014; Guynn, 2014; Guynn & Weise, 2014). Most major high tech companies (Apple, Yahoo, Google, Facebook, LinkedIn, and Twitter) have released results of demographic studies of their workforces. In all cases, White men are overrepresented in relation to their numbers in the labor force. Furthermore, in five of the six companies, about half the women employees are in non-tech jobs (Frank, 2014), and ethnic pay disparities exist for similar jobs (Guynn, 2014). In terms of the three steps outlined by Cox and Beale (1997), publication of these workforce studies indicates *awareness* of disparities that could indicate low diversity competence.

Some in these organizations also have some level of *understanding*; in fact, conduct and publication of these studies may indicate a high level of understanding by some company executives. Spokespersons have publicly stated that underrepresentation is due to a lack of individuals from underrepresented groups trained in the tech fields and that educational reforms are needed to address this gap. However, publicly available information shows that as many as 9% of graduates in computer science or engineering in 2012 were African American and about the same percentage were Hispanic, far more than the 2–4 % of employees reported by these companies (Weise & Guynn, 2014). One reason for disparate hiring is that recruiting seems to focus on a small number of prestigious universities instead of a wider net. Implicit bias has been mentioned as a factor limiting companies' ability to identify qualified graduates who may not resemble those typically hired.

Such information increases *understanding* of the issue. We cannot say from publicly available information whether *action* has been taken to assure equity, diversity, and inclusion. However, if this analysis is correct, one simple action would be to increase the range of educational institutions from which companies recruit. Companies such as Apple, Google, and LinkedIn have also described efforts to work with HBCUs to improve curricula and graduation rates in computer science (Weise & Guynn, 2014). African American tech executive Ken Coleman pointed out that half the jobs in tech firms do not require high levels of skill in information technology. He suggested that HR departments should be staffed partly by ethnic minority professionals and that companies should recruit at historically minority institutions. Managers must also learn to overcome the natural risk they experience in considering applicants different from the current workforce (della Cava, 2014).

Rev. Jesse Jackson's Rainbow Push Coalition has commissioned surveys and organized panels including executives from tech companies to draw attention to this issue and generate possible solutions (Swartz, Guynn, & della Cava, 2014). Major tech companies sell products or services related to computing. Of these major companies, Amazon is most focused on marketing a wide range of items to a very diverse clientele. Statistics provided by companies themselves show that Amazon reports the highest percentage of Black employees (15%) and is one of two with a representative percentage of Hispanics in its workforce (9%) (Swartz et al., 2014). This could be taken as evidence of the business case for diversity at Amazon. Is the potential clientele of other tech companies equally diverse, and will these companies follow the employment pattern set by Amazon?

Many employers already offer one or more specific program or technique like mentoring or training to advance D&I in an organization. However, the ideal way to proceed is to consider D&I program development as *organizational development (OD)*, requiring broad and careful analysis and articulation of why D&I work is desirable or appropriate, areas to be targeted, and how to proceed and monitor progress.

The term OD refers to an approach to organizational change that is (a) planned, (b) integrated, (c) system-wide with management support, (d) long-term, (e) based on behavioral science, and (f) designed to improve organizational functioning and the development of individuals (Anderson, 2015; Cummings & Worley, 2015). The traditional OD approach is collaborative rather than an "expert" model. That is, although consultants may be involved in implementing an OD program, the eventual aim is to collaborate with organization members to develop their knowledge and skill so they can continue improvement even after consultants have left. The OD approach is entirely consistent with the goals and philosophy of a good program for managing D&I. The system-wide nature of successful D&I efforts is emphasized by Church, Rotolo, Shull, and Tuller (2014) when they say "practicing inclusive OD means applying a diverse and inclusive mindset and framework to every core HR, I-O, or OD process" (p. 262). D&I should not be seen as a separate change effort but instead should be incorporated into all efforts to measure and improve the organization.

Diversity Training (DT) is probably the most common aspect of a D&I program and often starts with a focus on preventing or responding to harassment or discrimination. In a survey of 108 DT providers, researchers identified nine characteristics of DT that had moved anti-discrimination training to planned organizational change (Bendick, Egan, & Lofhjelm, 2001). These were: (a) top management support; (b) training designed for client's particular needs; (c) links between DT and organization's goals; (d) trainers with managerial or OD backgrounds; (e) training provided for all levels of employees; (f) presentation of discrimination as a broad process rather than narrowly dealing mainly with race or sex; (g) focus on behavior as well as awareness and attitudes; (h) training along with changes in HR practices; and (i) training that impacts the organization's culture. This approach is advocated here.

Changing an organization is not easy. Mature organizations are systems with a network of interlocking and mutually reinforcing procedures, policies, and culture. Systems Theory reminds us that change in one part of a system brings about adjustments in other areas, sometimes in unexpected ways. Furthermore, many people have a vested interest in the *status quo* and may resist attempts to alter it. Legal, economic, and sociocultural factors in the organization's environment may also support things as they are and provide obstacles to significant change.

On the other hand, such factors can also facilitate and support change if they are well understood and used wisely. Dissatisfactions and frustrations with existing problems can motivate change. Internal or external constituencies may desire and support new ways of operating and provide collaboration opportunities. Change in one area can bring about change in other areas as well. Successful organizational change requires thorough understanding of (a) organizational environment, structures and processes; (b) sources of resistance and support; (c) techniques for bringing about change; and (d) realization that *making* change is not enough. It must also be *institutionalized* if the effort is to have lasting positive effects.

Action Research

Firm evidence-based recommendations for D&I initiatives are hard to make, partly because organizational research seldom yields unambiguous conclusions. Because D&I activities and contexts vary so much across organizations, generalizing from one setting to another is difficult. In an ongoing organization, many internal and environmental factors cannot be controlled as they might be in a laboratory. Changes in key personnel, technological improvements, competitors' behavior, and the general economy illustrate the many things that can affect outcomes of change efforts. Judgments about causality are always tentative, especially for large-scale systemic changes in organizations. Therefore, the *action research* framework is useful for implementing and evaluating effects of programs, including those to advance D&I.

Action research, usually attributed to Kurt Lewin, the "Father of Social Psychology," is a three-stage repeating cycle of (a) data collection and diagnosis; (b) planning and implementation; and (c) collection of new data and evaluation. Results are used for another cycle of further planning, redesign, and additional evaluation through collection of new data. Lewin also described three steps of *unfreezing, change,* and *refreezing* as a framework for changing an organization. Unfreezing occurs when something disrupts the ongoing equilibrium, such as a significant event or recognition of a problem through a routine survey. With things more fluid, changed procedures or understandings can be implemented. To have lasting effects, refreezing or institutionalization must occur, without which things will tend to revert to their original status (Locke & Golden-Biddle, 2004).

Data Collection and Diagnosis: Culture Audits and Strategic Analysis

A first step is identifying *why* D&I organizational change is desirable or necessary. Answering this question requires careful analysis of present and desired future state, both externally and internally. This analysis should suggest how and which differences can be *leveraged* to improve the organization's management of D&I (Davidson, 2011). In ordinary language, leveraging means using a tool, carefully placed for mechanical advantage, to influence or bring about movement in something else. In leveraging difference to create change, organization leaders consider relevant differences present (or missing) within the organization and its environment, and create a compelling rationale to show how these differences will help achieve the organization's goals. For example, an organization might identify demographic shifts in customer base and adapt hiring, training, and product development to this reality.

In one case, a company sold pharmaceuticals through retail stores, mail prescriptions, and nursing homes (Davidson, 2011). Using the opportunity provided by the construction of new facilities, a new upper manager had employees investigate how order fulfillment could be redesigned to suit older workers and those with disabilities. Collaborating with knowledgeable external partner organizations, the company made technological and process changes that benefited all employees and also improved profit margins. Here diversity was a tool leveraging other factors to accomplish good things for the organization based on a clear business rationale.

Often internal and external examination requires analysis of newly collected data to set D&I goals compatible with the employer's business strategy, just as needs assessment helps to set goals for training.

Understanding Internal Factors through a Culture Audit

The term *culture audit* refers to data collection to provide a current picture of individual, group, and organizational level factors relevant to D&I. Similar to a needs assessment for training, this audit should identify potential problem areas, possible ways of addressing them, people or processes that may be helpful or resistant, necessary resources, and other data useful for designing or improving a D&I program (see shaded box).

Exploring Resistance to Diversity

A culture audit might identify a major challenge for D&I professionals: resistance to diversity. What management and change agents see as growth and improvement may be viewed by others as unnecessary, threatening, or a waste of time. OD practitioners have long recognized that many factors can lead employees to react negatively to attempts to change their organizations, but few have addressed resistance in response to diversity initiatives in particular (for an exception see K. Thomas, 2008). Diversity resistance consists of *any work behaviors or practices that obstruct the use of diversity as an opportunity for the organization to learn and become more effective* (K. Thomas & Plaut, 2008). Resistance can take many forms, including avoidance, procrastination, argument, backlash, or manipulative responses. Thomas and Plaut have developed a typology of forms of diversity resistance. These may be *individual behaviors* or *organizational practices*, either of which can be *overt* or *subtle and covert*, as shown below.

Diversity Resistance	By Individuals	By Organizations
Overt Indicators		
Subtle Signs		

To illustrate, overt individual resistance may manifest in discriminatory or harassing behavior; graffiti, nooses, or offensive posters; violence; or complaints of *reverse discrimination*. Examples of subtle resistance by individuals are exclusion, avoidance, or distancing from members of other identity groups (Hebl, Madera, & King, 2008); ignoring comments or contributions made during meetings; or remaining silent in the face of others' discriminatory or harassing behavior. Examples of overt resistance by organizations include retaliation against those who complain of discrimination, continued use of exclusionary and discriminatory policies and procedures, and deception in management of AA and anti-discrimination policies. Illustrations of subtle resistance by organizations are practices of placing members of underrepresented groups only with supervisors of the same sex or race, or only in "minority" activities or departments; lack of support for D&I initiatives; or cultures of silence around complaints of discrimination.

What accounts for such resistance? At the individual level, resistance may be due to a sense of threat (including identity threat) or potential loss of status or resources as "others" become more advantaged; fear of the unknown as norms and relationships change from the comfortable *status quo*;

anxiety about interacting with unfamiliar others and being viewed as racist or sexist; or other reasons (Chrobot-Mason, Hays-Thomas, & Wishik, 2008). Some reasons for organizational resistance are difficulty and expense of changing established practices and procedures; reluctance to expose data that could lead to grievances or legal challenges; belief in the myth of meritocracy and the idea that discrimination no longer exists; or rejection of the business case for D&I.

Addressing Resistance

Diversity professionals should recognize that resistance is a typical response to organizational change efforts. Understanding areas and possible sources of resistance can help in counteracting or reducing it. Wide dissemination of information about benefits of D&I efforts and why they are being undertaken, knowledge and skill on the part of diversity managers and staff, honesty and transparency, and mechanisms for employee feedback can go a long way in minimizing resistance.

Specific actions to prevent or eliminate resistance cannot be recommended because its forms are so many and its causes so varied and complex. Instances of overt discrimination and harassment must be dealt with swiftly and fairly according to organization policies. In designing new programs or changes in policy or procedure, one should anticipate who might perceive threat or loss as a result and, where appropriate, take steps to minimize or compensate for possible harm. Principles of organizational justice should be incorporated into efforts wherever possible. Finally, recall that diversity management is intended to develop "an environment that works for all employees" (R. Thomas, 1991, p. 10). Resistance is likely to be minimized when program design and communications lead employees to believe that this is true.

R. Thomas (1991) defined a culture audit as identification of the organization's "roots" or fundamental corporate culture, usually done with in-depth interviews, document reviews, observation, surveys, and focus groups. Similarly, Cox (1993/1994) used this term to refer to a "comprehensive assessment of the organizational culture and human resource management systems of the organization" (p. 237). The culture audit should gather information about how demographic and other differences are related to hiring and structural placement in the organization, to processes such as training or mentoring, and to employee outcomes such as salary, promotion, satisfaction, or productivity. An excellent comprehensive example of a culture audit is provided by Qirko (2007), an anthropologist who described an ethnographic culture assessment in a business setting. This project used multiple methods to study formal and informal norms and cultural assumptions. Methods included interviews with key informants, participant observation, analysis of records and documents, and a survey developed from information gained in the other methods.

Use of a standard questionnaire is recommended because it allows identification of change over time and in some cases comparisons with other organizations. The survey should be administered to all or a representative sample of employees to assess perceptions of diversity culture. Survey questions may address perceptions of whether the experience of various demographic groups is equivalent, feelings of fairness, or experiences of discrimination or harassment. One measure that could be used or adapted for inclusion in a culture audit is *diversity climate* (DC).

Diversity Climate

DC is a shared employee perception of the degree to which an organization's policies, procedures, and structures indicate a priority on D&I through fair practices and social integration across differences. (See McKay, Avery, & Morris, 2008; and Pugh, Dietz, Brief, & Wiley, 2008.) A more complex definition of DC is "perceptions of six organizational conditions: (a) pluralism . . . (b) full structural integration . . . (c) full integration of the informal networks . . . (d) low cultural bias . . . (e) minimal intergroup conflict . . ." and (f) employee identification with the organization (Wolfson, Kraiger, & Finkelstein, 2011, p. 163; based on Cox, 1993/1994). DC becomes a baseline for comparing subsequent measurements (perhaps yearly) to determine whether progress has been made.

Diversity Attitude

A different concept, not to be confused with DC, is that of *attitude toward diversity* (van Knippenberg, Homan, & van Ginkel, 2013). In measuring climate, one assesses shared perceptions of how diversity is valued in an organization (team or group) as expressed in norms, systems, structures, and procedures. This differs from asking employees about their attitude, i.e., their personal thoughts and feelings about diversity. As van Knippenberg et al. have noted, some published instruments for assessing climate actually contain items representing attitude as well. Some scales that purport to measure DC may also measure attitude (e.g., Kossek & Zonia, 1993; Mor Barak, Cherin, & Berkman, 1998; Mor Barak, 2014).

Climate or Attitude?

Both measures would be useful in a culture audit: what employees see as the organization's perspective on D&I (DC) and what they themselves think and feel about D&I (attitude). Measures of DC give clues about whether the organization should examine and perhaps change its procedures and might also show that employees do not know about policies and procedures actually in place. In contrast, measures of diversity attitude suggest sources of resistance, persistent stereotypes, or exclusionary feelings to be addressed by D&I programming. The two concepts should not be confused.

In such surveys, anonymity and confidentiality are critical for respondents to feel able to answer honestly; for this reason an objective third-party individual or organization might be engaged to conduct the survey and compile results. Other information may come from focus groups or interviews with key informants in critical jobs or otherwise in a position to understand how well the organization is working. Some sample DC items for interviews in a culture audit are provided in Box 14.1.

Box 14.1 Sample DC Items for Culture Audit Interviews

Items adapted from R. Thomas (1991).

- What first attracted you to (this company)? Were your expectations met?
- What needs to be promoted here?
- Are mentors important for career progress here? Have you had a mentor?
- How do employees here receive feedback on their performance?
- Is pay connected to performance appraisals?
- Is training provided for management-potential employees? Special training programs for women or minorities?
- What factors hinder advancement of women/minorities here?

Other sample items

- Are you aware of discrimination or harassment of other employees? Have you experienced this based on your sex/age/race/religion/ability status?
- How are incidents of sexual or racial harassment handled here?
- How do people find out about opportunities for promotion?

A complete culture audit also includes analysis of data about operation of organizational systems and procedures such as recruitment, selection, performance evaluation, compensation, promotion, training, and dispute resolution. The analysis should show whether these systems work equally well for all employees and employee groups.

Understanding Internal and External Factors: Strategic Planning and SWOT Analysis

Most medium or large organizations conduct strategic planning, a systematic way of taking stock of current status and future directions, given certain information or assumptions about the environment. For the diversity professional, a strategic plan suggests how to tie D&I initiatives into business strategy by connecting D&I with things already been identified as important. If nothing in the strategic plan seems related to D&I, this should lead to discussions about whether the plan should be revised!

Next, armed with information from a culture audit and strategic planning, the diversity professional can conduct a *SWOT analysis*. This term from marketing and business uses the initial letters of *strengths, weaknesses, opportunities, and threats* as an acronym for identifying internal and external factors to consider in developing any proposal, such as a program for D&I (Goodrich, 2013). Strengths and weaknesses are positive and negative factors internal to the organization; opportunities and threats are positive and negative factors in its environment. SWOT analysis can also yield critical information about whether and how organizational systems and structures are in or out of alignment with organization goals. A basic SWOT analysis matrix is shown in Table 14.1.

To conduct a SWOT analysis for D&I, the diversity professional invites a group of knowledgeable people to participate in identifying internal and external factors likely to support or oppose a plan for D&I. Although SWOT analysis could be done by one or more individuals working separately, typically a group session is used. Participants should be chosen for expertise in several relevant areas. To increase the group's informational resources for the task they should bring somewhat non-overlapping viewpoints and knowledge. Participants should include persons occupying key positions with access to useful information or representing key constituencies or organization areas.

The analysis itself can be conducted in different ways; research on group process (see Chapter 8) suggests that participants should be asked to complete the task separately first, followed by a group session to generate a listing of strengths, weaknesses, opportunities, and threats. This could be done in a round-robin process with each participant contributing an item to the boxes in

Table 14.1 SWOT Analysis Matrix

	Internal Factors	External Factors
POSITIVE	**STRENGTHS**	**OPPORTUNITIES**
NEGATIVE	**WEAKNESSES**	**THREATS**

a matrix posted so it can be seen by all. After items are listed and there are no further ideas, a facilitator leads a discussion of the group's product. Examples for a D&I program might be:

- Strength: top management support for improving D&I programs;
- Weakness: lack of knowledge among employees about how to implement D&I initiatives;
- Opportunity: community presence of educational institutions with relevant courses and programs;
- Threat: growth of other nearby organizations that compete for employees and customers.

Can you generate a SWOT analysis for a project or program you would like to put in place?

Building Organizational Competence through OD

When a decision has been made to implement D&I change, how can this be done? We turn next to a sample of OD techniques often used to bring about planned organizational change. These techniques were developed by scientists and practitioners influenced by the Group Dynamics work of Kurt Lewin, largely before the contemporary emphasis on D&I. However, this work is applicable to bringing about the kinds of changes needed to move an organization toward greater diversity competency. Extensive discussion of the OD field is beyond the scope of this text but can be found elsewhere (e.g., Anderson, 2015; Cummings & Worley, 2015).

Survey Feedback (SF)

One of the earliest and most widely used OD techniques, SF starts with an organization-wide survey of factors affecting productivity and satisfaction. Developers (e.g., Mann, 1961) recommended that survey development and planning include members of top management and key personnel. However, today external organizational consulting firms commonly administer and score survey instruments to protect respondents' anonymity and confidentiality. The *feedback* part of SF involves systematic presentation of survey results through tiers of the organization, beginning with top management (Burke, 2002). Information cascades down through the formal structure, with sessions facilitated by either supervisor/manager or external consultants. Feedback sessions consist of an overall summary of results with discussion of their meaning and implications. In some cases subunits deal only with survey aspects involving their group. According to Burke, SF can be powerful because it is data-based, directly and widely involves people in the organization, suggests what to change and identifies priorities, and aims change efforts at the organization rather than individuals. This may reduce defensiveness and other sources of resistance to change.

SF alone is unlikely to alter organizational functioning unless the information it provides is sufficiently motivating and engaging. However, it is often a good way to start an organizational redirection or renewal effort. In a large organization SF can require considerable time and resources; it should not be undertaken unless management is prepared to follow through with results. SF does not generally deal with business influences or factors in the external environment potentially relevant to development of an effective D&I program.

Process Consultation (PC)

This procedure focuses on process within a group, team, or larger unit, often during meetings or other work sessions. PC is usually associated with Schein (1999), who defined it as creation of a client-consultant relationship that allows the client to "perceive, understand, and act on the process events . . . to improve the situation as defined by the client" (p. 20). This definition is so broad that it applies equally well to organization-wide activity as to work with a specific unit. In practice, however, most examples of PC focus on observable processes in interpersonal and small group interaction. For example, the consultant may observe a group in action and consider seating and physical arrangements, agenda management, procedures, and interaction process. PC generally targets member roles and functions, communication, development and operation of group norms, problem-solving and decision-making, and use of authority and leadership (Huse, 1980). From an OD perspective, the observer does not provide expert diagnoses or recommendations but instead asks questions based on his or her observations to facilitate the client's own diagnosis and process improvement. However, some consultants are more willing to provide diagnoses and suggestions in their attempts to assist a group. Although PC appears simple, its successful use requires skill, tact, careful observation, and a good understanding of dynamic processes within groups. Applying this technique in the context of improving D&I, the consultant might pay particular attention to demographic and other characteristics of those who are present, influential, active, and well-received by others—and those who are not. Forms of address, reactions to a speaker's contributions, and even the seating pattern are clues to the degree of inclusion as well as diversity within the group.

Team Building (TB)

In this intervention a facilitator addresses how a group or team functions with respect to its specific task or function in the organization (Dyer, 1987). Unlike PC or SF, this technique focuses primarily on the unit's work and on relationships and processes related to these tasks. This dual emphasis on task and interpersonal factors differs from earlier team development methods such as sensitivity training, encounter, or t-groups, which focused mainly on interpersonal dynamics. According to Beckhard (1972), there are four purposes for TB: (1) setting goals or priorities; (2) considering member roles and responsibilities with respect to the group's task; (3) investigating the group's norms, processes, decision-making, and communication; and (4) analyzing interpersonal relationships within the group. These are listed in the order in which they should be addressed, because clarity and agreement on the first item may reduce or eliminate some difficulties that appear on later items. For example, process or relationship problems may stem from differences in understanding of work priorities; once this is corrected, social process may improve without further specific attention.

Unfortunately the team building label has also come to be used for a variety of activities, often provided off-site and at considerable expense, that might better be called "team recreation." According to one critic, "research does not suggest that rock climbing, whitewater rafting, blind trust walks, or playing basketball on donkeys increases productivity in any way" (Wheelan, 2013, pp. 119–120). The hallmark of true TB is whether it is clearly targeted on the team and its task within the organization.

A meta-analysis of 20 selected studies including 60 separate analyses found support for TB as a potentially successful intervention (Klein et al., 2009). Overall, TB had positive effects on cognitive, affective (emotional), group process, and group performance outcomes, but process and affect were the most positively influenced. Of Beckhard's (1972) four components, focus on goal-setting and role-clarification produced stronger impacts than focus on interpersonal relations and problem-solving, but all four emphases showed positive effects. Larger teams benefited most although teams of all sizes improved.

This is good news for advocates of TB, although it is important to remember that studies in this meta-analysis were relatively few and probably represent the best rather than typical TB. Klein et al. (2009) advise that managers should identify characteristics of a team and the problems it is encountering before implementing a TB intervention. The activity should be designed to address issues of concern for a particular team, given its work.

In the context of D&I, TB might be used with a management team to clarify the priority placed on D&I projects compared to others. With those working in D&I, it could help sort out roles and responsibilities and how various aspects fit together. With a work team, TB could help identify how aspects of D&I may enhance or weaken the progress of its work.

Organizational Mirroring

If organizational issues include strained relations between or among interdependent units, this technique may be appropriate. After interviewing members of units separately to understand the nature of their conflicts, the consultant brings the groups together in a session to discuss these issues so that work relations can be improved. First one group shares its perceptions of the nature of the difficulties and of the other group, while the second group listens without comment. Next, roles are reversed with the second group sharing its perceptions of difficulties and of the first group while they listen. This mirroring is followed by conversations facilitated by the consultant to improve working relationships. Discussions may be held collectively or in smaller task forces constructed for this purpose. Considerable facilitation skill is needed to guide these sensitive discussions productively so that relationships do not become worse as a result (Jones, 2004).

In D&I work, this technique could be used to address faultlines among identity groups or cross-unit difficulties among units whose work is interdependent. The facilitator should be careful to lead discussions in constructive directions and away from statements that may be interpreted as evidence of discrimination against members of protected groups in any subsequent legal proceedings. (See discussion of the Lucky Stores case in Chapter 6.)

Appreciative Inquiry (AI)

Methods described above generally focus on identifying problems or sources of conflict and determining how they can be addressed. AI takes a different approach, emphasizing activities that can lead to positive and *transformational* change rather than identification and solution of problems (Cooperrider & Whitney, 2005). Transformational change, as opposed to incremental change, involves alteration in the very identity of an organization and its state of being (Bushe & Kassam, 2005). In a successful AI intervention, members develop new information or ways of thinking about their organization; *generative metaphors* emerge as expressions of a new way of thinking and acting as an organization. To illustrate, the term *green energy* can be understood as a generative metaphor implying emphasis on environmentally friendly thoughts and actions such as recycling and increased reliance on solar and wind power.

AI is based on several principles, some philosophical (e.g., positive approach focused on how members conceptualize the organization). Others are action-oriented (e.g., begin with positive aspects and accomplishments, collaborate with members of the system, create new ways of thinking that impel changed behavior, and develop outcomes that actually apply to the organization itself; Bushe & Kassam, 2005). A typical AI intervention begins by collecting anecdotes from employees about their best experiences in the area of focus, then moves to discussion of these positive experiences to generate enthusiasm for moving forward with new ways of thinking about the organization and its work.

Practitioners of AI generally use a four-phase process called the *4D cycle*: (a) *Discovery:* dialogues about strengths, accomplishments, positive experiences; (b) *Dream:* imagination of possible futures and development of visions; (c) *Design:* collaborative articulation of a new organizational state along with actions to move the organization in that direction; and (d) *Destiny:* construction of working groups of stakeholders with power and willingness to act toward this new future. AI identifies strengths and successes as the basis for imagining another organizational future instead of identifying deficiencies and developing action plans to remedy them (Anderson, 2015). Suggestions and advice have been offered about use of AI in the public sector (Schooley, 2012) and as a part of large-scale change efforts (Drew & Wallis, 2014).

In D&I work, AI might begin by collecting stories about good experiences with diversity and scenarios about feeling included and valued. In analyzing these experiences, participants can develop new patterns of thinking about D&I as well as ideas for what might be done to expand diversity and the sense of inclusion and who might be involved in these efforts.

Job Rotation and Job Redesign

Although they do not share the philosophical foundations of OD, these techniques may be helpful in an OD program focused on D&I. *Job rotation* refers to movement of employees through different specific job assignments. This is done to maintain motivation, ensure cross-training and flexibility within a work group, or provide learning opportunities for those in interdependent positions. In some cases managerial trainees rotate through assignments to learn various aspects of the work they will manage. Rotating employees may also provide new ways of looking at the work that may lead to improvements (Barbian, 2002; Blanchard & Thacker, 2013). In the context of D&I, job rotation could be used (if feasible based on skills required for specific jobs) in an occupationally separated work setting so that individuals experience and better understand challenges, rewards, and stresses of other employees' work. Rotation interactions would also allow workers who are usually separated to get to know one another. Managers might complete rotations through different jobs under their supervision in order to understand incumbents and their work better.

Job redesign involves changing the characteristics of work to increase motivation, satisfaction, and productivity of job-holders. Job redesign (sometimes called job enrichment) usually begins by assessing work from the perspective of people who do it as well as those who supervise or observe it. One popular approach, the Job Characteristics Model (Hackman & Oldham, 1980), uses the Job Diagnostic Survey (JDS) to measure such job attributes as variety of skills required, significance and unitary identity of the work, degree of autonomy, feedback from the job or from others, and interaction with others (Hackman & Oldham, 1975, 1976). This model proposes that these characteristics lead to psychological experiences of meaningfulness, responsibility, and knowledge of results, which are key to motivation and other outcomes such as satisfaction and effectiveness.

Other models of job and work design have also been developed (e.g., Campion & Thayer, 1985; Campion, 1988; Morgeson & Humphrey, 2006). For example, Morgeson and Humphrey expanded the Job Characteristics Model based on their review of the literature in work design. A meta-analysis of the work design literature (Humphrey, Nahrgang, & Morgeson, 2007) found support for the expanded model in explaining several work outcomes.

These approaches to work design/redesign could be part of a job-focused D&I effort. For example, studying jobs from incumbents' perspectives could increase their sense of inclusion and understanding of how their work fits in. Improving job attributes through redesign could increase inclusion as well as productivity. Work redesign could also lead to improvements in working hours, compensation, or other factors. Reorganization of work into self-managing teams might also have beneficial effects.

Putting It All Together

This review includes only a few techniques used by OD professionals, industrial-organizational psychologists, and others to improve psychological aspects of work. Church et al. (2014) recommended widespread integration of D&I focus into all personnel functions, particularly ongoing organizational surveys, 360-degree feedback systems, compensation and reward systems (also called performance management), and talent management (i.e., finding, developing, and moving talent). None of these was developed specifically to deal with issues of D&I, but all can be adapted to that purpose. According to Church et al., "the only way to truly drive D&I as a transformational change effort is to fully integrate it into every aspect of one's assessment and development efforts" (p. 262).

Although some OD procedures sound very simple and easy, some caution is prudent. There are many anecdotes of facilitators who caused more difficulty than they remedied by an approach that was unskilled, unnecessarily confrontational, or not sufficiently grounded in diagnostic information. There is a saying in the OD field that one needs *gray hair* to be successful at this work. This means not only that one should be mature, but also that success requires organizational experience, a background in social science and organizational processes, facilitation skills, and collection of sufficient preliminary data so that diagnosis is accurate and appropriate technique(s) are used. Some consultants have a *one size fits all* approach to organizational interventions, specializing in techniques that are used regardless of the problem. This is as misguided in organizational science as it is in medicine; no "aspirin" exists for organizational problems.

Successful implementation of a strong D&I program often does mean significant organizational change. In some cases an incremental approach is wise, beginning with small activities justified by results of a culture audit but unlikely to be controversial, and proceeding to more extensive work as interest and support develops. In other situations—for example, if D&I work arises from a discrimination lawsuit or is court-ordered—a comprehensive approach may be required from the beginning. Many things should be considered before starting a large-scale effort, including resources, employees' experience with earlier change efforts, and sources of support and resistance. No wonder gray hair is required!

The diversity professional should carefully consider whether he or she has the requisite knowledge, skill, and experience to undertake any of these change techniques. In some cases, others in the organization may be of help but sometimes a consultant and facilitator from outside the organization will be more appropriate. Besides OD techniques and procedures, another very important aspect of organization change for D&I is the structural location of responsibility for D&I change within the organization.

Structural Locus of Responsibility

Momentum for an organization's D&I efforts begins in varied ways. Someone in top management or on the Board of Directors may be informed about and personally committed to developing a D&I program. Professionals in Human Resources may realize the importance of these issues as they deal with grievances, recruiting and loss of employees, or through contact with professional or trade organizations. Sometimes interest arises from employees whose personal experiences have led them to advocate for a more inclusive and diverse climate. In some cases a lawsuit or consent decree, pressure from clients or other stakeholders, or pressure from competitors may lead to development of D&I emphases. Or, someone like yourself, whose academic preparation included coursework emphasizing the importance of D&I, may join the organization!

To be successful over time, D&I initiatives must be seen as a priority and part of the strategy for reaching organizational goals. In addition, different aspects of D&I work must be well coordinated in order to address the most significant issues and prevent duplication of effort. A "bird's eye" view of the organization is required along with capacity to influence decision-makers and managers in various areas. Clear responsibility and accountability for coordinated D&I efforts should be given to a specified position or office, ideally one at or near the top of the organization's structure.

The importance of structure was highlighted in a study of success of AA and diversity management in more than 700 private sector firms (Kalev, Dobbin, & Kelly, 2006). Researchers analyzed over 30 years of archival data reported on federal EEO-1 forms showing men and women, African Americans and Whites in management. Survey data were also collected from a sample of organizations whose HR managers reported on the history of their organization's use of various policies or programs. Kalev et al. identified three approaches used by employers to increase representational diversity in management: (a) positions with responsibility for achieving increased diversity; (b) training and feedback for managers to address bias and inequality; and (c) programs such as mentoring and networking to reduce isolation of managers from underrepresented groups. Management diversity over time was analyzed for organizations reporting use of one or more of these approaches.

Largest improvements in representational diversity were associated with "structures establishing responsibility (AA plans, diversity committees, and diversity staff positions)" (2006, p. 590). Less improvement followed use of networking or mentoring to reduce social isolation of women and African Americans. Managerial education and feedback to reduce stereotyping and bias were not associated with increases in ethnic and gender diversity. Kalev et al. also found that programs such as training and evaluation, mentoring, and networking were more effective when structural responsibility for diversity management was clear. Importance of accountability was also shown by the fact that organizations covered by federal AA compliance reviews were more successful in diversifying their managerial ranks; plans and reports without review and follow-up were not as effective. This study focused only on representational diversity, but it seems likely that accountability is also important for the success of broader D&I goals.

This research does not address where the responsible and accountable unit should be located in an organization. Much variability exists across employers in whether one person or unit is responsible and, if so, where in the organization's structure responsibility lies. In SHRM's survey of a sample of its members, about two-thirds of organizations reported that responsibility for leading or implementing D&I initiatives went to HR. The president/CEO was responsible in about one-quarter of the cases (SHRM, 2014). Sometimes senior management bore responsibility for leading (21%) or implementing (10%) D&I programs. Diversity committees or councils were also responsible for leadership or implementation (11% in both areas). Only 6% of respondents reported that a Chief Diversity Officer (CDO) led or implemented, and most (85%) reported their organization had no staff dedicated exclusively to D&I work. This was a small sample ($n = 292$) with a low response rate (10%), and respondents were all SHRM members, probably working in HR. Most organizations were small (one-quarter with fewer than 100 employees) or medium size (41% with 100–500).

Many larger organizations are likely to have a Diversity Department and/or Council and the Diversity Officer may be a member of senior management with responsibility for diversity strategy and planning, employee communication, company-wide policy development, and attraction/retention of underrepresented groups. Other responsibilities may include community relationships, measurement of diversity and its effects, and programs such as diversity training, mentoring, and affinity groups.

A single best way to organize D&I work across all organizations probably does not exist. Larger employers have more resources (as well as more work) and are more likely than smaller organizations to be able to dedicate staff to this function. However, responsibility should be given to one or more persons who have a broad perspective on the organization's systems and are placed highly enough in the organizational structure to have access to top management and resources as well as influence across the organization. Although D&I work is commonly associated with the HR function, arguments exist against this arrangement. Employees sometimes associate HR offices with compliance efforts and maintenance of the *status quo*; furthermore, management of grievances, disciplinary processes, and other functions may seem incompatible with goals and culture of D&I efforts. Employees may come to see D&I activities as just another name for AA and management of discrimination complaints. In addition, in some organizations the legal function is closely associated with HR. In such cases, another location should probably be sought, especially one reporting directly to top management. At this time, data do not recommend one structure over others and it is likely that various arrangements can be effective. However, a specific position or office should be responsible for D&I.

Building a D&I Management Program

For an existing organization, embarking on a program to advance D&I can be understood as OD. In a startup or new organization, D&I work can be built into structure and processes from the beginning. We have discussed many activities that are typically part of D&I programming. Which are chosen or devised should be based on issues identified in a culture audit, strategic planning, business plan, or other efforts to define data-based goals for the newly founded or existing organization. Programs should be implemented because they serve an identified need, not just because other employers are doing it, a consultant is selling it, or someone read or heard about it.

As with individuals, reaching organizational diversity competence is a process of awareness, understanding, and action. That is, in the organization there must be (a) *attention to and awareness of* how diversity affects work behavior and outcomes and the continual need for learning; (b) *understanding* based on knowledge about D&I, its effects, and possible steps for improvement; and (c) *action* to implement procedures, programs, and structural changes for managing D&I more effectively. Like action research, this learning process is a cycle, with examination of action leading to more awareness, understanding, and subsequent actions. Among components often found in D&I programs, diagnostic work such as culture audits and strategic analysis can increase *awareness* and draw *attention* to aspects of D&I management most significant for a particular organization. Effective diversity training, mentoring, and other learning programs can increase *awareness, understanding and capacity for action* by individuals.

Alignment

Another important factor about infrastructure is the *alignment* among various parts or processes of the organization. When functions are aligned, they all work in the same direction toward the same or compatible goals instead of operating at cross-purposes. Misalignment often limits the success of efforts to improve D&I management because different programs contradict one another. For example, an organization may broaden its scope of recruiting in an attempt to bring more diversity to its employee base. However, overly rigid or outdated requirements in performance evaluation and promotion systems may continue to favor majority employees, working in opposition to D&I. For example, the US military's early attempt to bring more women into its ranks was counteracted by promotion requirements emphasizing experience in combat or at sea, neither of which was open to women. As another example, equipment or work areas may be designed for persons of a particular stature because of cost or custom rather than technical necessity; this can create performance or safety challenges for those who are smaller (e.g., women or men of Asian ethnicity). Employees may be required or encouraged to participate in diversity training but without any accommodation in production schedules to take into account their required absence from the job. HR staff may be directed to present diversity training but budgets may not take into account the cost of hiring professional staff with qualifications and expertise to conduct effective training. These are all examples of misalignment in different aspects of organizational process or structure relevant to management of D&I. A model of D&I organizational change that explicitly directs attention to alignment among relevant aspects of structure and process was developed by Cox (2001).

Cox's (2001) Model of Organizational Change: The Concept of Alignment

Cox identified five elements of organizational functioning important for advancing D&I: Leadership, Research and Measurement, Education, Alignment of Management Systems, and Follow-Up. In the 2001 version of this model, the elements are drawn in a circle to indicate

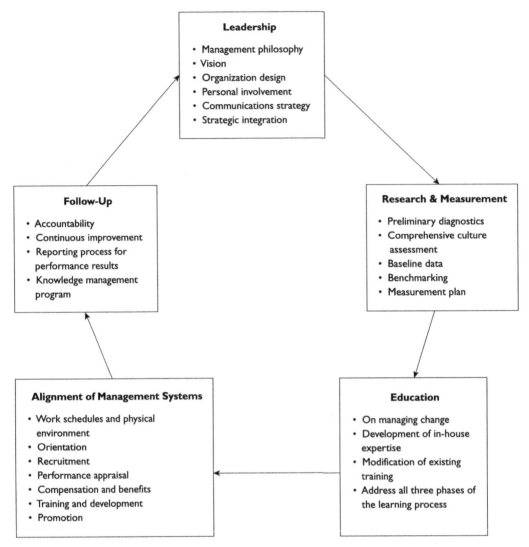

Figure 14.1 Change Model for Work on Diversity. Reproduced by permission from T. Cox (2001). *Creating the multicultural organization.* San Francisco, CA: Jossey-Bass, p. 19.

that they continue to interact over time as a system in a continuous loop. The model is shown in Figure 14.1.

According to Cox (2001), Leadership is the most critical element because it provides a vision of change and motivates others by emphasizing the importance of D&I and creating conditions to support change. The Research and Measurement element concerns data for planning, implementation, and evaluation. Education provides necessary information and skills as well as understanding of why change is undertaken. Cox stresses Alignment of Management Systems (e.g., scheduling and environment of work, recruitment, performance appraisal, promotion, compensation) partly because the need for it is often not understood. Seeing organizations as *systems* of interdependent parts makes it clear that managerial subsystems must work in the same direction if meaningful change is to result. Finally, the Cox model includes Follow-Up, which is critical for appropriate feedback and reinforcement as well as for continuous improvement.

Getting Started

No recipe or set of instructions exists for implementing a program for managing D&I, and every organization presents a different context and set of challenges. However, some initial questions include:

- Does the organization's strategic plan include D&I? How does D&I relate to strategic goals? Are there specific concerns (e.g., desire to diversify employee base, high turnover in certain groups, legal challenges, changing customer base or employment pools) relevant to D&I?
- Where are sources of support and who are potential allies for potential collaboration? Is top leadership committed? If not, what can be done to increase their knowledge, understanding, and motivation and secure this commitment?
- Has a culture audit or other organizational assessment been conducted that suggests areas of strength or concern, or issues that should be addressed? If not, can one be designed and conducted to guide further work?
- What programs or activities are currently in place that could be part of a coordinated approach to better D&I management? These might be found in areas of recruitment and selection, training and development (e.g., mentoring and networking), compensation and promotion, Employee Resource Groups (ERGs), or HR policies (e.g., family leave, flextime, benefit packages). Are managers of these programs likely to welcome collaboration with the D&I program or might concerns like territoriality, budgets, or possible legal ramifications impede cooperation?
- What is the structure of responsibility for a D&I initiative? Is someone in charge? If not, can this be altered so that someone at or near the top of the organization has clear responsibility for implementation and coordination? Is D&I responsibility structurally associated with compliance (legal HR) activities? Is this a problem, and if so, can the structure be changed?

Once these and other initial questions have been considered, what happens next? There is no one best way to proceed, but the person or unit with D&I responsibility may want to do some or all of these things:

- Develop a strategic plan for D&I activities integrated with the organizational strategic plan. Find ways in which D&I activities can support strategic initiatives.
- Collaborate with others whose work interfaces with or will benefit from expanded D&I activities. Look especially for people and programs that will be stronger and more successful with this collaboration. Work with others who may see D&I as competition so that areas of mutual interest can be developed.
- Secure budgetary and other support and resources from other people and programs, and consider ways to present the D&I program as an area with high-level administrative support and widespread benefit across the organization.
- Examine results of the cultural audit or other organizational assessments for guidance about areas of concern and success. If no such assessment has been conducted, sell the idea to highly-placed and influential members of management by showing how such data could benefit them. Determine whether the organization is capable of conducting such an assessment or whether an outside consultant should be secured for this work. Follow up by making use of results in ways that participants can see.
- Convene a group of knowledgeable people to examine various management systems, policies, and procedures to determine whether and in what ways they are aligned with the D&I effort or whether they may actually be impediments to D&I goals. If so, develop a plan to reduce or correct this misalignment.
- Conduct a preliminary needs assessment for D&I education and training. What is already being done, and with what effect? Develop a data-based plan for learning experiences, starting with

information about the D&I initiative and why it is being undertaken. Design additional learning experiences based on needs assessment.

- Decide whether to use a "start-small" or a comprehensive approach. For example, Valuing Diversity events could provide a low-cost and pleasant entrée into subsequent larger-scale efforts as financial, social, and other support increases. Informative communications can be added to existing channels to build support. Another starting point might be establishment of one or more ERGs which could later assist in developing ideas, motivation, and support. However, in some cases a comprehensive approach might be preferred. This will require more initial coordination and resources but may ensure alignment among the various initiatives.
- Implement a system for keeping track of results. Use simple metrics to see what is working and what is not. Review available data about hiring, promotion, satisfaction, turnover, and other routine HR functions and implement simple measures of how people react to and learn from D&I experiences. Solicit input widely.

These recommendations are all consistent with good OD practice and with Cox's (2001) model of D&I organizational change. Can you identify the five aspects of his model as they are reflected in these pointers?

Recapping Possible Components

Several different activities and programs are commonly found in comprehensive D&I initiatives. Expanded recruiting and outreach efforts sometimes incorporate scholarships or internships targeted at members of underrepresented groups as well as participation in community public service consistent with values of D&I. Many organizations review their suppliers and customer bases and reach out to more diverse groups if appropriate, making D&I part of external as well as internal operations. Routine monitoring of hiring, placement, and promotion practices is important for overall business success as well as the D&I effort. Also needed is an overall assessment of alignment among systems for hiring/placement/promotion, appraisal and reward, compensation, and training and development, as well as general HR policies and procedures and employee benefits. Valuing Diversity events, DT, Work & Family initiatives, and ERGs are frequently included and many organizations develop programs for employee networking and mentoring. Examination of structural and informal integration (Cox, 1993/1994) can guide the development of a D&I program. Some organizations assign ombudspersons to whom an employee can speak about concerns with an aim to mediate and resolve problems. Decisions about staffing and assignment of responsibility are critical and should include consideration of whether and how compliance and grievance processes should be related to proactive D&I work. Assessment is also necessary as part of planning and evaluation of D&I work.

What to Expect

Best practices are those followed by employers who are thought to be leaders in an area. For many topics covered earlier in this text, empirical data exist to guide action, but that is not the case with large-scale implementation of D&I programs. Organizations vary in history and culture, employee characteristics, external environment, competitive challenges, relevant expertise, and many other ways that can affect the success or failure of programs. Also, D&I programs are complex and usually involve many aspects so it is difficult to determine what accounts for success or lack of it. Furthermore, for most of those responsible for implementing D&I change, the demands of managing a program take precedence over attention to the design and measurement that are important to establish clear and generalizable data-based recommendations. Finally, it is unlikely that there is one best way to build a successful D&I program. Diversity professionals must therefore rely on expert opinion, their own experience and expertise, and consensus in the field to devise a plan that is workable and likely to be successful. The following sections present two types of information that may be helpful in planning and implementing a program of D&I management and anticipating what may happen as the program is put into place.

The Full Integration Model of Diversity Change

Agars and Kottke (2004) have developed a framework describing what is likely to happen as a program of D&I management is implemented. The model has not yet been empirically tested in its entirety and should be understood as a conceptual framework calling attention to issues of likely concern at different phases during implementation.

The model proposes that large-scale diversity management change occurs in three phases: (a) *Issue Identification*; (b) *Implementation*; and (c) *Maintenance*. Four processes underlie employee perceptions about the program, and the strength of each process varies from one phase to another. These processes are: (a) *social and identity* concerns; (b) perceptions of *threat*; (c) perceptions of *fairness and justice*; and (d) views of *utility or usefulness*. Diversity professionals should anticipate and try to manage these stresses so that each phase can progress successfully, resulting in a new equilibrium of structure and systems with the behavior of individuals. To summarize, the model proposes:

- Issue Identification phase: options are considered, top management becomes involved, and initial changes occur in organizational strategy and goals.

  o   Utility: convincing stakeholders of the benefits of a D&I program;
  o   Threat: factors (e.g., legal challenges, competitive pressures) leading to the D&I program; challenges to the *status quo* or to their interests.

- Implementation phase: changes occur in structure and systems/procedures, and in individuals' behavior and role modeling.

  o   Social: behaviors and identities challenged;
  o   Threat: to existing statuses and outcomes;
  o   Fairness: for different identity groups.

- Maintenance phase: some stability as cultural changes are accepted and support for D&I issues grows.

  o   Utility: need to show D&I program leads to valued business and social outcomes.

The model is presented as a three-phase linear process, but this dynamic probably recurs in repeated cycles of issue identification, implementation, and maintenance as the D&I program matures and parts of it are revised, dropped, or added. Not specifically mentioned in this model, but very important, is the process of monitoring the progress of change and evaluating its success overall and in its components. Data are needed to guide decisions about aspects to retain, expand, modify, or eliminate.

Benchmarks and Standards

The Full Integration Model analyzes what to expect as a program of D&I change is implemented. In contrast, the *Global Diversity and Inclusion Benchmarks* (GDIB) (O'Mara & Richter, 2016) are a set of standards described by 266 indicators in each of 14 categories (see Figure 14.2).

Three foundation or basic categories are shown at the base of the pyramid. Four internal categories of indicators, shown on the left side, are organizational programs or systems involved

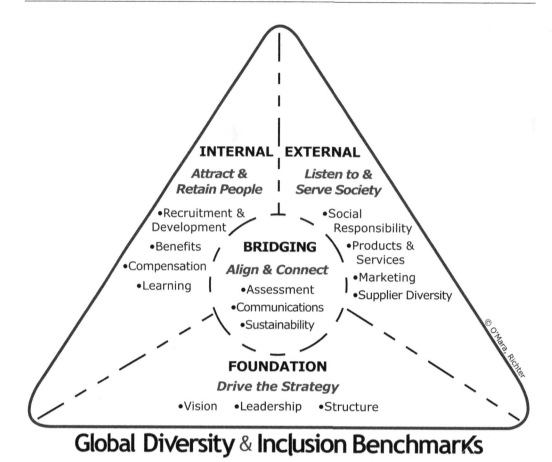

Figure 14.2 Global Diversity & Inclusion Benchmarks: Standards for Organizations Around the World
© 2016 Julie O'Mara and Alan Richter. Used with permission. All Rights Reserved.

with D&I change. Four external categories on the right show areas in which the organization interacts with its environment. Three bridging categories in the center link foundation areas with internal and external categories.

In each category there are several indicators or descriptions against which an organization's current status can be compared. These markers are organized into five levels (1–Inactive, 2–Reactive, 3–Proactive, 4–Progressive, and 5–Best Practices) showing the general degree to which the organization has progressed in a particular area. In each area "Inactive" indicates little or no D&I work. Focus only on compliance and symbolic actions would rate "Reactive." Level 3 "Proactive" indicates the beginning of a program and some movement, with "Progressive" marking a strong and systematic approach. An organization at the "Best Practices" level is seen as a leader in global best practices. Levels are ratings of the organization in the user's judgment as guided by specific indicators rather than precise or standardized measurements. To illustrate, in the foundation category of "Structure":

- Level 1: no infrastructure or budget; no one with formal D&I responsibility.
- Level 2: D&I an "add-on" to another department's duties; D&I structures without real power or resources.

- Level 3: D&I "champion"; manager, staff, council, chosen for competence and diverse ideas rather than demographic background; some budgetary resources; D&I staff respected and engaged with organizational groupings; unions, if any, engaged.
- Level 4: adequate D&I budget and staffing with knowledgeable and influential leader; D&I structures and functions respected and integrated throughout organization line and staff, and aligned with organization strategy.
- Level 5: D&I leader part of senior leadership; D&I leaders and networks advise on core systems, procedures, issues.

These benchmarks, including categories and indicators, have been developed and revised by O'Mara and Richter along with a group of 95 Expert Panelists who have included internal and external D&I practitioners and researchers with extensive international experience in the field of D&I. The model's first edition was based on government-funded research in the 1990s at the Tennessee Valley Authority. Benchmarks are based on Expert Panel judgments and consensus rather than on specific scientific research. Studies of reliability or validity have not yet been conducted. Although the benchmarks have not been formally adopted by professional organizations, they are sponsored by the Diversity Collegium, a nonprofit organization of professionals in the D&I field. Many topics in this textbook appear in the indicators and categories of this GDIB model, which appears to be the best guide currently available for determining overall quality of an organization's program of D&I management.

Another example of a framework for judging how well an organization addresses D&I issues is standards development (Hays-Thomas & Bendick, 2013). In manufacturing and other areas, agreed-upon standards facilitate commerce within and across national boundaries: for example, when sellers meet international standards, buyers can be confident of the quality of their purchases. Standards development for HR and D&I was initiated by SHRM under the auspices of the American National Standards Institute (ANSI) and its parent organization, the International Organization for Standardization (ISO) (ANSI, n.d.). In the area of D&I, SHRM organized task forces to develop three standards: D&I Programs, Diversity Metrics, and Lead D&I Professional. However, SHRM subsequently announced that it would withdraw from this work with the intent of transitioning the project to a collaborating organization (McIlvaine, 2014).

Wrapping Up

To become a knowledgeable and skilled diversity professional, one should have an interdisciplinary foundation of the kinds of concepts and information presented in this text: social sciences, especially psychology and sociology; human resource procedures and systems; measurement; legal issues related to fair employment; and training and organizational development and change. Management of D&I is a relatively new professional field, and many of those working in D&I began their careers in HR, psychology (particularly industrial-organizational psychology), management, or other fields. These are still good areas in which a young professional might start. Only in the last several years has it been possible to take formal coursework, academic concentrations, or degrees in D&I. For those with more general employment interests, knowledge about D&I is important in order to function successfully in an increasingly diverse work environment and because it is a significant issue in today's employment and in society at large.

The aspiring diversity professional should be aware of professional organizations that have become centers of expertise in the knowledge base and practice of D&I. A glance through the text's reference citations shows the breadth of scholarly and professional sources as well as nonprofit organizations and government agencies that have something to contribute to knowledge about managing D&I. At this time there is no single widely accepted certification for professionals in the field of D&I but such credentials now exist and are likely to increase. Each D&I professional must judge whether career advancement would follow completion of a particular certificate or degree program but continuous learning is surely needed as best practices evolve over time. Generalizations from research require updating as new studies are published and most critically, legal interpretations can change overnight as a result of new laws and court decisions.

This text has focused on the management of D&I in the US rather than globally. Individuals working in multinational contexts will find that knowledge about the practice of D&I work in other countries is extremely important. One obvious difference across countries is in relevant employment law, but other differences (e.g., work/life benefits) vary with the culture, customs, and laws of each country. This is well illustrated in the work of Mor Barak (2014).

Management of difference among people at work is both challenging and rewarding. Success requires a genuine respect for individuals and what they bring to the work environment. Also important are a system perspective, flexibility and creativity to function within a particular organizational setting, and the willingness to seek advice and help when needed. No textbook can teach all of these things, but a good text can help to increase awareness, understanding, and ability to act in ways that support the values of D&I. If this text helps you to develop in these ways, it will have been successful.

References

Agars, M. D., & Kottke, J. L. (2004). Models and practice of diversity management: A historical review and presentation of a new integration theory. In M. S. Stockdale & F. J. Crosby (Eds.), *The psychology and management of workplace diversity* (pp. 56–77). Malden, MA: Blackwell Publishing.

American National Standards Institute. (n.d.). *ISO programs—Overview.* Retrieved from www.ansi.org/standards_activities/iso_programs/overview.aspx?menuid=3

*Anderson, D. L. (2015). *Organization development: The process of leading organizational change.* Los Angeles, CA: SAGE.

Barbian, J. (2002). A little help from your friends. *Training, 39*(3), 38–41.

Beckhard, R. (1972). Optimizing team-building efforts. *Journal of Contemporary Business, 1*(3), 23–32.

Bendick, M., Jr., Egan, M. L., & Lofhjelm, S. M. (2001). Workforce diversity training: From anti-discrimination compliance to organizational development. *Human Resource Planning, 24*(2), 10–25.

Blanchard, P. N., & Thacker, J. W. (2013). *Effective training: Systems, strategies, and practices.* Boston, MA: Pearson.

Burke, W. W. (2002). *Organization change: Theory and practice.* Thousand Oaks, CA: SAGE.

*Bushe, G. R., & Kassam, A. F. (2005). When is Appreciative Inquiry transformational? A meta-case analysis. *The Journal of Applied Behavioral Science, 41*, 161–181.

Campion, M. A. (1988). Interdisciplinary approaches to job design: A constructive replication with extensions. *Journal of Applied Psychology, 73*, 467–481.

Campion, M. A., & Thayer, P. W. (1985). Development and field evaluation of an interdisciplinary measure of job design. *Journal of Applied Psychology, 70*, 29–43.

Chrobot-Mason, D., Hays-Thomas, R., & Wishik, H. (2008). Understanding and defusing resistance to diversity training and learning. In K. Thomas (Ed.), *Diversity resistance in organizations* (pp. 23–54). New York, NY: Lawrence Erlbaum Associates.

*Church, A. H., Rotolo, C. T., Shull, A. C., & Tuller, M. C. (2014). Inclusive organization development: An integration of two disciplines. In B. M. Ferdman & B. R. Deane (Eds.), *Diversity at work: The practice of inclusion* (pp. 260–295). San Francisco, CA: Jossey-Bass.

Cooperrider, D. L., & Whitney, D. (2005). *Appreciative Inquiry: A positive revolution in change.* San Francisco, CA: Berrett-Koehler.

Cox, T., Jr. (2001). *Creating the multicultural organization: A strategy for capturing the power of diversity.* San Francisco, CA: Jossey-Bass.

*Cox, T., Jr. (1993/1994). *Cultural diversity in organizations: Theory, research, & practice.* San Francisco, CA: Berrett-Koehler.

*Cox, T., Jr., & Beale, R. L. (1997). *Developing competency to manage diversity: Readings, cases, activities.* San Francisco, CA: Berrett-Koehler.

*Cummings, T. G., & Worley, C. G. (2015). *Organization development and change.* Stamford, CT: Cengage.

Davidson, M. N. (2011). *The end of diversity as we know it: Why diversity efforts fail and how leveraging difference can succeed.* San Francisco, CA: Berrett-Koehler Publishers, Inc.

della Cava, M. (2014, October 27). Diversity in Silicon Valley: An African-American pioneer speaks out. *USA Today/Pensacola News-Journal,* p. 4B.

Drew, S. A. W., & Wallis, J. L. (2014). The use of appreciative inquiry in the practices of large-scale organisational change: A review and critique. *Journal of General Management, 39*(4), 3–26.

Dyer, W. G. (1987). *Team building: Issues and alternatives.* Reading, MA: Addison-Wesley.

Frank, B. H. (2014, August 15). *Chart: This is how bad the gender gap is at tech companies.* Retrieved from www.geekwire.com/2014/chart-bad-gender-gap-tech-companies/

Goodrich, R. (2013, October 9). *SWOT analysis: Examples, templates, & definition.* Retrieved from www.businessnewsdaily.com/4245-swot-analysis.html

Guynn, J. (2014, October 9). *High-tech pay gap: Minorities earn less in skilled jobs.* Retrieved from www.usatoday.com/story/tech/2014/10/09/high-tech-pay-gap-hispanics-asians-african-americans/16606121/

Guynn, J., & Weise, E. (2014, August 15). *Lack of diversity could undercut Silicon Valley.* Retrieved from www.usatoday.com/story/tech/2014/06/26/silicon-valley-tech-diversity-white-asian-black-hispanic-google-facebook-yahoo/11372421/

Hackman, J. R., & Oldham, G. R. (1975). Development of the Job Diagnostic Survey. *Journal of Applied Psychology, 60,* 159–170.

*Hackman, J. R., & Oldham, G. R. (1976). Motivation through the design of work: Test of a theory. *Organizational Behavior and Human Performance, 16,* 250–279.

Hackman, J. R., & Oldham, G. R. (1980). *Work redesign.* Reading, MA: Addison-Wesley.

Hays-Thomas, R., & Bendick, M., Jr. (2013). Professionalizing Diversity and Inclusion practice: Should voluntary standards be the chicken or the egg? *Industrial and Organizational Psychology: Perspectives on Science and Practice, 6,* 193–205.

Hebl, M., Madera, J. M., & King, E. (2008). Exclusion, avoidance, and social distancing. In K. Thomas (Ed.), *Diversity resistance in organizations* (pp. 127–150). New York, NY: Lawrence Erlbaum Associates.

*Humphrey, S. E., Nahrgang, J. D., & Morgeson, F. P. (2007). Integrating motivational, social, and contextual work design features: A meta-analytic summary and theoretical extension of the work design literature. *Journal of Applied Psychology, 92,* 1332–1356.

Huse, E. F. (1980). *Organization development and change.* St. Paul, MN: West Publishing Co.

Jones, G. R. (2004). *Organizational theory, design, and change: Text and cases.* Upper Saddle River, NJ: Pearson.

Kalev, A., Dobbin, F., & Kelly, E. (2006). Best practices or best guesses? Assessing the efficacy of corporate Affirmative Action and diversity policies. *American Sociological Review, 71,* 589–617.

Klein, C., DiazGranados, D., Salas, E., Le, H., Burke, C. S., Lyons, R., & Goodwin, G. F. (2009). Does team building work? *Small Group Research, 40,* 181–222.

Kossek, E. E., & Zonia, S. C. (1993). Assessing diversity climate: A field study of reactions to employer efforts to promote diversity. *Journal of Organizational Behavior, 14,* 61–81.

Locke, K., & Golden-Biddle, K. (2004). An introduction to qualitative research: Its potential for industrial and organizational psychology. In S. G. Rogelberg (Ed.), *Handbook of research methods in industrial and organizational psychology* (pp. 99–118). Malden, MA: Blackwell.

Mann, F. (1961). Studying and creating change. In W. Bennis, K. Benne, & R. Chin (Eds.), *The planning of change* (pp. 605–613). New York, NY: Holt, Rinehart & Winston.

McIlvaine, A. (2014, December 24). SHRM stepping back from HR standards work. *HRE Daily.* Retrieved from http://blog.hreonline.com/2014/12/24/shrm-stepping-back-hr-standards-work/

McKay, P. F., Avery, D. R., & Morris, M. A. (2008). Mean racial-ethnic differences in employee sales performance: The moderating role of diversity climate. *Personnel Psychology, 61,* 349–374.

Mor Barak, M. E. (2014). *Managing diversity: Toward a globally inclusive workplace.* Thousand Oaks, CA: SAGE.

Mor Barak, M. E., Cherin, D. A., & Berkman, S. (1998). Ethnic and gender differences in employee diversity perceptions: Organizational and personal dimensions. *Journal of Applied Behavioral Sciences, 34,* 82–104.

Morgeson, F. P., & Humphrey, S. F. (2006). The Work Design Questionnaire (WDQ): Developing and validating a comprehensive measure for assessing job design and the nature of work. *Journal of Applied Psychology, 91,* 1321–1339.

O'Mara, J., & Richter, A. (2016). *Global Diversity and Inclusion Benchmarks: Standards for Organizations around the World.* Retrieved from www.diversitycollegium.org/downloadgdib.php

Pugh, S. D., Dietz, J., Brief, A. P., & Wiley, J. W. (2008). Looking inside and out: The impact of employee and community demographic composition on organizational diversity climate. *Journal of Applied Psychology, 93,* 1422–1428.

Qirko, H. (2007). Diversity and cultural assessments in business organizations. *The International Journal of Diversity in Organisations, Communities and Nations, 7,* 151–158.

Schein, E. (1999). *Process consultation revisited: Building the helping relationship.* Reading, MA: Addison-Wesley.

Schooley, S. E. (2012). Using appreciative inquiry to engage the citizenry: Four potential challenges for public administrators. *International Journal of Public Administration, 35,* 340–351.

Society for Human Resource Management. (2014, April 8). *SHRM survey findings: Diversity and inclusion.* Retrieved from www.shrm.org/research/surveyfindings/articles/pages/diversity-inclusion.aspx

Swartz, J., Guynn, J., & della Cava, M. (2014, November 11). How best to close tech diversity gap: Panel hits on education, recruiting. *USA Today/Pensacola News-Journal,* p. 4B.

Thomas, K. M. (Ed.) (2008). *Diversity resistance in organizations.* New York, NY: Lawrence Erlbaum Associates.

Thomas, K. M., & Plaut, V. C. (2008). The many faces of diversity resistance in the workplace. In K. Thomas (Ed.), *Diversity resistance in organizations* (p. 1–22). New York, NY: Lawrence Erlbaum Associates.

Thomas, R. R. (1991). *Beyond race and gender: Unleashing the power of your total work force by managing diversity.* New York, NY: AMACOM.

van Knippenberg, D., Homan, A. C., & van Ginkel, W. P. (2013). Diversity cognition and climate. In Q. M. Roberson (Ed.), *The Oxford handbook of diversity and work* (pp. 220–238). New York, NY: Oxford University Press.

Weise, E., & Guynn, J. (2014, October 13). Despite tech degree, minorities not hired: It's "just not the case" nobody is qualified. *USA Today/Pensacola News-Journal,* p. 1B.

Wheelan, S. A. (2013). *Creating effective teams: A guide for members and their leaders.* Thousand Oaks, CA: SAGE.

Wolfson, N., Kraiger, K., & Finkelstein, L. (2011). The relationship between diversity climate perceptions and workplace attitudes. *The Psychologist-Manager Journal, 14,* 161–176.

* Recommended for advanced reading.

Author Index

Note: only the first named author is indexed for references to multi-author works.

Subject Index

Abilene Paradox 162
ability 5, 239; older workers 259; sex differences 176
absenteeism 15; disabled employees 267; intimate partner violence 193–4; older workers 259; sexual harassment 186
access: access discrimination 210, 244–5; work-family benefits 301
Access-and-Legitimacy paradigm 23
accountability 320
acculturation 23, 25, 96
action research 310
activation 111–12, 113
active listening 292
actor-observer effect 55–6, 118
actual productivity 152, 154
ad hoc groups 150, 159
ADA Amendments Act of 2008 (ADAAA) 146
administrative procedures 133
adverse impact 134, 137, 138–9, 213; employment tests 215; first-generation and second-generation models 217; *Ricci v. DeStefano* case 229; sex differences 176; subgroup norming 144
advertising 14, 45
affinity groups *see* Employee Resource Groups
Affirmative Action (AA) 4, 6, 9, 15–16, 56, 97; Black women 95; blinding 113; Diversity-Validity Dilemma 215–16; elite recruitment 219; fairness 59; legal issues 134, 135, 136, 141–2; public opinion 142–3; quotas equated with 54; recognizing privilege 47; reviews 65, 141, 320; targeted recruitment 218; terminology 206; Thomas's three organizational conditions 22; for Whites 37; women 72
Affirmative Action Plans (AAPs) 27–8, 32–3, 72, 141
African Americans: adverse impact 217; Black History Month 108; demographic changes 10; desegregation 117; Ethnicity Paradigm 208; glass escalator 68; high tech industries 308; managers 13–14, 320; mentoring 296; occupational segregation 225; phantom diversity 97; race discrimination cases 228, 229; racial identity development 86; slavery 36; stereotype threat 110; terminology 206; US Census 28, 29; wage gap 77; *see also* Black people

age 239, 254, 257–63; demographic changes 10; generational differences 261–2; labor force participation 31, 32; law 132, 135, 144–5; population projections 30; retirement 262–3; social construction of 54; stereotype threat 110; stereotypes 259–60; US Census 29
Age Discrimination in Employment Act of 1967 (ADEA) 132, 133, 136, 144–5, 258–9, 260
Alaska Natives: employment research 209; labor force participation 31; population projections 30; unemployment rates 31; US Census 28–9
alignment 321–3
alternative workers *see* contingent workers
altruism 175
Amazon 309
ambivalent sexism 179
American Community Survey 27, 28, 264
American Religious Identification Survey 29
Americans with Disabilities Act of 1990 (ADA) 133, 136, 145–7, 184, 263, 265–6, 269
Amtrak 181
Anheuser-Busch Inbev (SB) 11
anxiety 110, 243, 250
appearance 94, 132, 254, 264–5, 267, 269–71
Apple 308
Appreciative Inquiry (AI) 317–18
Arabs 119, 224–5, 228, 257
ASA model 96–7
ascribed status 4
Asian Pacific American Heritage Month 108
Asians: Affirmative Action 141; demographic changes 10; employment research 209; employment tests 213, 214–15; Ethnicity Paradigm 208; frequency of discrimination 225; identity 88, 90, 91; labor force participation 30–1, 32; legacy issues 35; medical students 47; microaggressions 290; Model Minority stereotype 208–9; occupational segregation 225, 226; overweight 265; population projections 29; religion 257; skin color 52; terminology 207; unemployment rates 31; US Census 28, 29, 37; wage gap 226
assessment centers 211, 213
assimilation 21, 23, 24, 208
associated attributes 104
attendance 25

Made in the USA
Las Vegas, NV
20 June 2021

25099485R10201